New Zealand

The Complete **Residents'** Guide

Passionately Publishing...

EXPLORER

New Zealand Explorer 1st Edition ISBN 13 - 978-9948-03-382-0 ISBN 10 - 9948-03-382-5

Front Cover Photograph: One Tree Hill – Victor Romero.

Printed and bound by Emirates Printing Press, Dubai, United Arab Emirates.

Explorer Publishing & Distribution
PO Box 34275, Dubai
United Arab Emirates
Phone +971 (0)4 340 8805
Fax +971 (0)4 340 8806
Email info@explorerpublishing.com
Web www.explorerpublishing.com

Welcome

You've just made living in New Zealand a whole lot easier by buying this book. In the following pages you'll find out everything you need to know to get settled into – and then get the most out of – your new life in one of the world's most beautiful and laid-back countries. From finding a house to watching the All Blacks, we can tell you how and where to do it.

General Information (p.2) fills you in on New Zealand's history, geography and culture, and provides details of how to get around and where to stay when you first arrive.

The **Residents** chapter (p.66) takes away all the headaches involved in setting up your new home. With information on visas, residential areas in and around Auckland, Wellington and Christchurch, schools and red tape, this section will tell you how to deal with all the formalities.

After settling in, take a look at **Exploring** (p.198). This chapter guides you through the North and South Islands, telling you all about their many and varied natural attractions, museums, art galleries and sights of historical interest. There's also a checklist of must-dos to work through.

If you've still got time on your hands, move on to **Activities** (p.304). Here you'll find out where to practise whitewater sledging, how to join a hockey club, and where to learn Maori. If you'd prefer to indulge, there's also a wealth of well-being options to digest, from acupuncture to yoga, with a bit of spa in between.

Now that you're living in New Zealand, you'll also have full access to all the retail that the country's best **Shopping** cities have to offer (p.364). We've got a whole chapter dedicated to helping you discover the top markets, malls and designer boutiques in which to splash the cash.

Don't spend it all in the shops though – save some for the evening. Our **Going Out** chapter (p.426) gives you a detailed run-down on the premier places for eating, drinking and partying in Auckland, Wellington and Christchurch.

Nearly all of the places of interest have references that correspond to the detailed **Maps** in the back of the book – use these for everything from finding a bar in Wellington's Courtenay Place to navigating Auckland's CBD. At the end of the book is a pull-out map of the North and South Islands to help you navigate your new country.

And if you think we've missed something, please tell us. Go to www.explorerpublishing.com, fill in the Reader Response form, and share the knowledge with your fellow explorers.

The Explorer Team

About the Authors

Explorer's New Zealand

Wide-open spaces, inescapable beauty and some of the world's finest wines – what's not to like about New Zealand? These incredible islands come with a life-enhancing reputation; the endless variety of landscapes and their pure vitality make exploring an endless treat – even for hardened Kiwis. It's impossible to cover all of New Zealand's charms here, so why not start with a few simple pleasures: watch a rugby game, anytime, anywhere (p.347), quaff a pinot noir (p.339), enjoy Maori hospitality (p.22), surf off the North Island's west coast (p.221) and ski on Mount Ruapehu (p.232) in the same day, swim with fur seals at Kaikoura (p.231), tramp in a national park (p.318), enjoy the solitiude of Southland (p.288), and then settle back with a well-earned beer (p.429).

Brett Atkinson When he's not researching and writing guidebooks on a variety of countries, Brett writes about travel, entertainment and sports, and reviews the bars and restaurants of his hometown, Auckland. **NZ Must-do**: Auckland's vibrant Otara Market (p.410) – the past, present and future of the city. **Best place to drink with the locals**: Galbraith's Ale House (p.445).

Bronwyn Sell Though she's lived in London and Sydney, Bronwyn far prefers the open spaces, varied landscapes and laid-back atmosphere of her native New Zealand. A freelance writer and editor based in Auckland, Bronwyn is a regular contributor to *The New Zealand Herald* and edits travel books. **Best view**: The wild blue coastline on the North Island's East Cape (p.233).

Catherine Jarvie This book is a welcome chance for Catherine to reacquaint herself with the her Kiwi roots, resulting in a burst of national pride previously reserved for the Flying Nun back catalogue. A freelance journalist, Catherine writes for various international broadsheets, including *The Times* in the UK. **Best NZ memory**: A midnight picnic on Mount Eden with good friends and lashings of champagne.

Heather Ramsay The traditional Kiwi OE gave Heather a desire to explore new destinations. A former teacher, she is now a full-time freelance writer who contributes travel features to many publications in New Zealand and abroad, and has a weekly travel column in *The New Zealand Herald*. **Best view**: From her home office – gorgeous Mount Taranaki (p.238) over lush bush filled with native birds.

Jennie Scotcher Jennie came to New Zealand in 2005 with her partner and young family having never visited the country before. Now there is nowhere else she would rather be. After 20 years of teaching, public relations and marketing, Jennie is finally doing what she always wanted – writing and editing. **Must-do**: Carols by candlelight in the Westpac Stadium, Wellington. **Best view**: The Kapiti Coast (p.133) from Paekakariki Hill Road.

*Having trouble navigating your way around the City of Sails? Look no further than the **Auckland Mini Map**, an indispensable pocket-sized aid to getting to grips with the roads, areas and attractions of New Zealand's largest city.*

*Now that you've moved to New Zealand, it won't be long before you're playing host to wave upon wave of visiting family and friends – and we've got the perfect guide to help them get the most out of their sightseeing. Packed with information on all the attractions, you can't go wrong with the **New Zealand Mini Explorer**.*

John McCrystal A contributor to most of New Zealand's major newspapers and magazines, John has published more than a dozen non-fiction titles, and has won awards for travel writing and for short fiction. He spends as much spare time as he can on the 'Mainland'. **Best view**: The panorama over the countryside from any tramping track in the South Island (p.248).

Lois Watson An award-winning journalist who worked in the newspaper industry for 13 years, Lois recently took the plunge and went freelance. She still contributes regularly for New Zealand's leading Sunday publication, the *Sunday Star Times*, and is working on a number of book projects. **Favourite daytrip**: A drive over the Port Hills to the French settlement of Akaroa (p.264).

Rachel Taulelei Rachel owns food retailer Yellow Brick Road. She thinks about food, talks about it, writes about it, and sources it for chefs around the world. A born-and-bred Wellingtonian, Rachel is passionate about the vibrancy of the city and its culture of hospitality. **Best thing about New Zealand**: Friends, family, food and wine. **Must-do**: Wine tasting in Central Otago (p.275).

Soraya Nicholas Soraya has been creating stories since she was a small child. After completing a law degree, she rediscovered her passion and promptly put pen to paper. She now writes travel, lifestyle and entertainment pieces from her home base in Christchurch. **Favourite restaurant**: Pedros (p.468); particularly garlic prawns followed by lamb shoulder.

Thanks

As well as our talented team of authors, whose expert advice and exhaustive research have ensured the ***New Zealand Explorer*** is the most up-to-date and comprehensive guide to expat life in the country, there are a number of other people who have made contributions towards making this book a success. Thanks go to Kerrie-Anne Love, Jeanne Davies and Rob Jones for their sub-editing support and to our hard-working cartographers Noufal Madathil, Riyas Chembhan and Sudheer Mekkatu, as well as Tony and Anand from Emirates Printing Press. And last but not least, Hashim, Mimi and Jake for all their help and hard work.

Where are we exploring next?

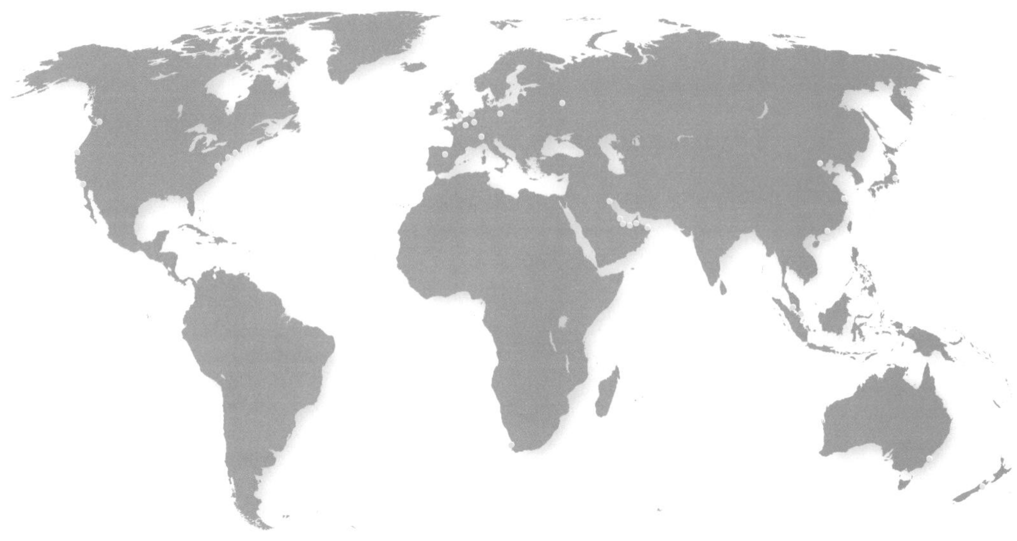

- Abu Dhabi
- Amsterdam
- Bahrain
- Barcelona
- Beijing*
- Berlin*
- Boston*
- Brussels*
- Cape Town*
- Dubai
- Dublin
- Geneva
- Hong Kong
- Kuala Lumpur*
- Kuwait
- London
- Los Angeles*
- Moscow*
- New York
- New Zealand
- Oman
- Paris
- Qatar
- San Francisco*
- Shanghai
- Singapore
- Sydney
- Tokyo*
- Vancouver*
- Washington DC*

* Available 2008

Where do you live?

Is your home city missing from our list? If you'd love to see a residents' guide for a location not currently on Explorer's horizon please email editorial@explorerpublishing.com.

Advertise with Explorer

If you're interested in advertising with us, please contact sales@explorerpublishing.com.

Make Explorer your very own

We offer a number of customisation options for bulk sales. For more information and discount rates, please contact corporatesales@explorerpublishing.com.

Contract Publishing

Have an idea for a publication or need to revamp your company's marketing material? Contact designlab@explorerpublishing to see how our expert contract publishing team can help.

www.explorerpublishing.com

Life can move pretty fast, so to make sure you can stay up to date with all the latest goings on in your hometown, we've revamped our website to further enhance your time in the city, whether long or short.

Keep in the know

Our Complete Residents' Guides and Mini Visitors' series continue to expand, covering destinations from Amsterdam to New Zealand and beyond. Keep up to date with our latest travels and tips by signing up to our monthly newsletter, or browse our products section for information on our current and forthcoming titles.

Make friends and influence people...

by joining our Communities section. Meet fellow residents in your city, make your own recommendations for your favourite restaurants, bars, childcare agencies or dentists, plus find answers to your questions on daily life from long-term residents.

Discover new experiences

Ever thought about living in a different city, or wondered where the locals really go to eat, drink and be merry? Check out our regular features section, or submit your own feature for publication.

Want to find a badminton club, the number for your bank, or maybe just a restaurant for a first date?

Check out city information on various destinations around the world in our residents' section – from finding a Pilates class to contact details for international schools in your area, or the best place to buy everything from a spanner set to a Spandau Ballet album, we've got it all covered.

Let us know what you think

All our information comes from residents which means you. If we missed out your favourite bar or market stall, or you know of any changes in the law, infrastructure, cost of living or entertainment scene, let us know by using our feedback form.

AMOUAGE

Contents

Contents

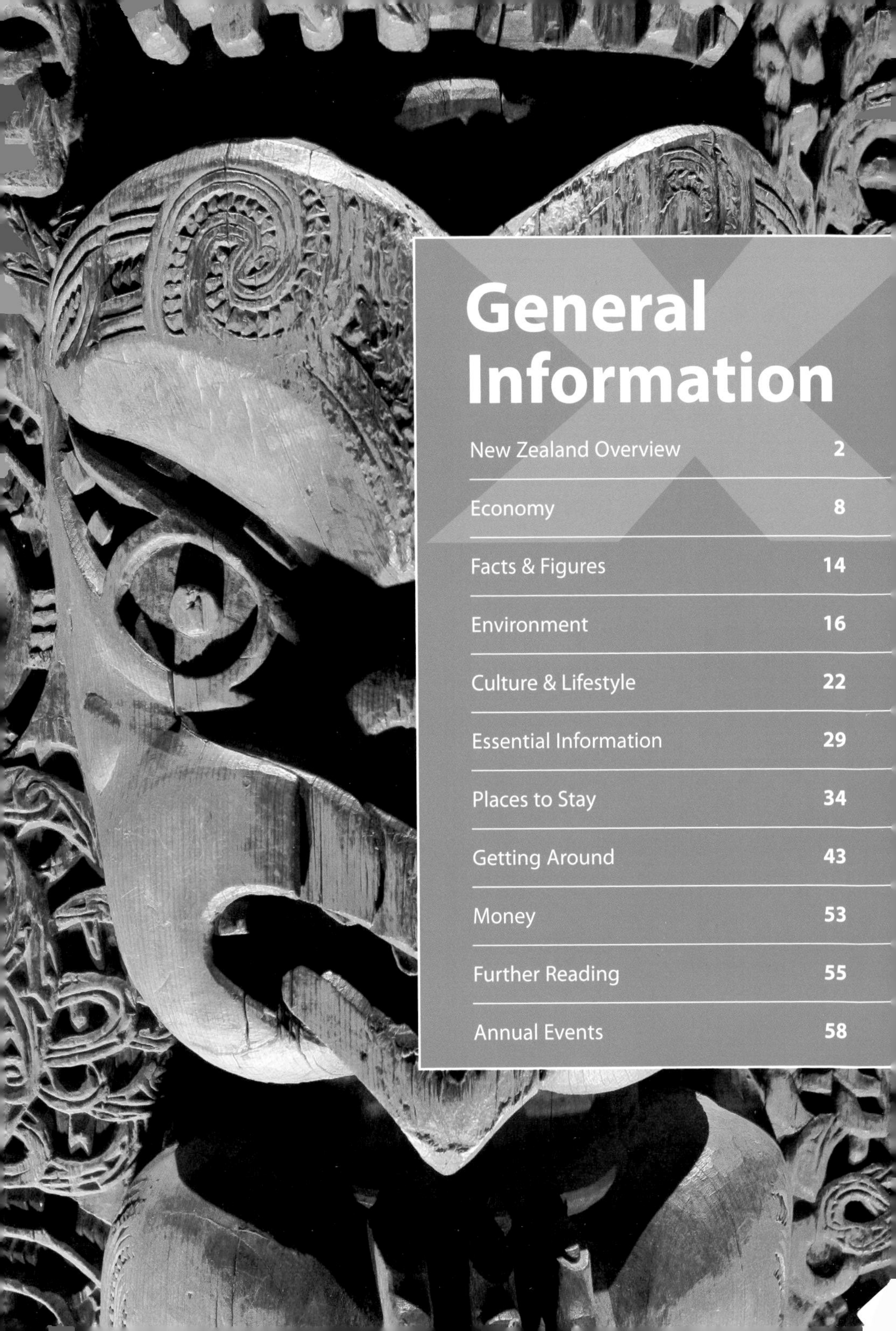

General Information

General Information

North & South

New Zealand's South Island is the 12th biggest island in the world – its northern neighbour comes in two places behind. No matter where in the country, you are always less than 128km from the sea.

Geography

New Zealand nestles in the region broadly known as the Antipodes, flanked on one side by the Tasman Sea, and on the other by the vastness of the mighty Pacific Ocean. Its nearest neighbour, Australia, is more than 2,000km to the west.

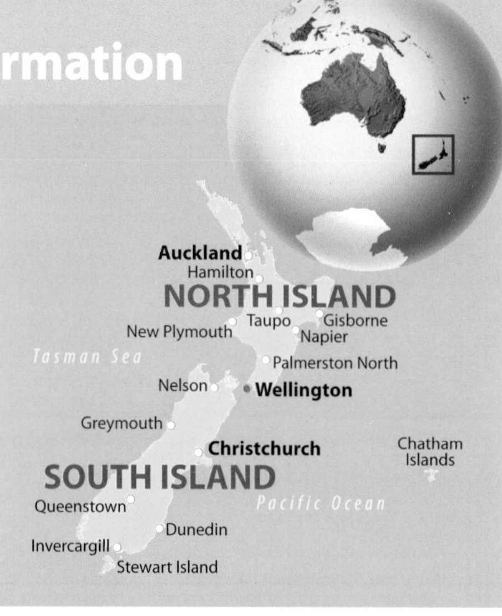

Covering a total area of 268,680 square kilometres (a little larger than the United Kingdom and slightly smaller than Japan), the country consists of two main land masses – the North and South Islands – divided by the Cook Strait. The considerably smaller Stewart Island, located towards Antarctica at the base of the South Island, and a series of smaller, satellite islands (including the inhabited Great Barrier and Chatham Islands, off the North and South Island mainlands respectively) also form part of the country.

The North Island (115,777 sq km and 829km long) is home to the capital, Wellington, and Auckland, New Zealand's largest city. Across Cook Strait lies the South Island, which, at 515,215 sq km, is New Zealand's largest land mass. Te Wai Pounamu (as the South Island is known in Maori) is renowned for its fiords and glaciers and is broadly divided along its length by the Southern Alps. It is also home to New Zealand's highest mountain, Mount Cook/Aoraki.

For such a relatively small country, the variety of lanscapes can appear wonderfully dramatic. The beautiful, windswept peninsula of Cape Reinga at the furthest tip of the North Island, which the Maori call 'the leaping place of the spirits' – the point from which the spirits of their departed leave for the spirit world – is in stark contrast to the rugged unpredictability of tiny Stewart Island (1,746 sq km), 30km south across the Foveaux Strait, home to Antarctic winds, dense coastal rainforest and the Stewart

Westhaven Marina, Auckland

Island tokoeka, a rare species of kiwi, New Zealand's native bird. A journey from sub-tropical Auckland in the narrow finger of the upper third of the North Island (Te-Ika-a-Maui) to its southern centre, home to the country's rich, volcanic landscape of hot springs, bubbling mud and dramatic geysers, offers the potential for trips that live up to the promise of New Zealand as a country where you can surf, sunbathe and ski all in one day. Raglan's surf-pummeled beaches along the west coast, for example, are only hours away from the geothermal splendour of the Tongariro Crossing (famously depicted in blockbuster film trilogy *The Lord of the Rings*, and the snow-capped peaks of nearby Mount Ruapehu (p.333), an active cone volcano that is the island's highest peak. In the South Island, Milford Sound was carved from rocks by prehistoric glaciers, and its surrounding alpine peaks are a world away from the main cities of Christchurch and Dunedin. The inhospitality of this and nearby regions has meant that many of the South Island's ancient landscapes have remained largely untouched by man, boasting plant – and even some animal – life that predates the dinosaur.

Bombay Hills

Aucklanders are regularly accused of being aloof, latte-supping snobs, or simply not caring what happens 'south of the Bombay Hills', a range 22km south-west of the city that naturally separates the region from the rest of the country.

Urban Geography

New Zealand has five main cities: Auckland, Hamilton and Wellington in the North Island, and Christchurch and Dunedin in the South Island. The country is divided into 16 regions according to the top tiers of local government. From the top of the North Island to the bottom of the South the regions are: Northland, Auckland, Waikato, Bay of Plenty, Gisborne, Hawke's Bay, Taranaki, Manawatu-Wanganui, Wellington, Tasman, Nelson, Marlborough, West Coast, Canterbury, Otago and Southland.

New Zealand remains a relatively sparsely populated country with more than a third of the nation's population concentrated in Auckland alone. As such, the country's urban landscape remains fairly uncluttered. Skyscrapers are largely limited to the central business districts of Wellington, Auckland and Christchurch.

What is rapidly changing the face of the landscape around New Zealand's major cities, however, is suburbia. A reluctance to build up has left town planners with only one way to move – out. In Auckland alone, rapid growth has seen the perimeters of the city expand exponentially over the past decade, swallowing farmland and small towns in its wake.

History

Legend has it that the first major settlement of New Zealand was a result of the arrival of the Great Fleet, a flotilla of seven double-hulled canoes in which the ancestors of the modern Maori travelled to Aotearoa ('Land of the Long White Cloud' in Maori), a literal description of what the country looked like as they sailed towards it in 1350AD. It's a powerful image, this vision of a fleet of Polynesian adventurers crossing the South Pacific in search of a new land, so it's hardly surprising that such a myth was for a long time accepted as established fact. Archaeological research, however, has revealed that the truth is more likely to be that New Zealand was settled over the course of several migrations between 1200AD and 1300AD.

Having arrived with provisions from home, including edible plants such as kumara and taro (potato-like tuber vegetables still widely eaten today), the Polynesians' migration was clearly planned.

They settled in the South Island, where the abundance of coastal marine life and indigenous wildlife, including the giant moa (a man-sized flightless bird that was eventually hunted to extinction), allowed the new settlers to not only establish a home but thrive in villages (kainga) and pa (fortified villages built to withstand attack between rival tribal groups).

Over time, the Maori began to explore their new country, crossing what is now known as Cook Strait to the North Island, where the considerably warmer climate gradually encouraged them to resettle. By the time the first Europeans arrived, 95% of the Maori were living in coastal settlements in the upper half of the North Island.

Gallipoli
The Australian and New Zealand Army Corps (ANZAC) expedition was New Zealand's first major foray into world war one. Allied troops landed on the shores of the Gallipoli peninsula on April 25, in what was hoped would be a bold and sudden strike to finally knock Turkey out of the war. Instead, the soldiers met huge resistance. The campaign lasted for nine long months before Allied forces were eventually evacuated at the end of 1915. More than 2,700 New Zealanders and 8,000 Australians lost their lives.

European Discovery & Settlement

Englishman James Cook was the first European to set foot on Aotearoa, in 1769. Over a century earlier, Dutch seaman Abel Tasman had 'discovered' the land mass when he anchored in Golden Bay. However, when his small rowing boats came under attack from a Maori war canoe, resulting in the death of four of his sailors, Tasman fled, but not before naming the country Staten Land (later rechristened Nieuw Zeeland after the Dutch province).

Cook's initial landing didn't fare much better. He first set foot in Gisborne, where conflict with the local Maori tribe resulted in several deaths, before also clashing with the native Ngati Kahungunu people after anchoring near Cape Kidnappers (p.234). But the English sailor wasn't going to give up so easily. Cook unfurled the British flag off the coast of the Coromandel Peninsula, claiming formal possession of the land against orders and without the permission of the Maori. New Zealand, as it has come to be known, was in its infancy.

The British were in no great rush to colonise a very foreign land miles from home. It took around another half a century for initial, early European settlement to occur – largely as the result of an 'overspill' from the Botany Bay penal colony in nearby Australia. By 1830 settlers' outposts were firmly established in what was widely recognised as a lawless land, focused around Kororareka (now Russell) in the Bay of Islands. 'Of all the vile holes I ever visited, this is the vilest,' said Matthew Felton, the first Surveyor General of New Zealand, of the region in 1840. This seemed to capture the mood of the place at the time, despite the presence of Christian missionary Samuel Marsden and his followers, who arrived in 1814.

Meanwhile, for the Maori, tribal structure began to crumble as European disease swept through their population and alcohol abuse became rife. Tribes relocated from their prime lands to insalubrious encampments near flax swamps in exchange for the guns that were fuelling inter-tribal wars. In desperation, a group of Maori tribal chiefs petitioned the British monarch to become 'friend and guardian of these islands' (despite Cook's actions in 1769, New Zealand was never declared as 'officially' British). James Busby was sent as British Resident in 1833 and, after a series of failures to regain peace and control, persuaded 35 northern chiefs to proclaim themselves the United Chiefs of New Zealand, in 1835. Later, as interest in New Zealand land as a valuable commodity began to grow, he encouraged the drawing up of the Treaty of Waitangi in 1840.

Over the next two decades, fallout from disagreements over the treaty escalated, eventually encouraging Maori to put aside inter-tribal animosities for the greater fight

Old Government Buildings, Wellington

– getting the Pakeha (as the European settlers were – and still – are called) to respect their ownership of the land. This eventually led to the New Zealand Wars of the 1860s, with brutal fighting throughout the North Island. And while fighting had largely finished by the end of that decade, peace wasn't officially declared until 1881.
Meanwhile, the number of Pakeha in NZ continued to grow. Between 1839 and 1843, the New Zealand Company, founded by Edward Gibbon Wakefield, had dispatched 19,000 people to planned settlements in Wellington, Wanganui, Nelson and New Plymouth. This number swelled from 60,000 to 470,000 between 1860 and 1881, with settlement increasing in the South Island (mostly as a result of the Gold Rush that began around Queenstown in the 1860s). And New Zealand's indigenous people were more and more marginalised.

Lost in Translation?
The Waitangi Treaty was drawn up in English and Maori, an alleged gesture of goodwill that has since become the focus of much dispute. A translation of both documents reveals inconsistencies and a change in emphasis between each version. Dissatisfaction over the treaty wasn't really addressed until the Waitangi Tribunal was established in 1975.

Establishing a New Society

Through the later decades of the 19th century and the first years of the 20th, New Zealand rapidly established itself as an ideal and egalitarian society – for the new settlers at least. Treasurer Julius Vogel set into motion a programme of public works, unifying NZ's series of provinces with improved roads and communication. Kiwis' much vaunted love of sheep began early, with wool the main export from these early years. It was joined in 1882 by meat exports, as the first shipment of refrigerated lamb was sent to Britain, establishing a reliable export market that was the mainstay of the economy for many decades. But momentous as these changes undoubtedly were, the best was yet to come.
From its unsettled beginnings, New Zealand might have seemed an unlikely place to lead radical social change, but lead it did. In 1890, the Liberal Pact (a left-wing political party made up of a Labour and Liberal alliance), led by John Ballance, began a series of sweeping reforms. Under Minister of Labour William Pember Reeves, workers' conditions and pay were radically improved, a trend that continued under new party leader Richard Seddon, who introduced graduated income tax, full female suffrage (NZ was the first country in the world to give women the vote) in 1893, and established an old-age pension in 1898.
Meanwhile, the Maori began to be re-establish themselves within society, with members serving in the New Zealand government. Their numbers steadily began to rise as resistance to European diseases grew.
By the time New Zealand was called upon to fight alongside the British in the first world war, it was a Dominion rather than a self-governing colony and locally born Pakeha outstripped the immigrant population. Nevertheless, 100,000 soldiers, including a significant number of Maori servicemen, signed up to fight in the trenches, 17,000 of whom failed to make it home. The worst loss of life was in Gallipoli, which is commemorated as Anzac Day right across New Zealand and Australia (see p.15).
Throughout the 1920s, NZ continued to grow, although the fallout of the Great Depression in the USA caused export income to drop and national debt to rocket, bringing Aotearoa's liberal social policies up short. Pensions and healthcare budgets were slashed, while unemployment soared, sparking a wave of poverty and deprivation the country hadn't seen before or since. Hopes that a new decade would turn things around were dashed when an earthquake hit the Hawke's Bay region on the morning of 3 February 1931, killing hundreds and destroying the town of Napier, a physical destruction to match the decimated NZ psyche. However, just as the people of Napier used the earthquake as a chance to rebuild and reinvent itself from scratch, so did the Labour Party. Its ascension to power in 1935 ushered in a new national mood. The birth of the world's first welfare state promised renewed prosperity to all, including, for the first real time, the Maori, who were recognised in welfare, farming and communal land ownership reforms.

New Allegiances

World war two's impact on the Pacific was felt with the bombing of Pearl Harbour in 1941, an act that brought New Zealand into military allegiance with the USA for the first time. It began a process of political repositioning that was cemented with the signing of the ANZUS alliance (a policy of mutual defence between New Zealand, Australia and the US), in 1951.

Back home, political changes led to huge social upheaval. The National Party sparked a wave of union protest following the establishment of its conservative government in 1949, culminating in 1951's Waterfront Lockout, the most widespread industrial dispute in the country's history. More than 20,000 workers went on strike in support of the dockers in a dispute that lasted 151 days, and eventually broke much of the power of New Zealand's mighty unions.

None of which stopped a wave of British immigrants moving to New Zealand. In the years between 1947 and 1975, 77,000 so-called '10 pound Poms' (named after the average cost of their passage) made their way to New Zealand to seek work and escape the restrictions of post-war rationing.

At the same time, promises of employment were luring Maori citizens into the cities like never before. But the struggle to find work equal to that of their Pakeha contemporaries created anger and disillusionment. Disparity and discrimination led to a rise in Maori gang culture and disproportionate representation in prison.

The Maori community became freshly politicised, staging occupations of traditional land at Raglan and Auckland's Bastion Point. In 1975, the Waitangi Tribunal was established to investigate Maori claims to land.

Race relations took on an international hue in the 1970s too, not only with the first major wave of immigration from Polynesia (namely Tonga, Samoa and the Cook Islands), but with the 1976 rugby tour of apartheid South Africa, where the All Blacks played against racially selected teams. African nations demonstrated their disapproval by boycotting the Montreal Olympics. The New Zealand government responded by signing the 1977 anti-apartheid Gleneagles Agreement, but falling foul of the public mood again by sanctioning the 1981 Springbok tour to New Zealand.

New Zealand's international reputation for social politics was more assured but was tested in 1985. The Rainbow Warrior, an anti-nuclear protest ship operated by Greenpeace, was bombed while docked in Auckland's Waitemata Harbour. The year before, Labour Prime Minister David Lange had refused US ships entry into NZ harbours unless they declared themselves nuclear-free. This stance had toppled the longstanding ANZUS defence pact and a year after the bombing, New Zealand was officially declared a nuclear-free Zone.

New Zealand Today

New Zealand has long prided itself on its biculturalism, but in truth that's a claim that has only recently been made with any real conviction. Maori is once again being taught in classrooms and Maoritanga (Maori culture and lifestyle) is widely celebrated. The pride felt in the country's mixed heritage might not be universally greeted, but is, perhaps for the first time in the country's short history, respectfully acknowledged on both sides.

The past decade or so has thrown up another dramatic shift in New Zealand's culture. Since the 90s, government policy has encouraged an influx of new immigrants, mostly from Asia, who now collectively make up 10% of the population.

There remains, overall, a willingness to welcome new people and new ideas. The mood is upbeat. New Zealand is finally becoming what it always wanted to be: a truly international country.

New Zealand Timeline

1200-1300AD	Polynesians first arrive in NZ
C1350	The 'Great Fleet' arrives from (the mythical land of) Hawaiiki
1642	Abel Tasman records location of New Zealand while navigating the southern oceans on behalf of the Dutch East India Company, but doesn't land
1769	James Cook lands and makes first contact with Maori
1814	Samuel Marsden, the first Christian missionary, arrives
1833	James Busby installed at Waitangi as British Resident
1835	The United Tribes of New Zealand proclaimed as independent
1840	Signing of the Treaty of Waitangi. Auckland established as capital city.
1852	The New Zealand Constitution Act – New Zealand becomes a self-governing colony
1860-65	New Zealand Land Wars fought between Maori and Pakeha
1860s	Gold rush fever hits the South Island
1865	Wellington takes over from Auckland as capital
1867	Maori men given right to vote
1893	New Zealand becomes the first country to give women the vote
1914-18	New Zealand enters world war one and suffers huge troops losses at Gallipoli
1920s	New Zealand suffers the fallout of the Great Depression
1931	New Zealand's worst-ever earthquake hits Napier, killing 256 people
1935	The world's first welfare state is established under the Labour government
1941	New Zealand joins fight in the Pacific during World War Two
1947	Full independence from Great Britain granted
1951	The ANZUS military alignment is established with Australia and the USA
1953	In a world first, New Zealand mountaineer Sir Edmund Hillary and Tenzing Norgay reach the summit of Mount Everest, the world's highest mountain
1959	Auckland's Harbour Bridge opens on 30 May connecting the city to its North Shore
1960s	First wave of immigration into New Zealand from the Pacific Islands
1974	Christchurch hosts the Commonwealth Games
1975	The Waitangi Tribunal established to investigate Maori claims for land
1975	Conservative leader Robert Muldoon adopts his 'think big' policies with mixed results
1977	NZ signs the Gleneagles Agreement; all sporting ties with Apartheid South Africa cut
1979	Spiralling international oil prices force the advent of car-less days; Britain's entry into the European Common Market curtails New Zealand traditional export routes
1981	South Africa's Springbok rugby tour of New Zealand sparks huge protests
1983	Australia and New Zealand sign treaty for Closer Economic Relations
1985	David Lange's Labour government's bans US nuclear warships from NZ harbours
1985	Rainbow Warrior bombed by French secret service while docked in Auckland harbour
1986-87	NZ resigns from the Anzus pact; the country declares itself a nuclear-free zone
1990-96	Privatisation and the dismantling of the welfare state begins
1996	Political infrastructure changed; first election under MMP system takes place
1997	Jenny Shipley becomes New Zealand's first female Prime Minister
1999	Helen Clark elected for first term as Prime Minister
2001	New Zealand wins yachting's America's Cup; Viaduct Harbour in Auckland transformed
2001	*The Lord of the Rings* is released, turning New Zealand into a tourism hotspot
2002	Second term for Helen Clark
2003	Maori grievances over foreshore and seabed take the political spotlight. New Zealand's population reaches 4m, following a government-backed immigration drive
2004	NZ supreme court established, taking criminal appeals away from the UK's Privy Council
2004	Maori party wins four out of seven possible parliamentary seats in general election
2005	Helen Clark narrowly wins a third term as Prime Minister
2006	New Zealand sends troops to East Timor to calm violence in the fledgling state

New Zealand Overview

New Zealand is currently in rude economic health – almost too rude, according to some. The New Zealand Dollar is strong against other major international currencies, which some economists fear may be its undoing if local goods become too expensive for foreign markets to purchase. This is because New Zealand is, in general, a small, but prosperous free-market economy that relies heavily on trade with overseas economies, namely Australia, the US and Japan. Annual GDP was $160 billion in 2006.

Trade & Industry

Since the mid 80s, the government has made a conscious effort to build a buoyant, independent economy. In the process, import regulations have loosened, exchange rates have been freely floated, and controls on interest rates, prices and wages have been eliminated. The former long-standing government subsidies in areas such as agriculture have been removed, which might explain why New Zealand's famous resident population of sheep has dropped by a third from its pre 80s peak of around 60 million to around 40 million today.

Even so, New Zealand's economy is still best known for its agricultural exports, including meat, fish and dairy products, fruit and vegetables and, of course, wool. Other valuable export assets include substantial reserves of natural gas. The country boasts extensive marine resources – over 15 times its landmass at an area covering more than 4m sq km – making it the world's seventh largest area for fishing rights.

Manufacturing in New Zealand, on the other hand, is at a post-war low. In recent years, tourism has boomed; a change in fortunes that's called the *The Lord of the Rings* effect for good reason (p.10).

Trade agreements have also boosted New Zealand's economy over the years, namely Closer Economic Relations (CER), a partnership forged with Australia that allows free trade in most goods and services between the two countries. More than 18% of all of New Zealand's exports now travel across the Tasman Sea, up from 14% in 1983. Elsewhere, the P4 agreement, offering free trade with Singapore, was extended to Chile and Brunei in 2005.

Leading Industries & Average Salaries

Information Technology Services	$55,565
Law Firm/Law Office	$41,623
Healthcare	$49,611
Manufacturing and Distribution	$42,340
Software Development	$54,572
Education College/University	$49,611
Education	$46,486

Growth

It has been a somewhat uncertain road for New Zealand to economic independence. As a small country, even one with a bountiful supply of indigenous goods and resources, it has often fallen prey to international economic events.

The 70s and early 80s were a difficult time, as spiralling international oil prices, magnified by the revolution in Iran, squeezed availability, while Britain's entry into the ECM cut NZ's traditional export markets drastically.

The result led to a series of economic reforms, beginning with Robert Muldoon's Think Big policy in 1981, a misguided attempt to make NZ self-sufficient by drawing on and utilising its abundant natural gases for energy supplies.

It was followed by a wave of privatisation and deregulation by David Lange's Labour government that saw the further erosion of New Zealand's much-loved social welfare policies. By the time Jim Bolger's National Party took power in 1990, the economy had been hit hard by 1987's stock market crash. Still, Bolger's free-market reforms continued unabated, cutting employment rights and welfare programmes, further widening the gap between the rich and poor. Two successive years of drought in 1997 and 1998, and the financial crisis in Asia, contributed to a sharp decline in the country's fortunes, from which it began to recover in 2000. Good weather led to improved agrarian production, and, with the value of the dollar still low, demand for exports grew.

Gross Domestic Product

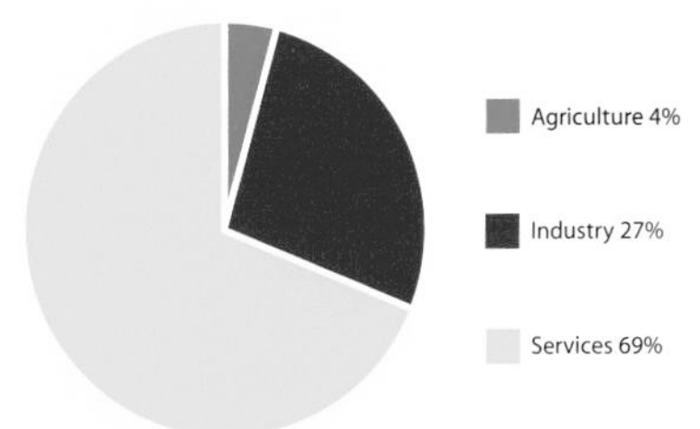

Largely, the country hasn't looked back since. The annual growth rate in 2006, for example was 2.4%, up from 1.8% the year before. However, high interest rates and the rising value of the New Zealand dollar are making the country's economists nervous. Interest rates have soared to some of the highest in the developed world (Westpac Bank's floating base rate in June 2007 stood at 10.05%) in a so-far futile attempt to curb housing prices and inflation. Current plans are for a 'soft' landing but it remains to be seen whether predictions of a crash will prove to be more accurate. New Zealand's recent policy of inviting overseas investment largely without discrimination has made it an oasis for foreign investors, but has left many of its citizens feeling nervous. The backlash, however, has begun. 'Kiwi owned and operated' is becoming a big selling point in local business – not a statement of xenophobia, but rather a reflection of the general population's increasing concern at foreign takeovers.

Income & Employment

According to the latest census results, the average income in New Zealand is NZ$40,000. When compared to the UK, where the average income is £24,500 (equivalent to NZ$66,000), this might seem low. But living costs in New Zealand remain relatively low and the country offers a generally good standard of living to its citizens (per capita GDP is $26,000 compared with $32,900 in Australia and $43,500 in the US), although the shifting economic culture has meant the unofficial gap between the rich and poor has continued to grow (18% of New Zealanders earn more than NZ$50,000 per annum, for example, while as many as 43% earn less than $20,000). Even so, in 2006 New Zealand was ranked 20th on the UN Human Development Index of the most liveable countries, two places behind the United Kingdom and one ahead of Germany. The criteria for calculating rankings are on factors including life expectancy, educational attainment, and income.

Unemployment peaked in 1992, at 10.4%, following the selling of government-owned enterprises in the late 1980s and early 1990s, but have been steadily declining since 1998. In 2005, just 3.7% (79,000 people) of the population was unemployed. Initiatives such as Skill NZ (www.skillnz.org.nz), which aims to develop employees' skills in the workplace, reflect the government's commitment to reduce unemployment further. Nearly 30,000 organisations and businesses have signed up to Skill NZ, with 160,000 workers taking part in industry training each year.

Tourism

The number of overseas visitors to New Zealand has been climbing steadily for the past four decades, but in recent years the rise has been dramatic. In 2006, more than 2.3m people visited the country – and they just keep on coming. March 2007, for example, saw a 5.4% increase in visitor numbers over the same period in 2005.

New Zealand attracts people of all ages and across every budget. The sheer range of activities available and the variety of the landscape means that this is a country as appealing to skiers as it is to those seeking to holiday by the beach.

According to the government's Tourism Satellite Account of 2005, tourism contributes 9% of New Zealand's GDP (both directly and indirectly) and is one of its largest export industries. All of which has a major impact on the country's citizens. Tourism supports one in 10 jobs in New Zealand, with more than 105,000 full-time positions provided directly through tourism, and another 71,000 indirectly.

Auckland CBD

Large chunks of the country have been designated Unesco World Heritage Sites, including Te Wahipounamu (south-west New Zealand), which includes Aoraki and Fiordland National Parks, and on the North Island, the glacial and volcanic landscapes of Tongariro National Park (p.230). In 2005, New Zealand was voted third best long-haul destination in the UK's *Guardian/Observer* Travel Awards. A year later and it had jumped two places to claim top spot, with judges declaring its blend of scenery, food and wine a winning formula.

The falling costs of long-haul air travel and the lure of Aoteroa's magnificent scenery have undoubtedly played a part, but one event has done more to promote New Zealand than any other.

The Lord of the Rings

When Kiwi filmmaker Peter Jackson got the green light to shoot *The Lord of the Rings* trilogy in his home country, the nation rejoiced. Not only because it gave virtually every underused actor and film technician the opportunity to work, but also because it would shine a spotlight on this quiet corner of the globe and finally show the rest of the world what Kiwis have known all along – that New Zealand is, mile for mile, one of the most varied and fascinating landscapes on earth.

Even so, the impact of the films came as a surprise. Foreign tourists started to pour into the country in their thousands, many wanting to follow in the footsteps of their hobbit heroes with visits to locations such as Tongariro National Park in the central North Island (which offered the spectacular backdrop to Mount Doom and Mordor) and the Kawarau River in Queenstown (p.280), where the Pillars of the Kings were shot near the bungee bridge.

More than 150 locations were used and sometimes it feels like every single one of them has been exploited for its film tie-in tourist potential. Jens Hansen jewellers in Nelson, for example, has become a place of pilgrimage to Ring devotees for having forged – sorry, designed – the 'one ring to rule them all'. Canny tour operators were quick to exploit this new gap in the market and there are now dozens of companies offering *The Lord of the Rings* packages. For a list of locations in New Zealand, visit www.newzealand.com/travel/homeofmiddleearth/

Tourism Developments

New Zealand is proud of its continuous efforts to grow, change and adapt. Plans are in place across both islands to improve what is already available to tourists, as well as to encourage new developments.

Eden Park

Reimers Av
Kingsland
Auckland
Map p.490 C4 1

www.edenpark.co.nz

In 2011, New Zealand will host the Rugby World Cup, and Auckland's most famous sports ground, Eden Park, is in line for a $385m makeover before hosting the final. The

tournament will be a huge boost to tourism, and is already eagerly anticipated among locals. See www.nzrugbyworldcupinfo.com for more information.
Completion 2011

Cnr Wellesley St & Lorne St
Auckland
Map p.488 A3 2

Auckland Art Gallery

www.aucklandartgallery.govt.nz/gallery2009

Auckland Art Gallery is preparing to undergo a $90m redevelopment that will result in 50% more exhibition space and better access for visitors. The historic 19th century building itself is being made earthquake-proof.
Completion 2009

Auckland
Map p.484 C7

Auckland International Airport

www.auckland-airport.co.nz

There are plans to build a second Auckland International Airport at Whenuapai Air Base. Passenger numbers are growing at the existing airport by 4% a year and it's hoped that a second airport will help ease traffic flow, both on the air and on the ground.
Completion Not known

12 Hickory Av
Auckland
Map p.484 A5

Henderson Valley Studios

www.hendersonvalleystudios.com

Waitakere City Council is developing a purpose-built soundstage (due to be the largest in New Zealand) on the site of existing Henderson Valley Studios in a bid to become the 'Hollywood of the South Pacific'.
Completion Late 2007

Hamilton
North Island Map G8

World Rally Championships

www.rallynz.org.nz

In 2006, the World Rally Championships (WRC) were extended to New Zealand as part of a three-year deal. The new leg, which takes place in Hamilton, is estimated to be worth around $12m in revenue. The New Zealand leg of the WRC is one of 16 rounds, 11 of which are held in Europe with the rest in Mexico, Argentina, Japan and Australia.

Wellington
Map p.498 E6

Weta Workshop

www.wetaworkshop.co.nz

Wellington-based Weta Workshop, the team behind the special effects in *The Lord of the Rings* is working with The Dinosaurs Aotearoa Museums Trust to develop the models for a $30m dinosaur park and museum at an, as yet, undisclosed location on the Coromandel Peninsula.
Completion Not known

Rutherford St
Nelson
South Island Map M3

Nelson Theatre Royal

Nelson Theatre Royal, built in 1878 out of native timber and corrugated iron, and the oldest functioning wooden theatre in Australasia, is undergoing a $4.5m renovation.
Completion August 2008

Christchurch
Map p.508 A3

Christchurch Airport

www.airportcity.co.nz

A $200m development is underway to upgrade Christchurch Airport, where work on the carpark has already finished. The next stage is the building of a dedicated precinct containing bars, restaurants and cafes, along with a large retail development.
Completion 2009

International Relations

As a small, fairly politically neutral nation, New Zealand has done little to cause offence on the world stage, and as such its citizens are pretty much welcomed everywhere. It's a state of affairs which is mirrored by the representation of most major foreign embassies and consulates in New Zealand (p.30).

There have been one or two exceptions to this rule. New Zealand's first real act of independent international relations was the forging of the Anzus Treaty in 1951.

The alliance between New Zealand, Australia and the USA was a commitment to defend each other against attack and became the cornerstone of the country's international relations. That was, until New Zealand banned nuclear-powered or armed ships from using its ports in the mid 80s, leading to a stand-off with the US that has strained relations ever since. The current war in Iraq has not helped matters; the New Zealand government remains defiantly opposed to the actions of its powerful one-time ally.

The country's only other major international contretemps occured when France started testing nuclear devices in French Polynesia, in 1966. There were immediate public protests in New Zealand, which grew over the next two decades and culminated in Greenpeace forming a protest flotilla in 1985.

The night before the boats were due to sail, the Greenpeace flagship, Rainbow Warrior, was hit by two bombs while moored in Auckland's Waitemata Harbour, killing onboard photographer Fernando Pereira. A couple posing as tourists were revealed to be members of the French secret service, and the act was declared by New Zealand as one of 'state-backed international terrorism'. Despite international outcry, the French spies, Dominique Prieur and Alain Mafart, were imprisoned on a French Pacific island, where they served only three years. In 1995, French president Jacques Chirac announced that his country would be testing in the South Pacific again. Following six weeks of testing, the project was halted. French and New Zealand foreign ministers only met for the first time since the Greenpeace bombing in 1998.

Helen Clark

Helen Clark has been nothing if not a controversial leader. She has been praised by many for leading New Zealand through a sustained period of economic growth, and her social reform agenda, such as steady increases of the minimum wage and child tax credits, remain popular, but detractors claim her to be too single-minded over policy (including, of course, the foreshore and seabed debate, p.13).

Government & Politics

New Zealand operates a parliamentary representative democratic monarchy, as it has done since becoming self-governing from Britain in 1852. Queen Elizabeth II remains as head of state, but the government is lead by a Prime Minister, who oversees a parliament drawn from elected representatives. The current PM and leader of the Labour Party is Helen Clark. Parliament comprises 120 democratically elected members (MPs), who can serve up to three years.

The Queen's representative in New Zealand is the Governor General (currently Anand Satyanand), who is appointed by the monarch on the advice of the Prime Minister and who in turn overseas the Executive Council, a formal committee made up of all ministers of the Crown (all are MPs and most are cabinet members).

Unlike its British counterpart, New Zealand's parliament has only one chamber, the House of Representatives. There are eight parties in the current parliament: ACT New Zealand, Green Party, Labour Party, Maori Party, National Party, NZ First, Progressive, and United Future. Elections take place every three years, with the next due in November 2008. While the system of government has broadly remained the same, New Zealand's voting system underwent a radical overhaul in 1993. The traditional first-past-the-post, Westminster-style voting process, which had been in place since 1852, was replaced by Mixed Member Proportional representation (MMP).

The biggest recent development in New Zealand politics has been the establishment of the Maori Party, in 2004. After a long-running dispute over whether or not the Maori have a legitimate claim to ownership of New Zealand's foreshore and seabed (the fishing and development rights for which are potentially huge), Labour Party member

Tariana Turia and Maori academic Pita Sharples formed the party in a bid to unite all Maori into a single political group. In the general election of 2005, the Maori Party contested all seven of the Maori seats reserved in parliament, winning four.

MMP

Traditionally two main groups, the centre-left Labour Party and the National Party at centre-right, have dominated New Zealand politics. It was a growing disillusionment at this stagnation, particularly during the economic slump of the early 90s, which led to a change in the country's voting system.

The idea with proportional representation is that smaller parties are given the opportunity for greater influence in parliament, as has been the case with the current coalition government. While Labour-led, it is made up of a mixed bag of support from the centrist New Zealand First and United Future parties and the only elected representative of the left-leaning Progressive Party.

Even if the jury is out as to whether or not MMP has been a success, the results have certainly been colourful. The first MMP election brought more Maori MPs into parliament than ever before (Maori voters can choose to vote for a countrywide Maori seat or for a combination of local government and party candidates within the general system), and subsequent elections have seen New Zealand vote for the world's first transgender MP, Georgina Beyer (Labour), and Nandor Tanczos, New Zealand's first Rastafarian MP, representing the environment-focused Green Party.

Foreshore & Seabed Debate

In 1975, a permanent commission of enquiry was established following the passing of the Treaty of Waitangi Act. Its role was to help investigate Maori claims of breaches by the Crown on any part of the Treaty, particularly regarding land rights.

The current debate began in 2003, following a ruling by the Court of Appeal that Maori could seek 'customary title' over some parts of the country's foreshore and seabed. Essentially, the ruling only opened up the possibility of making a claim and no land rights were appointed as such.

Prime Minister Helen Clark announced a plan in which the government would legislate to ensure public ownership of the foreshore and seabed. Her detractors claimed this was too favourable to Maori, who, according to Clark's proposals, would be heavily consulted over matters of debate. Many New Zealanders claimed that too many concessions were being given to the Maori, who in turn claimed this to be yet another example of Pakeha domination. At the peak of the debate, the opposing National Party pushed forward in the polls for the first time in 18 months.

The Waitangi Tribunal held an urgent enquiry into the government's policy and was highly critical of its approach. Clark, however, was determined to press forward with the legislation, which angered not only political opponents but some within her own party. The foreshore and seabed bill was eventually established in late 2004. Not long after, it was criticised by the United Nations' Committee on the Elimination of Racial Discrimination, who stated that it contained 'discriminatory aspects'. It remains a significant issue in New Zealand's ongoing race relations debate. With the popularity of the Maori Party increasing, history may well reveal it to have been a turning point in the nation's politics.

Breaker Bay, Wellington

Population

According to the 2006 census, the total population of New Zealand was 4,027,947. This figure represented an 8% rise in five years. More than half of the population (53%) lives in four main urban areas: Auckland, Hamilton, Wellington and Christchurch.
Nearly three quarters (73%) of the population is resident in the North Island, with around a third in Auckland (more than 1.4 million) and 448,959 in the Wellington region (179,466 in Wellington City itself).
Nearly a quarter of people in New Zealand were born overseas. The concentration of those born overseas varies across the country, accounting for more than a third (37%) of the population in Auckland and only 1 person in 13 in Southland.
Even so, there has been a marginal decline in the average household size over the past 10 years (from 2.8 to 2.7 persons per household between 1996 and 2006), and an increase in the number of one-person households.
There is roughly the same ratio of men to women in New Zealand (48.8% and 51.2% respectively). The average life expectancy is 77.6 for men and 78.8 for women.

Population by Nationality

3,000,000
2,500,000
2,000,000
1,500,000
1,000,000
500,000
0
Australian
British
Chinese
Cook Island Maori
Dutch
Indian
Korean
Maori
NZ European
Samoan

Population by Principal Language

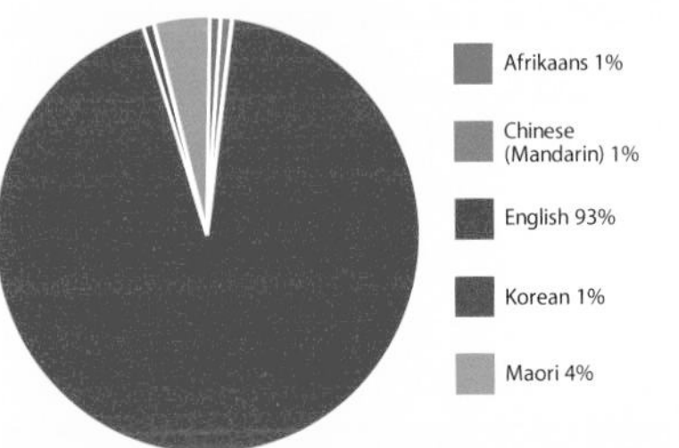

Education Levels

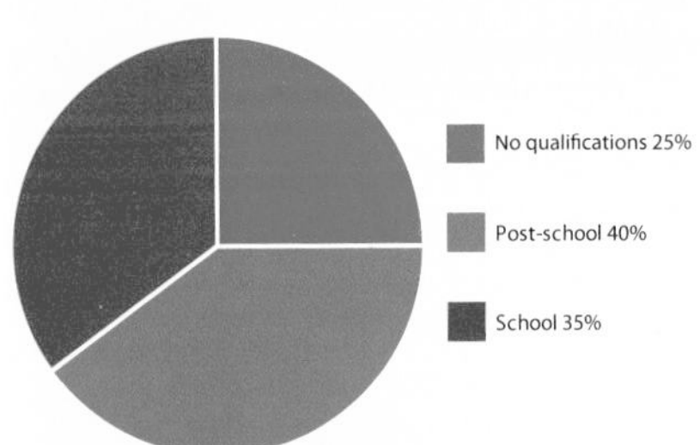

Source: Statistics New Zealand

Fern Favourite
Since 1998, when National Party Prime Minister Jenny Shipley backed a call for an alternative national flag featuring a silver fern on a black background, there have been intermittent rumblings about ditching the current design. A trust has been set up to encourage debate. See the arguments for yourself at www.nzflag.com.

National Flag

New Zealand's flag incorporates a Union Flag against a blue background and four stars that represent the Southern Cross (or Crux), the smallest constellation in the sky, and the most familiar in the southern hemisphere.
Its design is very similar to that of the Australian flag, which goes some way to explain why discussions to change the national flag have been ongoing for years. The presence of the Union Flag, a nod to New Zealand's colonial past, is another sticking point for some Kiwis keen to separate their country's identity from that iof the UK.
The flag is flown on important national occasions such as Anzac Day, and at Waitangi, where the treaty of the same name was signed. Alternatively, a red ensign of the official blue version is also flown during Maori events and on areas of Maori land. This too has a substitute in the form of a 1990 design, The Tino Rangatiratanga flag, which features a stylised white koru (a curl that represents the unfolding of new life) against a red and black background.

Time Zones

Adelaide	-2.5
Amman	-10
Athens	-10
Bangkok	-5
Beijing	-4
Beirut	-10
Brisbane	-2
Canberra	-2
Colombo	-6.5
Damascus	-10
Denver	-19
Dubai	-8
Dublin	-11
Hobart	-2
Hong Kong	-4
Johannesburg	-10
Karachi	-7
London	-10
Los Angeles	-20
Melbourne	-2
Moscow	-8
Mumbai	-6.5
Munich	-11
New York	-17
Paris	-11
Perth	-4
Prague	-11
Rome	-11
Singapore	-4
Sydney	-2
Tokyo	-3
Toronto	-17

Local Time

New Zealand's time zone is equal to UCT (formerly GMT) plus 12 hours. During summer months, the country is subject to daylight saving, so the clocks go forward one hour between the first Sunday in October and the third Sunday in March.

Social & Business Hours

While far from work-shy (they work an average 38 hour week), New Zealanders definitely work to live rather than the other way around.

Standard business hours tend to be Monday to Friday 09:00 to 17:00 (the same as government office hours), with an hour's break for lunch, usually between 12:00 and 14:00. Likewise, banking hours are weekdays only, from 09:30 to 16:30.

Retail hours are longer, particularly in the larger cities and towns, where shops tend to be open until 18:00 on weekdays, with late-night shopping until 21:00 in cities and larger retail outlets, including suburban malls, on Fridays. Weekend shopping is now commonplace, with many places open from late morning until early evening on Saturdays and, increasingly, Sundays (except in smaller towns and centres).

Retailers can open year-round, with one or two notable exceptions, namely Easter (Good Friday and Easter Sunday in particular) and Christmas (December 25 and 26). On Anzac Day (April 25), shops, bars and restaurants can open after 13:00, although it's worth noting that they often impose a surcharge of between 10% and 15% on public holidays.

While most formal restaurants operate only at lunch (typically 11:30 to 15:00) and dinner (18:30 to 23:00), many cafes serve food throughout the day. Bars can trade seven days a week and apply for 24 hour liquor licences, but in truth opening hours tend to be dependent on trade, particularly in smaller towns and cities.

Even in Auckland and Wellington many restaurants and bars choose not to open on Mondays, traditionally one of the quietest days of the week. Fridays and Saturdays are the big nights, with bars and clubs staying open until midnight and 03:00 respectively.

Public Holidays

New Zealand's annual public holidays reflect the country's colonial and Christian history, as well as a smattering of deeply felt, indigenous celebrations, such as Waitangi and Anzac Days.

Statutory holidays are honoured at the same time, if not always on the same day, every year. Most holidays have been moved to the nearest Monday to make them part of a long weekend. The exception is Easter, which varies with the lunar cycle in keeping with the rest of the world, and Waitangi and Anzac days, which take place on February 6 and April 25 respectively. In general, statutory holidays are celebrated nationwide, although each region also enjoys a provincial anniversary day, which varies from place to place throughout the year. Schools, universities and other educational facilities have additional holidays, roughly divided into four terms of about 10 weeks each with two to three weeks holiday between.

Public Holidays

New Year's Day	1 January
Day After New Year's Day	2 January
Southland	17 January
Wellington	22 January
Auckland	29 January
Nelson	1 February
Waitangi Day	6 February
Otago	23 March
Taranaki	31 March
Anzac Day	25 April
Queen's Birthday	1st Monday in June
Labour Day	4th Monday in October
Hawke's Bay	1 November
Marlborough	1 November
Chatham Islands	30 November
Westland	1 December
Canterbury	16 December
Christmas Day	25 December
Boxing Day	26 December
Good Friday	Varies (21 March 2008)
Easter Monday	Varies (28 March 2008)

Climate

New Zealand has a climate as complex as its beautiful landscape. It ranges from subtropical in the central and upper North Island to downright chilly in the south, where the gentle shift of all four seasons is more readily observed.

The mild, variable climate makes New Zealand ideal to visit at any time of year. Even during the wettest, coldest months of winter (May to September), clear, bright days are common, particularly in the milder north. Heavy snowfalls in the central North Island and the Southern Alps from June to October present some of the freshest opportunities for skiing and snowboarding anywhere in the world.

Peak summer temperatures during January and February in Auckland, for example, are around 23°C. In the winter months (May to September) it will rarely drop below 8°C. And while Auckland may be regarded as damp among locals, its maximum average rainfall of 145mm in July has nothing on that of Hokitika (p.285) in the South Island, which, at a maximum of 292mm, receives almost double.

New Zealand has one of the highest UV ratings in the world, with radiation levels a feature of many weather forecasts. The use of sunscreen is an absolute necessity, even on the most overcast of days.

Considering the variety of New Zealand's climate, it's no surprise that some places are better known for their weather than anything else. Gisborne (p.236), at the north-eastern tip of the North Island, is, during the summer months, the first city in the world to greet the sun.

Wellington, at the south-western tip of the North Island, will always be the 'windy city' to Kiwis, thanks to its exposure to wild weather patterns from across the Tasman. It is also the only capital city in the world situated in the notorious Roaring Forties (the name given to latitudes between 40°S and 50°S) that are infamous for their unrelenting winds.

Nelson, at the top of the South Island, boasts New Zealand's best climate. The sun shines on the town for an average of 2,400 hours each year (p.253).

Botanical Gardens, Christchurch

Flora & Fauna

There's more to New Zealand's wildlife than the Kiwi – a small, nocturnal, flightless bird that has long been the national symbol. The entire land is rich with native trees and plants, from the mighty kauri to the native ferns found in its vast expanses of bushland. Indigenous animals include beautiful of birdlife, thorny, jurassic throwbacks such as the tuatara (a lizard-like reptile) and the truly disconcerting weta, a kind of cockroach crossed with a cricket. In Maori, its name means 'god of ugly things'.

Indigenous Fauna

With no snakes and only one poisonous spider (the rarely seen katipo, found in coastal regions), New Zealand is safe from a biogeographical perspective.

One of the most impressive of its indigenous animals and insects is the lizard-like tuatara, whose lineage stretches back to the Mesozoic era of more than 200 million years ago. Sadly, loss of habitat and predators such as rats mean that tuataras are now an endangered species. It is hoped, however, that their recent introduction into the Karori Wildlife Sanctuary (p.244) will boost their numbers.

Temperature & Humidity – Auckland

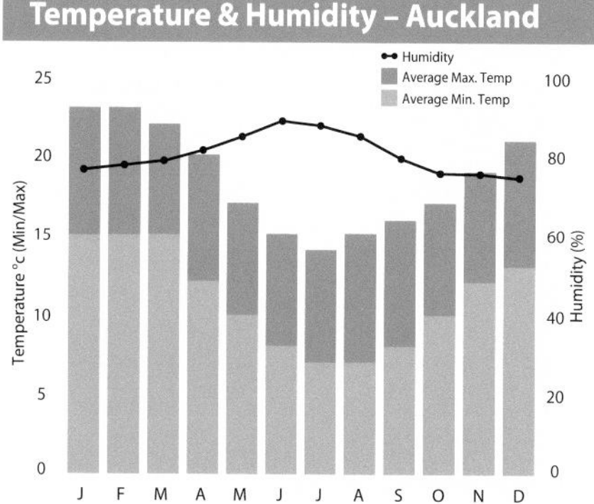

Temperature & Humidity – Christchurch

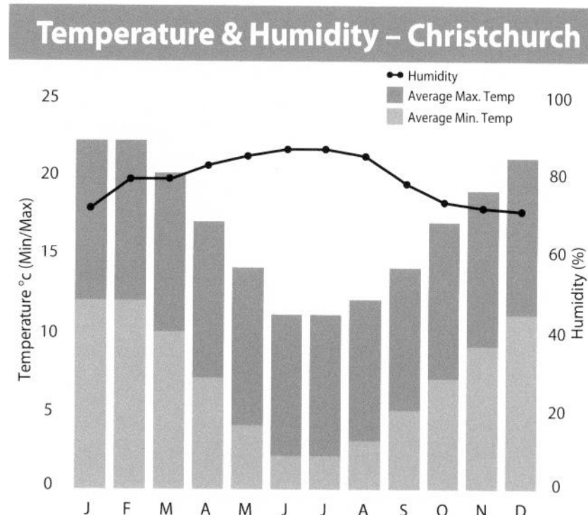

Temperature & Humidity – Wellington

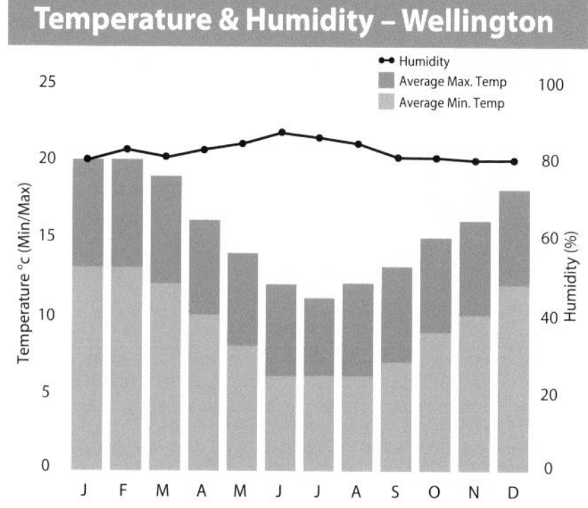

Rainfall – Auckland

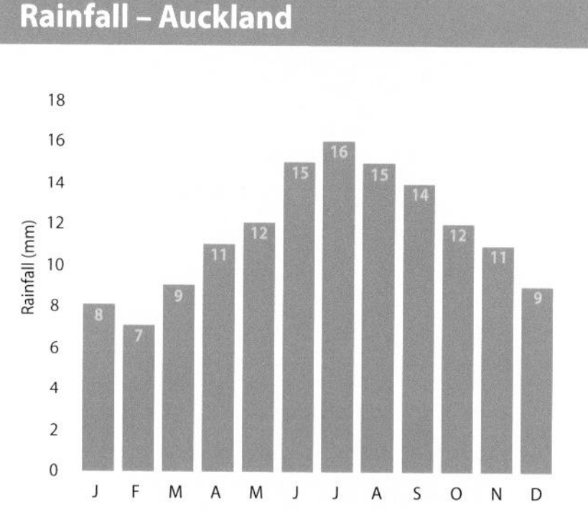

Rainfall – Wellington

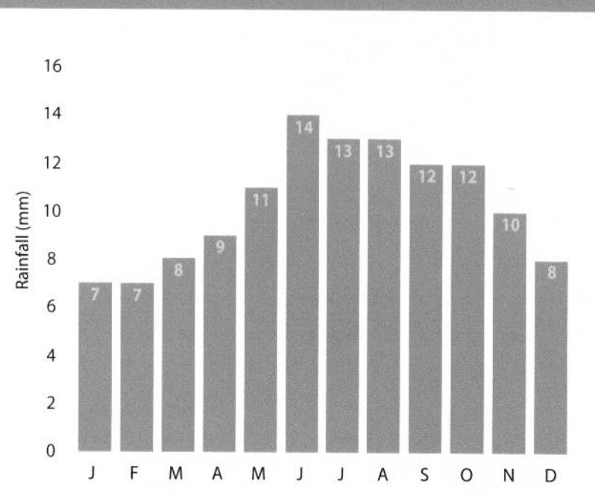

Radiation – Auckland

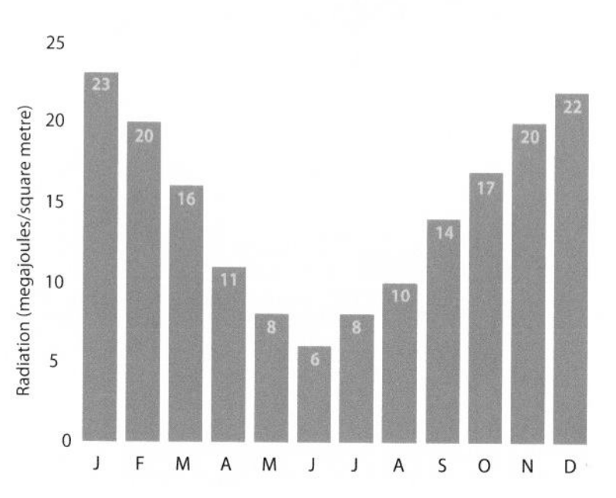

Source: Statistics New Zealand (www.stats.govt.nz)

Another prehistoric survivor found only in New Zealand is the weta (of which there are around 70 varieties). This stick-like insect, which looks like some sort of primordial grasshopper, is rumoured to have been the inspiration for the alien in Ridley Scott's movie of the same name – which says all you need to know about its attractiveness as a species.

Indigenous Flora

The kauri is probably New Zealand's most famous tree. Growing to a height of around 30m and notable for its broad trunk and long, straight branches, it was a favourite of both the Maori (who would carve out large canoes from a single trunk) and the European settlers who used the branches for everything from ship masts to housing.

The trees were last commercially harvested in the 1960s and are now a protected species, along with other native podocarps (members of the pine family) including rimu, miro and totara.

New Zealand's many native tree ferns include the ponga (or silver fern), which has been adopted by national sporting teams and as a motif on the 'alternative' New Zealand flag (p.14). Less well known outside the country, perhaps, but with a deep symbolism for every New Zealander is the beautiful pohutukawa tree. It comes ablaze with red flowers every December and has been adopted as the nation's Christmas tree.

Maori have a long tradition of using native plant life as natural medicines, a practice that has been adapted and is widely seen across New Zealand today. Manuka honey, for example, is praised for its medicinal properties, while the antiseptic properties of tea tree oil make it a medicine cabinet necessity.

Credere Non Possum

First introduced to New Zealand in the 1800s, possums were intended to help develop a fur industry, but soon became a threat to gardens and native trees. It wasn't until the 1930s that any attempt was made to curtail them. At more than 70 million, these pesky critters now outnumber New Zealand's sheep by almost two to one. In spite of increasingly drastic efforts to eradicate the population, possums are estimated to eat through 21,000 tonnes of vegetation every night, threatening the homes of indigenous birds and wildlife. Ironically, New Zealand possum fur has been granted 'ethical fur' status by the Worldwide Wildlife Fund and possum goods – from scarves and hats to woolly socks – have become a staple of the New Zealand souvenir industry.

Birds

New Zealand's native birds are a joy to behold. From the fantails that flit alongside walkers as they tramp through the bush to the kea – the world's only alpine parrot – you're never far from a beautiful, unique creature. The much-loved tui (voted Bird of the Year in 2005 by Forest & Bird) even has a beer named after it. Sadly, 22% of New Zealand's native birds are now globally threatened species, much of which is down to the introduction of species such as possums.

The authorities, however, are doing what they can to increase numbers by setting up wildlife sanctuaries such as Tiritiri Matangi (www.tiritirimatangi.org.nz) off the coast of Auckland, Kapiti Island (www.kapitimarinecharter.co.nz) near Wellington and the wonderful Ulva Island (www.ulva.co.nz), an open wildlife sanctuary two kilometres south of Oban on Stewart Island (p.294).

Of all the birds that you can see in New Zealand, the kiwi remains the most famous – and one of the hardest to spot. Rather shy, these flightless birds are nocturnal and while in theory the four main varieties (tokoeka, rowi, brown and little spotted kiwis) can all be seen in their natural environments, for a guaranteed sighting your best bet is the zoo. However, there are more than 30,000 tokoekas in the wild, many on Stewart Island and in Fiordland (p.290).

Marine Life

New Zealand's proximity to the Antarctic means that penguins, seals, sea lions and whales can all be seen off its coast, many all year round. The South Island is best for spotting marine life. Catch sight of yellow and blue-eyed penguins near Oamaru

(p.271), or visit Kaikoura (p.251) or the Catlins Coast (p.251) for a veritable menagerie of marine animals, including orcas, sperm and humpback whales (depending on the time of year). The Bay of Islands (p.208) in the North Island is your best bet for minke whales and dolphins.

If getting up close and personal with wildlife is more your style, you can swim with the tiny hector's dolphins at Akaroa (p.264) in Canterbury, or try seal swimming at Kaikoura. Keen divers, snorkellers and fishermen will enjoy the wealth of fish that New Zealand's warm waters attract, including game varieties such as marlin and barracuda and local species like the orange roughy. For anglers, the abundance of rainbow trout (found most famously in Lake Taupo) is reason alone to book a flight to New Zealand.

Environmental Issues

With its rich, natural habitat it should come as no surprise that New Zealand takes environmental conservation very seriously. To some degree this is an attempt to right some of the wrongs of the past, including the destruction of large sections of the country's forest cover. A parallel concern is that some of the introduced brush and scrub has, over time, overwhelmed parts of the native environment, strangling indigenous plant life and destroying food supplies for native animals and birds.

Saving Species From Extinction

New Zealand has one of the highest numbers of endangered species anywhere in the world. The introduction of predators, including the pesky possum (see p.18), along with ferrets, rabbits, rodents and wild dogs and cats, has decimated vast swathes of the bird population, including the beloved kiwi.

Over recent years, authorities have worked hard to save New Zealand's indigenous animals. Bird sanctuaries, such as those at Tiritiri Matangi, are seeing numbers steadily increase, while the purpose-built reserve for black stilts near Twizil is helping to restore levels of one of the world's rarest wading birds.

One side-effect of this belated rush to protect New Zealand's natural heritage is the hard line the country now takes with biosecurity. Visitors carrying anything from fresh fruit and vegetables to certain types of coral and wood can expect to pay hefty fines for breaching the rules.

Clearing the Air

Air pollution in Auckland, home to a full third of the nation's population, gets worse with every passing year. Its 1.5 million residents own half a million cars between them, which doesn't take into account the endless flow of tourists using the city's roads. The official government line is that New Zealand is committed to reducing overall emissions and meeting the environmental targets stipulated in the Kyoto agreement. However, plans to introduce emissions tests in 2006 were abandoned and a new date has not yet been agreed.

National Parks

In 1887, the Maori chiefs of the Tuwharetoa tribe offered their ancestral peaks of Tongariro, Ngauruhoe and Ruapehu to the people of New Zealand, creating the country's first National Park, Tongariro (p.230). Since then, a full 30% of New Zealand has been declared national park land.

There are 14 areas in total – the most recent being Rakiura National Park, which opened in 2005, and covers most of Stewart Island (p.294). In addition, there are hundreds of scenic reserves and forest parks, dedicated to preserving the local environment of specific regions. Most of this work is overseen or run in accordance with the Department of Conservation (DOC), a government body responsible for conserving New Zealand's forests, wetlands and volcanic areas. As well as protecting endangered species and encouraging breeding programmes, the DOC oversees pest control, which ensures increasing stocks of native species are allowed to flourish. The conservation of the land itself is also of primary importance with the reforestation of native trees, such as kauri and rimu, a key priority.

National Treasure
Tongariro National Park is the oldest national park in New Zealand. In 1993, it became the first property to be categorised as a cultural landscape on Unesco's World Heritage list, thanks to its deep significance for the Maori.

Conservation Bodies

The following organisations are committed to improving and preserving New Zealand's natural history and wildlife:

- Department of Conservation (www.doc.govt.nz) – The official government body entrusted with looking after New Zealand's native land and wildlife.
- National Parks (www.nationalparks.org.nz) – A privately funded, nationwide fundraising organisation endorsed by the DOC that's dedicated to, in its own words, linking 'the conservation estate with private individuals, businesses and visitors'.
- Forest and Bird Protection Society (www.forestandbird.org.nz) – One of the driving forces behind New Zealand's bid to save its endangered birdlife, this leading independent conservation organisation has been leading the charge to 'restore the dawn chorus,' since 1923.
- Save the Kiwi (www.savethekiwi.org.nz) – Does exactly what it says on the tin; a charity that aims to boost the numbers of New Zealand's favourite native bird.

Energy Concerns

New Zealand's location at the bottom of the globe means the country sometimes suffers with power supply problems. The nation first realised its vulnerability in the 1970s, when the spiraling cost of oil resulted in drivers being forced by law to stay off the roads for one day each week. Things have stabilised over the past few decades, but a rapidly expanding population and dwindling supplies of natural gas, combined with New Zealand's erratic weather patterns (unseasonable droughts affect hydro-dam levels, causing power black-outs), mean new solutions are required.

Around two thirds of New Zealand's electricity supply is provided by hydro and geothermal power. The latter is sourced mainly around the lower central North Island, where seven power stations are located near Taupo and Rotorua. Options beyond natural gas remain limited. Foreign oil is too pricey, nuclear goes against the country's policy, while the greenhouse gases released by the country's ample supplies of coal reserves would have an enormously detrimental environmental impact.

Wind farming has been mooted, particularly in the Wellington region, but it seems to involve amounts of planning and investment beyond the government's current capability.

Karori Wildlife Sanctuary, Wellington

Culture

New Zealand's relative youth makes it a vibrant and forward-thinking place. Its pioneer mentality and desire for fair play created an egalitarian society far more quickly than many of its western counterparts – it was the first country to give women the vote and the first to instigate a welfare state. And while these aspects of its political and social history have perhaps been overplayed at times (New Zealand's maternity laws provide rights for working mothers that lag way behind that of their UK contemporaries, for example), Kiwis retain the belief in the right for all members of society to be supported and looked after.

New Zealand's physical isolation from the rest of the world meant that for many years the country had a tendency to look outwards, first to Britain and then to the USA, and mimick cultural tips. With time, however, has come confidence.

The result is an optimistic outlook, with an admirable capacity for hard work and openness to new ideas. That's not to say that New Zealand doesn't remain a fairly conservative place. For all its bright ideas and young creative talent, it remains rather charmingly old-fashioned. This is still a country where the reopening of a local pie shop can make front-page news.

It's been a long and sometimes rocky road, and there's still a long way to go, but it's undeniable that Maori culture enriches New Zealand like never before, with a rebirth of interest in the language and history that is coming largely from a younger generation, keen to hold onto a heritage they feared might one day be lost.

It could be argued that part of New Zealand's willingness to embrace its bicultural heritage is related to recent population changes. An immigration policy aimed at bringing foreign money and skill into the country has seen the population swell by more than a third over the past decade or so. These new additions to the economy consist largely of Asian immigrants, predominantly from China, India and Korea (who number 147,570, 104,583 and 30,792 respectively, according to the 2006 census). New Zealanders have long been used to new arrivals from 'familiar' cultural territories such as Polynesia and Europe, less so immigrants from elsewhere.

It's fair to say that there is a degree of wariness among many Kiwis, particularly in the cities where most of the new arrivals have settled, about what this rapid population change will mean for the country in the long term.

Lord Abiding?

*New Zealand has always regarded itself as having a Christian culture (*God Defend New Zealand *is the national anthem, after all), and while ostensibly this is still true (the 2006 census saw more than 55% of the country affiliated with some form of Christianity), it's not really something that controls day-to-day life.*

Introducing the Maori

The customs and culture of New Zealand's indigenous people, the Maori, are known collectively as Maoritanga. It encompasses everything from rituals and behaviour on a marae (a settlement based around a traditional meeting house) to the myths and legends that help connect the Maori to the land.

The rise of biculturalism in New Zealand, in which both Maori and European heritage are recognised and celebrated, since the 1980s has seen a rebirth of interest in Maoritanga, from Pakeha and Maori, enriching the experience of both.

The Maori people are Polynesian in origin. They share a strong sense of family, which covers a large whanau, or extended family group. Few Maori now live on marae, but this sense of community that embraces not only immediate family but also cousins, nephews and nieces several times removed still exists.

Even so, perhaps the best place to see a concentration of Maori culture first-hand is at one of the many marae that are open to the public across New Zealand. Here visitors will not only experience the rituals of wero (a challenge to establish whether visitors are friendly) karanga (welcoming call) and powhiri (sung welcome), but can see and appreciate the intricacies of Maori culture and craftsmanship first-hand.

Here you'll find whare whakairo (carved houses) that were traditionally created from native timbers such as kauri and totara, from shells and sharp stones, and later pounamu (greenstone). Maori carving often tells a story, laid out in a distinctive cursive style, featuring organic swoops and spirals inspired by tree fronds and seashells. Motifs include the hei tiki, a highly stylised human form that represents the ancestor figure, alongside secondary figures such as the moko (lizard). Meeting house floors are still covered with whariki, patterned floor mats that traditionally feature natural dyes extracted from native trees.

The marae is also a good place to experience Maori dance, which is now taught in schools and playgrounds across the land. The most famous of these is, of course, the haka, a rhythmic chanting posture dance complete with foot stomping, thigh slapping and tongue poking, that's most famously performed by New Zealand's national rugby team, the All Blacks, before games. Other, less ferocious songs and dancing are just as widely performed, if not quite as well known. Poi dances (in which flax balls tied on the ends of long strings are swung in deft, rhythmic movements) are a staple of Maori concerts, while relatively modern (as in post-European) waita, or songs, such as the haunting Pokarekare Ana will have Kiwis everywhere – Maori and Pakeha – moved close to tears.

Myths & Legends

The New Zealand landscape is a source for many of the most beautiful Maori legends, including how the great Polynesian navigator Kupa (from the mythical land of Hawaiiki) discovered Aotearoa after a furious battle with a giant Octopus-like sea monster.

And long before that, the very story of creation involves the separation of the earth mother, Papatuanuku, and the sky father, Ranganui, by their children (later to become the Maori gods). The earth was created when the pair held each other close, allowing no light between them. When their children forced them apart, light was allowed in and the land and sea began to form.

The tales often involve taniwha (water spirits), such as Awarua who lived in Porirua Harbour many years ago. Awarua was friends with an albatross called Rereroa, who offered to help the water spirit learn to fly. According to Maori legend, the mishaps of her lessons shaped the land around Porirua Valley in the western North Island. The flat appearance of Mana Island, the legend states, was caused when Awarua crash-landed into it, while Onepoto Park was created in the huge gully that formed when the taniwha collided into nearby Whitireia.

Maori carving and street art

Language

Other options **Learning English** p.186, **Language Schools** p.320

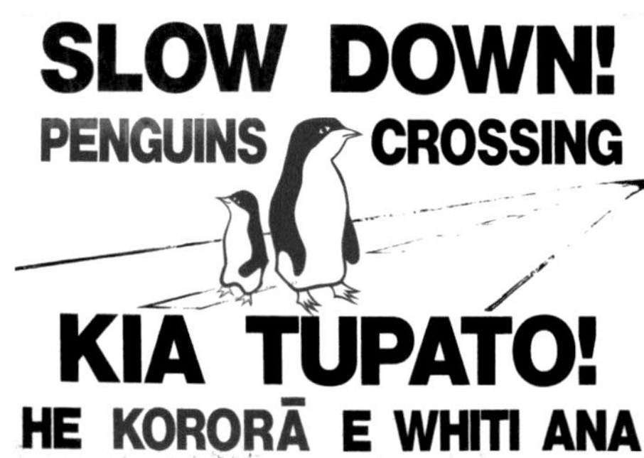

New Zealand's official languages

English and te reo Maori, the Maori language, are New Zealand's official languages. Most official documentation is bilingual and New Zealand citizens have the right to request to be addressed in Maori in a court of law. Place names, such as Aoraki/Mount Cook, which share Maori and English titles, tend to be written or referred to using both. The day-to-day language of the country is, however, resolutely English. For the most part it's all visitors will ever need, although an understanding of everyday Maori words, which now litter New Zealand English, will make life marginally easier – and more interesting. Pronunciation is easier than you might think; two rules worth remembering are that ng is pronounced as in 'ring' and wh sounds like 'wh' as in 'where' or 'f' as in 'off'. If you're keen to learn more, pick up a copy of *The Collins Maori Phrase Book*. Maori is spoken fluently by about 150,000 of the population (a third of whom are native speakers), but it's very much a living language and its popularity is growing. Pre-school children up to the age of four can learn Maori in kohanga reo (Maori language nests). The language is also taught as a subject in schools for children aged five to 16, or in dedicated education programmes at kura kaupapa Maori schools. Most universities and technical colleges across New Zealand offer Maori classes. Dedicated Maori television and various radio shows draw a small, but devoted following.

While English is the common tongue, at times it can feel like New Zealanders are talking a language known only to themselves. The following common Kiwi words and phrases will help you understand what they're saying.

Common Kiwi Terms

A holiday home, usually by the beach	Bach
A long way away/remote areas	Wop-wops
A pick-up truck or utility vehicle	Ute
Chewing gum	Chuddy/chuddy gum
Affectionate term for a friend	Cuz
Brilliant/fantastic	Choice
Cinema/movies	Flicks
Cool, fine	Bludger
Cool, fine	Sweet
Died (as in 'this car's carked it')	Carked it
Excellent (as in, good as gold)	Sweet as/good as
Flip-flops/thongs (footwear)	Jandals
Guided tour (often used disparagingly as taking the long way round)	Tiki tour
Have a go/try it	Give it a burl
Hoon	A lout
Insulated cool box for food	Chilly Bin
It'll work out fine	She'll be right
Kissing/snogging	Pashing
Large glass of beer	Handle
Local grocery shop/newsagents	Dairy
No way (a refusal to do something)	No fear
Overseas experience – one or two years spent abroad by twentysomething Kiwis	OE
Putting goods aside and paying for them in installments	Lay-by
Rugby	Footie
Sliding door onto a patio or garden	Ranch slider
Swimming costume	Togs
Takeaway food (fish and chips)	Greasies
To be exceptionally tired	Rooted
To buy a round of drinks or pick up the tab	Shout
To leave	Shoot through
To move (usually drive) quickly	Blat
To stare rudely	Gawk
To take a break (usually from work)	Smoko
To tell on someone/report them to the police	Dob in

Basic Maori

A Maori canoe	Waka
A Maori term to indicate status, authority or esteem	Mana
Ancient homeland of Maori people	Hawaiki
Assembly or gathering	Hui
Food	Kai
Goodbye (to the person going)	Haere ra
Goodbye (to the person staying)	E noho ra
Hello (to a group, formal, such as a greeting on a marae)	Tena koutou katoa
Hello (to one person, formal)	Tena koe
Hello or Hi (informal)	Kia ora
Indigenous inhabitants of New Zealand	Maori
Maori culture and custom	Maoritanga
Maori sub-tribe, a number of which make up an iwi	Hapu
Maori welcome by touching noses	Hongi
Meeting house	Marae
New Zealand greenstone	Pounamu
No	Kaore
Please	Koa
Sacred (usually refers to land)	Tapu
Songs	Waiata
Stomach – usually a well-covered one! (Term of endearment)	Puku
Sweet potato	Kumara
Thank you	Kia ora
The Maori language (te –j the; reo – language)	te reo Maori
Traditionally means an extended family, but has been adopted into Kiwi culture to mean the family	Whanau
Tribe	Iwi
Usually refers to European inhabitants of NZ, but really any non-Maori	Pakeha
Welcome (formal, such as on a marae)	Haere mai
Work or an activity	Mahi
Yes	Ae

Maori Geographical Terms	
Bay/harbour	Whanga
Beach/sand/soil	One
Big	Nui
Bird	Manu
Cave	Ana
Cloud	Ao
Earth/floor/flat	Papa
Hill	Puke
Home/village	Kainga
Island	Motu
Lake	Roto
Land	Whenua
Light	Tahu
Long/high	Roa
Man	Tane
Peak	Tara
River/channel	Awa
Road/path	Ara
Rock	Toka
Sea	Tai
Sea/lake	Moana
Sky/heavens	Rangi
Small	Iti
Stream	Manga
The	Te
Water	Wai

Maori Numbers	
One	Tahi
Two	Rua
Three	Toru
Four	Wha
Five	Rima
Six	Ono
Seven	Whitu
Eight	Waru
Nine	Iwa
Ten	Tekau

Race Relations

Whatever your colour or culture you're unlikely to experience overt discrimination in New Zealand. For the most part Kiwis are a welcoming bunch, curious rather than confrontational. That said, the country's recent influx of overseas immigrants – particularly in Auckland where 37% of the current population were born overseas – has led some to question the country's sense of identity in the long term.

It would also be wrong to say that there is no tension between Maori and Pakeha. It's no secret that Maori have for a long time been at an economic disadvantage to their Pakeha neighbours, resulting in everything from lower achievement in tertiary education to higher prison numbers. Disputes over land rights, of course, remain a contentious issue. In recent years, however, open debate at almost every level of society, along with a concerted embrace of biculturalism, has encouraged cooperation.

Religion

According to the 2006 census, New Zealand remains a predominantly Christian country, with 55% of the population aligning themselves with either Anglican, Catholic or Presbyterian faiths. This number is down 5% of the total from the 2001 census. In contrast, the number of citizens who classify themselves as Hindus, Muslims or Sikhs, while still small in real terms, has risen dramatically.

The major Christian dates, such as Christmas and Easter, are celebrated with statutory holidays. And more often than not, even the smallest town will operate some kind of church. On the whole, New Zealanders are pretty open-minded about religion, keeping an admirable 'to each his own' outlook. Faith-based lobby groups do exist and Christian political parties have surfaced in the past, but they have been largely unsuccessful in reinforcing their views. Schools tend to encourage inter-faith practices and customs in the classroom.

Places of Worship

Auckland			
Auckland Hebrew Congregation	108 Grey's Ave, (Centre)	09 373 2908	Jewish
Bhartiya Mandir Temple	252-254, Balmoral Rd, Balmoral	09 846 2677	Hindu
Buddhist Centre	381 Richmond Road, Grey Lynn	09 378 1120	Buddhist
Holy Trinity Cathedral	Parnell Rd (crn St Stephens Ave), Parnell	09 303 9500	Anglican
Ponsonby Mosque	17 Vermont Street	09 378 8200	Muslim
St Patrick's Cathedral	43 Wyndham Street (Centre)	09 303 4509	Catholic
Wellington			
Beth El Synagogue	80 Webb St (Centre)	04 384 5081	Jewish
Buddhist Centre	63 Cambridge Tce (Centre)	04 384 1334	Buddhist
Cathedral of St Paul	Crn of Molesworth and Hill St (Centre)	04 472 0286	Catholic
Sacred Heart Cathedral	21 Eccleston Hill, Thorndon	04 496 1700	Catholic
St Joseph	42 Ellice St, Mount Victoria	04 384 1975	Catholic
Wellington Mosque	7-11 Queens Drive, Kilbirnie	04 387 4226	Muslim
Christchurch			
Cathedral of the Blessed Sacrament	122 Barbadoes St (Centre)	03 377 5610	Catholic
Christ Church Cathedral	Cathedral Square (Centre)	03 366 0046	Anglican
Christchurch Jewish Synagogue	406 Durham St (Centre)	03 365 7412	Jewish
Diamond Way Buddhist Centre	22 England Stree, Linwood	03 381 3108	Buddhist
Hare Krishna Cultural Centre	83 Bealy Ave (Centre)	03 366 5174	Hindu
Masjid al Noor	101 Deans Ave, Riccarton	03 348 3930	Muslim

National Dress

Traditional Maori clothing is the closest New Zealand gets to a national dress. It consists of garments mostly made from harakeke, a flax that has been used in weaving by Maori since they first arrived in Aotearoa. Adornments such as greenstone and bone carvings, worn with threads as necklaces, are also popular. The most famous of these is the tiki, a highly valued symbol of fertility, which was passed down from generation to generation. Also popular is moku, an intricate form of facial tattooing. Grass skirts (pui pui) are traditionally coupled with intricately woven bodices and headbands, the designs of which vary from tribe to tribe. But the real star of Maori textiles is cloak weaving (whatu kakahu). This is done either with flax or feathers, which are still donned by tribal chiefs for ceremonies and formal occasions to this day. Pois are another familiar Maori accessory. These balls on ropes, now a feature of performances by kappa haka (Maori culture groups), were originally used by warriors to keep their wrists supple for battle.

Food & Drink

Other options **Eating Out** p.427

The fact that sheep have long outnumbered New Zealand's human population has meant lamb has always been a mainstay of the country's diet. Top quality meat is far from all New Zealand has to offer, however.

Fresh fruit and vegetables are plentiful, as is all manner of seafood and shellfish and, like the excellent dairy products, regularly prove good value for money both in supermarkets and restaurants.

As befits the country's reputation, health and well-being are prime concerns for many New Zealanders, so expect to find vitamin-packed extras such as spirulina (made from powdered seaweed) on many cafe menus.

What might stand out, however, is the nation's collective sweet tooth. Pineapple rings are routinely placed in hamburgers (to create, along with beetroot, the towering 'kiwiburger'), and honey is added to everything, from home-made fruit smoothies to some commercially brewed soft drinks. Even locally produced olive oil tends to be sweeter than its Mediterranean equivalent.

Despite a few local favourites (p.428) there is no defining New Zealand cuisine as such. What you'll be eating is fairly standard, if mighty flavoursome and well executed western fare. In recent years, New Zealand has been developing a sophisticated culinary palate. While the nation hasn't embraced fusion or pacific rim (a blend of Asian and western flavours) cooking with quite the gusto of Australia, expect to find influences from across Asia and the Mediterranean in even the most humble cafe cooking.

The rise in residents from China, Korea and India has also improved authentic offerings. Everything from the finest bento box to the tastiest biriyani can be found in larger urban centres. Maori cuisine, however, doesn't have a large presence in New Zealand. In fact, the closest you're likely to come to it is to attend a hangi, which are widely practiced within local communities (Maori and otherwise) as commercial tourist activities.

In brief, the hangi (pronounced 'hungi') is a method of slow cooking meat and vegetables by steaming them in an earth oven deep in the ground. Meanwhile meat, seafood and vegetables, including the ubiquitous kumara (or sweet potato) are wrapped in leaves and placed in baskets, which are lowered into a pit and covered with earth to seal in the steam and flavours. It usually takes several hours for the food to be properly cooked, at which point the oven's earthen seal is broken and the baskets of food raised from within. The result is a moist, delicious and slightly earthy-flavoured meal.

Dalmatian Drinks

West Auckland was the first area in New Zealand to produce wine, mostly thanks to the resident Croatian community. The vineyards around Kumeu and Henderson still feature names such as Babich and Brajkovich.

Wine

New Zealand's cool, moderate climate makes it one of the top wine-producing countries in the world. The white grape variety sauvignon blanc was the country's first real success story in the late 80s and 90s, and elite label Cloudy Bay, its first international wine superstar. Since then the industry has gone from strength to strength.

Reisling grapes and more recently those of gewurztraminer and viognier are the rising stars of the white wine industry. New Zealand reds, so long considered a poor relation, are now scooping up industry awards across the globe. New Zealand pinot noir, for example, now ranks among the best in the world, especially those from the Central Otago and Marlborough regions.

A visit to one of the country's outstanding wine-producing regions such as Marlborough (p.248) or Hawke's Bay (p.233) wouldn't be complete without a visit to a vineyard, many of which offer tastings and even B&B accommodation and fine dining.

Local Favourites

New Zealand has a wealth of native ingredients that are well worth seeking out. Here are some of the most popular:

Pipis and tuatua – small shellfish found along the seashore at low tide. Often coated in batter and served deep-fried in fritters at seaside fish and chip shops.

Paua – large (up to 15cm in length) shellfish which to eat requires a fairly strict routine involving a lot of pounding and discarding of much of the flesh. The paua is quite tough and rubbery and best known for its shell, a form of abalone with an iridescent sliver, blue and green hue, rather than its contents.

Pavlova – delicious meringue-based dessert filled with fresh fruit and cream. Kiwis and Aussies have been arguing for years about who produced it first.

Feijoa – an abundant, guava-flavoured green fruit which grows in back gardens everywhere. Its distinctive flavour and aroma is added to everything from vodka to ice cream, but the fruit itself is best.

L&P – Lemon and Paeora takes its name from the town in the Hauraki Plains where it was first made. A classic Kiwi soft drink.

Hokey Pokey icecream – the country's second most popular flavour (after vanilla) and rightly considered something of a national treasure. Small pieces of hard toffee are whipped into vanilla icecream, creating a rather dreamy caramel concoction.

Market offerings

In Emergency

In the case of an accident or serious, time-critical crime, dial 111 to be immediately connected to the emergency services of the Ambulance, Police or Fire departments. For calls made from GSM mobile phones, dial 112.

Access all Areas

Disability Resource Centre – General information and resources for the physically challenged. www.disabilityresource.org.nz
Disabled Persons Assembly – Information on tour operators and travel agencies that accommodate disabled travellers. www.dpa.org.nz
Enable New Zealand – Help and advice for all people with disabilities. www.enable.co.nz
Galaxy Autos – Auckland-based company offering a range of vehicles adapted for drivers with special needs. www.galaxyautos.co.nz

Medical Treatment

New Zealand's health service is excellent but it comes at a price. While all visitors can claim back the cost of some medical and hospital treatment following an accident via the accident compensation scheme, short-term visitors are advised to have full medical insurance to avoid a potentially hefty bill. Travellers from Australia and the UK, however, are covered by a reciprocal healthcare scheme that allows them the same access to publicly funded treatment, including free cover for most accident and emergency treatment at the country's public hospitals, including x-rays and tests. Note, however, that GPs operate as private practitioners and charge for the cost of a consultation, usually between $35 and $57. Prescription costs are extra (from $15). Visit the Ministry of Health website (www.moh.govt.nz) for more information.

Crime & Safety

Other options **In Emergency** p.29

The 'P' Problem

New Zealand is thought to have one of the highest methamphetamine addiction rates in the world. The biggest concern – it's dubbed an epidemic in the press – is with the drug known as 'P', or pure amphetamine. Its side-effects are often blamed for an increasing number of violent crimes.

New Zealand is relatively safe in terms of crime. Violent offences do, of course, occur, but according to the latest United Nations survey of crime trends there is less than one murder per 1,000 people. Far more common are petty crimes, such as bag snatching and muggings, especially in urban areas.

Recent years have seen a growing trend for personal theft, particularly from cars and holiday vehicles. Visitors and residents should take care of personal belongings at all times, keeping items secure whenever possible.

Women should avoid walking alone late at night in parts of the larger cities (Fort Street and Karangahape Road in Auckland, for example).

Emergency Numbers

Emergency Services	
Alcohol and Drug helpline	0800 787 797
Domestic Violence	05 0838 4357
Emergency	111
Gambling Helpline	0800 654 655
Kidsline	0800 543 754
Lifeline	0800 543 354
Mental Health (Auckland)	0800 800 717
(Wellington)	04 494 9169
Poisons Information Centre	0800 764 766
Rape Crisis (Auckland)	09 623 1700
(Wellington)	04 499 7532
(Christchurch)	03 364 8791
Samaritans	0800 726 666
Lost/Stolen Cards	
American Express	0800 722 333
Mastercard International	0800 449 1400
Visa International	0508 600 300
Support Services	
Gay/Lesbian Line	0800 802 437
Victim Support	0800 842 846

Traffic Accidents & Violations

New Zealand is a nation of car drivers, so it's no surprise that some of its highest crime statistics come from accidents on the road. Excessive speed is the biggest killer, particularly on rural roads. Drink-driving is another common cause of crashes and fatalities. Even so, the number of deaths on the country's roads has been

Embassies and Consulates

Argentinean Embassy	04 472 8330
Australian Consulate	09 921 8800
Australian High Commission	04 498 7103
Brazilian Consulate	09 521 2227
Brazilian Embassy	04 473 3516
British Consulate	03 374 3367
British Consulate-General	09 303 2973
British High Commission	04 924 2888
Canadian Consulate	09 309 3690
Canadian High Commission	04 473 9577
Chilean Embassy	04 471 6270
Chinese Embassy	04 472 1382
Fijian High Commission	04 473 5401
French Consulate (Auckland)	09 522 1410
(Christchurch)	03 355 4319
French Embassy	04 384 2555
German Consulate (Auckland)	09 375 8718
(Christchurch)	03 347 6729
German Embassy	04 473 6063
Greek Embassy	04 473 7775
Indian High Commission	04 473 7775
Indonesian Embassy	04 475 8697
Israeli Consulate	04 475 7622
Italian Consulate (Auckland)	09 489 9632
(Christchurch)	03 359 7372
Italian Embassy	04 473 5339
Japanese Consulate (Auckland)	09 303 4106
(Christchurch)	03 366 5680
Japanese Embassy	04 473 1540
Malaysian Consulate (Auckland)	09 361 0500
(Christchurch)	03 374 5361
Malaysian High Commission	04 385 2439
Mexican Embassy	04 472 0555
Philippine Consulate (Auckland)	09 303 2423
(Christchurch)	03 351 8602
Philippine Embassy	04 472 9848
Polish Consulate	09 533 5166
Polish Embassy	04 475 9453
Singapore High Commission	04 470 0850
Swedish Embassy (Auckland)	04 499 9895
(Christchurch)	03 377 0542
Swedish Consulate	09 373 5332
Thai Consulate	09 373 3166
Thai Embassy	04 476 8616
Turkish Embassy	04 472 1290
US Embassy	04 462 6000

dropping steadily over the past 10 years. There were 400 deaths in the 12 months up to April 2007, and the aim is to reduce this figure to 300 a year by 2010.

Speeding, drink- or drug-driving and failure of passengers to wear seat-belts are all against the law in New Zealand. The penalties depend on the severity of the infringement and its consequences, but in general, minor offences carry an instant fine ($150 if you fail to buckle up, for example).

Anyone caught driving over the legal drink-drive limit is arrested on the spot. The penalties, if caught, range from fines and temporary loss of licence to permanent disqualification from driving and prison sentences.

Any accident in which someone is injured or killed is thoroughly investigated by the police. If you are to blame, expect to be arrested. If there is enough evidence to press charges you will have to await trial and sentencing at a later date.

Getting Arrested

If you are arrested in New Zealand you'll be taken to the nearest police station, where you can expect to be questioned. A statement will be taken and, depending on the nature and severity of the alleged crime, you may be kept in custody or granted bail, with a commitment to attend court at a later date. If you are granted bail it's unlikely that you'll be able to leave the country until your case is settled.

New Zealand law is bound by both the Bill of Rights Act (1990) and the Human Rights Act (1993), which safeguards the civil and political rights of all citizens and visitors, and includes the right to a fair trial. The Human Rights Act includes the right of access to legal counsel. You do have the right to make phone calls and to appoint a lawyer (or, if you cannot afford one, the right to a state-appointed lawyer through legal aid).

Prison Time

New Zealand has a mostly modern, rehabilitative prison system. Along with custodial sentences, a number of other options are available to those convicted of crimes, including community service and periodic detention (in which offenders attend a centre to undertake community work). In general, inmates are treated well. Full meals and basic comforts are provided, and work, education and vocational training programmes are all available in a bid to discourage repeat offence. The length of a prison sentence determines whether or not a prisoner retains the right to vote. Prisoners serving less than 12 months are released on remission once half of their sentence is complete.

Victims of Crime

If you are a victim of crime in New Zealand, the first thing to do is to report it to the police station. Even petty crimes, such as bag-snatching, or the theft of individual items should be reported, not least to validate future insurance claims. If you need further support, The Crime Victims Hotline and other numbers on p.29 will offer both practical and emotional advice.

Police

There is more than 10,300 staff in New Zealand Police, of which 75% are police officers, including traffic police, undercover and uniformed officers, and 25% are support staff. Uniformed officers, who patrol on foot and in cars, are easy to spot, as they generally wear blue trousers, a light blue shirt, a tie and peaked cap. The country's police force is generally considered to be one of the least corrupt in the world, which isn't to say there aren't occasional reports of misconduct, but means that officers are easily approachable and willing to give advice.

Officers, while in possession of batons and pepper spray, do not carry firearms, although some special units are equipped with guns.

The force is divided into 12 districts across the country. The larger of these, in the Auckland and Wellington regions, have numerous stations and a regular presence on the streets, particularly in urban areas. In isolated rural communities with small populations, however, it's not uncommon for stations to be manned by a lone officer.

Female Visitors

In general, New Zealand provides a safe environment for female visitors. Men and women are treated equally and while sexism and episodes of sexual harassment and worse occur, these are largely frowned upon in Kiwi culture. Women should employ the same caution as they would elsewhere. Avoid the seedier parts of urban areas, particularly late at night, and if you're travelling on buses after dark, sit up front, close to the driver. Alternatively, taxis are a good and generally safe late-night option. Booking with a firm approved by the New Zealand Taxi Federation is recommended (see, p.50).

Travelling with Children

New Zealand is a child-friendly country. Most motels, hotels and campgrounds offer family rooms and, in the case of some holiday parks, kidzones and child-minding facilities. Restaurants tend to be fairly accommodating, with some larger venues offering special children's menus and games. The majority of tourist attractions are geared up for children, and most offer well-priced family tickets, although the country's more adventurous outdoor activities, such as bungee jumping and whitewater rafting, will restrict some users according to age and/or height.

People with Disabilities

People with disabilities are generally well provided for in New Zealand. Along with priority bays in car parks, there are roadside parking concessions for disabled drivers and a ticketing facility that allows anyone unable to use public transport half-price taxi fares (see www.transport.govt.nz/total-mobility-index).

In addition, all new hotels, motels and hostels must by law provide at least one room that offers full disabled access and has been designed or modified for disabled use. This is a practice that's been adopted by many existing accommodation providers. New Zealand airports accommodate disabled travellers with lifts, free gate transfers and wheelchair provision. Most taxi companies offer minivans with wheelchair access, although these are best booked in advance.

Wheelchair access

In general, restaurants do their best to accommodate disabled customers, although it's best to phone ahead to ensure access is available. Counters of banks and government departments are fitted with hearing loops to aid the hard of hearing.

Dress

Kiwis are a casual lot, more inclined to don shorts and a T-shirt than a two-piece suit. Much of this, of course, is to do with their laid-back lifestyle and love of BBQs in the summer sun. This is the country, after all, for which items of iconic clothing include the swanndri (a kind of plaid all-weather bush shirt made from NZ wool) and gumboots (waterproof footwear, similar to Wellington boots).

Style does not entirely pass Kiwis by, however. New Zealand fashion has made it onto the world stage thanks to Auckland designer Karen Walker (p.381), who is famous for offering a modern twist on, you guessed it, the swanndri.

The relatively mild climate means that even in the depth of winter there is little need for more than jumpers or a moderately heavy jacket. An umbrella or waterproof jacket, however, is a good year-round essential as getting caught in anything from a drizzle to a downpour is a routine hazard.

In the summer months, the greatest threat is the sun. Don't be fooled into thinking moderate temperatures mean you're safe from burning. New Zealand has thin ozone layer coverage, meaning high radiation and fast burn times (as little as 10 minutes during spring and summer). Wear a hat, regularly apply cream and stay out of the sun during the middle of the day.

NZ Tourism Offices Overseas

Australia	Sydney	+61 2 8220 9000
China	Hong Kong	+852 2522 0088
China	Shanghai	+862 1 6279 7368
Singapore	Singapore	+65 6738 5844
UK	London	+44 207 930 1662
UK	London	+44 207 930 1662
USA	New York	+1 866 639 9325

Dos & Don'ts

Smoking is banned in public places, including all shops, bars, restaurants and office buildings, throughout New Zealand. Alcohol bans have been introduced in some town centres and holiday spots on weekend evenings and some public holidays (such as New Year's Eve) in a bid to prevent anti-social behaviour. Likewise, drink-driving is not only socially unacceptable but can result in hefty fines, and a prison sentence for repeat offenders. Drugs are illegal. 'Pure' (known as 'P') is an amphetamine-based narcotic that is particularly notorious (especially in urban areas) and its use is heavily frowned upon, with prison sentences not uncommon, even for casual users. And while marijuana use is fairly commonplace, don't be lulled into thinking that it's condoned; being caught with even a small amount could still see you arrested.

Lost/Stolen Property

Contact the relevant company if you lose anything on public transport. Or contact the local police station. Websites such as www.stolen-lost.co.nz and www.lostandfound.co.nz have been set up to help track lost and stolen items and can provide an alternative means of finding missing goods.

Tourist Information Offices

Crn of Shotover and Camp Sts	Queenstown	03 442 4100
Cathedral Sq West	Christchurch	03 379 9629
Crn Victoria and Wakefield Sts	Wellington	04 802 4860
43 The Octagon	Dunedin	03 474 3300
49 Hurstmere Road	Auckland (Takapuna)	09 486 8670
Sky City Atrium	Auckland (CBD)	09 367 6009

Tourist Information

i-SITE is New Zealand's official network of visitor centres – every major city and most large towns have one. Visitors can pick up leaflets for tours and destinations.

Places to Stay

Finding somewhere to stay while in New Zealand should be easy enough – unless you're travelling at high season (December to March), when it's advisable to book ahead. The savings can be remarkable if you travel outside peak times: easily up to a third of what you might pay in the height of summer.

With a wide selection of options available at almost every level, from five-star luxury to boutique B&Bs and cosy home and farmstays, the country is very well equipped to meet the needs of travellers.

Travellers, however, don't simply mean foreign visitors. New Zealand's geographical remoteness, along with its natural beauty, means that its residents are, to some extent, its best tourists. During school holidays, particularly the summer break over December and January, motels and Department of Conservation (DOC) campsites across the country fill up with families.

In general, accommodation standards are high. Whatever your budget, rooms should be comfortable and well maintained (although city centre cheapies have to cut corners somehow and it's usually on room size and extras). You can pay as little as $50 per night, but more realistically $80 to $110 for a good B&B.

Budget-conscious travellers will find Kiwi backpacker hostels are a good alternative to main hotels. They are likely to offer individual rooms alongside dorm accommodation and maybe even a bar and/or restaurant on-site. At the other end of the scale, 'super lodges' have sprung up. These speciality dwellings in some of the most beautiful locations across the country, range from mountain and lakeside properties to eco-resorts and spas in native forests, offering everything from helicopter transfers to private golf-courses and award-winning fine dining.

Qualmark (www.qualmark.co.nz) is the official hotel accreditation system and rates hotels according to the internationally recognised star system (from one to five). At the last count, more than 1,000 hotels were registered and rated using the system, but there are many, many more who remain unregistered by choice and are just as good and in some cases even better.

Wellington CBD

Villa Alexandra, Sumner

Hotels

Other options **Main Hotels** p.36

If you want to stay in your favourite chain of luxury hotel then you won't be disappointed by the choice in New Zealand's major cities; Hyatt, InterContinental and Sheraton all have a presence. Those looking for more interesting stays will find a growing number of boutique properties, often in historic and characterful buildings. Local mid-range chains such as Kingsgate and Pacifica are reliable mainstays.

Budget Hotels

New Zealand isn't bad for budget hotel accommodation – if by budget you're thinking around $100 per night. Cities can deliver much better than anywhere else; the sheer volume of travellers passing through means that occupancy rates are higher. All of this can add up to cheaper rates for customers. Standards, however, may be slightly lower. Ask to see a room before you put your money down if you're not sure, and bear in mind that what's considered 'budget' cost-wise is likely to creep upwards outside Auckland and Wellington. It's worth noting that in New Zealand some of the best hostels and upmarket motels are as good as budget hotels in other countries.

City Hotels

Five Star	Area	Phone	Website	
Bolton Hotel	Wellington	04 472 9966	www.boltonhotel.co.nz	Map p.502 C1
InterContinental	Wellington	04 472 2722	www.intercontinental.com	Map p.503 D3
Langham Hotel	Auckland	09 379 5132	auckland.langhamhotels.com	Map p.492 A1
The George	Christchurch	03 379 4560	www.thegeorge.com	Map p.512 A4
Four Star				
Chateau on the Park	Christchurch	03 348 8999	www.chateau-park.co.nz	Map p.510 C4
Crowne Plaza	Christchurch	03 365 7799	www.crowneplaza.co.nz	Map p.512 B4
Duxton	Wellington	04 473 3900	www.duxton.com	Map p.505 D1
Hilton	Auckland	09 978 2000	www.auckland.hilton.com	Map p.488 A1
James Cook	Wellington	04 499 9500	www.ghihotels.com/hgc	Map p.502 C3
Novotel Ellerslie	Auckland	09 529 9090	www.novotel.com	Map p.484 D5
Sky City Hotel	Auckland	09 363 6000	www.skycity.co.nz	Map p.487 F3
Three Star				
Copthorne Hotel	Christchurch	03 358 8129	www.commodore.net.nz	Map p.508 A3
Esplanade Hotel	Auckland	09 445 1291	www.esplanadehotel.co.nz	Map p.484 D4
Mercure Hotel	Wellington	04 385 9829	www.mercure.com	Map p.504 B2
Mercure Hotel	Auckland	09 377 8920	www.mercure.com	Map p.488 A2
Rydges Hotel	Christchurch	0800 446 187	www.rydges.com	Map p.516 B2
Shepherd's Arms	Wellington	04 472 1320	www.shepherds.co.nz	Map p.502 B1
Spencer on Byron	Auckland	09 916 6111	www.castleresorts.com	Map p.484 C4
Two Star				
Abel Tasman Hotel	Wellington	04 385 1304	www.abeltasmanhotel.co.nz	Map p.504 C1
Aspen House	Auckland	09 379 6633	www.aspenhouse.co.nz	Map p.488 B2
Auckland City Hotel	Auckland	09 303 2463	www.aucklandcityhotel. co.nz	Map p.488 C3
Cambridge Hotel	Wellington	04 385 8829	www.cambridgehotel.co.nz	Map p.505 E2
City Central	Auckland	09 307 3388	www.citycentralhotel.co.nz	Map p.488 A3
Elms Hotel	Christchurch	03 355 3577	www.elmshotel.co.nz	Map p.508 C3
Halswell Lodge	Wellington	04 385 0196	www.halswell.co.nz	Map p.505 E2
Pavilions Hotel	Christchurch	03 355 5633	www.pavilions.co.nz	Map p.511 F2
Rainbow Hotel	Auckland	09 356 7272	www.rainbowhotel.co.nz	Map p.487 F3
Boutique				
Huntley House	Christchurch	03 348 8435	www.huntleyhouse.co.nz	Map p.508 B5

Main Hotels

State Highway 48
Mount Ruapehu
North Island
Map H10

Bayview Chateau Tongariro

07 892 3809 | www.chateau.co.nz

Bayview, built in 1929 to provide accommodation for New Zealand's early skiers, offers luxury accommodation on the doorstep of New Zealand's 'volcanic playground'. Situated at the foot of Mount Ruapehu, this alpine treasure has recently been awarded a Category 1 status by the New Zealand Historic Places Trust.

Lake Wakatipu
Glenorchy
South Island
Map D10

Blanket Bay Lodge

03 441 0115 | www.blanketbay.com

Surely the most super of New Zealand's new breed of 'super lodges', Blanket Bay has been sitting proudly on best hotel lists across the world since it opened in 1999. Alongside fine food and luxurious pampering, the hotel offers some of the country's most spectacular scenery from its position on the edge of Lake Wakatipu.

Waiheke Island
Auckland
North Island Map G6

The Boatshed

09 372 3242 | www.boatshed.co.nz

Upmarket settlers used to visit Waiheke in full Victorian regalia and enjoy grand picnics on its craggy foreshores. These days, the island is better known for its boho-chic atmosphere and fine vineyards. You can get the best of both worlds at this gorgeous five-bedroom, owner-operated seaside hotel.

Milburn St
Caversham
Dunedin
South Island
Map H12

Corstorphine House

03 487 1000 | www.corstorphine.co.nz

Built in 1863, this fine example of classical grandeur, art nouveau and colonial comfort has been given Category 1 status by the New Zealand Historic Places Trust. Featuring all the trappings of a five-star experience, the fine-dining Conservatory Restaurant uses fresh produce grown on its 12 acre estate.

Marine Parade
Queenstown
South Island Map E10

Eichardt's Private Hotel

03 441 0450 | www.eichardtshotel.co.nz

A recent top-to-toe refurbishment has made this stunning lakefront property a fine place to stay. The hotel seamlessly blends state-of-the art technology with old-fashioned charm, and overlooks Lake Wakatipu and The Remarkables, whose craggy heights provided some of the spectacular backdrops in *The Lord of the Rings*.

103 Bealey Av
Christchurch
Map p.512 B2 14

Historic Hambledon

03 379 0723 | *www.hambledon.co.nz*
With its many original features, antiques and art-lined walls, this boutique B&B in one of Christchurch's oldest historic mansions is a must-stay for history lovers. Original owner George Gould, one of the city's founding fathers, initiated the planting of trees in nearby streets, and in doing so, helped give Christchurch its 'Garden City' tag.

30 Hobson St
Auckland
Map p.488 A2 15

Heritage Hotel

09 379 8553 | *www.heritagehotels.co.nz*
This four-star hotel in the heart of Auckland was built from the shell of what was once Auckland's iconic Farmers department store. Heritage is a favourite of visiting sports teams, and has spectaular views over Waitemata Harbour. Be sure to visit Hector's Restaurant – named after Farmers' famous in-store parrot – for liquorice icecream.

Huka Falls Rd
Taupo
North Island Map J9

Huka Lodge

07 378 5791 | *www.hukalodge.co.nz*
Just a little upstream from the spectacular Huka Falls on the shores of the Waikato River, lies one of the first – and still one of the best – of New Zealand's luxury lodges. It has been a stopover, at one time or another, for everyone from Microsoft founder Bill Gates to the Queen of England.

Dickens St
Christchurch
Map p.508 C5

Jailhouse Accommodation

0800 524 546 | *www.jail.co.nz*
This friendly hostel and backpackers lodge was once a fully functioning prison. Benjamin W Mountford, architect of Christchurch Cathedral, oversaw the building of this Gothic Revival jailhouse, completed in 1874 and constructed in 60cm thick concrete. Needless to say, it remains an imposing and impressive structure today.

83 Symonds St
Auckland
Map p.492 A1 18

Langham Hotel

09 379 5132 | *auckland.langhamhotels.com*
This three-time winner of New Zealand's 'best hotel in tourism' industry award has also been accredited as a 'leading hotel of the world'. Expect excellent service and extravagant extras, such as the heated rooftop pool. Langham's signature afternoon tea, served daily in the lobby bar, is a favourite treat among locals.

Kauri Cliffs
Matauri Bay Rd
Matauri Bay
North Island Map E2

The Lodge at Kauri Cliffs

09 407 0010 | *www.kauricliffs.com*

A three-hour drive from Auckland, this 'super lodge' and its 11 surrounding guest cottages offer vacationers a top notch golf course, nature-infused spa and personalised service. Kauri Cliff's position on top of an elevated peninsula grants loungers incredible views of the Pacific Ocean.

Havelock North
Hawke's Bay
North Island Map K11

Mangapapa Lodge

06 878 3234 | *www.mangapap.co.nz*

Given its location in the heart of New Zealand's oldest wine-growing region, it's no surprise that Mangapapa's star turns are wine and fine dining. Facilities at this 120 year old historic country house include a swimming pool, a grass tennis court and on-site sauna and spa.

10 Elizabeth Rd
Napier
North Island Map K11

The Master's Lodge

06 834 1946 | *www.masterslodge.co.nz*

The two suites at this beautifully appointed hilltop hotel are named after Kidnapper Bay (where Cook first landed) and the city's famous art deco buildings. Once the home of Gerhard Husheer, the house was designed by Louis Hay, architect of the town's National Tobacco Company building (of which Husheer was director).

11 View St
Stewart Island
South Island Map D14

Sails Ashore

03 219 1151 | *www.sailsashore.co.nz*

This hotel, finished in native Rimu timbers, is the perfect spot from which to explore Rakiura, New Zealand's latest national park. The hotel offers road tours, during which you can explore the haunting beauty of this isolated landscape, and guided eco-tours of nearby wildlife sanctuary, Ulva Island (p.294).

285 Tinakori Rd
Wellington
Map p.502 B1 23

Shepherd's Arms

04 472 1320 | *www.shepherds.co.nz*

This hotel first opened its doors to customers in 1870, when it still served as a coach terminus for the surrounding area. This lovingly preserved building has been fully refurbished with a careful nod to its past. It is reputed to be New Zealand's oldest lodging house and offers a fine taste of Wellington history.

44 Rhine St
Wellington
Map p.498 B7

Tapu Te Ranga Marae

04 970 6245 | *www.taputeranga.maori.nz*

Manuhiri (visitors) are welcomed onto Tapu Te Ranga with a powhiri (traditional Maori greeting). The backpacker-style accommodation is low-key, but thread counts aren't what is important here. At this heritage-listed living marae, the spirit of Manakitanga (hosting, sharing, respecting others) is what counts.

351 Kearoa Rd
Rotorua
North Island Map J8

Treetops Lodge

07 333 2066 | *www.treetops.co.nz*

Located in the heart of thermal New Zealand, Treetops sits in 2,500 acres of native forest. Guests can hike, mountain bike, try clay pigeon shooting, fish for trout and try their hands at many more adventurous activities. They can also, of course, just sit back and take in the view, with a plate of fine food and a glass of wine.

State Highway 12
Dargaville
North Island Map E4

Waipoua Lodge

09 439 0422 | *www.waipoualodge.co.nz*

Overlooking the majesty of Waipoua Kauri Forest Sanctuary and home to the world's largest kauri tree, this is one stunning eco-lodge. Accommodation is in a carefully restored late 19th century kauri villa. Be sure to book into a night tour of nearby Trounson Kauri Park. If you're lucky, you may spot a native kiwi.

2-8 Maginnity St
Wellington
Map p.503 D2 27

The Wellesley

04 474 1308 | *www.thewellesley.co.nz*

This magnificently restored heritage building is one of the capital's finest examples of neo-Georgian architecture, and boasts the only remaining open fire in Wellington's CBD. If that all sounds too cosy, why not book a night on floating sister hotel, The Wellesley Cruise Ship (04 474 1308).

Western Lake Rd
Palliser Bay
Featherston
North Island Map G14

Wharekauhau Lodge

06 307 7581 | *www.wharekauhau.co.nz*

Relatively close to Wellington, Wharekauhau serves as a good getaway for the outdoors type looking for the finer things in life. Quad bike safaris and jetboat rides round out the large list of activities, while an award-winning restaurant consistently serves some of the best food in the whole region.

Hotel Apartments

A viable alternative to standard hotels is the myriad self-catering hotel apartments that have sprung up in recent years. Found in greatest concentration in the main cities, they can be rented by the day, week or longer and are as good for lone travellers wanting a more 'homely' experience as they are for families who want to avoid separate rooms and eating out every night. Accommodation ranges from glorified hotel rooms to luxury suites and even whole apartments that sleep anything up to eight people. Expect to find them furnished with kitchen basics including hobs, glassware and cutlery, and often dishwashers. Many offer customers the choice of serviced rooms, which are cleaned daily or weekly.

Apartments in Lighter Quay, Auckland

Hotel Apartments

High Standard	Area	Phone	Website
At Home Wellington City	Wellington	04 802 0858	www.athomewellington.co.nz
Chamber Towers Apartments	Christchurch	03 377 1025	www.fleur-de-lys.co.nz
Elliot St Apartments	Auckland	09 308 9334	www.esapts.co.nz
Poplars Apartment Hotel	Christchurch	04 365 4220	www.thepoplars.co.nz
Quest	Auckland	09 980 9200	www.questauckland.co.nz
Quest Atrium	Wellington	04 931 1000	www.atriumtowers.co.nz
The Quadrant	Auckland	09 984 6000	www.thequadrant.com
Medium Standard			
Aitken on Mulgrave	Wellington	04 473 1870	www.wellingtoncityhotel. co.nz
Central City	Wellington	04 385 4166	www.centralcityhotel.co.nz
Chateau Blanc Suites	Christchurch	03 365 1600	www.chateaublanc.co.nz
Oaks Smartstay Apartments	Auckland	09 337 5800	www.theoaksgroup.com.au
Waldorf Bankside	Auckland	09 974 0600	www.auckland-apartments.co.nz
Budget			
Apollo Lodge	Wellington	–	www.apollolodge.co.nz
Livingspace	Christchurch	03 964 5212	www.livingspace.net
Orange Apartments	Wellington	04 913 6442	www.orangeapartments.co.nz
Sapphire Apartments	Auckland	0800 569 888	www.sapphireapartment.co.nz

Bed & Breakfasts

There is a plentiful supply of B&Bs and homestays in New Zealand. Homestays (and their rural equivalent, farmstays) typically offer a guestroom in an ordinary house, and a more intimate Kiwi experience than that of a larger hotel. B&Bs tend to be owner-operated, and usually only have a handful of rooms. *The New Zealand Bed & Breakfast Book* (www.bnb.co.nz) is your comprehensive guide. For more information on farmstays, see www.truenz.co.nz/farmstays.

The standard B&B ranges in price from about $80 to $150 per double room. Expect to pay much, much more than that for the many boutique and luxury options that have sprung up in recent years. The lodges, which are a staple at many of the country's most popular resorts, are a step up again. They are more likely to be run by a company and vary in price – from well under $100 for a double room to triple figures for those that offer spas and high-end leisure activities.

Bed & Breakfasts

Auckland	Area	Phone	Web
Amitee's	Ponsonby	09 378 6325	www.amitees.com
Ascot Parnell	Parnell	09 309 9012	www.ascotparnell.com
Colonial Cottage	Ponsonby	09 360 2820	http://bed-and-breakfast.co.nz/
Great Ponsonby Bed & Breakfast	Ponsonby	09 376 5989	www.greatpons.co.nz
Number One House	Devonport	09 480 7659	http://nz-homestay.co.nz
Peace and Plenty Inn	Devonport	09 445 2925	www.peaceandplenty.co.nz
The Ridge	Puhoi	09 426 3699	http://theridge.co.nz
Wellington			
Admiral's Breakfast	Seatoun	04 934 5913	www.admiralsbreakfast.co.nz
Booklovers B&B	CBD	04 384 2714	www.booklovers.co.nz
Frinton by the Sea	Eastbourne	04 562 7860	www.frintonbythesea.co.nz
Manley Terrace	CBD	04 389 3011	www.manleyterrace.com
Tranquillity Homestay	Upper Hutt	04 526 6948	www.tranquilityhomestay.co.nz
Christchurch			
Anselm House	Riccarton	03 343 4260	www.anselmhouse.co.nz
Eliza's Manor on Bealey	CBD	03 366 8584	www.elizas.co.nz
The Charlotte Jane	Papanui Rd	03 355 1028	www.charlotte-jane.co.nz
The Windsor Hotel	CBD	03 366 1503	www.windsorhotel.co.nz
The Worcester of Christchurch	CBD	03 365 0936	www.worcester.co.nz
Villa Alexandra	Sumner	03 326 6291	www.villaalexandra.co.nz

Lodges

Name	Area	Phone	Web
Azur Luxury Retreat	Queenstown	03 409 0588	www.azur.co.nz
Bixley House Country Retreat	Kapiti	06 364 3969	www.bixleyhouse.co.nz
Blanket Bay Lodge	Glenorchy	03 441 0115	www.blanketbay.com
Huntaway Lodge	Porirua	04 234 1428	www.huntawaylodge.co.nz
Mill Cottage	Akaroa	03 304 8007	www.millcottage.co.nz
The Lodge at Kauri Cliffs	Bay of Islands	03 355 9902	www.kauricliffs.com

Motels

The motel is a Kiwi institution, loved equally by businessmen on the road and families travelling en masse. They are usually located just out of town on main routes, are functional rather than fashionable, and have good facilities. Most units come fully equipped with towels, bed linen, a full kitchen and TV (usually with satellite or cable). Expect to pay from $80 for a studio or from $90 for a one-bedroom unit. Family suites can sleep up to six or eight, and are usually charged at the same basic rate as one bedroom, with an additional cost of $10 to $20 per extra person.

Motels

Auckland	Phone	Web
Acabo on Jervois	09 360 3850	www.acabo.co.nz
City of Sails Motel	09 486 9170	www.cityofsailsmotel.co.nz
Cornwall Park Motor Inn	09 638 6409	www.cornwallpark-motorinn.co.nz
Parnell Inn	09 358 0642	www.parnellinn.co.nz
Siesta Motel	09 520 2107	www.siestamotel.co.nz
Wellington		
Airport Motor Lodge	04 380 6044	www.airportmotorlodge.co.nz
Apollo Lodge Motel	04 385 1849	www.apollo-lodge.co.nz
Halswell Lodge	04 385 0196	www.halswell.co.nz
Johnsonville Motor Lodge	04 939 0039	www.jvillemotorlodge.co.nz
Sharella Motor Inn	04 472 3823	www.sharella.co.nz
Christchurch		
Akron Motel	03 366 1633	www.akronmotel.co.nz
Aloha Motel	03 343 9911	www.alohamotel.co.nz
Bella Vista Motel	03 377 3363	www.bellavista.co.nz
Diplomat Motel	03 355 6009	www.diplomatmotel.co.nz
Tuscana motor lodge	03 377 4485	www.tuscana.co.nz

Hostels		
Auckland		
Bamber House	09 623 4267	www.hostelbackpacker.com
Base Auckland (two hostels)	09 358 3877	www.basebackpackers.com
BK Hostel	09 307 0052	www.bkhostel.co.nz
City Garden Lodge	09 302 0880	www.citygardenlodge.co.nz
The Fat Camel	08 0022 0198	www.nomadsworld.com
Verandas	09 360 4180	www.verandahs.co.nz
Wellington		
Barnacles Seaside Inn	04 902 5856	www.seasideyha.co.nz
Cambridge Hotel	04 385 8829	www.cambridgehotel.co.nz
Coachman on the Square	04 377 0908	www.coachmanbackpackers.co.nz
Dorset House	04 366 8268	www.dorsethouse.co.nz
Downtown Backpackers	04 473 8482	www.downtownbackpackers.co.nz
Moana Lodge	04 233 2010	www.moanalodge.co.nz
Wellington City YHA	04 801 7280	www.yha.co.nz
Worldwide	04 802 5590	www.worldwidenz.co.nz
Christchurch		
The Marine	03 326 6609	www.themarine.co.nz
The Old Countryhouse	03 381 5504	www.oldcountryhousenz.com

Hostels

Good, clean hostels are widely available across New Zealand. There is a range of options, from dorms ($20 to $25 per night) to individual rooms ($40 to $60 for a twin/double). Hostels are still mainly the preserve of backpackers, although budget travellers find them good value. Boutique backpacker outfits that offer hotel-style extras – individually decorated rooms and luxury touches – are an increasingly attractive option. There are around 400 self-catering options across New Zealand, around one in six of which are official Youth Hostel Association (YHA) Hostels, or YHA-affiliated. Many of the rest are aligned with Budget Backpacker Hostels (BBH) and are listed in the *BBH Accommodation Guide*, available from hostels and visitor centres.

Campsites

Other options **Camping** p.310

Camping is a popular option in New Zealand, particularly in the summer, when rain is less likely. As such, campsites tend to be pleasant, well-equipped places, well positioned on the outskirts of towns or, if you're lucky, by the sea. Prices start from $10 to $15 per person. For a little more ($30 to $40 for two) you can opt to stay in one of the basic wooden cabins that are often found on-site.

The more upmarket campsites also offer cabins with en suite and cooking facilities (from around $60) and the shared facilities are generally of a high standard, with fully equipped kitchens and plenty of hot water. You may even get a games room and a pool. Orere Point (09 292 2774, www.orerepointholidaypark.co.nz) is a good option on the Pacific Coast Highway – an hour's drive from central Auckland – and provides access to Coromandel and Rotorua.

Auckland North Shore Top 10 Holiday Park (www.top10.co.nz) is New Zealand's first Qualmark-rated 4 Star holiday home. Near Wellington, Hutt Park (04 568 5913, www.huttpark.co.nz) is located just 12km from the Interlsland Ferry and offers good access into town, while Christchurch's Meadow Park (03 352 9176, www.meadowpark.co.nz) is only five minutes walk from local cinemas, restaurants and bars. It's well equipped for kids. Visit www.topparks.co.nz for a full list.

Perfect for nature lovers are the Department of Conservation (DOC) campsites, 240 of which are dotted around New Zealand in national parks and reserves. These tend to be very basic. There should be toilets, and running water – but don't expect it to be hot. However, the beauty of your surroundings – deep within native bush and close to stunning maritime scenery – will more than make up for any inconveniences.

Fullers Ferries (www.fullers.co.nz) make the two-hour trip from Auckland to Great Barrier Island daily during the summer. Here, visitors can take advantage of no less than six DOC campsites. For a full list, see www.doc.govt.nz. Prices start from free (for sites with little more than running water) up to $18 per person for the few serviced sites.

Getting Around

By far the most popular and easiest way to travel around is by car. New Zealand has one of the highest car ownership rates in the world: a staggering 2.5 million cars to a little over four million people, with a full fifth of those clogging up Auckland's roads. All of which says a lot about Kiwis' love affair with being the drivers of their own destiny – or at least their daily commute.

Visitors planning to tour the country will make good use of the State Highway network, which comprises 100 main roads across the North and South Islands. The star of the show is State Highway 1 (SH1), which runs the full length of the country (with a quick break for the InterIsland ferry service), from Cape Reinga in the north to Bluff in the far south, and connects New Zealand's five biggest urban areas.

State Highway 1 also includes New Zealand's busiest stretch of road, just south of the Auckland central motorway junction, which has upwards of 190,000 vehicles passing through it each day.

All other forms of transport are available to a greater or lesser degree. Domestic flights to main centres are frequent and fairly reasonable in price (particularly if booked in advance), with Air New Zealand being the main carrier. For long-distance, inter-city travel, buses are more reliable and cover considerably more of the country than trains, which, sadly, operate only for tourists along scenic routes, although city commuter services fare better.

Good ferry services operate between the North and South Island (see p.198), and to the various islands (Stewart, Great Barrier, Waiheke) off the mainlands, carrying more than four million passengers a year.

Air

New Zealand's geographical isolation means that the majority of visitors arrive by air. Direct flights operate from most international cities, with flights from Europe stopping in the US or Asia to refuel. Auckland is the main port for international flights, although an increasing number of airlines, including British Airways, Korean Air, Singapore Airlines and Qantas also fly into Christchurch.

The only direct route from north America is from Los Angeles to Auckland. Some carriers, including Emirates and Qantas, have incorporated New Zealand into their Australian routes and will stop in Sydney or Melbourne, both on inbound and outbound journeys.

Air New Zealand is the national carrier and operates daily flights to many international destinations, including London and Los Angeles, but focuses particularly on Australasia and the South Pacific. The airline is a Star Alliance member, and has a

Auckland Harbour Bridge

points system that allows flyers to collect miles for use with affiliated airlines, including United and Royal Thai. Air New Zealand picks up the majority of the business on domestic routes, although low-cost carrier Freedom Air is nipping at its heels. Qantas is the other major domestic rival.

Security

New Zealand takes great care to protect its native landscape and wildlife. Measures include a long list of 'banned' items such as fruit, plants and animal products. Footwear and camping gear may be inspected and disinfected before being given clearance. In addition, all arriving passengers must complete a Quarantine Declaration Form.

Flight of Fancy
Never mind no frills airlines, Air New Zealand plans to camp up its flight from San Fransisco to Sydney in celebration of mardi gras, one of the world's most popular gay and lesbian festivals. Passengers can enjoy drag queens, pink cocktails, and a cabaret – the pilot is even wearing angel's wings to mark the occasion.

Checking In

Electronic check-in facilities are available at all three of the country's major airports and are located near the check-in desks. You can also check-in online with most airlines. Dedicated fast lanes are available with the appropriate airline's check-in desks. All departing international passengers must pay a $25 departure tax (payable to the BNZ Bank) before reaching the departure gates.

Airlines

Aerolineas Argentinas	09 379 3675	www.aerolineas.com/ar
Air New Zealand	09 336 2400	www.airnz.co.nz
Air Pacific	09 379 2404	www.airpacific.com
Air Vanuatu	09 367 2324	www.airvanuatu.com
Asiana Airlines	09 256 6681	http://us.flyasiana.com
British Airways	09 966 9777	www.ba.com
Cathay Pacific	09 379 0861	www.cathaypacific.co.nz
Emirates	09 377 6004	www.emirates.co.nz
Freedom Air	0800 600 500	www.freedomair.com
Garuda Indonesia	09 366 1862	www.garuda-indonesia.com
Great Barrier Airlines	0800 900 600	www.greatbarrierairlines.co.nz
Korean Air	09 914 2000	www.koreanair.com
Malaysia Airlines	09 373 2741	www.malaysiaairlines.com
Origin Pacific	0800 302 302	www.originpacific.co.nz
Pacific Blue Airlines	0800 670 000	www.flypacificblue.com
Polynesian Blue Airlines	0800 670 000	www.polynesianblue.com
Qantas	09 357 8900	www.qantas.com.nz
Royal Brunei Airlines	09 302 1524	www.bruneiair.com
Singapore Airlines	09 303 2129	www.singaporeair.com
Thai Airways	09 377 3886	www.thaiair.com

Auckland Airport

New Zealand's largest and busiest airport is still small by international standards, which makes it easy to navigate even for first-time visitors. The main international terminal is located next to two domestic terminals (operated by Air New Zealand and Qantas), which makes connections easy. It's a 10 minute walk between terminals, but there's a shuttle bus every 20 minutes. For flight information, visit www.auckland-airport.co.nz. For lost property, phone 09 256 8968.
A taxi from Auckland airport into the city centre costs about $60 and is a 21km drive.

Wellington Airport

Wellington Airport, which is 10km south-east of the city centre, is an important hub for domestic flights, serving 20 destinations across the country through a single terminal.

It handles around four and a half million passengers each year. Between 12:00 and 16:00 daily, airport ambassadors are on hand to offer assistance and answer queries. For flight information, visit www.wlg-airport.co.nz. For lost property, phone 04 385 5124. Taxis into town cost around $25.

Christchurch Airport

Christchurch Airport services both international and domestic flights. More than 5 million passengers passed through in 2005, and it's anticipated that this will rise to 7.4 million by 2013. To meet this growing demand, a $200 million development is underway to upgrade the existing terminal building (p.11). On completion in 2009, the airport will offer 40% more bays. The Antarctic Visitor Centre (p.260) is only a five-minute walk from the domestic and international terminals and offers a good opportunity for travelling families to pass some time. Flight information can be found at www.christchurch-airport.co.nz. For lost property, contact the travel information centre, or email travelinfo@cial.co.nz

A taxi from the airport to the city centre costs $35 to $40. Red Bus City Flyer runs a shuttle service, twice an hour from the airport into town. Alternatively, hop on one of the door-to-door shuttle buses from outside the terminal. Rates vary, from $15 per person, less for groups.

The train station is roughly two kilometres south west of Cathedral Square, on Clarence Street (corner of Hagley Park). This is your point of take-off for the beautiful TranzAlpine (p.51) and TranzCoastal railway journeys. The InterCity bus terminal is centrally located at 123 Worcester Street, but note that most long-distance bus companies will drop off at, or near, the city's major hotels and hostels.

Airport Transfer

Auckland: Your options are the AirBus (every 20 minutes until 22:00; $15 one way, $22 return) or a door-to-door minibus that operates like a shared taxi waiting until enough people are heading in one direction before departing (usually about 15 to 20 minutes). Expect to pay around $22 for one person and an additional $5 for every extra passenger travelling together. For destinations beyond Auckland, long-distance buses leave from the InterCity Bus Terminal at SkyCity (102 Hobson St). Trains arrive and depart from the Britomart Transport Centre near the harbour on Queen Street.

Wellington: Take the Stagecoach Flyer bus (every 30 minutes until 20:00) from outside the terminal for the 15 minute trip into town. Shuttle buses charge from $15 per person for a door-to-door service. Additional passengers to the same address cost $4 extra.

Christchurch: The Red Bus City Flyer runs a twice-hourly (06:30 to 01.00) shuttle service from the airport into town. Alternatively, pick up one of the door-to-door shuttle buses (from $15 per person, less for groups) from outside the terminal.

Boat

Passenger ferries operate between the mainland on both the North and South Islands and the outlying islands, including between Auckland and Great Barrier Island ($105 return adults; see www.fullers.co.nz), and from Bluff to Stewart Island ($102 return adults; see www.stewartislandexperience.co.nz). Auckland offers a range of passenger ferry services, including commuter trips to North Shore suburbs Devonport and Northcote/Birkenhead, along with regular waterbuses to Waiheke and Rangitoto Islands (contact www.fullers.co.nz for details of times and prices). Pleasure cruises

Devonport ferry

operate from both the North and South Island, taking passengers on sightseeing trips to enjoy whale watching or dolphin swimming, while in the Marlborough Sounds, water taxis operate around the Queen Charlotte Track (p.250).
In addition, some of the country's many wildlife sanctuaries, such as the beautiful Tiritiri Matangi, off the coast of the Whangaparaoa Peninsula at Gulf Harbour, are easily reached by boat from Auckland's downtown ferry terminal. Check out 360 Discovery (0800 888 006, www.360discovery.co.nz).

Dolphin Watch
So long as the wind isn't whipping up, the journey from North to South Island across Cook Strait is a memorable one. Just before you approach Marlborough Sounds, head out on deck and you should be lucky enough to spot a school of diving dusky dolphins.

The Interlslander

Boat travel across Cook Strait – the 92km stretch of water that separates the North and South Islands – can be a disconcerting experience. Thanks to the Strait's placement in the Roaring Forties (the name given to the notoriously windy locations found at latitudes between 40°S and 50°S) the going can be pretty choppy, even on the large passenger-and-vehicle ferries that ply the route.
If you're travelling by car, however, this route will be your only option. And even if you're not, the temperamental weather conditions are compensated by the beauty of the journey itself. Only half the trip is on open water, giving you the rest of the three-hour crossing to take in the majesty of the Marlborough Sounds (p.248).
Be sure to book in advance, particularly in the summer months when the ferries fill up quickly. Travelling in winter is not only quieter it's also considerably cheaper – a one-way ticket costs from just $45 for an adult and $110 for a car with Interlslander (0800 802802, www.interislander.co.nz), the main company that works the route from the Interlslander Ferry Terminal, one kilometre north of Wellington's train station. In summer, a fully flexible fare will cost about $70 for adults, $230 with a car. Alternatively, book with smaller outfit Bluebridge (0800 844844, www.bluebridge.co.nz), which offers a year-round flat-rate fare of $55 for a one-way adult journey, $185 with a car.

Bus

Bus services in New Zealand's main cities are pretty reliable. In Auckland, the free City Circuit bus, which leaves from the Britomart Transport Centre, runs in a loop along Queen Street, up to the university and back around to the bottom of town. The Link ($1.50), which follows a circuit through the city centre, Ponsonby and Parnell, runs every 10 to 15 minutes from early morning until late at night.

Electric bus, Wellington

Auckland

Auckland buses are operated by a number of different companies, each offering slightly different fare options and means of paying. Fares can be paid in cash, and there are a number of passes available, including the one-day Discovery Pass (available for use on local ferries and trains, as well as buses) and weekly and monthly travel passes. These can be bought on-board from bus drivers. Visit www.maxx.co.nz for more information. Stagecoach, the largest bus operator, issues the GoRider card, similar to a credit card in size and shape, which can be loaded with credit, either on the bus or at various ticket agencies across the city, such as at the Britomart Transport Centre and from selected newsagents. Visit www.stagecoach.co. nz/auckland for a full list of agents.

Maori Migration

New Zealand's government is keen for Maori expatriates to return home. One in seven Maoris lives across the Tasman Sea in Australia, calling themselves 'mozzies', Maori Australians. More than 100,000 indigenous Maori now live and work outside New Zealand.

Wellington

Wellington offers distinctive trolley buses, as well as an extensive network of standard buses in and around the city centre, all of which start at the Lambton Interchange. Inner city fares cost $3. The best route for those new to town is definitely that taken by the bright yellow City Circular buses, which travel in a loop between Parliament and Te Papa Museum of New Zealand (p.245), taking in all the major sights along the way. Multiple-trip tickets offer savings of 20% on standard fares, while one-day passes start from as little as $6. Multiple-trip tickets can be purchased in advance from newsagents and foodmarkets across Wellington, or from the Tranz Metro ticket office at Wellington station. Visit www.stagecoach.co.nz/wellington for more information.

Christchurch

The relatively new City Exchange bus station on the corner of Colombo and Lichfield streets is the hub of Christchurch's transport network. From here, the bright yellow, environmentally friendly shuttle runs between the town hall and Moorhouse Avenue, every 10 to 15 minutes. Christchurch is a small, pedestrian friendly city, so this useful free service might well be all you need, especially if you're staying in the city centre. Visit www.metroinfo.org.nz for more information.

Cross Country

New Zealand's long-distance buses offer an easy, affordable and largely hassle-free way to see the country, with routes to most places. The two main coach companies are InterCity (09 623 1503, www.intercitycoach.co.nz) and Newmans (09 603 1504, newmans.co.nz), owned by the same firm. Both share a timetable and operate from the same stations. InterCity passes are often transferable to Newmans (which offers excursions and sightseeing tours).

Tickets tend to be cheaper the further they're booked in advance – a limited number of super saver fares offer 50% off the standard price. InterCity's fixed-route passes are another good deal, as is the Flexi-Pass, for which travel is booked by the hour. Phone or visit their websites for more information, or pick up a timetable from any visitor centre (many of which take bookings too).

Car

Other options **Transportation** p.187

The car is the best and most popular way of getting around New Zealand. With the notable exception of rush hour in Auckland (p.212), and, to a lesser degree, Wellington, traffic is generally light and the going mostly easy.

Cars are driven on the left, and, in general, New Zealand road laws share much in common with those in Australia, the UK and the US. There are one or two notable exceptions, however. Cars turning left must always give way to traffic crossing or approaching from the right, a red light means a red light (there is no left turn rule), and you must always park in the direction that you're travelling. Drivers must carry their licence or other permit with them at all times while driving. You can legally drive in New Zealand with a foreign or International Driving Permit for up to 12 months after your arrival in the country, after which you'll need to convert to an New Zealand licence. All licences must be in English or translated into English.

There is a maximum speed limit of 100kph on the open road and 50kph in urban areas. Distances are marked in kilometres and signposting follows standard international symbols. Speed limits are rigidly enforced by traffic police, with fines starting at $80 and increasing in line with the scale of the offence. This hard-line approach applies to the compulsory wearing of seatbelts by all passengers and there are regular random breath tests aimed at discouraging people from drinking alcohol before driving. This is because for many years NZ had one of the highest death-tolls per capita in the west, a trend that has been steadily reversing in recent years. Latest figures reveal New Zealand's annual road deaths per 100,000 of population now stand at 10, compared to 6 per 100,000 in the UK and 15 in the USA and Spain.

As yet, there is no charge for driving on New Zealand's roads, although commercial vehicles and heavy trucks are levied an RUC – Road User Charge. Congestion charging, however, has been mooted for Auckland and Wellington and busier routes. It is likely that when the State Highway 1 (SH1) Northern Motorway extension opens in Auckland in a few years it will be the country's first toll road. Public opposition to the idea, as you might imagine, is strong.

On the Road
New Zealand is a driver's paradise, packed full of iconic touring routes. For a good overview and no little inspiration, pick up a copy of New Zealand Driving Holidays, *written by respected travel writer Donna Blaber.*

State Highways

State Highway 1 (SH1) is the spine of New Zealand's road network and covers the whole country, stopping where the ferry service connects Bluff in the South Island to Stewart Island. Because of its great length, SH1 suffers every weather hazard New Zealand can throw at it, from melting tarmac under Northland sun to the perils of snow and ice during winter, including on the spectacular Desert Road (between Waiouru and Turangi), which passes through much of the country's most beautiful volcanic scenery. In the South Island, the 120km journey from Te Anau on SH94 to Dunedin, is one of the country's most scenic (p.291). Take great care around the Homer Tunnel, however. With only a single lane, it is notorious for head-on collisions.

Most New Zealand roads are sealed and well maintained. The notable exception to this rule is the 'metal' roads, which are covered with gravel and prone to wash-outs after heavy rainfall. If you do come across them (around the Coromandel say, or the former gold-mining region of Skippers Canyon outside Queenstown), drive under 60kph and slower still during or after rainfall. Much of New Zealand is rural, so beware of other hazards such as livestock crossing on the roads.

Auckland Traffic

Talk to any Aucklander for any length of time and you can be sure that the subject of the city's traffic will find its way into the conversation. Locals are obsessed with it, and it's easy to understand why.

More than 190,000 people pass along the country's busiest road, just south of the Auckland central motorway junction on SH1, every day. During rush hour (from 07:30 to 09:30 every morning and 16:30 to 18:30 each evening) traffic along the city's motorways slows to a virtual standstill at times – not unheard of in other, more heavily populated parts of the world, but an odd state of affairs for a nation with the population-to-land ratio of New Zealand. Aucklanders living on the North Shore suffer much of the worst of it. The fastest (in theory at least) way of getting from 'the Shore' to the city is travel over the Harbour Bridge, but with only eight lanes open, the result is a major traffic headache. Work is underway to build better bus lanes and to expand the motorway network where possible. Congestion charging is hugely unpopular with the city population, the public transport system outside the city and inner suburbs is woeful and, when it comes down to it, locals feel passionate about their right to drive. With Auckland's population increasing at a rate of 2% each year and the number of cars going up by 4% over the same period, something will have to done; whether it's car-sharing, congestion charging or government investment in Auckland's road network remains to be seen.

Welly Central
Residents' parking permits are required in some parts of Thorndon (p.131), Te Aro (p.130) and Newtown (p.124). These are available from Wellington City Council or online at www.wellington.govt.nz.

Parking

As you might expect in a country with so many cars, parking can be a problem, particularly in central Auckland. Park and ride schemes have been set up on the North Shore to shuttle commuters by bus to the city.

On average, it costs between $2 and $4 per hour to park on the street, and between $5 and $12 per hour in a public carpark.

Measures such as pay & display ticketing machines that enable drivers to pay for their parking by text message are gradually being introduced across larger cities. A useful tip is to use a carpark of one of the bigger department stores or malls, many of which offer free or reduced-cost parking providing the ticket has been validated with a purchase in-store.

The price of long-term parking varies, but as an indicator it costs $13 a day for uncovered parking at Auckland airport ($16 covered), $25 for the first day and then $8 per day after that at Wellington airport, and a maximum charge of $19 a day and $57 a week for uncovered parking at Christchurch Airport.

Hiring a Car

Major international companies such as Avis, Budget and Hertz are represented in New Zealand, along with a good sprinkling of local firms. Prices range from $30 to $60 a day for a 1.3 to 1.8 litre small car in high season, depending on the age of the model. Be aware that although smaller companies are often cheaper they might not provide the same level of breakdown or insurance cover as a larger international firm.

Car Rental Agencies

A2B Rentals	09 377 0824	www.a2b-car-rental.co.nz
Ace Rental Cars	09 303 3112	www.acerentalcars.co.nz
Apex	03 379 6897	www.apexrentals.co.nz
Auto Rentals	0800 736 893	www.autorentals.co.nz
Avis	09 526 2847	www.avis.co.nz
Bargain Rental Cars	09 444 4573	www.bargainrentals.co.nz
Britz	0800 831 900	www.britz.co.nz
Budget	09 529 7784	www.budget.co.nz
Europcar	0800 800 115	www.europcar.co.nz
Ezy	09 374 4360	www.ezy.co.nz
Hertz	09 256 8695	www.hertz.co.nz
Kea Campers	09 441 7833	www.keacampers.com
National	03 366 5574	www.nationalcar.co.nz
New Zealand Rent a Car	09 262 1296	www.nzrentacar.net
Omega	09 377 5573	www.omegarentals.com
Pegasus	03 548 2852	www.rentalcars.co.nz
Thrifty	03 359 2720	www.thrifty.co.nz
USave	0508 112 233	www.rental-car.co.nz
Vroom Vroom	–	www.vroomvroomvroom.co.nz

Most types of vehicle are available for rent, including camper vans for longer-term touring. If you are planning to hire in the summer months, book well in advance. Winter is a better time for last minute deals. It's worth noting that it can be cheaper to rent if you're traveling South to North. Most traffic goes the other way and lower rentals may be used as an incentive to get cars back to Auckland where there is more demand. Longer-term rentals of a few weeks or more can also lead to lower prices.

Cycling

Other options **Cycling** p.312

In the major cities, good roads and a generally light traffic flow (except in certain parts of Auckland) make cycling relatively straightforward, so it is surprising that only around 3% of the population uses a bicycle for its daily commute. Dedicated cycle lanes, however, are thin on the ground. In Auckland, a cycle route can be found on part of the north-western motorway extension, along Tamaki Drive (p.217) and in city centre suburbs such as Mount Albert.

Wellington offers a number of shared footpaths (such as those along Oriental Parade and the Mount Victoria Tunnel) and dedicated lanes in the city centre, including one around the busy train station on Bunny Street.

Christchurch is probably the most cycling-friendly city. Not only is it largely flat, with a large number of dedicated cycle lanes, but the police and local council are committed to increasing the number of cyclists on the roads and keeping them safe under its 'share the road' campaign.

All cyclists are required by law to wear a helmet, and for good reason. While most of New Zealand's main roads are sealed and in good condition, minor roads are often unsealed, pot-holed or 'metal' (composed of a loose cover of small stones with a shifting surface that can be difficult to navigate).

Cycle touring is becoming an increasingly popular way to see the country (p.312). Whether you opt for a one-day hire to get around a town or city, or sign up for a two-week adventure tour across one of the islands (such as those offered by www.cycletours.co.nz), the mild climate, fine scenery and relatively short distances between destinations make travelling on two wheels a pleasant way to get around. For the adventurous, dedicated mountain biking trails are plentiful (p.323). See www.tourism.net.nz (follow the link through attractions and activities).

Taxi

Taxis throughout New Zealand are run by private companies, many of which are approved by self-appointed quality-controllers, the New Zealand Taxi Federation. In general, taxis are metered, although for some journeys (those over particularly long distances, or in smaller towns) you may be able to negotiate a price beforehand. Available cars can be flagged down on the street, but it's more common to either queue at a designated taxi rank or call ahead and get one to pick you up.

To know if a car is available for hire, look for the illuminated 'taxi' light on the top of the vehicle. Ranks are usually only available in city centres and large towns but all hotels, restaurants and bars will be able to provide you with a number to call. Smaller towns may have only one or two cars operating so book as far in advance as possible. Lone women travellers should have nothing to fear from riding in taxis late at night, though booking with the larger New Zealand Taxi Federation-approved companies is recommended.

Taxi Companies

Auckland	
Alert Taxis	09 309 2000
Auckland Co-op Taxis	09 300 3000
Elite Tour Connections	09 275 7377
President Taxis	09 309 0700
Western Cab Society	09 838 9199
Wellington	
Combined Taxis	04 384 4444
Hutt & City Taxis	04 570 0057
Porirua Taxis	04 237 6099
Christchurch	
Blue Star Taxis	03 379 9799
Corporate Cabs	03 379 5888
Gold Band Taxis	03 366 1001

Train

The standard of New Zealand's national passenger rail service has declined steeply in recent decades. What's left is a small number of slow, if rather scenic routes, more commonly used for sightseeing than for shuttling people efficiently up and down the country. The three remaining are: the Overlander, a 12 hour journey from Auckland to Wellington; the TranzCoastal, a five-hour, part-coastal run between Picton and Christchurch, and the TranzAlpine, between Christchurch and Greymouth. Tickets for all three are cheaper outside the summer months. In winter, a one-way trip on the TranzAlpine can cost as little as $69, rather than the standard $99 ($149 return). Alternatively, Scenic Rail Passes (0800 827467, www.tranzscenic.co.nz) offer value with unlimited travel across the network over a set period of time.

Commuter Services

Commuter train services operate in Auckland and Wellington, but not, in any real sense, in Christchurch. Auckland has a rather tired and run-down operation that is subject to cancellations and frequent problems with rolling stock. It is hardly surprising then, that only an estimated 1% of the city's population uses the network, which runs from Queen Street's Britomart Transport Centre to the western suburbs. However, there is talk of an upgrade in time for the 2011 Rugby World Cup. In Wellington, by contrast, the local service is superb. Efficient and well serviced trains leave for outlying towns and suburbs from the station on Bunny Street, every half hour, with single fares from just $2 off-peak and $3.50 at peak times (04 498 3000, www.transmetro.co.nz). The difference in usage between Auckland and Wellington is stark – the number of passenger trips on the capital's trains during peak times was up 11% in the year ending June 2006.

The TranzAlpine

The most southern of New Zealand's passenger railway services – and its most spectacular – leaves Christchurch railway station at 08:15 sharp every day. The 231km coast-to-coast journey to Greymouth travels into the heart of the South Island's spectacular Southern Alps. After an initial run over the flatness of the Canterbury Plains, the landscapes flashing past begin to change. The train gently up chugs up

Britomart, Auckland

through the rugged mountains to Arthur's Pass, where the relative dryness of the landscape around Craigieburn gives way to luscious beech forests. The addition of an extra locomotive at Arthur's Pass offers a brief moment to take in the full beauty of the Alps, against the backdrop of the 920m pass. You're then taken underneath it, into the Otira Tunnel, before beginning your descent to the rain-swept west coast, passing through verdant forests of native hardwoods and finally, gliding down the Grey Valley into Greymouth, arriving at around 12:30.
The return journey starts about an hour later, gliding back into Christchurch by early evening. What's truly incredible is that what was once an arduous two-day trek by horse-drawn carriage (so tough, in fact, that it reduced the life-span of the draught horses to just 18 months) is now such a pleasant ride. Complimentary morning or afternoon tea is served and an open-sided observation car allows you to take in the full majesty of the dramatic alpine landscape. During winter, the snow-dusted mountains are particularly imposing, but whatever the time of year, this is a journey you'll be glad to repeat.

Tram Scram
If you'd like to make a night of it on the tracks, dine in the tramway carriage restaurant, or hire the whole thing out for a special occasions (p.462).

Tram

Trams only operate in Christchurch. And they are a delight; both an efficient way to move about, and, with beautifully restored carraiges from 1905 plying much of the route, wonderfully easy on the eye. The tramway runs a 2.5km circular loop through the city centre, taking in many of its most famous sights, including Cathedral Square (p.262) and the Botanical Gardens (p.262). Tickets are valid for two consecutive days at a cost of $12.50. Local residents can purchase a discounted pass. For more information, phone 03 366 7830 or visit www.tram.co.nz.

Walking

Other options **Hiking** p.319

With so many people on the road, it's easy to forget that New Zealand's city centres tend to be compact, and easily navigable by foot. Christchurch, with its largely unbroken flatness and grid-like layout of streets, is a city that could have been designed for pedestrians. Each major city centre has pedestrianised areas, including Manners Mall in Wellington and Poplar and Ash streets in Christchurch.
The least pedestrian-friendly city is Auckland, where the tiny Vulcan Lane is one of the few genuine car-free places in the centre of town. All of this will soon change, however, as first-stage approval has been granted to create a pedestrian mall on Alfred Street. But even in Auckland, where the hills can prove daunting to the unfit, the relatively small distances between locations in the CBD and inner-city suburbs make walking a pleasure rather than a chore. A stroll around Parnell or Ponsonby, for example, will probably get you around faster than a bus, and will offer plenty of distractions.

Christchurch Tramway

Money

Cash and cards are pretty much interchangeable in New Zealand. Even the smallest shops have Eftpos, a widely used electronic payment system that debits money directly from NZ bank accounts, and which can usually handle credit card transactions as well. Many shops, service stations and other outlets often offer a cashback service on debit cards. The only accepted currency is the New Zealand Dollar.

Queen Street banks, Auckland

Anzac Dollar?

A survey in April 2007 revealed that 49% of Kiwis and 41% of Aussies were in favour of a united Australian and New Zealand dollar. It's argued that a single rate of currency would make importing and exporting of goods more straightforward and boost tourism, but so far Prime Minister Helen Clark is yet to be convinced.

Local Currency

The New Zealand dollar, or 'buck', is made up of 100 cents, and comes in five denominations of bright polymer banknotes and two gold coins. These are $100, $50, $20, $10 and $5 notes, and $2 and $1 coins. The other coins – 50c, 20c and 10c – are silver and come in varying sizes.

Although prices are not rounded to the nearest 10c on menus and labels, this is done at all till transactions automatically and balances out in the end. Note that most items come with GST (Goods and Services Tax) included, a 12.5% surcharge similar to VAT in the UK.

Banks

Every town centre has a bank of some description, probably one of New Zealand's big five: The National Bank, ANZ, ASB, BNZ and Westpac, all of whom are affiliated with foreign banks. In addition, there are a number of smaller local banks and overseas operations. New Zealand banks offer a full range of financial services. Larger branches usually have a dedicated area for money exchange, and smaller branches will usually change foreign currency into Kiwi dollars if you ask. Opening hours are generally 08:00 or 09:00 until 16:30. For more detailed information on opening a bank account, see p.82.

ATMs

Every high street has at least one ATM (usually marked 'cashpoint'). Foreign credit cards and some debit cards can be used at most machines. Cirrus and Maestro are the most widely accepted. ATMs in New Zealand are mostly safe. However, in 2006, BNZ admitted to losing $47,000 after a skimming scam (in which card details are read at an ATM machine and later used to make purchases). It was the first known skimming operation to have affected the country's 2,300 strong ATM network. Treat money withdrawls in New Zealand with the same care you would anywhere else.

Exchange Rates

Foreign Currency(FC)	1 Unit FC = x NZ$	NZ$1 = x FC
Australian Dollar	1.12	0.90
British Pound Sterling	2.62	0.38
Canadian Dollar	1.24	0.81
Euro	1.77	0.57
Hong Kong Dollar	0.17	5.93
Japanese Yen	0.01	93.48
Singapore Dollar	0.86	1.17
South African Rand	0.19	5.38
South Korean Won	0.0014	694.52
UAE Dirham	0.359	2.77
US Dollar	1.32	0.76

**Rates from October 2007*

Money Exchanges

Auckland and Christchurch airports both offer currency exchange services that are open for all incoming international flights. As well as banks, larger hotels typically operate a money exchange, although the rates aren't that competitive. Bureaux de change are another option. Available throughout main centres, they tend to open late, often until 21:00, and offer similar rates to those of banks.

Exchange Centres

American Express	0800 722 333	www.americanexpress.co.nz
Travelex	0800 200 232	www.travelex.com/nz

If you need to wire money, the best option is to have it sent directly from your home bank to its New Zealand equivalent. Western Union's wire transfer service is also available, as is MoneyGram (www.moneygram.com), although these services are more expensive than standard bank transfers.

Credit Cards

New Zealand is a country drowning in electronic debt – in excess of $4.5bn at the last count. With average interest rates on cards at 18.8%, it's estimated that New Zealanders paid around $540m in interest charges during 2006. No surprise than that all major credit cards are accepted in New Zealand. In general, anywhere that operates Eftpos will be able to take credit cards, although smaller retail outlets may charge a nominal fee or around 5% of a transaction to offset costs. You may even be able to use them at larger, established markets (such as Victoria Park Market in Auckland, p.411). You can also use a credit card to withdraw cash from ATM machines. If a credit card is lost or stolen, report it to the appropriate company immediately.

Tipping

Tips are not expected in New Zealand although they are always appreciated by hard-working staff. Some of the more upmarket restaurants and hotels may add a service charge of 10%, but usually it's at the customer's discretion.

The only other exception is on public holidays. Venture out to a restaurant on Anzac or Waitangi Day and your bill will come with a 15% surcharge. Surcharges are handled in the usual upfront Kiwi way – before your order is taken you'll be asked if you're aware of the extra fee.

Waitakere Ranges

Metro *Test*
In Auckland, the self appointed arbiter of the city's restaurant scene is Metro *magazine, an opinionated 'must read' for locals and visitors. In areas such as Mount Eden Village, Ponsonby Road and Kingsland, keep your eyes peeled for* Metro's *signature 'We like it here' window stickers.*

Newspapers & Magazines

New Zealand's press is an oddly disjointed affair, heavy on local, regional newspapers but with only one national broadsheet, *The Sunday Star Times*, which hits shelves once a week. As a result, you can feel oddly removed from other parts of the country at times.

The main newspapers in each of the three main cities feature a good enough selection of national news, but only cursory and syndicated international updates.

The New Zealand Herald ($1.50 Monday to Saturday, $2.00 Sunday), the country's only seven-day publication, is produced in Auckland and readily available throughout most of the North Island.

Much of the printed press is now owned by Australian media company, Fairfax, including *The Press*, Christchurch's main daily ($1.10, weekdays, $2.00 Saturday), available across the South Island, and Wellington's *The Dominion* ($1.10 weekdays, $1.80 Saturday), available through much of the southern centre of the North Island.

The Sunday Star Times (awarded Best Weekly Newspaper and Best Weekly Magazine in the Qantas Media Awards 2007), is based in Auckland and has news bureaus in Wellington and Christchurch. New Zealand doesn't really do tabloids in the UK sense, but *The Sunday News* ($1.50) is as close as it gets.

The weekend papers are the best for local listings. Alternatively, pick up a copy of *The Listener*, New Zealand's only nationwide current affairs and listings magazine. It costs $3.80 and is published on Saturdays.

Newspapers and magazines are available to buy from newsagents (such as the Magazino chain), dairies, service stations and all major bus and train stations.

A good selection of international newspapers and magazines (mostly in English) is available. Australian publications arrive in New Zealand at pretty much the same time as they're available across the Tasman. For magazines from further afield, however, it can be six weeks to three months from the original publication date before they arrive in New Zealand – unless you're willing to part with as much as $15 to have a UK title delivered earlier.

Books

Other options **Websites** p.56

New Zealand has an honourable if little-known literary heritage; occasionally its authors make an impact overseas. Katherine Mansfield is still the country's most famous literary export thanks to her connection with Virginia Woolf and the famous Bloomsbury set, while Keri Hulme won the prestigious UK-based Booker Prize in the 1980s for her novel *The Bone People*.

Elsewhere, Kiwi novels have found fame via the big screen, including the award-winning adaptation of Janet Frame's *An Angel at My Table*, and *Once Were Warriors*, by Alan Duff, which painted a passionate and brutal (though far from universally agreed upon) picture of disaffected urban Maori. Many of the country's other top-class authors may have failed to make an impact further afield, yet are well worth seeking out. Virtually anything by Witi Ihimaera, one of the country's finest Maori authors (he wrote *Whale Rider*, which also made it to the big screen), is worth a look, but *The Matriarch* is the best introduction to his work. For a taste of old-fashioned New Zealand, Barry Crump's blokey and highly amusing tales of the bush can't be beaten, while Emily Perkins' collection of short stories, *Not Her Real Name*, offers a wry and insightful look at young Kiwis finding their way in the world.

The Penguin History of New Zealand, by Michael King, offers a clear, well-rounded insight into the country's past, while A K Grant's *Corridors of Paua* is a light-hearted look at modern Kiwi politics from the mid 1980s to the present day. *A Cook's Tour of*

Further Reading

New Zealand, by chef, author and broadcaster Peta Mathias and Laurence Belcher is a good traveller's companion to the country's food, as is Michael Cooper's *2007 Buyer's Guide to New Zealand Wines*.

Elsewhere, the Department of Conservation produces brochures on everything from national parks and activities to factsheets on native wildlife, which are available from its website (www.doc.govt.nz) and local offices.

Websites

According to international usage statistics, almost 75% of the population uses the internet. The greatest Kiwi online success story is Trade Me – New Zealand's answer to auction site eBay. The site, set up in humble circumstances in 1999, sold for $700m to Australian media empire, Fairfax, in 2006. It is the most popular website in the country, with more than 50% of New Zealand's entire web traffic passing through its portals. In a country of a little more than 4 million people, 1.5 million of them are registered on the site. Alongside the usual buying and selling, many virtual communities have been established, making it a very friendly affair.

It's not all buying and selling, however. Like most places, New Zealand has a website to support almost every activity, from informative government resources to a host of engaging restaurant and bar reviews.

Blogs

Many blogs follow the standard form of diary entries and personal musings, such as *A Brit in the Boonies* (www.britintheboonies.blogspot.com), which explores the pros and cons of starting a new life in New Zealand. Others, such as *Morph Blog* (www.blog.morph.net.nz) and *Psychowreckers* (www.psychowreckers.blogspot.com) combine dairy-style entries with links to local and world news.

Fairfax site www.stuff.co.nz ran a blog competition in early 2007, Blog Idol, where 10 writers competed for the title and a chance to join the website's writing team. More than 50,000 votes were cast, with librarian Moata Tamaira declared the winner. You can read her musings at www.stuff.co.nz/blogs/moata.

Websites

Business/Industry	
www.convention.co.nz	Christchurch Convention Centre
www.dhl.com.nz	DHL Worldwide Express
www.moneycorp.com	Foreign Exchange
www.newzealand.govt.nz	New Zealand Government website
www.nzchambers.co.nz	New Zealand Chambers of Commerce
www.nzexporters.co.nz	Links local and international buyers and sellers
www.nzte.govt.nz	New Zealand Trade and Enterprise
www.nzx.com	New Zealand Stock Exchange
www.the-edge.co.nz	Auckland Convention Centre
www.wellingtonconventioncentre.com	Wellington Convention Centre
Country Information	
www.aucklandnz.com	Guide to living in Auckland
www.christchurchnz.net	Official visitors' guide to Christchurch
www.creativetourism.co.nz	New Zealand crafts and culture
www.doc.govt.nz	Department of Conservation
www.nz.com	Online guidebook
www.purenz.com	Online travel guide and visitor information
www.tourism.net.nz	Visitor information and travel guide
www.wellingtonnz.com	Wellington City guide

Websites

Culture	
www.aucklandartgallery.govt.nz	Auckland Art Gallery
www.christchurchartgallery.org.nz	NZ's newest art gallery in Christchurch
www.historic.org.nz	New Zealand Historic Places Trust
www.maori.org.nz	Information about Maori culture and heritage
www.nzballet.org.nz	New Zealand Ballet Company
www.nzff.telecom.co.nz	Auckland and Wellington International Film Festivals
www.nzopera.com	The NBR New Zealand Opera
www.tepapa.govt.nz	Wellington's Te Papa Museum of New Zealand
www.the-edge.co.nz	Auckland entertainment facility, including Aotea Centre
Directories	
www.accessnz.co.uk	Online directory
www.nzmaps.co.nz	Street maps
www.police.govt.nz/district/phonebook	Listings of all NZ Police stations
www.whitepages.co.nz	Online phone book
www.yellowpages.co.nz	Online business phone book
Living and Working	
www.emigratenz.org	Official advice and practical tips
www.escapeartist.com/nz	Resources to help you move
www.expatwomen.com ▶ p.xiv	Advice for women living overseas
www.immigration.govt.nz	Department of Immigration
www.migrationbureau.co.nz	Professional immigration services
www.uk2nz.co.uk	Emigration advice tailored to UK residents
www.workingin-newzealand.com	Guide to moving to NZ
News & Media	
www.nzherald.co.nz	*The New Zealand Herald*
www.scoop.co.nz	Independent news outlet
www.stuff.co.nz	Fairfax-owned regional newspapers, including *The Press* (Christchurch) and the *Dominion Post* (Wellington)
www.thelistener.co.nz	Entertainment and current affairs
Nightlife	
www.dineout.co.nz	NZ-wide restaurant reviews
www.entertainmentnz.com	Nationwide entertainment listings
www.localeye.info	Entertainment listings for Canterbury region
www.menulog.co.nz	Eating out in Auckland, Wellington and Christchurch
www.nzcinema.co.nz	Guide to New Zealand cinemas
www.ticketek.co.nz	Online booking facility
www.viewauckland.co.nz	Auckland listings information
www.wgtn.wotzon.com	What's on in Wellington
www.whatson.org/nightlife	Online guide to Christchurch nightlife
www.wr2eat.co.nz	Auckland's largest online dining guide
Online Shopping	
www.foodtown.co.nz	Supermarket deliveries
www.newzealandmall.co.nz	Online shopping centre
www.realgroovy.co.nz	Music and books
www.trademe.co.nz	Auction site
Other	
www.metservice.co.nz	Weather reports
www.police.govt.nz	New Zealand Police
www.traffic.transit.govt.nz	Auckland traffic reports
www.wotif.com	Cut-price rates on NZ hotels

Annual Events

Waipu
1 January

Highland Games

www.highlandgames.co.nz

Scotland comes to the North Island. Or so it has seemed every New Year's Day since 1871, when the whole town of Waipu erupts in the spirit of Caledonia in a big festive nod to the town's Scottish roots. Expect piping, drumming, Highland dancing and the odd athletic event. And lots and lots of tartan.

Great Barrier Island
Auckland
First weekend January

Mussel Festival

Around 3,000 people descend on Great Barrier Island to gorge on the fare fresh from the island's mussel farms – more than a tonne will be put away in a single day. Not that the party ends there. There's live music and dancing until long after the last mussel is shucked and served.

Blenheim
Hastings and Mount Maunganui
Mid-late January

Blues, Brews and Barbeques

www.bluesbrews.co.nz

Annual celebration of all things that are held dear to the traditional Kiwi summer – music, ale and food cooked over an open fire. The festival is spread over three venues (Blenheim, Hastings and Mount Manganui) and over three weeks, featuring some of the county's finest musicians.

Various Locations
8-9 February

Coast-to-Coast Multi-Sport Race

www.coasttocoast.co.nz

A gruelling 243km journey in which contestants start from just outside Greymouth on the edge of the Tasman Sea and end beside the Pacific in the Christchurch suburb of Sumner; cycling, running and kayaking their way through the Southern Alps along the way. The race is usually split into a two-day event, but elite multisporters try to complete it within 24 hours, a competition aptly titled 'the longest day'.

Blenheim
8-9 February

Marlborough Food and Wine Festival

www.wine-marlborough-festival.co.nz

In the time it has been running – 25 years in 2008 – the Marlborough Food and Wine Festival has become the South Island's premier food and wine event, if not the premier fixture on the summer calendar. It's well-supported by the region's many excellent wineries, features great food and live music in the reliably blazing Blenheim sunshine and is hopelessly popular with the public: tickets sell out within hours of going on sale, months in advance.

War Memorial Park
May Rd
Auckland
Mid-late February

Auckland International Cultural Festival

www.aucklandcity.govt.nz

Held on a Sunday in mid- to late-February, the Auckland International Cultural Festival actually begin life as Refugee Day. Now it's an annual opportunity for newcomers from more than 30 countries to share their food, music and culture. It's the only place in Auckland you can have a DIY banquet of Cambodian, Chilean and Kurdish food to a soundtrack of Burundi drummers. Entry is free and the festival runs from 10:00 to 17:00. Each year, there's a seven-a-side Ethnic Soccer Cup.

Albert Park
Auckland
Late February

Auckland Lantern Festival

www.aucklandcity.govt.nz

Auckland has a significant Chinese population from China, Hong Kong and Taiwan. The annual Auckland Lantern Festival celebrates the end of Chinese New Year across three days in late February. Entry is free and each night the festival runs from 17:30 to 22:00. The pretty surroundings and trees of Albert Park are decorated with hundreds of lanterns, many imported from China especially for the festival. Diverse food stalls satisfy the biggest appetite, and there's always plenty of entertainment, including fireworks, fortune telling and martial arts displays. Parking is difficult so consider catching a bus into the city.

Various Locations
Napier
February

Art Deco Festival

www.cubacarnival.org.nz

When downtown Napier was devastated by an earthquake in 1931, the city was rebuilt in the art deco architectural style which was popular at the time. For many decades the city's stunning design unity was largely ignored by locals and outsiders, but now Napier's art deco heritage is respected and treasured. Every February it's used as an excuse for a good old party featuring jazz concerts, costume balls and vintage car rallies. Dressing up 1930s style is virtually mandatory. When things get a bit quieter you can join special walking tours exploring Napier's art deco past. Accommodation books out well in advance.

Waitangi
February

Harvest Hawke's Bay

www.harvesthawkesbay.co.nz

The region's winemakers throw open their cellar doors to reveal the latest vintages for a weekend of fine wine sampling. A jump-on-jump-off bus service takes punters around the vineyards, stopping at a selection of the area's top food producers along with way.

Christchurch
February

Festival of Flowers

www.festivalofflowers.co.nz

It's reckoned to be pretty romantic to be poled along the placid waters of the Avon and Heathcote rivers when Christchurch (the 'Garden City') is in bloom. The city's adminstration has treated this as the only invitation they needed to establish another annual event, namely the Festival of Flowers and Romance. It's slightly artificial, needless to say, but the attractions along the way – the wearable flower art competition, the photographic and art exhibitions, the annual celebrity debate on the nature of love – are a lot of fun. Bring your hayfever medication.

Devonport
Auckland
16-17 February

Devonport Food and Wine Festival

www.devonportwinefestival.co.nz

Fine wine, good food and chilled-out music are the order of the day at this charitable two-day celebration by the sea, which attracts more than 12,000 to Auckland's North Shore. Among the many food exhibitors are a few familiar faces from the popular Devonport Farmers' Market. And to make you feel better after all that over-indulgence, all the money raised is put back into the local community, with nearly $2 million being raised since the innagural festival in 1990.

Cuba St
Wellington
20-22 February

Cuba St Carnival

www.cubacarnival.org.nz

Funky Cuba Street shows off its bohemian roots at this three-day street festival that's held every two years (20-22 February 2009 is the timing for the next festival). Across a variety of stages in Cuba Street and adjacent roads and lanes, there's everything on offer from DJs and dub bands to outdoor screenings of classic music movies. Most years it's a moving feast, as roving street performers and buskers surprise and delight passers-by. It's also a good chance to see up-and-coming bands in Wellington's eclectic music scene. Admission free.

Wellington
Late February to late March

International Arts Festival

www.nzfestival.telecom.co.nz

It's entirely fitting that New Zealand's best arts festival is held in the nation's capital. Wellington's arty black-clad types flock to the three-week extravaganza that's held every two years. High-profile international performers also draw arts fans from around the country, and accommodation is often booked out months in advance. Theatre, opera and classical music form the bulk of the festival line-up, but a surprising number of more contemporary and challenging artists also perform. Past acts have included jazz trumpet legend Wynton Marsalis, performance artist Laurie Anderson and Senegalese world music supergroup, Orchestra Baobab.

Masterton
First week March

Golden Shears Sheep-Shearing Competition

www.goldenshears.co.nz

A visit to New Zealand wouldn't be complete without taking in a little competitive sheep-shearing. All joking aside, these are highly skilled and immensely popular competitions; if you do plan to come along, it pays to book early.

Northland
Mid March

Te Houtaewa Ninety Mile Beach Challenge

www.newzealand-marathon.co.nz

Staged in honour of the Maori legend Te Houtaewa, who stole kumara from his enemies and made his escape along Te Oneroa a Tohe (Ninety Mile Beach), this is a series of races on sand and sea, from the 6km Walk For Life charity event to the 60km Ultra Marathon.

Auckland
Mid March

Pasifika Festival

www.aucklandcity.govt.nz/whatson/events/pasifika

Auckland is the world's biggest Polynesian city, and in early March the annual two-day Pasifika Festival showcases food, music and entertainment from across the South Pacific. The culture of countries as diverse as Samoa, Tonga, Fiji and Niue is on display, lakeside at Western Springs. Pasifika is easily Auckland's biggest festival, and each day around 200,000 people visit the busy combination of four entertainment stages, special 'cultural villages' from nine different Pacific islands, and more than 150 food stalls offering everything from fresh coconuts to food cooked in a traditional earth oven or umu.

Pasifika Festival

Auckland
Mid March

Round the Bays

www.roundthebays.co.nz

What began as an event for little more than 1,000 participants on its first outing in 1972 has grown into one of the world's largest fun runs, with an estimated 70,000 people taking part in the 2007 event. It is an 8.4km flat course around the picturesque Waitemata Harbour, made all the more fun with street parties and barbeques lining the route.

Hokitika
Mid March

Wildfoods Festival

www.wildfoods.co.nz

This event, which began in 1990, has become an iconic Kiwi festival. Loosely based on the opening of the whitebait season, it's widened to become a celebration of the West Coast's rugged individuality, as symbolised by an intrepid willingness to eat anything for a dare. Dishes range from the lesser-eaten end of the mammal family – possums, rabbits and hares feature heavily – right down to the invertebrate world, where even earthworms and insects find themselves surprise additions to the human foodchain. For the squeamish and the fainthearted, there's plenty more conventional fare on offer, from the Blackball Salami Company's superb goods to Monteith's Brewery's excellent beer.

Near Hamilton
Saturday nearest 17 March

Ngaruawahia Maori Regatta

Maori canoes take to the water manned by rowers in traditional dress in what is one of the most spectacular annual displays of Maori culture. The Regatta has been held annually for more than 120 years; as well as boat racing, the event features traditional singing, dancing and food.

Wanaka
Late March

Five Day Festival of Colour

www.festivalofcolour.co.nz

Wanaka is surrounded by exotic deciduous trees, from the venerable poplars along the lakefront to the willows on the banks of the Clutha, and every autumn these ignite in every shade of red, gold and yellow. To capitalise, the township hosts a spectacular annual arts festival celebrating colour and what you can do with it. Participation is especially encouraged, and local artists are on hand to facilitate the flow of creative juices. Meanwhile, there's usually a strong line-up of visiting artists, writers, film-makers and photographers, musicians and performers to complement the happy amateurism.

Waiheke Island
Auckland
Easter Week

Waiheke Island Jazz Festival

www.waihekejazz.co.nz

The lovely, laid-back island of Waiheke (p.111), only a 35 minute boat ride from Auckland, is the ideal setting for a lovely, laid-back jazz festival. You can look forward to fine food and wine benefitting one of the country's more rarefied island retreats and three days' worth of highy polished parping.

Auckland
Easter Week

Royal Easter Show

www.royaleastershow.co.nz

New Zealand's largest family festival turns 165 in 2008, and it's still bringing in the crowds in their thousands. What began as an agricultural event now boasts a host of attractions from the notable to the bizarre, including a competition to find the finest Easter bunny. The big attraction here, however, is the fairground packed with dozens of thrill-seeking rides.

Wanaka
Easter Week

Warbirds Over Wanaka International Airshow

www.warbirdsoverwanaka.com

This biennial airshow (it takes place each even-numbered year) has steadily grown from year to year, and it's now one of the South Island's most popular events. Vintage civilian and military aircraft from all over New Zealand, and a surprisingly large part of the wider world, attend and there's all kinds of events and amusements besides the static and aerial displays to keep you entertained.

Bluff
19-20 April

Bluff Oyster & Southland Seafood Festival

www.bluffoysterfest.co.nz

After closing for five months to let the critters get on with breeding, the Bluff oyster season reopens in April. The arrival in town of the first boat-loads has always been celebrated one way or another, and what started out as just a clutch of cake and craft stalls accompanying all that shucking and slurping has become a red-letter day on the calendar of all New Zealand gourmands. Highlights include a shucking competition, as well, of course, as lots of oysters in the menu. The culinary catchment has widened to include finfish as well – the South Island's legendary blue cod, and greenshell mussels, salmon, paua and scallops, too. Wine features, and so does beer. For two days a year, you'd almost believe there's life in Bluff.

Northland
Mid June

Matariki Maori New Year

www.taitokerau.co.nz/matariki

Maori New Year is marked by the rise of Matariki, the cluster of stars otherwise know as Seven Sisters or Pleiades that are taken as a symbol of rebirth and renewal. The New Year occurs at the time of the following full moon and is celebrated with more than 40 events across Northland that focus on traditional Maori culture and practices, including indigenous music and crafts.

Queenstown
Late June/early July

Queenstown Winter Festival

www.winterfestival.co.nz

There's always a degree of anxiety around Queenstown at the beginning of June, as the town takes a gamble on the official opening of the ski season coinciding with its actual opening. No worries in 2007: the cold arrived with a vengeance, so much so that the fireworks display that kicks off the event was postponed because, er, it was too cold. The town fills up for the event, and most of those people were trapped by frozen runways and snowbound alpine passes. Never mind, they had the Speight's Dog Derby on Coronet Peak, and the annual business leader's drag race to enjoy, besides the prospects of a flying start to the ski season.

Various Locations
Mid July to early August

New Zealand International Film Festivals

www.enzedff.co.nz

New Zealand's largest cities host this showcase of worldwide cinematic talent, which includes everything from feature-length dramas to animated shorts. Following the main events in Wellington, Christchurch, Auckland and Dunedin, a selection of the best films are shown in a further 10 cities across the country.

Queenstown
Mid July

Element Peak-To-Peak Race

www.southerntraverse.com

A true multisport event, this annual race takes competitors from The Remarkables, through Queenstown and up to Mount Coronet. Those taking part have to ski (or snowboard), paddle, run *and* cycle their way to the finishing line.

New Plymouth
Late July-early August

Taranaki International Festival of the Arts

www.artsfest.co.nz

Featuring more than 250 acts performing over two weeks, this exuberant two-yearly celebration promises to brighten up winter days with everything from circus acts and classical music to visual arts and cabaret.

Buskers Unite

The dazzling arts precinct in the centre of Christchurch (p.260) is pretty well-populated by buskers at the best of times, so it was a stroke of genius to emulate similar festivals overseas and draw even more there for 10 days each January. See www.worldbuskers festival.com for more information.

Dunedin
Early September

Moro Marathon

www.moromarathon.co.nz

A highlight of the early spring sporting calendar, this annual running event celebrates 30 years in 2008. If you're not up to the gruelling full-length race, you could try the half-marathon or half-marathon recreational walk. Or just watch from the sidelines at beautiful Otago harbour.

Wellington
Last week in September

World of Wearable (WOW) Art Awards

www.worldofwearableart.com

Spectacular is the only word for this surreal event that attracts around 30,000 people each year. What began a decade ago as a promotion for a Nelson art gallery and museum (p.254) has become one of the highlights of New Zealand's creative calendar. Part dance, part music and pure theatre.

Bay of Plenty
Mid-late October

Tauranga Arts Festival

www.taurangafestival.co.nz

This twice-yearly gala of the arts runs for 10 days from its opening on Labour Day weekend. Expect a good line-up of Kiwi theatre, music, art and dance alongside a host of community events. The 2007 event featured two photograhic shows that have won worldwide acclaim: Earth from Above and World Press Photo. Tauranga was the only city in New Zealand to see the latter, which has been visited by more than two million people in some 45 countries.

Christchurch
8-18 November

New Zealand Cup and Show Week

www.nzcupandshow.co.nz

Agricultural and Pastoral (A&P) Societies all over New Zealand hold annual shows, and none is bigger and better than the Canterbury A&P Show. It happily coincides with the week in which two of the biggest events on the national horse-racing calendar are held, the New Zealand Cup and the Christchurch Casino Trotting Cup. These furnish an excuse for a 10 day-long fashion parade and a celebration of the bountiful and bucolic hinterland of Christchurch. The horse-racing kicks off with Ladies Day – New Zealand's answer to the Melbourne Cup, a high-stakes and high-fashion affair.

Martinborough
Third Sunday in November

Toast Martinborough Wine, Food & Music Festival

www.toastmartinborough.co.nz

In summer, it's hard to turn around without discovering a wine and food festival somewhere in New Zealand, but Toast Martinborough is one of the best. The various vineyards are very close together, so rather than spending half the day going around by bus, you can quite easily walk to each venue. The quality of the wines (especially the pinot noir) is matched by excellent food and some of the country's best DJs and bands. Special trains run across the Rimutaka Ranges from Wellington so you can make a day of it.

Caroline Bay
Timaru
26 December

Caroline Bay Carnival

www.carolinebay.org.nz

The natural attractions of Timaru's lovely Caroline Bay – the safe swimming beach, children's paddling pool and playground, the open grassland, mini-golf and the maze – are supplemented each summer for three weeks by fairground rides, stalls, amusements and musical and theatrical events. It is the summer event of the South Island, very well-attended by locals and folks from further afield. Highlights include a talent contest and the amazing New Year's Eve fireworks display.

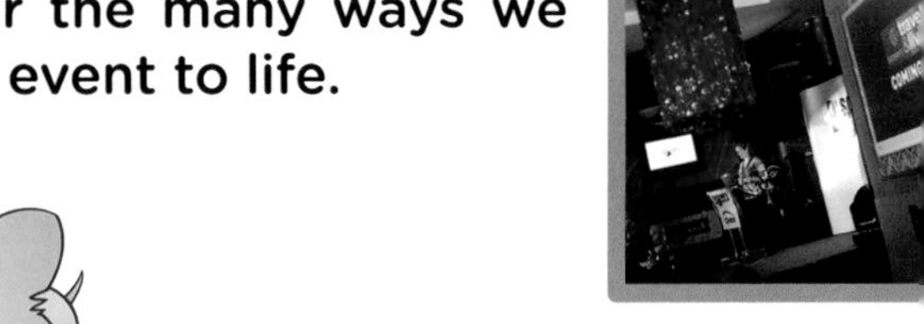

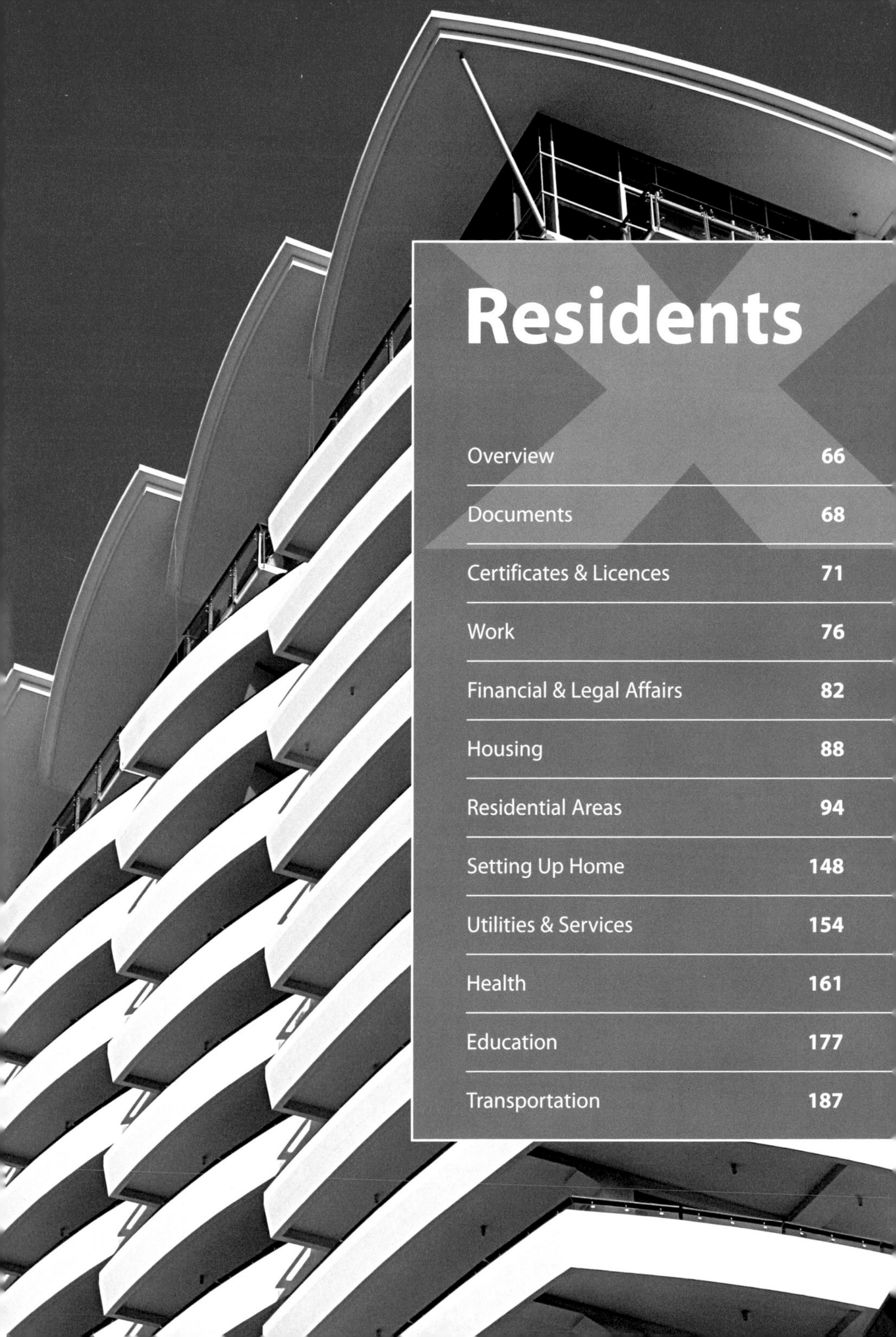

Residents

Residents

Overview

New Zealand might be a small and isolated country but is has a history of punching above its weight. With a population of just over four million, it has fewer people than many big cities around the world, and can offer an enviable quality of life (Auckland ranked 5th and Wellington 12th in Mercer's 2007 survey of the world's most liveable cities).

Since its settlement by Europeans in 1810, New Zealand has attracted immigrants from around the world. All are drawn to its far-flung shores by the promise of wide-open spaces, a free and democratic society, and high standards of living. Internationally, New Zealand has a reputation for its forward-thinking and liberal approach. It was the first country in the world to introduce a welfare state and is a leading proponent of green policies. Employment in New Zealand is at a record high, with demand for skilled workers still outstripping supply, and, with Kiwis renowned for their friendliness, newcomers typically receive a warm welcome to Aotearoa.

Sheep Jibe

The often quoted statistic that New Zealand has 20 sheep for every human residing on its isles might have been true at one stage in the country's history but these days it's an urban myth – New Zealand is home to about 40 million sheep; that's roughly 10 sheep per person.

Considering New Zealand

To most people, the pros of living and working in New Zealand far outweigh the cons. By international standards, wages in New Zealand may be low, but so too is the cost of living, so your money tends to go further. Most New Zealanders can afford to own their own home, although soaring property prices in recent years have meant that some now struggle to get onto the first rung of the property ladder. The country's isolation means it's largely free from the effects of the 'war on terror', and the familiarity of western political, legal, financial and business systems all make it an enviable place to live, especially for English-speaking expatriates. English is by far the most widely spoken language, although te reo Maori (the Maori language) is also recognised as an official language of New Zealand.

The country's economy is robust and employers are always on the look-out for skilled workers, particularly in the high-tech and health sectors. Employers regularly recruit overseas and may be able to help with your journey through the red-tape. Check employment sites such as www.jobstuff.co.nz and www.seek.co.nz for current vacancies. Seasonal jobs (p.79) are also available for those prepared to work in New Zealand's vineyards and orchards.

While the country's isolation and size brings benefits, it also has disadvantages. If you've become accustomed to living in fast-paced cities such as New York and London the quietness here could drive you to distraction. And if you don't share New Zealand's obsession with sport, you soon will.

Before You Arrive

Once you've made the decision to move to New Zealand, you'll probably think of 101 things you need to do before booking that flight. Make yourself a list and start with the basics. You'll need a passport and a visa to get into the country. More details on visa requirements can be found on p.68 and at www.immigration.govt.nz. Tell your bank about your plans as it should be able to help you set up an account in New Zealand, enabling you to access funds from the minute you arrive in the country. If you want to invest in property in New Zealand, you should do some homework. Sites such as www.myplace.co.nz will give you an idea of what money will buy. If you have children, you will also need to swat up on schools. The Education Review Office monitors schools in New Zealand and its website (www.ero.govt.nz) includes details of every school and its performance. Finding a job will also be high on your list of priorities. There are a number of recruitment agencies and websites that can help with your search for the ideal job. These will be discussed in more detail later (p.78).

When You Arrive

The to-do list gets even longer when you set foot in New Zealand. Obviously, you'll need somewhere to live. If you're planning to rent, be aware of the fact that most places come unfurnished. Unless you had the foresight to ship a container of your possessions ahead of you, you might have to put up with the basics.

Once you've got a roof over your head, you'll need to contact the Inland Revenue Department (www.ird.govt.nz) and get an IRD number. Without this, you won't be able to open a bank account (unless you set one up before you left) and any wages you might earn will hover in limbo. You should also register with your local medical centre, so that if you're unfortunate enough to fall ill, you won't have to fill out too many forms before you are seen by a doctor.

You can drive in New Zealand for up to 12 months, using either an International Driving Permit or your current overseas driving licence. After that, however, you will need to get a New Zealand driving licence (p.71).

Hooking up to the electricity and phone networks in New Zealand is relatively simple – most companies just require proof of identification, proof of residence, and one payment upfront. You should also register with your embassy (p.30).

Open all Hours

The lights don't go out in New Zealand at midnight any more. These days, the pubs and clubs are going well into the small hours of the morning (p.426). Stick to the main cities, though; the only wildlife you're likely to find elsewhere will be of the four-legged variety.

Essential Documents

Your passport will be your most valuable possession when you first arrive in New Zealand – you will constantly be asked for it as proof of identification. Make sure you have multiple copies (and other photo ID) and get them signed by a lawyer, Justice of the Peace or your embassy, who will attest that they are genuine. Also, get copies made of your birth and marriage certificates, and anything that relates to your children.

Very soon after arrival you'll find yourself needing documents that show your address in New Zealand, such as utility bills, bank statements or tenancy agreements. Keep a record of your IRD number because your employer and your bank will want it for tax purposes. Take plenty of passport photos and keep them with you.

When You Leave

If you decide to leave New Zealand you will need to notify the Inland Revenue Department (www.ird.govt.nz) and your bank. It would also be advisable to get in contact with immigration officials at least one month before your departure as they will be able to advise you if anything needs to be done. If you have been renting a property you will need to give the full notice required on your rental agreement if you want to claim back your bond. Utility companies will also require notice of your plans to leave, so provide them with a forwarding address where they can send final bills. Remember too that New Zealand is a long way from anywhere, so if you have possessions to ship home you will need to organise it well in advance because it can take up to three months (p.367).

Auckland from the North Shore

Documents

Whether applying for a visa or arranging a wedding, it's always wise to get an idea of how long any administrative procedure will take and leave plenty of time for bureaucratic machinations.

Be prepared to fill in plenty of forms and make sure that you have everything the Immigration Service asks for, as you can be turned away if you have missed something. Patience is a key requirement. If you're being sponsored by a company, then much of your paperwork should already have been completed. Either way, your original passport, valid for at least six months from your date of arrival in New Zealand, is absolutely essential. And you're almost certain to need the following in the first couple of months: birth certificate, marriage or civil partnership certificate, proof of employment, proof of address and driving licence.

It's a good idea to make copies of all your documents and take plenty of passport photos.

Newcomers
New Zealand is increasingly popular with immigrants. The top five countries for migrants in the five years to 2006 (the last New Zealand census) were: the United Kingdom (10,460), Fiji (2,321), India (1,987), Japan (1,740) and Germany (1,463).

Entry Visa

When you enter New Zealand, your passport needs to be valid for three months after your departure date.

If you are visiting for three months or less, you won't need a visa if you are from the following countries: Andorra, Argentina, Austria, Bahrain, Belgium, Brazil, Brunei, Canada, Chile, Cyprus, Czech Republic, Denmark, Estonia, Finland, France, Germany, Greece, Hong Kong, Hungary, Iceland, Ireland, Israel, Italy, Japan, South Korea, Kuwait, Latvia, Liechtenstein, Lithuania, Luxembourg, Malaysia, Malta, Mexico, Monaco, the Netherlands, Norway, Oman, Portugal, Qatar, San Marino, Saudi Arabia, Singapore, Slovak Republic, Slovenia, South Africa, Spain, Sweden, Switzerland, United Arab Emirates, USA, Uruguay or Vatican City. You will however, have to provide travel tickets or proof of travel if asked. Australian citizens do not need a visa and British passport holders are granted six-month visas automatically on arrival. Any citizens of countries not listed above must apply for a visa before coming to New Zealand. It costs between $80 and $120 to obtain a visitor visa, depending on which country you are applying from.

If residency has already been arranged, your passport will be stamped accordingly when you arrive at immigration. Alternatively, you can arrive on a visitor visa and then apply for residency within three months.

If you have been recruited by a company from New Zealand, you apply for a work visa before arriving. If you have not been sponsored by a company, the best idea is to arrive on a visitor's visa and then apply for a work visa.

If there is a question mark over whether a friend or family member qualifies for a visa, they should apply in their home country. They need to provide evidence of good health (a medical certificate from a doctor), good character (no police record) and intentions for visiting a friend or family. See www.immigration.govt.nz for more information.

Health Card

You do not need a health card to access health services in New Zealand. Provided you are a New Zealand resident, health services are provided free or at a subsidised cost. For more information, see Health (p.161).

Residence Visa

To become a resident of New Zealand, you need to obtain a residence visa, either by applying outside the country or when you are on a visitor visa. You can apply through an office of the New Zealand Immigration service while in the country or at a New Zealand diplomatic mission overseas. You can also apply for some visas online at www.immigration.govt.nz. The site also gives you handy hints on how to apply and answers to the most popular questions asked.

There are several types of residence visas. The procedure for applying is the same if you are employed or unemployed, however a letter from your company will assist you in the application. Once you are a permanent resident, you are entitled to buy property. All migrants to New Zealand have to undergo a medical examination that involves chest x-rays, a physical examination and blood tests. These health checks are at your own expense. Health checks can be done at any medical practice by any registered doctor. Make sure you bring the completed medical and chest x-ray certificate (NZIS Form No.1007), passport, three passport pictures and details of any medical conditions. Allow up to three weeks before your certificate is issued.
In order to prove that you and your accompanying family members are of good character, the Immigration Service requires you to supply police certificates if you are applying for residence or will be working, visiting, or studying in New Zealand for longer than two years. These have to be from your home country and should prove you have no criminal record that could affect your entry into NZ.
Visas that grant permanent residency are listed on the New Zealand immigration website (www.immigration.govt.nz). These include **skilled and business migrant**, **work to residence** and **family quota**. Residence visas are valid for 12 months. After that time you may apply for permanent residency, otherwise known as a resident permit. This allows you to live and work in New Zealand indefinitely. It is valid for the time your passport is valid. When you renew your passport, you must renew your permit. After being a permanent resident for five years, an application for citizenship, which takes about two weeks to process, can be made.

Panel Doctors

If you'd prefer to have your medical check completed outside of New Zealand, you must visit a New Zealand Immigration Service approved panel doctor. A list, searchable by city and country, is available at: www.immigration.govt.nz.

Family Quota & Family Category

This type of visa enables families to be reunited by granting residence to a number of family members of New Zealand citizens or residents who are not eligible for residency under any other category. Otherwise each person may apply individually for residency. You are able to sponsor family members if you are an eligible sponsor and if your family meets the requirements for residence under the family quota category; see www.immigration.govt.nz.
Spouses of New Zealand citizens must prove their relationship is genuine and ongoing and that the couple has been together for at least a year. You may need to show photos of you as a couple, and provide letters and other keepsakes. Immigration can interview you both, asking anything from the colour of your partner's toothbrush to the colour of their eyes. Apart from requiring a sponsor under this category, medical and chest x-ray certificates are needed, as is a police certificate to prove you are of 'good character'.

Sponsored Employees

If you are coming here to work and are sponsored by a company or organisation then you will have to show correspondence with your New Zealand sponsor including letters of acceptance and work contracts, including start dates. You will have to provide medical and chest x-ray certificates and a police certificate. The chest x-ray is to prove that you are tuberculosis free.

Children

If your child is born in New Zealand they automatically gain New Zealand citizenship (and hence New Zealand residency). If you bring children with you they will need to enter on a visa; see www.immigration.govt.nz. If they are children of a New Zealand citizen born overseas, you can apply for a New Zealand passport with an overseas embassy or consulate.

Student

If you are coming to New Zealand to study for three months or more, you will need a student visa or permit. You can get a visitor visa if you need to study for less than three months. To get a student visa/permit, you will need an offer of a place from a school, university or college. You need to provide the name of the course and the minimum time required to complete it. The course must be approved by the New Zealand Qualifications Authority (www.nzqa.govt.nz). The cost of a student visa is $140. You must provide proof that you can support yourself; this includes evidence you have enough money to cover living costs, tuition fees and travel costs.

Work to Residence

This category of visa allows you to get a temporary work visa and/or permit as a step towards gaining permanent residence. Applicants may be qualified in occupations that are in demand in New Zealand, or may have exceptional talent in sports or the arts. After two years you can apply for residence.

Skilled Migrant

The skills shortage across New Zealand means that the government is keen to recruit people into certain industries. There's a comprehensive list on the New Zealand immigration website, but the broad categories are: education, health and medical groups, information and communications technology, agriculture and farming, engineering and trades.

The Immigration Department has a useful tool for assessing whether you have the necessary credentials to apply for this visa.

ID Card

New Zealand has no official ID or residence card. The accepted, standard form of ID is a driving licence with photograph. It does not hurt to carry your passport as well, especially if you know you'll need to produce identification.

Auckland CBD

Devonport beach

Too Young to Drive?
New Zealand has the lowest legal driving age of any country in the developed world, something which is often blamed for the high the number of fatal accidents. In September 2007, the Prime Minister Helen Clark backed a draft bill to raise the legal driving age to 16.

Driving Licence

Other options **Transportation** p.187

Getting a driving licence is relatively straightforward and should be made a priority if you intend to stay in New Zealand for longer than 12 months. You are legally able to drive on your overseas licence when you first arrive. Before 12 months has elapsed you need to apply for a New Zealand licence. You will have to pass a theory test and, depending on the country you are from, may also be required to pass a practical test. You need to carry your driving licence with you at all times. If you are stopped by the police while driving and not able to produce a licence, you can be fined. Normally, they give you 24 hours to take it into the nearest police station as proof. The legal age to start driving in New Zealand is 15. There are three types of licences: learner, restricted and full. You can apply for your licence at www.landtransport.govt.nz.

Full Licence

Anyone who holds an overseas driving licence or international driving permit is qualified to drive in New Zealand for up to 12 months. If your overseas licence isn't in English, you must carry an accurate translation. If you cannot produce your existing licence you must get a letter from your home country's licence issuing authority confirming the details, but be aware that this can take months.
To change to a New Zealand driving licence you will need to visit a Land Transport New Zealand driver licensing agent. These can be found at the offices of The Automobile Association, Vehicle Testing New Zealand (VTNZ), Vehicle Inspection New Zealand (VINZ) and On Road New Zealand.

Driving Schools			
AA Driver Training	Various Locations	0800 223 748	www.aa.co.nz
Driving Solutions	Christchurch	03 366 9978	www.csbec.co.nz
Excel Driver Training	Auckland	09 834 1313	www.excel-drivertraining.co.nz
Freedom Driving School	Wellington	04 977 5005	www.freedom.net.nz
Kiwi Driving School	Auckland	09 377 7802	www.kiwidrive.co.nz
Mainland Driving School	Christchurch	0800 438 542	www.driveschool.co.nz
Stephens Driving School	Wellington	0800 425 423	www.stephensdrivingschool.co.nz
Takapuna Driving School	Auckland	09 476 3603	www.takapunadrivingschool.co.nz

Here, you will have to take an eye test, pass a theory test (requiring a minimum 32 correct answers out of 35) and take a driving test if you are *not* from one of the following countries: Australia, Austria, Belgium, Canada, Denmark, Finland, France, Germany, Greece, Ireland, Italy, Luxembourg, the Netherlands, Norway, Portugal, South Africa, Spain, Sweden, Switzerland, the UK or US.
You will also need to complete an application form, provide proof of identification, evidence of address and, if needed, a medical certificate. The cost of a full licence is $115. There's full details of how and where to apply at www.landtransport.govt.nz.

Restricted Licence

You can apply for a restricted licence after you've held a learner licence for six months. You will have to pass a practical driving test in order to get the licence. You need to take an eye test and provide evidence of your current address. When you get a restricted licence, you can drive on your own, but not between the hours of 10:00 and 17:00. Between these times you must be accompanied by a supervisor, who must sit in the front passenger seat beside you. Your supervisor must hold a current, full New Zealand driving licence and have held it for at least two years. You are not allowed to carry passengers unless you have a supervisor with you. It costs $39.30 for the application and $48.90 for the practical driving test.

Learner Licence

You must be aged 15 or over to apply for a learner licence. You must pass an eye test and pass a theory test (you must have at least 32 correct answers out of 35), as well as fill out the application form and provide passport pictures and proof of your address. You can apply for a restricted licence after six months.

Driving Test

Although you're not required to take lessons from professionals before any driving test, it is advisable. The average cost of a lesson is $50. If a parent or friend takes the lessons they can use the Practice programme, devised by Land Transport NZ to provide learner drivers and their instructors with a structured plan of two or more hours' driving tuition a week. For more information about Practice, visit www.practice.co.nz or phone 0800 772 284. To get a full driving licence, if you are under 25, you need to have been a learner and to have been on a restricted licence for 18 months. If you are over 25, you need to have been on a restricted licence for six months. You can book a practical driving test for the restricted and full licence by phone or online at www.landtransport.govt.nz. The test costs $48.90 and $70.80 respectively.

Motorcycle Licence

The system works in much the same way as for cars. You must be at least 15 before applying for a learner's licence. After six months you can apply for a restricted licence and then a full version. The learner licence fee is $39.30, learner test $39.70 and a full licence test is $70.80.

Jack the Lad

According to the Department of Internal Affairs, the most popular name for a newly born boy in New Zealand in 2007 was Jack; for a girl it was Charlotte.

Birth Certificate & Registration

A child born in New Zealand automatically becomes a citizen if either parent is a citizen or permanent resident. Otherwise a child is not eligible for citizenship. Once your baby is born you have two months to register the birth. A Notification of Birth Registration form is typically provided to parents shortly after birth at the hospital where the child was born. This has to be be completed and returned to Births, Deaths and Marriages (address available at www.dia.govt.nz). This registration is free, but you pay $26 for a birth certificate, which you can order on the registration form. The Department of Internal Affairs keeps all birth, death, marriage and civil union details, so you can ask for duplicate copies of the birth certificate at any stage. There are no specific religious laws regarding childbirth and parents do not have to be married.

Passports

Babies and children under 16 must have their own passports in order to travel. To apply for a New Zealand passport, you must fill out a separate form for each child, and consent is needed from at least one parent named on the child's registration form. Application forms for a New Zealand passport can be downloaded from www.citizenship.govt.nz. The cost is $80 for a child under 16. You have to include the child's birth certificate, photo identification and fee when you submit the application form. If neither parent is a New Zealand citizen they must be lawfully and permanently living in the country.

To qualify for a visa, the child must either be born before the parents applied for residency and have been declared on the application for residence, or be born after the parents applied for residency.

The child is also eligible for a visa if it has been adopted by the parents, either in New Zealand or overseas in an adoption recognised under New Zealand law. The child must be in good health and a birth certificate must be provided. Either the mother or father can apply for a visa soon after the birth.
If you're in New Zealand on a temporary basis, you should consult your embassy in order to arrange getting a passport for your child from your home country.

Adoption

When a person has been legally adopted, the birth certificate that is normally issued is the post-adoptive birth certificate, which shows the details of the adoptive parents.
If you are born in New Zealand and adopted in New Zealand, you may wish to apply for a copy of your original, pre-adoptive birth certificate, showing the details of your birth before you were adopted. Under New Zealand law, you can do this once you turn 20, by writing to Births, Deaths and Marriages (www.dia.govt.nz).
It is a rigorous procedure to adopt in New Zealand. You will need to provide names of two people who know you well and will provide references. Child, Youth and Family (CYF), a part of the Ministry of Social Development, will obtain medical information from your family doctor about your health and you will be required to give permission to CYF for them to request a police certificate on you.
The Adoption Information and Services Unit (AISU) provides support to all parties in what can be a trying business. You have to sign a Consent to Adoption form in front of a solicitor, but this cannot be signed until the baby is at least 12 days old. Once you have signed the form, it is virtually impossible to have the adoption reversed.
To adopt a child overseas you have to lodge an application with the AISU or CYF. It holds a list of countries which are compatible for adoption under New Zealand law. There will then be interviews with social workers and education and preparation programmes. An assessment report is sent to the child's country of origin. Each country determines whether adoption will occur in its court or in the New Zealand Family Court. Adopting overseas can take from three months to two years.

Christenings & Naming Ceremonies

Both christenings and naming ceremonies are popular in New Zealand. Christenings are performed in churches and the ceremony is typically a formal one, which includes the naming of godparents who, along with the parents, pledge to bring up the child according to religious teachings. Naming ceremonies are much less formal and can be performed at the parents' house or any other venue.

Marriage Certificate & Registration

Marriage is still the most common option in New Zealand for couples looking to stay together long term. The country is also one of the most popular places to get married for overseas couples because of its weather and choice of picturesque venues. As these venues are often not on consecrated grounds, religious ceremonies cannot take place. Instead, marriage celebrants (individuals authorised by law to conduct the service) perform the ceremony.
If you have a religious service in mind, contact the relevant religious body. For example, the Catholic Church of New Zealand (www.catholic.org.nz), the Federation of Islamic Councils of New Zealand (www.fianz.co.nz), or the Hindu Foundation of New Zealand (www.asianz.org.nz). Most weddings in New Zealand follow the practices of a Christian culture but you're likely to come across a diverse range of services. See p.406 for a list of wedding items.

St Mary of the Angels, Wellington

Civil Partnerships

Since 2004, same sex couples and couples of different sexes over the age of 16 have been able to enter into Civil Union in New Zealand. You can also register for a union in New Zealand if you live overseas. For further information, see www.bdm.govt.nz. Couples in a Civil Union have the same status as marriage in terms of tax, benefits and immigration status.

Frosty Reception
Alpine and glacier wedding packages are available throughout New Zealand. One of the most spectacular settings is Tasman glacier (reached by ski plane), the country's largest. To find out more about traditional – and adventurous – weddings go to www.kiwi weddings.com or www.nzwedding services.co.nz.

The Paperwork

The Department of Internal Affairs records all marriages in New Zealand.
Couples need to complete a Notice of Intended Marriage form. These are available from your nearest Births, Deaths and Marriages office (you will find these listed in the blue 'Government listings' in the front of your telephone directory or online at www.bdm.govt.nz). One of you must appear in person before a Registrar of Marriages to sign a statutory declaration, which is when you pay a fee. If you wish for your marriage to be conducted by a Registrar of Marriages at the Registry Office, you must pay $170 when you send in or hand over the completed form. This includes the fee for the marriage licence and the ceremony.
Discuss with the registrar at the office where you plan to have the marriage ceremony, including the date and time. Remember to supply your contact details in case the registrar needs to get in touch. There are two types of marriages: a civil ceremony held by a registrar in a registry office and a ceremony conducted by a marriage celebrant, such as a priest or vicar.
If you wish for your marriage to be conducted by a Marriage Celebrant, you must pay a fee of $120 when you send in or hand over the completed Notice of Intended Marriage form. This includes the fee for the marriage licence but does not include any costs the celebrant may want covered. Three days later you will receive a marriage licence and copy of particulars of marriage, which you need to give to the celebrant. The licence is valid for three months after being issued.
You have to marry at the place stated in your application.
Some women choose to adopt their husband's surname. This is not a legal requirement but if you decide to, you need to complete a statutory declaration form and pay a fee of $45. A copy of the change of name form costs $20. Again, call 0800 22 52 52.
This can be used when changing your name on your driving licence or passport.
Overseas couples marrying in New Zealand need to fill out a Notice of Intended Marriage form and send the notice to a registry office close to where they are getting married (find a list at www.bdm.govt.nz). In general, any marriage overseas is recognised as legitimate in New Zealand.
A typical marriage ceremony involves the bride and groom signing declarations that they are over 16 years old, not legally married to others and not directly related to each other. After exchanging vows, the Certificate of Marriage is signed by the bride, groom and two witnesses.

Residence Status After Marriage

Spouses of New Zealand citizens, whether married, in a civil union, or de facto, do not have an automatic right to citizenship. To be eligible, the spouse must be a permanent resident for a certain period of time. Requirements for citizenship changed in July 2007. Applicants will need to have been a permanent resident in New Zealand for five years. See www.immigration.govt.nz for the latest information.

The Location

The advantage of marrying in New Zealand is the vast array of choice. You can opt for indoor, outdoor, traditional or non-traditional. If you want a registry office wedding you'll need to book at least a month before the ceremony. If you choose a traditional wedding in a church, you will also need to book well in advance, especially during spring (September to November) and summer (December to February). Beaches and country gardens are popular locations. Then there are the daring options: a balloon wedding or tieing the knot while bungee jumping. Another idea is to fly by helicopter to the top of The Remarkables (p.282) mountain range near Queenstown.

Death Certificate & Registration

Most deaths occur in a hospital or other care facility and those facilities can look after the formalities. If the death occurs elsewhere, call the person's doctor. A doctor must certify that death has occurred, determine the cause and time, and sign and issue a medical certificate with the cause of death. An ambulance will then take the body to the mortuary. The deceased's next of kin should be told as quickly as possible, and arrangements made with a funeral director, who, as well as organising the funeral or cremation, will act as a guide through the process of registering a death.
The family has almost absolute choice when it comes to the type of funeral service it wants. The only exception is if the death led to a coroner's investigation. Then the authorities might only allow a burial in case the body has to be exhumed for further investigation. In New Zealand, cremations now outnumber burials. A body must be cremated or buried in an area permitted by law. If you haven't employed the services of a funeral director, you must get permission from the local council to conduct the burial or cremation. You can find contact details of funeral directors from the New Zealand Funeral Directors Association (www.fdanz.org.nz). Funerals can be organised within a few days. Once the doctor has signed and issued a Certificate of Death, a funeral company can take charge of the body and prepare for the service.

Sure Thing
For a list of companies who can offer life and medical insurance, see p.162.

Claiming Life Insurance

Contact the deceased's insurance policy provider, who will require a doctor's Cause of Death Certificate, a certificate from the Department of Internal Affairs (to register a death is free but you pay $26 for a death certificate), your own proof of identification and, if applicable, a copy of the coroner's report.

Registering a Death

A death must be registered within three working days of the burial or cremation. There is no charge for this. If a funeral director is in charge of the arrangements, they will collect all the information required and forward it to the Births, Deaths, and Marriages at the Department for Internal Affairs for registration. Within the three days, two forms must be sent to the department: Notification of Death for Registration, and either a Medical Certificate Cause of Death or order of Disposal of Body under the Coroners Act of 1988. If you do not use a funeral director, you are required to notify the department of the death. Death certificates are issued by the Department of Internal Affairs (www.dia.govt.nz). A certificate costs $26 and you will need to fill out an official form, obtainable online or from your nearest office.

Investigation & Autopsy

A coroner is called if a doctor can't determine the cause of death or the death has occurred in unnatural circumstances. The Governor General appoints coroners who will then investigate. The coroner orders a post-mortem (autopsy) which is carried out by a pathologist. The coroner then opens an inquest into the death. A post-mortem may delay the release of the body for burial or cremation. When a body is removed from the place of death, the person in charge of the body is required by law to sign a Transfer of Charge of Body.

Working in New Zealand

New Zealand's economy is currently in good heart and there are very good opportunities for migrants. As long as you have marketable skills, speak good English, and have a positive can-do attitude you should have no trouble picking up work, as the shortage of skills in New Zealand is acute.

The volume of newspaper and internet job ads continues to run at all-time highs, with many employers having to readvertise positions they cannot fill. Jobs within the health, IT and education sectors are plentiful but lower skilled positions, such as plant and machine operators, are also proving difficult to fill. There has even been discussion of bringing in unskilled but willing Pacific Islanders to help with New Zealand's planned road building programmes.

Public Sector Jobs
All public sector vacancies are listed on the government's comprehensive website (www.jobs.govt.nz), where you can search for jobs by type and region, and apply online.

Kiwis are hard-workers, they rarely refer to people by their title, dress more informally than you are probably used to, and like to mix socially with their colleagues. They tend to be very technology-savvy and they like employees who show initiative.

In New Zealand there's a real recognition of the importance of work-life balance and most employers recognise the need for some flexibility in working arrangements. Non-standard employment options, giving people the flexibility (in negotiation with their employer) to choose the hours they work, are not uncommon. Flexible work arrangements, part-time work, job sharing, home-based work and paid parental leave have all been introduced to help workers in New Zealand achieve a better balance between their work and personal lives. If you're reluctant to tie yourself down to a nine-to-five job discuss the options with potential employers – they may be happy to make some allowances if it means they get your skills.

New Zealand's economy has traditionally been based on agricultural exports, such as meat, dairy and forest products, fruit and vegetables, fish, and wool. The economy though has diversified dramatically in the past two decades and tourism is now one of the biggest economic drivers in the country. New Zealand also has strong manufacturing and technology sectors.

According to latest Department of Labour figures, the average Kiwi male works 38.5 hours a week but earns about 1.3 hours paid overtime to take his total wages to $920 per week. Despite recent large strides towards pay equality, women in New Zealand still tend to get paid less than men. The average New Zealand woman earns about $735 a week. (Pay rates for women in New Zealand still lag behind those of men

Civic Square, Wellington

despite equal employment opportunity legislation. The disparity between wages paid to men and women is lessening though).

Graduates in the education sector earn relatively attractive salaries by New Zealand standards. For example, experienced school teachers with no management responsibilities earn $56,000 per annum. University research fellows can expect an initial $50,000 and can earn $73,000 once they reach a senior level. In general, the salaries offered in Wellington and Auckland tend to be higher than those offered in other parts of the country because the cost of living is also higher. For example, a chartered accountant in Auckland or Wellington might earn between $105,000 and $110,000 but only between $80,000 and $85,000 elsewhere. New Zealand's highest paid chief executive has a salary package of around $3 million but around $100,000 per annum is the norm for those in corporate management positions.

If you are going to be job hunting in New Zealand make sure you get your qualifications approved by the New Zealand Qualifications Authority as not all overseas qualifications will be recognised in New Zealand. You don't want to turn up expecting to walk into a job only to find your qualifications aren't acceptable. You will also need good references from previous employers and, in most cases, a valid work permit or residence permit. Some employers may be happy to deal with immigration procedures if it means getting a good, experienced worker on board but some will be reluctant to tackle the paperwork.

Most employers will be welcoming and take steps to help you adjust to life in a new country. Some will organise short-term accommodation for you on your arrival and some will help cover cost your moving costs – particularly if they have specifically recruited you for a position. These 'extras' should be detailed in any employment contract you sign. If you have skills that are in demand you can afford to be a little bit aggressive when it comes to negotiating your contract – push your employer a little and see whether there are any extras he can throw in. Some bigger companies will have their own superannuation schemes which you can join and some will offer subsidised healthcare. What you get will ultimately depend on your negotiating skills.

Remember when you are considering work opportunities in New Zealand that it is only a small country and that most of its companies are, by international standards, small. This means the environment will probably be more laid-back and informal than you are used to. However, Kiwis pride themselves on being hard-working and employers expect similar from their workers. The plus side of working for small companies is that often you get greater freedom and more responsibility. On the down side, there may be fewer opportunities for promotion.

The business sector within New Zealand is fairly close-knit so it doesn't pay to burn too many bridges. Everyone knows everyone else so if you upset one employer don't be surprised if there are repercussions when you come to apply for your next position.

Working Hours

Most employees in New Zealand start work at 08:30 and finish at 17:00, but working hours will vary depending on the sector. For example, government departments and local authorities often don't expect their employers to start until 09:00. Most people get paid for working a 40 hour week; for any extra hours worked they may get paid time and a half, or double time, depending on the terms of their employment contract.

Business Councils & Groups

Australia New Zealand Business Council	www.nzbcsd.org.nz
British New Zealand Trade Council	www.bnztc.co.nz
French New Zealand Business Council	www.fnzbc.co.nz
Korea New Zealand Business Council	www.koreanzbc.co.nz
Latin America New Zealand Business Council	www.lanzbc.co.nz
New Zealand Pacific Business Council	www.nzpbc.co.nz

Finding Work

The best course of action, not only for your peace of mind but also for your residence application, would be to get a confirmed job offer from a New Zealand employer before you arrive. But if you choose to come to New Zealand without one, the country's major newspapers are full of executive and general employment vacancies, and there are a multitude of recruitment agencies and online job sites where you can search vacancies, register your details and upload your CV.

It is a good idea to contact the New Zealand Qualifications Authority (www.nzqa.govt.nz) before you arrive, to ensure your qualifications are on a par with those in New Zealand. In some instances you may need to consider extra study or training in order to get the job you want.

WorkSite (www.worksite.govt.nz) provides information on most aspects of employment and training in New Zealand, including information on public holidays and New Zealand employment legislation.

The Whole World is Your Home

The Explorer Residents' Guides series is expanding, with new titles for locations as far flung as Los Angeles and Beijing in the pipeline. So if you fancy living abroad check out the complete list of current and upcoming Explorer guides on our website ***www.explorer-publishing.com*** Remember life's a trip... all you need to do is pick a destination.

Finding Work Before You Come

Even if you work in one of the areas where New Zealand is currently short of staff, such as the health and IT sectors, leaving the job hunt until you arrive in New Zealand might be inviting trouble. It's not uncommon for it to take up to six months for a migrant to find an appropriate position; there are many examples of extremely well qualified immigrants being forced into unskilled and menial jobs because they have been unable to secure a job in their field. The best way to get a handle on the job market is through websites such as www.seek.co.nz, www.jobstuff.co.nz and www.ubd.co.nz. The latter has a comprehensive directory of New Zealand businesses.

Make sure your curriculum vitae (CV) is user-friendly for potential employers. Remove any slang/terminology that is specific to your country and ensure that the contact details for your referees have international calling codes. Also include email addresses because of time zone differences. Give background information on the companies that you have previously worked for, such as the size of the organisation and its areas of expertise, as many companies will be unfamiliar to New Zealand employers. Always make sure you follow to the letter any guidelines on how to apply.

Recruitment Agencies

You can sign up with a recruitment agency but don't sit back and think they'll take care of everything for you. They will probably gush about your qualifications and promise you that work is just around the corner, but experience suggests you will need to be proactive and keep them on their toes if you want to secure your ideal position. Among the biggest general recruitment agencies in New Zealand are Adecco, Drake and Ryan Recruitment.

Companies that specialise in education sector recruitment include: Education Personnel Limited (www.edperson.co.nz), Oasis Education (www.oasis-edu.co.nz) and Select Education (www.selecteducation.co.nz). For jobs in the health sector, it's worth

Recruitment Agencies

Adecco	09 309 7572	www.adecco.co.nz
Bridge Personnel-Recruitment	09 479 9499	www.ubd-online.co.nz/bridgepersonnel
Coverstaff International	03 377 3992	www.coverstaff.net.nz
Drake	09 379 5610	www.drakeintl.com
Enterprise Recruitment	09 306 2160	www.enterprise.co.nz
Ryan Recruitment	03 365 0294	www.ryan.co.nz
Team Recruitment Ltd	09 525 6400	www.teamrecruitment.co.nz
The Ultimate Recruitment Company	04 472 7092	www.ultimaterecruitment.co.nz

contacting Med Call (www.medcall.co.nz) and Nursing Careers Allied Health (www.ncah.com). Other specialist recruitment agencies include Acorva (www.acorva.co.nz), who deal with technical design and planning staff; Ready Workforce (www.readyworkforce.co.nz), specialists in industrial recruitment, and Status Recruitment (www.statusrecruitment.co.nz), which concentrates on accounting, finance, legal and office support.

Finding Work While You're Here

The newspapers are probably the best source of job leads once you arrive in New Zealand. Saturday's newspapers (www.nzherald and www.stuff.co.nz) normally have the most classifieds but keep an eye out on other days of the week, too. It's worth reading news stories to find out about companies and organisations that might be expanding and looking for new staff. Cold calling and talking to human resources departments to find out about potential jobs is perfectly acceptable and can be successful.

Voluntary & Charity Work

There are plenty of opportunities to do voluntary or charity work in New Zealand, from helping prepare food parcels for the poor to planting trees in conservation areas (p.315). To work with some organisations, such as children's charities, you may need to undergo security or police checks, but for most charity work all you need is an altruistic streak. Most of the main cities in New Zealand have volunteer recruitment agencies. Alternatively, contact your nearest Citizen's Advice Bureau (www.cab.org.nz), who should be able to put you in touch with those groups looking for new recruits. Volunteering New Zealand (www.volunteeringnz.org.nz) is an umbrella organisation of national volunteer groups and is a useful resource.

Going it Alone

To set up and operate a business in New Zealand you will need to apply for a Long-Term Business Permit via the Immigration Department in Wellington. New Zealand is a popular country in which to set up a business because of its free-market philosophy and stable political system.

Working as a Freelancer/Contractor

In New Zealand's ever-changing economy there are plenty of opportunities for freelancers and contract staff, but you will need an appropriate visa, even if you only want to work temporarily. There is particularly high demand for contract workers in the horticulture and viticulture industries. If you are interested in working in these sectors you may qualify for a Seasonal Work Permit (SWP), which will allow you to undertake seasonal work for any employer in specific regions where a labour shortage has been identified by the Ministry of Social Development. Those looking for freelance positions in the media or creative sectors can get a handle on the market at www.thebigidea.co.nz. If you are seeking contract work in other professions or industries, you will probably need a temporary working permit. Check the New Zealand Immigration Service's website (www.immigration.govt.nz) for more information.

Employment Contracts

Once you've found the job you want and convinced the employer to hire you, you should receive a formal letter offering you the position. If you accept the offer, then you and the employer will begin negotiating the terms of your employment contract. Once you have signed that contract you are locked in and could be sued for breach of contract if you decide against taking the position.

In New Zealand, employers must offer their workers either an individual or collective (normally negotiated by a union) agreement written in plain English. Don't sign the contract until you've read it thoroughly.

It should include:

- Minimum wages for employees aged 18 or older
- Minimum wages for employees aged 16 to 17

- The same rate for the same job for male and female employees
- Four weeks' paid annual leave after 12 months in the job
- 11 public holidays per year, when those fall on days of the week when an employee would otherwise work
- After 6 months' employment, 5 days of special leave for the next year, which can be used as sick leave, domestic leave or bereavement leave
- After 12 months' employment, up to 12 months' parental leave

Your employment contract is likely to also include conditions relating to duties and responsibilities, the term of the agreement, pay rates, pay day, hours of work, health and safety, company policy, redundancy, and restraint of trade. Don't be afraid to haggle a little – there is almost always some room for negotiation.

Some employers may insist on a three-month probationary period but this is relatively unusual. If your contract does include a probationary period make sure you discuss the implications of this with your employer so you have a clear understanding of the standards you will be expected to meet.

Employment contracts in New Zealand are normally set for a fixed-term period and there is no automatic right of renewal. If your contract only provides for three months employment then that's all you should bank on getting. Employers, however, are always reluctant to lose good members of staff so if you do a good job it's possible a more permanent role will be found.

If the job's not you, you can resign at any time as long as you do so within the conditions of your employment agreement.

If your boss wants to get rid of you there must be good reason for your dismissal and the process must be conducted fairly. An employer can insist on a probationary period but this must be clear in your written employment agreement. If you feel that you have been treated unfairly, you can take legal action against your employer in the form of a personal grievance (see www.ers.govt.nz/problem/pg.html for more information). Another, more extreme, option is to take your case to the Human Rights Commission (www.hrc.co.nz).

If you decide to take a personal grievance case against your employer it will be costly. Lawyers don't come cheap and there is no government subsidy to help you mount your case. If you are a member of a union, it might pick up some or the entire tab, but that will largely depend on whether it thinks you have a strong case or are fighting a losing battle.

Employee Relations

If you have a grievance at work or would just like peace of mind on current rules and regulations, visit the website of the government's Employment Relations Service, www.ers.govt.nz.

Labour Law

The Department of Labour oversees employment laws in New Zealand and its website (www.dol.govt.nz) is full of useful information on worker's and employer's rights. The department also offers a free telephone information service (0800 20 90 20).

If you are dismissed from your job, ask for a written statement setting out the reasons why. You must make this request within 60 days of the dismissal and your employer must respond within 14 days. Then, if you still feel aggrieved, you can lodge a personal grievance case with the Employment Relations Authority (www.ers.dol.govt.nz). You will need to employ a lawyer to represent you, which can be costly and time-consuming. Disputes are often settled through mediation. If the outcome is in your favour, you may be reinstated or reimbursed lost wages. In some cases, compensation might also be awarded.

Under New Zealand's employment laws a person who is aged between 16 and 17 must be paid a minimum wage of $9 an hour. That minimum jumps to $11.25 for people over 18. Most jobs are based on a 40 hour working week.

By law you are entitled to four weeks' paid annual holiday after 12 months' service. Even if you don't last the year, you should still get holiday pay. For example, if you leave the job after six months your holiday pay should be the equivalent of 8% of your gross earnings. After six months with an employer, you will be entitled to five days' paid sick leave during the next 12 months of employment. You will also be entitled to paid bereavement leave of up to three days.

Looking for a job

On the birth of a child or adoption of a child under five years of age you can apply for parental leave, but you must have worked at least an average of 10 hours each week, including at least one hour per week or 40 hours per month, for the same employer for either six or 12 months before the expected date of birth or adoption. You may also be entitled to up to 14 weeks' paid parental leave.

Career Break
If you're thinking of a complete change of direction at work, have a look at the government's careers website, www.kiwicareers.govt.nz.

Changing Jobs

If you want to change jobs while in New Zealand you need to be aware that it could affect your immigration status.

If you're in the country under a working holiday scheme, changing employers does not affect your status. However, if your employer is named on your work permit, then you need to inform the Immigration Service (www.immigration.govt.nz) that you've changed employer. You will need to apply for a new permit when you have a job offer, and you should not start work in your new job until you have the permit.

If you gained your permit because you secured a job with an accredited New Zealand employer, you'll only be able to remain in New Zealand if you're working for another accredited employer. Even if this is the case, the Immigration Service will still need to approve the arrangement.

Company Closure

Whether you get any redundancy payment when a company you are working for closes will depend on the terms of your employment contract. If you are joining a start-up or relatively new company make sure there is a redundancy provision in your agreement, as there is no right to redundancy compensation unless employers and employees and/or their union have agreed to it. In addition to the financial ramifications of redundancy, you could also find your immigration status affected. If your employer is named on your work permit, then you need to inform the Immigration Service that you're no longer working for that employer. You will need to apply for another work permit and in some cases there will be restrictions on which company you can join. For example, if you gained your permit because you secured a job with an accredited New Zealand employer, you'll only be able to remain in New Zealand if you can get work for another accredited employer. Even if you find work with one, immigration authorities will still need to approve the arrangement. Visit www.immigration.govt.nz for more advice.

Bank Accounts

Setting up a bank account in New Zealand is relatively easy. All you will need is proof of identification and an IRD number from the Inland Revenue Department – and some money (typically around $2,000) to deposit.

Most banks open at 09:00 and close at 16:30, and are open weekdays only. Kiwibank is part of New Zealand's post office network and opens earlier than other banks. ASB and some others have been trialling weekend opening but this is the exception rather than the norm. You will find cash machines everywhere; if the cash machine is owned by a bank different to yours you may be charged a small transaction fee.

Banking Comparison

Name	Phone	Web	Online Banking	Tele-Banking
ASB	0800 803 804	www.asb.co.nz	✓	✓
BNZ	0800 240 000	www.bnz.co.nz	✓	✓
HSBC	0800 802 380	www.hsbc.co.nz	✓	✓
Kiwibank	0800 000 654	www.kiwibank.co.nz	✓	✓
National Bank	0800 181 818	www.nationalbank.co.nz	✓	✓
PSIS	04 495 7700	www.psis.co.nz	✓	✓
TSB	0508 872 2265	www.tsb.co.nz	✓	✓
Westpac	0800 400 600	www.westpac.co.nz	✓	✓

Most banks in New Zealand charge you for transactions, including writing cheques and making cash withdrawals. Charges can be as much as $1.50, but they vary from bank to bank, so it pays to shop around.

Some banks offer a flat monthly account fee or will waive the charges if you keep significant sums of money in your account(s) or have a mortgage with them. For example, KiwiBank and TSB Bank offer free banking so long as you keep between $4,000 and $5,000 in your account. All major banks offer online banking.

New Zealanders are savvy when it comes to banking and many use telephone or internet banking. Carrying large sums of cash around is unusual as most people use credit cards or Eftpos cards to pay for goods in shops. When you use an Eftpos card the money is transferred out of your bank straight into the shop's account.

How Much?
If the costs in the table opposite mean nothing to you, refer to the currency exchange table (p.53) to work out the equivalent in your home country's currency.

Financial Planning

There are several ways to profit from investments in New Zealand. The absence of a capital gains tax and the availability of high, tax-free dividends make it an attractive place to invest, but only if you obtain the services of a good financial planner or adviser.

Financial Advisers

Auckland	Phone	Web
AMP	0800 808 267	www.amp.co.nz
LifeTime Financial Group	09 418 5000	www.life-timefinancialgroup.co.nz
Money Matters	09 366 1672	www.moneymatters.co.nz
NZ Financial Planning	09 309 3680	www.invest.co.nz
NZ Guardian Trust	09 375 9453	www.nzgt.co.nz
Tower Finacial Services	0800 486 937	www.tower.co.nz
Wellington		
MacQaurie Financial Services	04 462 4914	www.macquarie.co.nz
The Terrace Financial Group	04 472 3322	www.tfg.co.nz
Christchurch		
Forsyth Barr	03 365 4244	www.forsythbarr.co.nz
Strategic Financial Planning	03 377 8046	www.strategicfp.co.nz

Cost of Living	
1.5l water	$2.39
Apples (1kg)	$1.89
Bananas (1kg)	$1.99
Bottle of house wine (at restaurant)	$27
Bottle of wine (off-licence)	$15.99
Burger (takeaway)	$4.50
Bus	$3
Camera film	$10.95
Can of dog food	$1.75
Can of soft drink	$1.50
Cappucino	$3.50
Car Rental	from $25 per day
Carrots (per kg)	$1.69
CD	$30
Chocolate bar	$1.20
Cigarettes	$10.60
Cinema ticket	$14
Dozen eggs	$3.50
Film developing	$19.95
Fresh beef (per kilo)	$9.99
Fresh chicken (per kilo)	$12.99
Fresh fish (per kilo)	$17.99
Golf (18 holes)	$35
House wine (glass)	$7
Large takeaway pizza	$12
Loaf of bread	$2.20
Local postage stamp	50c
Milk (per litre)	$1.89
New release DVD	$34
Newspaper (international)	$5.50
Newspaper (local)	$1.10
Orange juice (per litre)	$2.79
Pack of 24 aspirin	$3.89
Petrol (per litre)	$1.59
Pint of beer	$5
Postcard	$1.20
Rice (1kg)	$3.89
Salon haircut	male $25/female $45
Six pack of beer (off-licence)	$8.99
Strawberries (a punnet)	$3
Sugar (2kg)	$2.44
Taxi (10km journey)	$30
Text message (local)	20c
Tube of toothpaste	$3.99

The downside is that the financial planning and advisory industry in New Zealand is largely unregulated at present. As a result, financial advisers do not require a licence or registration, nor do they have to belong to an industry body. However, more than 1,400 financial advisers are members of the Institute of Financial Advisers (IFA) and, as such, voluntarily subscribe to a code of ethics and provide a written disclosure document that must declare any conflicts of interests.

The IFA website (www.ifa.org.nz) has a list of its members and advice on how to select a financial planner, including some suggested questions you should ask. The website also details its complaint procedure should you run into problems.

In recent years, residential property investors have done well in New Zealand. New Zealand's favourable tax regime has led to property investment becoming the preferred method for many people attempting to build their riches, especially as there is no tax to pay when you sell a property for a profit. Be warned though, there are rumours that the government is considering a change to these rules. If the Inland Revenue Department believe you are trading in property (buying and selling *frequently* for a profit) your profits will be taxed as part of your income. Most banks look favourably on borrowers wanting money for an investment property and are happy to provide mortgages provided you have sufficient equity.

Stock market investors have also done well in New Zealand in recent years. The major index, the NZX50, rose by more than 80% in the three years to May 2006, while the MidCap index rose by almost 100%. There are some tax exemptions on overseas holdings for new residents, so you should check with the Inland Revenue (www.ird.govt.nz). If you are living in New Zealand you don't have to pay tax when you sell your investments in New Zealand or Australia for a profit.

Buying and selling shares is relatively easy and you don't need to be a financial mastermind to play the stock market. For a fee of about $30 shares can be bought or sold over the internet. Most major banks, such as ASB and National Bank, also offer online share-trading facilities. The small size of the New Zealand stock exchange means it can take several days to obtain shares in some of the smaller companies. This is because there are generally fewer buyers or sellers than in larger financial markets such as New York and London. You can find out more about the New Zealand stock exchange at www.nzx.com.

Pensions

You will be entitled to a New Zealand pension at the age of 65 if you have lived in the country continuously for at least 10 years, five of them after the age of 50. At current levels, this is worth $249 per week after tax if you're single or $383 per week after tax for married couples. If you are receiving a pension from an overseas government you will need to declare it as it will probably be deducted from your NZ pension. If you think you will need more money than the state pension provides, there are plenty of private plans from which to choose, and many employers also offer contributory plans. The government has recently introduced a new retirement saving scheme called Kiwisaver, which is designed to encourage people to save more for their old age. See www.kiwisaver.govt.nz for more information.

Taxation

Double Trouble

If you are resident in both New Zealand and another country you could be at risk of double taxation. To avoid this, check the list of countries that New Zealand has tax agreements with; they include the UK, US, France, Germany, Australia, Canada, the United Arab Emirates and Japan.

You will have to pay tax on all the income you receive while in New Zealand whether it is generated in the country or overseas. This means you will need to apply to the Inland Revenue (www.ird.govt.nz), the government department that collects taxes, for an IRD number. An IRD number is generally issued within a few days and is required before you start a job or open a bank account.

Personal income tax rates vary but you can expect to pay 19.5% if you earn up to $38,000, 33% if you earn between $38,001 and $60,000, and 39% if you earn more than $60,001.

In addition to these payments, you also pay 1.2% of your wage for accident insurance (ACC levy). The levy covers the cost of medical treatments in the event that you have an accident in New Zealand (see p.164).

Most people pay these taxes as they earn their income. This is called PAYE and employers deduct tax on salary and wages. Banks and other financial institutions deduct tax on interest. If you do not pay tax on your income as it is earned (in which case you're probably self employed) you will need to file tax returns at the end of the tax year (31 March) to work out how much tax you owe the government. The New Zealand tax year runs from 1 April to 31 March.

One tax that you won't be able to escape paying is Goods and Services Tax (GST). It is charged at 12.5% and applies to everything you buy except for financial services and the rent or purchase price of residential property. Price tags in shops always include GST.

If you are running a business in New Zealand and it is a limited company, the company is taxed 33% of its profits. If your business has sales of $40,000 or more, you must register and charge a sales tax, GST, on sales. If you register for GST, you can reclaim any GST you are charged by other businesses.

The amount of accident insurance your business pays to the government depends on whether it has any employees. If it does, you pay insurance at the employer rate of 90c per $100 of payroll. Otherwise, you pay the self-employed rate of $1.79 per $100 of liable earnings.

Property Tax

Councils and regions raise money by levying property taxes, called rates in New Zealand. This money goes towards services such as street cleaning, and the upkeep of roads and community facilities. Each house or building has a 'rateable value.' The rateable value is normally dictated by the capital value of the property and it determines the amount of local tax that you as owner pays.

Need Some direction?
The ***Explorer Mini Maps*** pack a whole city into your pocket and once unfolded are excellent navigational tools for exploring. Not only are they handy in size, with detailed information on the sights and sounds of the city, but also their fabulously affordable price mean they won't make a dent in your holiday fund. Wherever your travels take you, from the Middle East to Europe and beyond, grab a mini map and you'll never have to ask for directions.

The more valuable your home, the more you will pay in rates. In some areas the rates will include charges for water and sewage disposal but in other cities, such as Auckland, these are charged separately. Rates in rural areas are generally lower than in urban areas because fewer services are provided to residents. An average suburban home in New Zealand can expect to pay somewhere between $1,000 and $2,000 in council and regional rates each year. Bills are sent out quarterly and you can find out how much you can expect to pay by contacting your local council; see www.localcouncils.govt.nz.

Legal Issues

The legal system in New Zealand closely mirrors that of the United Kingdom. The judicial system is independent from the Government and judges are appointed by the Governor-General, the Queen's representative in New Zealand.

The Supreme Court is the highest court in New Zealand. The court was only established in January 2004, and hears appeals on both civil and criminal cases. Before the Supreme Court was set up, the Judicial Committee of the Privy Council, which sits in London, was the highest court in New Zealand.

The Chief Justice of New Zealand sits on the Court along with four other Supreme Court judges. It is the role of the Supreme Court to determine the law on issues of particular public or legal significance. The Court of Appeal hears civil and criminal appeals and its role is to determine the law of New Zealand and resolve conflicting court decisions.

The High Court is made up of the Chief Justice and 37 other judges, who are based in Auckland, Hamilton, Wellington and Christchurch. They travel on circuit to 14 other cities around the country. The High Court deals with major crimes and larger civil claims. It also hears appeals from lower courts and tribunals.

New Zealand has 66 District Courts located throughout the country, which have extensive civil and criminal jurisdiction. Court proceedings are generally conducted in English, although the Maori language is officially recognised by the courts.

High Court, Auckland

Getting a Divorce

In New Zealand, irreconcilable differences is the only ground for legally dissolving a marriage or civil union. The only way of proving that your relationship has broken down irreconcilably is by living apart for two years. It is only then that your marriage or civil union can be dissolved.

Even if you both agree to the dissolution of the marriage, you have to wait for two years for the divorce to come through.

You must apply to the courts for an order to dissolve the marriage and one of you must be living in New Zealand. You will need to complete an application form, an affidavit and an information sheet. There are different versions of these forms depending on whether you are making the application together (joint application) or on your own (one party application). The filing fee is $175 and you will need to supply the court with a copy of your marriage certificate. If your marriage certificate is not in English, you will need to file a certified English translation with it.

Making a Will

If you are aged over 18 you can draw up your own will in New Zealand. But without proper legal advice it is easy to produce an invalid will, therefore it is advisable to consult a private lawyer or the Public Trust (www.publictrust.co.nz), who will draw up your will for free, provided it is named as executor.

Adoption

If you want to adopt in New Zealand you need to go through the government agency Child Youth & Family (CYF). CYF is part of the Ministry of Social Development (www.msd.govt.nz). If you are considering adoption, you can get more information from an adoption social worker, or from meetings arranged by the CYF. Contact the Adoption Information and Services Unit (AISU) in your area for more information. Adults over 18 years of age who are judged suitable to be parents are eligible to adopt.

Text in Touch

If you travelling in remote areas, you can send updates about your location and travel movements via text message to 7233 [SAFE] to let others know where you are. These details are kept on a database, which can be accessed by New Zealand Police if necessary. Call 111 if you are in any sort of trouble.

Crime

By international standards, New Zealand is generally regarded as a safe and law-abiding country. In 2005, there were more than 407,000 offences recorded by New Zealand Police, who resolved 43% of these. The overall recorded crime rate in New Zealand has fallen since 1992, with the 2005 rate being comparable to that of 1982. The media focus heavily on violent crime, but with between 40 and 70 murders each year, the number of serious offences isn't considered high compared with other western nations. It is dishonesty offences, including theft, burglary, car conversion, fraud and receiving, which account for more than half of all reported crime. Drugs and anti-social offences are the next biggest categories, followed by violent offences, property damage and abuse, administrative and sexual offences.

Poorly lit, sparsely populated areas can be unsafe after dark so stick to areas where there are lots of people as there is normally safety in numbers. If you are a woman think carefully before you walk city streets alone at night. While New Zealand isn't considered a dangerous country, it's not impervious to violent crime so you should take sensible precautions. Keep an eye on your belongings and don't leave valuables in your car as these are a favourite target for opportunistic thieves. According to the Ministry of Justice there is a higher risk of burglary and vehicle crime in Auckland, but risks for other offences are similar to other areas of New Zealand. New Zealand police has taken a tough stance in recent years on domestic violence – rates are among the highest in the developed world – and responds immediately to calls for help.

The Parliament

Driving Under the Influence

Drink-driving is a serious offence in New Zealand. Third and subsequent offenders face maximum fines of $6,000, prison terms of up to two years, and a minimum of one-year disqualification from driving. If you cause injury or death while drink-driving, you can be fined up to $10,000 for driving carelessly while under the influence (no breath or blood test needed); and up to $20,000 where a breath or blood-alcohol test shows you were over the limit.

Drugs Possession

If you're caught with illegal drugs in New Zealand, even cannabis, you could theoretically be sent to jail. Possession of class C drugs, including cannabis carries a maximum three-month prison term and/or a $500 fine. If you're caught with harder drugs such as heroin or cocaine you could be sentenced to up to 10 years in prison for serious offences and six months for possession.

Public Nuisance

If you're drunk and causing a public nuisance don't be surprised if you get thrown into a police cell to sober up. If police decide to charge you, you will have to appear in court and are likely to be given a fine if convicted.

Arrest

If you do get arrested you will be offered the opportunity to seek legal advice. If you can't afford a private lawyer, one will be provided by the courts for you. Depending on the seriousness of the offence you will either be granted bail or remanded in custody until your next court appearance.

Prison

Conditions in New Zealand prisons are basic but humane. They have a booking system for visits; you'll need to apply to the prison manager. Once you have been approved as a visitor you must book a time to visit with the prison/corrections facility. If you arrive at the prison without an approval letter, form of identification or a time booked, you may not be able to enter.

If you are convicted of a serious crime, New Zealand authorities may opt to have you deported to your country of origin. If you were convicted of a crime or crimes before you arrived in New Zealand this will show up on your police check and may affect your chances of gaining permission to enter the country. Most New Zealand employers will also ask if you have any criminal convictions.

Law Firms		
Auckland		
Duncan Cotterill	09 309 1948	www.duncancotterill.com
Kensington Swan	09 379 4196	www.kensingtonswan.com
Simpson Grierson	09 358 2222	www.simpsongrierson.com
Turner Hopkins	09 486 2169	www.turnerhopkins.co.nz
Wellington		
Bell Gully	04 473 7777	www.bellgully.com
Buddle Findlay	04 499 4242	www.buddlefindlay.com
Minter Ellison Rudd Watts	09 353 9700	www.minterellison.co.nz
Christchurch		
Anderson Lloyd	03 379 0037	www.andersonlloyd.co.nz
Cavell Leitch Law	03 379 9940	www.cavell.co.nz
Wynn Williams & Co	03 379 7622	www.wynnwilliams.co.nz

Housing

For most Kiwis, home ownership is an attainable dream and most would rather own than rent. However, property prices have risen steeply in the past few years and many first-home buyers are struggling to get onto the property ladder. That said, the rate of home ownership in New Zealand is among the highest in the world, so rental properties are at a premium in some areas. Prices vary greatly from city to city, suburb to suburb, so don't rush in and buy or rent the first place you see. Allow yourself time to get to know the local market in the main cities (p.96).

Fair Deal
The Department of Building and Housing has a useful list of average rents throughout the country, which is updated each month. The figures are based on what a 'willing tenant might reasonably expect to pay for the tenancy'. See www.tenancy.govt.nz/market-rent

Renting in New Zealand

With mortgage rates and property prices rising, renting is becoming a more popular option in New Zealand. You can rent anything from bedsits to executive family homes, but be prepared to pay a premium for properties in sought-after areas where you're close to good schools and amenities. It is unlikely that any accommodation will be provided as part of your employment package, so the job of finding somewhere to live will fall to you.

How much rent you will pay will be influenced by the area, the condition the house or apartment is in and its size.

Homes are described as 'apartments', 'units', 'houses', or 'townhouses'. An apartment is normally in a block, with others above and/or below it. A 'unit' or 'flat' is a semi-detached or terrace house. A 'house' is normally a detached, standalone structure. A 'townhouse' can be either detached or attached to another house. Townhouses are usually reasonably modern and tend to have smaller gardens than houses.

The vast majority of homes for rent in New Zealand are unfurnished – they'll have carpets, curtains or drapes and a cooker or stove, but that's it.

Most newspapers include listings of rental properties (especially on Saturday and Wednesday), but it might be easier to sign up with an agency that can show you multiple properties. If you do find a rental property through a real estate agent, you will have to pay them a fee – typically an amount equal to one week's rent. If you find a rental property in the newspaper classifieds, be prepared to act fast, particularly if the property is in a popular area.

Rental Contracts

There are two common types of rental contract in New Zealand – the fixed term and the periodic tenancy. These will be explained in detail further on in this chapter (p.90).

Once you've signed a tenancy agreement you will be expected to pay a bond (deposit). A landlord can ask you to pay up to four weeks' rent as bond, but two weeks is the norm. By law, the landlord has to deposit your bond with the Bond Centre at the Ministry of Housing within 23 days. Receipts are then sent to you and the landlord.

You will need your receipt to claim your money back from the Bond Centre when your tenancy ends. Provided you haven't damaged the house or its contents in any way, you should get all your bond money back. Rent is normally paid fortnightly, in advance. It does not normally cover the cost of electricity or phone, so make sure you budget extra for essential utilities.

Real Estate Agents

Finding a real estate agent in New Zealand is easy – they're everywhere. Make sure you chose one who is a member of the Real Estate Insitute of New Zealand. The institute regulates

Real Estate Agents		
Barfoot & Thompson	09 638 9158	www.barfoot.co.nz
Bayleys	09 375 6868	www.bayleys.co.nz
Harcourts	09 520 5569	www.harcourts.co.nz
Harveys	09 375 7550	www.harveys.co.nz
LJ Hooker	0800 447 060	www.ljhooker.co.nz
Ray White	09 377 5069	www.raywhite.co.nz

Kiwi housing styles

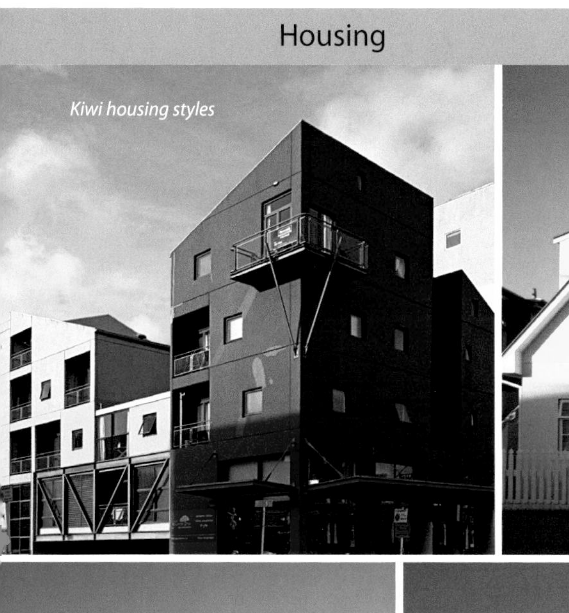

Housing Abbreviations

Br	Bedroom
Bthrms	Bathrooms
C/yard	Courtyard
Cas din	Casual dining
D.washer	Dishwasher
Dbl	Double
Dn. rm	Dining room
Ens	Ensuite – bedroom has private bathroom
F.ds	French doors
Fam hm	Family home
Gdn	Garden
Gge	Garage
HRV	Heat recovery ventilation – a system that provides an exchange of air and better climate control
Htg	Heating
Int.acc	Internal access, typically from a garage to the kitchen
L/s	Landscaped
Lge	Large
Liv.	Living
Neg.	Negotiable
O.n.o.	Or near offer
O.s.p.	Off-street parking
O/p kit/liv	Open-plan kitchen/living area
P/mats	Permanent materials
Sep	Separate
Spec'd	Specified
T/house	Townhouse
TLC	Tender loving care
U/floor	Underfloor heating
W.I.R.	Walk-in-wardrobes, walk-in closet
WCs	Toilets

the real estate industry and offers the consumer a degree of protection. Most real estate agents are paid a percentage of the sale price (normally around 3.5%) by the vendor when they sell a property, but some charge a flat fee. Discuss commission with an agent before you sign anything.

The Lease

When you've found the house you'd like to rent you will need to negotiate with the landlord as to whether you sign a fixed-term or periodic tenancy. If you sign a fixed-term tenancy, you are agreeing to rent the property for a set period, say six months or a year. The advantage of this type of tenancy is that your rent cannot be increased unless there is a clause to that effect in the lease. Read the fine print carefully before you sign. A periodic tenancy is more common and does not bind you to renting the property for any set amount of time. To end your lease you simply need to give the landlord three weeks' notice. But if he wants to turf you out, he needs to give you six weeks' notice, and 60 days' notice in the event of a rent increase. A periodic tenancy is probably the best option if your circumstances are likely to change, as it allows you to keep your options open.

Main Accommodation Options

Renting a flat

If you value your own space, then you're probably best off renting a flat or apartment. Rents vary significantly, from city to city, suburb to suburb. Expect to pay a premium for flats or apartments that are close to amenities and in good condition. Most flats come unfurnished so you will have to source furniture from friends, buy new, or ship some over from home.
Most New Zealanders choose to live in detached houses with their own private garden. Such properties are popular with families and students because they offer plenty of space. The size, location and condition of the house will determine the rent.

Flatting

If you don't know many people in New Zealand and have no children, sharing a flat might be an option for you. It's a good way to meet others and it tends to be less expensive than renting or buying a property on your own. Most newspapers include to let or flatmate wanted sections that list rooms available for rent. Prices for a room range from about \$60 a week in a basic student flat to around \$200 a week for a room in a luxury pad. Flatmates normally split the cost of electricity and phone bills and often pool money to buy groceries.

Serviced Apartments

You'll find serviced apartments in all the main cities. Most of these are located within the central business district (CBD) and often have extra facilities such as gymnasiums and swimming pools. They don't come cheaply, but if you're not good at housework and like everything laid on for you, they're a good bet. Expect to pay anything from \$300 to \$700 a week.

Other Rental Costs

When calculating your housing costs, remember that most rentals do not include the cost of utilities such as electricity and a landline. And while water is included within your rates in many parts; in some areas, including Auckland, you will have to pay for what you use. Most utility companies will ask you to pay a bond (a deposit) and a connection fee (p.154). If you found your rental property through an agent, you may also have to pay them commission, which is normally the equivalent of a week's rent.

Final Offer?

For average real estate prices, go to www.reinz.co.nz. To peruse the market, start with www.realestate.co.nz, www.trademe.co.nz and www.open2view.com. In Auckland pick up a copy of the local Property Press *at real estate agencies.*

Buying Property

A buoyant property market has seen house prices in New Zealand soar in recent years, with many overseas investors joining the throng of local buyers looking for their own slice of paradise. Property along New Zealand's coastline, in particular, has skyrocketed in value and now even simple beachfront baches (a Kiwi term for a beach cottage) can fetch prices in excess of $1 million. If you're a permanent resident, there are no restrictions on the property you can buy in New Zealand. If you have any other status, you are limited to buying a home on less than five hectares (12.5 acres) of land.

In New Zealand 'open homes' are popular with both sellers and buyers. Normally held at the weekend, and lasting for half an hour to an hour, an 'open home' is when anyone is allowed to look around the property without first making an appointment. Even if you're undecided about buying, a visit to an open home gives you a good idea of the market in your area. If you're short on time though, your best bet might be to have a real estate agent take you around. Agents are usually happy to do this, particularly if you are a cash buyer as they stand to earn significant commission if you purchase a home through them.

Once you've found the right place, done your sums and made sure you can afford it, you need to make an offer. Most New Zealand property is offered at a fixed asking priced or within a price band. It's normal to offer less than the asking price; how much less will depend on the state of the housing market and your desire to own that particular property. Quotable Value NZ (www.qv.co.nz) can help you find out what other properties in the area have sold for, so that you can make an appropriate offer.

Auctions have become a popular way of selling property, particularly in recent years when the property market has been hot. People usually opt to auction their properties when they think buyers will bid the price up.

Auctions cost the seller more, and are a more lucrative marketing option for real estate agents because even if the house doesn't sell, they still earn auction fees. This means that real estate agents will often try to persuade homeowners to sell by auction, but think carefully before you agree to it and make sure you know exactly how much it will cost you.

The Process

If the house you've fallen in love with is selling at a fixed price, you will normally make an offer through the real estate agent who showed you the property. This is where the negotiation begins. Your offer might be met with a counter-offer. Be prepared to negotiate until you reach an agreement with the seller. And be aware that even if the seller accepts your conditional offer, you can still be gazumped: if someone comes along with an unconditional offer, the seller can accept it. Once your offer is agreed upon, you will be expected to pay a deposit – normally about 10% of the purchase price. If the house is being auctioned, you can make an offer before auction day but you need to be sure that it is the property for you because your offer has legal status as an auction bid. This means that your offer cannot have any conditions attached to it and if it is accepted, you will have to go through with the purchase.

The seller can accept or reject your offer and continue with the planned auction. If a house goes to auction and bidding is light, you could find yourself bidding against the sellers. Here, an agent is allowed to make bids on the seller's behalf. If you suspect you're in a bidding war against the sellers themselves, you are advised to stop bidding. If the house doesn't reach its reserve price at auction, it's normal practice for the seller to then start negotiations with the highest bidder.

If you do buy a house at auction, you need to have funds available immediately for settlement – there really is no room for second thoughts.

Buying to Rent

Buying property is considered a sound investment, and a growing number of New Zealanders own not only their home but also an investment property that they rent out. If you plan on following suit, make sure it's in an area where rental accommodation is in high demand, such as near a university or in the inner city. If you don't want the hassle of managing the property yourself, you can employ the services of a property management company who will ensure the property is adequately maintained – for a fee, of course.

Selling Property

While most houses in New Zealand are sold through a real estate agent, a growing number of property owners are adopting a do-it-yourself approach, using websites such as trademe.co.nz to market property themselves. Private property sales avoid the need to pay real estate agent commission, which, at around 3.5% of the selling price, can be quite a sizeable sum. Agent commission varies so shop around and find out from the outset what expenses they expect you to bear.

Mortgages

If you've met the government's requirements to work or live in New Zealand, you will almost certainly be eligible to get a mortgage from a bank or lending institution. It's relatively easy to get a mortgage, with all the major banks offering home loan services. How much the bank will loan you, and under what terms and conditions, varies so it's worth shopping around. A mortgage broker can help you with this process (normally at no cost to you as they recover their fees from the banks) saving you considerable time and effort. Find recommended companies from the New Zealand Mortgage Brokers Association (www.nzmba.co.nz).

In general, lenders will offer around four and a half times your gross household income, provided that you have no significant debts. If you're a couple and both employed, some lenders will finance mortgages of five times your gross joint income. It is possible to get mortgage certificates from banks prior to purchasing a property which state how much the bank is willing to lend you, and this can help speed up the buying process.

Table mortgages are the most common type in New Zealand. Repayments do not change over the lifetime of this type of loan, which means that in the first few years you're really only paying back the interest. That might not sound very appealing but the advantage is that it is easy to plan ahead because you know the exact amount of your mortgate repayments. As the years pass, you will start repaying more of the principal amount.

Another possibility to consider is a reducing mortgage. Here, you pay off the same amount of principal with each payment so that interest charges fall with time, as do your payments. Whether you take a table or reducing mortgage, you will also be able to choose between a variable or fixed-rate mortgage.

Mortgage Providers

ASB	0800 803 804	www.asb.co.nz
BNZ	0800 240 000	www.nationalbank.co.nz
HSBC	0800 802 380	www.hsbc.co.nz
Kiwibank	0800 000 654	www.kiwibank.co.n
National Bank	0800 181 818	www.nationalbank.co.nz
PSIS	04 495 7700	www.psis.co.nz
TSB	0508 872 2265	www.tsb.co.nz
Westpac	0800 400 600	www.westpac.co.nz

With a variable-rate mortgage, the interest rate will change whenever the Reserve Bank raises or lowers interest rates (of late the former has been occurring on a regular basis). Or you can fix the rate for anywhere between six months and five years. If interest rates go up during the term of your loan, your repayments remain the same. But naturally your repayments also stay the same if the interest rate drops.

Other Purchasing Costs

Buying a house in New Zealand, like anywhere else, is an expensive business. You will probably need to pay several hundred dollars for a valuation report on the property, which is required before a bank will approve a mortgage. You should also budget a couple of thousand dollars for legal costs, for things such as obtaining a Land Information Memorandum (LIM) report from the local territorial authority. The LIM contains information about a property's zoning, boundaries and building consents. It often pays to have a professional building inspector check the property before you finalise the contract, to ensure you're not buying a two-storey lemon. This is particularly important in the wetter parts of the North Island, in particular.

Leaky Homes
Auckland has been dogged with a problem of leaks appearing in new housing developments in recent years. It pays to get an independent builder's report; the damage has been known to cost buyers thousands of dollars in unexpected repair bills.

Real Estate Law

Before entering into any agreement to buy property, you should appoint a lawyer. In general, real estate agents act for the vendor and, while they may appear friendly, it's wise to remember that it's not your interests they have in mind. Once you've chosen a property, the real estate agent will draw up a sale and purchase agreement. This outlines your offer, the date of settlement, and any conditions that must be met before the sale goes ahead. Before you sign this agreement, you should go through it with your lawyer. There are two kinds of offers: unconditional and conditional. An unconditional offer is an outright offer to buy the property. You need to be completely sure that it is the property you want, and that you have sufficient funds, before you make an unconditional offer as once it has been accepted, you are legally obliged to go through with the sale.

A conditional offer is also a binding contract, provided that all your conditions are satisfied. You can back out of this type of contract if one or more of your conditions are not met. Conditions may include:

- Subject to valuation: This means the sale will only go ahead if the valuation is acceptable to you and your bank.
- Subject to title search: The sale will only go ahead if there are no ownership, access or other claims recorded on the property title.
- Subject to a Land Information Memorandum (LIM) report: The sale will only go ahead if the property (including any alterations) complies with all building regulations.
- Subject to a builder's or engineer's report: The sale will only go ahead if you are satisfied that the house and the land it is on are sound.

You can set other conditions. For example, you may want to insist that certain repairs are carried out on the property before your offer becomes unconditional. You should discuss these things with your lawyer and make sure you are happy with the conditions before you sign the sale and purchase agreement. The vendor can accept your offer, reject it, or make a counter-offer. If a counter-offer is made, the real estate agent acts as the go-between until an agreement has been reached or one of the parties calls it quits. If you cannot agree on a price, you can withdraw your offer.

On signing a sale and purchase agreement you will typically be expected to pay all or part of your deposit to the real estate agent, who will place that money in a trust account until all the conditions of the agreement have been met. The sale and purchase agreement will state the amount of time you have to settle the conditions. Once that has occurred the offer becomes unconditional and there's no backing out.

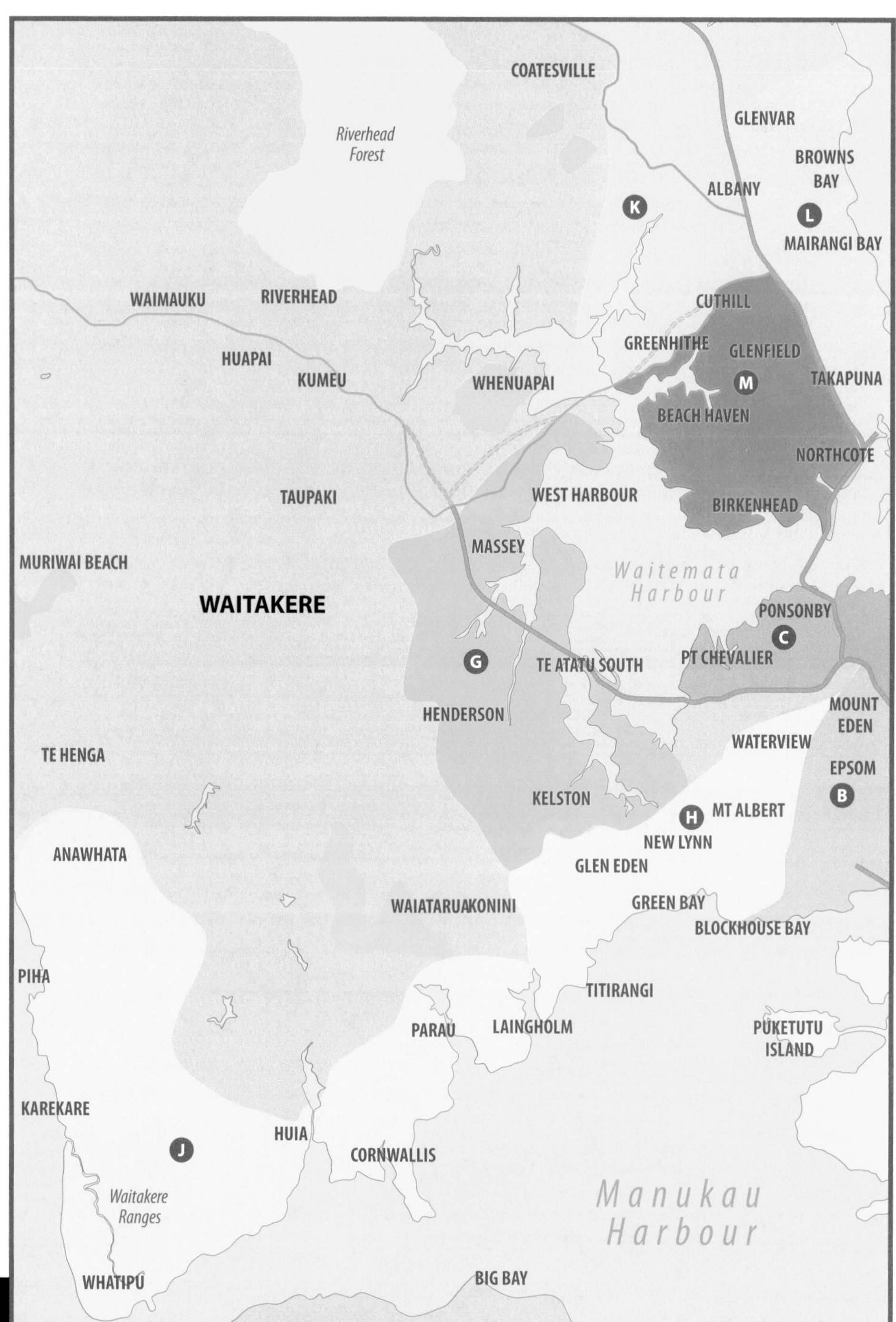
COATESVILLE
Riverhead
Forest
GLENVAR
BROWNS
BAY
ALBANY
K
L
MAIRANGI BAY
WAIMAUKU
RIVERHEAD
CUTHILL
GREENHITHE
GLENFIELD
HUAPAI
KUMEU
WHENUAPAI
M
TAKAPUNA
BEACH HAVEN
NORTHCOTE
TAUPAKI
WEST HARBOUR
BIRKENHEAD
MASSEY
MURIWAI BEACH
Waitemata
Harbour
WAITAKERE
PONSONBY
C
PT CHEVALIER
G
TE ATATU SOUTH
HENDERSON
MOUNT
EDEN
WATERVIEW
TE HENGA
EPSOM
B
KELSTON
H
MT ALBERT
NEW LYNN
ANAWHATA
GLEN EDEN
GREEN BAY
WAIATARUA
KONINI
BLOCKHOUSE BAY
PIHA
TITIRANGI
PARAU
LAINGHOLM
PUKETUTU
ISLAND
KAREKARE
HUIA
J
CORNWALLIS
Manukau
Harbour
Waitakere
Ranges
WHATIPU
BIG BAY

Residential Areas – Auckland

RANGITOTO ISLAND
HAURAKI
Hauraki Gulf
ONEROA
Q
ONETANGI
OSTEND
MOTUIHE ISLAND
DEVONPORT
BRAWNS ISLAND
WAIHEKE ISLAND
PARNELL
MISSION BAY
F
A
ORAKEI
NEWMARKET
MEADOWBANK
REMUERA
GLEN INNES
HALF MOON BAY
E
MELLONS BAY
ELLERSLIE
D
OMANA
N
PANMURE
BOTANY DOWNS
PENROSE
PAKURANGA
ONEHUNGA
WEST FIELD
EAST TAMAKI
MANGERE BRIDGE
WHITFORD
OTARA
MANGERE
P
PAPATOETOE
FLAT BUSH
MANUKAU
BROOKBY
CLEVEDON
AUCKLAND INTERNATIONAL AIRPORT
WIRI
TOTARA HEIGHTS
MANUREWA
0 Scale 1:23,000 10km
N
WEYMOUTH

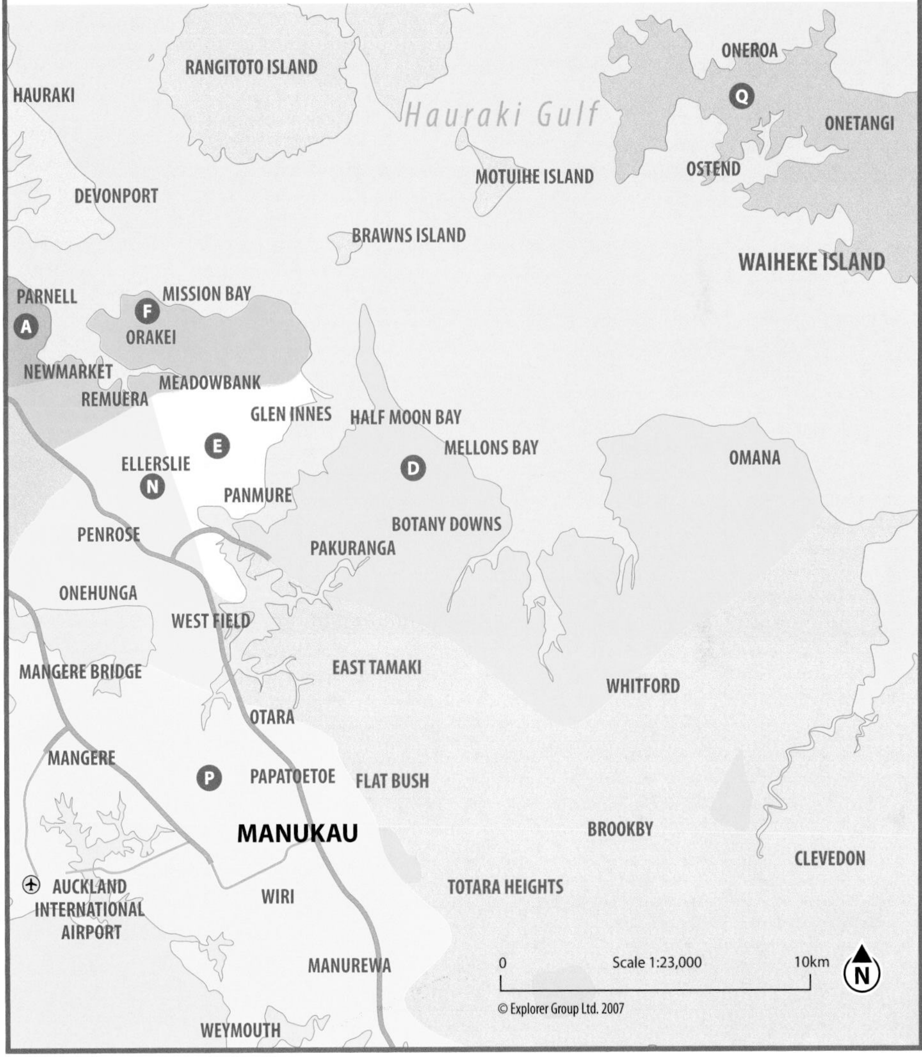

The Plot Thickens
Throughout the Residential Areas pages you'll see mention of 'sections'. These refer to the plots of land that come with an individual property.

Auckland & Further Out

With several great beaches, two large harbours and a relaxed lifestyle, Auckland is a great spot for a city – if you don't mind idling in congested traffic. Certainly plenty of New Zealanders and immigrants think so; greater Auckland attracts about 100 new residents every day and hosts the bulk of New Zealand's immigrants. The population is 1.3 million and counting, so it's still a small city by international standards, though it does house a third of New Zealand's population.

The bulk of Auckland's residents are New Zealand Pakeha – mostly descended from migrants from the UK and Europe – but a whopping 37% were born overseas, most in Asia and the Pacific Islands.

Auckland's popularity is making it an increasingly vibrant, international and colourful city, but this has also brought problems: traffic congestion, inadequate public transport and rising house prices.

It might make sense to put off deciding where to live in Auckland until you've landed a job. It is a sprawling city and you won't want to be commuting from Whangaparaoa, 40km north of the city, to Papakura, 30km south, in rush-hour traffic.

Map p.488, 489, 492
Area A p.94-95

Central Auckland: City, Parnell & Newmarket

Auckland inner-city living was once the preserve of grungy students. Now high-rises are shooting up all over and are especially popular with immigrants, though locals too are cottoning on to the benefits of city life. To the east, the gracious and arty suburb of Parnell is the domain of the wealthier city dweller, while the shopping haven of Newmarket is sprouting apartment complexes.

Best Points
Great shopping, eating, drinking and entertainment.

Worst Points
Noise, parking hassles and cheap and ugly high-rise apartments.

Accommodation

An inner-city building boom has created a glut in the apartment market, which means there are bargains to be found, especially for renters, although some places are pokey and noisy. Apartment prices vary from less than $100,000 for a tiny leasehold student studio, to $10 million for a Princes Wharf stunner. On the city fringes, Eden Terrace, Grafton and Newton, there are smaller, low-rise apartments. Parnell has grand old homes and new mansions priced in the millions, but also cheaper apartments and terraced houses. Newmarket has myriad brand-new apartments to buy for $250,000 to $500,000 and also to rent. Rents range from less than $300 per week for a studio apartment in the city to $2,000 for a penthouse with views.

Shopping & Amenities

You won't be short of places to spend your money here, with Queen Street's chain stores, High Street's designer clothing, the quirky shops of Karangahape Road and Symonds Street, Parnell's galleries and boutiques, and Newmarket's chain stores and boutiques. Neither will you be short of things to do, with the Auckland Museum and Auckland Domain, art galleries, Parnell's Rose Gardens, and swimming pools in Parnell, Newmarket, and the Viaduct. There are also cinemas in the city and in Newmarket. Auckland City Hospital (p.164) is in Grafton.

Eating & Drinking

It could take you years to get around every eatery in the city centre, from top gourmet restaurants, to cheap ethnic food halls. There's also no shortage of bars, from big, brash waterfront offerings, to dark, 'cool' hangouts, hidden all over the city. Parnell has lively bars, restaurants and cafes. Newmarket is littered with food and drink establishments too, though it has less charm than Parnell and less energy than the city.

Parnell

Education

Parts of this area fall into the zones of Auckland Girls' Grammar School, Western Springs College, Auckland Grammar School and Epsom Girls Grammar School. Younger children can attend Ponsonby's primary schools. There's a private secondary school in the inner city, a couple of international colleges and a Jewish school. Parnell has a private year 1-13 school. The University of Auckland and the Auckland University of Technology are in the central city.

Transport

From the city you can catch a bus, ferry or train to almost anywhere in Greater Auckland or the Hauraki Gulf. The regular Link buses connect the city, Parnell, Newmarket and Ponsonby. The airport bus leaves from the city and the northern, southern and north-western motorways intersect here. Newmarket has a railway station on the city to Pukekohe route. If you have a car, make sure you have off-street parking. Parnell is 3km from the city, Newmarket is 4km.

Safety & Annoyances

Like any international city, central Auckland has its problems with drunks and crime, but it's probably safer than most. Before you move in, visit the neighbourhood at night to check its safety and noise levels.

Central Auckland: South to Manukau Harbour

Map p.484, 496, 497
Area B p.94-95

Best Points
Quaint Mount Eden Village, cool Kingsland and affordable properties to the south.

Worst Points
Grammar-zone snobbery, peak-hour gridlock and rundown rental properties in the outer suburbs.

Mount Eden and Epsom are the king suburbs of this area, with their gracious old wooden villas and mansions, and Auckland's most sought-after state secondary schools. The suburbs at their edges have also risen in popularity as Auckland's property market has boomed. Mount Albert is now not that far behind in popularity or price.

Accommodation

The most exclusive streets of Mount Eden and Epsom are lined with gated million dollar-plus mansions, and there are many villas, bungalows and large new houses from $700,000. Though they're still rough in places, Mount Albert, Kingsland, St Lukes, Sandringham, Balmoral and Morningside are attracting young professionals and families who have been priced out of Mount Eden and Epsom. Further south, the traditionally working-class suburbs of Mount Roskill, Three Kings and Hillsborough are also going up in the world. Prices start at less than $300,000 for a small apartment or unit in St Lukes, and $300,000 to $500,000 for a unit in Mount Eden.

Shopping & Amenities

Mount Eden Village is a small but pleasant stretch of shops. Kingsland has a few boutiques and quirky stores and Epsom is known for its antiques. There are several comparatively shabby shopping strips elsewhere. For chain-store shopping and blockbuster movies, head for Westfield's busy St Lukes mall. As for open space, there's Mount Eden Domain or, for cricket and rugby fans, Eden Park (p.45). There's an arthouse cinema (Lido, 09 630 1500) in Epsom, a golf course on St Lukes Road and public swimming pools in Mount Albert and Mount Eden.

Mount Eden

Eating & Drinking
Mount Eden village is probably the most pleasant place for a coffee, a drink or a bite to eat, though Kingsland is the most hip. There are plenty of ethnic restaurants and takeaways throughout the area. Molton, at 422 Mt Eden Road, is the area's most acclaimed restaurant.

Education
Most of Epsom and Mount Eden, and parts of the other suburbs, lie in the coveted Auckland Grammar School and Epsom Girls Grammar School zones. The alternatives – Mount Albert Grammar School, Avondale College, Western Springs College and Mount Roskill Grammar – are also pretty good. Epsom has the private girls' schools, St Cuthbert's College and Diocesan School for Girls. There are several Catholic schools in the area. Kingsland has no primary schools, but there's a pedestrian bridge over the motorway to Newton Central School. Unitec University of Technology is based in Mount Albert.

Transport
Mount Eden offers the quickest commute to the city and the most regular bus services, and some residents even walk in. Residents in suburbs further out face longer trips and less regular services. The Western Line Train stops in Kingsland, Morningside, Mount Eden and Mount Albert. Kingsland and St Lukes back onto the North-Western Motorway and Epsom and Mount Eden are near the Southern Motorway. A planned Western Ring Route motorway will carve through Mount Roskill and Mount Albert. Mount Eden is 3km from the city, Mount Albert is 8km and Hillsborough is 9km.

Safety & Annoyances
The area is generally safe though some parts are slightly rough. There are several main roads in the area that get congested at peak times.

Central Auckland: West, Ponsonby to Point Chevalier

Map p.484, 486, 487
Area C p.94-95

Best Points
Lovingly restored old homes, great cafes, pubs and restaurants, proximity to the city.

Worst Points
Cramped sections, parking woes and speedway noise.

Until a generation ago, much of this area was run down and considered undesirable. Today, the situation couldn't be more different. The charm of the area has been restored along with its characteristic old kauri villas, which are filled with young professionals and middle-class families. All relish living so close to the city, and close to many great cafes. There's also a sizeable Pacific Islander population.

Accommodation
Almost all of the villas in Ponsonby, St Mary's Bay and Herne Bay have been beautifully restored to a standard they wouldn't have known even when new. They're not cheap, ranging from about $800,000 to $2m or more. You can still find cheaper options in the suburbs, further west, as well as affordable newer houses and apartments. The cheapest apartments are $200,000 to $300,000 – but don't expect anything grand. There's a lot of good rental property, popular with young professionals who work in the city.

Shopping & Amenities
Ponsonby and Jervois roads have great boutique clothes and homewares stores but, like the real estate, it isn't always cheap. There are appealing clusters of shops at West Lynn on

Ponsonby villa

Richmond Road and in Westmere. Grey Lynn and Point Chevalier have shabbier but interesting shopping strips. Western Springs hosts Auckland Zoo, the Museum of Transport and Technology (MOTAT), a small lake, a stadium and a speedway track.

Eating & Drinking

Ponsonby and Jervois roads are among Auckland's most popular night-time destinations. The area hosts a lot of up market bars and there's a variety of restaurants and cool takeaway bars, too. Ponsonby Road, especially, is famous for its thriving daytime cafe scene. The road's institutions include the restaurants SPQR(09 360 1710) and Prego (09 376 3095), the cafes Dizengoff (p.440) and Bambina (09 360 4000) and the cake shop Rocket Kitchen (09 360 8834). The quieter West Lynn shops are also near to a few great bars, restaurants and takeaways.

Education

Auckland Girls' Grammar School and Western Springs College are two perfectly good public secondary schools in the area, but some streets have the added benefit of being in the zones of Auckland Grammar School, Avondale College, Epsom Girls Grammar and/or Mount Albert Grammar, all of which are highly regarded. Some residents without all this choice send their children to private schools. There are several Catholic primary and secondary schools around.

Transport

It's a quick and cheap bus trip into the city, especially from the eastern parts, and the buses are frequent. Many residents walk into the city. The area is bounded by both the North-Western and Southern Motorways, making it easy to dash off to other parts of Auckland in off-peak times. The handy circular Link bus route links Ponsonby with the city, Parnell and Newmarket. Ponsonby is 2.5km from the city and Point Chevalier is 7km.

Safety & Annoyances

The area is generally safe, although Ponsonby can be noisy at night. Parking can be a problem close to the city as a lot of houses don't have off-street parking. The speedway can be heard throughout the area on a still night, as can the odd rock concert at Western Springs Stadium.

East Auckland: Eastern Beaches

Map p.484 E5
Area D p.94-95

Best Points
A quieter pace of life and a pleasant environment.

Worst Points
Characterless new housing developments and commuter traffic.

On the eastern side of the Tamaki River lies a collection of quiet, largely middle-class suburbs – Pakuranga, Howick, Half Moon Bay, Botany Downs, Farm Cove, Bucklands Beach, Eastern Beach and Mellons Bay and, further south, East Tamaki, Dannemora and rural Whitford. It's a pretty area, with several nice beaches and bays, which has seen intense residential and commercial development in recent years. It's popular with immigrants from Asia, Europe, South Africa and the UK. Further out, the former holiday towns of Beachlands and Maraetai have been discovered by Auckland commuters.

Accommodation

The average price of a house is around $550,000. The highest prices are generally found in million-dollar-plus coastal and cliff top properties, and the lowest in the sprawling, new Botany Downs and Dannemora apartments, townhouses and older, more basic Pakuranga homes and units that start at about $350,000. In between is block after block of large new Mediterranean-style homes, priced from about $650,000. Many former farms are being divvied up for even more new housing in Beachlands and Maraetai.

Shopping & Amenities

Pakuranga has a Westfield mall, featuring the usual chain stores, but the new Botany Town Centre (p.411) outdoor mall is more pleasant, and also has cinemas. Nearby is The Hub, a cluster of homeware stores. Highland Park has a shopping centre, with supermarket and cinemas, and Howick Village has a small parade of shops. There are several safe beaches and golf courses at Bucklands Beach, Pakuranga, Whitford and just south of Beachlands. Whitford Forest is a short drive east. Pakuranga's Lloyd Ellesmore Park has sporting facilities and several pools.

Eating & Drinking

Botany Downs has the biggest selection of cafes, but the most picturesque are on The Parade at Bucklands Beach. There are plenty of restaurants throughout the area, many offering ethnic food, but most don't make the 'Best in Auckland' lists. An exception is Aunty Fong Chinese Restaurant (09 533 8923) in Howick.

Education

Macleans College in Bucklands Beach has the best reputation of all the area's secondary schools, but Howick College and the new Botany Downs Secondary College are also good. Pakuranga has Pakuranga College and Edgewater College (Pakuranga College has had better recent reviews from the Education Review Office), and private St Kentigern College. Buses take students from Beachlands and Maraetai to Howick College. There is a dearth of primary schools in Botany Downs and Half Moon Bay.

Transport

The best way to commute to the city is by ferry from Half Moon Bay or Beachlands. Otherwise, it's a gridlocked car trip or a long bus journey. The south-eastern motorway has improved the traffic flow in recent years but Pakuranga has one of Auckland's worst peak-hour congestion problems. Almost all residents have their own transport. Pakuranga is 16km from the city, Howick is 23km and Maraetai is 40km.

Safety & Annoyances

In general, the area is regarded as safe. Commuter traffic is the biggest annoyance.

Map p.484 D5
Area E p.94-95

Best Points
Affordable housing and good train links.

Worst Points
New developments lacking in atmosphere.

East Auckland: Inland

The neighbours of Remuera in Meadowbank would probably be horrified to be grouped with Glen Innes and Point England. Indeed, Meadowbank has a far more gentlemanly reputation. But, though they still struggle with an image problem, Glen Innes and Point England are slowly coming up in the world. St Johns, Mount Wellington and Panmure are somewhere in between and make good options for affordable suburban living.

Accommodation

Though some properties in Meadowbank are akin to Remuera in price, the suburbs behind the Eastern Bays – Meadowbank, St Johns, Glen Innes and Point England – are far more modest and affordable than their coastal neighbours. Meadowbank and St Johns have brick and tile units for less than $300,000 and townhouses and bungalows from about $500,000. Mount Wellington and Panmure are not renowned for attractive architecture, but basic homes and new townhouses sell here for as little as $350,000. Glen Innes and Point England offer modest but sturdy family homes, some with water views, on decent-sized sections from about $350,000. There is also a high concentration of state and rental housing.

Tractor Factor
Aucklanders love their sports utility vehicles (SUVs). They've earned the nickname 'Remuera tractors' because they're rarely driven off-road and are mostly brought out for the school run.

Shopping & Amenities

Mount Wellington's enormous new Sylvia Park mall (p.412) has more than 180 stores (boutiques as well as chain stores), three supermarkets and a cinema complex. There's a Mega Centre that sells mostly homewares in Mount Wellington and the Eastridge shopping complex, with supermarket, on Kepa Road near Meadowbank. There are good sports facilities in the area, including a golf course, and a few decent estuary walks.

Eating & Drinking

Glen Innes has some interesting food stores, including a great gourmet market called Nosh (09 521 1115) that draws people from all over Auckland. This area isn't renowned for its fine dining or upmarket drinking, though there are plenty of good, cheap takeaway outlets and ethnic restaurants, especially in Panmure.

Education

Tamaki College is the only secondary school in the area. It has a good reputation, though children also have the option of nearby Glendowie and Selwyn colleges, and Penrose High School. Auckland University has a satellite campus in Tamaki. Some primary schools in the poorer areas have a high proportion of children with social problems but, according to the Education Review Office, cope well.

Transport

There are train stations to the city and south at Meadowbank, Glen Innes, Tamaki and Panmure. On buses, it can be a long haul into the city at peak times. Otherwise, the car reigns. The busy Ellerslie to Panmure and south-eastern highways link southern parts of the area to the motorway. Panmure has an infamously confusing roundabout. Meadowbank is 10km from the city and Glen Innes is 14km.

Safety & Annoyances

Some of the poorest neighbourhoods of Glen Innes and Point England have bad reputations among some residents.

East Auckland: Remuera & the Eastern Bays

Map p.484 E5
Area F p.94-95

Remuera, with its grand homes and central location, has long been Auckland's most exclusive and expensive suburb. The Eastern Bays of Orakei, Mission Bay, Kohimarama, St Heliers and Glendowie are also sought-after locations. Hugging a strip of white-sand coastline, they attract the moneyed middle class. Mission Bay, with its summer holiday feel, is the focal point of life.

Best Points
The pleasant waterfront and the views.

Worst Points
Overdevelopment in parts, with cramped sections.

Accommodation

Housing is mostly in the upmarket – and more expensive – range, especially on Remuera's northern slopes and near the coast. Think in the millions. But there is cheaper housing, mostly inland, including former state houses, basic but sizeable 70s style houses and leasehold homes. There are also decent rental properties available. Entry-level is about $500,000 to $650,000. Orakei's Paratai Drive has long been *the* address in Auckland.

Shopping & Amenities

Remuera has a good strip of shops, but there isn't a lot in the way of shopping in the Eastern Bays, apart from the odd neighbourhood spot, a small strip at St Heliers and Eastridge Mall, with supermarket, on Kepa Road, behind Mission Bay. People flock to Mission Bay on summer weekends to swim, eat and drink, run, cycle, hire a kayak or rollerblade along the waterside footpath. Its Berkeley Cinema is also worth a visit. Kids will love Kelly Tarlton's Antarctic Encounter and Underwater World (p.216). The best green spaces are Michael Joseph Savage Memorial, high above Tamaki Drive, and Remuera's Mount Hobson.

Eating & Drinking

Mission Bay has plenty of cafes and restaurants, some with nice views, though the food and atmosphere often doesn't live up to the location. Sage Pasta Restaurant (09 528 4551) gets the best reviews. On a sunny day, grab a burger or fish and chips and eat it on the beach or reserve. Café on Kohi (09 528 8335) in Kohimarama is recommended. The best restaurants are Hammerheads Restaurant (p.437) and Mikano (09 309 9514), both along the waterfront, and Banque (09 522 6688) and The Maple Room (09 522 1672) in Remuera. There are cosy pubs in Mission Bay and Remuera village.

Education

Remuera is within the Auckland Grammar School and Epsom Girls Grammar School zones and has several leading private schools and a Catholic girls' secondary school. In the bays, multicultural Selwyn College and Glendowie College are the state secondary schools and both have positive Education Review Office reports. There are two Catholic primary schools in The Bays.

Transport

New bus lanes at peak traffic times along Tamaki Drive will mean a quick trip into the city for those on public transport, but more of a crawl for drivers. A train service to the city skirts these areas, with stops in Meadowbank (south of Mission Bay) and Orakei. Public transport is infrequent on weekends. Traffic gets heavy on Saturdays and Sundays in summer and it can be a bit slow to the Southern Motorway. Remuera is 8km from the city.

Safety & Annoyances

In general, the area is very safe. Central Mission Bay residents will have to put up with noise, gridlocked traffic and a fight for parking on summer weekends.

Remuera

Map p.484 A5
Area G p.94-95

West Auckland: Henderson, West Harbour & Te Atatu

Best Points
Affordable housing, rural serenity.

Worst Points
Less salubrious areas in Te Atatu, Henderson and Ranui. Traffic hold-ups.

There are two West Auckland stereotypes: 'westies' – lovers of loud cars and loud parties – and the self-explanatory 'greenies'. Henderson is the 'westie' capital and a working-class stronghold, as is Te Atatu South. Further out, Ranui, Massey, Waitakere and Swanson reputedly wave the eco-friendly banner. Newer developments in West Harbour, Henderson Heights and the Te Atatu Peninsula are attracting young professionals, wealthier young families and empty nesters. To the northwest, rural areas such as Kumeu are being divided up into lifestyle blocks for luxury homes.

Accommodation
Henderson, Te Atatu South, Massey and Ranui have lots of basic 50s and 70s housing. Many are on decent sections and cost about $350,000 (cheaper in Ranui). There is a lot of rental accommodation. Swanson, swathed in bush, and the country town of Waitakere are a bit more expensive. West Harbour and Te Atatu Peninsula are reasonably affordable for coastal Auckland – $450,000 will buy a large, new home and $700,000 will get a mansion with sea views. The peninsula has a lot of older, basic housing for less than $400,000. Small rural lifestyle blocks with modest houses start at $600,000. An upmarket, high-density housing development is planned for Massey North.

Shopping & Amenities
Henderson's West City mall (p.414) is the shopping hub, followed by Massey's Westgate complex. Both have cinemas. Other areas have small shopping centres. Henderson has a sports stadium and a good swimming pool complex. Waitakere Hospital is in Henderson. West Auckland is a boutique winery region. There are golf courses at Waitakere, Massey and Swanson, and good walks around the Te Atatu Peninsula and West Harbour.

Eating & Drinking
There are plenty of cheap ethnic restaurants, but for the best restaurants and cafes, head to the winery region. Try Curry Leaf (09 636 9666) and Soljans Café in Kumeu and BeesOnline Honey Centre and Café (09 411 7953) in Rodney. Servo (09 834 0222) is a popular cafe on Te Atatu Peninsula.

Education
Several multicultural secondary schools serve the area, though there are none in West Harbour. Henderson High School has recently been criticised by the Education Review Office for some very poor quality teaching. Other options are Massey High School, Rutherford High School and Waitakere College. There are several Christian schools, a Hare Krishna primary school in Riverhead and a special school in Henderson.

Transport
Buses are regular at peak times and less so at other times, meaning the trip into the city can be a long one. Most people have their own transport. The area gets congested at peak times – especially the Northwestern Motorway, but dedicated bus lanes are being installed. The Northwestern Motorway will eventually hook up with the North Shore and Auckland Airport via the Western Ring Route. A cycleway runs alongside the motorway. West Harbour has a commuter ferry to the city, but it's not cheap. The Western Line train stops at Waitakere, Swanson, Ranui and Henderson. Te Atatu South is 14km from the city, Henderson is 18km, Kumeu is 27km.

Safety & Annoyances
There are rough pockets, especially in the poorer areas. Westies have a reputation for loud cars and even louder parties.

Map p.484 B5/6
Area H p.94-95

Best Points
Affordable housing, Avondale College and the proximity to the city and the west coast.

Worst Points
Dodgy in pockets, cramped infill housing.

West Auckland: Inner West

The working class and middle class suburbs of the inner west (Avondale, Waterview and Blockhouse Bay) are becoming popular with young professionals and families, as houses closer to the city have become more expensive. It's a culturally diverse area, with comparatively high Maori, Pacific Island and Indian populations.

Accommodation

Avondale and Waterview have some old villas, Blockhouse Bay, New Windsor and Lynfield are mostly 1960s and 1970s bungalows, Green Bay is largely an ode to the 1970s and there are higher density developments in New Lynn and Glen Eden but overall there's a real mixture of housing. The most expensive homes are those in Lynfield, Blockhouse Bay and Green Bay that overlook Manukau Harbour, some of which squeak into the million-plus bracket. Avondale and Waterview prices are creeping up, though you can still find decent three-bedroom homes for less than $450,000, while the median house price in New Lynn, Glen Eden and Kelston is $340,000. There is a lot of rental housing in the area and pockets of state housing.

Shopping and Amenities

Lynnmall in New Lynn is the biggest shopping mall and there are smaller shopping centres in almost all the other suburbs. Avondale has a racecourse that hosts colourful markets on Sundays. There are several parks around and there's a golf course in New Lynn/Green Bay, a public pool in Glen Eden and a wetland reserve in New Lynn. Tidal Blockhouse Bay is the best spot for a swim.

Eating and Drinking

There are plenty of good local ethnic restaurants, as you'd expect in such a culturally diverse area, and some nice cafes – Maxim Café (09 827 7300) in New Lynn is one of the best, but there's little in the way of fine dining or sophisticated drinking, though Bricklane Restaurant in New Lynn is pretty good. New Lynn also has a good food store called Taste.

Education

Avondale College has a great reputation and is a drawcard for the area. Not that there's anything wrong with Kelston Boys High School, Kelston Girls College or Lynfield College. Green Bay High School is recovering from a troubled recent past. There are several Christian schools around, a good private school, Hill Top School in Blockhouse Bay, and a special school and a school for the deaf in New Lynn.

Transport

Bus links into the city are fairly good but, as with any commuter suburb, traffic can back up at peak times. At other times there's usually a good traffic flow. Residents can hook up with the Northwestern Motorway through Waterview and skirt around the harbour to the Southwestern Motorway, which is being extended into a Western Ring Route that will pass to the north-east. The Southern Motorway is a long trawl away. A city-west train link stops at Avondale, New Lynn, Kelston South and Glen Eden. Waterview is 9km from the city centre, Blockhouse Bay is 13km, and Green Bay is 16km.

Safety and Annoyances

It's mostly a safe area but there are rough patches. The Western Ring Route will cause some disruption.

Map p.484 A6
Area J p.94-95

Best Points
Isolation, peace and nature.

Worst Points
Isolation, a lack of services, few schools.

West Auckland: Manukau Harbour Suburbs & West Coast Beaches

If city living is not for you and you don't mind commuting along a winding bush road, consider the stunning wild west coast beaches – Piha, Karekare, Bethells (Te Henga) and Muriwai. The isolation is not for everybody, but nature lovers will adore the lifestyle. The bush-covered suburbs overlooking Manukau Harbour – Titirangi, Laingholm and Huia – are a great compromise for those who want a bit of peace and nature, as well as the comforts of civilisation.

Shopping & Amenities

Titirangi has a small, pleasant village shopping area, a gallery and a monthly market, while the other settlements have little more than a general store – but people don't move here for the shopping. The black-sand surf beaches are wild – and wildly popular among Auckland residents in summer. The Waitakere Ranges offers great bush walks. Woodhill Forest, north of Muriwai, is popular for four-wheel driving, mountain biking and canyoning. There are golf courses at Muriwai and Waitakere.

Eating & Drinking

Titirangi has some good cafes and restaurants – the most popular is the Hardware Cafe. Piha has an excellent takeaway hut, and the local surf club serves up a good meal in a prime location. Muriwai has two cafes, and a caravan sells takeaway at Bethells.

Accommodation

The typical Titirangi house is made of wood and surrounded by bush, but newer properties are less rugged and more suburban. Decent family homes cost between $350,000 and $600,000. Nearby Huia and Laingholm are less developed and a bit cheaper. The west coast beaches used to be dominated by modest weatherboard holiday homes. Now, luxury beach houses and permanent homes are taking their place. Basic old holiday homes on small sections start at about $400,000; beachfront luxury will set you back more than $1 million.

Education

There are no secondary schools in this area; students take the bus to secondary schools in more built-up suburbs. Bethells and Te Henga are in the Massey High School zone. There are no primary schools at the western beaches, except for Karekare's Lone Kauri Community School, a cute rural outpost. Piha has a pre-school. There are several primary schools in and around Titirangi, including a Rudolf Steiner school, but none at Huia.

Transport

Buses head into the city from Titirangi. Other areas are devoid of public transport, so you'll need your own wheels. Parking spaces can be hard to find at Piha during summer weekends. Titirangi is 18km from the city, Piha is 41km, Muriwai is 45km.

Piha beach

Safety & Annoyances

The most dangerous part of this area is the surf. Swim between the flags and keep a close eye on children. Care must be taken on the winding bush roads, especially in bad weather. And the usual rules apply in the bush. Otherwise, the area is very safe.

Map p.484 B3
Area K p.94-95

Best Points
Greenhithe's serenity, Whangaparaoa's beaches and parks.

Worst Points
Albany is a work in progress and suffers from a lack of atmosphere.

North Auckland: Albany & Beyond

Extensions to Auckland's Northern Motorway have opened up intense settlement in commuter suburbs, which once seemed far from the city. Albany has been the biggest benefactor, with block after block of shiny new houses, shops and offices. The rural enclave of Greenhithe has also grown in popularity, but is still peaceful. Further north, the picturesque Whangaparaoa Peninsula, which has a dozen beaches, is also filling up.

Accommodation

Want a big flash concrete house in a block of big flash concrete houses? Or a new apartment? Then Albany is the place for you. The formerly quiet village has been developed beyond recognition in the last decade, and median house prices have zoomed up past $600,000, though you can buy a small apartment for $250,000. In Greenhithe, a nice house on a large section costs $700,000 upwards. Whangaparaoa has a lot of older, former holiday homes and new housing, including a canal development, where prices start at $400,000. There's also lot of rental housing, aimed primarily at the student market.

Shopping & Amenities

Albany has plenty of shiny new shops, with a 100 store mall, including a cinema, a supermarket and a Mega Centre (with homeware and fashion stores) near the North Harbour Stadium. The original Albany village still has a few shopkeepers holding out against the invaders. Whangaparaoa offers a mall with a cinema, as well as three golf courses, a leisure centre with a pool and the Shakespear Regional Park.

Eating & Drinking

Albany and Whangaparaoa are not known for their cuisine, though there are a couple of good cafes and restaurants in Albany's original village. There are numerous cafes spread throughout the new office developments. Whangaparaoa has a smattering of bars and eateries.

Education

Albany has two private schools – Pinehurst School and Kristin School – both catering to all ages, but there's no state secondary school. Secondary school students can take a bus to Long Bay, Rangitoto or Glenfield colleges. The Palmerston North-based Massey University has a large satellite campus in Albany. Whangaparaoa has a new state secondary school, Whangaparaoa College, and a new private school, Wentworth College.

Transport

Most residents have cars. Whangaparaoa has a commuter ferry to Auckland city, but driving in at peak times isn't recommended. The peninsula has one main road that regularly gets clogged. Albany is a quick bus trip from the city, along the motorway express lane, but peak-time drivers should take a large cup of coffee for what could be a long journey. There is a new Western Ring Route planned to better link Albany with West Auckland. Albany is 18km from the city, Greenhithe is 22km and Whangaparaoa is 40km.

Safety & Annoyances

In general, the area is safe. Albany and Whangaparaoa residents have to put up with a lot of construction and roadworks. There's a maximum-security prison at Paremoremo on the outskirts of Albany.

Map p.484 D4
Area L p.94-95

North Auckland: North Shore East

With miles of sandy coastline, the laid-back suburbs stretching from Devonport to Takapuna and up the East Coast Bays are among the most popular in Auckland. Devonport, with its pretty villas and village atmosphere, is easily the most coveted suburb on 'The Shore'. Takapuna is the economic, retail and social hub of the area and boasts what is arguably Auckland's best beach. Stretching north is the well-heeled suburbia of The Bays, popular with British and South African immigrants.

Best Points
Plenty of beaches and a laid-back seaside atmosphere.

Worst Points
Peak-hour motorway traffic, bored teenage mall rats and conspicuous alcohol consumption.

Accommodation

Wealthy east coast bays residents like their houses modern and impressive; the most expensive homes in older Takapuna and Devonport are usually older and more restrained. There is plenty of more affordable housing around, especially further north around Browns Bay, in the inland suburbs (Sunnynook, Forrest Hill and inland Milford), and in Takapuna's many brick and tile units. Average house prices are around $800,000 in Devonport, $650,000 in Takapuna and Milford and $550,000 in the East Coast Bays.

Shopping & Amenities

Takapuna is the retail capital of the North Shore, with a mall full of the usual chain stores, as well as a gym. It also has a swimming pool, a cinema and a theatre complex, and there's a Sunday morning market. There are smaller shopping centres scattered around. Devonport has nice boutiques and galleries. Long Bay Regional Park and Devonport's North Head Reserve are good for picnics and walks. North Shore Hospital is in Takapuna.

Eating & Drinking

Perhaps the best dining experience on the North Shore is to grab a kebab or pizza from a Takapuna takeaway, and eat it on the beach. Takapuna also has the widest choice of bars and restaurants. Devonport has arguably the best cafe in the area – the Stone Oven Bakery and Café (09 445 3185) – as well as one of the best restaurants, the casual Manuka (09 445 7732) in Victoria Road. There are a couple of cosy pubs too. Several pleasant spots can also be found in the East Coast Bays, mostly huddled in Browns Bay and Mairangi Bay.

Education

The huge and well-resourced Rangitoto College, in Mairangi Bay, is a drawcard for The Bays. Not that there's anything wrong with the alternatives: Takapuna Grammar, Westlake Boys High School and Westlake Girls High School and Long Bay College. In Browns Bay, there's the private Corelli School of the Arts.

Cheltenham housing

Transport

Public transport is good in Takapuna, which is served by regular and quick buses to the city. Devonport and Bayswater each have a ferry to the city, which both take about 15 minutes and cost around $5 – quicker but slightly more expensive than a bus trip. Northern Motorway bus lanes have quickened the peak-hour trip to the city from The Bays, but most residents have their own transport. Thus, the motorway and its tributaries get badly congested at peak times. Takapuna is 9km from the city, Devonport is 13km and Long Bay is 23km.

Safety & Annoyances

The North Shore has the least crime per capita of any Auckland region.

Map p.484 B4
Area M p.94-95

Best Points
Modestly priced housing and peaceful village life in Northcote Point.

Worst Points
Onewa Road congestion. Uninspiring, infilled housing in Glenfield.

North Auckland: North Shore West

The western side of the North Shore is far less glitzy than its eastern counterpart, but is wrapped in a long coastline and has several parks and bush walks. And you can probably find a home to suit your budget, be it a multimillion dollar cliff-top mansion in Northcote Point or a little wooden bungalow in Beach Haven.

Accommodation

There are loads of comparatively affordable homes (about $400,000) in suburbs such as Birkdale and Beach Haven, many near the water and with decent backyards. Here you can get waterfront properties for less than $1 million. Northcote Point and Birkenhead Point, with their quiet streets of renovated villas, are the pick of the suburbs. Inland are the suburban sprawls of Glenfield and Hillcrest – some houses have views across to the city. There's a lot of rental property, especially in the cheaper areas. A two-bedroom flat in Glenfield, Beach Haven, central Northcote and Birkdale costs about $250-$350 a week; in Birkenhead and Northcote Point expect to pay a little more.

Shopping & Amenities

There are basic shopping malls in Glenfield and Highbury, and a shopping centre in Northcote, which is dominated by Asian food stores. You'll find a factory shopping complex in Northcote, a cluster of large homeware stores on Link Drive in Glenfield, and a small neighbourhood shopping centre in Beach Haven. Glenfield has a good leisure centre, with a pool and gym. There are good walks around the Chelsea Sugar Refinery and in Kauri Park in Birkenhead. The best place to spend an evening is probably the Bridgeway Cinema (09 481 0040) in Northcote Point.

Eating & Drinking

Birkenhead Point and Northcote Point have the best cafes and fine dining in an area that is otherwise lacking such luxuries. The Northcote Tavern is a popular, if shabby, watering hole. Considering it's a comparatively low-socio economic suburb, Birkdale is the surprise culinary highlight of the area, with a good cafe, Verrans Espresso & Food (09 481 629), and restaurant, Verbena Restaurant & Bar (09 483 9571).

Education

The secondary schools – Northcote College, Birkenhead College and Glenfield College – have a reputation for being rougher than those on the more expensive side of The Shore, but the Education Review Office seems happy with them. There is a Catholic primary school in Northcote, a Christian school in Glenfield and a special school in Wairau Valley. Some areas are in the zones for well-regarded Ponsonby primary schools.

Transport

Onewa Road, which leads onto the motorway in Northcote, has a reputation as one of the worst arterials in Auckland. The best way to commute to the city is by ferry from Northcote Point or Birkenhead Point. By bus it's a quick trip from Highbury and Northcote, but if you live in the outer suburbs it can be a long haul. Northcote Point is 8km from the city centre, Beach Haven is 14km. Most residents have cars.

Northcote Point

Safety & Annoyances

The North Shore is generally safe, but there are pockets of social problems.

Map p.484 C6
Area N p.94-95

Best Points
Affordable accommodation, access to motorways, Cornwall Park.

Worst Points
Motorway congestion, unsightly industrial areas, some rough spots.

South Auckland: South-East

One Tree Hill has always had pockets of exclusive housing, especially near Cornwall Park. Otherwise One Tree Hill, Ellerslie, Greenlane and Royal Oak are refuges for the middle class, and benefit from the reflected glory of their more affluent neighbours, Mount Eden, Epsom and Remuera. The traditional working-class suburb of Onehunga is slowly transforming, as young professionals and families head south to find more affordable accommodation within commuting distance of the city.

One Tree Hill

Accommodation

One Tree Hill and Greenlane's large renovated character homes are about the most expensive real estate in the area, some reaching a couple of million dollars. Many properties around Cornwall Park are on leasehold land, which lowers the price, though the leases can be expensive. Ellerslie, Royal Oak and other parts of Greenlane and One Tree Hill have a mixture of housing, from beautifully renovated old villas to basic units and newer townhouses, with prices starting at $350,000. Historic Onehunga, which has some great Ponsonby-style villas and more basic state housing, has a median property price of $400,000. There's plenty of rental housing around.

Shopping & Amenities

Apart from a booming factory shop outlet in Onehunga, the shopping centres are mainly small local strips that offer the basics. Cornwall Park and One Tree Hill Domain are the leisure drawcards of the area. Greenlane Hospital and National Women's Hospital are near Cornwall Park. Greenlane Racecourse hosts the ASB Showgrounds, where a lot of large commercial exhibitions are held, including the Auckland Home Show.

Eating & Drinking

There are some great restaurants and bars scattered throughout this area. Try One Tree Grill (09 625 6407) at Greenwoods Corner, Claret (09 622 2988) in Onehunga, the Abbey (09 524 6190) in Greenlane, Lube bar (09 525 2522) in Ellerslie and Francoli Bar & Restaurant (09 579 2303) in Ellerslie. Onehunga has a good assortment of cafes.

Education

A few streets of One Tree Hill and Greenlane sneak into the Auckland Grammar School and Epsom Girls Grammar School zones. The other options are multicultural Onehunga High School, which has a business school and a building and construction school (although parts of the campus are dilapidated, according to the Education Review Office), and Penrose High School, which is improving after being criticised for variable quality of teaching and some poor student performance.

Transport

In general, the area has good peak time bus services into the city, though traffic can get congested, especially on the Southern Motorway. Most people have their own transport. A city-to-Pukekohe train stops at Greenlane, Ellerslie and Penrose. Onehunga's train line to the city is due to be reconnected in 2008. Greenlane is 7km from the city, Onehunga is 11km.

Safety & Annoyances

In general the area is regarded as safe, although there are rough pockets in Penrose and Onehunga.

South Auckland: Weymouth, Flat Bush & Beyond

Map p.484 D7/8
Area P p.94-95

Best Parts
Cheap housing, colourful communities.

Worst Parts
Rough areas, burglaries, Southern Motorway congestion.

South Auckland is the poorest part of Auckland, has a comparatively high crime rate and the worst reputation. It's also the most colourful area, with a large Pacific Island population, and has some of the cheapest real estate. Several suburbs – Mangere Bridge, Weymouth, Flat Bush, Totara Heights, Wattle Downs, Manurewa East and rural Karaka – are particularly popular. Although prices are rising, there are some good lifestyles and views to be bought for a comparatively low price.

Accommodation

You can get waterfront real estate for less than $1 million in places such as Weymouth, Wattle Downs and Mangere Bridge. Mangere Bridge is an established middle-class enclave in a working-class area. Sparkling new subdivisions at Goodwood Heights, Wattle Downs and Flat Bush have comfortable new homes for $450,000 to $700,000, with older homes for less than $400,000. Totara Heights and Manurewa East are older and cheaper areas, but with some large new homes. At the time of writing, Manurewa boasted the cheapest house for sale in South Auckland – for $219,000. There is a huge rental market, but many properties are dismal.

Shopping & Amenities

Manukau City is the shopping hub, and has a large Westfield mall. Otara hosts a popular Saturday market (p.410). There are several good nature reserves, including Whitford Forest, Hunua Ranges Regional Park and the Auckland Regional Botanic Gardens. Middlemore, Wattle Downs and Papakura have golf courses and Manukau has a sports centre, velodrome and theme park. South Auckland's hospital is at Middlemore.

Eating & Drinking

If it's cheap ethnic food, greasy takeaways and basic pubs and steakhouses that you're after, there's no shortage in South Auckland. Anything more sophisticated is harder to find. Try the Villa Maria Vineyard and Restaurant (09 255 0660) in Mangere, the Latin Coffee cafe in Mangere Bridge, Bracu (09 236 1030) in Bombay, Palazzo Roma Restaurant (09 294 7440) in Drury or Vin Alto (09 292 8845) in Clevedon.

Education

Most of South Auckland's schools cope admirably well with the challenges of being in lower socio-economic areas but wealthier parents often send their children to private schools, notably King's College in Otahuhu. Of the state secondary schools, Papatoetoe High School, Rosehill College and Alfriston College have the best reputations. There are new secondary schools planned for Flat Bush. There's a school for the blind in Manurewa, a Muslim girls' college and a Muslim school serving all ages.

Otara Market

Transport

Buses and trains serve the area adequately but most residents have private transport. The city-to-Pukekohe train has 10 stops in South Auckland. The Southern Motorway cuts through the area and gets very congested at peak times. The Southwestern Expressway links Manukau with Auckland Airport, in Mangere. Mangere Bridge is 14km from the city, Karaka is 35km.

Safety & Annoyances

South Auckland has a high crime rate compared with most other areas of Auckland. Burglaries are a particular problem. The airport disturbs the peace of many residents.

Map p.484 F4
Area Q p.94-95

Best Points
A laid-back lifestyle, good weather, great restaurants and vineyards.

Worst Points
The sometimes tricky logistics of life on an island.

Waiheke Island

Waiheke Island

Once the domain of hippies, artists and humble holiday homes, Waiheke Island is now largely a commuter suburb of Auckland – and many of the holiday homes are far from humble. The friendly 93 sq km island enjoys a slightly warmer climate than the city, a relaxed environment, a beautiful landscape and some great restaurants and wineries.

Accommodation
There are a lot of empty sections for sale from about $150,000, holiday units for $200,000 and basic holiday homes from $300,000. The median house price is in the early $500,000s, and has been driven up by numerous multimillion dollar properties on the waterfront, many with incredible sea views. Even a basic holiday shack can go for $2 million if it's on one of the best beaches – Oneroa or Onetangi. There is some long-term rental accommodation available, especially in the winter months.

Shopping & Amenities
Shops here cover the basics and little else. There's a supermarket and large hardware store at Ostend, a strip of shops and banks at Oneroa and a few other shops scattered elsewhere. Ostend hosts a morning market on Saturdays. Boating, fishing, beaches and vineyards are the big attractions. Much of the island is covered by bush and farmland and there are some great bush walks. There's a golf course near Rocky Bay.

Eating & Drinking
Waiheke has some of Auckland's finest eateries, including Mudbrick (09 372 9050), Te Whau (09 372 7191) and The Shed at Te Motu (09 372 6884), all vineyard restaurants. There are several great cafes and bars; try the Lazy Lounge Café Bar and Cortado Espresso Bar in Oneroa, Caffe da Stefano at Surfdale, Sticki Fingers at Palm Beach and Nourish and Eleven at Ostend. Oneroa has a good fish and chip shop.

Education
There are several primary and intermediate schools on the island. The high school has been having run-ins with the Education Review Office for years over poor management. It might have turned the corner since appointing a new principal in 2006, although most parents send their children to the mainland for secondary schooling.

Transport
Besides private boats, the passenger ferry to Auckland and Devonport, and car ferry to Half Moon Bay are the island's lifelines. It's a 35 minute, $15 trip to the city, making it a fairly easy – and scenic – commute, and 45 minutes to Half Moon Bay ($15 per passenger, $70 per car). Buses circle the island and meet the ferries. Taxis can get booked up quickly in summer, especially at weekends. The car ferry isn't that cheap so many residents have one car on the island, and another parked in a city car park for quick getaways and mainland chores.

Safety & Annoyances
Waiheke is very safe, but being a boat ride from anywhere and having to rely on the ferry can make life a little more complicated. On summer weekends the island is packed with tourists, Aucklanders and wedding guests.

Hamilton

North Island Map G8

Best Points
Central location, comparatively affordable housing, the Waikato River.

Worst Points
A reputation for dullness, rough in patches.

Hamilton is the thriving hub of rural Waikato. A local reporter once wrote of Hamilton that 'it's a great place to live but you wouldn't want to visit'. And, true there isn't a lot in the way of tourist attractions in the city of bustling commerce, university students, families, retirees and endless flat suburbs. It has a reputation for being a bit dull but has everything a city of 130,000 should have – decent shopping and schools, plenty of bars and some nice parks and activities. Auckland is about 130km north and Rotorua and Tauranga are both about 110km away.

Hamilton's real estate is mostly a sprawl of modest three and four bedroom homes for around the city's median house price, $340,000. Development has surged in the last decade, with sparkling new suburbs popping up, but there are also a lot of older villas and bungalows in varying conditions.

Most of the shopping is along Victoria Street, where you'll also find cinemas. There's a big mall at Chartwell and smaller centres dotted around the city. Te Rapa has factory shops and homeware stores. Frankton has a good Saturday morning market.

Hamiltonians have the newish Waikato Stadium in which to worship their rugby heroes. The nearest beach is at stunning Raglan, which is also worth considering as a place to live for its windswept scenery, good surf and village atmosphere. Cambridge is a sleepy town 24km away with a good craft shop.

This being a student city, and one in which there's little else to do, there are plenty of bars, most of which line Victoria Street. Popular choices are The Bank, the Loaded Hog and Cazbar. The best cafes are also in the city, including Scott's Epicurean (07 839 6680) and Metropolis (07 834 2081). For fine dining, try Balcony Restaurant (07 838 3718), Canvas (07 839 2535) and Palate (07 834 2921).

Hamilton has half a dozen state secondary schools, including two single sex schools. All but Melville High School have very good recent Education Review Office reports. There are a few good private schools – Southwell School, Waikato Diocesan Schools for Girls and, in Cambridge, St Paul's Collegiate – and several Catholic schools and a Rudolf Steiner School. The biggest tertiary providers are the University of Waikato and Wintec Institute of Technology.

Hamilton's public transport is really buses, which provide an adequate service even if most residents have their own transport. The city's road system isn't keeping pace with its growth, so the traffic can get unduly congested for a city of its size.

The city is generally safe but has a few problems with gangs and there are rough areas. Those areas with the worst reputations are Glenview, Nawton and Poets Corner in Fairfield.

Napier housing

Napier

North Island Map K11

Best Points
Great wineries, good climate, affordable housing and a relaxed atmosphere.

Worst Points
Relative isolation.

An attractive and laid-back coastal city, with a warm climate, surrounded by vineyards and orchards, Napier's relative isolation – 420km from Auckland and 320km from Wellington – keeps the population (57,000) down. It is, however, growing slowly. It has a higher proportion of retirees and a lower proportion of people aged 20-45 than the rest of New Zealand, and about 7% of its residents were born in the UK or Ireland. The local council has been actively marketing the city to prospective immigrants from the UK in recent years. Napier was flattened by an earthquake in 1931, and its town leaders had the vision to rebuild it in art deco style, giving it a unique and attractive appearance.

The median property price is $300,000. The most sought-after and most expensive properties are the large homes on lifestyle blocks in the wider, Hawke's Bay region and large renovated or new homes on the city's hills – Napier Hill, Bluff Hill and Hospital Hill – as well as Bay View and seaside Ahuriri. Ahuriri is in a big development phase, with many apartment complexes and shops springing up. There is plenty of housing in Marewa, Onekawa, Tamatea and Napier South for less than $250,000.

The small but pleasant city centre hosts the main shopping area. There's a great open-air seaside hot pool complex, an aquatic centre, a museum, a cinema, a theatre, an aquarium and a small theme park called Marineland, with penguins, sea lions, dolphins and fur seals. There are several good golf courses in the Napier region. Napier Beach isn't particularly safe for swimming – try Westshore, or go further out to Waipatiki Beach and Ocean Beach.

The best eating and drinking experience is a long lunch in one of the region's superb wineries. Try Te Awa, or Vidal Estate, near Hastings, or Terroir at Craggy Range near Havelock North. In town, there's a cluster of restaurants and bars at the West Quay development at Ahuriri. Ocean Boulevard has several takeaways outlets and Hastings Street is a good spot for a pub crawl.

There are four state secondary schools in Napier, including two single-sex schools – all of which have good Education Review Office reports – as well as several Catholic and other Christian schools and a Rudolph Steiner school. The Eastern Institute of Technology is the local tertiary education provider.

Napier's public transport is rudimentary – most residents have their own transport and it's an easy city to get around. It tends to be very safe, although there are a few rougher patches, including Maraenui.

North Island Map J7

Tauranga

Best Points
Relaxed lifestyle, great beaches.

Worst Points
Suburban sprawl.

Tauranga's image is changing from a conservative retirement spot to a fast-growing city full of young professionals, families – and retirees. All are moving to take advantage of the city's great beaches and relaxed environment. Its population is now 110,000, which is only a few thousand less than Dunedin's.

The city's housing is a mixture of 1970s suburban sprawl, some older housing and more recent developments, including apartments that are extending the town's boundaries. The most sought-after spots – and the most expensive – are along the surf beach from Mount Maunganui to Papamoa, and on a lifestyle block in the city's semi-rural outskirts. Central Tauranga, positioned around the harbour, is also popular. The cheapest beach houses go for several million dollars. But the median house price is around $370,000, so there's plenty of cheaper housing, particularly in Greerton, Papamoa and Welcome Bay, which start at about $250,000. There are also a lot of sections for sale in the city's fast-developing outskirts.

Tauranga's biggest shopping precinct is downtown – which is pretty small for a city this size – where you'll find a mixture of chain stores and boutiques. Mount Maunganui has a pleasant but basic shopping strip, and the Bayfair mall, with an array of chain stores, is on the road towards Papamoa. There are smaller shopping centres in Papamoa, Gate Pa, Greerton and Fraser Cove.

The beaches are the number one leisure attraction in the area, while sailing and fishing are also popular pastimes. For green spaces, try Mauao, the extinct volcano in Mount Maunganui, McLaren Falls in the Wairoa River valley and the Kaimai-Mamaku Forest Park. The nearby Coromandel Peninsula (p.223) is a great place to spend a weekend.

There are several aquatic centres dotted around the city and Papamoa, a theatre complex called Baycourt, and several cinemas. There's a good selection of cafes, restaurants and bars along Devonport Road and the Strand in the downtown area and on Mount Maunganui's main street. In Bethlehem, try Mills Reef Winery Restaurant and Somerset Cottage.

Tauranga has three large secular state secondary schools – two single-sex and one co-ed – and one in Mount Maunganui but none in Papamoa. All have good recent Education Review Office reports, though Tauranga Boys' College has arguably the best reputation. There are several Catholic and other Christian schools, a Rudolph Steiner School in Welcome Bay and a private primary school. The main tertiary providers are the Bay of Plenty Polytechnic and a small University of Waikato campus.

Tauranga is a city of cars and has limited public transport. There are a lot of roadworks as the transport system tries to keep pace with the city's growth. In general, Tauranga is a safe city although there are rough spots and teenagers can get rowdy on the beaches. Take care in the pounding Mount Maunganui surf.

North Island Map F4

Whangarei

Best Points
Cheap housing, stunning scenery, good cafes and restaurants.

Worst Points
Some parts are rough and dingy.

The small laid-back city of Whangarei (population 48,000) is 170km north of Auckland and close to some stunning scenery and great beaches. Nearly one-third of the city's residents are Maori and it's largely a humble working-class city. It has a pleasant town basin with a marina, some good cafes and is close to a beautiful harbour. But the best spot is out on a small block of land at Whangarei Heads.

European settlement began here in the mid 19th century, but most of the housing dates from 1965. The city's median house price has only recently crawled past $315,000, with a nice three-bedroom home costing about $350,000 to $500,000. The median for the surrounding area is hovering around $400,000, with small, bare lifestyle blocks starting at about $125,000.

The best city suburbs are Maunu, Riverside and Central Whangarei. At Whangarei Heads, a waterfront home goes for between $750,000 and $1 million. More modest homes with sea views can be bought for less than $500,000. There is a lot of cheap rental housing in the city and there are some good value winter rentals on the coast.

Whangarei has all your basic chain stores, supermarkets, banks and a cinema (most of which are based at the Cameron Street mall in the town centre), plus a few boutiques, craft shops, museums and galleries in the town basin. There's a golf course in Tikipunga and an aquatic centre on Ewing Road. Whangarei Heads offers great walks and fishing and there are superb beaches on the east coast where you can take your pick of water-based activities.

The city has some great casual restaurants, cafes and bars, many of which are clustered around the town basin. The best restaurant in town is undoubtedly A Deco (09 459 4957) in Kensington. Also try Tonic (09 437 5558) in Kamo Road and Reva's on the Waterfront (09 438 8969). A longtime favourite is Killer Prawn (09 430 3333) in Bank Street, which is also home to the popular cafe Bob (09 438 0881) and also has good takeaway outlets.

There are four secondary schools in the area: Kamo High School, Tikipunga High School, Whangarei Boys' High School and Whangarei Girls' High School. All have good Education Review Office reports, except Whangarei Boys', which has problems with bullying and under-achievement. There are primary schools at Whangarei Heads but students travel to Whangarei for secondary school. There are several Christian schools in Whangarei. NorthTec is the biggest provider of tertiary education, and the University of Auckland has a small satellite campus here.

There is a rudimentary network of buses in the city but it's best to have your own transport, especially to get to the beaches. Whangarei doesn't have a big congestion problem and there shouldn't be any problems with parking.

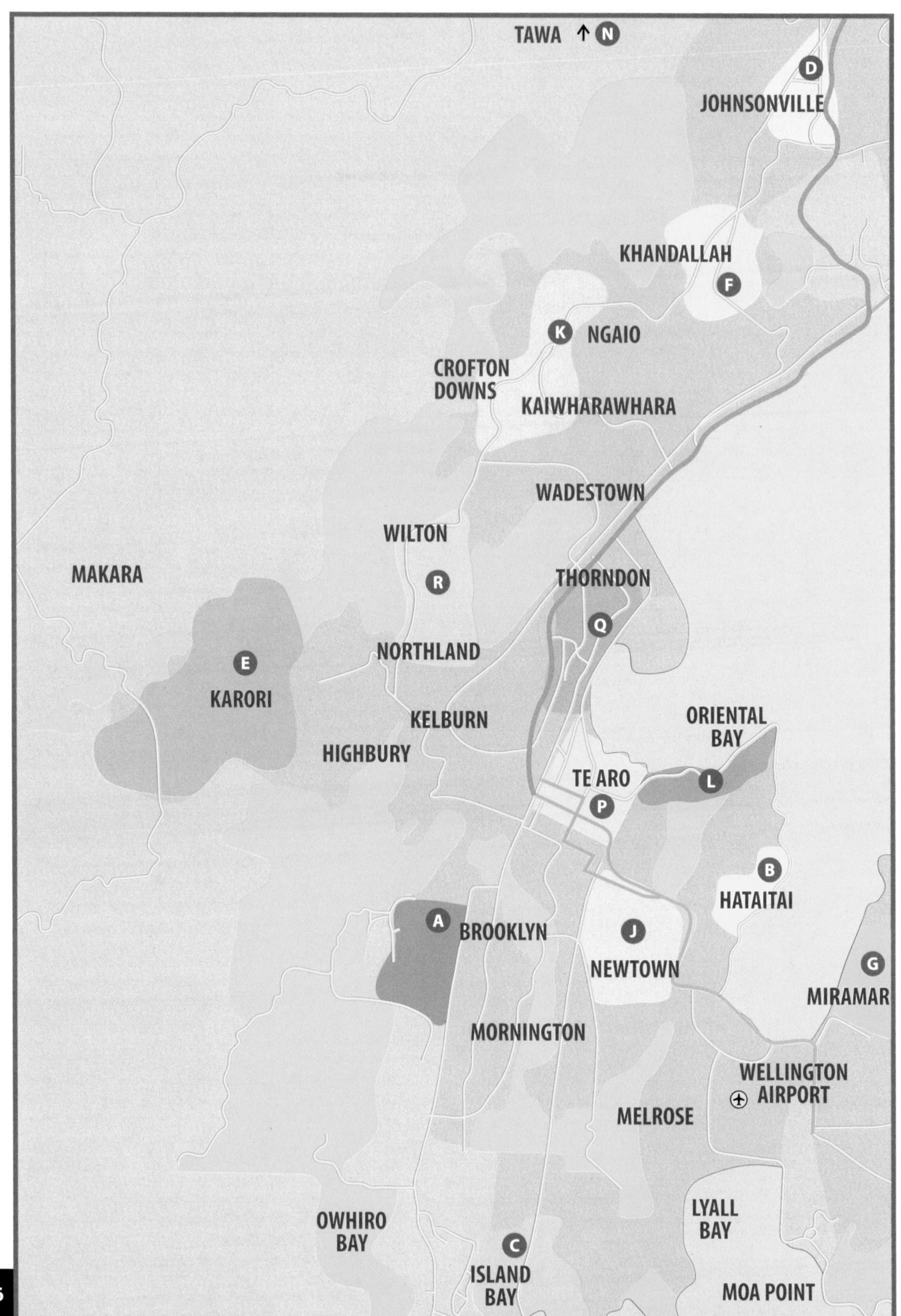
TAWA
N
D
JOHNSONVILLE
KHANDALLAH
F
K
NGAIO
CROFTON
DOWNS
KAIWHARAWHARA
WADESTOWN
WILTON
MAKARA
R
THORNDON
Q
E
NORTHLAND
KARORI
KELBURN
ORIENTAL
BAY
HIGHBURY
TE ARO
L
P
B
HATAITAI
A
BROOKLYN
J
NEWTOWN
G
MIRAMAR
MORNINGTON
WELLINGTON
AIRPORT
MELROSE
LYALL
BAY
OWHIRO
BAY
C
ISLAND
BAY
MOA POINT

PAPARANGI
ALICETOWN
NEWLANDS
H
PETONE
MATIU/SOMES ISLAND
MAUPUIA
KARAKA BAYS
MURITAI
M
SEATOUN
BREAKER BAY
0
Scale 1:8,000
2km
N
© Explorer Group Ltd. 2007

Wellington & Further Out

As the self-proclaimed cultural, creative and coffee capital of New Zealand (as well as the political capital), Wellington has all the benefits of cosmopolitan city living. Just under a quarter of residents in the region were born overseas, with the largest numbers coming from Europe, Asia and the Pacific Islands. Increasing numbers are coming from North America and Africa, which is adding to the city's multicultural appeal. Wellington is a compact city set around a harbour, and surrounded by bush and green rolling hills. It has good transport links and the main retail and entertainment areas are all within 30 minutes of the city's suburbs. From colonial villas spilling down the hillsides to new multi-storey apartments, Wellington has a wide choice of accommodation. Most have sea, bush or hill views and access to beaches, watersports and great expanses of open countryside.

State education provision is good but the most popular schools have introduced enrolment schemes (zoning), which specify geographical boundaries for each school (www.schoolzones.co.nz). Victoria (p.185) and Massey universities (p.184) have large campuses in Wellington and there are also two polytechnics in the region.

Map p.498, 506
Area A p.116-117

Brooklyn

Best Points
Strong community feel.

Worst Points
Houses can be damp, unless they're in the sun all day.

Brooklyn is close to the city and borders Central Park, making it popular with families. Settled by Europeans in the 1860s, it is probably best known today for the nearby wind turbine, installed in 1993 to harness the strength of the notorious gusts coming off the Tasman.

Accommodation

Accommodation ranges from municipal state housing blocks near Central Park to grand old houses and executive pads with glorious views of the harbour. Panorama Heights, a new sub-division behind Karepa Street, is chipping away at the green space in the area. Most styles of property are available for sale and to rent. Three-bedroom homes typically cost $500,000 plus, while weekly rental is around $420.

Shopping & Amenities

All essential shops can be found within the village, along with a busy community centre and library. Brooklyn also boasts its own cinema, the Penthouse (04 384 3157). The *Brooklyn Tattler* is a monthly community newsletter full of information for residents.

Eating & Drinking

The cafe at the Penthouse cinema is popular, as is the Windmill Bar and Café (04 385 6465). There are also a few takeaway places and a Thai restaurant.

Education

For pre-schoolers, there is a free kindergarten, creche and childcare centre. Primary school education is offered at Brooklyn School (zoned) or St Bernard's Catholic school. Secondary boys are zoned for Wellington Boy's College and girls can choose from Wellington Girl's College or Wellington East Girl's College, if they live in central Brooklyn.

Transport

It is a five-minute drive into the city centre, and there's also a frequent bus service. The hospital and Massey University are within easy walking distance.

Safety & Annoyances

The southern landfill on Ohiro Road is not far from Brooklyn, but it doesn't cause day-to-day problems for residents.

Map p.498 D6
Area B p.116-117

Best Points
Sea views, a beach and close to the CBD.

Worst Points
Small sections and traffic bottlenecks.

Hataitai

An upmarket eastern suburb, Hataitai is a five-minute drive into the city and has a village feel. It is popular with professional couples, particularly from European backgrounds. The name originates from the Maori, whataitai, a mystical snake-like creature whose back, according to legend, makes up the Miramar peninsula.

Accommodation

Most houses have sea views over Hataitai beach and Evans Bay, and out towards Maupuia – some residents have their cars parked on wooden jetties built into the hillsides. There are some lovely wooden character-villas around, together with more surprising builds, including a blue-roofed apartment block, complete with towers, near the Mount Victoria Tunnel. Proximity to the city makes prices higher than in neighbouring Kilbirnie. Typical rent for a three-bedroom house is $420, and there are plenty of new apartments and executive townhouses available. Property prices start at $500,000.

Shopping & Amenities

Hataitai has its own village shops, with a bakery, dairy, takeaways, pharmacy and specialist herbal dispensary. The larger shops of Kilbirnie are a few minutes away. There is a beach at Hataitai and plenty of secluded spots along Evans Bay Parade. Hataitai Park hosts sports fixtures all year round.

Eating & Drinking

As well as the ubiquitous fish and chip shop, Hataitai has a cafe, Thai restaurant and takeaway, plus a pub that serves food.

Education

A community creche and free kindergarten are available for pre-schoolers. Hataitai Primary School accepts pupils living within one kilometre of the school, which covers most of the suburb. Alternatively, pupils can choose Kilbirnie School. Secondary schooling is at Rongotai for boys, and Wellington East Girls' College.

Transport

Hataitai is well served by buses. Walking and cycling are also options, with a walk into the CBD taking just 30 minutes; go via Oriental Parade rather than the fume-filled Mount Victoria Tunnel, with its narrow cycle and pedestrian path.

Safety & Annoyances

Traffic delays in peak times can mean driving takes nearly as long as walking. Plans are in place to create more bus lanes.

Apartments in Hataitai

Island Bay character

Island Bay

Map p.498 C8
Area C p.116-117

Best Points
Gorgeous seaside village.

Worst Points
Windy.

Island Bay enjoys an idyllic setting around a tiny sandy cove, and is so named because of the rocky island, Taputeranga, just offshore. Originally settled by an Italian fishing community, the area is now home to many artists and creative types. In 2005, the naval frigate, F69, was sunk in the nearby marine reserve as an attraction for divers. It is now one the most popular dive spots in New Zealand.

Accommodation

Many properties are older character houses, particularly from the turn of the century and 1930s. Homes with sea views fetch premium prices. There are few affordable starter homes and hardly any choice below $500,000.

Shopping & Amenities

The Parade has all the essential shops, including a popular butchers and New World supermarket. Just off the main street is a community centre and small library. The Learning Connexion art school is based here, as is Victoria University's marine research centre. Island Bay's Empire cinema, which shut in the 1960s, has recently been restored and has three small screens and a cafe.

Eating & Drinking

Island Bay has some nice cafes and a couple of low-key restaurants. Café Zilli (04 383 5933) is a good Turkish eatery. The Original Thai Restaurant is a BYO with a handy liquor store opposite. A good range of takeaways is available.

Education

Pre-schoolers can attend a free kindergarten, creche, and childcare centre or Playcentre. Island Bay School is a school for years 1 to 6 and St Francis De Sales school provides Catholic education. Years 7 and 8 pupils from Island Bay usually attend South Wellington Intermediate School. Secondary girls are zoned for Wellington East Girl's College and boys attend unzoned Rongatai.

Transport

Buses run every ten minutes to the hospital, Courtney Place and the station.

Safety & Annoyances

A 10 minute drive to the city at the weekend can be a 40 minute drive during weekday peak times.

Johnsonville

Map p.498
Area D p.116-117

Best Points
Good community and retail facilities.

Worst Points
Not one of Wellington's most picturesque areas.

Johnsonville is a relatively large, characterless suburb. Good road, rail and bus links into the city, 7km away, make it popular with commuters. It has experienced rapid growth in the last few years, including big retail expansion.

Accommodation

The majority of houses in Johnsonville are owned, but there are lots of rental properties available. It is one of the more affordable suburbs, with plenty of choice in the $300,000 to $500,000 bracket. With lots of undeveloped land to the west, there are plenty of sections for sale. Most properties are modern townhouses.

Shopping & Amenities

There are branches of all the usual chain stores here, including The Warehouse (p.380), Countdown and Woolworths. Johnsonville Mall is set to double in size over the next few years. The community centre provides lots of classes and is home to a craft co-operative, an opportunity shop that sells second-hand goods, and local Citizens Advice Bureau. The decent-sized library is well-stocked. The Keith Spry Pool (04 478 9237) has excellent facilities.

Eating & Drinking

Jays Bar (04 9200 310) is popular with locals, especially for sports events. Otherwise, there are a number of takeaways, a foodcourt within the shopping mall, several decent cafes and Indian, Chinese and Malaysian restaurants.

Education

Johnsonville has a wide range of early childhood options, including Montessori, free kindergartens and a Playcentre. There are two state primary schools and an intermediate. Johnsonville School is zoned, West Park is not. There is also St Brigid's Catholic School for years 1 to 8. State secondary education is zoned for Onslow College in Johnsonville. Pupils living north of Broderick Road may also able to choose Newlands College.

Transport

Johnsonville is commuter heaven; it takes just 20 minutes to get to Wellington on the Tranz Metro. There are also regular buses. The suburb lies just off State Highway 1, which means it's well positioned for a quick escape from the city.

Safety & Annoyances

This is one of the few suburbs with no easy access to the sea.

Karori

Map p.498 A5
Area E p.116-117

Best Points
Great facilities.

Worst Points
A 15-minute journey to the sea.

The largest suburb in Wellington, Karori, is set in a valley surrounded by Karori Wildlife Sanctuary, scenic reserves and farmland, but is still close to the western edge of the city. With good schools and facilities, it is popular with families and older people.

Accommodation

Most styles of houses are available in Karori – at a price. Properties are cheaper on the western side of the suburb. Homes often have bigger sections and greater privacy than those in neighbouring Kelburn. Nearly three quarters of homes are owner-occupied and rental properties are quickly snapped up. Expect to pay upwards of $560,000 for a three-bedroom property.

Shopping & Amenities

Karori has plenty of shops, although they are divided into several separate areas along Karori Road. The main shopping area, around Karori Mall, has everything residents need, from a library to small supermarkets. Munro's shoes, in the Mall, is one of the two shoe shops in Wellington, which will measure children's feet and fit shoes, including Clarks (the other being Gubbs in central Wellington). Mud Cycles, at the eastern end of Karori Road, repairs and hires bicycles – handy for nearby Makara Park mountain bike park. A community centre in Karori Road holds popular youth sessions and lots of activities for older people. Two large parks with good play and sports facilities, and an excellent swimming pool add to an abundance of amenities.

Karori

Eating & Drinking

For such a large neighbourhood, Karori has surprisingly few good restaurants. Boutique Dining Café (04 476 3354), which offers excellent French bistro food, is a notable exception. There are a few cafes and takeaways. The Terawhiti Arms (04 920 0254) and The Quiet Lady are dedicated drinking holes.

Education

Karori has a range of pre-school options, including free kindergartens, private childcare centres and community creches. There are three state primary schools: the large Karori Normal School, which has a good reputation, the smaller, more multicultural Karori West Normal School, and St Teresa's, a catholic school. Secondary school pupils are zoned for Wellington College for Boys and Wellington Girl's College. The Samuel Marsden Collegiate School is a private girl's school.

Transport

Buses run frequently from Karori to the city centre, and take 10 minutes on a good day. Travelling by bus or car can take considerably longer in peak times.

Map p.498 D3
Area F p.116-117

Best Points
Glorious views and good facilities.

Worst Points
Expensive.

Khandallah

The suburb was named after the old Khandallah Homestead, which was built in 1884 by Captain James Andrew on his return from India. As a result, many of the streets have Indian names. This is a trendy, popular suburb, just 10 minutes drive from the centre of Wellington. Good facilities, great transport links and wonderful harbour views make it one of the more expensive places to live.

Accommodation

The typical Khandallah house is sleek, modern and designed to make the best of the stunning harbour views. There are also some neat Victorian villas. Nearly 80% of homes here are owner-occupied, making rentals competitive. Many properties command prices in excess of $1 million.

Shopping & Amenities

Excellent facilities include a number of small shops, New World supermarket and library. The best of the several open spaces is Khandallah Park, which has an outdoor swimming pool (open November to March), community centre, tennis and squash courts and a grand old town hall.

Eating & Drinking

Aside from the pizza and Chinese takeaways, Khandallah also has Taste (04 479 8449), a family friendly pub and restaurant that serves sophisticated New Zealand cuisine.

Education

Khandallah is well served by two childcare centres, two free kindergartens and a community creche for pre-schoolers. Primary school pupils can attend Khandallah Primary or the more popular Cashmere Avenue School, whose zone covers the majority of the eastern side of the suburb. Catholic primary education is available at St Benedict's. Khandallah is zoned for Raroa Normal Intermediate School for years 7 and 8. Choice for secondary education favours girls who can attend Wellington Girl's College or Onslow College. Boys attend Onslow College.

Transport
Khandallah has its own train station on the Johnsonville line, meaning a journey of 15 minutes into town. Frequent buses take around the same time to reach the city, and can also take passengers to Wellington Hospital, or the eastern suburbs of Kilbirnie and Miramar.

Safety & Annoyances
Khandallah has a reputation for being rather an elite neighbourhood, and is one of the least multicultural of Wellington's suburbs.

Map p.498 E6
Area G p.116-117

Miramar
Miramar means 'sea view' in Spanish, and many residents enjoy ocean vistas and access to the pretty little beaches at Worser and Scorching Bays. Miramar has found recent fame as the home of *The Lord of the Rings* director Peter Jackson's studios. Wellington Airport separates the area from the central city suburbs.

Best Points
Family-friendly with good facilities

Worst Points
Noise from the planes is loud and frequent during the day, even though few international flights use Wellington Airport.

Accommodation
Although there are some expensive houses that command great views, many of the homes here are in the lower price bracket. Streets are lined with typical single-storey wooden houses with iron roofs. Homes on the hillsides have wonderful views but can have very sloping sections, with steep drives and little usable land. Three-bedroom rentals in the better streets cost around $400 a week; similar properties can be bought from $430,000.

Shopping & Amenities
Miramar has great facilities. The shopping centre in Miramar Avenue has a large New World supermarket, post office, garden centre with a good cafe, specialist Mediterranean foodstore, library and community centre. On the peninsula, there is another garden centre, golf course and tennis courts.

Eating & Drinking
No fine dining here, but some great cafes including the Chocolate Frog (04 388 8233) at Palmers Garden Centre, Eva Dixon's and Moyses Greek Taverna. All the takeaway options are here, including a choice of fish and chip shops. Miramar also has The Cutting Sports Cafe, a great sports and gaming bar.

Education
There are good pre-school facilities in Miramar, including a community creche and free kindergarten. There are five primary schools: Miramar North and Central (decile 6), which are both zoned, Miramar Christian School, Holy Cross Catholic School, Miramar South (decile 2) and Worser Bay (decile 10). Secondary pupils attend nearby Rongotai (boys) or Wellington East Girl's College.

Transport
Frequent buses take just over half an hour to reach Wellington station.

Safety & Annoyances
Noise from nearby Wellington Airport is loud and frequent during the day.

Looking down on Miramar

Newlands

Map p.498 E2
Area H p.116-117

Best Points
Close to the city.

Worst Points
Limited amenities.

Situated on hills on the opposite side of State Highway 1, Newlands' residents enjoy the facilities of Johnsonville and the close proximity to central Wellington. It's favoured by younger commuters and Asian families.

Accommodation

Newlands is more affordable than Johnsonville and has lots of properties for sale between $300,000 and $400,000. Although nearly three quarters of the homes are owned, there is a good rental market, particularly for house-sharers. Most houses have been built in the last 25 years. Houses on the hilltops have views over the entire harbour and city, including the airport, but consequently are battered by fierce winds.

Shopping & Amenities

There are plans to invigorate the shopping and community facilities in Newlands, but at the moment there is little except for a few dairies, a petrol station and pharmacy. Residents drive five minutes to the shops and amenities in Johnsonville.

Eating & Drinking

Getting a meal is limited to takeaways: fish and chips, Chinese or Hell Pizza (0800 666 111). The Innkeeper of Newlands is the only pub.

Education

Early childhood centres include two free kindergartens and a Playcentre. Primary school pupils have a choice of three schools, all unzoned. There is also an intermediate school for pupils attending Bellevue and Newlands Primary Schools. Secondary age students are zoned for Newlands College, (a co-educational school).

Transport

Residents either drive, use the frequent bus service (15 minutes to the city centre) or cycle to Johnsonville train station.

Safety & Annoyances

Driving onto the State Highway 1 northbound can be hazardous. The on-ramp from Newlands is one of the three worst traffic hotspots in Wellington.

Newtown

Map p.506, 507
Area J p.116-117

Best Points
Handy location for CBD, Massey University and the hospital.

Worst Points
Higher crime levels than most other suburbs.

Set on the fringes of the city and within walking distance to the CBD, Newtown was one of the first suburbs to be developed by European settlers, and is now one of the Wellington's most multicultural. It has a significant number of Victorian and Edwardian commercial and residential properties, and is also home to Wellington Hospital (p.165) and Massey University (p.184). In keeping with its cosmopolitan make-up, Newtown is home to Wellington's annual gay and lesbian fair (p.430).

Accommodation

From small turn-of-the-century villas to new apartment blocks and townhouses, Newtown has accommodation for most budgets. The area is undergoing slow gentrification, which is reflected in the number of new apartment and townhouse developments. There are several social housing developments around Constable and Daniell Streets. Larger family homes can be keenly priced. Around a third of homes are owner-occupied, making it a competitive rental area. Small apartments can be bought for $250,000 upwards, with three-bedroom homes costing from $400,000.

Shopping & Amenities
Newtown is particularly good for food shopping and offers a large number of ethnic specialists, including the Mediterranean Food Warehouse (04 939 8100), Asian supermarkets and fresh fish shops. Riddiford Street is the main shopping area and includes pharmacies, bookshops, a supermarket, a jeweller, florist, several antique stores, hairdressers and fabric retailers. Newtown Community and Cultural Centre houses lots of classes and regular groups, as well as Newtown Citizens Advice Bureau. There is a public library in Constable Street and free internet access and computer classes next door at the Smart Newtown Project. The sprawling Wakefield Hospital (p.165) is situated in Newtown.

Eating & Drinking
Reflecting its cosmopolitan community, Newtown has a wide range of restaurants, cafes, takeaways and bars centred on Riddiford Street. Indian, Chinese, Turkish and Malaysian cuisine is available, as are South American delicacies at the Amigos Chilean Restaurant and Mexican Café (04 939 0310). Romantic, intimate dining can be found at Eateria De Manon (p.449), which serves French dishes. Other popular restaurants include Beijing and Jewel of Nepal. For a different cafe experience, try Eva Dixon's (04 389 6222) at the entrance to Wellington Zoo – it has a window onto a meerkat enclosure.

Education
Plenty of choice exists for pre-school education. St Anne's is a Catholic primary school. Children attending Newtown Primary go to South Wellington Intermediate in years 7 and 8. Secondary state education is available for boys at the unzoned Rongotai College in Kilbirnie, or, for only the most northern parts of Newtown, the more popular Wellington College. Girls are zoned for Wellington East Girl's College.

Transport
Newtown is within walking distance of the city centre. Buses run frequently and take 10 minutes to the CBD.

Safety & Annoyances
Walking the streets alone at night, particularly near the hospital, can feel uneasy. Development of the hospital will mean construction noise for some years to come.

Boathouses in Evans Bay

Newtown

Map p.498 C3
Area K p.116-117

Best Points
Close to city facilities and greenery.

Worst Points
Winding Ngaio Gorge Road and no buses from Crofton Downs.

Ngaio & Crofton Downs

Ngaio and Crofton Downs are north and north-west of the city centre and share facilities. Crofton Downs backs on to Otari-Wilton's Bush, a beautiful botanic garden dedicated to native plants, while Ngaio borders Khandallah. Ngaio was originally a logging community and is situated on the slopes of Mount Kaukau.

Accommodation

All sorts of accommodation is available, but there's an abundance of 60s weatherboard houses. Sub-divisions on Mount Kaukau have some stucco 'leaky homes' built in 2000 (see www.dbh.govt.nz/weathertightness-index). Infill housing is an issue in Ngaio, making sections smaller and less private. Three bedroom rentals start at $350 per week, and there are plenty of houses to buy between $450,000 and $600,000.

Shopping & Amenities

There is a small shopping centre at Crofton Downs, with a Woolworths, pharmacy, toy store and a handy Mitre 10 DIY store. Community facilities are based in Ottawa Road, Ngaio, a short distance away, and include a small library, town hall, post shop, cafe and shops. Trelissick Park, which runs alongside Ngaio Gorge Road, is a beautiful spot for a picnic.

Eating & Drinking

There is Cafe 26 in Crofton Downs, but Ngaio has all the takeaways. Cafe Villa (04 479 5707) in Ngaio has a real neighbourhood feel and a loyal following.

Education

Ngaio has several private childcare centres, a free kindergarten and Playcentre. Primary pupils in Crofton Downs usually attend the small Chartwell School or St Benedict's Catholic school in nearby Khandallah. Ngaio School is zoned and excludes residents of Crofton Downs. Intermediate pupils normally go to Raroa Normal Intermediate in Johnsonville. Secondary school pupils are zoned for Onslow College.

Transport

Crofton Downs is one of the few Wellington suburbs without a bus service, although residents continue to campaign for one. Crofton Downs and Ngaio are on the Johnsonville Tranz Metro line and trains to the city take just seven minutes. Ngaio has a frequent bus service.

Safety & Annoyances

There is relatively little crime, but theft from unlocked cars is a problem.

Map p.498
Area L p.116-117

Best Points
City centre living by the beach.

Worst Points
Only for the rich.

Oriental Bay

Living in the most expensive suburb of Wellington, Oriental Bay residents have got the lot: beautiful views across the harbour and city, a sandy beach, an easy walk to work and play and a marina for their yachts. The area is popular with professional couples and retirees, nearly all of whom have European backgrounds.

Accommodation

The median price of properties here is more than $1 million, but there are still some apartments available for $600,000 plus. Just over half the properties are owner-occupied so rentals are easy to find, although expensive. Underground parking can be included with high-end properties, but off-street parking is rare. Most accommodation is penthouse or apartment-style, but there are still some turn-of-the-century houses to be found. These are gradually being demolished and replaced by apartment blocks. There are some grand art deco buildings on the main road.

Shopping & Amenities

City centre shopping is close at hand, and there are small convenience shops dotted around the bay. Cinemas, theatres and other entertainment options are within walking distance. Freyberg Pool (04 801 4530) offers swimming, health and fitness facilities and classes, together with stunning views over the water. On the way towards Mount Victoria you'll find plenty of green space in Charles Plimmer Park.

Eating & Drinking

There are a few recommended dining options, including the casual Fisherman's Table (04 801 7900), which has one of the best locations in Wellington, and the upmarket White House (p.453) and Martin Bosley's Yacht Club Restaurant (p.454), both of which specialise in seafood. Cafes include Kaffe Eis (04 385 1727), which serves authentic Italian gelato icecream.

Education

Pre-schools, a community creche and free kindergarten facilities are available in Mount Victoria, a short distance away. The nearest primary schools are Clyde Quay School, which is zoned for most of Oriental Bay, or the small Roseneath School, just around the bay and unzoned. Secondary pupils are zoned for Wellington College (boys) and Wellington East Girl's College. Alternatively, the only private Anglican co-educational school, St Mark's, is situated close to the colleges. This enrolls students up to 14 years and offers the International Baccalaureate.

Transport

Oriental Bay is on two bus routes and is within walking distance of the CBD and the city's main retail spots.

Safety & Annoyances

City centre liquor restrictions have led to youths drinking in the area and minor vandalism. Temporary liquor bans for public holidays have been granted and permanent bans in the area are being considered.

View across the harbour at Oriental Bay

Map p.498 F7
Area M p.116-117

Best Points
Seaside holiday village feel.

Worst Points
Rather elite neighbourhood.

Seatoun

Until the Seatoun Tunnel was built in 1907, this most eastern suburb could only be reached by boat. A century later, Seatoun retains its exclusivity and reputation as a classy seaside resort for the affluent.

Seatoun property

Accommodation

Seatoun is one of the most expensive areas in Wellington and property is at a premium. There is practically nothing for sale for less than $1 million. With 80% of property owner-occupied, rentals are rare. Many houses used to be weekend cottages, but have either been expanded over the years, or replaced by large, modern family homes. Smaller, traditional wooden places with iron roofs are still around, but fetch prices in excess of $950,000, especially if they have sea views. Houses with good-sized gardens are rare.

Shopping & Amenities

There is a small area of shops including a dairy and bookshop. Watersports and a yacht club can be found at Worser Bay, a few minutes away. There is also a memorial park built for the 151 people who died on the Wahine inter-island ferry, which sunk in heavy storms off Seatoun in 1968.

Eating & Drinking

Seatoun boasts Breakers Café (04 388 5566) and Solstice (04 388 8299), which both serve Mediterranean cuisine. Chocolate Fish Café (p.455) – where staff cross the road to serve customers on the waterfront – is a five-minute drive away at Scorching Bay.

Education

Seatoun School moved to impressive new grounds in 2002, and has a free kindergarten attached. St Anthony's offers Catholic schooling. The nearest secondary schools are Rongotai for Boys and Wellington East Girl's College. Independent boy's day and boarding school, Scot's College, is nearby in Strathmore and Catholic secondary schools are in Kilbirnie.

Transport

There is a regular bus service into the city and driving takes around 20 minutes. Road access is via the Seatoun Tunnel or the coast roads in either direction. The airport is five minutes away.

Safety & Annoyances

Wind from every direction hits Seatoun, covering the houses in salty spray and making gardening a challenge.

Map p.498 C1
Area N *p.116-117*

Best Points
Excellent facilities

Worst Points
Not the most sunny or scenic of suburbs.

Tawa

The most northern of Wellington's suburbs, Tawa is set in a valley between Wellington and Porirua, and is split in two by the State Highway 1. It has more churches per capita than anywhere else in New Zealand and, until recent times, was a teetotal neighbourhood. Good transport and a wide range of facilities make it very popular with families.

Accommodation

Although there are some older character properties, the majority of houses have been built in the last 50 years. Because Tawa is set in a valley, low cloud often hangs over the area, making some properties feel damp. Plots with several acres of land, known as lifestyle blocks, are available on the hillsides around Tawa. These often have more sun and fetch higher prices, as do those in Redwood. Cheaper properties can be found at the northern end of town around Linden. Rentals are available, from single units to large family homes, with prices typically 20% lower than inner city suburbs. A three-bedroom rental costs around $335 per week, and there are plenty of houses available to buy for $300,000 upwards.

Shopping & Amenities

Tawa has a good range of shops and a community centre, and has quite a village feel. The swimming pool complex (Tawa Pool) has one of the best toddler pools in Wellington and is set in a pleasant reserve. Wellington's only outlet mall, Dressmart (p.417), is at the southern end of town, together with Chipmunks, an indoor soft play centre. There's a library on the main street, along with several large second-hand shops.

Eating & Drinking

Tawa is not known for its restaurants or bars. Liquor licences are approved by local referendum, and the conservative population did not grant any until 1999, making Tawa one of the last places in New Zealand to allow the purchase of alcohol. There are the usual takeaways and a couple of cafes. Locals frequent the Roundabout, which serves well-priced pub grub.

Education

Parents have lots of choice for pre-school, from private childcare centres to free kindergartens. Tawa has six primary schools, none of which are zoned. Pupils attend Tawa Intermediate before moving to Tawa College for secondary education. Although highly regarded by parents, Tawa College does less well academically than nearby Newlands and Onslow Colleges.

Teetotal Tawa

Transport

Three railway stations and regular bus services make public transport a good option. Tawa is located just off State Highway 1, making travel to the city and other areas of the lower North Island straightforward.

Safety & Annoyances

Tawa is home to Arohata Women's Prison, and inmates have occasionally escaped into the local community.

Map p.504, 505
Area P p.116-117

Best Points
Entertainment centre of Wellington.

Worst Points
Loud, late-night noise.

Te Aro

Te Aro is in the centre of Wellington's entertainment and nightlife district and is one of the city's liveliest suburbs. It is popular with students, young professionals and business people, many of whom work in the area.

Accommodation

Apartment living is the norm in Te Aro, although there are some streets with period villas. Many commercial buildings have been converted into loft-style apartments, most of which are rented. Sharing is common. Off-street parking and garages are at a premium. Most streets require resident parking permits, but parking is allowed after 18:00 on weekdays and during weekends.

Shopping & Amenities

There is a large New World supermarket in Wakefield Street and several larger convenience stores dotted around. Cuba Street (p.414) is the destination for more bohemian options, including vintage clothing, local designer-wear, second-hand bookshops and music stores. Specialist stores in Te Aro include Commonsense Organics (p.388) and Cool Britannia, which sells mostly food items to British expats. Central Library is well-stocked and has lots of information about events and activities. Te Papa (p.370), the National Film Archive, City Gallery, the Opera House, Town Hall and Michael Fowler Centre (home to the New Zealand Symphony Orchestra), and the large multiplex cinemas are all nearby. Green space is almost non-existent in Te Aro, but the harbourside around Frank Kitts Park is popular with skaters and joggers.

Eating & Drinking

There's no end of good cafes and takeaways. Restaurants are concentrated around Courtney Place, where there's something for all budgets and tastes. Vegetarians are well catered for at Real Earth Organic Café (04 470 7752), Aunty Mena Vegetarian Café (Asian) and Hare Krishna Higher Taste (Indian). Families are welcomed at many venues, including One Red Dog (04 918 4723). Top-end restaurants include Logan Brown (p.452) and Citron, which is famous for its nine-course degustation menu. Zibibbo (p.451) serves Mediterranean food. Nearly all the decent, popular nightclubs and bars are also found here. Live music venues include San Francisco Bath House (04 801 6797) and Bar Bodega (04 384 8212). There are several sports bars, wine bars and some more traditional pubs.

Education

There is no dedicated early childhood education provision in Te Aro, which could explain why there are few families in the area. There is a small primary school. It has around 200 pupils from more than 40 different countries, special classes for those with English as a second language, and a class for the deaf. Secondary pupils are zoned for Wellington College (boys) and Wellington East Girl's College. Wellington High School is located on Taranaki Street.

Transport

Most residents walk to work. Buses run frequently to other areas of the city. It's a bus ride or 20 minute walk to Wellington train station.

Safety & Annoyances

Thursday nights are cheap drinking nights for students, so there can be minor street violence, broken bottles and vandalism. Friday and Saturday nights see the streets busy with noisy revellers. There have been issues with homeless people around Cuba Street in the past, but any problems are minor compared to other capital cities.

Thorndon apartments

Map p.500, 501
Area Q p.116-117

Best Points
The business heart of the city, with attractive residential areas and great schools.

Worst Points
Expensive daytime parking and lack of sun in the afternoon.

Thorndon & CBD

As the home of parliament, law courts, the national library, foreign embassies and educational establishments, Thorndon/CBD has the best transport links in Wellington, and great facilities. There are many historic buildings here, including two cathedrals and the largest wooden structure in the southern hemisphere, which used to house the parliament buildings. Popular with politicians and high earners, the area offers excellent schools and the convenience of city centre living.

Accommodation

Some of the city's oldest houses are situated in the northern end of Thorndon and Tinakori Road, which has a welcoming, village feel. The Terrace, which is the main commuter road, has apartment blocks overlooking the motorway. There are still family houses available for less than $1 million and plenty of properties for sale or rent. Off-street parking is very desirable.

Shopping & Amenities

The amenities here are probably the best in Wellington. Thorndon has a large New World supermarket and lots of small specialist shops. Tinakori Road is known for its antiques shops. The department store, Kirkcaldie & Stains (p.414), is nearby on Lambton Quay. World-class sporting events at the Westpac Stadium are within walking distance, and Thorndon even has an open air swimming pool in the summer. There is plenty of green space to explore to the west, in the Western Slopes Reserve, and Northern Walkway to Wadestown. Access to the Botanical Gardens is just over the motorway. Harbourside facilities include kayak and skate hire at Fergs Kayaks (p.402). If you fancy a workout during your lunch break, there are several gyms on The Terrace.

Eating & Drinking

Cafe culture is cut-throat here and even extends to the poaching of popular staff. There are a number of good restaurants too, including Tinakori Bistro (04 499 0567) and Maria Pia's Trattoria (04 499 5590). Good pub grub can be found at the Shepherd's Arms Hotel, the oldest hotel in New Zealand. There are also some great restaurants at the harbour with views across the water.

Education

There are several early childhood centres and private creches based in Thorndon. Primary education is offered at Thorndon School and Sacred Heart Catholic School. Secondary pupils are zoned for Wellington Girl's College in Thorndon or Wellington College (boys). Girls also have the option of Queen Margaret's College, which offers private education from ages 3 to 18. Kimi Ora is a special unit based at Thorndon School for the disabled, aged between 5 and 21.

Transport

Residents have access to all bus and train services, as well as the Interlslander ferry to Picton, and services across the harbour to Days Bay and Eastbourne (p.244).

Safety & Annoyances

Much of the CBD and the area around parliament are dead at night. Residents have to head to Tinakori Road, or further east to the waterfront to find anything open.

Wilton

Map p.498 B4
Area R p.116-117

Best Points
Surrounded by plentiful native bush.

Worst Points
The lack of amenities.

Surrounded by native bush and parks, Wilton is on the fringes of the city and home to Otari-Wilton's Bush, the only public botanical garden in the country dedicated to native plants. Residents, who include a number of Green Party activists, have plenty of pleasant walks from which to choose.

Housing on the hills in Northland

Accommodation

Most types of accommodation can be found in Wilton, but availability is limited. There is some state housing in Hampshire and Shropshire Avenues. Two thirds of the homes are owner-occupied. A typical three-bedroom home can be bought for $450,000 upwards and rented for $380 per week.

Shopping & Amenities

Wilton has no amenities of its own, other than a bowling club and a dairy that stocks essentials, but it's only five kilometres from the city centre and a shorter distance to the many facilities at Karori (p.121) or Crofton Downs (p.126).

Eating & Drinking

Wilton residents have a Chinese takeaway, which also serves fish and chips. For everything else, they go to Crofton Downs or Thorndon.

Education

Pre-school options are limited to a Montessori school, a childcare centre and Playcentre. Otari Primary School for years 1-8 has a majority of Maori pupils, who are offered total Maori immersion classes. It also provides Montessori teaching, as well as standard national curriculum. There have been some concerns about the school's performance, which are being addressed. Catholic education is provided at the Cardinal McKeefry School. Wilton is zoned for Wellington College (boys), Wellington Girl's College and Onslow College (co-ed).

Transport

Wilton is served by a frequent bus service into the city.

Safety & Annoyances

The lack of amenities means travelling for just about all supplies.

Eastbourne

Map p.498

Best Points
Parks, beaches, galleries.

Worst Points
Cost.

Eastbourne, including Lowry Bay, York Bay, Days Bay and Muritaiis, is the largest settlement on the sparsely populated eastern side of Wellington harbour. Although a little isolated, it is a popular area and offers access to huge expanses of regional parks and reserves, while still being 20 minutes to the city by ferry and 45 minutes by bus. It is an exclusive area with swimming beaches, speciality shops and art galleries. Properties costing less than $500,000 are rare and on the small side. Rental properties are available and are typically $450 plus, per week for a three-bedroom house with sea views. The facilities of Petone and Lower Hutt are 10 minutes by car. Primary schools include private Wellesley College for boys, San Antonio Catholic School and Muritai School. Two Playcentres and a free kindergarten are available for pre-schoolers. Secondary pupils attend Hutt Valley High (zoned) or Wainuiomata (unzoned).

North Island Map G14

The Hutt Valley & Petone

Best Points
Affordable housing and family-friendly facilities.

Worst Points
Identikit suburbs.

The Hutt Valley offers some of the most affordable housing in the Wellington region. Lower Hutt is a large sprawling city 14km from Wellington CBD, with excellent shopping and good amenities including swimming, sports, schools, an art centre and community groups. Most streets are based on a grid system, centred on the recent Westfield Queensgate retail development, which has around 140 stores, a multiplex cinema and foodcourt.

This is a family focused areas with good schools and childcare options. There are several smaller suburbs within Lower Hutt, the majority of which are single-level houses, built in the last 30 years, and set on long streets with no distinguishing features. Notable exceptions are properties on the western side of State Highway 1, including those in Belmont and Maungaraki, which can have good views against the backdrop of Belmont Regional Park.

Petone was the original European settlement in Wellington and is now enjoying a growth in popularity. Its main drag, Jackson Street, is home to some good speciality shops, including an Asian supermarket, bookshops, and galleries. Popular cafes, bars, takeaways and restaurants line the road. Locals make good use of their free artesian water supply in Buick Street.

A 20 minute drive or train journey from Lower Hutt takes you to Upper Hutt and its surrounding suburbs, including Trentham, Silverstream and Heretaunga. It has adequate shopping facilities and amenities including supermarkets, cinemas, parks, golf courses, schools, childcare and sporting facilities. Commuting to Wellington is easy by train (maximum 45 minute journey) or car. Upper Hutt offers good access to the Wairarapa region through the nearby Rimutaka Range.

North Island Map G14

Kapiti

Best Points
More than 30km of beautiful beach.

Worst Points
Somewhat tricky commute.

Extending north from Paekakariki, the Kapiti Coast is popular with families and retirees. Many city workers take the 55 minute train ride from Paraparaumu, or drive into Wellington along State Highway 1, enjoying some breathtaking ocean views. This road has a high accident rate, however, and plans to either expand the coastal highway or develop a new inland route have been under discussion for decades. The area offers a seaside community, with a 30km stretch of sandy beach, and good retail and leisure facilities. House prices and rental costs are typically 20% to 30% lower than popular inner city suburbs. The schools are good and there are two respected secondary colleges in the area.

Kapiti Coast in Autumn

Porirua

North Island Map G14

Best Points
Cheap property in places.

Worst Points
Some sub-standard secondary schools.

Porirua is situated to the north of Wellington, around two arms of Porirua Harbour and connected by Mana Esplanade. It has excellent shopping facilities, including the North City and Mega shopping centres, as well as a large museum, art gallery and performance venue, Pataka (04 237 1511).

The area is popular with commuters. A trip to the city takes about 30 minutes. Pre-schools and primary schools are good but the area's secondary school doesn't enjoy a favourable reputation. Many residents send their children to colleges outside the region. Rental prices average $260 per week for a three-bedroom house but rentals in more sought-after areas such as Plimmerton can be considerably higher. Although house prices in Porirua are the cheapest in the greater Wellington region, in the popular areas they are significantly higher than in nearby Tawa. Eastern Porirua, particularly Canons Creek, is a comparatively high crime area, with resident members of the Mongrel Mob gang regularly arrested for violence or drug offences. In contrast, the favoured and picturesque seaside communities of Whitby, Camborne, Pukerua Bay and Plimmerton have luxury properties, high-income residents and little crime.

Palmerston

North Island Map H13

Best Points
Plenty of indoor and outdoor activities.

Worst Points
John Cleese thinks it the dullest place in New Zealand.

Located in the Manawatu region of the lower North Island, Palmerston North is a sizeable city, 140km north of Wellington. It is home to Massey University (p.184), good schools and several government research facilities. The city is arranged in a grid around a central square and is noticeably flat. 'Palmy', as it is known, is two hours' drive to Hawke's Bay, Taranaki, Martinborough, Wellington and the ski fields, making it a great base for exploring the lower North Island. It has a reputation, however, for being a bit dull. British comedian John Cleese described it as the 'suicide capital of New Zealand'. Residents responded by naming a rubbish tip after him. Outwardly, the city doesn't look anything special, but there's plenty to do. There's the great museum, gallery and science space, Te Manawa (06 355 5000, www.temanawa.co.nz), two theatres, an indoor and outdoor swimming pool complex and good sports facilities. The surrounding areas of Manawatu Gorge and the Tararua Range offer great recreational tramping and kayaking. House prices are significantly lower than Wellington with plenty of choice from $200,000. Palmerston has 17,000 Massey students in term time, meaning there's plenty of reasonable rental property available.

Wairarapa

North Island Map H14

Best Points
Wine, wine and more wine.

Worst Points
A fair stretch from Wellington.

For some years the expansion of Wellington has been creeping across the Rimutaka Range into the wine-growing region of the Wairarapa.

Most accessible for commuters are the villages of Featherston and Greytown, but the train line runs all the way from Wellington to Masterton, with a 90 minute journey time. Several years ago, large period villas could be bought for between $100,000 and $200,000, but the increasing popularity of the area has pushed prices up. It is still significantly cheaper than Wellington, thanks largely to the long commute and isolated nature of the Wairarapa, but true housing bargains are now rare. A three-bedroom rental is around $230 per week. Greytown is a particularly attractive village that retains much of its 19th century history. The area is popular for weekend wine breaks, and is packed come the annual Toast Martinborough Food and Wine Festival (p.59).

Mana Island at sunset

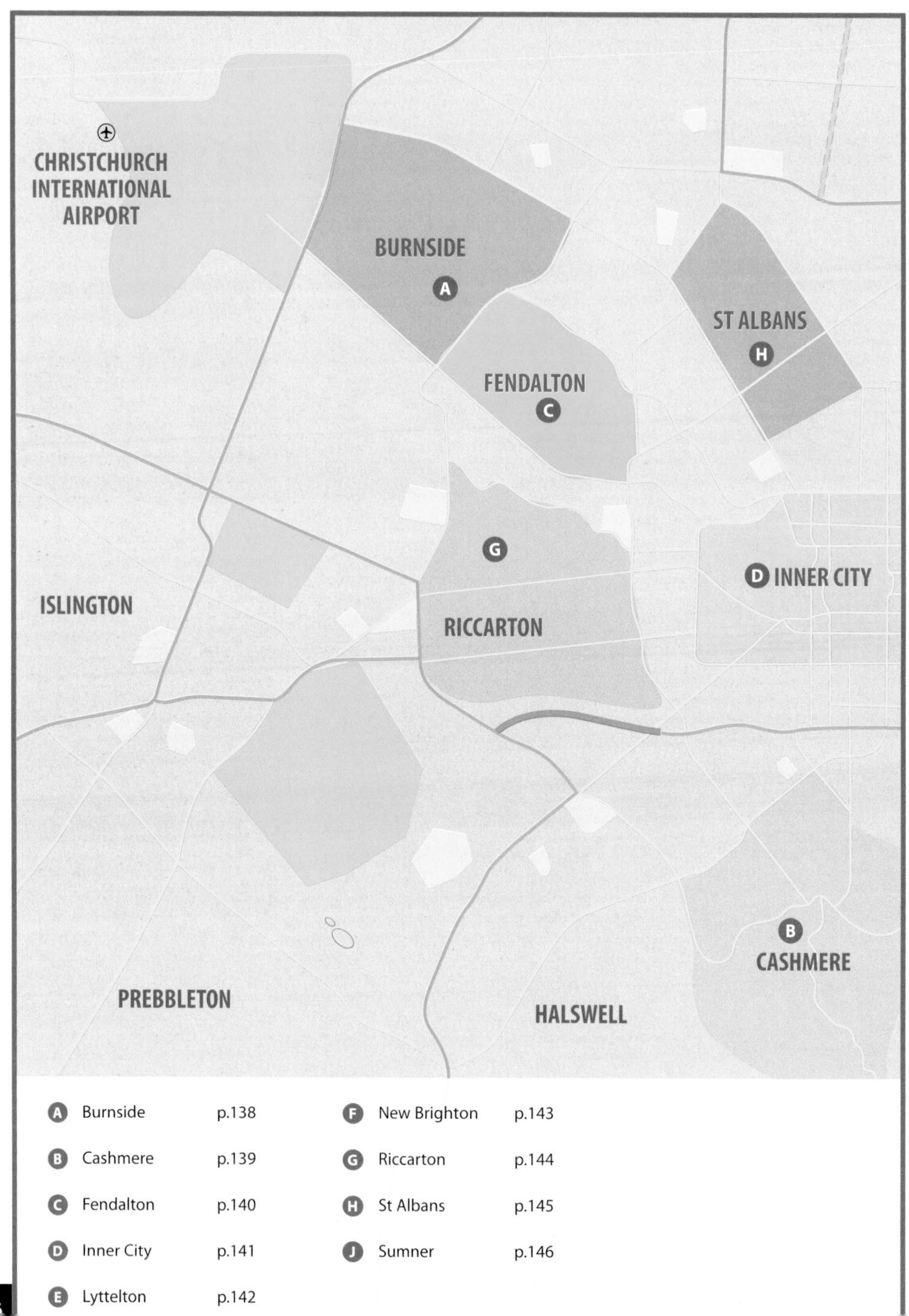
CHRISTCHURCH INTERNATIONAL AIRPORT
BURNSIDE
A
ST ALBANS
H
FENDALTON
C
G
D INNER CITY
ISLINGTON
RICCARTON
B
CASHMERE
PREBBLETON
HALSWELL
A Burnside p.138
B Cashmere p.139
C Fendalton p.140
D Inner City p.141
E Lyttelton p.142
F New Brighton p.143
G Riccarton p.144
H St Albans p.145
J Sumner p.146

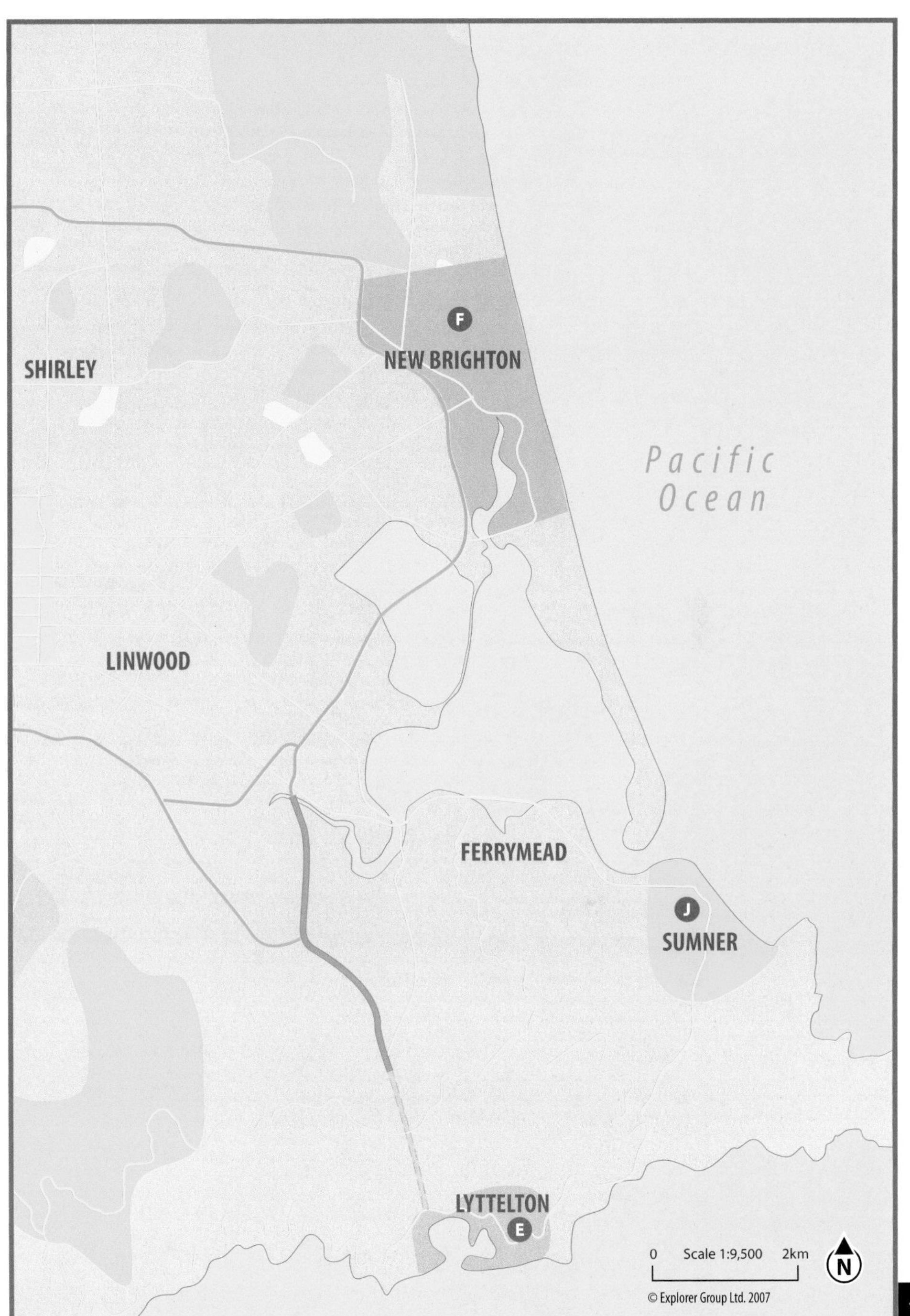

F
NEW BRIGHTON
SHIRLEY
Pacific
Ocean
LINWOOD
FERRYMEAD
J
SUMNER
LYTTELTON
E
0 Scale 1:9,500 2km
N
© Explorer Group Ltd. 2007

Christchurch & Further Out

With tree-lined streets, lush parks, meandering rivers, good schools, beautiful coastline and access to ski fields, it is not hard to understand why Christchurch is such a popular place for families to live. The city was founded by English settlers who wanted to recreate a slice of home in far-flung New Zealand. They largely succeeded, but in recent years Christchurch has shrugged off some of its English conservatism to become a cosmopolitan city. One notable feature of its population however is that it is conspicuously monocultural compared to other New Zealand regions, particularly the North Island. The Maori presence here was small compared with the North Island, and they were swiftly and heavily outnumbered by European settlers.

Christchurch is the largest city in the South Island and is the retail, commercial and cultural hub of the 'Mainland'. It is home to two universities and a polytechnic, boasts an impressive array of art galleries, theatres, and museums, and is easy to navigate, particularly for pedestrians and cyclists. The barren Port Hills flank the southern edge of the city and act as an adventure playground for the city's residents. And with mountains only an hour or so away, Christchurch is the ideal base for people who love the outdoors but still want the benefits of city living. The city's suburbs offer a diverse range of housing, schools and amenities.

Burnside

Map p.508 B3
Area A p.136-137

Best Points
It's a safe family suburb, well positioned between the airport and the city centre.

Worst Points
The constant drone of planes flying overhead can get tiresome.

If you're looking for a slice of middle-class suburbia, buy in Burnside.

Situated on the north-western side of the city, near to Christchurch International Airport, the suburb is dominated by detached family homes and new townhouses. Burnside was considered to be on the outer edges of the city's boundaries, but rapid housing development over the past couple of decades has seen the green belt erode, and more homes built to the west. There are excellent facilities and good transport links, so family homes here are highly desirable.

Accommodation

Modern family homes line the streets of Burnside. While many of the bigger sections have been subdivided in order to accommodate more housing, most homes still come with a sizeable amount of land. New properties tend to be two-storey townhouses, designed for low maintenance. Some residential complexes for the over 60s are beginning to spring up. You'll be lucky to find any property for less than $400,000.

Shopping & Amenities

With parks, tennis courts, bowling clubs, sports grounds, golf courses, shops and a performing arts centre, Burnside almost has it all. There are lots of small shopping precincts where you can stock up on basics, and Northlands Mall (p.421) – one of the largest indoor shopping centres in Australasia – is in the nearby suburb of Papanui.

Eating & Drinking

For five-star dining you will have to venture into the city centre, but there are a number of surprisingly good restaurants dotted around Burnside. Don't be fooled by their run-of-the-mill appearances – the food is delicious and the service good. Try Le Petite in Kendal Avenue (03 358 8810) or Cousinns Resaturant in Harris Crescent (03 352 222). Neighbourhood taverns will ensure you won't die of thirst, but if you're looking for sophisticated watering holes you will have to head into town.

Education

Burnside High School is one of the biggest secondary schools in the country and has a good reputation. Its particular strengths are music and arts. The school sits in the heart of the suburb, and properties within its school zone are highly sought after. There are also a number of well-regarded primary schools (Westburn, Christ the King and Burnside primary) and pre-schools, which explains Burnside's popularity with families.

Transport

The main route from the airport to the central city dissects Burnside, providing easy access to the ring road system and other parts of the city. The public transport system servicing the suburb is probably one of the best in Christchurch, with both normal bus services and the Orbiter operating in the area.

Safety & Annoyances

Burnside is regarded as one of the city's safer suburbs, but you still should still think twice about walking through its parks after dark. The only things likely to annoy you are the planes flying overhead.

Cashmere

Map p.508 C6
Area B p.136-137

Best Points
Most of the houses lie above the smog and enjoy spectacular views of the city and the coast.

Worst Points
Even going to collect the mail in the morning can constitute a serious workout.

For fantastic views, and to escape the thick smog that often carpets Christchurch in the winter, head to the slopes of Cashmere. The hillside suburb is home to some of Christchurch's most expensive property, and some of the city's best walking and mountain-biking tracks. Nearby Victoria Park is a favourite playground for Christchurch residents. From the hills of Cashmere, you get stunning views from the Southern Alps to the Kaikoura coastline.

Accommodation

Those views don't come cheaply. Property prices start at around $400,000 at the bottom of the hill and rise steeply the higher you go. Sprawling, executive homes dot the hills of Cashmere and can easily command in excess of $1 million. Most of the houses are detached and multi-level, and make the most of the views over the city and the Canterbury plains. Most of the land in Cashmere has already been snapped up for housing but there is still the odd section available.

Shopping & Amenities

There are a handful of local shops, including a bakery and greengrocers, but you'll have to head further out to find a supermarket and into town for any real retail therapy. On the plus side, you have a pleasant park (Victoria Park) on your doorstep, in which to spend the weekends soaking up the sunshine and breathing the fresh, smog-free air.

Eating & Drinking

Cashmere has gone for quality rather than quantity. There is only a handful of cafes and restaurants in the suburb, but they are all recommended. Best bets include Jack Flash Bar and Restaurant (03 964 2880), The Cup (p.470), and Coffee Culture (03 331 8100). For gourmet takeaway burgers, it's hard to look past Burger Wisconsin (p.462).

Housing in Cashmere

Education

The collective wealth of Cashmere is reflected in the quality of its schools. Cashmere Primary and Thorrington Primary both have excellent reputations, while the local secondary school, Cashmere High, is also well regarded.

Transport

You'll need a car – or strong calf muscles – if you're going to make Cashmere your permanent home. Bus services do operate, but not very regularly at weekends or late at night. They are also suspended at least a couple of times each winter because of ice or snow on the roads.

Safety & Annoyances

You won't have too many safety concerns if you buy or rent here. The crime rate is fairly low. You will need to keep an eye out, however, for speeding mountain bikers, who come careering down the hill at alarming rates.

Map p.510 B4
Area C p.136-137

Fendalton

Best Points
Grand property and some of the best schools in the city.

Worst Points
You need to get dressed up, even for a trip to the supermarket.

If you want to mix with high society on a day-to-day basis, buy property in this leafy green suburb, long home to Christchurch's elite. Grand mansions once sat side-by-side with small, non-descript state houses, but these days, the state houses are virtually all gone, and have been replaced with pricey new townhouses. The area boasts arguably the two best state secondary schools in the city and lies only minutes away from prestigious private schools such as Rangi Ruru Girls' College, St Margaret's College and St Andrew's College. Fendalton is equidistant to the city centre and airport.

Accommodation

There is no such thing as cheap in Fendalton – even a tiny flat is likely to set you back in excess of $400,000. The suburb is dominated by standalone family homes. You'll need at least $700,000 to buy a decent-sized place and in excess of $1 million if you want one bordering the Avon River. Rental properties are in short supply and command very high prices.

Shopping & Amenities

You won't have to travel far to fill your kitchen shelves. There are two local shopping centres in the area, each with a supermarket, chemist and other essential shops. But if you want trendy clothes, you'll need to take a five-minute drive into the city centre or to the shopping mall in the neighbouring suburb of Merivale. There is a public library in Fendalton, bowls and croquet clubs, and plenty of picturesque parks – if your backyard isn't quite big enough to play cricket.

Eating & Drinking

For post-work drinks, most people head to Misceo (p.463). It does great food but is about the only watering hole in Fendalton. There are plenty of decent cafes in the area.

Education

Fendalton is home to some of the best schools in Christchurch, which is partly why house prices in the area are so high. The pre-schools and primary schools in the area, including the exclusive Medbury School for Boys, have excellent reputations. Places in the suburb's state secondary schools – Christchurch Girls' High and Christchurch Boys' High – are highly sought-after, and students living within the suburb are given preferential entry. Canterbury University (p.184) also has its campus in Fendalton.

Transport

If you can afford to live in Fendalton, you probably won't need to use public transport, which is good because it is limited. You can catch a bus into town, or out to the airport, but that's about it.

Safety & Annoyances

The only thing likely to annoy you is the busloads of tourists, admiring your tree-lined streets, posh homes and immaculately kept gardens.

Map p.512, 513, 516
Area D p.136-137

Inner City

Few people lived in Christchurch's inner city twenty years ago, but its popularity has soared in recent times, as more people realise the benefits of living so close to the city's bars, restaurants and shops. Christchurch City Council has been investing heavily in the area, while apartment blocks and townhouse complexes are cropping up in record numbers.

City centre living

Best Points

The city's shops, galleries, theatres, bars and restaurants are on your doorstep.

Worst Points

The morning-after mess on Saturday and Sunday mornings after drunken revellers have partied their way around town.

Accommodation

The standard varies, from multi-million dollar penthouses with amazing views over Hagley Park to small studio units tucked into any spare nook or cranny. Apartments and townhouses close to Hagley Park and the area's cultural precinct command the highest prices – to rent and buy – while accommodation on the eastern side of the city is more affordable. Prices for apartments start at around $300,000.

Shopping & Amenities

As one would expect, there is no shortage of shops in the inner city, from boutique designer stores to large department and chain stores. This is also the heart of Christchurch's cultural scene, so there's an enticing mix of museums, galleries, theatres and public spaces.

Eating & Drinking

Three words: spoilt for choice. Christchurch's nightlife is centred on Oxford Terrace, otherwise known as The Strip. Adjacent to the picturesque Avon River, The Strip is home to the city's best bars and restaurants and offers a European atmosphere, with alfresco dining and stunning river views. The area south of Lichfield Street is also developing into a trendy spot, with new bars and restaurants springing up all the time.

Education

The inner city is home to the Christchurch Polytechnic Institute of Technology, where students can study anything from jazz and circus performance to car mechanics and hospitality. There are a number of primary and secondary schools in the area, as well as an alternative high school called Unlimited (www.unlimited.school.nz), where each student has a tailored learning plan.

Free-ish Parking

The council-run parking buildings in the Inner City offer free parking for the first hour for those wanting to make a quick dash to the shops.

Transport

Much effort has gone into making the Inner City pedestrian friendly, and you can pretty much walk everywhere. If you do need public transport, head to the Bus Xchange, the main terminal for all the city's bus routes. Trams and a free shuttle bus circuit the Inner City, but these are aimed more at tourists than residents.

Safety & Annoyances

By day, the Inner City feels pretty safe, but at night it is a different story. Alcohol-fuelled crime is not uncommon and you do need to exercise caution. Boy-racers using the streets as a racetrack are the biggest annoyance, with their presence most felt on Friday and Saturday nights.

Lyttelton

Map p.508 F7
Area E p.136-137

Best Points
Lyttelton is full of character and has a distinct cosmopolitan feel.

Worst Points
It can get bitterly cold, and it's a long trip into town.

Fruit and Veg
On Saturday mornings, Lyttelton hosts a popular farmers' market that is great for stocking up on fresh produce.

When the European settlers arrived in Christchurch, they docked at Lyttelton Harbour and then trekked over the Bridle Path to establish Christchurch as we know it now. Separated from the city by the Port Hills, Lyttelton is still dominated by the port, which is the major deep-water port in the South Island. More recently, the town's great bars and offbeat vibe have made it a trendy place for young professionals and arty types.

Accommodation

Lyttelton is dotted with charming workers' cottages, many of which have been lovingly restored. Property prices on this side of the Port Hills tend to be slightly cheaper than on the city side, but most of the bargains have already been snapped up. A two-bedroom cottage will cost you around $300,000, while a larger family home is likely to set you back between $400,000 and $500,000. Rental accommodation is in high demand, so you can expect to pay around $300 a week for a three-bedroom place.

Shopping & Amenities

A smattering of shops along Lyttelton's main street will ensure you won't go hungry or run out of toilet paper, but if you want retail therapy, you'll need to make the trip through the road tunnel, to the city. Public amenities in Lyttelton are also in short supply, so be prepared to travel if you want an indoor swimming pool, golf range or cinema.

Eating & Drinking

It's at night that Lyttelton comes into its own. It has a great selection of bars and cafes. The Wunderbar (03 328 8818) is wonderfully offbeat – dolls heads adorn the walls – and attracts punters from all over. Expect to share the bar with foreign seamen from one of the many ships docked at the port. The bars are closely packed, so it's easy to stumble from one to the other. Just watch the steep steps.

Education

One of the reasons why Lyttelton is less popular with families is its lack of educational facilities. There are a couple of primary schools but secondary school age children have to make the trek over the hill into Christchurch.

Offbeat Lyttelton

Transport

You really need a car if you live in Lyttelton, or muscly legs so you can pedal your way over the hill (you're not allowed to cycle through the road tunnel). There is a bus, which runs regularly between Lyttlelton and the city on weekdays, but services are limited at the weekends and weeknights.

Safety & Annoyances

One of the downsides of living in Lyttelton is the coal dust from the port's coal facility, although steps have been taken in recent years to address the problem. With so many foreign sailors visiting the port after being at sea for prolonged periods, safety can at times be an issue.

Map p.508 F4
Area F p.136-137

Best Points
Sun, sea and surf on your doorstep.

Worst Points
The cutting easterly wind frequently takes the gloss off trips to the beach and leaves a fine coating of sand in your backyard.

New Brighton

Ferrymead

Despite millions of dollars being spent on a new pier and improvements to its beach, New Brighton remains in Sumner's (p.146) shadow. You can blame it on the cold easterly wind that cuts through the area, or the towering sand dunes that provide a buffer between the sea and the houses, but New Brighton still sits as a faded jewel in Christchurch's crown.

Accommodation

New Brighton offers an eclectic mix of housing. Property developers, crossing their fingers for a change in New Brighton's fortunes, have started erecting apartments, but the bulk of the accommodation is detached housing. There is a high percentage of rental accommodation. The harsh coastal conditions can take a toll on properties and some of the houses have seen better days. For people who want seaside living on a budget, it's still possible to buy property here for between $200,000 and $300,000.

5 November
On Guy Fawkes night, 5 November, the sky over New Brighton is lit up by Christchurch's biggest annual fireworks display.

Shops & Amenities

New Brighton's heyday as a shopping haven is long gone. Repeated efforts to attract retailers back to New Brighton Mall have met with little success and the area offers slim pickings for those wanting a retail fix. There is a supermarket though, so you can keep the kitchen shelves stocked. On the plus side, New Brighton has a superb ship-shaped public library, where you can sit and read books, surf the internet or simply gaze out to sea.

Eating & Drinking

If you're happy to settle for a cheap pub meal, New Brighton can satisfy your needs, but if you're looking for sophisticated dining, head elsewhere. Some of the suburb's bars have a reputation for being 'lively'.

Education

If finding good local schools for your children is a top priority, you should probably bypass New Brighton. The suburb is in one of Christchurch's lowest socio-economic areas and that is reflected in the quality of its schools. The nearest secondary school is in Aranui, regarded as one of the most deprived suburbs in Christchurch.

Transport

There is a regular bus service between New Brighton and the city centre. The Orbiter bus also provides a link between New Brighton and the main suburban shopping hubs around Christchurch.

Safety & Annoyances

Safety can be an issue in New Brighton, so don't take unnecessary risks. The easterly wind is annoying but the beauty of the coastline makes up for it.

Map p.514 B5
Area G p.136-137

Best Points
Close to everything – town, shops, the university, and wonderful open spaces.

Worst Points
The traffic at peak hours is horrendous and cars crawl along Riccarton Road at a snail's pace.

Riccarton

Just to the west of the city centre is the bustling suburb of Riccarton. Popular with students because of its close proximity to Canterbury University, it is one of the oldest suburbs in Christchurch. Home to one of the city's largest shopping centres, its main street is lined with hotels and motels. Riccarton is also popular with families as many of its streets lie within the zone for Christchurch Girls' High and Christchurch Boys' High Schools.

Accommodation

From cheap bedsits and student flats to modern townhouses and stately old homesteads, Riccarton pretty much has it all. The average house price in the suburb is around $340,000. There is a fair amount of infill housing, as many of the larger sections have been carved up and sold off to eager property developers. Pockets of state housing sit alongside an increasing number of retirement villages. The suburb is very popular with students and as such, has good rental potential.

Shopping & Amenities

At the centre of Riccarton lies Westfield Riccarton (03 983 4500, www.westfield.co.nz), a covered shopping mall with 150 shops and parking for 2,300 cars. Retail and commercial premises line both sides of Riccarton Road, one of the main thoroughfares into town. Historic Deans Bush, the site of the first settlement in Christchurch, lies at one end of the suburb and Hagley Park is at the other, meaning there is plenty of green space in which to enjoy your leisure time. Riccarton also has its own indoor swimming pool and multiplex cinema.

Eating & Drinking

Westfield Riccarton boasts a foodcourt and a number of cafes for quick snacks, but if you want more sophisticated dining there's a host of places to choose from on the surrounding streets. You can get everything from Japanese to Italian – and at prices to suit all budgets. There is no shortage of pubs either, but if you want to party late you're best to take the short walk into town.

Education

The big plus for Riccarton is that many of its streets lie within the catchment zone for the prestigious state schools, Christchurch Girls' High and Christchurch Boys' High. The suburb also has excellent state primaries, Ilam & St Teresa's, and a good intermediate school, Kirkwood, and lies within a few minutes' walk of the Canterbury University campus.

Transport

Riccarton Road is a main route into town and is crammed with cars and buses, seven days a week. You won't have to wait long to catch a bus, but you might have to sit in traffic for a while once you're on it.

Safety & Annoyances

Traffic congestion is probably the biggest annoyance for residents, although there are plans to address the problems, particularly on busy Riccarton Road. The area is safe during the day, but you need to be careful where you venture after dark.

Suburb Stats
Based on census information, Statistics New Zealand (www.stats.govt.nz) publishes demographic reports on all neighbourhoods – a useful background to your suburb search.

Map p.508 C4
Area H p.136-137

St Albans

St Albans was once one of the cheaper suburbs in Christchurch, but it has soared in value and popularity in recent years as people have discovered its benefits. The area borders the inner city, which means it lies within stumbling distance of the city's pubs and clubs. This has made the suburb a popular haunt with young people. Years ago there were plans to dissect the area with a motorway, but now they have been indefinitely shelved, families are once again settling in St Albans.

Best Points
It's close to the inner city, affordable, and full of character homes and tree-lined streets.

Worst Points
Educational options are limited.

Accommodation

It is still possible to find the odd bargain property, but most of the old villas have already been renovated, their sections subdivided, and new townhouses built beside them. Property developers who have seen the suburb's potential have started to erect terrace housing and apartments. All this new development has helped push the average price of a property in the area to around $300,000, which still makes St Albans one of the more affordable suburbs in the city.

Shopping & Amenities

St Albans is well served by local shops selling fresh fruit and vegetables, meat and all the basics. It's also only five minutes from town, and five minutes to the large Palms Shopping Centre in Shirley, which has hundreds of outlets under one roof. Like most suburbs in Christchurch, St Albans has plenty of green, open spaces.

Eating & Drinking

St Albans isn't renowned for its eating establishments, but with The Strip in Christchurch's central city just five minutes to the south, and the cafes and wine bars of Merivale five minutes to the north, there are plenty of options for eating and drinking. If you're just after a good coffee and some cake, try Meshino Espresso (03 355 2449) in Rutland Street.

Education

The lack of school facilities is probably the area's biggest downfall. The suburb is home to St Albans Primary School, which does have a reasonably good reputation, but that's about the extent of its educational facilities. There are a number of pre-schools in the area, however.

Transport

Buses connect St Albans to other parts of Christchurch, but one of the reasons why so many people enjoy living here is that they can walk to most places. And getting a taxi home from town, at any time of day or night, won't break the bank.

Hagley Park

Safety & Annoyances

While it's safe to wander the streets of St Albans during the day, care should be taken at night, when alcohol-fuelled crime can be a problem. The biggest nuisance is the number of impatient motorists, who use the suburb's side streets as a short cut to Christchurch's outlying northern suburbs.

Beachside apartments in Sumner

Sumner

Map p.508 F6
Area J p.136-137

Best Points
The beach is beautiful, the air is crisp and clean, and the village has a laid-back feel.

Worst Points
Television and radio reception is patchy, but if you can afford to live in Sumner you can probably afford satellite TV.

In this picturesque suburb it's all about leisurely lunches, strolling along the promenade and long summer evenings on the beach. During the summer months, the beach is packed (by New Zealand standards) but there's still room to pitch your umbrella and spread out your towel. When the sun gets too much, there are plenty of cafes, bars and restaurants. The area is popular with young professionals and retired people, but a lack of school facilities means it is not the ideal base for families.

Accommodation

The growth in demand for coastal properties has seen apartments springing up all over Sumner. While some are hardly big enough to swing a cat, they're a tempting proposition for property owners and investors because they're only metres from the Pacific. People build up to make the most of the views, so three-storey homes are not unusual. Properties tend to get snapped up quickly so be prepared to pay generously for your laid-back lifestyle. While you might pick up a tiny apartment without sea views for around $400,000, you will need at least $700,000 for any substantial property near the beach.

Shopping & Amenities

There's not much you can't get in the quaint shops that make up Sumner village. There's a grocery store, wine shop, bookshop, bakery, chemist, as well as a smattering of gift shops and galleries. There's also a charming old-fashioned cinema (Hollywood Cinema, 03 326 6102), where you can catch all the latest releases. For your big weekly grocery shop, however, you will need to head to nearby Ferrymead.

Eating & Drinking

One of the reasons why Sumner is so popular with the young professionals and discerning oldies is that it has a wonderful array of beach-front restaurants and bars, where you can get anything from Indian food to good Kiwi tucker. The Ruptured Duck Pizzeria & Bar (03 326 5488), and JDV Sumner (03 964 3860) are particularly popular with locals. The restaurants are busy over the summer months so it does pay to book ahead. There are a couple of fine takeaways – try Indian Sumner (03 326 4777) in Wakefield Avenue or the Sticky Rice Thai Restaurant & Café in Nayland Street.

Cliffhangers
If you're buying a property which backs onto a cliff, make sure you get a geological survey done to ensure the land is stable – rock falls have been known to occur.

Education

With only one primary (Sumner School) in the suburb, education facilities are in short supply, which explains the area's limited appeal to families. The nearest state high school, Linwood High, is a good 10 to 15 minute drive, depending on rush-hour traffic.

Transport

The biggest drawback to living in Sumner is that there's really only one road in and one road out. Getting to and from work can be a slow process. The situation doesn't improve much at the weekends either, when beach-lovers flock to the area. There are bus services between Sumner and the city but you really need a car.

Safety & Annoyances

The area tends to be populated by the well-heeled, so crime isn't a big problem. Boy racers make the occasional visit, but finding a parking space at the weekend is a bigger problem.

South Island Map H12

Dunedin

Best Points
Relatively cheap housing and good city living.

Worst Points
Can be cold; crammed with students.

Dunedin is a university town. The city is built around its tertiary institutions like no other in New Zealand. It has a deserved reputation as the country's premier seat of learning and is home to a student population of 25,000, who give the city a special character. Dunedin (p.272) is the second largest city in the South Island and is an important retail and business hub. Institutions such as the Dunedin Public Art Gallery (p.273) and the Otago Museum (p.272) bring a touch of cultural sophistication. Schools, sporting facilities, supermarkets and shopping centres are located within easy travelling distance of the city centre. Property prices tend to get cheaper the further south you move, which in part explains why the average house price in Dunedin is a paltry $240,000.

There is plenty of choice in terms of accommodation, although rental properties are in short supply during the university year when students are in residence. Winters can be very cold in Dunedin, so you'll need a good supply of thermals. Apart from the antics of a few boisterous students, Dunedin is regarded as a safe, family friendly city. Otago Boys' and Otago Girls' High are regarded as the best state secondary schools in the area.

South Island Map M3

Nelson

Best Points
More sunshine than anywhere else.

Worst Points
Too laid-back for some.

Situated at the top of the South Island, Nelson (p.253) is renowned for its sunshine, strong artistic community and family friendly beaches. In the summer, its population swells dramatically as what feels like half of Christchurch heads north to enjoy its warmer climes and pristine beaches.

There has been a lot of residential building activity in recent years, and the average cost of a house is now in excess of $300,000. New subdivisions at Ngawhatu, Saxton and Nayland are proving very popular with families, while Richmond is said to be the fastest growing suburb in New Zealand.

The city has excellent educational facilities, including The Nelson Marlborough Institute of Technology (www.nmit.ac.nz), a well-regarded polytechnic. Nelson is very popular with retirees and those seeking warmer climes and a quieter pace of life. It has all the shops, restaurants, bars and amenities you would expect from a city, but a more laid-back feel than Christchurch and Wellington. Public transport is limited to buses, so if you really want to make the most of the area, you will need a car.

South Island Map E10

Queenstown

Best Points
Great wine, good skiing and beautiful surroundings.

Worst Points
Overrun with 'adventure' tourists and thrill-seekers.

Nestled beneath The Remarkables mountain range, and alongside stunning Lake Wakatipu, the Central Otago resort town of Queenstown (p.280) is one of the most picturesque spots in New Zealand. It is a favourite retreat for the rich and famous and a tourist hotspot. In the winter, the snow-covered peaks provide ideal conditions for skiing, while in the summer, Lake Wakatipu is a playground for watersports enthusiasts. Tourism is the backbone of Queenstown, and its shops, bars and restaurants are all geared towards bringing in as much money as possible. Venues are open around-the-clock, but you'll have to be prepared to pay tourist prices for your pint.

The cost of living is extremely high and affordable accommodation is in short supply. The average house price in Queenstown is just over $550,000 and waterfront properties command far more. The town has its own primary (Queenstown Primary, www.queenstown.school.nz) and secondary schools (Lake Wakatipu High, www.wakatipu.school.nz) and has excellent recreational facilities.

Because the town is so compact, you can walk to most places. But if you're a skier you'll need a 4WD as the roads in the winter are very icy.

Most of the jobs are within the hospitality sector, so the town has a high proportion of young people, many of them foreigners on working holidays.

Setting up Home

Finally you can lay the property pages aside, offload the real estate guides and, safe in the knowledge that you've tackled the major administrative tasks, start settling down into New Zealand life. It's time to set up home and start making the most of the services available to help ease you into functional and satisfying day-to-day life in your new country.

Moving Services

There are relocation specialists that can help oversee the process of your move and who will advise you on legal and logistical issues. There are also international shipping companies that can assist you in getting your prized possessions to New Zealand. Although having a company transport your goods from overseas is costly, the benefits of having the experts deal with the bureaucratic processes often justifies it. And you're also likely to save money by having your furniture shipped over, as your style and budget choices locally may be more limited.

Relocation Companies			
Affordable Worldwide Movers Ltd	Auckland	09 820 6060	www.worldmoving.co.nz
Crown Relocations Ltd	Auckland	0800 227 696	www.crownrelo.co.nz
Kiwi Relocation & Settlement Consultants	Auckland	09 533 4312	na
Relocations International	Wellington	04 479 3765	www.relocate.co.nz
Transworld Logistics	Auckland	09 828 0213	www.transworld.co.nz
Woburn International	Wellington	04 569 4861	www.woburn.co.nz

With New Zealand's strict agricultural regulations, expect to deal with Customs officials extensively and to provide detailed lists of everything that you're importing. Ministry of Agriculture and Fisheries (MAF) officials will target the following for inspection: any used vehicles (looking for dirt); sporting and gardening equipment; wooden furniture and ornaments, and food that could potentially compromise the farming and forestry industries, so vital to New Zealand's economic survival. See www.biosecurity.govt.nz for further information.

Moving your personal effects within a main centre of the country is an easy, relatively inexpensive process. You may choose a premium service or simply make use of the friendly services of a man with a van – you can expect to pay around $40 an hour or $300 for a full day – and your goods will be insured for the move. Try www.manwithavan.co.nz. There's seldom a waiting time for these services, and you'll probably enjoy the Kiwi can-do approach.

Removal Companies			
Backload Moving Company	Auckland	0800 321 000	www.backloadmoving.co.nz
Horizon Moving & Storage	Auckland	0800 800 247	www.horizonmoving.co.nz
Stokes DW Shipping & Travel	Christchurch	03 218 7364	www.dwstokes.co.nz
United Relocations	Auckland	09 622 9042	www.unitedcarriers.co.nz
Walker Logistics	Auckland	09 275 7803	www.walkerlogistics.co.nz

Alternatively you can do it yourself by hiring a truck or trailer – available at most service (gas) stations for a charge of around $10 an hour. If you're moving between the islands, you can take your vehicle packed with goods on the ferry service.

Furnishing Your Home

Rental properties are typically unfurnished, although there will be a cooker. Very few rentals are fully- or even semi-furnished. Semi-furnished indicates the inclusion of what's called 'whiteware' – a washing machine, fridge and possibly a dishwasher.

You'll find furniture shopping options for any budget. The Warehouse and Big Save Furniture are at the lower end of the scale in terms of price, Freedom Furniture is an example of a mid-scale supplier and there are boutique options at the higher end that can also tailor-make items to your specifications. (See Home Furnishings & Accessories, p.389, and Second-Hand Items, p.400, in Shopping). Stores provide a variety of payment plans including lay-by and hire purchase options where you can pay the goods off in installments.

Buying Second-Hand

The second-hand market is a fantastic resource for furnishing your home. In general, quality is good. Many local furniture stores have second-hand goods, or you can visit www.trademe.co.nz – New Zealand's answer to eBay.

Garage sales from residential homes are commonplace at the weekend, as are organised car boot sales that are held in parks or large carparks. Check your local newspapers for details.

Tailors

If the range of ready-made curtains and soft furnishings don't take your fancy, there are plenty of tailors who can run up these items for you. You'll find them willing to tackle (almost) any project you have in mind. The same can be said for having furniture re-upholstered. You'll find tailors in standalone stores, associated with dry cleaners or within furniture stores themselves, as well as, of course, in the *Yellow Pages*.

Household Insurance

Despite its safe reputation, New Zealand is not crime-free. Petty theft and home burglaries do occur, so insuring your belongings is a must. Fortunately, there's a healthy insurance market and brokers will help you find the most appropriate cover for your needs.

Insurance companies are helpful to deal with and will provide a quote free of charge. The type of cover you choose will depend upon the value of assets you wish to ensure. Often there's an overall sum insured, while items of exceptional value must be detailed separately. Most policies have a maximum payout for specific items such as jewellery. Obviously, insurance companies will want to ensure that you have adequate security precautions, so depending on where you live you may have to install an alarm system if you don't already have one.

Household Insurance		
AA Insurance	0800 500 221	www.aainsurance.co.nz
AMI Insurance	0800 100 200	www.ami.co.nz
NZI Insurance	0800 694 276	www.nzi.co.nz
Sovereign Ltd	0800 500 108	www.sovereign.co.nz
State Insurance	0800 802 424	www.state.co.nz

Home owners are advised to take house and contents insurance, while renters can insure the contents of their home alone. Basic home insurance will cover you against any sudden or unforeseen events such as fire and flooding. Contents insurance protects your belongings when they are at home or temporarily moved elsewhere in the country. The policies have a mix of replacement and indemnity (market value) coverage.

You're likely to save money if you use one company for your various insurance needs – household and vehicle insurance, for instance.

Laundry Services

Most Kiwi homes have their own clothes washing facilities and people expect to do their own washing, so self-service laundrettes are not commonplace. However, dry-cleaning services are readily available and are often used for speciality cleaning needs or by those with a hectic lifestyle. Dry cleaning a suit may cost around $20, a shirt $5 and a winter coat $15.

Domestic Help

Typically New Zealanders do not employ live-in domestic help, although many do rely on the weekly services of a cleaner or gardener. You'll find a number of agencies that will help you source the household help you require in the *Yellow Pages*. Your local stores and libraries often display adverts on their noticeboards, offering anything from spring-cleaning to walking your pets. The rates you pay will vary from centre to centre; in the bigger cities, expect to pay around $50 for someone to clean the house once a week.

Babysitting & Childcare

Employing babysitters to look after your children is a way of life in New Zealand. A national body called Plunket (www.plunket.org.nz) organises parent groups, among other things, which are a good forum to find out about safe and reliable babysitting services in your area. It's also not uncommon for parents to pay a trusted teen from a neighbouring family to mind the children for an evening. Some entrepreneurial youths organise themselves into babysitting clubs and advertise in local stores.

You can also employ the services of experienced and qualified day nannies; you'll find contact details in the *Yellow Pages* or by approaching your child's nursery staff.

Babysitting & Childcare			
Complete Nanny Services	Auckland	04 939 5522	www.completenannyservices.net.nz
Home Grown Kids	Tauranga	0508 445 437	www.homegrownkids.co.nz
Kids Campus Childcare	Auckland	09 630 1454	na
Nannies of Canterbury	Christchurch	03 339 0833	www.canterburynannies.co.nz
Welllington Playcentre Association	Auckland	04 237 7827	www.wgtnplaycentre.school.nz

Qualified nannies will hold a minimum qualification of the New Zealand Certificate in Nanny Education. Some agencies, for example www.nanny.org.nz, differ in the qualifications they require of their nannies, and it's up to you to ensure that you're comfortable with the childcare qualification a caregiver holds. To find out if you're eligible for government childcare funding, check with the nanny agencies.

Shopping malls are not likely to have creche facilities, although these services are often found at gyms and larger hotels. Many local shops, restaurants and cafes have a children's play area, but remember that parents are responsible for supervising their children in these places.

Domestic Services

New Zealand is rich in domestic service providers; you'll never find yourself short of information on local plumbers, carpenters or electricians. You can gain a wealth of information through talking to neighbours and shop owners, who will invariably be happy to recommend their favourite 'chippy' or 'sparky'.

The *Yellow Pages* also provides a plethora of information – search under 'plumbers', 'builders', 'building contractors' and 'electricians'. When choosing someone, make sure you opt for those with a master qualification or full registration with a professional body. This will protect you against shoddy workmanship and give you the security of recourse should problems occur down the line.

Domestic Help Agencies			
Absolute Domestics	Auckland	0800 663 987	www.absolutedomestics.co.nz
Bill McDonald Cleaning	Hamilton	07 847 8275	www.bmcleaning.co.nz
Florence Nightingale Agency	Christchurch	03 348 7600	florence2care.co.nz
Mr Green Home Services	Various	0800 663 783	www.mrgreen.co.nz

Most tradespeople charge by the hour – expect to pay around $70 an hour, plus a call-out fee and the cost of any parts. It's worth shopping around and asking for a quote before you get the job done. You can find most services 24-7 but expect to pay a premium after-hours and at weekends.

Pest control issues in New Zealand are reasonably limited. Main offenders are rodents, wasps, ants, fleas and crawling insects. Birds or small animals don't often become a real problem. While pest control is the resident's responsibility, your local council will provide best practice advice. Extermination and pest control management companies are easily found in the *Yellow Pages* and usually affordable.

Your landlord is responsible for repair and maintenance of your rental property including structural maintenance, plumbing, electrics and gardens. If you have a dispute with your landlord over this, or any other issue for that matter, visit www.tenancy.govt.nz.

DVD & Video Rental

DVD & Video Rental

Blockbuster	09 625 5511	www.blockbuster.co.nz
Civic Video	09 447 1900	www.civicvideo.co.nz
Fatso	0800 232 876	www.fatso.co.nz
Movieshack	na	www.movieshack.co.nz
Video Ezy	na	www.videoezy.co.nz

As DVD or video players can be bought at competitive prices at discount warehouses or electronics stores, most Kiwi households have one. It follows that DVD rental shops are numerous and generally found on most main streets and in shopping malls. Online and mail order options are also popular. New Zealanders consider themselves quite technology savvy, so video rentals are less commonplace.

To become a member at a rental store, you'll need to show personal identification such as a driving licence or passport and usually a utility bill in your name. This will enable you to hire movies and games. To hire a new release overnight costs around $8. Older releases cost less and are often hired out for three-day periods. Larger national rental companies include Video Ezy and Blockbuster. Speciality boutique film stores, such as Aro Video in Wellington (04 801 7101, www.arovideo.co.nz can), can be found tucked away in some neighbourhoods, and many have real gems amid their shelves. Don't forget to experience some iconic New Zealand films including *The Piano*, *The Whale Rider* and *Came a Hot Friday*.

Pets

Kiwis love their pets. They are an important factor of life in Aotearoa and are considered part of the family. Cats and dogs are by far the most common, but rabbits, guinea pigs, fish and birds, and the occasional sheep (never mind the jokes) are also popular.

Big-hearted New Zealanders prefer to look to pet rescue agencies, such as The Royal New Zealand Society for the Prevention of Cruelty to Animals or Auckland Cat Rescue (www.aucklandcatrescue.org), to acquire their pets. But there are also pet stores aplenty, offering a range of furry friends for you to purchase, as well as pet care and accessory items. These shops are governed by legislation and are usually of a high standard – if not, they don't last long as Kiwis cannot abide cruelty to animals.

Landlords and apartment building boards have the final say on whether pets are allowed in their rental properties. New Zealanders assume that their cats and dogs need time outdoors and require space to run around in, so they tend not to keep them in small apartments.

There are plenty of annual pet shows and exhibitions that showcase the fine form that most New Zealanders keep their pets in, and top prizes are often hotly contested.

Cats and Dogs

Companionship, protection and help on the farm are all reasons that Kiwis keep four-legged friends. Dogs need to be registered with the local authority by the time they're three months old (if not sooner) and annually thereafter. Failure to do so might result in a fine. To register your dog, visit your local council authority where you'll need to fill in a form and pay a fee of less than $100. Apart from those that work on a farm, dogs also have to be micro-chipped.

Dogs must be kept under control at all times and when on a road they must be on a leash. They can be exercised off the leash as long as they're kept under effective control. Council-owned reserves are abundant and provide suitable areas for enjoying some fun with rover. Owners are in charge of the immediate removal and disposal of dog waste and you'll find bins in most parks.

Unlike dogs, cats don't have to be registered but owners often put tags on their pets with contact information in case they stray.

Pets Boarding/Sitting

Bunny Lodge	Christchurch	03 347 8835	Animal Holiday Resort
Guardians (NZ) Ltd	Auckland	09 580 2981	Pet minding/sitting
Hamilton Vet Service Cattery	Hamilton	07 849 2963	Boarding kennel/cattery
Mr White's Place	Wellington	06 364 3522	Cattery

Fish & Birds

If you're into low maintenance pets it's hard to look past goldfish or their more tropical cousins. The only restrictions on the tropical fish you can keep will be those imposed by the size of your wallet.

Most New Zealanders prefer birds outside in their natural environment but your local pet shop will have some budgies and parakeets in stock. It will also be able to supply you with all the necessary accessories.

Feline Fare

Once you've got your new moggy, you'll need to feed him. *See p.399 for details on pet shops.*

Pet Shops

The Royal Society for the Protection of Animals or RSPCA (www.rspca.org.nz) is the leading pet-rescue organisation and a popular choice for homing an animal.

That said, pet stores are widespread, offering a range of animals and the necessary items. Alternatively, you can browse your local newspapers and community notice boards to find a pet, or visit sites such as www.petsonthenet.co.nz which lists animals for adoption, sale and breeding, as well as events and retails outlets for petcare equipment.

Vets & Kennels

Lots of pets means many vets. You'll have no difficulty finding a qualified, approachable individual to see to your pet's health needs. There are vets for all breeds and sizes and of all specialities. You'll find they're quite used to being brought the odd stranded bird or confused hedgehog to nurse back to health too.

Expect to pay around $70 for a basic consultation, with costs for further treatment and medication on top. Telephone directory listings will provide contact details.

You'll usually find kennels and catteries on the outskirts of a town or city. The average cost of a night's stay for a dog is $20; cats cost less. If you book your pet in for a long stay, you usually get a discounted rate. Local vets often house pets temporarily, but will be more costly. Vets will also be able to advise you on boarding options.

You'll find noticeboards at your local vet or store advertising the services of a pet sitter who will look after your animals in your own home. They'll either stay over, or visit your home each day. Of course you may be lucky and find an obliging neighbour who's willing to care for your pet while you're away.

Pet Grooming

Auckland	
Bark 'N' Bubbles	09 473 0352
Pampered Pets Grooming Parlour	09 521 1717
Pet Grooming Parlour	09 265 2570
Wellington	
Dapper Dogs	04 472 7921
DoG Zone Grooming Salon	04 939 8909
Posh Pets	04 236 7407
Christchurch	
Grooming Room	03 355 5838
Paws in Puddles	03 385 0500

Grooming & Training

Grooming, training and walking services are widely available, while special services such as cat and dog spas are increasing in popularity.

Dogs are expected to be trained, and professional help with training – in the form of puppy pre-school or obedience classes – can greatly improve your dog's behaviour. Another benefit of joining a class is that dogs learn to socialise with other dogs – not to mention the opportunity it provides for owners to meet. Visit www.doglinks.co.nz for a list of dog trainers in New Zealand. The site also has play ideas for you and your dog.

Importing and Exporting Pets

Bringing a pet into the country can be a costly and time-consuming process. If you're coming from a country where rabies still occurs, you need to begin the process at least six months prior to your arrival; your pet will be quarantined for four weeks once it enters New Zealand. Animals from low-risk countries, such as Australia and the UK, will not need to be quarantined. In all cases, however, animals will require health certificates; see www.biosecurity.govt.nz for information on travel tickets and the paperwork that needs to be done. As bringing your pet to New Zealand can be a complicated process, it's a good idea to use a pet exporter in your own country. Exotic pets will be considered on a case-by-case basis.

Animals being exported from New Zealand need an Animal Welfare Export Certificate (AWEC) to ensure that they can travel and will arrive in good health. Pet owners are advised to contact a registered pet exporter to deal with the protocols and procedures. Two of these are Pets By Air (09 520 6297, www.petsbyair.com) and Katz 'n K9z (03 325 2243, www.katznk9z.co.nz). If you're not using a pet exporter, contact a verification agency to arrange for an accredited veterinarian to sign the export certificate and AWEC. You can find a verification agency via the New Zealand Food and Safety Authority (04 894 2500).

Veterinary Clinics

After Hours Veterinary Clinic	Christchurch	03 366 1052
AnimalZ	Various	0800 473 822
Howick Veterinary Clinic	Auckland	09 537 1002
Island Bay Veterinary Clinic	Wellington	04 383 6012
Karori Veterinary Clinic	Wellington	04 476 3555
Mangere Veterinary Clinic	Auckland	09 636 6732

AnimalZ Veterinary Care

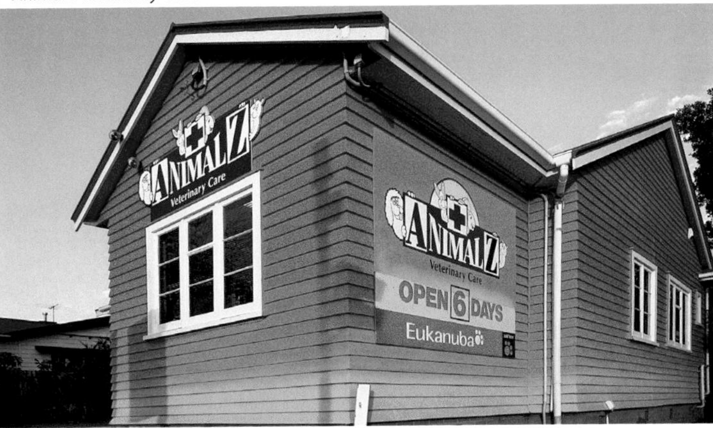

Electricity & Water

Mention electricity supply in New Zealand and you're bound to generate a debate. The country is grappling with ways to meet an increasing demand for power, and while the supply is generally reliable, there have been one or two embarrassing glitches, including one that saw Auckland virtually shut down for several days because of power cuts. The electricity sector was deregulated in the 1990s, and there are now several electricity retailers and wholesalers operating in the country. In the main cities, you will have a choice of electricity retail companies, but in many rural parts of the country there will only be one supplier operating.

The Electricity Commission oversees the industry and handles complaints from consumers about electricity and gas companies. Most of the power companies offer tips on energy conservation, as does the government-funded Energy Efficiency Conservation Authority (www.eeca.govt.nz). The water supply is generally excellent in urban areas, but in some rural areas you may have to rely on private water tanks or bores. The Ministry of Health, which monitors drinking water quality in New Zealand, judges that 85% of the population has a certifiably safe water supply.

If you're renting a property, the cost of electricity is not normally included in the rent, so you will need to budget extra for this.

Switched On
The Consumers' Institute of New Zealand has a handy website, www.consumer.org.nz/powerswitch, which allows you to compare electricity company prices.

Electricity

In most cases, the procedure for getting electricity connected is simple and just requires a phone call to your chosen electricity company, or filling out a form online. If you are a new customer, the power company will probably ask you to pay a bond. You will also need to produce proof of residence. Power companies tend to bill monthly and offer customers a range of billing/payment options. For example, some companies will just bill you based on a guesstimate following an initial meter reading. Others offer you the opportunity to pay a flat monthly fee, which allows you to avoid the peaks and troughs over the summer and winter months. Shop around for the deal that will best suit you. Details of electricity retailers and their offices can be found in the Telecom *Yellow Pages*, under Electricity Supply – Retail.

Plugs & Electrics

The New Zealand electricity supply is 240 volts, 50 hertz. If you come from the UK, continental Europe, South Africa, South Korea, India, UAE, China, Russia or Malaysia, your electrical equipment should work in New Zealand. You will, however, have to fit new plugs or buy an adaptor because New Zealand plugs are shaped differently. It would also be wise to bring some four-socket extension boards with you. You can then get a New Zealand plug fitted to each board and use the existing plugs in the extension board. If you come from the US, Canada, Japan, Taiwan and most Latin American countries your electrical equipment will need to be modified. It might be more straightforward – and cheaper – to buy afresh in New Zealand.

Hydroelectricity at Lake Pukaki

Water

Local councils oversee water supplies. In 90% of cases, the property you buy will already be connected to the mains water supply. If it isn't, you will need to contact the local council and apply for a new connection. Most councils charge around $500, and getting connected can take up to 10 working days.

The water you do get is generally of a very high standard and safe to drink from the tap. Only 5% of New Zealand's population uses water supplies, with which the Ministry of Health has concerns. The taste and purity of the water in New Zealand does vary. In Christchurch, the supply is sourced from spring-fed underground aquifers, and is therefore pure and untainted. But in other parts of the country, the water is chemically treated. Controversially, fluoride is added to the water in some main centres – however this is not the case in Whangarei, Tauranga, Wanganui, Napier, Nelson, Blenheim, Christchurch, Timaru and Oamaru. In the few areas where the water supply is of questionable quality, it is still fine for cooking or boiling the kettle. While water dispenses are a common sight in offices in New Zealand, people rarely have them in their homes.

Each council uses a different system for charging. In Christchurch, for example, people pay a flat fee for their water, as part of their rates bill. In Auckland, however, people are charged according to how much water they use. The water charge is kept separate from the rates bill and averages around $800 a year, although proposed hefty increases could soon see that figure rise to closer to $1,000. Check with your local council to find out how they charge for water.

Gas

There is no mains gas supply in the South Island, but it is available in some parts of the North Island. The costs for mains gas varies and depends on the plan you choose. An average bill for the year ranges between $700 and $900. The Consumers' Institute website (www.consumer.org.nz) has a gas price calculator, which will help you get an idea of costs. Bottled gas is also available for those who prefer cooking on gas stoves or who like the warmth and convenience of gas heaters.

Gas Suppliers	
Auckland Gas Company	0800 438 427
Bay of Plenty Electricity	0800 500 710
Contact Energy	0800 809 000
Energy Direct NZ	0800 567 777
Genesis Energy	0800 300 400
Mercury Energy	0800 101 810

Trash & Treasure

Two landfill sites accept unwanted items in Wellington. They can be great places to not only dispose of your own things without paying tip fees, but find replacement parts such as microwave turntables and window catches.

Sewerage

In urban areas most homes will be connected to sewerage mains, but in some more remote parts of New Zealand you may have to use septic tanks. These are normally buried on a property and take wastewater from the kitchen and bathroom. Tanks need to be pumped out every three to five years. As for water, councils have a variety of means of charging for sewerage disposal. Most will simply include the cost in your general rates bill, but some councils charge separately for wastewater. In Auckland, for example, wastewater is charged based on 75% of your metered water use. In general, Aucklanders receive a bill four times a year.

Rubbish Disposal and Recycling

Local authorities are responsible for rubbish disposal and recycling. They are guided, however, by a long-term government strategy, which aims to help reduce and better manage waste in New Zealand. The strategy contains 30 targets for improved waste management, waste minimisation and resource efficiency.

In the main centres, councils run kerbside recycling schemes to encourage homeowners to recycle plastics, glass, cardboard and other materials that can be re-used. In most cities you will also find resource recovery centres, at which you can drop off unwanted items for recycling. There are several regional landfills around the country, which hold waste that cannot be recycled. Check with your local council for more details on recycling schemes in your area.

Telephone

Telecom is the main provider of telephone landline services in New Zealand. It had a virtual monopoly on the market until December 2006 when the government cleared the way for other service providers to have access. Up until then it was only possible to get a landline through rival telecommunications company Telstra-Clear, in parts of Christchurch, Wellington and the Kapiti Coast.

The phone service in New Zealand is efficient and Telecom is one of the country's top performing corporates. Other players are likely to enter the market now the way has been cleared for them, but Telecom's stranglehold on the industry will probably last for some time. Each year, Telecom produces *White Pages* and *Yellow Pages* directories for each district. These list residential and business phone numbers respectively. Directories are delivered to each household and business but are also available online (www.whitepages.co.nz and www.yellowpages.co.nz).

Telephone Companies

Telecom	0800 000 000	www.telecom.co.nz
TelstraClear	0508 888 800	www.telstraclear.co.nz
Vodafone	0800 800 021	www.vodafone.co.nz

Once you're settled in New Zealand and are ready to get a phone connection, you can simply call Telecom on 123, or fill out an online form at www.telecom.co.nz. If you join over the phone, you will have to allow between 20 and 30 minutes to complete the application process. You will need the address for connection and some personal identification. It will also speed up the process if you know the previous phone number and or/Telecom account holder of the same address. Provided there is already a live Telecom phone line connecting your home to the network, Telecom should have your phone working within 24 hours. Expect to pay a minimum of $48.99 for the reconnection; more if they have to physically install a phone line.

Once connected, you'll be charged a monthly line rental of around $40. Calls made locally from your home phone should be free. You will be charged for national and international calls, however. Charges vary but toll calls are normally cheaper, as are calls at weekends and between 19:00 and 07:00. Often Telecom runs special offers, where you can call certain countries for a set amount (normally around $5 or $8) and talk for as long as you like. These are normally well advertised on television and radio.

Extra services available from Telecom include call minder, which will answer and take calls for you when you can't, call waiting, which signals when there is a second incoming call and allows you to switch between calls, caller display, which allows you to see the number of the person calling before you answer, and call diversion, which automatically redirects incoming calls to another nominated number. For other services offered by Telecom, see its website at www.telecom.co.nz.

Mobile Phones

It's not uncommon to see New Zealanders with two or more mobile phones. This is usually because they're taking advantage of the specials offered by the two competing mobile network operators, Telecom and Vodafone. Both companies offer a range of pay monthly and pay-as-you-go options.

Mobile Service Providers

Telecom	0800 651 000	www.telecom.co.nz
Vodafone	0800 800 021	www.vodafone.co.nz

It's hard to separate the two companies in terms of the quality of service they offer; in some parts of the country the Vodafone network signal is stronger than that of Telecom's, but in other parts the roles are reversed.

Signing up to either network is relatively simple – you will have to fill out a couple of forms and produce proof of ID, but that's about all. Telecom runs a special call centre for new customers from overseas wanting to organise mobile phones. Call +64 3 374 0253 between 07:00 and 21:00 any day of the week. Vodafone also has a helpline (+64 9 355 2007 from overseas, 0800 800 021 from within New Zealand).

Public phone boxes

Nuisance Calls

If you receive harassing or nuisance calls on your home phone on an on-going basis, you should report them to Telecom. If the call is of a threatening or abusive nature, phone the police. The investigation centre (0800 809 806) will follow up. You will need to provide the date, time and nature of the call. It is likely the phone company representative will advise you to keep a log of nuisance calls over a period of time. If they consider the calls a breach of the Telecommunications Act, they will investigate further. You should be aware however, that even if it's found that a breach has occurred, you will not be given the number of the offending caller. The phone company will deal with the situation on your behalf.

Talk Isn't Cheap

Despite competition between Vodafone and Telecom, the cost of mobile phone calls in New Zealand is among the highest in the developed world, according to the latest figures from NZ's Commerce Commission (www.comcom.govt.nz).

Public Phones & Calling Cards

Public phone boxes are a little harder to find these days (a few years ago they were painted bright red), although there are still plenty around. Most take coins, but gobble them up quickly, so it's probably better to buy a Telecom calling card. You should be able to pick up Telecom cards at most bookshops and convenience stores. You can buy cards of various values, ranging from $5 to $50.

Hotel Phones

If you want to make calls from your hotel, check first to see how much they cost. Even though local calls are normally free, some hotels will charge you for these. It may also charge you a premium for national and international toll calls, so it might pay to use the nearest public phone box.

Cheap Overseas Calls

Cheap Overseas Calls		
Go Call	0800 646 444	www.gocall.co.nz
Simply Calling	0800 422 554	www.simplycalling.co.nz

Calling cards can be a good option if you want to save money on toll calls. They're mainly imported from Asia or Australia, they're easy to find at retail stores and even corner dairies, and their rates tend to be cheaper than those offered by the main telecommunications companies. To make a call you simply scratch the back of the calling card to reveal a card number. You then ring an access number that connects you through to a platform. This gives you a series of prompts asking you to enter your card number and the place you wish to call. Make sure you get a rate sheet because some have hidden charges.

Internet

Other options **Websites** p.56

Internet Service Providers	
Actrix	www.actrix.co.nz
Ihug	www.ihug.co.nz
Maxnet	www.maxnet.co.nz
Quicksilver	www.quicksilver.co.nz
Slingshot	www.slingshot.co.nz
Woosh	www.woosh.com
Xtra	www.xtra.co.nz

New Zealanders are pretty tech-savvy and most homes have computers connected to the web. Some internet service providers (ISPs) will send you out a starter kit, containing software and/or written instructions on how to get set up, while others will take you through the process over the phone. Some ISPs also offer support in your own home, but this usually costs extra.

Net Gains
You can compare the prices of various ISPs by using a helpful tool on the Consumers' Institute webiste, www.consumer.org.nz.

Because your computer connects to the internet through the phone network, ISPs have to provide enough lines for customers to get through. If they don't, you'll get an engaged signal, an error message, or no connection. Check that the ISP you select can provide a reliable connection. Ask them whether they monitor use and will add more lines before things start to get too busy. Consult your friends and workmates about which ISP they use and which they recommend.

In New Zealand, you pay a regular fee for access to an ISP, usually based on the time you use, but sometimes on the quantity of material you access or download. In addition to this, some ISPs charge a one-off connection fee. There are three types of time-based charging plans:

Prepaid hours: you pay for a set number of hours over a given period (usually one month), with a charge per extra hour used.

Hourly or **per-minute** rate.

Unlimited: a flat rate or fixed charge, usually per month.

Flat rates are popular, and many good deals are available. Each provider has a different fee structure and service options. Some ISPs also offer 'email only' plans. Some of these are true email only plans, but others offer a limited amount of web access, as well. Check with the ISP concerned.

Broadband

If you want a fast internet connection, you should sign up for broadband. There are four main types of broadband connection available, but ADSL is the most commonly used. ADSL is available to around 95% of New Zealand homes and allows you to talk on the phone at the same time as surfing the net. Interestingly, despite its high availability, use of broadband in New Zealand is low, with most people having dial-up connections. Prices for broadband start from $30 a month.

Surfing in Auckland

Bill Payment

Phone and internet bills are normally paid on a monthly basis. You can either pay by cheque or via direct debit from your bank account. If you bank online, you can also pay your bills over the internet. Companies such as Telecom offer a variety of phone and internet packages for the home and office, so shop around and choose a plan that meets your needs. In general, it's worth remembering that if you forget to pay your bill and are disconnected, you will be charged a reconnection fee.

Post & Courier Services

New Zealand has a very efficient postal service. The service is operated by New Zealand Post and it costs just 50c to post a standard letter within the country. In most instances, the letter will arrive at its destination within two to three days. There is also a fast-post service available for $1, which should ensure your letter arrives at its destination the next day. Post from Australia normally takes three to five days to arrive, while post from the UK and the US normally takes a week to 10 days.
Posting a medium-sized letter to Australia costs around $1.50, and posting to most other parts of the world will cost around $2. The cost of posting packages overseas depends on the weight of the package and the speed at which you want it delivered. New Zealand Post delivers mail to householders six days of the week, and you can buy stamps at most supermarkets, bookshops and all New Zealand Post shops. If you do not want your mail sent to your home address, you can organise a post office box through your nearest New Zealand Post store. Check out www.nzpost.co.nz for more details.

Courier Companies

New Zealand Post offers a courier service, CourierPost. It is reliable, but it comes at a premium; couriering a standard letter within New Zealand will cost you around $5. If you want items delivered over the weekend, you will normally have to pay extra. The quicker you want your letter or package delivered, the more it will cost. A number of other companies also offer courier services at the local, national and international destinations.

Courier Companies		
CourierPost	0800 501 501	www.courierpost.co.nz
DHL	0800 800 020	www.dhl.co.nz
Fastway	09 634 3704	www.fastway.co.nz
Gateway Express	0800 920 2000	www.gatewayexpress.co.nz
New Zealand Couriers	0800 800 841	www.nzcouriers.co.nz
TNT	0800 275 868	www.tnt.co.nz
Urgent Couriers	09 307 3555	www.urgent.co.nz

Tune In
National Radio broadcasts on AM and FM in most areas of the country. See www.radionz.co.nz for the exact frequency in your region.

Radio

If there is one thing New Zealand has plenty of, it's radio stations. You can tune into any number of them throughout the country, offering everything from talk radio and classical music to edgy rock and wall-to-wall sports coverage. Radio New Zealand is the state-funded national broadcaster and has two commercial-free stations: National Radio and Concert FM. If you're a news junkie and like to keep abreast of what's happening in the world, National Radio (101.1 FM) is the station for you. It provides comprehensive news coverage from throughout the country and the world. *Morning Report*, which airs from 06:00, is its flagship programme. Similar to the BBC in the UK, National Radio (www.radionz.co.nz) offers an excellent online service, as well as a range of 'listen again' and podcast options.

The Radio Network runs a number of radio stations throughout the country called NewsTalk ZB. As the name implies, these stations are largely talk radio stations but most have their own locally staffed newsrooms so listeners can find out what's happening in their backyard. RadioLive, which is broadcast nationally, is another talk radio station. There are dozens of commercial radio stations in the country such as MoreFM, the Edge, and 91ZM, playing a wide range of music. Twiddle the dial and you will soon find a station that suits your tastes. If you're sports-mad, you might find your ears fixed on Radio Sport, which provides round-the-clock sports coverage.
Ruia Mai (www.ruiamai.co.nz) became the country's first Maori-owned, Maori language radio station when it launched a little over 10 years ago.

Television

There are five free-to-air stations in New Zealand, including two state-funded television channels, imaginatively entitled TV One and TV2. Both are operated by state broadcaster, Television New Zealand, as commercial channels. TV One has more British programming, news and documentaries than TV2, which features famous NZ soap *Shortland Street*, American imports and, in general, is aimed at a younger audience. There is a third, privately funded channel called TV3 and a spin-off channel called C4 – essentially a music channel aimed at young viewers.
A new digital service called Freeview is now available in New Zealand. The service is free and allows all New Zealanders to watch their favourite programmes in crystal clear, high resolution digital quality. Viewers need to pay for a set-top box (around $300) and, if necessary, a satellite dish but there is no monthly charge for programming.
Viewers can also tune into Prime Television, which is broadcast from Australia and includes a mix of programming, from *Who Wants to Be a Millionaire?* to endless re-runs of *Midsummer Murders*. In addition to the three main television channels, there are regional television stations in some parts of the country that provide local, community-oriented programming.
To truly immerse yourself in Kiwi culture, there's a Maori station, Maori Television, which is partly funded by the Government.

Satellite TV & Radio

If you want round-the-clock news and sport, plus the best of British programming while in New Zealand, you'll need to hook up to satellite TV. Sky Television is the main provider, with its digital service offering viewers endless channels from which to choose. You will need to pay an initial fee of around $99, which covers the cost of installing the satellite dish, then a minimum charge of around $47 a month. For that rate, expect a start-up package with a mixture of more than 20 channels covering news, kids' programmes, documentaries and sport. You can then add on extra channels, at fees ranging from about $5 for Sky digital music to $17 for the three dedicated Sky Sports channels.
Most hotels and motels in New Zealand now have Sky installed in guest rooms and most pubs around the country are also hooked up. There's always a demand for watching the All Blacks, or for catching up with the English and European football leagues.

Satellite & Cable Providers

Sky Television	0800 759 759	www.sky.co.nz
TelstraClear	0508 888 800	www.telstraclear.co.nz

Telstra-Clear

People living in Wellington, Kapiti and some suburbs of Christchurch can get satellite television services from Telstra-Clear. It offers similar programming choice to Sky Television, but to hook up to it you must have a Telstra-Clear phone line. The starting price for the phone line and digital TV service is around $70 a month.

General Medical Care

Despite ongoing reforms and a workforce crisis, New Zealand's public health care system is still widely regarded as one of the best in the developed world.

New Zealand citizens are entitled to a range of free and subsidised services, including free hospital care. The government subsidises the cost of visits to the doctor and prescriptions for the most vulnerable groups: children, those who require frequent healthcare, and people on low incomes.

The public health system provides free healthcare during pregnancy and childbirth and free dental checks for children until they leave school or turn 18.

New Zealand's network of private hospitals and clinics provides a range of services, which include recuperative care and general surgery through to specialist procedures such as heart and lung operations. There are also private radiology clinics and testing laboratories.

If you're visiting the hospital because of an injury sustained during an accident it is likely that your costs will be covered by ACC. This accident compensation scheme provides personal injury cover for all New Zealand citizens, residents and temporary visitors in the event of an accident. It is financed through taxes (p.84).

The scheme will cover your treatment costs, but there is a catch – you have to waive the right to sue for personal injury, other than for exemplary damages.

With minor exceptions, such as some kinds of cosmetic surgery, hospital treatment in public hospitals is provided free of charge. If you are not a New Zealand resident, you may have to pay for some services. If you can't afford to pay, hospitals will arrange a payment plan with you. You will not be refused emergency care if you haven't got the funds. Waiting times for essential surgery vary from hospital to hospital. If your case is urgent, you will be put on an urgent waiting list.

If you need treatment at an emergency clinic outside normal working hours be prepared to pay a premium as these visits are subsidised at a lesser rate than routine visits to your GP.

When you or someone in your family is unwell, the first point of contact is usually a primary healthcare provider such as a general practitioner (GP), so it is important you register at your local medical centre. In urban areas there are GP practices in nearly all suburbs and registering is free and easy. All you have to do is give the clinic your address, phone number, and the names and ages of your family. If you can provide them with any medical records (in English) and details of any health problems it is wise to do so.

Finding a GP

Doctors are listed in the green pages at the front of your telephone directory. GPs can also be found on the Royal New Zealand College of General Practitioners website, www.rnzcgp.org.nz.

Registering With a Doctor

Which GP you register with is entirely up to you. Some people choose the doctor that is closest to their home, but if you want a woman doctor or a GP who shares your national or ethnic background then you can shop around. Talk to locals about which doctor they use – as is the case with most professions, standards can vary and they'll be able to advise you on who has a good reputation. You can

Mobile medical care in Otago

change your doctor at any time if you are unhappy or your circumstances change. You do not need to explain why you want to change doctors. Most surgeries are open from 08:30 to 17:00, Monday to Friday. Some practices are also open one or two evenings a week, and sometimes on Saturday mornings, but outside of those hours you will have to go to your nearest 24 hour clinic. Expect to pay a premium for being seen by a doctor at these clinics.

In rural areas, GPs are in short supply and you are unlikely to have much choice about who you see, or when you can see them, as one doctor may service several communities. Your local GP and community-based accident and medical centres can treat many injuries and complaints but if your condition requires hospital care your GP will give you a letter of referral to see a specialist (either in a public hospital or private clinic depending on your circumstances).

Health Insurance

There can be long waiting lists for treatments and surgical procedures, particularly in cities, in the public system, so many New Zealanders opt to take out health insurance, which provides access to private hospitals for the immediate treatment of non-urgent but often debilitating conditions. Even if you have private health insurance, you are still entitled to free public health services. Several insurance companies offer a range of health policies – from basic care to fully comprehensive cover. Policy premiums vary widely. See opposite for a list of providers.

Pharmacists

Pharmacists in New Zealand are a good first point of contact if you are feeling unwell. They will either advise you on the best over-the-counter remedy for your ills or recommend that you visit your doctor. Another option, if you are unsure as to whether you need medical help, is to call Healthline on freephone 0800 611 116. Healthline is a national service that provides access to a registered nurse any time of the day. The service is free and confidential and the staff will advise you what action you should take. Healthline incorporates PlunketLine, which offers advice on children under five years of age.

Emergency Services

Most public hospitals have accident and emergency departments, although the level of care they are able to provide will vary. In some cases a transfer to another, better equipped hospital may be required. This is often the case if you live in a small city or town without its own tertiary hospital.

For all serious injuries and complaints you should go to a public hospital emergency department directly or by ambulance (111 is the emergency number for ambulance, police and fire emergencies). Ambulances are provided by non-profit, community-based services in most parts of the country. The services are free in some regions but in others there may be a part-charge for emergency call-outs. Charges vary according to location; the highest rate that can be charged is $67.50. You will not be expected to pay this fee upfront.

Health Insurance

New Zealand's public health service, while good, cannot cope with the demand for its services and there are long waiting lists for some non-urgent treatments. This is why many people chose to buy health insurance, as it gives them the option of seeking private treatment rather than sitting on a waiting list for months, or possibly even years. Having health insurance means you can choose your doctor and the time and place of your treatment.

If you're a non-resident, you are not entitled to free government healthcare, so you will definitely need health insurance. Some of the larger companies offer health insurance as part of salary packages. Sometimes the policy will cover you, your spouse and your children.

There are three main types of health insurance policies available:

- Hospital and surgical only policies (HSO)
- Hospital and specialist cover policies (HSO-plus)
- Comprehensive policies

Your premium is based primarily on your age. If you're looking at a range of plans, don't simply choose the least expensive. The reason a plan is cheaper than others might be because it's harder to make a claim – this is sometimes why the insurance company can afford to offer a cheaper price. Try not to get caught in the trap. Read the terms of your insurance carefully and make sure you understand the fine print. At the other end of the scale, some plans offer optional add-ons that are plainly unnecessary. Some plans in New Zealand will only ever cover 80% of your costs so check carefully before you sign up.

Health Insurance Companies

AXA NZ	0800 106 652	www.axa.co.nz
Southern Cross Healthcare	0800 800 181	www.southerncross.co.nz
Sovereign	0800 500 108	www.sovereign.co.nz
Tower Health & Life	0800 754 754	www.tower.co.nz
Vero	0800 800 786	www.vero.co.nz

Donor Cards

New Zealand does not have a donor card system as such, but when you fill out your driving licence application form, you'll be asked if you would be willing to donate organs in the event of your death. If you tick the 'No' box, you will not be recorded as a donor on the database. By ticking the 'Yes' box and signing a form, all you are agreeing to is having the word 'donor' printed on your licence card. It does not automatically mean that your organs or tissues will be donated in the event of your death. In practice, your family will always be asked for their agreement. You can reconsider your decision every time you renew, replace or change your licence.

Giving Blood

Less than 5% of New Zealanders donate blood annually, yet more than 80% of the population will require blood products at some stage in their life.

You may donate up to four times a year, with a gap of at least 12 weeks between donations. Before you give blood you will have to fill out a health questionnaire. If you are accepted as a donor, you will then be issued with a blood donor card that indicates your blood group. This card is important as it has an identification number that will speed up the process when you donate again. If you have lived in the UK, France or the Republic of Ireland for a total of six months or more between 1980 and 1996 your blood will not be accepted. This is because of the presence of Creutzfeldt-Jakob Disease in those countries during that period.

The New Zealand Blood service is responsible for collecting blood donations and has donor centres in all the main cities, and it also runs mobile clinics. It sometimes issues public appeals for donors if stocks of a particular blood type are running low. For more information, visit www.nzblood.co.nz.

Giving Up Smoking

For those wanting to stop smoking and make a fresh start in New Zealand, the Ministry of Health funds a range of smoking cessation initiatives and programmes. These include:

- Quitline, a freephone nationwide service (0800 778 778) that provides counselling and offers NRT (nicotine replacement therapy) to those attempting to give up. Most of the advisors are ex-smokers and can offer advice, support, resources and low-cost nicotine patches and gum.
- Smokestop (www.smokestop.co.nz) is an online programme that supports people through the quitting process. Using an interactive process and email, it prepares a person for giving up smoking in eight simple sessions. It can be completed alone or with support from a friend or health professional.
- Subsidised nicotine replacement therapy (NRT) is available; it costs between $5 and $10 for a four-week supply.

Some district health boards fund their own stop smoking programmes.

Main Government Hospitals

New Zealand has 85 public hospitals, which are run by District Health Boards. The hospitals provide a range of services – from emergency medical and surgical to maternity – and some have facilities specifically for the elderly or people with disabilities. Their primary aim is to provide good-quality acute care, and then to ensure that as many people as possible have access to elective services.

Access to hospital services can be as one of the following: as an inpatient, where you are admitted to hospital and stay overnight; as a day case, where you are admitted and discharged later that day; or as an outpatient, where you attend a clinic for specialist care, without being admitted to hospital.

With some exceptions, such as for cosmetic surgery, hospital treatment is provided free of charge to residents and to non-residents in the case of an emergency. Many of the bigger public hospitals provide an interpreter service for patients whose first language is not English.

Other Government Hospitals		
Burwood Hospital	Christchurch	03 383 6836
Hutt Hospital	Wellington	04 566 6999
North Shore Hospital	Auckland	09 486 8900
Porirua Hospital	Wellington	04 385 5999
Princess Margaret Hospital	Christchurch	03 337 7899
Waitakere Hospital	Auckland	09 839 0000

2 Park Rd
Auckland
Map p.492 B1 1

Auckland City Hospital

09 367 0000 | *www.adhb.govt.nz*

As befits the country's largest city, Auckland City Hospital is the largest in New Zealand. Located in Grafton, east of the central business district, the hospital opened in its current form in 2003, and combines the services of the Auckland, Green Lane and National Women's Hospitals in one large building. The old Auckland hospital is linked to the new one by means of a glass atrium, and is now known as the Support Building.

For a public hospital, the Auckland City is light and airy, and refreshingly welcoming. All the wards benefit from natural light and a large internal courtyard dominates the building. But it's not all about the architecture – the hospital has 710 beds and is also a research and teaching facility. Many complex cases from around the country and the South Pacific are referred here for specialist treatment.

Riccarton Av
Christchurch
Map p.515 F2 2

Christchurch Hospital

03 364 0640 | *www.cdhb.govt.nz*

Treating more than 65,000 patients a year, Christchurch Hospital's emergency department is the busiest in Australasia. With 650 beds, it's also the largest hospital on the South Island, and one of the country's four teaching hospitals. As such it provides the full range of services on an acute, elective and outpatient basis, and its doctors and specialists often travel across the South Island, setting up specialist clinics in remoter parts. The institution also has telemedicine facilities, which means that patients don't always have to leave their hometown to receive treatment.

201 Great King St
Dunedin
South Island Map G12

Dunedin Public Hospital

03 474 0999 | *www.otagodhb.govt.nz*

The second largest tertiary and research hospital in the South Island, Dunedin Public Hospital, located in Dunedin's CBD, serves the lower half of the South Island (the Southland and Otago regions). It's a teaching hospital and is closely aligned with the Otago University School of Medicine. It has 350 beds and is operated by the Otago District Health Board.

Hospital Rd
Auckland
Map p.484 D7

Middlemore Hospital

09 276 0000 | *www.cmdhb.govt.nz*

Situated near Auckland Golf Course, Middelmore offers secondary level care and a range of community services for people living between Otahuhu and Port Waikato in Auckland. The hospital also offers specialist orthopaedic, plastic surgery, burns, spinal injury, renal dialysis and neonatal intensive care services and patients are referred here from all over the country. Some of its other facilities (which are not located at Middlemore) include the Kidz First Children's Hospital and dedicated mental health, maternity and rehabilitation units.

2 Park Rd
Auckland
Map p.492 B1 5

Starship Children's Health

09 367 0000 | *www.adhb.govt.nz*

Starship was the first specialist children's hospital in the country (it opened in 1991), and remains the largest. Although a separate facility, it's located on the same grounds at Auckland City Hospital (p.164). The name was chosen to appeal to children and due to the design of the building – although some say it looks more like a cake. Following the intention to make the hospital as child-friendly as possible, a place where a wide range of complex medical, surgical and mental health services can be provided to children and young people, the building's interior is bright and colourful.
Starship is a major teaching hospital and a leading New Zealand paediatric training and research centre. Its facilities include inpatient, outpatient and community-based services and outpatient clinics across the country.

Riddiford St
Newtown
Wellington
Map p.507 D3 6

Wellington Hospital

04 385 5999 | *www.cdhb.govt.nz*

Serving the lower half of the North Island and the upper half of the South Island, Wellington Hospital is the region's main emergency hospital and its only trauma unit. It has a helicopter service that covers most of the country, bringing in emergency surgical, intensive care and neonatal intensive care patients. The hospital is situated just south of the CBD in Newtown.

Main Private Hospitals

There is a large number of private hospitals across the country. Many of the medical professionals who work in the public health sector also work in private hospitals. Equally, many Kiwis have private health insurance as this allows them to bypass the public health system's lengthy waiting lists for the treatment of non-urgent conditions. People who have private health insurance are still entitled to free public health services.

Other Private Hospitals

Bowen Hospital	Wellington	04 479 2019
Gillies Hospital & Clinic	Auckland	09 631 1947
Wakefield Hospital	Wellington	04 381 8100

90 Greenlane East
Remuera
Auckland
Map p.484 C5

Ascot Hospital

09 520 9500 | *www.ascot-hospital.co.nz*

Ascot Hospital in Auckland provides a broad range of surgical and medical services. The hospital has 12 operating theatres, a dedicated intensive care facility, coronary facilities unit and a short-stay unit with six single bedrooms. It also has a day surgical facility that can accommodate up to 26 patients. Some of the country's leading surgical and medical specialists have their consulting rooms here. Famous patients treated here include Rolling Stones guitarist Keith Richards.

Private Health Centres & Clinics

Auckland	
Blockhouse Bay Medical Centre	09 627 9176
Ponsonby Medical Centre	09 378 7916
Titirangi Medical Centre	09 817 8069
White Cross Accident & Medical Centre	09 524 5943
Wellington	
Karori Medical Centre	04 920 4562
Newlands Medical Centre	04 478 9858
Wakefield Specialist Medical Centre	04 381 8120
Christchurch	
Christchurch South Health Centre	03 322 0108
Oxford Clinic	03 379 0555
St Albans Medical Centre	03 355 9119

666 High St
Wellington
North Island Map G14

Boulcott Hospital

04 569 7555 | *www.boulcotthospital.co.nz*

The only private hospital in the Hutt Valley, Boulcott sets out to create a relaxing environment for its patients. Currently undergoing expansion, the hospital has two operating theatres and an endoscopy suite. Specialties include orthopaedics, gynaecology, general surgery, plastic surgery, urology and gastroenterology.

98 Mountain Rd
Dunedin
South Island Map G12

Mercy Hospital

03 464 0107 | *www.mercyhospital.co.nz*

Founded by the religious order, the Sisters of Mercy, in 1936, Mercy Hospital is Dunedin's only private surgical hospital. Today, it is a modern, fully equipped and accredited hospital that provides a wide range of advanced surgical and medical services. Adjoining it is The Marinoto Clinic, a 22 suite facility where more than 50 specialists and health professionals offer a comprehensive range of diagnostic and treatment services.

131 Bealey Av
Christchurch
Map p.512 B2 10

Southern Cross Hospital Christchurch

03 379 4433 | *www.southerncross.co.nz*

The Southern Cross network consists of 13 private hospitals across New Zealand. The group is a not-for-profit organisation, which means that any extra funds are reinvested in the hospitals, their equipment, facilities and staff. Of the group's hospitals, Southern Cross Hospital Christchurch is the largest and is currently being expanded. Patients who are admitted can expect fairly luxurious facilities (including flat-screen TVs once the development is completed). The seven operating theatres are also to be upgraded and fitted with state-of-the-art equipment.

Dermatologists

Auckland	
Auckland Dermatology	09 631 0088
Skin Surgery Clinic	09 828 6438
Skinsite	09 368 9062
Wellington	
Dermatology Plus	0800 400 420
The Skin Centre	04 479 2060
Wellington Dermatology	04 475 8664
Christchurch	
Anne Davis	03 365 5378
Christchurch Dermatology	0800 242 433
Deramtology Associates	03 371 9138
Grant Bellany	03 356 0214
Ken Mcdonald	03 379 9467

Birthcare Hospital, Auckland

Maternity

The maternity services offered in New Zealand are highly regarded. Provided you have New Zealand residency or hold a work permit, you are entitled to free care during your pregnancy and the birth. The first thing you will need to do, once you've got over the shock of discovering you're expecting, is to choose a lead maternity carer who will be responsible for providing and coordinating your maternity care, developing your care plan with you, and attending your labour and birth.

A lead maternity carer can be a midwife (independent or hospital-based), a general practitioner, an obstetrician or a hospital team. To some extent the choice will depend on where you live, as the full range of options is not available in every area. You can choose to have your baby at home, but most babies in New Zealand are born in hospital. There is no charge for hospital stays, which generally last from two to five days. Women who have miscarriages are also cared for without charge. Approved abortions are free.

Most women are cared for throughout their pregnancy and at the birth by an independent midwife, though some women choose a local maternity hospital, or a GP who provides maternity care. If women need specialist care they can choose to be referred to a free hospital clinic or to a private specialist. If you choose a private specialist, you will have to pay all fees.

Even in private maternity hospitals the care is provided free – provided you meet the eligibility criteria – until you are clinically fit for discharge. This is approximately 48 hours after delivery. You may stay on for further rest and support, which will be charged for, but your insurance should cover the cost of this extended stay.

Labour

The pain relief you will receive during labour is discussed during the preparation of your birth plan. Gas, drugs or an epidural are usually only used when all other methods of pain relief, such as relaxation and breathing techniques, have been exhausted. As elsewhere in the west, a growing number of women in New Zealand are having elective caesareans, but natural child-birth is still the preferred option of most lead maternity carers (LMCs).

When you go into labour, it's common practice to have your partner with you in the delivery room. Other family and friends can also be present for the birth if you wish. Once you've had your baby, the hospital (or your LMC, if you had your baby at home) has to notify the Registrar of Births within five working days of the birth. The hospital will give you a copy of the birth registration form. It is compulsory for you to complete it and return it to the Births, Deaths and Marriages Central Registry (PO Box 10526, Wellington) as soon as possible after the birth.

The Ministry of Health's website (www.moh.govt.nz) has an extensive guide to maternity services in New Zealand, including a detailed brochure on what mums-to-be can expect. There's also the Maternity Helpline: 0800 686 223.

Going Back to Your Home Country

If you want to return home for the birth of your child you will need to check with the airline as to how far into your pregnancy they will allow you to fly. The rules vary, but typically, if you're having a normal pregnancy, all your travel must be completed by the end of the 36th week. There must be 28 days between the date travel is completed and the date on which you're due to give birth. You must also carry a letter from a registered medical practitioner stating that your pregnancy is progressing normally and specifying your expected due date. If you've had a complicated pregnancy, medical clearance will be required before you are allowed to board a plane. You should take your maternity care records with you.

Antenatal & Postnatal Care

Your LMC will recommend antenatal classes to you. These are intended to teach you and your partner (or support person) what to expect during pregnancy, labour and birth. After the birth, you can expect between five and 10 home visits from your LMC or midwife. You should not receive less than five consultations, unless you request less. If you had your baby in hospital, you will receive your first visit within 24 hours of arriving home from hospital.

The postnatal care you will get from your LMC includes assistance with, and advice about, feeding and caring for your baby, as well as suggestions about your nutritional needs and contraception. Your LMC will be able to tell you about any support groups in your area such as La Leche League (www.lalecheleague.org.nz), Parents Centre (www.parentscentre.org.nz) or Home Birth Association (www.homebirth.org.nz).

Four to six weeks after your baby's birth, your LMC will give you a final maternity check. While the check officially marks the end of your maternity care, you are still able to contact your LMC regarding any maternity related problem until six weeks after the birth.

At six weeks you should take your baby to your GP for a further check and for vaccinations. This visit falls under the subsidised primary health care for children from newborns to 6 years old, but you may be charged a part payment for it.

You and your child have the right to free Well Child Tamariki Ora care (www.wellchild.org.nz). This support is different from standard subsidised medical care and is more about child development and prevention of illness.

Maternity Hospitals & Clinics

Auckland		
Botany Downs Maternity Unit	09 534 6063	Public
National Women's Hospital	09 367 0000	Public
North Shore Hospital	09 486 8930	Public
Waitakere Hospital	09 389 0000	Public
Wellington		
Kapiti Health Centre	04 298 6069	Public
Kenepuru Hospital	04 237 6015	Public
Wellington Hospital	04 385 5999	Public
Christchurch		
Christchurch Women's Hospital	03 364 4699	Public
St George's Hospital	03 355 9179	Private

Maternity Leave

If you have been in continuous employment in New Zealand for 12 months, you are entitled to 14 weeks' paid parental leave. You first need to apply to your employer for parental leave, then to the Inland Revenue Department for parental leave payments. This paid leave must be taken at the same time as any unpaid leave you decide to take. Extended leave of up to 52 weeks, unpaid, is available for employees with 12 months' eligible service.

Postnatal Depression

Postnatal or maternity blues are very common and involve the mother feeling down and in the week after her baby is born. This feeling typically passes after a few days. Also common is postnatal depression, a much more serious condition. In this instance, mothers become seriously depressed in the first months following the baby's birth. While some particular personality types may be more likely to develop depression, the vast majority of women who experience postnatal depression have been previously healthy. If you're concerned about postnatal depression contact your GP.

Gynaecology & Obstetrics

Finding a gynaecologist you feel comfortable with is difficult, particularly if you're new to the country. The best method is to ask your GP or your friends. Almost all gynaecologists in New Zealand are also obstetricians. You will have to make it clear if you would prefer to be seen by a female gynaecologist.

You don't need to see a gynaecologist to get contraception, as your GP can give you a prescription. You can also obtain contraceptives from family planning clinics. The Telecom *White Pages* will list your nearest clinic.

Breast Cancer

Approximately 2,500 women a year are diagnosed with breast cancer in New Zealand. Mammography is not failsafe (some 10% of abnormalities might not be detected), but it is the best test available to find a lump when it is still very small. You should, however, also have a doctor give you a physical examination when you have a mammogram.

It's recommended that women aged between 40 and 50 have a mammogram annually, while women over 50 should have mammograms twice a year. Breast Screen Aotearoa (www.nsu.govt.nz) provides free mammograms for women aged between 45 and 69. If you're a resident you can register with them by calling 0800 270 200.

Abortions

Under New Zealand law, women of any age have the right to terminate a pregnancy at any stage if two doctors agree that the pregnancy would seriously harm your mental or physical health, or that the baby would have a serious disability. The safest time to end a pregnancy is between eight and nine weeks. Most abortions are carried out before 12 weeks.

Fertility Treatment

There are fertility clinics in Auckland, Hamilton, Wellington and Christchurch. Each offers donor insemination (DI), intra-uterine insemination (IUI) with ovarian stimulation, ovulation induction, in vitro fertilisation (IVF), intracytoplasmic sperm injection (ICSI) and egg donation. You can have blood tests and ultrasound scans done locally to cut down on travel, and most of the clinics offer initial and follow-up consultations in other cities.

Gynaecology & Obstetrics

Chris Heron	Auckland	09 443 0367
Christchurch Obstetrics & Gynaecology Associates	Christchurch	03 375 4040
Dr Neil Buddicom	Auckland	09 520 9520
Dr Philip Beattie	Auckland	09 630 8270
Dr Renuka Bhat	Auckland	09 271 3344
H B Koya	Wellington	04 381 8134
Howard Clentworth	Wellington	04 569 7555
John Doig	Christchurch	03 379 0557

Contraception

Condoms can be bought at most supermarkets, service stations and pharmacies, and many pubs have condom vending machines in their bathrooms. Your GP or a family planning clinic can write you a prescription for the pill, or fit an intrauterine contraceptive device (IUD). Depo Provera, which is a three-monthly injection of progesterone, is available for women who tend to forget to take the pill. The emergency contraceptive pill, also known as the 'morning after pill', is available from sexual health clinics, your doctor, accident and emergency medical centres and pharmacies.

Paediatrics

Most healthcare for children is provided by GPs, but in some cases you may be referred to a paediatrician. If you rely on the public health system you will not have much choice in who your child is referred to, but if you have health insurance a visit to a paediatrician in the private sector is likely to be covered.

Starship Hospital in Auckland (p.165) is New Zealand's only specialist paediatric hospital, and a seriously ill child may be transferred there for specialist care. Children in New Zealand typically receive their first vaccination shots at six weeks of age. The injections, for diptheria, tetanus, whooping cough, and polio, are repeated at five months, 10 months and four years. At 10 months, children are also vaccinated against meningococcal B and at 15 months against measles, mumps and rubella. Booster shots are given at the age of 11.

Paediatricians		
Dr Guy Bloomfield	Auckland	09 489 3012
Dr Jan Sinclair	Auckland	09 585 0190
Dr Robyn Shaw	Wellington	04 920 0870
Dr Rodney Ford	Christchurch	03 377 7196
Dr Terry Casely	Christchurch	03 365 7766
Dr Vaughn Richardson	Wellington	04 385 5265

There is a vaccine for chickenpox, but it doesn't fall under the government's free vaccination programme so you'll need to pay for it. If you come from a country with a high incidence of tuberculosis, you can also have your child vaccinated against the disease.

If you have a child with disabilities or learning difficulties, your paediatrician will refer you to an appropriate community agency for access to support services. As your child approaches school age, the Ministry of Education's special education service will help you with schooling arrangements.

Dentists & Orthodontists

Dental care for adults is not publicly funded and paying the bill for a filling may be more painful than the procedure itself. For an adult, a basic dental check-up can cost anything from $50 to $90. An amalgam filling will set you back between $60 and $122, while a crown can cost up to $1,100. A half-hour visit to a dental hygienist will cost you between $45 and $120. Oral care providers – dentists, oral surgeons, orthodontists, hygienists and dental therapists – are listed in the *Yellow Pages*. The Dental Council (www.dentalcouncil.org.nz) also has an online directory of registered New Zealand dentists.

Dentists & Orthodontists		
A+ Dental Group	Auckland	09 534 7916
AA Dental Centre	Wellington	04 473 9283
Accident & Emergency Unit	Auckland	09 270 0200
Gentle Dental Centre	Wellington	04 384 6046
Great Teeth Dental Care	Wellington	04 473 7573
Northwest Dental Centre	Christchurch	03 359 8300
St Albans Dental Centre	Christchurch	03 355 9380

Luckily, primary school children receive free dental care from School Dental Service therapists who operate out of mobile clinics. Routine preventative and restorative treatments are covered but children requiring specialist care, such as teeth straightening or surgery, are usually referred to a private dentist. Once children leave primary school they are still entitled to free dental care, provided by private dentists but funded by the local district health board, until they are 18. Again, most of this is free but you will need to pay for some specialist services.

Opticians & Ophthalmologists		
Anstice & Associates	Christchurch	03 334 3909
Eden Eye Optometrists	Auckland	09 309 3900
Eye Pro	Christchurch	0508 393 776
Eyecare Cottage	Auckland	09 575 5568
Focal Point Optometrists	Wellington	04 474 6662
Local Eyes Optician	Auckland	09 626 7713
Sercombe & Matheson	Wellington	04 472 4261

Opticians & Ophthalmologists

Most routine eye care in New Zealand is not publicly funded. You will need to see an optometrist if you need glasses. Optometrists are trained to conduct eye examinations and prescribe glasses or contact lenses. Most stock frames and can have lenses for glasses or contacts made for you. They can also detect conditions such as cataracts, glaucoma or diabetes. A standard consultation will cost between $45 and $75. If you need glasses, the cost will depend on how fashion-conscious you are and the style and brand of frames that you choose. You'll find a range of opticians and optometrists at shopping malls, or you can ask your GP or local pharmacy to point you in the right direction.

If you have an eye complaint or a problem requiring greater specialist knowledge, you will probably be referred to an ophthalmologist or eye specialist who is qualified to carry out eye surgery in the event that it is necessary.

Children have their eyes tested during their first year at primary school. The check is fairly rudimentary and is designed primarily to identify problems with a child's distance vision, as this can affect their learning. If you're concerned about your child's eyesight you should take them to an optometrist. Telltale signs that your child might need glasses include: headaches, rubbing of eyes frequently, shutting one eye when reading, holding a book very close, poor concentration, reversing letters or numbers or copying things down incorrectly from the blackboard at school.

Shopping for sunglasses

Cosmetic Treatment & Surgery

While cosmetic surgery has grown in popularity in recent years, it's still seen largely as a luxury for the rich, famous and vain. Still, you can have any one of the following procedures done: breast augmentation or reduction, liposuction, liposculpture, abdominoplasty, rhinoplasty, otoplasty, browlift and blepharoplasty. Members of the New Zealand Foundation for Cosmetic Surgery are registered by the New Zealand Medical Council as specialists in plastic surgery. The foundation has a website, www.cosmeticsurgery.org.nz, that's worth checking out if you're considering a particular procedure.

A number of clinics that offer non-surgical treatments, such as botox and chemical peels, have sprung up in recent years.

Cosmetic Treatment & Surgery		
Caci Clinic	Various Locations	0800 438 438
Christopher Porter	Christchurch	03 366 5623
Dr Julian Lofts	Auckland	09 520 3906
Janek Januszkiewicz	Auckland	09 529 5002
Plastic Surgery Masters	Wellington	04 499 4775
Stewart Sinclair	Christchurch	03 355 6815

Alternative Therapies

New Zealanders are not averse to turning to alternative therapies to treat their ailments – in fact they place a great deal of faith in them. A 2005 study by Otago University found that nearly two-thirds of Kiwis believed that complementary therapies could be beneficial when used alongside conventional medical treatments for cancer.

Acupuncture, acupressure, aromatherapy, healing meditation, and homeopathy providers can all be found in the *Yellow Pages*. The national accident compensation scheme (ACC), subsidises acupuncture, chiropractic and osteopathy services by specified providers. With the influx of Asian migrants into the country, the popularity of acupuncture has grown markedly in the last decade. There are many Chinese medicine practitioners to be found, especially in Auckland.
Complementary and alternative medicines can be bought at standard and homoeopathic pharmacies, health food stores and supermarkets (p.387). You can also buy some products directly from practitioners – herbal tonics from herbalists, for instance. You can also obtain products by mail order or over the internet.

Alternative Therapies	
Alternative Health Titirangi	09 817 2702
Jet Therapy	03 359 0280
Nourishe Natural Therapies	04 569 7832
Release Massage Therapy	03 355 5080

Acupressure/Acupuncture

A form of traditional Chinese medicine, acupressure predates acupuncture by about 2,500 years. Practitioners believe a person's energy (known as chi) travels through the body along pathways called meridians. A block in the flow of chi results in discomfort or disease. To release the blocked energy, or to promote energy flow to a certain area, the practitioner presses an acupoint. More than 300 acupoints have been identified in the body and practitioners believe that by applying moderate to penetrating pressure for up to several minutes they can right most ills.

Acupressure/Acupuncture		
Acupuncture & Herbal Centre	Auckland	09 52 2087
Acupuncture Associates Ltd	Wellington	04 473 9005
Auckland Acupuncture Centre	Auckland	09 630 9388
Christchurch Acupuncture Centre	Christchurch	03 354 2398
Japanese Acupuncture	Wellington	04 938 1017
Karori Acupuncture	Wellington	04 476 2765
Natural Health Acupuncture Clinic	Christchurch	03 343 3280

Addiction Counselling & Rehabilition

There is a myriad of self-help organisations for people battling drug, alcohol or gambling addictions in New Zealand. If you have a problem with addiction your GP will be able to steer you towards appropriate support services.
Alcoholics Anonymous (AA) Aotearoa-New Zealand runs a 12 step programme for people who want to stop drinking. It has a free helpline (0800 229 6757), and you'll find meeting times and venues at www.alcoholics-anonymous.org.nz. Narcotics Anonymous is also an active network for people with drug addictions. As with the AA, 12 steps form the core of NA's programme, and addicts help each other to recover. If you require help you can call 0800 628 632 and leave a message and someone will call you back.

Addiction Counselling & Rehabilition		
AA Auckland Analytical Hypnotherapy Consultancy	09 307 1123	na
Alcoholics Anonymous	0800 229 6757	www.alcoholics-anonymous.org.nz
Asian Problem Gambling Helpline	0800 862 342	na
Higher Ground Drug Rehabilitation Trust	09 834 0017	www.higherground.org.nz
Narcotics Anonymous	03 365 0686	www.nzna.org
Problem Gambling Foundation of NZ	0800 646 262	www.gamblingproblem.co.nz
Salvation Army Bridge Addiction Centre	03 338 4436	www.salvationarmy.org.nz

There are a number of support services available for those addicted to gambling, including a national helpline. The Gambling Helpline (0800 654 655) offers ongoing motivational support, referral and information services. It helps people who are, or have been gambling, family and friends concerned about someone else's gambling and anyone interested in the impact the problem has had in the country. Overeaters Anonymous, for people with food addictions, also operates in New Zealand's main centres, and it has a helpful website, www.oaregion10.org. There are a few residential alcohol and drug treatment centres throughout the country. The National Addiction Centre, which is at the forefront of drug and alcohol treatment in the country, is based in Christchurch, and forms part of the Christchurch School of Medicine and Health Sciences (03 364 0530, www.chmeds.ac.nz).

Aromatherapy

Aromatherapy		
Absolute Essential Aromatherapy	Various Locations	0508 277 658
Healing Hands	Auckland	09 410 0588
Life Essentials	Wellington	02 7223 9777
Nicola Quinn Beauty & Day Spa	Christchurch	03 355 6400
Spa Parnell	Auckland	09 300 7157
Wellpark College of Natural Therapies	Auckland	09 360 0560

Aromatherapists believe they can use essential oils to enhance physical and emotional well-being. A registered aromatherapist will compile a case history and at each consultation will review your current symptoms and formulate a blend of essential oils that are appropriate. You may be given a cream or blend to use between visits to enhance the healing process. Like homeopathy, aromatherapy has recently grown in popularity in New Zealand. The New Zealand Register of Holistic Aromatherapists (03 379 2710, www.aromatherapy.org.nz) oversees the industry.

Healing Meditation

Healing Meditation		
Self Realization Meditation Healing Centre	Christchurch	03 359 8507
Self Realization Meditation Healing Centre	Auckland	09 441 9446

Followers of healing meditation believe that when the mind, body and spirit work together, the result is a balance of thought, awareness and well-being, and the ability for the body to heal itself. The New Zealand Spiritual Directory (www.spiritualdirectory.co.nz) provides a comprehensive list of companies offering healing meditation.

Homeopathy

Homeopathy in New Zealand dates back to 1849, but it's only in the last decade that it's really taken off, as Kiwis discover the benefits of using homeopathic treatments. Where once there were only 11 professional homeopaths registered with the governing body, the New Zealand Council of Homeopaths (www.homeopathy.co.nz), there are now around 150. Homeopaths in New Zealand do not have to have a medical licence to practice. There are four colleges in New Zealand providing training in homeopathy: The Wellington College of Homeopathy (04 232 7942), the Bay of Plenty College of Homeopathy (09 849 4436), which has faculties in Tauranga, Auckland and Christchurch, and the Auckland College of Classical Homeopathy (09 377 2214). These colleges often offer discounted treatments.

Homeopathy		
Auckland College of Classical Homeopathy	Auckland	09 377 2214
Back to Health	Auckland	09 361 3616
Essence Homeopathy	Auckland	09 292 9561
Gingko Tree Natural Health Centre	Christchurch	03 379 7181
Natural Health Matters	Wellington	04 569 5136

Reflexology & Massage Therapy

Other options **Well-Being** p.353

Reflexology & Massage Therapy		
Bien-Etre Beauty Therapy	Christchurch	03 356 2685
Bliss Reflexology	Auckland	09 368 4698
Elementa	Auckland	09 520 4015
Natural Health Centre	Wellington	04 385 4342
Reflexology 4 U	Christchurch	03 981 2004
Wellington Group of Reflexology	Wellington	04 387 2929

If you're looking for a reflexologist in New Zealand, the best place to start is the Reflexology New Zealand website (www.reflexology.org.nz). Reflexology NZ is the professional body responsible for ensuring standards are maintained. By choosing a professional member of their list you will have some reassurance that your care is being provided by a qualified practitioner. Reflexology works on the premise that there are reflex areas in the feet that relate to all organs and systems within the body. By applying pressure or massaging these areas you can find out which areas are out of balance. Treatment can then be given to rebalance the body by stimulating its own healing mechanism.

Rehabilitation & Physiotherapy

Sports-mad Kiwis always seem to be visiting physiotherapists for one reason or another. The Accident Compensation Corporation (ACC) system in the country means that seeing a physiotherapist for an accident-related injury is normally free. The ACC (www.acc.co.nz) has a network of endorsed physiotherapists at clinics around the country for which it pays an increased fee, in exchange for them agreeing not to charge ACC claimants. You may, however, be charged for services provided outside normal working hours, for materials used in treatment or a 'no show' fee if you fail to keep your appointment. Your first consultation will usually last between 30 to 45 minutes and cost between $40 and $70 (if not covered by the ACC). The physiotherapist will take a detailed case history and conduct a physical assessment, and then work with you to devise an individual treatment programme, which commonly involves exercise and massages. Subsequent visits may be cheaper, depending on the time required.

Rehabilitation & Physiotherapy		
Canterbury Neuromuscular Clinic	Christchurch	0800 700 755
Capital Sports Medicine	Wellington	04 499 5732
City Med Physiotheraphy	Auckland	09 377 5525
In Touch Phsyiotheraphy	Christchurch	03 385 1526
Ponsonby Physiotherapists	Auckland	09 378 6890
SportsMed	Christchurch	03 366 0620
Te Aro Physiotherapy	Wellington	04 384 6460

Back Treatment

Each year the Accident Compensation Corporation (ACC) subsidises more than three million visits to physiotherapists, chiropractors and osteopaths. Of these, more than 1.3 million are for bad backs. A first visit to a chiropractor will involve a case history being taken and physical examination. It will usually take between 45 minutes and an hour, at a cost of anything from $45 to $120 (if unsubsidised). If an x-ray is required, the cost can jump by anything from $50 to $150. A consultation with an osteopath usually costs between $45 and $50, and lasts for 15 to 35 minutes. If you require physiotherapy, expect to pay between $40 and $70. If your injury is as the result of an accident though, the ACC will subsidise the cost. The Pacific Association of Craniosacral

Back Treatment		
Back to Living Chiropractic	Wellington	04 997 7755
Bealey Chiropractic Clinic	Christchurch	03 366 3881
Chiropractic Edge	Newmarket	09 378 8011
Hammond Family Chiropractic	Albany	09 414 2225
Happy Spine	Christchurch	03 348 3536
Kelburn Clinic	Wellington	04 475 8312

Therapists has a comprehensive list of therapists around the country on its website, www.craniosacral.co.nz.

Nutritionists & Slimming

As in much of the rest of the world, business is booming for nutritionists and slimming clubs, as New Zealanders look to lose weight and tone their bodies. Many of the private gyms in New Zealand offer combined healthy eating and exercise programmes and there are dietitians attached to many of the community medical centres. Most will tailor programmes specifically to your needs. Popular weight loss programmes such as Weight Watchers, Jenny Craig and Sure Slim are also available in most of the larger towns, and your GP will be able to advise you on how best to achieve a healthy weight.

Nutritionists & Slimming	
Jenny Craig	03 348 6436
Nutrition Fit Consultans	03 381 6222
SureSlim Wellness Clinic	0508 787 375
Weight Watchers	0800 009 009
Zone Nutrition	0800 727 472

Counselling & Therapy

Health authorities in New Zealand have worked hard to overcome the stigma often associated with mental illnesses, and campaigns encouraging people to seek professional help for conditions such as depression are common. Former All Black John Kirwan, who suffers from depression, is among the high-profile New Zealanders fronting such campaigns, which are run by the Mental Health Foundation (www.mentalhealth.org.nz). If you think you're suffering from mental health problems, your GP should be the first port of call. GPs can prescribe anti-depressants and refer you to specialist mental health service providers such as a psychiatrist or a psychologist. Mental health services are provided free as part of the public health system, but if your condition isn't considered urgent you may to wait some time for an appointment. If you don't want to wait you can pay to go privately (if you have health insurance, your policy should cover the costs).

Counsellors/Psychologists		
Alcoholics Anonymous	Various Locations	0800 229 6757
Capril Alcohol Drug Gambling Treatment Trust	Auckland	09 527 6090
Gambling Helpline	Various Locations	0800 654 655
Home & Family Society Counselling Services	Auckland	09 630 8961
Kilpan & Associates	Auckland	09 529 2210
Men's Talk	Auckland	0508 636 782
Mount Eden Counselling & Psychotherapy	Auckland	09 623 2660
Petersgate Counselling Centre	Christchurch	03 343 3391

Psychiatrists		
Anxiety Associates Clinic	Auckland	09 520 2576
Child & Adolescent Psychiatrist	Auckland	09 638 9804
Dr Greg Young	Wellington	04 973 4818
Dr Harvey Williams	Christchurch	03 355 0336
Dr Robin Moir	Auckland	09 520 5468
Mental Health Education & Resource Centre	Christchurch	03 365 5344

While sometimes medication is needed, often just talking to someone can make a big difference to your mental health. Relationship Services (www.relate.org.nz) offers a professional counselling service throughout the country. Its particular speciality is dealing with relationships, both personal and professional. There are psychiatric hospitals around the country for people who require hospital treatment.

Support Groups

While New Zealand is a relatively easy place in which to live – the locals are friendly and the pace of life relaxed – settling into a new country does pose its challenges. Bouts of homesickness and culture shock are inevitable. Luckily, there are many organisations and clubs you can join that can help you settle into your new life. Kiwis enjoy helping others, so don't be afraid to ask for help if you're feeling lonely or isolated.

Your embassy should also be able to put you in touch with other expats in the country and, in the main cities there are refugee and migrant support services available to help you with the adjustment process. Details of these groups can be found on council websites or call your local Citizens' Advice Bureau, who should be able to help.

Support Groups	
Auckland Regional Migrants Services	09 625 2440
Migrant Support Services	09 636 7334
National Network of Stopping Violence Services	04 802 5402
New Settlers Centre	04 589 3700
Parents Centre	04 233 2022
Refugee & Migrant Centre	03 372 9310
Wellington's People Centre	04 385 8596

If you need support for a particular issue, for example if you're struggling with your first baby or have recently suffered a bereavement, help is usually just a phone call away. There are thousands of support groups operating in New Zealand, for people with issues ranging from a fear of the outdoors and a fear of flying to victims of crime. Local libraries are a good place to start if you're looking to find out which groups operate in your area. Check out the noticeboards or ask a staff member for assistance. The schools in your area can be a good source of information too, as many clubs and groups base their activities there.

Social Groups

One of the best ways to settle into a new country is to throw yourself in, boots and all. Becoming involved in clubs, sports and group activities is a great way of meeting people and establishing a new network to replace the friends and family you've left behind. If you're an active, outdoor person there are any number of tramping (hiking) clubs and walking groups, and sports clubs galore. Many companies have their own sporting teams and social clubs too, so check and see what your employer offers. Local ethnic communities have their own societies or associations where people can gather, and joining one of these groups can really help you get through those bouts of homesickness. Another way to meet people is through volunteer work or church groups. See the Activities chapter (p.303) for more details.

Super tramping

Education

School Reports
Read the latest government reports on individual schools and childcare centres in your area at www.ero.govt.nz.

New Zealand's state-funded education system is highly regarded, with the country's literacy and numeracy rates among the highest in the world. Schooling is compulsory from the age of 6 to 16 (15 with the parents' and the school's permission). Children with special educational needs may remain at school until the end of the year in which they turn 21.

University of Auckland

While there are many private pre-school centres, most children start going to school at the age of 5. Primary schools usually teach Year 1 to Year 6 and intermediate schools, Years 7 and 8. There are some 'full' primaries that teach children from Year 1 all the way to Year 8. Secondary schools teach Year 9 to Year 13. Class sizes depend on the nature and location of the school, but normally there are about 30 children to a class.

Schools are governed by a board of trustees. The board is elected by parents, and establishes the rules by which the school is run. School rules usually mean that uniforms are compulsory, particularly at secondary schools. In addition, pupils are usually not allowed to wear make-up, too much jewellery or have unusual facial piercings. The use of mobile phones during school hours is also often limited.

In the Zone
Check what school zones a neighbourhood is in at www.schoolzones.co.nz. Not all schools have zones, and even those with zones usually save an allocation for out-of-zone students.

Zoning

In general, your children will attend the local school for which they are zoned. If you live outside the zone of your preferred school, your children might not get a place there – particularly if the school is a popular one with a good reputation. Spare places at popular schools are allocated by ballot. There are exceptions to zoning rules, for instance, schools of a particular religion or that have other special characteristics. The Education Review Office regularly publishes reports on all schools which can be read online at www.ero.govt.nz.

School Fees & Decile Ratings

While state education is meant to be free, there are costs involved. Uniforms, stationery and extra-curricular activities are at the expense of parents, but textbooks are usually provided without charge.

Most state schools charge an 'activity fee' of around \$100 to \$200 per year per child – although some charge considerably more – to cover the cost of extras. Technically, payment of the fee is voluntary, but most parents pay, and schools have been known to employ debt collectors to try and recoup the money. The fee pays for extra resources for your children's school and is tax-deductible.

The government provides more money to schools in socially deprived areas than it does to schools in more wealthy ones. Each school has a decile rating of between 1 and 10 – the higher the rating, the less money the school will receive from the government. In order to make-up the funding differential, schools in wealthier areas tend to charge higher 'voluntary' fees than schools in poorer areas.

While state sector schooling is generally well regarded, New Zealand also has a strongly developed private education sector.

If you chose to educate your child at a private school you can expect to pay anywhere from $1,500 to $10,000 a term, depending on your choice of school and whether your child boards or lives at home. Most private schools offer a limited number of scholarships and your child may or may not be eligible for one of these.

Grammar Zones
Auckland Grammar School (p.181) and Epsom Girls Grammar School (p.182) are so sought-after that property prices have soared in their catchment areas. You'll often see the abbreviation GZ (grammar zone) in property ads.

The National Curriculum

The New Zealand curriculum is based on acquiring essential academic and practical skills. The Ministry of Education has identified seven academic or 'essential learning' areas that schools must focus on:

- Language and languages
- Mathematics
- Science
- Technology
- Social sciences
- Arts
- Health and physical education

These are balanced by eight practical or 'essential' skills:

- Communication
- Numeracy
- Information
- Problem-solving
- Self-management and competition
- Social and co-operative
- Physical
- Work and study

Schools are expected to report back to parents regularly on their children's progress. Most schools prepare written progress reports each term and hold parent-teacher evenings where parents can meet with teachers. Parents are often encouraged to participate in school activities, and can request a meeting with a teacher at any time if particular concerns arise. Many schools have anti-bullying programmes in place.

School Days & Terms

School days are Mondays to Fridays. Primary schools usually start at 09:00 or a little earlier, and finish at 15:00. Secondary schools usually start at around 08:30 and finish at around 15:00 or 15:15. The school year runs from the end of January or beginning of February to December. There are four terms, each roughly 10 weeks long. Summer holidays last about six weeks for primary schools and about a week longer for secondary schools. The autumn, winter and spring holidays each last two weeks. Some schools run after-school programmes for children whose parents work, and some also offer holiday programmes.

Nurseries & Pre-Schools

Most New Zealand children attend some form of kindergarten or pre-school prior to officially starting school at age 5. Early education is considered essential to children's learning, and services are provided by a range of operators, from private businesses to community church groups and voluntary agencies. Parents are usually encouraged to be involved in these childcare centres and getting involved is an excellent way of meeting other families and making friends in the area, particularly if you don't know many people. Playcentres are popular early childhood education centres that are run as parent co-operatives. There are more than 450 nationwide. See www.playcentre.org.nz for your nearest one and how you can get involved.

Unlike primary and secondary schools, nurseries and pre-schools don't automatically receive funding from the government. State funding is generally only provided if the service is licensed and has a 'charter' that formally sets out educational policies that are in line with those approved by the Ministry of Education.

The Ministry sets licensing standards that include minimum ratios of staff to children and restrictions on class sizes. Check that your chosen early childhood centre is licensed before you enrol your child as this guarantees a minimum standard of care. The centres are regularly monitored by the Education Review Office and their reports are avaiable. The MOE (www.minedu.govt.nz) can provide local contacts and free advice on the range of early childhood services available in your area, but it's also worth talking to neighbours or your local Plunket group, a not-for-profit organisation that provides support services for children under 5 (www.plunket.org.nz).

Kindergartens provide early childhood education for children from the age of 3 to 5. It is quite usual for kindergartens to have waiting lists so the earlier you register your child, the better. Children can be placed on the waiting list from the age of two years. Children attend either morning or afternoon sessions. Morning sessions are usually held five times a week and afternoon sessions usually three, although this will vary. The sessions tend to be informal and parental involvement is encouraged. The philosophy is learning through play and the emphasis is on developing children's social skills. Kindergartens don't formally charge fees, but a donation and help with fundraising and activities is generally expected.

Education and care centres offer full-day or half-day (up to four hours a day) care and are normally open for up to eight or nine hours (between 07:00 and 18:00). Some centres offer care in morning or afternoon sessions but usually require children to attend for a minimum time period. Usually, care is charged on the basis of a weekly or daily fee. The best facilities have waiting lists so if you want a place for your child get your name down quickly. Centres are licensed to take either under two year olds, over two year olds or a mix of both age groups. These include both standard facilities and specialist childcare centres such as those run by Montessori and Rudolph Steiner schools. Fees usually start at about $20 for a short afternoon up to $45 for a full day, or $200 for a full week of care.

Various Locations

ABC Learning Centre

09 269 0077 | *www.abclearningcentres.co.nz*

This pre-school is part of an Australian-based franchise that has 89 members in New Zealand. The ABC Learning Centre in Manurewa East, Auckland, is licensed for 100 children. Fees range from $175 per week for nursery to $145 per for pre-school. The centre has one staff member for every four children under the age of 2, and one staff member for every eight children over the age of 2.

30 Cook St
Auckland
Map p.484 E5

Howick Montessori Pre-School

09 533 0397 | *www.montessori.org.nz*

The name Montessori has not been trademarked, which means that any centre or school may call themselves 'Montessori'. For that reason it's worth checking the Montessori Foundation of New Zealand website, www.montessori.org.nz, to find out which pre-schools are part of the foundation. The Howick Montessori Pre-School in Auckland is a member of the foundation and ensures that the environment created is true to the movement's principles. Howick caters for children from two-and-a-half to 6 years of age. It's a relatively new pre-school, having opened only in 2004, and accommodates about 52 children. A growing number of the children stay on past their 5th birthday, while others move on to a local Montessori primary school.

Karori Childcare Centre

47 Beauchamp St
Wellington
Map p.498 A5

04 476 3621 | www.karorichildcare.org.nz

Karori Childcare Centre celebrated its 20th anniversary as a childcare facility in 2007. Managed by a parent committee, it provides an all-day education and care service for children aged from 9 months to 5 years, and accommodates up to 22 children. The centre is open from 07:00 to 17:45, Mondays to Fridays, for full or part-time care.

Kiwikids Nursery & Preschool

32 Annex Rd
Christchurch
Map p.508 B5

03 338 5179 | www.kiwikids.org.nz

Kiwikids is run by a married couple and has a relaxed, family feel. The centre is licensed to care for 12 children under the age of 2, and 32 over the age of 2. In the nursery, there's one staff member for every three children, while in the pre-school there's one staff member for every eight children. Fees are about $200 per week.

Roydvale Nursery & Preschool

139 Roydvale Av
Christchurch
Map p.508 A3

03 358 3000 | www.roydvalepreschool.co.nz

Roydvale's pre-school section sets out to provide a stimulating, creative environment with a strong emphasis on parental involvement. It is licensed to accommodate 30 children under the age of 5. The nursery section, which can accommodate 20 children, from infants to 2 year olds, has a warm, nurturing atmosphere. Roydvale is open from 07:30 to 17:30, Mondays to Fridays. Fees range from $27 for a morning, $38 for a full day, to $170 for a full week, and this includes hot meals, as well as morning and afternoon tea.

Primary & Secondary Schools

In New Zealand, children aged six to 16 must attend school. Most children actually start school when they are five. You don't need to wait until the beginning of a term or school year to start your child at school; most start on or very close to their fifth birthday. Schooling is free at state schools but parents are expected to meet some minor costs, including the cost of school books, stationery and uniforms. Costs vary widely depending on individual school requirements

Students are classified in year levels, beginning at Year 1 and moving up one class each year to the final Year 13. Years 1 to 3 are often referred to as 'primers' or 'juniors' and Years 4 to 6 as 'standards'. Years 7 and 8 are known as 'forms 1 and 2' and Years 9 to 13 as 'forms 3 to 7'. Class sizes are set by the school in accordance with Ministry of Education guidelines. Some junior classes may include children of different ages and year levels in the same classroom.

Students 16 years and over may choose not to finish their secondary education and leave in Year 11 or 12. By contrast, students can also attend school until the end of the year in which they reach 19 years of age, if they choose. State schools are co-educational at primary and intermediate level, although some schools have been experimenting with offering single-sex classes at intermediate levels because of concerns that boys learn better when they are not in the same class as girls. At secondary level, a single-sex

Strathmore Community School

Auckland Grammar School

education is available through the State but you may have to move into the right 'zone' to get it. If your child is not yet 16 but wants to leave school you can apply to the Ministry of Education for a special exemption and these are normally granted if your child is going onto work or another form of training.

A strong emphasis is placed on sport and physical activity at New Zealand schools and even in heavily built-up urban areas most schools have large playgrounds and sports fields.

Children must be enrolled at primary school by their sixth birthday. You can opt to home-school your children but you will still need to register with the Ministry of Education. Many schools have waiting lists so you should pre-enrol children before their fifth birthday. Depending on local options, children in their seventh and eighth years will either continue to attend primary school or move to a separate intermediate school till they are ready to start secondary school.

From age 12 or 13 through to 17 or 18 (Year 9 to Year 13), students attend secondary school (also known as high school or college). Students are usually grouped in form classes, but generally have different teachers and go to different classrooms for different subjects. Some secondary schools enrol students early and it is advisable to contact schools at least six months before the official enrolment date. The main qualification students work towards is the National Certificate in Educational Achievement.

In general, students need to obtain this to gain entry into university.

In rural areas, where there are only small numbers of school-aged children, it is common to find area or composite schools which combine primary, intermediate and secondary schooling in one location.

The Education Review Office monitors the performance of schools in New Zealand, auditing them at least once every three years. Copies of their reports are public and can be found on their website www.ero.govt.nz. You can search for schools by location. While this is a good place to start searching for a school for your child, also take the time to visit schools in your area and talk to other parents.

25 Mountain Rd
Epsom
Auckland
Map p.492 A3 16

Auckland Grammar School

09 623 5400 | *www.ags.school.nz*

Auckland Grammar School is a state secondary school for boys, and caters for students from Forms 3 to 7 (Years 9 to 13). Day students must reside in the 'grammar zone', but the school does also have a hostel that caters for 120 boys from outside Auckland. Students are expected to participate in sport and cultural activities. The school has a very strong academic record and places are highly sought-after.

Straven Rd
Christchurch
Map p.508 B5

Christchurch Boys High School

03 348 5003 | *www.chbs.school.nz*

Christchurch Boys' High School, founded in 1881, is a state school for boys, with a roll of approximately 1,350 students, and reputation for high academic achievement. The school boasts a modern library, a wide range of specialised laboratories, art studios, a music suite, technical workshops and four computer suites. The sports facilities include two gymnasiums, a weights training centre and an all-weather training pitch.

10 Matai St
Christchurch
Map p.510 B4 18

Christchurch Girls' High School

03 348 0849 | *www.chgirls.school.nz*

Christchurch Girls' High School, established in 1877, is the second oldest secondary school for girls in New Zealand. It is a modern and progressive school with a good academic and sporting reputation. Set in beautiful surroundings, the facilities include an art block, technology centre, drama room, music technology and practice rooms, computer centres and a gymnasium. A well-resourced library is the ideal place for students and staff to conduct research from books and the internet. The school has a roll of just over 1,000 students. There is an enrolment scheme in place and competition for out-of-zone placements is fierce.

Silver Rd
Epsom
Auckland
Map p.496 C1 19

Epsom Girls Grammar School

09 630 5963 | *www.eggs.school.nz*

Epsom Girls, opened in 1917, is now one of the largest secondary schools for girls in the country. It has a boarding house that accommodates around 120 girls from outside the Auckland area. Among the facilities are two gymnasiums, a dance room, six fully equipped IT rooms and a magnificent arts centre. The school offers a broad and balanced curriculum. Most students at the school go onto university or further tertiary education.

Golf Rd
Auckland
Map p.484 D6

King's College

09 276 0699 | *www.kingscollege.school.nz*

Considered one of the country's top schools, King's College in Auckland educates boys from Form 3 (Year 9) and girls from Form 6 (Year 12). It's a private school for both day students and boarders. There's a strong emphasis on academic, cultural and sporting achievement. King's College is one of a number of schools that offers an outdoor pursuits training camp where outdoor skills and, for those in Form 6, leadership qualities, are taught. Tuition fees are around $18,000 per year.

15 Dufferin St
Wellington
Map p.505 E4 21

Wellington College School

04 802 2320 | *www.wellington-college.school.nz*

Wellington College, a boys' school, was founded in 1867, and now has a maximum roll of 1,500 students, with a teaching staff of approximately 80 and a support team of around 20. In Years 9 to 11, English or ESOL (English as a second language), mathematics, science, social studies, physical education, design technology, music and health are compulsory subjects. Students may then select up to three additional subjects, with an emphasis on learning another language. Programmes in Years 12 and 13 offer a wide range of academic choices designed to prepare students for university and polytechnic studies.

Pipitea St
Wellington
Map p.501 D4 22

Welllington Girls College

04 427 5743 | *www.wellington-girls.school.nz*

Founded in 1883, Wellington Girls' College has about 1,200 students. The college is situated in Thorndon but its students come from all over the greater Wellington area. Students wear uniform in Years 9 to 12 but in Year 13 they wear mufti, or civvies. The New Zealand curriculum is taught and students are also encouraged to participate in cultural and sporting activities.

Polytechnics
New Zealand has 24 polytechnics, offering a wide range of academic, vocational and professional courses. As well as three and four-year degrees, polytechnics also offer short full-time and part-time courses.

University & Higher Education

The first university in New Zealand opened just over 130 years ago. Today there are seven universities and 24 polytechnics in the four main cities (Auckland, Wellington, Christchurch and Dunedin) and other provincial centres.

There are academic entrance requirements for all tertiary institutions. The National Certificate in Educational Achievement (NCEA) is the entry standard for university. To gain entry, students must achieve at least 42 credits at Level 3. Of these, 14 credits must be in mathematics at Level 1 or higher, and 8 in English or te reo Maori (4 in reading, 4 in writing). It is also possible to apply for discretionary entrance by achieving at least 80 credits at Level 2 in your best four subjects. Many universities require students to submit a recommendation from their school principal and some ask applicants to write a covering letter outlining their reasons for undertaking university study. These requirements are waived once you are 20 years old, however. Admittance to some courses, such as medicine and law, is keenly competitive and in these instances, only students with strong academic records are accepted.

Tertiary institutions are open to students who haven't attended school in New Zealand. Each university, polytechnic and college of education has its own entry requirements for students educated overseas and they will require a certain level of proficiency in English. However, many do offer intensive language programmes to prepare students for classes.

All universities offer general undergraduate and graduate degrees and diplomas in arts, sciences and commerce, as well as specialist degrees in particular disciplines. Undergraduate degrees such as a BA (Bachelor of Arts) or a BSc (Bachelor of Science) generally take three to four years to complete. Each university publishes an annual calendar detailing the courses scheduled during the academic year, as well as fees and entry requirements. These are held in the reference sections of most public libraries and can also be purchased from bookshops. Term dates vary between universities.

In general, tertiary institutions begin their academic year in February. Closing dates for applications vary so check with the institution concerned. For courses starting in February, it's advisable to apply by September of the previous year, particularly for more popular courses. Half-year courses generally begin in July. Application forms are available directly from each individual institution and sometimes an application fee of up to $150 will apply. Certified translations should be provided for all educational certificates in any language other than English.

University & Polytechnic Fees

Tertiary education is funded by a combination of government subsidies and student fees. Students who are permanent residents can access student loans and allowances to assist with fees and living costs (see www.workandincome.govt.nz). There is also a hardship grant for those already enrolled on a course but who have an urgent need for financial assistance.

Standard yearly fees are between $4,000 and $5,000. These figures are not based on the student's ability to pay. Fees can be paid via a training incentive allowance, scholarship or sponsorship.

Tertiary education institutions have been criticised recently for their high fees. It's also been pointed out that funding has not kept pace with costs or inflation. Some say this is the reason behind the skills shortages in the country, as graduating students head off for well-paying jobs in other countries to pay off their student loans. As a result of the criticism, education funding has come under review, and in 2006 the interest component on student loans was scrapped for students who remained in New Zealand.

Adult Education

Many secondary schools also run community classes in the evenings for adults wanting to acquire new skills. Details of these can often be found in the local community newspaper or by contacting the school directly. There are also several thousand private training providers in New Zealand, about 900 of whom are registered with the New Zealand Qualifications Authority. You can learn more about them by visiting www.nzqa.govt.nz.

Universities

Auckland University of Technology

Wellesley St
Auckland
Map p.488 A4 23

***0800 288 864** | www.aut.ac.nz*

Originally called the Auckland Institute of Technology, this place has been providing training in the trades for more than a century. In 1989 it became the first polytechnic in the country to offer degrees and masters courses, and now it has university status – making it New Zealand's latest university. Renamed the Auckland University of Technology, it specialises in health studies, tourism, engineering, communications and hotel management.

Lincoln University

Cnr Springs & Ellesmere Junction Rds
Christchurch
Map p.508 A6

***0800 101 610** | www.lincoln.ac.nz*

Lincoln University specialises in agriculture, horticulture and natural resource management. The campus is set in farmland about 20 minutes from Christchurch. Although it is one of the smallest universities in New Zealand, more than a third of its student population comes from overseas. With these international students representing more than 55 different countries, Lincoln is one of the most multicultural of the country's universities.

Massey University

Albany Expressway
Albany
Auckland
Map p.484 B3

***04 350 5599** | www.massey.ac.nz*

With campuses in Palmerston North, Auckland and Wellington, Massey is the only university in New Zealand that offers distance learning in a wide range of courses. Its specialisms include agriculture and horticulture, aviation studies, business studies, design, food technology, social sciences and veterinary science. The university has almost 40,000 students.

Otago University

Cumberland St
Dunedin
South Island Map G12

***03 479 7000** | www.otago.ac.nz*

The University of Otago excels in dentistry, law, medical laboratory science, medicine, physical education, physiotherapy, surveying and theology and has earned an international reputation for the quality of its research and teaching. It is the oldest university in New Zealand and today has around 17,000 students. Its campus is located in the heart of the city.

University of Auckland

Anzac Ave
Auckland
Map p.488 B3 27

***09 373 7999** | www.auckland.ac.nz*

Ranked among the top 50 universities in the world, the University of Auckland is also the largest university in New Zealand with around 40,000 students. It specialises in architecture, planning, engineering, medicine, optometry, the fine arts and law. The university is located in the centre of the city. It has a comprehensive website where potential students can find out more about its courses, facilities and extra-curricular activities.

Ilam Rd
Christchurch
Map p.508 B4

University of Canterbury

0800 827 748 | *www.canterbury.ac.nz*

The University of Canterbury is particularly well-known for its degrees in engineering, forestry, the fine arts, film and journalism. The university recently merged with the Christchurch College of Education and now provides training for pre-school, primary and secondary school teachers. The student body totals around 14,000.

Hillcrest Rd
Hamilton
North Island Map H8

University of Waikato

07 856 2889 | *www.waikato.ac.nz*

The University of Waikato's particular areas of expertise are law and Maori studies. Situated in Hamilton, in what is largely considered to be one of the most attractive settings among New Zealand's universities, it has a reputation for welcoming international students. Of the 15,000 enrolled students, more than 3,500 come from approximately 60 countries. The University of Waikato also has a number of older students – more than 40% are aged 25 years or older – and over half are women. Academic and general staff number some 1,300.

Kelburn Parade
Wellington
Map p.502 B4 30

Victoria University

04 472 1000 | *www.vuw.ac.nz*

The courses for which Victoria University in the capital is best-known include architecture, criminology, design, public administration, social work and law. Spread over several campuses in Wellington, the university has about 16,000 enrolled students and a staff of some 3,000. The Wellington College of Education merged with the university two years ago and, together with Massey University, Victoria has established the New Zealand School of Music (www.nzsm.ac.nz).

Special Needs Education

It is against the law for any education provider in New Zealand to discriminate against a student because they have a disability. Services for children and young people with special needs are provided by the Ministry of Education's Special Education Service. There are 28 special needs day schools in New Zealand, but many parents opt to 'mainstream' their children at local schools. A range of support is available to ensure that students with special needs can access the national curriculum. For example, all schools receive a grant called the special education grant (SEG) and can employ specially trained staff, called resource teachers.

Regional Health Schools provide a national service for students with greater health needs from bases in Auckland, Wellington and Christchurch. There are also two residential special schools (in Auckland and Christchurch, see below) to support students who have hearing impairments, and one to support students who are visually impaired. Teachers at these schools also provide support to pupils in local schools. Details of these and schools for students with other social needs, and entry criteria, can be found at www.minedu.govt.nz. Support agencies such as IHC (Interactive Health Communication) can also help you select a suitable school for your child. Visit its website at www.ihc.org.nz.

Special education offices in your area are listed under the Ministry of Education in the Government Phone Listings section at the front of the *Yellow Pages*.

131 Browns Rd
Manurewa East
Auckland
Map p.484 E7

Homai National School for the Blind and Vision Impaired

09 266 7109

Homai National School for the Blind and Vision Impaired is a co-educational special school and national resource centre. It provides teaching and support services to blind and visually impaired students, their families or whanau (kinsfolk) and staff at the schools that the students attend. The school has residential facilities and provides a range of on-site educational programmes for pre-school, primary and secondary aged pupils.

Maori language school

Truro St
Christchurch
Map p.508 F6

Van Asch Deaf Education Centre

03 326 6009 | *www.vanasch.school.nz*

This is a residential special school for hearing-impaired children. It also provides services and support for mainstream students and their teachers. Students are taught in small classes by qualified, experienced teachers. Programmes are based on individual education plans developed with input from the student and his or her family. Students can receive specialised one-to-one assistance with spoken language and literacy if they wish. The curriculum is delivered in sign language, signed supported English and oral and aural modes. In addition to the New Zealand Curriculum, students also have access to a local curriculum; programmes include deaf studies, literacy and speech and language. All classrooms are equipped with a range of computers, giving students access to excellent IT facilities.

488e Don Buck Rd
Takapuna
Auckland
Map p.484 C4

Westbridge Residential School

09 832 4918 | *www.westbridge.school.nz*

Westbridge Residential School is a co-educational special school for students whose ongoing behavioural, learning, emotional and social difficulties mean that their educational and social needs cannot be met in their local community. The school offers fixed-term residential learning and behaviour programmes for students from Years 3 to 8. It has room for 24 live-in pupils and eight in its day school. Class sizes range from four to eight children. The school's extensive grounds also include a gymnasium, bike track and obstacle course.

Learning English

Other options **Language Schools** p.320

There are plenty of options available to you if you need to brush up on your English skills – anything from one-on-one tutoring to a full-time English language course. There are hundreds of English language schools across the country from which to choose. Many schools also offer night-time English language courses, so you should be able to find one that suits your requirements. Your local polytechnic, university or schools are likely to be able to tell you which courses are available in your area. If you'd like to learn Maori, find a list of providers at www.tetaurawhiri.govt.nz.

Learning English		
The Campbell Institute	04 803 3434	www.campbell.ac.nz
Christchurch College of English	03 343 3790	www.ccel.co.nz
English New Zealand	09 379 3777	www.englishnewzealand.co.nz
Interlingua	09 523 3856	www.interlingua.co.nz
Kiwi English	09 309 0615	www.kiwienglish.co.nz

Transportation

Other options **Getting Around** p.43
Car p.47 **Driving Licence** p.71

With limited public transport networks in and between the main cities, the only option for many in New Zealand is to travel by car. Despite this, traffic is generally light, apart from in Auckland where the main highways become congested at peak hours and during holiday weekends (p.48).

If you're used to driving in the city, you will need to take care when using New Zealand's country roads; the varied weather, terrain and narrow secondary roads and bridges require motorists to be extra vigilant.

Roads are built to a high standard but the number of hilly, narrow and winding routes means that journeys may take longer than expected.

If you're unsure how long your journey will take, talk to a local – they will steer you in the right direction and tell you the best places to stop along the way. You will find multi-lane motorways and expressways on the approaches to the larger cities, with most roads being dual carriageways. Some cities, such as Christchurch, have a one-way street system in the centre, which can be confusing for first-time users.

Main roads are sealed and even those in rural locations are signposted, although at times haphazardly. Distances on road signs are given in kilometres. On the open road the speed limit is 100kph while in most urban areas it is 50kph. A special 40kph speed restriction operates outside some schools during the morning and afternoon, but these are normally very clearly signposted.

Driving Times

From **Auckland** to:
Christchurch:14hrs 20mins plus ferry crossing* from Wellington to Picton
Hamilton: 1hr 55mins
Wellington: 9hrs 20mins
Napier: 6hrs 30mins
Tauranga: 3hrs 20mins
Whangarei: 3hrs

From **Christchurch** to:
Auckland: 14hrs 20mins plus ferry crossing* from Picton to Wellington
Blenheim: 4hrs 35mins
Dunedin: 5hrs
Nelson: 6hrs 20mins
Picton: 5hrs
Queenstown: 7hrs 15mins
Wellington: 5hrs plus ferry crossing* from Picton to Wellington

From **Wellington** to:
Auckland: 9hrs 20mins
Christchurch: 5hrs plus ferry crossing from Wellington to Picton*
Hamilton: 7hr 20mins
Napier: 5hrs 10mins
Tauranga: 7hrs 35mins
Whangarei: 12hrs 15mins

*Ferry crossing time is normally 3hrs or 2hrs 15mins using The Lynx, a fast catamaran.

Drinking & Driving

In New Zealand it is illegal for adults aged over 20 to drive with more than 80 milligrams of alcohol for every 100mls of blood. If you are under 20 you shouldn't drink any alcohol before you drive; your limit is just 30 milligrams for every 100mls. Penalties for drink driving range from imprisonment and loss of licence to disqualification and fines.

Driving in New Zealand

New Zealanders love their cars. With 2.5 million cars for just over 4 million people, including children, the country's car ownership rate is one of the highest in the world. Kiwis enjoy the freedom of jumping into a car and heading out into the great outdoors (in New Zealand you're never more than two hours' drive from the coastline). Car prices, particularly for vehicles imported from Japan, are reasonable and the cost of petrol is cheaper than in some other parts of the world.

Cabs in the capital

Driving Habits

New Zealanders aren't the best drivers in the world, as the country's relatively high death toll from road crashes attests. In the UK, six people die for every 100,000 on the road. In New Zealand, 10 people die per 100,000. The extremes in weather can make driving conditions treacherous so you need to adjust your speed accordingly. New Zealanders have a reputation for being somewhat discourteous on the road and often forget to signal when they are changing lanes. Many accidents occur at intersections when drivers turning left forget to give way to those turning right.

Route Master
To get a full list of driving directions and distances throughout the country go to www.wises.co.nz or www.yellowpages.co.nz/maps.

Traffic Rules & Regulations

The maximum speed you can travel on New Zealand roads is 100kph. In urban areas the speed limit is normally 50kph. Police can issue instant fines for people caught travelling over the posted speed limit. Speed cameras are also sited on roads around the country so you may not be aware you've been caught speeding until an infringement notice arrives in the post. You will then have 28 working days in which to pay the fine. Some of the speed cameras are signposted but police also use mobile cameras hidden in the back of unmarked cars.

Parking

You will have to pay parking costs in the centre of most cities. Charges per hour can vary from $12 for covered off-street parking in Auckland to around $2 for on-street parking in the centre of Dunedin.

Accidents

All accidents that result in injury must be reported to the police. There is no requirement to report other accidents, although you might need to call the police if you and the other party involved cannot decide who is at fault for insurance purposes. In New Zealand, third-party insurance is not yet mandatory and many people, particularly youngsters, are driving vehicles that are uninsured. If you are hit by someone who is insured you should obtain their name, phone number, driving licence number, car registration number and their insurance company's details.

Pedestrians & Cyclists

A white diamond painted on the road means that there is a pedestrian crossing ahead. You must slow down and be ready to stop for pedestrians, regardless of what side of the road they are on (unless the crossing is divided by a raised traffic island, in which case you only need to stop for pedestrians on your side of the road). Watch out for pedestrians and cyclists at other busy places, such as at schools and bus stops, around parked cars, shopping malls and when you are turning into a driveway.

Petrol Stations

The price for a litre of petrol is around $1.55, so a gallon costs around $5.40. Prices do fluctuate though and the cost of petrol tends to be cheaper in cities than in rural areas, where there is less competition. Most petrol stations are self-service. The main suppliers are BP, Shell and Mobil. Many petrol stations also sell a basic range of groceries. Some have carwash facilities but you have to pay extra to use them.

Brooklyn Wind Turbine

Vehicle Leasing

If you're unsure how long you plan to be in the country, leasing a vehicle might be the best option. In New Zealand, leasing is a popular choice for self-employed people because the arrangement can be tax deductible. The lease price can include all maintenance and service costs, as well as Warrant of Fitness and registration fees (p.191). If not, you can opt to pay a lower monthly rental and cover the running costs yourself. Make sure you check the lease deal for any annual mileage limits and to see if you're responsible for insurance, and be aware that leaving the lease early will also mean extra fees.

A lease-to-buy arrangement gives you the option of buying the vehicle at the end of the contract. At the start of the lease you agree a residual price. This is the estimated market value of what the vehicle will be worth at the end of the contract. If you decide not to buy the vehicle at the end of the contract and the dealer can't get the agreed residual price you'll have to pay the difference. This happens quite often.

Company Cars

Normally only those in executive positions get company cars in New Zealand. If you are entitled to a company car it will be negotiated as part of your employment contract. Company cars are normally lease vehicles and restrictions may be placed on their use outside of working hours, for example you may not be able to take the car away when you are on holiday. If you would rather buy your own car haggle with your boss during your contract negotiations – you may be able to get a bit of extra money if you forego the perk of a company car.

Vehicle Leasing Agents

Autoselect	09 570 3933	www.autoselect.co.nz
Avon City Ford	03 348 4129	www.avoncityford.co.nz
Fleetsmart	0800 727 863	www.fleetsmart.co.nz
Lease Direct	03 366 9002	www.leasedirect.co.nz
Lease Plan NZ	0800 822 213	www.leaseplan.co.nz
MD Fleet Management	04 478 9690	na

Buying a Vehicle

New Zealand has one of the highest car ownership rates in the world and you won't have to go far to find a dealership. To get a feel for what is out there start your search online. Some websites you might find useful include www.turnersauctions.co.nz, www.trademe.co.nz and www.aacarfair.co.nz.

The classified ads in the country's main newspapers (www.nzherald.co.nz and www.stuff.co.nz) include numerous ads for new and used cars.

Once you've got an idea of the make and model you want you should check out the car fairs, yards or auctions. When you hit the car yards it is a good idea to take someone with you who knows a thing or two about motoring. They'll act as a second pair of eyes and allow you to concentrate on how the car feels to drive. Always insist on a test drive – include some speed driving and hill work so that you can really take the vehicle through its paces. Before you race off in your potential new motor, check that you will be covered by insurance should you have an accident.

If the car passes your vigorous road testing, there is still lots to check before you sign on the dotted line. Every vehicle in New Zealand sold by a dealer must have a Warrant of Fitness less than one month old. Private sellers have the option of selling without a warrant, but the car must be clearly identified for sale 'as is where is'. A dealer is required to attach to every motor vehicle displayed for sale a 'supplier information notice' (SIN).

Information that must be disclosed in the SIN includes:

- The name and business address of the dealer.
- Whether the dealer is a registered motor vehicle trader.
- The cash price of the vehicle.

- Whether any security interest is registered over the vehicle.
- The year in which the vehicle was manufactured (or the manufacturer's designated 'model year').
- The make, model, engine capacity and fuel type of the vehicle.
- The year in which the vehicle was first registered in New Zealand, or, if the vehicle was first registered overseas, the year of that first registration.
- The odometer (distance travelled) reading, or a statement that the odometer reading is or may be inaccurate.
- Whether the vehicle is recorded on the motor vehicle register as having been damaged when it was imported.

If you buy the car, you must be given a copy of the SIN.

New Car Dealers

Area	Name	Brands	Phone	Web
Auckland	Archibald & Shorter	Jaguar	09 917 9417	www.archibaldandshorter.com
Auckland	Giltrap City Toyota	Toyota	09 378 0261	www.gct.co.nz
Christchurch	Euromarque	Alfa Romeo & Fiat	0800 888 100	www.euromarque.co.nz
Christchurch	Christchurch BMW	BMW	03 363 7240	www.christchurchbmw.co.nz
Christchurch	Armstrong Motors	Chrysler, Jeep, Subaru	03 366 6939	www.armstrongmotorgroup.co.nz
Christchurch	Avon City Ford	Ford	03 348 4129	www.avoncityford.co.nz
Wellington	Team European	Audi & Porsche	04 384 8779	www.teameuropean.co.nz
Wellington	Honda Cars Wellington	Honda	04 385 9966	www.honda.co.nz
Wellington	Lexus NZ	Lexus	0800 453 987	www.lexus.co.nz

Before you buy, it normally pays to take the vehicle for an independent mechanical check. Some dealers may have already arranged a check of the vehicles they offer for sale. If you want to rely on this, make sure you know when the test was done, what was checked, who carried it out and what the results were. The Automobile Association (www.aa.co.nz) is often used to assess vehicles before purchase.

If you buy privately, be aware that your new car could be repossessed if there are any outstanding debts on it. Use a car history checking service to find out if the car is clear of debt. If you buy from a registered dealer, you won't be liable for any such debts, unless you were told about them.

The Certificate of Registration, which you should be shown, lists the current registered owner of a car. This should be the company or person – whether dealer or private – you are buying the car from. If you're in any doubt about the ownership of a vehicle, you can always call the police and check the vehicle is not listed as stolen.

If you're buying from a dealer, it must provide you with a written sale agreement and the SIN which you have signed. Don't sign an agreement until you have read and understood all the clauses, particularly those regarding interest rates and warranty costs. Also beware of documentation fees charged by the dealer.

Used Car Dealers

Name	Area		
Armstrong Peugot	Wellington	04 801 7222	www.armstrongpeugeot.co.nz
Buy Right Cars	Auckland	09 532 8010	www.buyrightcars.co.nz
City Cars Ltd	Auckland	09 360 4111	www.citycars.co.nz
Direct Import – Autos	Auckland	09 296 5477	na
El-Cheapo Cars	Wellington	04 570 2077	www.elcheapo.co.nz
King Toyota	Wellington	04 920 7770	www.king.toyota.co.nz
Lifestyle Vehicles	Various locations	09 295 0180	www.LifestyleVehicles.co.nz
The Clean Green Car Company	Various locations	0800 326 227	www.cleangreencar.co.nz
Turners Auction	Christchurch	03 343 9850	www.turnersauction.co.nz

Both the buyer and the seller have to fill out forms available from a Land Transport Safety Authority agent (such as New Zealand Post). The buyer pays the fee and is ultimately responsible for the changeover.
If you're selling privately, make sure the changeover has happened before you release the car; you don't want speeding or parking tickets turning up addressed to you.

Vehicle Finance

If you can't afford to buy a car outright there is no shortage of companies willing to offer you finance. While convenient, dealer finance is often expensive so you should shop around the banks as you will probably getter a better loan rate from them. As with any loan offer, check the time to repay, the monthly payments and the total cost of credit over the term of the loan. This information must, by law, be provided by all lending organisations so that you can compare the deals they offer.

Vehicle Finance		
AA Financial Services	0800 500 555	www.aa.co.nz
GE Money	0800 022 646	www.gemoney.co.nz
Marac	0800 262 722	www.marac.co.nz
MoneyMart Direct	0800 111 225	www.moneymartdirect.co.nz
UDC	0800 269 100	www.udc.co.nz

If a deal looks too good to be true, check that there are no extra hidden fees and that the asking price hasn't been inflated. Interest rates range from about 9.5% up to 15%, though this will vary depending on market conditions.

Vehicle Insurance

Vehicle insurance is not compulsory in New Zealand but it is advisable to at least have third-party insurance, as this provides cover against any damage you cause to someone else's vehicle in the event of an accident. It is the least expensive type of car insurance and the government plans to make it compulsory in the near future.

Vehicle Insurance		
AA Insurance	0800 500 213	www.aa.co.nz
AMI	0800 100 200	www.ami.co.nz
Tower	0800 808 808	www.tower.co.nz

A comprehensive car insurance policy covers you against accidental loss of, or damage to, your vehicle. It also covers you for any damage to other people's vehicles or property, whether it was your fault or someone else's, and for other costs such as salvaging your car from the accident scene and towing it to a garage. As well as the standard policy, companies offer a wide variety of options and benefits, such as free windscreen repair. As a general rule the more extensive the cover, the more expensive the policy. Insurance for young male drivers is priced at a premium as they are over-represented in accident statistics. You can get either cover for the market value of your vehicle or for an agreed value. Vehicle insurance is normally renewable every 12 months and premiums will be more expensive if your policy allows others, particularly teenagers, to drive the vehicle. If you are taking out a loan to finance purchase of the vehicle, banks may insist that you also take out insurance.

Registering a Vehicle

All vehicles must be registered before they can be legally driven in New Zealand. Vehicles can only be registered after they have been checked to ensure they are safe to be on the road and given a Warrant of Fitness (WoF). Approved garages and testing stations (WoF agents) carry out inspections. There are around 3,500 WoF agents in New Zealand. To find one near you, look in the *Yellow Pages*. Vehicles less than six years old must have WoF inspections every 12 months; all other vehicles must have them every six months.

Registration Service		
On Road New Zealand	04 495 2585	www.onroad.co.nz
The Automobile Association	0800 500 222	www.aa.co.nz
Vehicle Inspection NZ	0800 468 469	www.vinz.co.nz
Vehicle Testing NZ	04 495 2500	www.vtnz.co.nz

Vehicles must be re-registered every 12 months. If your car does not have a current registration certificate displayed on its windscreen you can be automatically fined $200. There is normally a grace period of one calendar month but some local authorities are more rigorous than others in enforcement. Registration costs about $180 for 12 months. You can register your car at all New Zealand Post shops and at WoF testing stations that act as agents for the Land Transport Safety Authority. You must produce proof that your car has a current Warrant of Fitness.

You will need to cancel your vehicle's registration if your vehicle is destroyed or rendered permanently useless, permanently removed from New Zealand roads, or written off by an insurer.

Traffic Fines & Offences

New Zealand's relatively high death toll on the roads has led police to take a tough stance on drivers who drive dangerously or flout the rules. If you are caught breaking the law, your punishment could range from an automatic fine to a prison sentence, depending on the severity of the breach. Common offences which could land you in trouble include:

- Driving at speeds in excess of the speed limit.
- Driving without an appropriate licence.
- Failing to produce a licence when stopped by police.
- Driving under the influence of alcohol or drugs.
- Driving an unregistered vehicle or a vehicle that does not have a current Warrant of Fitness.
- Driving dangerously.
- Failing to stop after a crash where someone has been injured or killed.
- Not wearing a seat belt.

Drivers and passengers must wear a seat belt in both the front and back seats. All children under the age of 5 must be properly restrained by an approved child restraint when travelling in cars or vans. Drivers must carry their driving licence with them at all times; if you get stopped by police and don't have your licence, you will receive an instant $200 fine.

Accident blackspots

Recovery Services/Towing (24 hour)	
AMI Assist	0800 100 200
Automobile Association	0800 500 222
Roadside SOS	0800 242 628
SOS Towing	0800 767 869
State Roadside Rescue	0800 101 112

Drink-driving is a serious offence in New Zealand. Third and subsequent offenders face maximum fines of $6,000, prison terms of up to two years, and a one-year minimum disqualification from driving. If you cause injury or death while drink-driving, you can be fined up to $10,000 for driving carelessly while under the influence (no breath or blood test is needed); and up to $20,000 where a breath or blood-alcohol test shows you were over the limit.

Speeding fines increase progressively from $30 for speeds less than 10kph over the limit, to a maximum fine of $630 for speeds up to 50kph over the limit. If your speed is more than 50kph over the limit you could be charged with careless, dangerous or reckless driving, and at more than 40kph above the speed limit you could also get a 28 day licence suspension.

There are strict rules covering tinted vehicle windows. The only overlays allowed on windscreens are anti-glare bands that extend no lower than the bottom of the sun visors. Windscreens must have a visible light transmittance of 70% or more. This will be checked as part of your Warrant of Fitness.

A full run-down of New Zealand's road rules can be found in the Road Code, which is available online at www.ltsa.govt.nz.

Wrecks in Peace

Finding a good resting place for your car can be tricky. Some local authorities in New Zealand provide car disposal yards for old wrecks – check with your local council. Otherwise your best bet is to look in the Yellow Pages *under 'recyclers of scrap metals' or 'scrap metal dealers'.*

Break downs

If your car breaks down on an isolated road you may have to wait some time for help to arrive. Most people in New Zealand carry mobile phones with them for such emergencies, but in some parts of the country coverage can be poor.

Check your car before you go on long trips and make sure you keep a close eye on the fuel gauge.

If it is dark and you break down in an isolated spot you may have to consider spending the night in your locked car. If possible, plan your travel so that you are not driving in remote areas at night. If you do break down, you'll have to decide whether it is safe to leave the car to call for assistance. If in doubt, stay put. If you don't feel that it's safe to leave and go for assistance, put your hazard lights on and raise the bonnet. Wait in your locked car until someone comes to your rescue.

Road authorities in New Zealand advise that on long trips you should carry bottled water and some emergency snacks just in case you do break down and face a long wait for help to arrive. This is definitely advisable in winter, when roads can quickly become impassable and you could find yourself stuck for a long time.

A number of motoring organisations and insurance companies offer nationwide 24 hour roadside assistance to their customers for an annual fee.

Traffic Accidents

Other options **Car** p.47

A love of cars, a propensity for violating traffic rules and some tricky road conditions adds up to lots of traffic accidents in New Zealand. It's not unusual to see white crosses on the side of the roads in memory of people who have been killed in crashes. More than 35,000 people have lost their lives on the roads since New Zealand's first known fatal crash in Christchurch in 1908. In 2006, 346 people were killed. Driving too fast for the conditions and drink-driving were the two biggest factors in those fatal crashes. Nearly a quarter of those killed in 2006 were not wearing seat belts.

Warning signs have been posted at some accident black spots to remind people of the dangers, but special care should always be taken at intersections and railway level crossings where accidents frequently occur.

Drivers in New Zealand aren't the most patient and incidents of road rage aren't uncommon. Most incidents are minor and simply involve impolite gesturing, but there have been occasions when road rage has led to serious violence. Be courteous on the road and avoid getting into confrontational situations with other road users.

Running repairs in Wellington

Demerit points are given for some traffic offences and for speeding infringements (except those recorded by a speed camera). If you get a total of 100 or more demerit points within any two-year period, you will be suspended from driving for three months. Failing to observe a give way sign will earn you 20 demerit points, breaching the conditions of your learner licence will earn you 25 points, while exceeding the speed limit by between 21kph and 30kph will earn you 35 demerit points. For a full list of offences and penalties check the New Zealand Road Code at www.ltsa.govt.nz.

Vehicle Repairs

The process for getting your car repaired after an accident will differ slightly depending on your insurance company. You should contact your insurer and report the accident as soon as possible. Most insurance companies will insist on getting photos of the damage to your vehicle before any repair work is done. Some may stipulate where you should take your car to be fixed but others will leave that choice up to you. If you are uncertain, ask the firm to recommend someone. If you were not at fault and the other party involved was insured the repairs should not cost you anything. However, if the accident was your fault you will have to pay the excess amount stipulated in your policy. You will also lose your no-claims bonus, which is likely to drive your premium cost up next time you renew.

For ongoing car maintenance and repairs, either take your car to your local neighbourhood garage or use the manufacturer's dealer. If your car is under warranty there will be strict rules about the servicing of the vehicle. Make sure you understand these before you drive the vehicle out of the sales yard or you could find your warranty isn't worth the paper it is written on.

Vehicle Repairs		
D E McMillan	Wellington	04 939 9243
European Vehicle Servicing	Auckland	09 444 9876
Kendal Vehicle Services	Christchurch	03 358 5381
Manukau Vehicle Servicing	Auckland	09 262 2783
Mount Eden Vehicle Care Centre	Auckland	09 638 6620
Team Hutchinson Ford	Christchurch	03 374 2620
Vehicle Repair Services	Auckland	09 525 2048

Exploring

Exploring

North Island

The North Island of New Zealand may be only two-thirds the size of its southern neighbour, but it's still home to three out of four Kiwis; a figure that is growing every year, especially in Auckland, the country's de facto economic capital. But despite having a population of more than three million, nobody is ever going to call the North Island crowded. After all, it is the 14th largest island on the planet, and no other North Island city has a population which comes close to the million-plus sprawl of Auckland. Even Wellington, the nation's capital, barely tops the 400,000 mark. Auckland is the country's most cosmopolitan and exciting city. It's New Zealand's essential business hub and the preferred destination for international shows and performers. And after working hard, Aucklanders love to take to the water or head to the beach and make the most of their maritime home on two harbours. At the opposite end of the island, formerly dowdy Wellington has been reborn with an innovative and arty spin. Some of the country's best bars and restaurants play host to locals fresh from the latest gallery opening or CD release party, and Peter Jackson's success with *The Lord of the Rings* trilogy has earned the city the nickname, 'Wellywood'.

More tourists head to the spectacular lakes and alpine landscapes of the South Island, but the North Island's other very livable provincial cities frame diverse regions with distinctive appeal for visitors. In Hawke's Bay, Napier and Hastings are the gateways to the region's winemaking diversity. Just further north-east, Gisborne is a relaxed surfing town, and, along the broad expanse of the Bay of Plenty, Tauranga is a 'let's move there' favourite for newcomers to New Zealand. Near the centre of the island, Rotorua, and to a lesser degree Taupo, are unashamed tourist hubs trading on their proximity to the incredible volcanic landscapes of the Central Plateau and Tongariro National Park. Along with the stunning coastal scenery of the Bay of Islands in the north, this is the region of the North Island which most people choose to visit.

The 'Middle Island'

In its history, the South Island also been known as the 'Middle Island' and (briefly) as 'New Munster'. It's colloquially referred to as 'the Mainland' by New Zealanders today, especially those who live there.

South Island

The South Island was known to the Maori as Te Wai Pounamu, which refers to the presence in its cold southern waterways of the highly prized greenstone (pounamu). It was the first part of New Zealand encountered by Europeans, sighted in December 1642 by the Dutch navigator Abel Tasman. It was left to the Englishman James Cook, in 1769, to prove that what Tasman had discovered was in fact the largest in a group of islands. Cook gave the South Island its present, rather prosaic, name.

For the first part of New Zealand's history, the South Island was, thanks to sealing and whaling, the nation's economic powerhouse. The major gold rushes from 1861 turned the trickle of immigration to a torrent and enriched many of the South Island's principal towns. If the 19th century was a boom time for the South Island, the 20th century was a period of stagnation. Today, the South Island's population is a sparse 900,000 – it's the most immediately conspicuous feature of the South Island's human geography, and one of the principal reasons most 'Mainlanders' give for living there.

But if the South Island is noted for anything in particular, it's for the range and spectacular beauty of its physical geography.

It's often said by foreign visitors that scenery exactly like every part of the South Island can be found elsewhere in the world, but nowhere else in the world can so many and varied natural attractions be seen in so small an area. You can appreciate the dramatic truth of this most effectively by taking a scenic flight, or by tramping through it and experiencing those contrasts first-hand. At its northern extremity, it features the drowned river valley system of the Marlborough Sounds, with their maze of sheltered waterways flanked, for the most part, by bush and inaccessible by road.

Arising just south of Nelson, the Southern Alps determine the character of much of the rest of the South Island. As their alternative name, the main divide, suggests, they delimit two starkly different landscapes. To the east, sheltered by the Alps from the prevailing westerlies, lie the arid plains of Marlborough, sustaining the largest and most prestigious wine-growing region in New Zealand.

Otago's provincial capital, Dunedin, is 'the Edinburgh of the south', a university town at heart, with little to give it much vitality when school's out for the 'scarfies'.

Beyond the Alps, the West Coast is a very different proposition. It hosts several local records for sustained rainfall, a fact that most visitors will find it easy to believe.

South Westland comprises some of the most scenic landforms in the world, and is a Unesco World Heritage area. It's the most sparsely populated region in New Zealand, and the deserted and scenic south coast is a rewarding destination for those seeking a refuge from crowds and commercialism. Taking this notion to extremes involves travelling across Foveaux Strait to the third of New Zealand's main islands, Stewart Island, where birds that are endangered elsewhere in the country practically outnumber the people.

The special character of some areas of the South Island – notably Golden Bay, Nelson and Central Otago – has sparked a sharp rise in property prices nationwide, and caused a mild panic among New Zealanders who fear they are becoming tenants in the most desirable parts of their own country. As for the rest, primary industry is still its backbone, and even the South Island's largest city, Christchurch, retains the flavour of the rural service town from which it grew. Change is overtaking the 'Mainland', but like the pace of life, it's doing it slowly.

Cape Reinga

Drive the East Cape p.236

Drive back in time along the Pacific Coast Highway (State Highway 35) from Te Kaha to Tologa Bay. Don't try to do it in record time, because the wonderfully windy road hugs the coast in many places. The predominantly Maori locals are usually in no hurry either, driving cars of ill-defined vintage or riding horses to get from bay to bay.

Auckland's West Coast p.218

Known locally as 'Westies', the proud folk of West Auckland are an independent and fun-loving bunch. It's all due to having a backyard that's fringed by dramatic surf beaches and criss-crossed with hiking trails in the rugged native bush landscapes of the Waitakere Ranges.

Ski the South Island p.265

With all due respect to the North Island's ski facilities, the South Island is the place to be with skis (or a snowboard) strapped to your feet, on or off piste. There are skifields everywhere and for the most part, they are wide open and varied in their terrain. New Zealand's best fields – Mount Hutt, Coronet Peak, Treble Cone and Cardrona – are all here, as is the country's only developed Nordic ski area in the Cardrona Valley.

Hawke's Bay Food & Wine Trails p.234

With plenty of sunshine and the country's most diverse soil types, the vineyards of Hawke's Bay are New Zealand's most versatile. The region's bordeaux-style red wines and oaky chardonnays are world renowned, but you'll also find excellent versions of other wine varietals.

Live Dangerously in Queenstown p.280

First it was whitewater rafting and bungee jumping, now there's any number of ways in the region you can look eternity in the eye without blinking – from jetboating and rafting to paragliding, skydiving, canyoning and riding the world's fastest survivable flying fox.

Waitomo Caves p.222

Locals claim that many caverns and underground cave systems at Waitomo are yet to be discovered. Until then enterprising folk keep devising increasingly exciting ways to explore the labyrinth of limestone and underwater rivers. Gentle subterranean strolling is allowed, but much more fun is had by floating on inner tubes, abseiling or sweeping through the inky darkness on a flying fox.

Visit Fox & Franz Josef Glaciers p.287

Seeing as they're a couple of the very few genuine glaciers in the world lying within easy view of the road and within a short walking distance of a carpark, it'd be an act of supreme ingratitude not to experience them, especially given how rare glaciers of any sort are predicted to become quite shortly. Get in while you can.

Whanganui River p.241

The 329km Whanganui River was once a main conduit of trade and transport for Maori and European settlers. Roads and rail diminished its importance, and now most river transport is canoeists and kayakers exploring its bush-lined and meandering course – all great ways to embark on a leisurely discovery of this scenic waterway.

Drive the Southern Scenic Route p.291

The best time to visit the places on the Southern Scenic Route is paradoxically the worst time. In winter, when it's cold as ice and there's no one about, you can appreciate the solitary splendour of the beautiful beaches, the rugged headlands, and the silent bush without distractions. Across Foveaux Strait, take a detour to Stewart Island – one of the nation's neglected gems, great for tramping and for fishing the way it used to be.

Rotorua p.227

The traditional tourist appeal of Rotorua is built on the considerable attractions of Maori culture and the steaming and bubbling energy of the region's volcanic terrain. Now 'Roto-Vegas' is an equal opportunity tourist town, and backpackers flock to test their mettle in an eclectic display of adventure sports activities. Somewhere in the middle are the Agrodome's highly entertaining performing sheep.

Bay of Islands p.208

There are nearly 150 islands in the Bay of Islands. After spending a few days in the Northland's most popular spot you may think there are almost as many ways in which to explore the region's endless array of bays. Cruise to the famed Hole in the Rock or drop anchor in a sailing ketch and explore hidden coves in a kayak.

Enjoy a South Island Wine Tasting tour p.300

So much wine, so little time. Sauvignon blanc in Marlborough, pinot noir in Waipara and Central Otago, chardonnay in Nelson – there's a star varietal in each region, and a whole bunch of pretenders. You can get around the vineyards yourself, but the best way to relax and enjoy is to join a tour and let someone else do the driving.

Visit the Chatham Islands p.269

Not even the national television weather forecast remembers that the Chathams are part of New Zealand. They're an outpost, and while similar to bits and pieces of the mainland, they're also different enough to let you feel you've travelled overseas. They're hardly a leisure spot – unless hunting or fishing are your chief pleasures –but you can hardly say you've seen all of New Zealand unless you've experienced the Chatham Islands hospitality and bleak charm.

Do a South Island Great Walk p.300

There are any number of superb tramping experiences, but a few are iconic: the Queen Charlotte Track in Marlborough, the Abel Tasman National Park in Nelson, the Heaphy and the Wangapeka in north Westland, the Rees-Dart, the Routeburn and the Milford tracks in south Westland and the Hump Ridge Track in Southland are all justly internationally famous.

Visit Farewell Spit & Bluff p.257 & p.289

There's an irresistible magnetism about the extremities of land masses, and the top and bottom respectively of the South Island are the long, sandy strand that is Farewell Spit, and Bluff, the windswept vantage from which you can contemplate the emptiness between yourself and Antarctica.

See Punakaiki (Pancake Rocks) p.284

Punakaiki is a unique landform, and one of the most photographed parts of the South Island: it looks like a whole bunch of flat, pancake-shaped rocks stacked where the Tasman Sea swell can hammer them – and it does. Standing at the observation point above the blowholes when the sea is really running is a lesson in the force of nature, and our place in it.

Hahei & Cathedral Cove p.225

With a combination of weather-aged limestone cliffs, native bush and white sand beaches, the area around Hahei and Cathedral Cove on the Coromandel Peninsula takes some beating. Most visitors opt for a balance of kayaking and walking. Don't miss the underwater snorkelling trail at Gemstone Bay.

Experience the South Island's Unique Wildlife p.222

There are whales in Kaikoura, and a number of points about the coastline where you might see hector's dolphins. There are penguins great (yellow-eyed, at Oamaru, Dunedin and Curio Bay in Southland) and small (little blues, at Oamaru). There's royal albatross at Taiaroa Head, Otago, kea in the high country, and white herons and kiwi at Okarito (and even more kiwi on Stewart Island), takahe at the Te Anau Wildlife Centre, and kakapo on Ulva Island.

Visit the Church of the Good Shepherd p.268

It often gets miscalled the Church of the Lonely Shepherd because of its location, stuck out on the shores of Lake Tekapo just before you cross the outlet and haul into the township on State Highway 8. There are many memorial churches dotting New Zealand's landscape, but it's hard to think offhand of another quite so pretty.

Pasifika p.60

Once you've settled into New Zealand, you owe it to yourself to explore the nearby nations of the South Pacific. But while you're saving up the airfare, let the Pacific come to you each March at Auckland's annual Pasifika festival. Two days of music and cultural performances and 150 different food stalls provide an excellent insight into Auckland's role as the world's biggest Polynesian city.

Hide in the Moeraki Boulders p.271

Like the Pancake Rocks, the Moeraki Boulders are a geological curiosity and a massive tourist drawcard. They don't look natural – and if they're not natural, they're a mystery. Everyone loves a mystery though, and it helps if the subject of the intrigue is located on a beautiful, secluded beach close to a fantastic restaurant. All that marveling and photography gives you an appetite.

Soak in Hanmer Springs p.259

Sure, the North Island has natural mineral hot springs. But does it have them way up in the mountains, where you can loll about in the water and look at the snow on the peaks, even on the ground about you? Hanmer has been beautifully developed to ensure that a soak is as much a therapeutic as a recreational experience.

Surf in Raglan p.221

The west coast surf town of Raglan has always drawn outsiders. Originally it was intrepid surfers drawn to the uniform and reliable waves of nearby Manu Bay and Whale Bay. Now the town's got a relaxed bohemian vibe, and you're likely to discover trendy galleries, cool little cafes and relaxation spas amid the aromas of suntan lotion and surf wax.

Switch off in Milford Sound p.292

The mountains rear straight out of the mirror-calm water, often shrouded in mist, and even more often with rain feeding hundreds of waterfalls. You can get a look at the undersea wonders at the observatory, and appreciate the Sound's beauty above the water on a cruise or by kayak, most likely escorted by dolphins as you go. There's nowhere quite like it on earth.

Tongariro National Park p.230

New Zealand's first national park was created in 1887 as a gift by the local Maori tribe to the nation. To experience the best of the park's rugged volcanic scenery, trek the Tongariro Crossing track. You'll complete it in around eight hours, but don't be surprised if the spectacular vistas have you quickly plotting a return visit to do a longer trek.

Te Papa, Museum of New Zealand p.245

New Zealand's national museum incorporates 36,000 square metres of innovative and state-of-the-art displays in a spectacular building on Wellington's waterfront. In English Te Papa translates to 'Our Place'. You should also regard it as 'your place' because there's no better place to fasttrack your understanding of New Zealand history and culture.

Bike the Central Otago Rail Trail p.275

You've been warned: the time to ride the 151km of level, well-graded track that skirts the great Maniototo Plain, full of light and history, is now, before the secret gets out. It's easy riding, and you can break up the pedaling with stops at some of the best little pubs in the South Island, either to stay, to have lunch, or just to refuel.

Tramp or Climb in Mount Cook National Park p.268

Mount Cook contains several of New Zealand's highest and most formidable peaks, including New Zealand's loftiest, Aoraki/Mount Cook. It's brilliant walking, climbing and tramping territory – even on the short walks, you're right in among the alpine environment, and can experience its unique silence, accentuated by the rattle of rockfall and the occasional distant boom of an avalanche.

North Island Overview Map

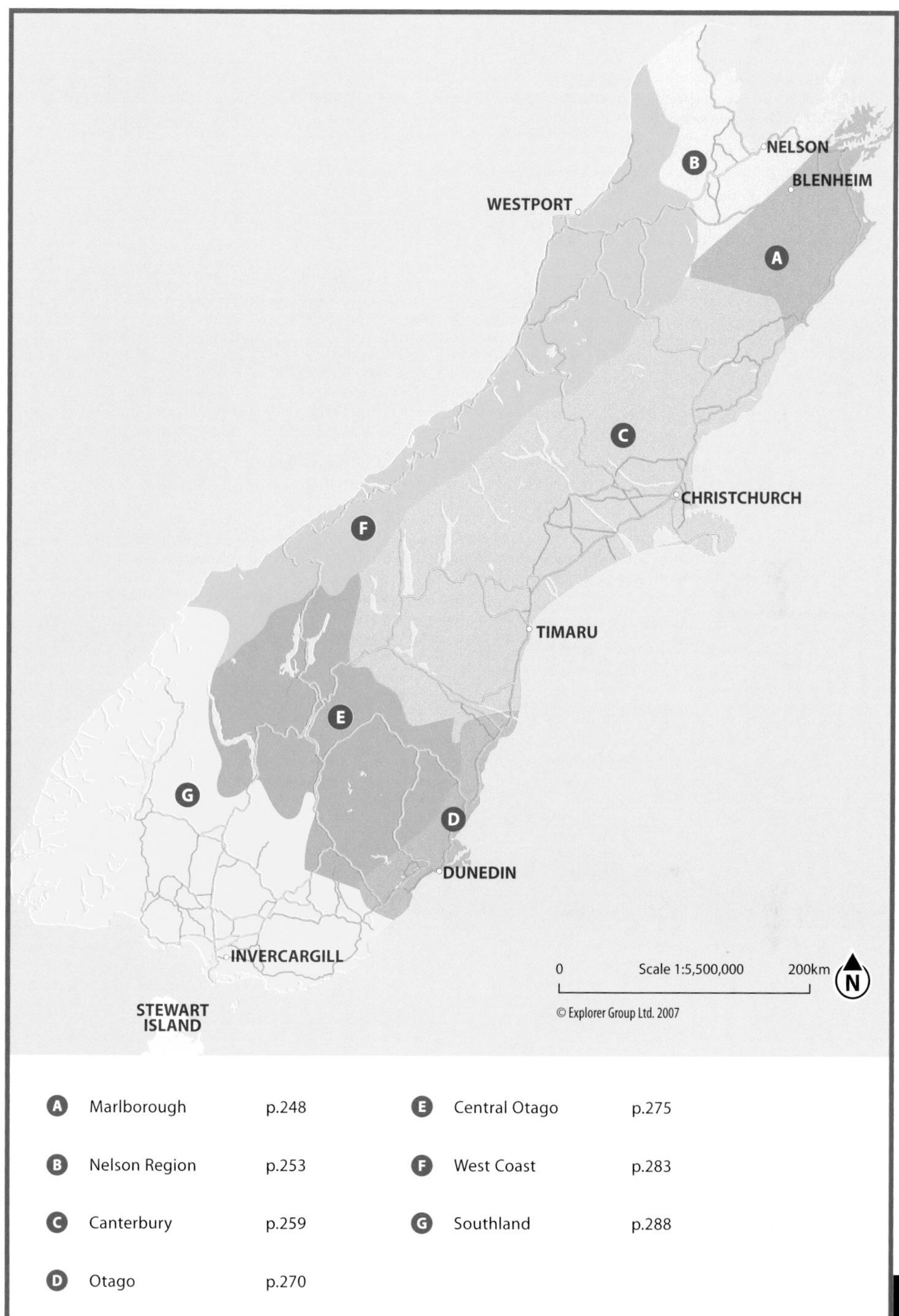
NELSON
BLENHEIM
WESTPORT
CHRISTCHURCH
TIMARU
DUNEDIN
INVERCARGILL
STEWART ISLAND
A
B
C
D
E
F
G
0
Scale 1:5,500,000
200km
N
© Explorer Group Ltd. 2007

On Tour
One of the best ways to get close to some of New Zealand's more remote natural attractions is with the help of a guided tour company (p.296).

At a Glance

The following pages are your invitation to explore the best of New Zealand. From the northernmost tip of the North Island to the edge of Stewart Island at the foot of the South, this chapter covers the country in all its glory. We've split the islands into easily digestible chunks, showcasing our authors' picks of the best things to see, do and savour along the way.

The North Island has been naturally divided into the following regions, also shown on the Overview Map on p.204: Northland, Auckland Region, Waikato & King Country, Coromandel, Bay of Plenty, East Coast & Hawke's Bay, Taranaki & Wanganui and Wellington Region.

The South Island comprises Marlborough, Nelson Region, Canterbury, Otago, Central Otago, West Coast and Southland.

Under each region we've included guides to the urban and rural areas that you'll want to visit, as well as a range of must dos; these cover the staggering variety of the country's natural attractions, as well as its most innovative and thought-provoking cultural draws.

Now that you live here you've got plenty of time to explore and discover every corner of New Zealand for yourself, but if you're in the mood for a specific secluded beach, a five-day tramp or a bungee jump in Queenstown, you'll find all the attractions listed by type below. Where relevant, all the places in the Exploring chapter have been given a map reference in order for you to easily locate the parks, galleries and heritage sites – those in the three major cities (Auckland, Wellington and Christchurch) can be found between p.484 and p.517. For the rest of the country, see the detailed pull-out map of the North and South Islands at the back of the book.

At a Glance

At a Glance

Area A p.204

Northland

Lowdown

Northland is called the 'Winterless North', and while that's a slight exaggeration there's nowhere else in New Zealand more likely to provide perfect beach weather. In the Bay of Islands there nearly 150 islands to choose from, so you should be lucky and find one you like.

Essentials

Historically hellraising Russell is now a seaside haven, and Kerikeri's heritage buildings bear witness to twin foundations of trade and rebellion.

With a sub-tropical climate that's (usually) warmer than the rest of the country, it should come as no surprise that New Zealand's earliest European settlers made their home in Northland. It was already densely settled by Maori though, and throughout the early decades of the 19th century the two races' co-existence was often tested.

Northland's Maori are still staunchly independent, and any visit to the region is bound to include exposure to their unique culture.

Ahipara

At modern New Zealand's birthplace, the Waitangi Treaty Grounds, proud local Maori now welcome visitors warmly to their marae (meeting place). The country's founding document, the Treaty of Waitangi, was signed here in 1840, and throughout this historic region there are many memories of the fledgling nation's development. Bearing witness to Northland's and New Zealand's development is stunning coastal scenery. The Bay of Islands is certainly visited the most, but 19th century trading hubs such as Kaipara and Hokianga Harbours are quieter and just as special. Compared with the bustling Bay of Islands, there aren't as many tour companies in these towns, but you can usually find a yacht, launch or kayak with which to explore hidden coves and bays. In the peaceful fishing port of Mangonui in Doubtless Bay, you can be sure your fish and chips at the Mangonui Fish Shop will be supremely fresh.

Further north, New Zealand narrows considerably, and the best way to approach Cape Reinga, the country's spiritual, windswept northernmost tip, is along the audacious sandy expanse of Ninety Mile Beach (p.211). OK, the beach is only 55 miles long, but after a few minutes of enveloping yourself in the scene of pounding surf and imposing sand dunes, you won't notice the difference.

North Island Map F3

Bay of Islands

The Bay of Islands is the crucible of New Zealand's history. In pre-European times, a pleasantly warm climate and the bay's rich bounty of seafood made it a popular settling place for Maori. Fast forward several centuries to the arrival of the first European settlers in the late 18th century, and the Bay of Islands witnessed the beginnings of European colonisation.

Read On

Find out more about the area and its offerings on www.bay-of-islands.co.nz.

In the 21st century, colonisers take the form of the steady streams of international tourists lured by the promise of boat trips around almost 150 islands. During summer it's a favourite refuge for holidaying Kiwis keen to discover their relaxed birthright with a spot of fishing, sailing or kayaking. Near the bustling tourist town of Paihia, Waitangi is where modern New Zealand was founded. Signed in 1840, the Treaty of Waitangi (p.4) still provokes healthy debate and controversy (p.13), and on Waitangi Day, every February 6, the people of New Zealand gather to recognise their country's past and future. Across the bay, Russell was briefly the capital of New Zealand, but is now a sleepy seaside village that comes alive every New Year's Eve for a legendary party.

North Island Map F3

Russell

The seaside village of Russell is a peaceful and relaxed spot, but in its early days in the 19th century it was known as the 'hellhole of the Pacific'. It was then a haven for whalers, convicts, sailors and prostitutes, and today's quiet tree-lined promenade was a hotbed of boozing and brawling. Originally known as Kororareka ('Sweet Penguin'), Russell is one of New Zealand's most historic settlements. For a brief period, from 1840 to 1841, it was actually the country's capital, and the early history of British and French settlers and eager missionaries keen to reform the rowdy locals is on display at the local museum (09 403 7701). Christ Church (the country's first church) was built here in 1836, and was where New Zealand was first declared a British colony. Along the waterfront is Pompallier House, which was built in 1842 by French Roman Catholic missionaries, and houses a printing factory. Once you tire of history and Russell's prim array of souvenir shops and cafes, walk 1.5km over the hill to nearby Long Beach. Visit www.russell.gen.nz before you visit the town itself to find out more and to book accommodation.

North Island Map F3

Paihia & Waitangi

Across the inner harbour from Russell, Paihia's array of motels, cafes, restaurants and tour operators encompasses everything the traveller needs. Two kilometres around the bay, New Zealand's early colonial history comes to life at Waitangi. In 1833, the country's first British resident, James Busby, established a home near the Waitangi River. Seven years later, the Treaty of Waitangi, which ceded authority of New Zealand to Britain, was signed by Queen Victoria's representative William Hobson and almost 50 Maori chiefs from around New Zealand. The Waitangi Visitor Centre and Treaty House (open daily from October to March, 09:00 to 18:00 and April to September from 09:00 to 17:00) includes an excellent 15 minute audiovisual presentation. Admission is $12. From October to April on Mondays, Wednesdays, Thursdays and Saturdays, a sound and light show (www.culturenorth.co.nz) takes place in the Treaty Ground's beautifully carved Maori meeting house. The two-hour show commences at 19:30 and costs $50. On February 6 every year, the Treaty Grounds are the location for commemorating Waitangi Day – New Zealand's national day.

North Island Map F3

Kerikeri

With two important heritage buildings, Kerikeri is one of New Zealand's most historic towns. On the Kerikeri Basin, the young country's oldest stone building and oldest wooden building sit side by side. The Stone Store was completed in 1836 and, in its early years, housed provisions for missionaries and ammunition for British garrisons fighting the local Maori chief Hone Heke. Now the store is an interesting museum showcasing the country's often turbulent early history. The nearby Mission House (also known as Kemp House) was built in 1821 and is New Zealand's oldest wooden building. It's the only structure that dates from the 'Musket Wars', a series of battles that pitted well-armed Maori tribes from Northland against each other in the early 19th century. The garden at Mission House has been continuously cultivated since 1820, and old-style preserves made from the garden's produce are for sale at the Stone Store. Both buildings (www.historic.org.nz) are open daily from 10:00 to 17:00 in the summer months, and from 10:00 to 16:00 the rest of the year. The combined admission fee is $7.50. For another informative look at local history take an hour-long cruise (09 407 9229, www.steamship.co.nz) up the Kerikeri Inlet on the compact *Eliza Hobson* steamboat. Tickets are $30 for adults and $15 for children.

Boat Trips

Explorer Captain James Cook was somewhat lacking in imagination when he coined the name the Bay of Islands, but with almost 150 islands you really can't blame him for stating the obvious. Walking along Paihia's waterfront you might think there are as many boat companies offering to help you explore the bay. The main firm is Fullers

Waitangi Day
You'll find more details about the events for the day, and information on the town and its history at www.waitangi.net.nz

(09 402 7421, www.fboi.co.nz), which operates the popular Cream Trip that traces the original journey supply boats took to pick up milk and cream from dairy farms around the area. Other popular destinations include Cape Brett and the nearby Hole in a Rock, a giant rock arch which the boats will go through if weather conditions are suitable. King's Tours & Cruises (09 402 8288, www.kings-tours.co.nz) runs similar trips, and if you want to combine thrills with your sightseeing, the Excitor (www.excitor.co.nz) and Mack Attack (09 402 8180, www.mackattack.c.nz) can zip you around the bay in high-speed jetboats.

Diving

On 10 July 1985, while preparing to set sail for a protest against nuclear testing at French Polynesia's Mururoa Atoll, Greenpeace's flagship Rainbow Warrior was bombed and sunk by French government agents. The sabotaged boat has been sunk off Matauri Bay (www.matauribay.co.nz) in memory of the crew member and photographer Fernando Pereira who drowned as a result of the explosion. This is now a popular dive site where, at a depth of around 25m, the visibility is typically up to 30m. Diving around the skeletal remains of the former protest boat is an eerie experience, especially when moray eels are sighted in its nooks and crannies. There are also other popular Northland dive sites, such as the nearby Cavalli Islands. Paihia Dive (09 402 7551, www.divenz.com) arranges dive trips to the wreck of the Rainbow Warrior. A single dive including gear hire costs $199.

Dolphin Swimming

It's not only bottlenose and common dolphins that you'll see in the waters of the Bay of Islands: other marine mammals also occasionally sighted include orca and minke whales. Because the water is relatively warm, trips run all year round, and while tour operators don't guarantee you'll see dolphins or whales, they'll take you out for free on another day if the marine mammals don't show. Wetsuits and snorkelling gear are provided so that you can swim with the amazing creatures, and operators donate part of the cost to the Department of Conservation for marine mammal research. Note that if dolphins are feeding or have younger dolphins with them (something that can happen year round), swimming is not allowed. The two main operators are Dolphin Discoveries (09 402 8234, www.dolphinz.co.nz) and Dolphin Adventures (09 402 7421, www.fboi.co.nz). Most trips run for three to four hours and cost $105 for adults and $60 for children.

Sailing & Sea Kayaking

The best way to experience peace and solitude in the Bay of Islands is to switch the motor off. Sailing around the bay is popular because the leisurely trips usually include other activities such as sunbathing, snorkelling and kayaking.

The most impressive boat is the *R Tucker Thompson* (09 402 8430, www.tucker.co.nz), a beautiful 26m long schooner with 179 sq m of billowing sails. Day sailings include a barbecue lunch and cost $120 for adults and $60 for children.

Carino (09 402 8040, www.sailingdolphins.co.nz) combines sailing on a catamaran and swimming with dolphins. Its six-hour trips include an onboard barbecue and cost $90 for adults and $50 for children. Carino's two-hour sunset sail around the inner harbour includes wine and cheese and is a relaxing way to end the day.

Ecocruz (www.ecocruz.co.nz, see p.298) offers longer three-day trips that include kayaking around deserted coves and islands. But if it's kayaking alone that you want, Coastal Kayakers (www.coastlkayakers.co.nz, see p.297) have trips from half a day to two days in length.

North Island Map G3

Tutukaka & the Poor Knights

Diving and big game fishing are the two main drawcards for visitors to Tutukaka (www.discovertutukaka.co.nz). Just 25km off the coast, the Poor Knights Island Marine Reserve has New Zealand's biggest diversity of underwater species. Because run-off from the islands is minimal, the water is exceptionally clear and you'll find visibility of up to 30m. The highlight is a series of vertical rock faces teeming with sub-tropical species, some of which are unique to the Poor Knights. The underwater bluffs descend to 100m and are punctuated with a network of caverns and arches. The rich waters of the Poor Knights are also a favourite refuelling spot for migrating whales, including the massive humpback and blue whale. The reserve features two wrecks that have been deliberately sunk, and the former naval ships Tui and Waikato now have new purposes as artificial reefs. Diving trips can be arranged through Poor Knights Divers (09 434 4678, www.pkdive.co.nz).

Fishing is not allowed within one nautical mile (1.8km) of the reserve, but outside the perimeter sport-fishing species such as shark, marlin and tuna are fair game. However, the biggest game in Tutukaka is afternoon drinks at the Deep Sea Anglers Club (09 4343 818, www.sportfishing.co.nz) when the boats dock at the Tutukaka Marina to weigh the day's catch. The friendly fisherfolk at the club can also arrange trips to catch your own big game.

North Island Map D3

Ahipara & Ninety Mile Beach

The friendly coastal community of Ahipara is the gateway for trips along the impossibly straight stretch of sand that is Ninety Mile Beach. The beach is actually only 55 miles (88km), but a journey along its straight expanse is never the less an essential Kiwi experience. The beach was the landing point for the earliest Australia-New Zealand airmail services, and even now it's an official part of the New Zealand State Highway network (although most rental car companies forbid you to drive on the sand). Major tour companies advertise bus trips from the Bay of Islands and other, more eclectic forms of transport are also on offer. Harrison's Cape Runner (ahipara.co.nz/caperunner/) runs half-day trips in robust four-wheel drive Unimogs that take on the giant sand dunes and win, and also include a spot of sandboarding and sand toboganning. Ahipara (www.ahipara.co.nz) is growing as an adventure sports hub, and the quiet town features everything from quad bike riding to blokarting, racing along the sand in a personal land yacht.

North Island Map C1

Cape Reinga

At the end of Ninety Mile Beach, Cape Reinga is the northernmost point of New Zealand. The nation's capital, Wellington, gets a hard time for its windiness, but the exposed headland of Cape Reinga is usually wilder and windier than Wellington. A lighthouse stands sentinel as the Pacific Ocean and the Tasman Sea swirl together, and an iconic New Zealand road sign measures the distances to the world's great capitals. Cape Reinga has spiritual significance for local Maori. An 800 year old pohutukawa tree marks the spot known to Maori as Te Rerenga Wairua – 'the leaping place of the spirits'. According to Maori mythology, this is where the souls of the dead complete their time on earth before journeying across the sea to the ancestral Polynesian homeland of Hawaiki. You can read more about the area on wwww.topofnz.co.nz.

East of Cape Reinga, the gentle seven-kilometre curve of Spirits Bay is New Zealand's northernmost beach.

Motuopao Island

Area B p.204

Auckland Region

Lowdown

The past home of yachting's prestigious America's Cup has the planet's highest incidence of private boat ownership. Your friendly neighbour could be your passport to exploring the Hauraki Gulf.

Essentials

Head west for a trio of ultimate Auckland experiences: start the day with a brisk bush walk in the Waitakere Ranges, refresh in the surf at Piha, and end the day sampling excellent wine.

Aucklanders are often accused of not caring about what happens 'south of the Bombay Hills', the natural division between Auckland and the rest of the country. But when you're living in a cosmopolitan metropolis built on two expansive harbours, overlooking the rest of New Zealand is understandable. One in four New Zealanders live in the 'City of Sails', named after Aucklanders' love affair with boating.

It's not the official capital, but the country's economic powerhouse is more important to New Zealand than some of the people in the provinces often accept. Most newcomers to the country arrive in Auckland, and many are perfectly happy to settle there. Nowhere else in New Zealand is there such a cosmopolitan mix of cultures and nationalities, and nowhere else in the country is as tolerant and forgiving of people's differences.

Framed by Waitemata and Manukau harbours, the ocean is important to the million-plus people living on Auckland's sprawling isthmus. The rugged beaches of the west coast, the islands of the Hauraki Gulf, and the waterfront bars and restaurants of Viaduct Harbour (p.217) are all good reasons to enjoy a relaxed and easygoing lifestyle. And when they tire of swimming, surfing or just mucking around in boats, residents enjoy a busy calendar of concerts, sports events and festivals.

More personal pleasures include the most diverse restaurant scene in the country, either in central suburbs such as Kingsland, Ponsonby and Parnell, or in more distant neighbourhoods where New Zealand's proximity to Asia is made deliciously real. And while most Aucklanders are happy with a few chilled beers and a barbecue, the region's vineyards in West Auckland, Matakana (p.218) and Waiheke Island produce some great alternatives. Maybe Aucklanders should care more about the rest of New Zealand, but can you really blame them for being a little short-sighted?

Map p.484

Auckland & Around

Map p.484 D4

Devonport

Just 15 minutes by ferry from downtown Auckland, the charming seaside suburb of Devonport is an excellent daytrip if your idea of a good time includes exploring eclectic second-hand bookshops, poking around arts and craft galleries, and having to choose between fish and chips on the beach or lunch in a cosy cafe. Devonport was one of the first areas to be settled in Auckland, and Victorian and Edwardian heritage buildings still line its main street, Victoria Road. On summer weekends the streets and beaches are busy with tourists and locals, but most head back to the CBD on an afternoon ferry. It's definitely worth missing the ferry if your idea of a good time also includes a few drinks in friendly pubs, and watching the lights of downtown Auckland from a quaint Devonport bed and breakfast.

'The Shore'

The short ferry ride from Viaduct Harbour to the North Shore takes you to some of the city's most-sought after suburbs, not to mention many of its most popular beaches, including arguably the city's best at Takapuna. For more information on Devonport and its neighbours, see p.107.

North Island Map H5

Great Barrier Island

If Auckland's nearest island neighbour Waiheke is inching towards gentrification, Great Barrier Island remains a rugged and remote rebel. You're only 88km from the mainland, but landing here by ferry or by plane is like stepping back a couple of decades. A lack of banks and streetlights – and patchy mobile phone coverage – forces visitors to relax at all costs. Nightlife is limited to the local boat club or a single Irish pub, but that's not really a problem. After a day hiking on more than 100km of well-maintained tracks, or mountain biking, partying will be the last thing on your mind. And despite Great Barrier's relative isolation, you can expect to sleep in surprisingly sophisticated accommodation.

One Tree Hill

Beach at Manukau

Auckland Domain

Albert Park

St Heliers Bay

North Island Map G6

Waiheke Island

Waiheke is the most populous island in Auckland's Hauraki Gulf, and while its traditional population of creative types is being infiltrated by richer newcomers building flash clifftop houses, it's still a unique haven worth at least a day of your time. Parts of the formerly sleepy island are now almost suburbs of Auckland, but the 35 minute ferry ride ensures that even the most stressed of commuters switch off well before docking at Waiheke's Matiatia Wharf. Traditionally Aucklanders flocked to the rolling landscape of Waiheke to swim in its picturesque coves, hike through the island's forests or along its ragged coastline. Now the appeal is more leisurely. More than 30 wineries dot the island, many complete with excellent restaurants. Every February the island's energy levels are revved up with the Waiheke Wine Festival (www.waiheke wine.co.nz), and a couple of months later the Easter Jazz Festival (www.waiheke jazz.co.nz) draws performers from around the world, and visitors from around New Zealand. Among the best accommodation is the Boatshed (p.36).

Read More
To keep an eye on what's happening on the island, visit www.touris mwaiheke.co.nz.

Cnr Wellesley St & Lorne St
Auckland
Map p.488 A3 **1**

Auckland Art Gallery

09 307 7700 | *www.aucklandartgallery.govt.nz*

New Zealand's first permanent art collection, the Auckland Art Gallery opened in 1888 but is still keeping pace with the times. Built in French chateau-style, the Main Gallery was closed for redevelopment in late 2006. When it opens again in 2010, exhibition space will be increased by 50%, and the building will integrate better with nearby Albert Park. In the interim, many of the gallery's 12,500 works are on display in the New Gallery, including the renowned photo-realistic paintings of 19th century Maori by CF Goldie and Gottfried Lindauer. Open daily from 10:00 to 17:00. Admission is adults $7, and concessions $5. Children under 5 enter for free.

Various Locations

Auckland Farmers' Markets

Whether it's an impromptu barbecue with friends and family, or a seafood meal at Viaduct Harbour, eating well is an essential part of the Auckland lifestyle. Growing in popularity across recent years, Auckland's farmers' markets provide locals with convenient access to tasty, healthy produce and gourmet foods from across the wider Auckland region. The City Farmers' Market (www.cityfarmersmarket.co.nz) is located in the re-energised Britomart Precinct near the wharves, and every Saturday from 08:30 to 13:30 it's a good place to pick up artisan breads, organic fruit and specialty meats. A similar market is held on Sundays from 09:00 to 13:00 in the seaside suburb of Devonport (www.devonportfarmers market.co.nz). La Cigale's is Auckland's longest running farmers' market, and it has a distinct French ambience. Organised by Parnell cafe, La Cigale

Auckland Art Gallery

(www.lacigale.co.nz) is an eclectic collection of stallholders offering everything from freshly baked Turkish bread to hand-made cheeses and Breton crepes. Arrive with an appetite; even if you don't buy anything there are loads of tasty samples on offer. La Cigale's French Farmers' Market operates every Saturday from 08:00 to 13:00, and there's a smaller mid-week market on Wednesdays from 12:30 to 18:30.

Domain Rd
Auckland
Map p.492 C1 3

Auckland Museum

09 309 0443 | *www.aucklandmuseum.co.nz*

With an imposing location atop a hill in the expansive and green Auckland Domain, the Auckland Museum can easily fill a visitor's morning or afternoon. Constructed in Greek Revival style, the hushed interiors contain an excellent Maori collection, including an 85m long Maori waka (war canoe) carved from a single log. The ground floor also contains a diverse collection of artefacts from all over the South Pacific, reflecting Auckland's role as the world's biggest Polynesian city. Natural history is the focus on the first floor with interactive and child-friendly displays of the seas surrounding New Zealand, and the country's turbulent volcanic beginnings. Don't miss the skeleton of the extinct moa, New Zealand's giant, flightless bird. On the top floor, the poignant Scars of the Heart traces the history of New Zealanders at war from the 19th to the 21st century. Open daily, 10:00 to 17:00. Admission is by donation ($5 is the suggested amount).

Greenlane Rd and Manukau Rd
Auckland
Map p.484 C6

Cornwall Park and One Tree Hill

09 630 8485 | *www.cornwallpark.co.nz*

The extinct volcanic cone of One Tree Hill (Maungakiekie) was once a terraced marae that housed 5,000 people, but now it's a prime viewing spot that overlooks Auckland's energetic urban sprawl. Adjoining the One Tree Hill Domain is Cornwall Park, which comes alive on summer weekends with immigrants from many countries enjoying picnics and barbecues. And while relaxation is on the minds of some, others walk, run or cycle around the park's oak-lined roads and paths. Cornwall Park was gifted to the people of Auckland in 1901 by the 'Father of Auckland', Sir John Logan Campbell, and it's still a working farm with cattle and sheep grazing its 81 hectares. Visit during spring and your leisurely stroll will be perfected with the sight of scores of newborn

Auckland Museum

lambs bouncing across the park's spacious pastures. Acacia Cottage (located in the heart of the park) is Auckland's oldest building and was Logan Campbell's home from 1841. Cornwall Park is open from 07:00 until dusk and admission is free.

23 Tamaki Dr
Orakei
Auckland
Map p.484 D5

Kelly Tarlton's Antarctic Encounter & Underwater World

0800 805 050 | *www.kellytarltons.co.nz*

Perspex walk-through tunnels have now become commonplace in aquariums around the world, but the unique system was first used here. Treasure hunter Kelly Tarlton transformed obsolete sewage tanks into a 120m cavalcade full of sharks, stingrays, moray eels and more than 40 other species of fish. Brave types can even sign up for a swim with the sharks and stingrays. Kelly Tarlton's newest unique attraction is the Antarctic Encounter, where you're transported in a heated snowmobile through an icy landscape that's home to a colony of curious king and gentoo penguins. While you may find this all totally alien, they're feeling right at home because the zero degree environment is built to replicate that of their homeland, night and day, each season, even down to the biting Antarctic winds. Open daily from 09:00 to 18:00. Entrance for adults is $28 and children, $14.

Newbury Lane
Auckland
Map p.484 D6

Otara Market

Auckland's ethnic diversity is changing faster than anywhere else in New Zealand. By 2016 it's projected that a third of the city's population will be of Asian descent, and less than 50% of Aucklanders will be of European stock. The future of the city is best experienced at Otara Market in south Auckland. Every Saturday morning from 06:00 the market brings the Pacific Islands to the city. Get there for an early breakfast of organic coffee and still-warm Polynesian coconut buns before exploring the cultural mosaic that is the market. Delicate Maori bone carvings, traditional food, and Middle Eastern rugs compete for your attention with paper-thin tapa panels made from the bark of mulberry trees. Chinese and Korean stallholders sell shiny eggplants and spindly okra to shoppers wearing Muslim headscarves or Sikh turbans. A constant soundtrack of eclectic Pacific beats keeps the commerce ticking over nicely, with CDs featuring Maori reggae, Samoan hip-hop and Rarotongan steel guitar music all on sale. It's a great celebration of a city that welcomes new residents from many different cultures and countries.

Cnr Federal St & Victoria St
Auckland
Map p.487 F3 7

Sky Tower

09 363 6400 | *www.skycityauckland.co.nz*

When the Sky Tower was first built in 1997, more than a few Aucklanders were not thrilled with the ostentatious 328m addition to the city's skyline. Now the southern hemisphere's tallest tower is a proud symbol of the country's biggest and brashest city, and most Aucklanders would miss it if it was gone. If you're trying to imagine Auckland's geography including two harbours and multiple extinct volcanic cones, the view from the main observation deck is a good place to start. If that's not high enough, ascend another 34m to the Sky Deck to make the most of the views stretching up to 80km into the distance. After dining at the revolving restaurant, Orbit, most visitors catch the lift down again, but a few brave types take the plunge with the Sky Jump (www.skyjump.co.nz), a thrilling bungee jump from 192m. Open Sundays to Thursdays, 8:30 to 22:30 and until 23:30 on Fridays and Saturdays. Adults pay $25, children $8.

91 Small Rd
Auckland
Map p.484 1B

Snowplanet

09 427 0044 | *www.snowplanet.co.nz*

Auckland's weather can be changeable, but no one expects snow on Mount Eden or One Tree Hill any time soon. Snowplanet is the convenient alternative to a five-hour drive to Mount Ruapehu's ski slopes, and the indoor ski slope has snow 365 days of the year. Inside, the temperature is a chilly -5°C, so you'll to need to come well wrapped up. You can hire ski gear and equipment if you don't have your own and, if you're a novice, the Snowplanet Academy can teach you some basic downhill skills before you venture on to the real thing. On Friday nights a DJ rocks the icy slopes from 19:00 to 22:00, and on Saturday nights the attached Mountain View Cafe & Bar makes for a particularly social apres-ski scene. Open daily, 10:00 to 22:00. Day passes costs $49 for adults and $44 for children. Family discounts and annual passes are also available.

Various Locations

Tamaki Drive

Stretching eastwards from central Auckland to St Heliers, scenic Tamaki Drive is fringed by the spectacular Waitemata Harbour as it wends its ways to the city's swankiest suburbs. It's a 10km stretch from the city to St Heliers, a journey that's popular with runners, rollerbladers and cyclists. Every March more than 70,000 participants run and walk the tree-lined esplanade in the annual Round the Bays Fun Run (www.roundthebays.co.nz). A more leisurely journey around Tamaki Drive involves a beach-side barbecue and a swim at pretty Okahu Bay. There are more than 20 bars and restaurants at energetic Mission Bay (www.missionbay.co.nz), or if it's peace and quiet you're after, try the delightful village-by-the-sea ambience of St Heliers. In summer, Auckland's oceanfront showcase comes alive with swimmers and picnickers, and events such as the Mission Bay Jazz & Blues Streetfest (www.jazz andbluesstreetfest.com). Between Okahu Bay and Mission Bay, Bastion Point provides excellent views of the islands of the Hauraki Gulf.

Hobson Wharf & Quay St
Auckland
Map p.488 A1 **10**

Viaduct Harbour

www.viaduct.co.nz

Auckland's central waterfront used to be a scruffy wasteland, but after New Zealand won yachting's America's Cup in 1995, the area was transformed into a ritzy enclave of restaurants, bars, super yachts and luxury apartments. The Viaduct can be tourist-central, but the array of squares and promenades is also very popular with locals, especially those keen on celebrating in a big way on a Friday or Saturday night. Lunch in the summer sun is also a popular form of relaxation, Auckland style. If you get the yachting bug, Sail NZ (09 359 5987, www.sailnz.co.nz) runs harbour races in a couple of the boats actually used in the 1995 America's Cup. Don't worry if you can't tell the difference between a spinnaker and a mainsail, because the match racing is designed for total landlubbers. After the race, visit the National Maritime Museum (09 373 0800 www.nzmaritime.org.nz) to further understand the City of Sails' heartfelt connection with the sea.

Various Locations

West Auckland Wine Trail

West Auckland's wine industry began in the early 20th century with settlers who originated from the Dalmatian coast in present-day Croatia. The vineyards around Kumeu and Henderson still feature names such as Babich and Brajkovich. In typical New Zealand style most of the wineries also feature excellent restaurants where you can partner the luscious results of previous vintages with good food. The Hunting Lodge restaurant at Matua Valley (09 411 8301, www.matua.co.nz) has the uncanny ability to be equally enjoyable for a formal dinner or a leisurely lunch, and Soljans (09 412 5858, www.soljans.co.nz) is perfect for Sunday brunch. All the West Auckland wineries produce excellent wines, but the chardonnay produced by Michael Brajkovich at Kumeu River (09 412 8415, www.kumeuriver.co.nz) is rated exceptionally highly internationally. For an overview of the area's wine offerings, visit www.kumeuwinecountry.co.nz.

North Island Map F6

West Coast Beaches

The rugged beaches of the West Coast are a favourite escape for busy Aucklanders. Karekare (www.karekare.org.nz) is fringed by steep, dramatic cliffs, and was where the opening scenes of Jane Campion's *The Piano* were filmed. Further north, popular Piha (www.piha.co.nz) is punctuated by the distinctive Lion Rock, and is a year-round magnet for keen and hardy surfers. Te Henga or Bethell's Beach (www.bethells beach.com) is reached after a brisk stroll through undulating dunes, and when you've tired of romantic walks along its windswept expanse, there's a hidden lake to discover. Afterwards, treat yourself to coffee and freshly baked carrot cake at the tiny caravan that doubles as a perfect little cafe. Continue north to Muriwai (www.muriwai.com), perennially popular with surfers and kiteboarders, and busy with swimming and picnicking families in summer. At the beach's southern end, more than 4,000 gannets nest from August to March. Note that all of the west coast beaches are surf beaches and care should be taken to swim between the lifeguards' flags. Bordering the rugged coast is the Waitakere Ranges Regional Park which conceals 250km of walking tracks amid its valleys and waterfalls. See www.arc.govt.nz for more information.

Map p. 484 C5

Western Springs

Aucklanders love to spend time in their backyards and Western Springs is one of the biggest and best. The lake was the city's original water source for early European settlers, and immigrants old and new discover their inner Kiwi in the park close to the city's centre. Throughout the year they jog, rollerblade or play touch rugby here. In summer they fire up barbecues for sunset picnics and a few cold ones. At the Pasifika festival in March, thousands of Auckland families with Pacific and New Zealand roots crowd the lakeside to celebrate their diversity. Western Springs' Museum of Transport and Technology (www.motat.org.nz) is an underrated attraction that displays Auckland's growth from Pacific outpost to burgeoning international city. Lots of interactive displays will keep the kids busy. At the nearby Auckland Zoo (www.aucklandzoo.co.nz) you can meet New Zealand's national icon, the shy and retiring kiwi, in the native fauna Encounter.

North Island Map F6

Matakana

For decades, the sleepy farming district of Matakana, one hour north of Auckland, was off the radar, but now it's a must-visit destination for anyone interested in great Kiwi food and wine.

Matakana's Saturday morning farmers' market kicks off around 09:00, and the busy riverside market is a great place to grab local artisan chocolate, specialty meats and freshly pressed olive oil. Once you've got armfuls of goodies, take a break and have an alfresco breakfast beside the river. Nearby Hyperion Wines (09 422 9375, www.hyperion-wines.co.nz) produces wines with grapes from two local vineyards. With a compact winery in an old cowshed you'd expect rustic, everyday tipples, but the Hyperion range is complex and elegant. Ascension Vineyard (09 422 9601, www.ascensionvineyard.co.nz) operates on a larger scale, and the lush estate with its echoes of Tuscany is a great spot for a Mediterranean-style lunch. Another good lunch stop is the Leigh Sawmill Cafe (p.436), where you'll find local wines, or a selection of its own microbrews if you can't make your mind up. In summer, the beaches here provide the opportunity to waste the rest of the afternoon in the best possible way. Matheson's Bay is a pleasant tree-lined cove that's safe for families, and Tawharanui is a wilder surf beach with a dramatic rocky coastline.

For more information on Matakana and surrounding areas, check out www.matakana wine.com and www.matakana.com.

Read More
Check out www.matakana wine.com and www.matakana coast.com to plan your assault.

Area C p.204

Waikato & King Country

The Lowdown
Discover New Zealand's unique wildlife at the Otorohonga Kiwi House and the Maungatautari Ecological Island. After coming all this way you deserve to see something a little different. Look out for the kiwi, New Zealand's national bird, or the prehistoric tuatara.

The Essentials
New Zealanders are an adventurous bunch, and at Raglan you can learn to ride the waves at one of the best left-hand surf breaks in the world. Further south at the Waitomo Caves, the water-borne thrills are underground – but no less exciting.

South of the big smoke of Auckland, the Bombay Hills mark the transition from the City of Sails' urban energy to the rural and laid-back atmosphere of the Waikato region. The ever-increasing suburban sprawl of south Auckland gives way to vivid green farmland, kept irrigated by the might of the 420km Waikato River that flows from Lake Taupo to the south.

Mountain biking, Castlerock

New Zealand's longest river flows through Hamilton, and although derided by some cynics as a little too ordered and organised, the country's fourth largest urban area is reinventing itself for the 21st century, armed with the energy of its large student population. Farming is still the biggest game in town, but a surprising number of innovative high-tech industries are also taking root here amid the city's academic heritage. Auckland is less than 90 minutes away, and Hamilton's cafes, bars and restaurant do a good job in keeping up with their urban big brother up State Highway 1. Elsewhere in the region, the rolling pastoral lands surrounding Hamilton morph into wilder, more exciting landscapes made for exercising the quintessential Kiwi sense of adventure.

On the west coast, Raglan is a surf town that's quickly becoming a slightly new age but supremely relaxing oceanside community. Raglan draws bohemian and creative types from around New Zealand, and a surprising number of immigrants too.

Further south in the dramatic landscapes of the King Country, one of New Zealand's oldest tourist attractions is undergoing a transformation as locals invent new ways to explore the subterranean labyrinths of the Waitomo Caves. And just when you think the region can't provide any more iconic New Zealand experiences, you can introduce yourself as a new Kiwi to a gathering of the real, feathered kind.

North Island Map H8

Hamilton & Around

183 Brymer Rd
Dinsdale
Hamilton

Hamilton Zoo

07 838 6720 | *www.hamiltonzoo.co.nz*

With more than 400 different species on 25 hectares of well-manicured gardens and walkways, Hamilton Zoo is an enjoyable way to spend a leisurely morning or afternoon. For a provincial city, Hamilton is host to a surprising range of animals including white rhinos, giraffes, cheetahs and chimpanzees. The zoo's proud feline stars are Jake and Mencari, a brother-and-sister pair of endangered Sumatran tigers. The walk-through free-flight aviary is the biggest in Australasia, and combines native plants with a variety of local and imported birdlife. If you've ever wanted to see a gangly ostrich side by side with brash and colourful macaws, here's your chance. Hamilton Zoo provides excellent resource material for younger visitors, and if the kids get hungry they can be fed and watered at the Safari Cafe. If you're able to plan ahead, there are also picnic and barbecue tables. Open daily, 09:00 to 17:00.

6 Minifie Rd
Hamilton

Kiwi Balloon Company

02 162 3595 | *www.kiwiballooncompany.co.nz*

Every April, Hamilton hosts the Balloons Over Waikato Festival (www.balloonsover waikato.co.nz). Ballooning enthusiasts from around the world take part in competitions, but more important is the display of a huge variety of balloons of different shapes, sizes and colours. Most popular are the balloons in the shape of giant cartoon characters, and the culmination of the five-day festival is the Hamilton Nightglow, an after-dark collage of fireworks, live music and an orchestrated (and illuminated) balloon show. If you're not in town in mid-April, the Kiwi Balloon Company offers one-hour flights above Waikato's fertile farmlands. The trips last four hours in total ($275) and you can expect to spend at least an hour in the air. On a clear morning it's possible to spy the mountains of Tongariro National Park to the south. A champagne breakfast is served upon landing.

64 Alpha St
Cambridge

Maungatautari Ecological Island Trust

07 823 7455 | *www.maungatrust.org*

For centuries, New Zealand's geographic isolation created a haven for unique birds and reptiles, but following the introduction of pests such as rats and stoats, many of the country's native species have become endangered. Established in 2004, the Maungatautari Ecological Island Trust is a project that aims to reintroduce endangered native wildlife to the rugged slopes of Mount Maungatautari, a forested volcanic cone that rises above the Waikato basin near the town of Cambridge, south-east of Hamilton. An area of 3,400 hectares is encircled by 47km of predator-proof fence, and threatened birds like the kiwi, the stichbird and the saddleback have been reintroduced. The tuatara, an ancient reptile that hasn't had a makeover for 200 million years, is now thriving here, along with other native lizards. Many of these species were previously restricted to predator-free offshore islands, and the Trust is ensuring that New Zealand's unique natural heritage is preserved. A network of well-maintained walking tracks provides excellent access. Open daily, dawn to dusk. Admission by donation.

Memorial Park
Memorial Rd
Hamilton

MV Waipa Delta

0800 472 335 | *www.waipadelta.co.nz*

In the 19th century, the Waikato's European settlers journeyed to fertile farming country up the Waikato River on the Waipa Delta, a paddle steamer built in 1876. In a new century, a replica of the original boat now runs popular cruises that leave from leafy Memorial Park on the river's edge near the city centre. The MV Waipa Delta doesn't venture as far as the original boat did, but the leisurely cruises are still a great way to learn about the history of the country's longest river. One hour coffee cruises leave daily at 15:00 ($20) and include freshly baked scones with cream and jam. If you're wanting something more substantial, join a 90 minute lunch cruise ($45) which departs at 12:30, or a two hour dinner cruise ($59) that leaves the river bank at 19:00. On Friday and Saturday nights the boat stays on the river until 22:00, and after a four course meal and wine for $69, there's the opportunity for dancing. Don't go expecting anything too sophisticated, and you'll have a good time.

1 Grantham St
Waikato

Waikato Museum

07 838 6606 | *www.waikatomuseum.co.nz*

The excellent Waikato Museum has four main collections. The visual arts collection of 2,500 works dates from the early years of European settlement to today, and the talents of contemporary artists across the nation are encouraged with the museum's annual Contemporary Art Award. The Tangata Whenua collection showcases the crafts and history of the local Tainui Maori tribe, and includes a 200 year-old carved waka (canoe). The science collection has loads of interactive push-me-pull-me displays for children to understand the natural world, and the museum's social history collection covers the changing fabric of Hamilton's population, including an award-winning exhibition on recent immigrants from Somalia. When you've exhausted the viewing possibilities, you can recharge at the museum's courtyard cafe, or at the classier Canvas Restaurant & Bar. The express lunch ($10 in 10 minutes) is excellent value. The museum is open daily from 10:00 to 16:30. Admission is by donation.

North Island Map G8

Raglan

On the rugged western edge of the North Island, Raglan is on the road to nowhere. You don't arrive in Raglan en route to somewhere better. The creative types in this bohemian haven will tell you there's nowhere else that's better anyway. Raglan used to be an isolated surf town, but now it's packed with artists, musicians, and other urban refugees seeking a simpler life. Raglan is also a big music town and, if you visit during summer, chances are you'll catch a gig from one of the hot local bands. Year-round, local musicians get together on Thursday nights at the Salt Rock Cafe (07 825 8022), and you'll see Maori reggae musicians jamming with Californian folk singers who've chosen Raglan as their home. The next morning, you can kayak around Raglan's sheltered harbour or head to the area's surf beaches. Swimming and bodysurfing is excellent at Ngarunui Beach, and further round the coast Manu Bay has pristine, uniform waves, and the longest left-hand surf break on the planet. Nearby Whale Bay has more good surfing, and cosy beachfront cottages for rent. If you find yourself humming Beach Boys songs, sign up for surfing lessons with the Raglan Surfing School (www.raglansurfingschool). Consider staying at the funky, converted railway carriages overlooking the ocean (Solscape, 07 825 8268, www.solscape.co.nz), where Hawaiian-style massages are on offer.

Read More
To find out more on Raglan and its attractions, see www.raglan.net.nz

North Island Map G8

The King Country

With its landscape dotted with sheep farms, and a ragged coastline punctuated with sheltered, isolated harbours, the King Country is a quintessential slice of no-nonsense New Zealand. The area is named after the Maori King Movement that began in the nearby Waikato region in the 1850s to combat land sales to Europeans, and to promote Maori authority. King Tawhiao and his followers were defeated by British troops in 1864 and took refuge in the King Country's craggy terrain. Three years later, a local Maori chief, Tane Tinorau, showed the Waitomo Caves to Fred Mace, an English surveyor, and before long Tane was running tours through the caves. His descendants now provide the same service to 21st century travellers, and the Waitomo experience has grown to reflect New Zealand's obsession with providing visitors with the best in activity-based adventure tourism. In the pleasant nearby farming town of Otorohonga, travellers can tick off another essential New Zealand experience at the Otorohonga Kiwi House & Native Bird Park. Find out more about what this region has to offer at www.kingcountry.co.nz.

585 Waitomo Caves Rd
Waitomo

The Legendary Black Water Rafting Company

0800 228 464 | *www.blackwaterrafting.co.nz*

This lot sparked Waitomo's adventure travel scene in 1987, and in many ways the original is still the best. Thoroughly professional guides with just the right amount of laconic Kiwi humour lead adventurous travellers on inner tubes along the Ruakiri Cave's underground river. On the black labyrinth tour ($90), there are a few crawlspaces and a waterfall jump to keep adrenaline levels up, and travellers float from the cave into the dappled light of native rainforest. The total trip time is three hours with an hour underground. The more adventurous black abyss tour ($175) takes five hours with at least two hours underground, and incorporates a 30m abseil into Ruakiri Cave before getting down to the serious business of cave tubing and cave climbing. After either trip it's back to the Long Black Cafe for a hot shower followed by soup and bagels.

Alex Telfer Dr
Otorohonga
North Island
Map H8

The Otorohonga Kiwi House & Native Bird Park

07 873 7391 | *www.kiwihouse.org.nz*

A diminutive, shy, flightless bird is probably the last creature you'd nominate as a country's national symbol, but human Kiwis wouldn't have it any other way. The best place to see this long beaked icon is the Otorohonga Kiwi House & Native Bird Park. To minimise contact with predators, the birds are defiantly nocturnal in the wild, so to ensure visitors can spy a kiwi, day and night are reversed in the Kiwi House. As well as seeing kiwis in their indoor abode, visitors can also join a kiwi watch outing after dark ($25). Viewing in small groups takes place from a hide in a nearby forest and lasts two hours. Bookings are essential. Other New Zealand birds are also on display including cheeky and inquisitive keas and kakas (native parrots), and the kereru, New Zealand's wood pigeon. All interesting birds, but in Otorohonga it's the shy and retiring kiwi that is the reluctant star of the show. Open daily from 09:00 to 16:00. Entrance fees are: $15 for adults and $4 for children.

Waitomo Caves Rd
Waitomo

Waitomo Adventures

0800 924 866 | *www.waitomo.co.nz*

Many of the cave systems in the Waitomo area are yet to be discovered, but that hasn't stopped the resourceful team at Waitomo Adventures coming up with exciting ways to explore the caverns which are known about. Tumu Tumu toobing ($95) involves donning wetsuits, and walking, climbing, swimming and floating in inner tubes through the spectacular Tumu Tumu cave. Travellers looking for a real adventure buzz can join the haggis honking holes ($165) tour for underground rock climbing and abseiling down subterranean waterfalls, and on the lost world tour ($225) you get to stay dry as you abseil 100m down into a massive vaulted cavern. All three tours last four hours with two hours spent underground. Dependent on the tour, minimum age limits from 10 to 15 years apply. The ultimate Waitomo Adventures experience is the lost world epic ($355) which combines abseiling and river caving for a breathtaking seven hours. And just when you think the inventive crew has exhausted ways to explore the caves, you can also traverse through the stunning St Benedict's Caverns on an underground flying fox ($120). Only in New Zealand...

21 Waitomo Caves Rd
Waitomo

Waitomo Caves

0800 474 839 | *www.waitomo.com*

Since 1889, the surreal subterranean caverns and underground rivers of the Waitomo Caves have been a major tourist attraction, and the childhood memories of most New Zealanders include a visit to this quirky limestone landscape. Guided tours along well-maintained walkways explore three main caves. The most popular is the easily accessible Glowworm Cave, which is reached on a silent boat ride through inky darkness. On the roof of the cave thousands of tiny glowworms create an effect like the night sky. Nearby Aranui Cave was discovered in 1910 when a local, Te Rutuku Aranui, lost his dog while out hunting. Inside the cave is a riot of delicate pink and white limestone, from robust centuries-old formations, to gossamer thin 'straw' stalactites suspended from the cave's roof. Reopened in 2005, the Ruakiri ('Den of Dogs') Cave is named after the wild dogs that used to guard its entrance. Entry is down a spectacular spiral walkway, and the experience continues for 1.6km, making it the country's longest underground guided tour. Tours for all three caves leave throughout the day year-round. Bookings are recommended for the Aranui and Ruakiri Caves, especially during summer and the school holidays. Tours include free entry to the excellent Museum of Caves (07 878 7640, www.waitomo-museum.co.nz) which is open daily in March to December from 08:00 to 17:00, and in January to February from 08:00 to 20:00.

Area **D** *p.205*

Coromandel

The Lowdown
When driving around the Coromandel Peninsula, don't be deceived with distances on your map. Many of the roads are windy and narrow, and getting around may take you longer than you plan. Just relax and enjoy the sublime scenery.

The Essentials
Explore some of New Zealand's loveliest coastline. At the peninsula's tip you can traverse the Coromandel Coastal Walkway, and near Hahei you can kayak around stunning Cathedral Cove.

It's a perfect irony. Many Coromandel residents have moved to the spectacular area to escape the urban rat race, but during the summer holiday season the population of some beach resorts can increase tenfold. Beachside towns inhabited by quiet retirees suddenly find themselves welcoming a younger crowd of families and surfing teenagers, while on the peninsula's northern tip, neo-hippies forging alternative lifestyles are joined by walkers enjoying stunning hikes through native forest and along deserted beaches.

Bordered by Auckland and the Hauraki Gulf to the west and the unfettered expanse of the South Pacific to the east, the Coromandel Peninsula's rugged and forested mountainous spine offers many opportunities for challenging hiking and mountain biking.

The west coast highlights the region's lustrous past when settlements such as Thames and Coromandel Town (p.224) drew enthusiastic gold prospectors from around the world. Gold was first discovered in 1852, and while the gold rush has long since expired, it's easy for visitors to recreate the old days in interesting museums and mines amid restored Victorian architecture.

The peninsula's east coast is more about looking ahead, and, from December to March, the area's beaches are a favourite holiday escape for urban refugees from across the North Island. The contrasting aromas of suntan lotion and barbecues drift on gentle sea breezes, along with the telltale sounds of summer – buzzing cicadas and beach cricket. In resort towns such as Whitianga and Whangamata (p.226), the quieter days of winter and spring give way to annual festivals and a packed schedule of summer events. Like all of coastal New Zealand, the stunning bays and coves are becoming dotted with flash new houses that belie the phrase 'holiday home', but with an adventurous spirit it's still not too hard to discover a remote and sandy patch of paradise.

North Island Map H6

Thames

Situated on the broad expanse of the Firth of Thames, this town of around 10,000 was a centre of the region's 19th century gold rush (www.thames-info-co.nz). Now there's a slightly forlorn melancholia to the town's wooden houses, old pubs and storehouses. It's a good base for bushwalks in the nearby Kauaeranga Valley, but once you've explored Thames' gold-mining history, the scenic wonders of Coromandel's beaches and forests hold more attraction. North of town, State Highway 25 winds leisurely along the Firth of Thames through charming bays such as Te Puru and Tapu. Travel the road in summer and it will be lined with the crimson blooms of the pohutukawa, New Zealand's unofficial Christmas tree.

Coromandel Forest Park

Department of Conservation Visitor Information Centre
Kauaeranga Valley Rd
Coromandel

07 867 9080 | *www.doc.govt.nz*

Stretching from Waihi in the south to Coromandel Town in the north, the Coromandel Forest Park is a major drawcard in the area. The entire peninsula is dotted with walking trails and hiking tracks through rugged, forested terrain, and a popular area for more accessible hiking is the Kauaeranga Valley. The valley conceals 22 walking trails. You can sample the area on a short 30 minute outing, or get to know it well on the Kauaeranga Valley loop track. The latter is a relatively easy journey with accommodation in well-maintained huts and Department of Conservation camping areas. Especially popular in summer is the Pinnacles track. From the trailhead it's four hours up (sometimes slippery) tracks and essential ladders to the 759m peak. You'll need to be pretty fit for this hike, but the views are worthwhile. Around one hour down from the peak, the Pinnacles hut has basic self-catering facilities. You'll need to book with the Department of Conservation Visitor Information Centre. From the hut, the three-hour Webb Creek trail and the four-hour Billy Goat track provide alternative routes back to the trailhead.

Cnr Moanataiari Rd & State Highway 25
Thames

Gold Mine Experience

07 868 8514 | *www.goldmine-experience.co.nz*

The 40 minute guided tour at the Gold Mine Experience is a great way to fast-track your understanding of Thames' golden past. Bring along a waterproof jacket, and be prepared to get your shoes muddy as you walk through an underground tunnel that first gave up its golden bounty in 1868. By the 1920s Thames was a mecca for prospectors from around the world, and now, nearly a century later, the hard-working members of the Hauraki Prospectors Association are knowledgeable and enthusiastic guides. As well as exploring the gold mine tunnel, the tour also includes a stamping battery that's used to crush rock, and the opportunity to pan for your own tiny piece of bling. An attached museum and video presentation puts everything you've seen in context. Open daily, 10:00 to 16:00 during summer, and weekends in winter. Entrance fees: $10 for adults, $4 for children (New Zealand currency is preferred but gold is also accepted).

101 Cochrane St
Thames

School of Mines & Mineralogical Museum

07 868 6277 | *www.historic.org.nz*

Not everyone is born with the skills to be a successful gold miner, and in the 1880s more than 30 mining schools sprouted to provide practical instruction to wannabe millionaires working the gold fields. One of the largest was The Thames School of Mines, established in 1886. It also survived the longest and, after the gold rush expired, the school's curriculum was broadened to include engineering, pharmacology and agriculture. The school closed in 1954, but the Mineralogical Museum that dates from 1900 remains open. The museum's important collection includes a significant number of indigenous rocks and minerals, and an eclectic array of scales and other vintage gold-mining equipment. It might sound dull, but it's actually an interesting way to spend an hour or two. In 1979 the heritage buildings were acquired by the New Zealand Historic Places Trust. Open Wednesday to Saturdays, from 11:00 to 15:00. Entrance fees: $4 for adults, children get in for free.

North Island Map H6

Coromandel Town

More than anywhere on the Coromandel Peninsula, Coromandel Town provides a window on the region's past and future. At the height of the gold rush, the town had a population of 10,000 hopeful prospectors and their families, and many Victorian wooden buildings from that area still stand – such as the Star & Garter pub (07 866 8503), which is a great lunch stop. Today, Coromandel Town is a sleepy place of just 1,800 people, and the main town in the north of the peninsula. The north-west of Coromandel is popular with alternative lifestylers – New Zealand's Green Party usually enjoys election success here – and the population of Coromandel Town is becoming more eclectic and cosmopolitan. You'll see the usual small town array of a couple of good pubs, but don't be too surprised to also spy cool cafes serving organic soy lattes. Check out the options on www.coromandeltown.co.nz.

Coromandel

Coromandel Coastal Walkway

North of Coromandel Town, a windy road continues to the small settlement of Colville, a haven for alternative lifestylers. From Colville, an unsealed but well-maintained road continues north to Cape Colville, the northernmost tip of the Coromandel Peninsula. The journey is windy but travellers are rewarded with superb forest and ocean views. From Fletcher Bay on the very tip of the peninsula, the Coromandel Coastal Walkway winds for three to four hours to Stony Bay. One of New Zealand's best walks, the accessible and well-signed track meanders gently along the coast and through pleasant farmland. It's not too strenuous but your eyes are in for a good workout thanks to the sublime scenery, including expansive views of Great Barrier Island and the Mercury Islands. There's also a mountain bike track for two-wheeled adventurers. If you're not keen to drive on the area's winding, unsealed roads, Coromandel Discovery Tours (07 866 8175, www.coromandeldiscovery.co.nz) have full-day trips for $90, leaving Coromandel Town daily at 09:00.

410 Buffalo Rd
Coromandel

Coromandel Goldfield Centre & Stamper Battery

07 866 7933

Originally opened in 1900, the Coromandel Goldfield Centre & Stamper Battery was the last gold stamper battery to crush rocks in New Zealand. More than a century on, it's still in working order, and visitors can experience the entire gold mining process. Once you've seen the country's biggest water wheel in action, you can try your luck with gold panning, or walk on well-marked paths to a forest lookout. Guided one-hour tours run every hour from 10:30 to 15:30, daily. Adults are charged $6, children $3.

380 Driving Creek Rd
Coromandel

Driving Creek Potteries & Railway

07 866 8703 | *www.drivingcreekrailway.co.nz*

New Zealand's lone narrow-gauge mountain railway only came about because well-known potter Barry Brickell discovered the clay on his land was perfect for his ceramic work. Accessing the clay at the top of a steep hill was difficult, so the industrious Brickell built a compact railway. The toy train system built out of necessity and incorporating two spirals, three tunnels, and several viaducts has now expanded to become a public railway that wends its way through kauri forest, with superb views of the islands of the Hauraki Gulf. The hour-long train trips run at 10:15 and 14:00 daily with additional departures at 12:45 and 15:15 during the summer months. After travelling through sculpture gardens filled with Brickell's work, the journey ends at the aptly named Eyeful Tower. If the weather's clear, you'll be able to see Auckland's Sky Tower in the distance. Profits from the railway are used for a reforestation programme. Driving Creek is very popular and bookings are recommended. Adults cost $20 and children $11.

North Island Map H6

Whitianga

Whitianga is the provincial hub of the eastern Coromandel and makes a good base to explore nearby attractions such as Hot Water Beach and Cathedral Cove. During the winter it's a sleepy town of leisurely retirees, but in summer it's a popular resort full of families taking advantage of quintessentially Kiwi activities such as kayaking, bushwalking and swimming. The area's traditional Maori name is Te Whitianga a Kupe, (the Crossing Place of Kupe), and it's reputed to be where the legendary Polynesian explorer Kupe landed around 925AD. The town is built on the edges of Whitianga Harbour. Travelling across the harbour to Ferry Landing and Cook's Beach can involve either a 45 minute drive, or a more straightforward two-minute trip on a passenger ferry. Every August the biggest game in town is the Whitianga Scallop Festival (www.scallopfestival.co.nz) when more than 6,000 visitors discover just how many different ways there are to cook the tasty bivalve mollusc. If you're looking to stay, consider the secluded self-catering cottages on private farmland (www.pitoone.com).

North Island Map J6

Hahei & Cathedral Cove

It's hard to know what's more impressive: Hahei's pink and white sand beaches or the spectacular limestone arch at Cathedral Cove. The limestone formations and small offshore islands comprise the Te Whanganui a-Hei Marine Reserve, and after visitors have tired of Hahei's seaside charm, they move on to exploring the beautiful coastline on kayaking and boat trips, or underwater with snorkels or scuba. From Hahei to Cathedral Cove is a one-hour walk along cliff tops and around pretty coves. Along the route, Gemstone Bay is the best snorkelling spot. Hahei is a 40 minute drive from Whitianga. For a small town it packs in a surprisingly sophisticated range of boutique accommodation, art galleries, and good restaurants. A special place for families to stay is Purangi Garden (07 866 4036, www.purangigarden.co.nz). Rustic cabins are set on a quiet estuary that can be explored in kayaks or rowing boats. Visit www.hahei-newzealand.co.nz for more details.

North Island Map H6

Matarangi & Kuaotunu

Built around the entrance to pretty Whangapoua harbour, the two settlements of Matarangi and Kuaotunu are contrasting slices of life on the Coromandel Pensinsula. Matarangi is a planned real estate development, complete with luxury villas, all-weather tennis courts and The Dunes golf course. Nearby Kuaotunu was once a gold mining town of 1,000 people, and now it's a sleepy hamlet with a family friendly camping ground, a couple of backpacker hostels, and beach cottages for rent. To the east and west of Matarangi and Kuaotunu are other superb beaches. From Kuaotunu turn left at the Coffee Lala caravan to sprawling Opito Bay, and west across the harbour from Matarangi is New Chums Beach. In 2006, the arcing cove fringed by native forest was named as one of the 20 best deserted beaches in the world by the British newspaper *The Observer*. It's about a 40 minute walk to get there, but unlike Matarangi, it's a pristine slice of untouched Coromandel. See www.coromandeltown.co.nz for directions and www.matarangie.co.nz for more information.

Whenuakite
North Island Map J6

Hot Water Beach

www.hotwaterbeach.co.nz

Visiting Hot Water Beach presents a real dilemma. Do you swim in the pristine ocean, or do you dig a hole in the sand and bathe in the warm water welling up from beneath? A combination of the two suits most visitors as they come armed with a garden spade and dig themselves their own personal seaside hot tub. Underpinning the rugged Coromandel Range is a volcanic fault, and just a few inches under the sand there is a layer of hot water (beware, it can be very hot). The best time to dig your own alfresco spa pool is either side of low tide. That's when the beach resembles some strange archeological dig, except one where all the archeologists have become bored and are now sitting in the sand with warm water welling up around them. Once the tide rolls in again, the informal thermal baths are washed away, and bathers head into the Pacific surf to cool down. Note that the surf at Hot Water Beach can be dangerous and you should always swim between the lifeguards' flags.

North Island Map J7

Whangamata

Read On
For more information, see www.whangamata.co.nz

For decades 'Whanga' has been the preferred New Year's Eve haunt for teenagers from across the upper North Island. Around the Christmas/festive period, the town gets mighty crowded and the resident population of 3,500 can rise to 35,000. In the past this increase has eventuated in social problems like excessive teen drinking, but a recently introduced ban on drinking alcohol in public places means the town is again a safe and enjoyable choice for families. Surfing or swimming along Whangamata's four kilometre-long beach and bush walking in the Coromandel Forest Park are popular attractions, and in April and May the annual Beach Hop (www.beachhop.co.nz) is one of the world's biggest celebrations of 1950s and 60s music, fashion and culture. Expect cool retro music, a cavalcade of hotrods, and more than a few guys that vaguely resemble Elvis.

Area E p.204

The Lowdown

Ignore the strong smell of sulphur in the air and dive into the North Island's most diverse array of travellers' experiences.

The Essentials

Believe the hype. The sublime volcanic lakes and landscapes you'll experience while traversing the Tongariro Crossing will easily fulfill your pre-conceptions of the world-beating beauty of New Zealand. Expect to share it with a few like-minded souls during summer though.

Bay of Plenty & Central Plateau

No other region in New Zealand showcases the violent volcanic forces that shaped the country as well as the Bay of Plenty and Central Plateau regions.

The tourist town of Rotorua is literally built on a vast underground network of geothermal activity, and it doesn't take too much effort to feel the power and the heat of the earth below. Since Rotorua's global appeal as a tourist attraction kicked off in the 19th century, local Maori have been both guides and guardians of the unique landscape, and the proud sharing of their culture has been as important as the region's spectacular geysers and hot springs. Rotorua continues to be an unabashed tourist town, but now the emphasis is also on freewheeling international backpackers pushing their mental and physical limits in adventure activities that could only come from the resourceful minds of the Kiwis.

Further south, nature's immense power is also on display at the massive Lake Taupo (p.230) and the trio of volcanic peaks that make up the Tongariro National Park (p.230). Summer and winter in the park are both essential experiences – just make sure you pack the right seasonal combination of skis and snowboards or hiking boots. The lakeside town of Taupo parallels Rotorua as an adventure sports hub, but more relaxed travellers can enjoy its family atmosphere, or don waders to test the area's international reputation for trout fishing.

After all this activity a restful beach holiday should be on the cards. Kick off in Tauranga (p.229), a relaxed but increasingly cosmopolitan port city, before moving on to the string of white-sand beaches that line the Bay of Plenty's Pacific Coast. And you're not quite done with the area's volcanic legacy just yet – take a boat trip over to White Island, where you can walk on a live volcano.

North Island Map J8

Rotorua

For more than a century, Rotorua has been the North Island's premier tourist destination, and the city, known colloquially as 'Roto-Vegas', is showing no sign of slowing down. Most visitors come to experience traditional Maori culture and the bubbling, steaming legacy of the region's violent volcanic past, but amid the laden tour buses, there's a steady flow of backpackers keen to tick off the next item on their New Zealand adventure sports checklist. Often overlooked in the rush from mud pools to bungee jumping is pretty Lake Rotorua, where leisurely trips by paddle steamer (www.lakelandqueen.co.nz) are available to explore the water and its place in local Maori legends. For more information, see www.rotoruanz.co.nz.

Whakarewarewa Thermal Reserve

Western Rd
Ngongotaha

The Agrodome

0800 339 400 | *www.agrodome.co.nz*

A show consisting of sheepdogs and rugged Kiwi blokes parading various woolly species may not sound very exciting, but there's a reason why the Sheep Show at the Agrodome is so popular. The interesting and informative hour-long shows are held daily at 09:30, 11:00 and 14:30, and include a shearing display and photo opportunities of super-cute lambs being bottle-fed. Then the whip-smart sheep dogs head outside to round up slightly confused looking sheep into pens. One of New Zealand's favourite shows on television was one that featured sheep dog trials, so this is essential heartland Kiwi stuff. In close proximity to the Agrodome there's a unique skydive simulator (www.freefallxtreme.com) in a vertical wind tunnel, a bungee jump and 'The Swoop' (both www.rotoruabungy.com), where willing participants are strapped into a hang-glider harness and then 'flown' through the air – at 130km per hour. You can then round off an adventurous afternoon by rolling down a hill inside a zorb (www.zorb.com), a giant transparent ball.

Fairy Springs Rd
Rotorua

Skyline Skyrides

07 347 0027 | *www.skylineskryrides.co.nz*

After the excitement of whitewater sledging or zorbing (p.229), the gentler thrills of the Skyline Gondola may be just what you need. Running for 900m up the side of the extinct Mount Ngongotaha, it affords you great views of Lake Rotorua and the geothermal activity at Whakarewarewa in the south. At the top, the Cableway Restaurant has a good value buffet. Thrillseekers can then descend the mountain in a three-wheeled luge on a choice of three different concrete tracks that travel up to two kilometres through redwood forests. When your run is over, there's a chairlift to take you to the top, so you can ease into the advanced one-kilometre track that ups the ante with tighter corners and steeper gradients. Back on ground level, the Rainbow Springs Nature Park (07 350 0440, www.rainbowsprings.co.nz) has pretty walking trails around pools stocked with huge trout, and there's another opportunity to spy a national icon at the Kiwi Encounter (07 350 0440, www.kiwiencounter.co.nz).

Waimangu Rd
Rotorua

Waimangu Thermal Valley

07 366 6137 | *www.waimangu.com*

Before 1886 the Waimangu Thermal Valley didn't even exist, but after the catastrophic eruption of nearby Mount Tarawera, the steaming, bubbling valley was created beside the shores of Lake Rotomahana. Lush native bush is now reclaiming the tortured landscape and the result is a unique combination of verdant forest, hot springs and billowing steam. The terrain includes wonderfully named attractions such as Frying Pan Lake, the world's largest hot spring at 100m in diameter, and the huge Inferno Crater that undergoes a fascinatingly regular cycle of filling, overflowing and emptying. Explore the valley on a self-guided walking tour (stay on the well-marked paths), and then join a 45 minute cruise on Lake Rotomahana to spy on native birdlife and learn about the havoc wrought by the 1886 eruption. Alternatively, settle in for a mud bath and a hot soak at the on-site spa. A few kilometres further south the colourful Wai-O-Tapu Thermal Wonderland (0800 768 678, www.geyserland.co.nz) features the stunning turquoise and orange Champagne Pool, and the grumbling, bubbling mud pools of the cannily dubbed Devil's Ink Pots.

Hemo Rd
Rotorua

Whakarewarewa Thermal Reserve

0800 837 842 | *www.tepuia.com*

In Rotorua you don't need to go far to discover the thermal activity the area is renowned for – just a stroll around town will present you with bubbling mud pools and

sulphurous odours. But for real appreciation of the spectacle, head three kilometres south to the Whakarewarewa Thermal Reserve. Here are more than 500 hot pools and 65 different geyser vents. The most famous geysers (pronounced 'guy-sers' by the Kiwis) are the spectacular 10m Prince of Wales' Feathers and the Pohutu ('Big Splash') that spouts up to 20m on four days out of five. The hour-long guided tours showcase the best of the spectacular activity.
The reserve is divided into two areas. Te Puia is an outlet for the New Zealand Maori Arts & Crafts Institute, and has regular Maori cultural performances and a kiwi house with New Zealand's national bird. The Thermal Village (www.whakarewarewa.com) also has a replica Maori village from pre-European times where visitors are shown how the Maori harnessed the power of the geothermal activity for cooking.

811 State Highway 33
Okere Falls
Rotorua

Whitewater Rafting & Sledging

0800 723 822 | *www.raftabout.co.nz*

Visitors can go whitewater rafting in several places around New Zealand (p.328), but the most intense thrills are reckoned to be on various rivers in close proximity to Rotorua. The Rangitaiki River offers Grade 4 thrills along 14km of rapids and scenic interludes, while the Wairoa River raises the intensity level significantly with Grade 5 rapids. To gain a sense of perspective, Grade 6 rapids are only attempted by rafting experts. On the Kaituna River (the name worryingly means 'eel food'), the attraction is rapids and waterfalls. Rafts plunge across three waterfalls and 14 rapids, including a seven-metre cascade that is the highest commercially rafted waterfall on the planet. Intrepid sorts can also take on the Kaituna on personal whitewater sledges that you ride headfirst like a toboggan. Full training is given and wetsuits and flippers are provided.

North Island Map J7

Tauranga & Mount Maunganui

Staying in Tauranga?
Then consider The Sebel Trinity Wharf (07 577 8700), designer cool right on Tauranga Harbour and just a 10 minute walk from the bars and restaurants on The Strand

The Tauranga and Mount Maunganui area is one of the sunniest regions in New Zealand. With its relaxed coastal lifestyle, it's one of the fastest-growing areas of the country, and a popular destination for cashed-up retirees moving from bigger cities. Growth has made Tauranga increasingly cosmopolitan, and the city's shipping and agricultural focus is now trumped by its new waterfront bars, cafes and restaurants. Across Tauranga Harbour is the extinct volcano of Mount Maunganui, known simply as 'The Mount' to the thousands of visitors who flock here for summer holidays. Welcome to the future of New Zealand beaches. Traditional beachside cottages or baches are being replaced by high-rise apartment buildings and multi million-dollar private homes. A newly built artificial reef produces uniform waves ideal for surfing, and trendy cafes line the main street. But despite the upmarket moves, Mount Maunganui still retains an honest Kiwi appeal. Walk around the 3.5km track at the base of Mount Maunganui, then have a swim in the surf and a well-deserved serving of fish and chips on the boardwalk, and you'll discover why 'The Mount' is one of New Zealand's most popular beaches.

North Island Map K8

Whakatane & White Island

Ever wanted to walk on a live volcano? Just 50km from the quiet harbour town of Whakatane (www.whakatane.com), White Island (Whakaari in Maori) bubbles and hisses to keep up its reputation as New Zealand's most active volcano. It's the nearest most people will ever get to another planet with ash, steam and sulphurous gases rising from a crater that's actually 60m below sea level. The island is privately owned and visitor numbers are restricted. Because the island has no jetty, boats must land directly on the beach, and trips are cancelled in poor weather. White Island Tours (07 308 9588, www.whiteislandtours.co.nz, also known as PeeJay Tours) operates an excellent six-hour outing.

North Island Map J9

Taupo

Formed almost 27,000 years ago by a volcanic eruption that's reckoned to have been more than 10 times bigger than Krakatoa, Lake Taupo is the country's biggest lake and is now a mecca for keen trout-fishermen from around the world. On State Highway 1 between Rotorua and Tongariro National Park, it's also a handy stopping-off point for international travellers and holidaying Kiwis. Pretty beaches such as Acacia Bay are recommended for swimming (although the water can be cold), and to fulfill a regular influx of backpackers, there's an ever-increasing range of adrenaline-fuelled adventure activities, including skydiving, bungee jumping and quadbiking. If the town's summertime energy verges on volcanic, during winter Taupo returns to being a quiet gateway to the snow capped mountains further south in Tongariro National Park.

Lake Taupo

Fishing

www.taupofishing.com

If you're a fan of trout, you'll be disappointed to discover that it isn't featured on restaurant menus in New Zealand. Selling the plump and tasty fish is illegal here, although catching it isn't. So you'll need to catch your own and either make like Jamie Oliver, or speak nicely to the cooks at your fishing lodge.

To catch it though, you need to get yourself to Lake Taupo, where brown and rainbow trout abound. You'll easily find space on a fishing boat (see www.fishlaketaupo.co.nz or call 07 378 2196) on the lake all year round, but from March to September – when the mature rainbow trout make their way upstream to spawn – you should be fly-fishing the streams and rivers that flow into the lake. There are many local fly-fishing guides who can show you why Taupo's trout fishing is world-renowned.

State Highway 1 & State Highway 5
Taupo

Wairakei

07 378 0913 | *www.wairakeiterraces.co.nz*

As you approach Taupo from the north you'll spy an agglomeration of curved silver pipes – that's if you can see them through the clouds of steam wafting across the road. Established in 1958, the Wairakei Geothermal Power Project was only the second place in the world where steam was harnessed to produce electricity. Before the 1950s the Wairakei area had 20 geysers, springs, and fumaroles producing about 30,000 tonnes of hot water daily. Now the network of bores and pipelines produces up to 7% of New Zealand's total electricity needs. The valley is also the site of the Wairakei Terraces, an ambitious man-made attempt to create the spectacular pink and white terraces that were destroyed by the 1886 eruption of Mount Tarawera. It's still early days, but once the blue, pink and white silica terraces are fully formed they will be equally spectacular, albeit on a smaller scale. The nearby Craters of the Moon is a sulphurous *Forbidden Planet* vista that was formed when construction started on the geothermal project. You'll need closed shoes for this one.

North Island Map H10

Tongariro National Park

In 1887, Maori chief Te HeuHeu Tukino IV gifted his tribe's three sacred mountain peaks to the people of New Zealand on the express condition that the land surrounding them would never be developed or settled. The protected area subsequently became New Zealand's first national park and the peaks of Mount Ruapehu, Mount Tongariro and Mount Ngauruhoe were protected for future generations. Tongariro National Park is now one of New Zealand's favourites, drawing thousands of visitors to ski on Mount Ruapehu in winter and hike amid the spectacular volcanic scenery and lakes during summer (www.visitruapehu.com). The park's volcanic peaks are still active and Mount Ruapehu last erupted in headline fashion in 1995 and 1996. In 1991, the park was granted Unesco World Heritage status

Waipunga Falls

Craters of the Moon

Lake Rotorua

En route to Taupo

acknowledging its place in the myths and legends of local Maori. More recently the conical peak of Mount Ngauruhoe played the part of Mordor's Mount Doom in the blockbuster *The Lord of the Rings* trilogy.

Mount Ruapehu

Skiing

www.mtruapehu.com

You've got a choice of ski fields on Mount Ruapehu. The two main areas are Whakapapa on the mountain's northern slopes and Turoa on the southern side. To the north-east is Tukino, a smaller, lower-key area, but that's probably because it's also relatively inaccessible. At Whakapapa and Turoa there's usually enough snow to warrant a trip from late June to late October. And because the mountain is just four hours from Auckland and Wellington, you'll have plenty of company on the slopes on weekends and during the school holidays. Whakapapa has more than 30 runs and the versatile terrain caters to everyone, from total newbies to advanced skiers. Across at Turoa, the expansive groomed trails are recommended for intermediate level skiers. Turoa also has the significant advantage of being nearer to the village of Ohakune, the mountain's best spot for raucous apres-ski action. Note that all accommodation on the mountain is owned by private clubs, so most visitors stay at Whakapapa Village, Ohakune, Tongariro National Park, or further afield in Taupo or Turangi.

Tongariro National Park

The Tongariro Crossing

www.tongarirocrossing.org.nz

Rated the best one-day hike in New Zealand, the spectacular Tongariro Crossing showcases the best of the park's volcanic landscapes. The total distance is 17km, and hikers of moderate fitness usually complete the task in seven to eight hours. You certainly don't need to be a mountain goat, but a couple of sections will make you dig deep. Highlights along the way include the volcanic ash expanse of Tongariro's South Crater and the vibrant turquoise palette of the Emerald Lakes. New Zealand's 'most beautiful country in the world' tag is sometimes used too glibly, but the otherworldly terrain of the Tongariro Crossing truly lives up to the hype. During summer the hike is very popular and handy shuttle buses run to either end on a regular basis. If you're feeling inspired and not too fatigued after the Tongariro Crossing, you can graduate to the Tongariro Northern Circuit. There are well maintained huts along the way, and most hikers complete the track in three to four days.

Huka Falls

Area F p.204

East Coast & Hawke's Bay

The Lowdown

Hawke's Bay is a popular retirement destination. Take plenty of sunshine, add in the region's excellent wines and a rapidly expanding gourmet food scene, and you might want to move there as well.

The Essentials

When Hawke's Bay heats up, locals cool off in the surf at Ocean Beach or Waimarama Beach. Further north – at Tokomaru Bay and Tologa Bay – you can also immerse yourself in traditional Maori culture.

Perched on the easternmost tip of the North Island, the good people of the east coast and Hawke's Bay don't let their relative isolation get them down. The scenery, together with the region's bustling provincial cities, a buoyant agricultural industry and excellent beaches enjoyed best in sultry summers, can render Auckland and Wellington relatively trivial distractions.

The locals are a diverse bunch. Around the East Cape's gloriously windy roads, traditional Maori communities inhabit a roll-call of stunning coves and bays, where getting around by horse is still common practice, whereas in Hawke's Bay, the moneyed folk of pretty Havelock North are more likely to park a shiny Range Rover at their children's private school.

There's plenty of natural beauty here, where fertile plains and meandering rivers are fringed by rugged mountains and the rolling surf of the South Pacific. Beautiful Lake Waikaremoana and the imposing profile of Te Mata Peak (p.236) are the equal of anywhere else in this photogenic country. And who says New Zealand's attractions are limited to scenic grandeur? The natural forces responsible for the Napier earthquake of 1931 created the opportunity for the city to be reborn in grand art deco style.

In a new century the region's laid-back cities continue to evolve. Napier's Ahuriri Port is now dotted with lively dockside bars and restaurants. Hastings is becoming the heart of the region's gourmet food scene, complemented by a local wine industry that began in 1851 and grows in scope and quality with every vintage. Further north-east Gisborne (p.236) is languidly making itself known for its surprising mix of sophistication and surfing.

Hawke's Bay

North Island Map K11

Hawke's Bay promotes itself as 'Wine Country', but that's really selling the region short. A wildly diverse combination of terrain, soil and climate does make it the country's most versatile wine-producing region, but there's more on offer than elegant Bordeaux-style red wines and complex chardonnays. Napier's immense pride in its distinctive art deco architectural heritage grows every year, and along the city's elegant tree-lined Marine Parade there are enough interesting attractions to keep kids of all ages occupied for a couple of days. Nearby Hastings doesn't have Napier's glam, but as the central marketplace of the fertile Heretaunga Plains the city is fast becoming the Kiwi foodie capital. Sophisticated winery restaurants and casual cafes serve the best produce from the soil and the ocean, and spontaneous picnics are easily assembled at local wineries and gourmet food shops. Take your pick of beaches to enjoy your purchases. Tucked under the audacious profile of Te Mata Peak, Havelock North is Hastings' better looking and richer cousin, where the flow of Audis and BMWs contributes to the moneyed ambience of this town of leafy gardens.

Napier

Art Deco Napier

06 835 0022 | *www.artdeconapier.com*

Following the Napier earthquake in 1931 the city centre was rebuilt in the art deco architectural style that was in vogue at the time. As well as being fashionable, the art deco style was also cheap to produce – a vital pre-requisite during the era's Great Depression – and its simple unadorned nature meant there was less to fall from buildings in the event of another quake. More than seven decades on, Napier now boasts some of the world's best preserved examples of the art deco style. Standout buildings include the wonderful Daily Telegraph Building (cnr Tennyson St & Church Lane) which incorporates an eclectic selection of art deco design elements such as sunbursts and zigzags, and the beautiful Rothmans Building (Bridge St) near the city's wharf area.

The best way to explore Napier's architectural heritage is on a guided walk. One-hour excursions ($10 per person) depart at 10:00 daily, and two-hour walks ($15) leave at 14:00 daily from the Napier Visitor Information Centre, come rain or shine. From 26 December to 31 March, there's also the option of a 90 minute outing ($12) at 17:30. The classiest way to see the sights is in a vintage car ($99 for an hour). After a few decades of relative indifference, Napier now embraces its art deco heritage, and in mid-February every year, Art Deco Weekend brings the city alive with jazz concerts, a vintage car rally, and lots of dining and dancing, 1930s style dress is highly recommended, and quite possibly mandatory.

Cape Kidnappers

Cape Kidnappers Gannet Colony

Gannets aren't small birds. An adult can weigh two kilos and has a wingspan of two metres, so when 2,000 breeding pairs gather in one place, it's quite a scene. From May to mid-July the birds are at sea, but by the end of July the first gannets return, and from August onward the Cape's narrow spine is covered by busy birds throwing themselves into energetic courtship rituals. Nests crafted from driftwood form havens for eggs in October and November, and by March the fluffy chicks have graduated to adolescent birds ready to try out their flash new wings. By April, the colony has returned across the Tasman to Australia, and the annual cycle of migration, courtship, breeding and birth is again complete. Walking to the Cape and back takes around six hours, and you'll also need to be wary of tides. Possibly more enjoyable are the trips with Gannet Beach Adventures (www.gannets.com) where you get to ride on a trailer behind a tractor, or Gannet Safaris' four-wheel drive expeditions (www.gannetsafaris.com).

Various Locations

Harvest Hawke's Bay

www.harvesthawkesbay.co.nz

Across the first weekend in February (Waitangi Weekend), the annual Harvest Hawke's Bay Wine Festival includes celebrations at more than 20 of the region's vineyards. As well as showcasing their wines, each vineyard offers food – often from some of the region's best restaurants. Live music of many genres keeps energy levels high. The best (and most responsible) way to get around is on the regular shuttle buses, which leave from nearby Hastings, Napier and Havelock North's various visitors' centres. But if you know a teetotal driver, classic cars and Harley Davidson motorcycles are available for rent. Hawke's Bay is also building a reputation for superb food, and in recent years the programme has included stops at artisanal food producers. On the Saturday evening, the annual Church Road Jazz Concert is held in the gardens surrounding the Church Road Winery (www.churchroad.co.nz), one of New Zealand's oldest vineyards.

Various Locations

The Hawke's Bay Food and Wine Trails

www.hawkesbaynz.com

If you decide to move to Hawke's Bay purely because of the region's excellent food and wine, you probably wouldn't be the first new resident to be seduced by nature's tasty bounty. And even if you're only in 'The Bay' as a visitor, exploring the area's many wineries, orchards and boutique food producers will be an essential highlight. Hawke's Bay Tourism produces an excellent wine trail map for travelling wine buffs. Wineries that should not be missed include: Mission Estate Winery (www.missionestate.co.nz), established in 1851 by Catholic missionaries from France; Te Awa (www.teawa.com), with a restaurant that's a favourite haunt of Hawke's Bay chefs and winemakers; and Craggy Range (www.craggyrange.com), which is housed in spectacular buildings under the vertiginous profile of Te Mata Peak. Also worth a visit are Church Road Winery (www.churchroad.co.nz), established in 1897, and Clearview Estate (www.clearviewestate.co.nz), which is located near the surf at Te Awanga.

A couple of days spent tasting wine should also include visits to Hawke's Bay's growing network of food producers. Hawke's Bay Tourism's food trail map details 20 different outlets for innovative produce from the Te Mata Cheese Company (www.tematacheese.co.nz) to Roosters Brew House (1470 Omahu Rd, Hastings, 06 879 4127). Many of these companies have stalls at the weekly farmers' markets. These are held in Napier on Saturday mornings from 08:30 to 12:30 at the Daily Telegraph Building on Tennyson St, and in Hastings on Sunday mornings from 08:30 to 12:30 at the Hawke's Bay Showgrounds off Kenilworth St. You can find out more about the essential food and wine stops on www.savourhawkesbay.co.nz and www.winehawkesbay.co.nz.

65 Marine Parade
Napier

Hawke's Bay Museum

06 835 7781 | *www.hawkesbaymuseum.co.nz*

Hawke's Bay Museum is an excellent place to understand the Napier earthquake. The multimedia exhibition combines old newspapers and photographs with *Survivors Stories*, a poignant 35 minute film about the tragic events of 1931.

Earlier eras in the region's past are also explored with the interactive Once Were Dinosaurs exhibition and an interesting array of art and artefacts from the Ngati Kahungunu tribe of Hawke's Bay. Napier's post-earthquake renaissance is illuminated in the art deco-style display, which features a fascinating range of homeware, furniture and architecture – a reminder of the grace and elegance of earlier times. The museum complex includes the Century Cinema, which has a reputation for showing entertaining and intelligent art house films. Museum admission is $7.50 for adults and children enter for free. Open daily, 10:00 to 17:00 from March to September and until 18:00 from October to February.

290 Marine Parade
Napier

Marineland of New Zealand

06 834 4027 | *www.marineland.co.nz*

Napier's Marineland showcases a collection of marine creatures straight from *Finding Nemo*. Children will love getting close to dolphins, seals, sea lions, otters and penguins, as well as New Zealand's roll call of sea birds featuring gannets and cormorants. Marineland opened in 1965, and while there are still dolphin and seal shows everyday at 10:30 and 14:00, there is also a wider range of activities and attractions. Visitors can swim with dolphins, feed seals and penguins, and go on behind-the-scenes tours to understand Marineland's role in rescuing and rehabilitating injured marine wildlife. At the Penguin Recovery Workshop visitors can have a hands-on experience with rescued penguins from the Hawke's Bay coastline. Marineland is very popular with local and international visitors and bookings are essential, especially during school holidays. Family passes (for two adults and one child) start at $24.50, and dolphin swims cost $50. Open daily, 10:30 to 16:30.

546 Marine Parade
Napier

National Aquarium of New Zealand

06 834 1404 | *www.nationalaquarium.co.nz*

Opened in 1964, this complex has grown to include a huge pool of 1.5 million litres of water filled with sharks, rays and turtles. For most visitors, the best way to immerse themselves in the marine environment is to stay dry and traverse the various exhibits on a moving walkway. But if that's not close enough, qualified divers can explore with the predators. Behind-the-scenes tours at 09:00 and 13:00 include the opportunity to feed marine creatures. The importance of the ocean to Hawke's Bay is showcased with environmental and ecological displays, including the gannet colony at nearby Cape Kidnappers. A couple of hours is enough time to explore the aquarium, but make sure you include the feeding sessions by divers at

10:00 and 14:00. And don't miss New Zealand's unique living dinosaur, the tuatara, and the much larger and more dangerous saltwater crocodiles. Open daily, 09:00 to 17:00. Entrance fees are $14 for adults, $7.50 for children.

Grove Rd
Hastings

Splash Planet

06 873 8033 | *www.splashplanet.co.nz*

If you're travelling with children, chances are they won't be as interested in wine and gourmet delicacies as you are so why not give them a treat at Hastings' Splash Planet waterpark. After traipsing around yet another vineyard, they'll relish the chance to ride water slides and assorted amusement park rides. With bumper boats, a ride-on pirate ship and mini golf, you won't mistake the low-key Splash Planet for Disney World, but in the middle of one of Hawke's Bay's notoriously hot summers you'll probably want to join the kids in the water. Open daily, 09:00 to 18:00. Entrance fees: $25 for adults and $19.50 for children.

Havelock North

Te Mata Peak

Te Mata Peak's spectacular profile is visible from most parts of Hawke's Bay, and there's probably no better place for a picnic than within its sight. There's a road to the top, but a popular alternative for energetic types is to hike or mountain bike to the 399m summit. A series of shorter one-hour walks take in the peak's interesting forests and limestone valleys. You can pick up maps at the Havelock North Visitor Information Centre (www.villageinfo.co.nz). During the day you're likely to see hang-gliders soaring above the Heretaunga Plains, and at night there are excellent views of the lights of Hawke's Bay. On a clear day in winter you can even see a snowy Mount Ruapehu in Tongariro National Park to the west. Te Mata Peak's silhouette is known as the Sleeping Giant, a reference to a local Maori legend.

North Island Map M9

East Cape & Poverty Bay (including Gisborne)

In 1769 when English explorer James Cook named the area surrounding Gisborne Poverty Bay, he couldn't have been more wrong. Staunch local Maori tribes may have forced him to depart without restocking his ship, but now the region is known for its warm hospitality, long, sunny summers and plenty of opportunities to enjoy local wine and fresh seafood.

Around East Cape, the winding Pacific Coast Highway (State Highway 35) meanders past stunning bays and remote Maori settlements, and is odds-on favourite to be New Zealand's most inspiring journey. And if any of the scenery looks familiar, you're probably a fan of the locally made film *Whale Rider*.

Gisborne is the country's easternmost city – the local slogan is 'First To See The Light' – and the city is quickly morphing into a bustling provincial hub with a casual ambience appropriated from the region's surf culture. And if you're wondering where to spend your first Kiwi Christmas, how about a few days on a Poverty Bay beach eating freshly caught crayfish (lobster) and drinking crisp Gisborne chardonnay?

Various Locations

Gisborne Wine

www.gisbornewine.co.nz

Gisborne is chardonnay country, and if you visit the annual Gisborne Wine & Food Festival held in October around Labour Weekend, you'll have plenty of opportunity to try the region's most famous export. Eastland's answer to Harvest Hawke's Bay is a little smaller, but it has an efficient system of minibuses to get you around and sampling the excellent food and music, and it becomes increasingly raucous as the day goes on. The festival is part of Gisborne's Wine Week, which also incorporates the International Chardonnay Challenge wine competition. But don't wait for the festival until you visit;

you can sample the luscious bounty of Gisborne's harvest at The Millton Vineyard (0800 464 558, www.millton.co.nz), New Zealand's leading producer of organically grown grapes, all year round. Or celebrate your move to New Zealand at the Lindauer Cellars at the Montana Gisborne Winery (09 336 8300, www.montana.co.nz). Lindauer is the country's most popular sparkling wine, and the cellars include a fascinating museum about the region's wine making.

18 Stout St
Gisborne

Tairawhiti Musuem

06 867 3832 | *www.tairawhitimuseum.org.nz*

If you've immersed yourself in the Maori culture of the rugged bays of the East Cape, this is an excellent place to put everything into context. The Kahurangi exhibition is a collection of sacred objects or treasures (taonga in Maori) that are revered by the tribes of the area, and a poignant collection of old photographs provides a glimpse into earlier times. The region's long maritime history stretches back to 1769 when James Cook called the area Poverty Bay, and the seafaring past comes to life in the tale of the *Star of Canada*, a cargo steamer that foundered on rocks in 1912. The ship's bridge and the captain's cabin were recovered and sit alongside Maori canoes. More recent marine adventurers are remembered in a retro collection of vintage surfboards. The museum includes the delightful Exhibit Cafe. Open Monday to Saturday from 10:00 to 16:00 and Sundays from 13:30 to 16:00. Admission is by donation.

Art deco flourishes, Napier

The promenade at Napier

Daily Telegraph Building, Napier

Area **G** *p.204*

Taranaki & Wanganui

For years the western edge of the North Island that thrusts out into the Tasman Sea was isolated from the cities of Auckland and Wellington. The people of the area have always been independent, and in 1840 Maori chiefs from the Taranaki refused to sign the Treaty of Waitangi. After peace was made between Maori and Europeans, trade and transport hugged State Highway 1, or the main trunk railway line, down the middle of the island, and the industrious folk of the Taranaki and Wanganui regions kept themselves busy with the important task of helping to drive New Zealand's dairy industry. In 1959 natural gas and oil were discovered in the South Taranaki Bight, and the dual industries of dairy farming and energy have ensured the area's economic well-being since.

The Lowdown

Throw away any preconceptions of New Plymouth being a dull provincial city and prepare to be impressed by the city's thriving array of contemporary arts and music events.

Almost 50 years on from the discovery of oil and gas, New Plymouth, Taranaki's capital, is now recognised as one of the country's most dynamic provincial cities. It enjoys one of the lowest unemployment rates and is an increasingly popular destination for local and international visitors alike. 'Just far enough away', claims the tourist literature, and now Taranaki's relative isolation is a benefit and a bonus.

The Essentials

Bag your first summit on Mount Taranaki. It's not a technical climb, but you'll need to be fit to conquer the 2,518m volcanic peak. If it's summer, celebrate by bodysurfing at one of the beaches along Surf Highway 45.

Visitors are attracted by an array of excellent beaches and the opportunity to explore the diverse wilderness of the Egmont National Park (the iconic volcanic cone of Mount Taranaki was previously dubbed Mount Egmont by Captain James Cook in 1770). South-east of New Plymouth, the Wanganui region (p.241) is steeped in Maori and pioneer European history. The quiet river city of Wanganui is the jumping off point for exploring the verdant labyrinth of the Whanganui River, and the challenging walking tracks of the Whanganui National Park. To the north, en route to the mountains of Tongariro National Park, the canyons of the Rangitikei River are an exciting adventure tourism hub.

North Island Map F10

New Plymouth

New Plymouth's tourist information office lures visitors and potential residents to the city with the slogan 'Like no other' and, for once, it's a catchphrase with tangible resonance. Nowhere else in the country has a hinterland comprising rugged surf beaches and a perfect volcanic cone. The population of Taranaki's provincial capital is just under 50,000, but its array of pretty parks and award-winning gardens outblooms most other Kiwi cities. And just when you've got New Plymouth pegged as a pleasant, but slightly dull centre of a thriving farming region, the city surprises with an innovative combo of museums and galleries, and an outdoor entertainment venue that regularly attracts major international performers.

For many years, New Plymouth was isolated from the North Island's traditional Auckland-Hamilton-Wellington axis, but now the city is one of New Zealand's fastest growing tourism destinations. With a regional economy that's insulated from economic downturn by the twin assets of dairy farming and the energy industry, New Plymouth's time in the Taranaki sun has arrived.

40 Queen St
New Plymouth

Govett-Brewster Art Galley

06 759 6060 | *www.govettbrewster.com*

A provincial New Zealand city might be the last place you'd expect to find the nation's premier contemporary art institution, but the coolly innovative Govett-Brewster Art Gallery in New Plymouth is just that. The gallery is home to a collection by modernist filmmaker and kinetic sculptor Len Lye. The Christchurch-born artist exhibited internationally, and, following his death in 1980, most of his work has returned home to New Zealand. Of particular interest are his experimental films and animation, and his kinetic sculptures demonstrating his theory of 'tangible motion'. Lye was one of the first New Zealand artists of European descent to appreciate traditional Maori and Pacific art, and the Govett-Brewster Art Gallery maintains this focus with a special commitment to the Pacific region. Complementing its dedication to the work of Len Lye, the gallery also showcases contemporary New Zealand art and sculpture, and hosts regular international visiting exhibitions. Open daily, 10:00 to 17:00. Admission by donation.

New Plymouth

Mount Taranaki & Egmont National Park

www.doc.govt.nz

Rising from the plains like a South Pacific version of Japan's Mount Fujiyama, Mount Taranki's 2,518m volcanic cone can be seen from across the region. That's if its shroud of mist and rain subsides for long enough. Formed 120,000 years ago, the volcano is still considered active, but its most recent eruption was in 1755. The allusion to Mount Fujiyama is not purely fanciful, and the mountain played the role of Japan's most famous peak in the 2003 Tom Cruise film *The Last Samurai*.

Numerous walking tracks criss-cross the mountain and the ultimate journey is a six to eight-hour return trek to the summit. Because it is so accessible, Mount Taranaki is New Zealand's most climbed mountain, but care must be taken as weather conditions can change quickly. Before embarking on any walks on the mountain, it's absolutely imperative that you register at the North Egmont Visitor Information Centre (2879 Egmont Rd, Inglewood, www.doc.govt.nz, 06 756 0990). It can provide walking maps and up-to-date information on weather and terrain conditions. The mountain has a small skiing scene at the Manganui ski area and the season runs from June to October. The Mountain House Motor Lodge (06 765 6100, www.mountainhouse.co.nz) near Stratford sells ski passes and rents ski equipment.

New Plymouth

New Plymouth Coastal Walkway

www.newplymouthnz.com

If you're new in town, one of the best ways to get your bearings is to walk or bike along the New Plymouth Coastal Walkway. Running for seven kilometres from Port Taranaki in the west to the mouth of the Waiwhakaiho River in the east, there's plenty to have a leisurely look at en route. Most of the expansive seafront promenade is paved, and there are pedestrian access points at regular intervals. At its eastern end, the walkway winds past the surf at Fitzroy Beach and East End Beach. If you're travelling with children, the playground at East End Beach will stop them from getting too restless. If that doesn't work there are another three playgrounds, a skateboard park and a mini-golf course to provide further distraction. The midway point of the walkway borders the New Plymouth CBD, where you'll find the excellent displays at Puke Ariki and the Govett-Brewster Art Gallery. Between Puke Ariki and the waters of the Tasman Sea, is the Wind Wand, a graceful, 45m high kinetic sculpture, designed by artist Len Lye.

1 Ariki St
New Plymouth

Puke Ariki

06 759 6060 | *www.pukeariki.com*

This excellent, self-described 'knowledge centre' incorporates New Plymouth's library, museum, and visitor information centre. The spectacular building is located on Puke Ariki ('Hill of Chiefs'), and it was a prominent Maori hilltop village until the end of the 19th century, when early European settlers made it the base for their fledgling township. Puke Ariki is now New Zealand's most innovative and interesting museum after Te Papa (p.245) in Wellington. The story of Taranaki is told via a range of displays and exhibitions from the early colonial days of the Land Wars through to more contemporary surfing culture. Interactive technology is used throughout the complex. In the Taranaki Stories area, visitors can access personal histories and memories on special 'infopods,' and the audiovisual Taranaki experience provides a snapshot of the region's history in a multi-screen theatre every 30 minutes. Children will love the interactive exhibits, and parents can recharge at the Daily News Cafe or Arborio restaurant while the kids are having fun. Puke Ariki is open from Mondays to Fridays, 09:00 to 18:00, until 21:00 on Wednesdays, and until 17:00 on weekends.

New Plymouth

Pukekura Park & Brookland Park

www.newplymouthnz.com

The 49 hectares of Pukekura Park and Brookland Park are undoubtedly the loveliest parks in New Zealand. Pukekura Park's combination of lawns, lakes and forest comes on like a perfectly compact version of New York's Central Park – there are even rowing boats for hire – and Brookland Park has the Bowl of Brooklands (06 759 6060, www.bowl.co.nz), an outdoor sound-shell that's hosted a large number of international performers including REM and Crowded House. Every March, The Bowl is the venue for the eclectic diversity of the Womad Festival (www.womad.net.nz). More traditional activities include Pukekura Park's gorgeous English-village style cricket oval – it's worth going to a match even if you don't understand the rules – and the annual Festival of Lights. From mid-December to mid-February, Pukekura Park's trees, gardens and waterfalls are illuminated with all colours of the spectrum, and there's live entertainment on two stages.
Taranaki is also renowned for its gardens, and the Taranaki Rhododendron and Garden Festival (www.rhodo.co.nz), held every October, showcases the best of them.

New Plymouth

Sugarloaf Islands Marine Park

www.windwand.co.nz/sugarloafmarine.htm

Normally you need to journey a significant distance out to sea to spy marine species in their natural habitat, but the Sugarloaf Islands Marine Park is a mere kilometre off the coast of New Plymouth. The islands were given their name by Captain James Cook in 1770, and by 1820 a whaling station had been established on Motoroa Island. Each crowned with a distinctive layer of guano from nesting seabirds, the seven islands cover an area of 749 hectares and were classified a Marine Protected Area in 1991. From June to November, the islands host New Zealand's northernmost fur seal colony, and underwater the spectacular terrain includes canyons and caves, and massive rock faces with crevices and overhangs. The islands are eroded volcanic remnants, and are home to 89 different species of fish, and oceanic seabirds including albatrosses. The best way to visit the islands is with Happy Chaddy's Charters (06 7589133, www.windwand.co.nz/ chaddiescharters). Fees: $30 for adults and $10 for children. Fishing and kayaking trips are also available.

Taranaki coast

Mount Taranaki

Various Locations

Surf Highway 45

www.taranaki.co.nz

The waves along the coast of Taranaki are well regarded by the Kiwi surfing community. So much so that the 105km of coastal road that skirts the region from New Plymouth to Hawera is known locally as Surf Highway 45. It's not just regular board riding that draws visitors to experience the pristine surf rolling in from the Tasman Sea. Just south of New Plymouth, Fitzroy Beach is good for bodysurfing, and further down the coast, Kina Road is the popular haunt of windsurfers. A clifftop track leads you to excellent kneeboarding at Opunake Beach. If you prefer to keep dry, most of the beaches are also ideal for fishing, horse riding, or just strolling and considering your good fortune in moving to New Zealand. In beachside settlements like Oakura (www.oakura.co.nz) there's a range of accommodation from luxury villas to more humble seaside cottages.

401 Ohangai Rd
Hawera

Tawhiti Museum

06 278 6837 | *www.tawhitimuseum.co.nz*

Acclaimed as the best private museum in the land, the Tawhiti Museum is an obsessive labour of love by local artist Nigel Ogle. The museum began when Ogle purchased the 70 year old Tawhiti cheese factory in 1975. At first making his incredibly realistic and life-size tableaux of south Taranaki history was just a hobby, but wide interest soon turned the private collection public. Even if your children aren't big fans of museums, the array of lifelike dioramas explaining the Maori and pioneer past of Taranaki should still have them enthralled. There's even a narrow gauge railway to transport visitors around the ever-expanding display. The museum's founder is a former art teacher and there's incredible attention to detail in the various displays. And if any of the faces look a little familiar, don't be alarmed. Ogle regularly uses friends and family as his models, and many of the faces in the displays have been moulded from real people. At the *Wind in the Willows*-themed Mr Badger's Cafe, the characters are slightly more fictional. The museum is open Friday to Monday from 10:00 to 16:00 between September to May, but only on Sundays in the winter months. Entrance fees: $10 for adults and $2 for children.

North Island Map G12

Wanganui

The historic river city of Wanganui (www.wanganui.co.nz) is the gateway for exploring the meandering Whanganui River and the isolated native forests of the Whanganui National Park. The Whanganui River (www.whanganuiriver.co.nz) is the country's longest navigable river, and historically was used by both Maori and Europeans for trade and transport. In these days of rail and road, traffic on the river now consists of travellers in canoes, kayaks and jetboats exploring an impossibly scenic procession of river landings and long-abandoned and isolated settlements. In the surrounding national park (www.whanganuinationalpark.com), days are spent on spectacular bush walks, and nights in a wide range of eco-friendly accommodation.

North Island Map H12

Rangitikei

For an area that's so close to New Zealand's State Highway 1, it's a surprise that the Rangitikei region is still an undiscovered tourism gem. It hugs the deep river gorges of the Rangitikei River, providing thrills ranging from river rafting and trout fishing to riding the world's highest and longest flying fox through the sublime Mokai Canyon (www.gravitycanyon.co.nz). Horse trekking and cultural tours by local Maori (06 3881444, www.hikoitreks.co.nz) provide the perfect balance. The best place to stay is at River Valley Lodge (06 388 1444, www.rivervalley.co.nz), an isolated and rustic lodge on a riverbend. Upstream from the lodge are international-class Grade 5 rapids, but downstream the paddling is more scenic and leisurely.

Area **H** *p.204*

The Lowdown
Wellington is a compact city, so forgo a car and use ferries, buses and the cable car to get around. In the centre of town you can easily walk between most places of interest and attractions.

The Essentials
Spend the morning at Te Papa, and the afternoon at the New Zealand Film Archive and you'll have downloaded all the essentials for becoming an authentic Kiwi.

Wellington Region

Not so along ago, Wellington was derided by the rest of New Zealand as a grey, faceless city inhabited by grey, faceless bureaucrats. Now the nation's capital is the last word in hip and cool.

For a capital, it's not a big city, but Wellington's population of 170,000 – tucked into the steep valleys and ridges that cascade down to the harbour – is large enough to sustain a surprising number of cosmopolitan galleries, theatres, bars and restaurants. On average, Wellingtonians are better educated and have higher incomes than the rest of New Zealand, and the locals celebrate this with an eclectic and diverse arts and cultural calendar. Wellington's recent metamorphosis from ugly duckling to cultural trendsetter has been partly fuelled by the international acclaim afforded to local filmmaker Peter Jackson, director of *The Lord of the Rings* trilogy and *King Kong*. Creative industries have sprouted up to support Jackson's vision, and the city's moribund political facade has been overtaken by companies such as Weta Workshop, the Oscar-winning special effects powerhouse. In Cuba Street's bohemian cafes Fidel's (p.456) and Ernesto's (p.456), the caffeine-fuelled talk now is more likely to be about entertainment than economics, while along Courtenay Place, the conversations continue long after dark in what is New Zealand's liveliest bar and restaurant scene.

All this work and play demands balance, and locals use mountain bikes and kayaks to make the most of their harbourside location. Wellington's challenging terrain produces equally challenging walks to scenic lookouts on the city's iconic Mount Victoria, and on weekends a less energetic alternative is to cross the Rimutaka Ranges to the vineyards, restaurants and boutique accommodation of the Wairarapa (p.246).

Cable Car Lane
280 Lambton Quay
Wellington
Map p.503 D3 **12**

Cable Car

04 472 2199 | *www.cablecarmusuem.co.nz*

Wellington's cable car, hidden down a quiet lane off busy Lambton Quay, takes six spectacular minutes to reach its terminus at Kelburn Park. For the best views of the CBD, the harbour and distant Hutt Valley, sit on the left-hand side as you ascend. Once you've reached the finish, spend a leisurely hour exploring the 25 hectares of Wellington's Botanic Gardens. Classified as a Garden of National Significance by the New Zealand Gardens Trust, the beautiful expanse includes lush native bush, and the lovingly tended Lady Norwood Rose Gardens. Nearby, the Carter Observatory (www.carterobservatory.org) has astronomy displays and videos during the day and viewing of the night sky in the planetarium after dark. Come back down to earth at the Cable Car Museum, which tells the story of one of Wellington's most popular attractions since its inception in 1902. The cable car runs every 10 minutes from 07:00 to 22:00 on Mondays to Fridays, and from 08:30 to 22:00 on weekends. Fees are $4.50 for a return trip; $2.50 for a single and $12 for a family return ticket.

Civic Square
101 Wakefield St
Wellington
Map p.505 D1 **13**

City Gallery

04 801 3952 | *www.city-gallery.org.nz*

Wellingtonians are an arty bunch, and black-clad creative types are regular visitors to City Gallery's exhibitions of innovative and challenging art, design and architecture. The emphasis is on New Zealand artists, but the gallery also features visiting shows from contemporary international artists. The best of Wellington artists is showcased in the Michael Hirschfeld Gallery, and the sunny courtyard at the attached Nikau Cafe (p.457) is the perfect place to ponder what you've just seen. Complementing the ever-changing array of art are regular events, including school holiday programmes for the kids, poetry readings and short films from up-and-coming film makers at Wellington's New Zealand Film School. City Gallery is open daily, 10:00 to 17:00. Admission is by donation but there may be a charge for international exhibitions.

The view from Brooklyn Hill

Fisherman's Table Restaurant, Oriental Parade

Cable Car

City to Sea Bridge

Evans Bay

Eastbourne & Days Bay

If the kids are getting restless trawling around Wellington's excellent historical attractions and museums, jump on a ferry and head across the harbour to Eastbourne and Days Bay. Locals flock to this seaside suburb for simple pleasures such as alfresco cafes, swimming and the challenge of finishing their icecreams before they melt in the summer sun. More active types can kick a football around Williams Park, or go on bush walks in nearby East Harbour Regional Park. Kayaks and bicycles are available from the Days Bay Boat Shed to increase your exploring radius. Some Eastbourne ferries stop at Matiu (Somes) Island. The island was once a quarantine station and a detainment camp for internees during the world wars, but is now administered by the Department of Conservation as a refuge for endangered birds and the tuatara, a small species of reptile that dates back 200 million years. You'll need around three hours to explore the island, so why not pack a picnic?

Waiapu Rd
Wellington
Map p.498 A5

Karori Wildlife Sanctuary

04 920 9200 | *www.sanctuary.org.nz*

A hidden valley of 252 hectares of native forest and protected endemic wildlife is not usually found within two kilometres of the centre of a capital city. The Karori Wildlife Sanctuary was opened in 1995 and, if you're pressed for time, it's an excellent opportunity to observe New Zealand wildlife in its natural state. The sanctuary is encircled by an 8.6km perimeter fence that keeps out domestic and wild predators, including cats, possums and mice. The long-term vision for the sanctuary includes the reintroduction of many endangered species that are now only found on isolated offshore islands. A significant area of wetlands is also being rehabilitated. Negotiating the sanctuary's walking tracks can be done independently, but you'll get more out of your visit on a two-hour guided tour. The sanctuary by night tour is your best chance to see the nocturnal kiwi and the elusive tuatara. Open daily, 10:00 to 17:00.

Queens Wharf
Wellington
Map p.503 E3 15

Museum of Wellington City & Sea

04 472 8904 | *www.museumofwellington.co.nz*

Located in the Bond Store, a wonderfully restored customs house, the collection at the Museum of Wellington City & Sea stretches back to cover the region's original Maori settlers, and the arrival of Europeans in the mid 19th century. Wellington's maritime history is brought to life with suitably salty sound effects, and two Maori creation myths are recreated with fascinating holographic imagery. More recent history is remembered in a moving documentary about the sinking of the inter-island ferry, the *Wahine*, which foundered in rough waters in Cook Strait in 1968 with the loss of 51 passengers. Wellington is known as a windy city, but the gusts on 10 April 1968 reached 240kph, and the accompanying storm was the most violent ever recorded in New Zealand. Open daily from 10:00 to 17:00. Admission is free.

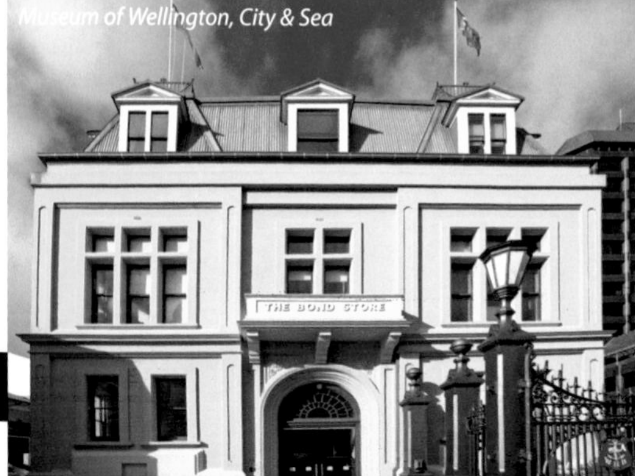

Museum of Wellington, City & Sea

The theatre at Te Papa

Cnr Ghuznee St & Taranaki St
Wellington
Map p.505 D2 16

The New Zealand Film Archive

04 384 7647 | *www.filmarchive.org.nz*

Following the global success of local boy Peter Jackson with *The Lord of the Rings* trilogy, Wellington has earned the affectionate and slightly ironic nickname of 'Wellywood'. The nation's capital is therefore the obvious place to find the New Zealand Film Archive. Established in 1981, the Film Archive is charged with the guardianship of New Zealand's moving image history. Dating back to 1895, films of every genre can be viewed including features, short films, historical footage, documentaries, TV programmes and advertising. It's a superbly managed resource and an essential asset for any newcomers to New Zealand wanting to fast-track their knowledge of the country. On at least five nights a week, the Film Archive's 120 seat cinema is used to show treasures from the vaults, including rarely seen local feature films, and thought-provoking international documentaries. Open from 09:00 to 17:00, Monday to Friday, and from 16:00 on Saturday.

Cnr Lambton Quay & Molesworth St
Wellington
Map p.503 E1 17

Parliament Buildings

04 471 9503 | *www.parliament.govt.nz*

The contrasting buildings that sit side by side to form New Zealand's official seat of government make up Wellington's most eclectic architectural sight. Parliament has been sitting on this spot since 1865 when the capital was moved from Auckland. The Victorian Gothic Parliamentary Library was completed in 1899, and in 1922 was joined by the Edwardian neo-Classical Parliament House. Next door is the incongruous executive wing, completed between 1969 and 1980, and which is nicknamed 'The Beehive'. The Beehive is not open to visitors but hour-long tours of Parliament House are available between 10:00 and 16:00, Monday to Friday, from 10:00 to 15:00 on Saturday and from 12:00 to 15:00 on Sundays.

You can watch the country's politicians verbally jousting in the wood-lined debating chamber from 14:00, Tuesday to Thursday. After you've finished at Parliament House, wander down the hill to New Zealand's original Government Buildings at 15 Lambton Quay. Built in 1876, the world's second-largest wooden structure was designed to look like it's made of stone. The interior is equally impressive with glorious staircases and wooden fittings. Open Monday to Friday from 09:00 to 16:30 and on Saturday from 10:00 to 15:00. Admission is free.

Cable St
Wellington
Map p.505 E1 18

Te Papa, Museum of New Zealand

04 381 7000 | *www.tepapa.govt.nz*

Dominating Wellington's re-energised waterfront, the national Museum of New Zealand was opened at a cost of $317 million in 1998. Since then, the striking building – which houses a collection of more than two million items – has been embraced by locals and visitors alike. Proud Kiwis like to refer to Te Papa as 'Our Place', and, as befits Wellington's reputation as an emerging hub for creativity and technology, the museum delivers world-class and cutting-edge interactive experiences.

In the time warp section, virtual reality technology transports visitors back 65 million years to the country's violent volcanic genesis, and the four discovery centres lead children on a variety of interactive 'learning trails'. Compulsory for all newcomers to New Zealand should be the poignant passports exhibition, which examines a millennium of immigration, while in the quirky Golden Days second-hand shop you can watch an entertaining film about the last century of Kiwi history. Te Papa really knows how to combine the high-tech with the heartfelt.

The Art of the Nation gallery has regular exhibitions showcasing treasured local artists such as Colin McCahon and Frances Hodgkins, and a superb Maori collection features a unique 21st century update of a traditional wharenui, or meeting house. Pacific

culture can also be experienced on Taonga Mataora evenings where cultural performances are combined with a menu of traditional Maori foods.
Open daily, 10:00 to 18:00 and until 21:00 on Thursdays. Admission is free.

Wellington

Wellington Waterfront & Oriental Bay

There's an oft quoted saying in the nation's capital: 'You can't beat Wellington on a good day.' It's true that the city can be very windy (be wary of the infamous southerlies and norwesters), but if you're here on a cloudless and wind-free day, a wander from the waterfront precinct to Oriental Bay will silence the harshest of critics from Auckland or Christchurch. With Te Papa as its hub, Wellington's waterfront offers opportunities for walking, cycling and rollerblading, or just stretching out on the grass watching the Cook Strait ferry start its journey to the South Island. West of Te Papa, Oriental Bay is Wellington's English-style seaside promenade, complete with band rotunda, ornamental fountain and the kids' favourite, the Freyberg Playground. Some of the cafes and restaurants aren't too bad either.

200 Daniell St
Wellington
Map p.498 C7

Wellington Zoo

04 381 6750 | *www.wellingtonzoo.com*

Founded in 1906 following the donation of a lion cub from a visiting circus, New Zealand's oldest zoo is now focused on conservation, research and education. Its captive breeding programmes for endangered species include chimpanzees, Sumatran tigers and Malaysian sun bears. More than 500 animals live in enclosures designed to recreate their natural environments as closely as possible. Boisterous primates get to hang out on monkey island, and shy red pandas live in their own Nepalese-style abode. The zoo's nocturnal house, Te Ao Maahina ('The Twlight'), is a good place to see native fauna such as the kiwi, the morepork (an indigenous owl) and the tuatara. Visitors can adopt animals through the zoo's parent programme, and, zoopreme sleepovers, an educational alternative to children's birthday parties. Open daily, 09:30 to 17:00.

North Island
Map G14

The Wairarapa

The first grapes were planted in New Zealand in 1819, but the Wairarapa has only been known as a wine-producing area for the last three decades. Centred on the pleasant town of Martinborough, the region's wine industry is already acclaimed internationally, particularly for its rich and peppery pinot noir. A gourmet food industry has developed around the vineyards, and on weekends the region's restaurants and classy boutique accommodation are popular with visitors from Wellington, just an hour's drive across the Rimutaka Ranges (www.wairarapanz.com).
At the Martinborough Wine Centre (www.martinboroughwinecentre.co.nz) you can sample and buy goodies from more than 30 local vineyards, and every November the Toast Martinborough Wine, Food and Music Festival (www.toastmartinborough.co.nz, see p.63) fulfils its promise as the country's best food and wine festival. With 11,000 visitors, it's mighty popular so you'll need to book well in advance. As well as trying world-beating wines, you'll get to hear top Kiwi music acts while picnicking in sunny gardens and vineyards. As the locals say: 'Sweet as...'

Wellington Zoo

Area A p.205

Marlborough

The Lowdown
Seafood, art, wine, seawater and wilderness – all the pleasures a middle-class income can buy.

The Essentials
Cruise the Marlborough Sounds, tramp or bike the Queen Charlotte Track, watch whales off Kaikoura, then get cheerful on a winetasting tour.

Marlborough broadly encompasses three distinct regions, as you appreciate when you reach the South Island by ferry, cruise through the Marlborough Sounds, and then drive south from the terminal at Picton.

The vast, convoluted and scenic waterways of the Sounds offers an altogether different experience from the river plains – mostly planted in grapes – and the arid hills of the Blenheim district, and both differ markedly from Kaikoura (p.252), crammed between mountains and the rocky margins of the sea.

The entire region is rich in history. Many places have associations with the turbulent inter-tribal warfare of pre-European Maori history. The site of the first permanent European settlement lies in the outer regions of the Marlborough Sounds, as do 'Kupe's footprints', supposed to be traces left by the first Polynesian explorer to visit Aotearoa. This heritage is preserved in a number of fine museums, from the Edwin Fox (p.250) on Picton's foreshore to the Marlborough Museum at Brayshaw Park (p.250) in Blenheim and the amazing Omaka Aviation Museum (p.257) just outside it.

Once a service hub to the struggling sheep farmers of the surrounding district, Blenheim (p.250) has, over the last 25 years, become the capital of the booming Marlborough winegrowing region.

With its super-abundant marine life, Kaikoura was an important resource for pre-European Maori. Today, it's the flagship of New Zealand's eco-tourism movement, and has acquired a distinctly new age, bohemian character.

South Island Map N3

Marlborough Sounds

The Marlborough Sounds is a maze of sheltered inlets, coves, bays, and rugged islands and peninsulas. There are three main waterways: Queen Charlotte, Kenepuru and Pelorus Sounds. With most of the best features of the Sounds inaccessible by road, the best ways to appreciate their charms is by boat (p.298), or on foot or by mountain bike on the Queen Charlotte Track (p.250). In any weather, boaties can find secluded anchorages where the water is millpond calm and a cathedral-like silence prevails. For those who don't have independent access to a boat, there are many excursions to the outer Sounds available. The water taxis to pick from are: Westbay Transport (03 573 5597, www.westbay.co.nz), Endeavour Express (03 573 5456) and Arrow Water Taxis (03 573 8266, www.arrowwatertaxis.co.nz). With abundant marine life, a bird sanctuary and a private wildlife preserve, the Sounds are a happy hunting ground for fishermen and the fledgling 'eco-tourism' industry. There's only one thing to beware: the water of the Sounds is very deep and icy cold, year-round.

View from the Interlslander

Anakiwa

Situated at the head of the Grove Arm of Queen Charlotte Sound, Anakiwa is a stop on the Queen Charlotte Track (p.250), and seems like a metropolis to walkers after the seclusion of the route's earlier stages. It features a number of accommodation providers, from backpackers to high-class establishments, and several private holiday homes for hire. The quiet, tidal cove is popular with boaties. Anakiwa makes a great base for exploring Kenepuru Sound, whether by car, on foot, or (the best way) by sea kayaks, (Sea Kayaking Adventures, www.seakayaking.com, 03 574 2765).

D'Urville Island

The largest of the islands of the outer Marlborough Sounds, D'Urville Island is mostly privately owned, but you can go fishing, diving, snorkelling, swimming, tramping, walking, mountain biking (trails are rated among the top 10 in the country) and sea kayaking – all can be arranged through the D'Urville Island Wilderness Resort (03 576 5268), which makes an attractive spot for an overnight stay.

The island is accessed by launch from Havelock. Points of interest nearby include French Pass, where the vicious tidal stream is reckoned to be among the fastest-moving seawater in the world, and the wildlife sanctuaries of Stephens and Maud Islands, both of which may be visited only with (rarely granted) permission of the Department of Conservation (www.doc.govt.nz).

Havelock

Havelock lies at the tidal head of Kenepuru Sound, and is the hub for most of the excursions and activities involving Kenepuru and Pelorus Sounds. It's noted as the birthplace of Ernest Rutherford, who pioneered the splitting of the atom, and to whom a memorial was opened in 2003. It's also the self-proclaimed 'Greenshell Mussel Capital of New Zealand', and a festival celebrates the marine delicacy annually (p.58). The town's situation is very pretty, backed by high, bushclad hills and overlooking the sheltered waters of the Sound.

Motuara Island

A short distance offshore from Ship Cove is the long, low Motuara Island. Sea kayak excursions operated by First Light Travel (09 360 3820, www.firstlighttravel.com) include it as a destination. Several species of bird that have vanished from the mainland, notably the saddleback (tieke) and the New Zealand robin (toutouwai) thrive here, and the island provides a protected habitat for others that are under pressure: the bellbird (korimako), the native wood pigeon (kereru) and the grey warbler (riroriro). A couple of rare native reptiles have been re-established, and a pod of the very rare hector's dolphins frequent the area. The walk to the island's summit is easy, but there is no water available. Visitors should check their belongings for mice before they leave; there are a lot about.

White's Bay

White's Bay is an attractive, sheltered beach on Marlborough's north-eastern coast, with excellent swimming and fishing off its hard white sand. It's an ideal location for a day trip, or a summer camping holiday. It's patrolled by a lifeguard in summer, and there's a Department of Conservation campground. The bay is a short drive on good roads from Blenheim.

Ship Cove

Even Yorkshiremen are susceptible to a nice bit of landscape, and the beautiful Ship Cove, with the bush overhanging the water, was one of the great English navigator James Cook's favourite places in the Pacific. He used it as his base on the first and both subsequent voyages. This was the site of the first extended transactions between the Maori and European cultures. The cove is not accessible by road, which has helped to preserve its charms. It is the beginning of the Queen Charlotte Track, and is serviced by water taxi and a number of the launch excursions operating out of Picton.

Tirohanga Walkway
Take this one and a half day walk on the hills behind Picton and be rewarded with panoramic views over the town and Queen Charlotte Sound. Find the start at Newgate Street in Picton.

Queen Charlotte Track

The Queen Charlotte is unique among New Zealand's Great Walks in that it doesn't have huts; accommodation is commercial, whether at campgrounds or in luxury lodges along the way. It's 71km in total, and mostly easy walking. You'll need to carry water between Punga Cove and Portage, as there is no source along the way. The views and the bush are magnificent. The Queen Charlotte can be done by mountain bike, and it can be walked in sections, with transport to and from entry points by water taxi. Guided walks are also available with several companies. Try the award-winning Dolphin Watch Ecotours (03 573 8040, www.naturetours.co.nz) or Tuatara Tours (0800 377 378, www.tuataratours.co.nz).

South Island Map N3

Picton

Although a good proportion of visitors to the South Island see Picton – the inter-island ferry terminal is here – the majority press on south rather stopping. Recent moves to create local attractions are intended to detain them. On Dunbar Wharf, there's an excellent aquarium, Seahorse World (03 573 6030, www.seahorseworld.co.nz), which stars the New Zealand potbellied seahorse, the largest species of this creature in the world, a tank into which brave visitors can dip their hands and touch the marine life, as well as audiovisual presentations on the area's whaling history. Best time to visit is at one of the two feeding times, 11:00 and 14:00 daily. Alongside it is the Edwin Fox Museum (03 573 6868), featuring the restored remains of one of the armada of vessels that brought British immigrants to New Zealand in the 19th century. Picton also has a small museum, which is of particular value to those with an interest in whaling. But if you have little more than an hour to kill, the town's foreshore is a magic spot for fish and chips.

South Island Map N3

Blenheim

It wasn't until the first grapevines were planted here in 1973 that Blenheim's fortunes really changed. What was once a dreary backwater has become quite a funky little town. Today, it attracts those in search of the good life. It's the focus of the annual Marlborough Food and Wine Festival (p.59), there's a thriving cafe and restaurant scene – including the nationally renowned Herzog winery and restaurant (03 572 8780) – and three excellent art galleries. The heart of Blenheim has been laid out with spectacular flower beds and fountains to complement the grand stone war memorial clock tower, raised to commemorate the fallen of Marlborough in the first world war. Protected by the Föhn effect from the prevailing westerlies, Blenheim typically enjoys some of New Zealand's hottest summer temperatures. The town also has one of the region's coolest boutique hotels, Hotel d'Urville (03 577 9945, www.durville.com).

The major attraction of the district is the vineyards; more than half of the national vineyard is here, there are over 70 wineries with open cellar doors, and tours are available by bus, bike and even horse and cart. Check out Marlborough Wine Tours (03 578 9515, www.marlboroughwinetours.co.nz) and Wine Tours By Bike (03 577 6954, www.winetoursbybike.co.nz).

Waihopai Valley Rd
Marlborough

The Diversion Gallery Grove Mill Winery

03 573 7376 | *www.thediversiongallery.co.nz*

Winemaker Grove Mill operates this gallery alongside its restaurant and cellar. Most media – paintings, drawings, sculpture and prints – are on display and for sale. Major recent exhibitions include leading New Zealand painters Michael Smither and Don Binney. Visitors are encouraged to view and sample the grapes at harvest time in the 'vine library'. All of it is a calculated attempt to get you to buy the wine, and it turns out that's not a bad idea, either. Open 11:00 to 17:00 daily, except public holidays.

Seymour Sq
Blenheim

Millennium Public Art Gallery

03 579 2001 | *www.marlboroughartsociety.com*

Blenheim may be a small town, but its municipal gallery punches above its weight in terms of the exhibitions it manages to attract from prominent international and national artists. The building, with its grand frontage on Seymour Square, was opened in 1999, in time for the millennium celebrations. Besides featured exhibitions, it also presents a good selection of the work of local painters, sculptors, jewellers and craftspeople. Entry is by donation. Open weekdays 10:30 to 16:30; weekends, 13:00 to 16:00.

Marlborough

Molesworth Station

This is the largest farm in New Zealand, covering 180,476 hectares and spanning much of inland Marlborough. Molesworth Station is now administered by the Department of Conservation as a 'farm park'. This was in recognition of the conservation values that were being trampled underfoot by the station's 10,000 head of cattle. The recreation possibilities include four-wheel drive touring, horse-trekking, cycling, rafting, kayaking, fishing and hunting. The three- to four-day rafting trip down the Acheron and Clarence rivers is rated as one of New Zealand's finest whitewater experiences. The roads in the north-western part of the park are four-wheel-drive only, and you'll have to pay for access. Camping is permitted only at specified sites along the roads. Several guided tour companies, including Molesworth Tour Company (03 577 9897, www.molesworthtours.co.nz), hold concessions in the park that give them year-round access. Permission to enter outside the summer months (December to the first weekend in March) can be negotiated with the Department of Conservation (www.doc.gov.nz).

79 Aerodrome Rd
Blenheim

Omaka Aviation Heritage Centre

03 579 1305 | *www.omaka.co.nz*

Thanks to the personal interest that movie mogul and vintage plane nut Peter Jackson has taken in this world-class aviation museum, the lifelike dioramas and the backdrops to the exhibits have been put together by some of the world's leading special effects technicians. Besides the machines, the inaugural feature exhibition 'Knights of the Sky' includes a remarkable collection of 'aerobilia', with bits of planes and flying gear used by world war one flying aces on display. It's not just for planespotters though; this is easily worth two or three hours of anyone's time. Open daily, 10:00 to 16:00.

South Island Map M5

Kaikoura

Kaikoura's Maori name literally translates as 'a feed of crayfish', and it's for its crayfish – along with just about anything else that lives in the ocean – that the area is famous. The presence of the undersea Hikurangi Canyon just offshore creates an abundance of nutrients, and the entire foodchain, from plankton to great whales, is represented. The town itself is small, but it enjoys one of the best locations in New Zealand, squeezed between the sea and the precipitous, snow-capped Kaikoura Ranges. A former whaling site, Kaikoura offers world-renowned and supremely well-organised whale-watching tours (03 319 6767, www.whalewatch.co.nz).

It is believed that the Kaikoura Peninsula has been continuously occupied for the last 1,000 years. The remains of many ancient Maori fortifications can be seen on a poke about the area. Evidence of its European past can also be found, in the shape of the whalebone picket fence that once surrounded a whaler's cottage and the whalebone headstone on a local grave. The views from the lookout at its highest point are impressive – out over South Bay, north toward Cape Campbell and west to the inescapable Kaikoura Ranges.

South Island Map N5

Hapuku

Hapuku, around 12km north of Kaikoura, boasts one of New Zealand's most interesting accommodation options, the treehouses at Hapuku Lodge (0800 524 56872, www.hapukulodge.com). Each treehouse is built from an eclectic range of materials and has panoramic views of sea and mountains. Just north of Hapuku at Half Moon Bay, a short walk off State Highway 1 brings you to a waterfall that a colony of local fur seals uses as a nursery; you can get within a couple of metres of seal pups at rest and play. Last but not least, the mouth of the Hapuku River is a popular and reliable surf break.

14 Ludstone St
Kaikoura

Kaikoura Museum

03 319 7440

This little museum has an extensive local history collection, detailing the natural, cultural and economic past of one of the oldest and most important sites of human habitation in New Zealand. You can browse fossilised Plesiosaur bones, many moa-hunter and Maori artefacts and plenty of relics of the district's whaling and farming days. Open 12:30 to 16:30 weekdays. Call ahead for weekend timings.

62 Avoca St
Kaikoura

Fyffe House

03 319 5835 | *www.historic.org.nz*

This cottage dates back to the 1850s, making it the oldest surviving building in Kaikoura and one of New Zealand's longest-standing houses. When Fyfffe was digging out the foundations, he discovered some pre-European adzes, a human skeleton and a moa's egg, which currently rests in Te Papa (p.245). Fyffe House has been preserved as a museum of sorts. Guided tours are available, or you can just wander through and imagine the lives of those who lived here in the days when the fishy stink of whale blubber hung over the whole town. Summer: open daily 10:00 to 18:00; winter 10:00 to 16:00.

Whale watching

Towards South Bay

Kaikoura

Area **B** *p.205*

The Lowdown
Sunshine, beaches and art; rivers, mountains, lakes and a long, long sandpit. The lifestyle capital of New Zealand.

The Essentials
Kayak Abel Tasman National Park, visit Farewell Spit, ski at Rainbow, learn to fly-fish, swim in the pure water of the Riwaka Resurgence.

Nelson Region

Given its climate, the quality of its beaches and the natural beauty of its landscapes, it's little wonder the region is very much a lifestyle capital. Something about the area draws an extraordinary number of artists – but they're brave; holding a mirror up to nature in these surroundings is a daunting task.

The Nelson region is physically diverse, ranging from the mountainous ranges of Richmond Forest Park to the broad coastal flats behind the great sweeps of Tasman and Golden Bays.

The west of the region gets pretty wild. First, there's Abel Tasman National Park (p.257), dividing Tasman and Golden bays. One of the iconic experiences to be had in the South Island is a kayaking holiday around its many bays and inlets. A reserve has been created centred on Tonga Island; marine life is abundant and it's not uncommon to share the water with inquisitive fur seals as you paddle past.

Between Abel Tasman and Kahurangi National Park, there are the unique karst landscapes of Takaka Hill, otherwise known as 'Marble Mountain' (p.256). This system includes the sublimely pure waterways of the Riwaka Resurgence and the Waikoropupu Springs, the second most optically pure water in the world.

At the region's western boundary, Kahurangi National Park (p.258) provides one of the few areas in New Zealand to find genuine wilderness, away from the crowds that even tramping tracks can bring.

North of Kahurangi National Park is the long, curving sandbar known as Farewell Spit. The tour to the lighthouse close to the end of the spit is a great day out, and best incorporated with a look at the gannet colony just beyond it, a visit to the historic sites at Puponga and a marvel at the massive granite arches on the coast at the base of the spit.

Several unique landforms in the area were used for locations in the *The Lord of Rings* trilogy of movies: Mount Owen, a weird outcropping of limestone, starred as Dimrill Dale, and Mount Olympus for the wildlands south of Rivendell. You can reach either on foot, or Nelson Helicopters (0800 450 350, www.nelsonhelicopters.co.nz) can set you down as part of a memorable scenic flight.

South Island Map M3

Nelson

Nelson enjoys the most sunshine hours of any town in New Zealand. Its location, sandwiched between wine-growing country and the magnificent coastline, combines with the climate to offer a pretty special lifestyle.

Nelson city itself occupies the flat land at the mouth of the Maitai River, which has a series of superb swimming holes just a couple of miles to the east. It's backed by hills that offer fine views over the city and the harbour enclosed by the naturally formed Boulder Bank – a great place for a stroll of a summer evening. The city has a number of pleasant open spaces, including the Victorian splendour of Queens Gardens, and there's a thriving cafe and restaurant scene. Lambretta's (20 Hardy Street, 03 545 8555) is a funky spot that does a good line in pizza. The top two restaurants, The Boatshed (350 Wakefield Street, 03 546 9783) and The Cut (94 Collingwood Street, 03 548 9874) are among the best in the South Island. Besides the small wineries out of town, it'd be worth your while visiting Founders Brewery (03 548 4638), which produces Tall Blonde lager, arguably New Zealand's finest beer.

Trafalgar St
Nelson

Nelson Cathedral

The present cathedral, a striking combination of gothic and modern styles realised in beautifully figured grey Takaka marble, is the third church on the site. This one was built in 1930, with the distinctive square steeple opened in 1965. There's a labyrinth in the eastern transept, which is open from 08:00 to 17:00 daily. The cawthron stairs in front of the cathedral are a popular spot for a picnic.

Cnr Hardy St and Trafalgar St
Nelson

Nelson Provincial Museum

03 548 9588 | *www.museumnp.org.nz*

The forerunner to Nelson Provincial Museum – and New Zealand's first ever museum – was the Literary and Scientific Institute of Nelson, which was founded in 1841 by a group of gentlemen enjoying a snifter in the stateroom of the New Zealand Company ship that was carrying them across the Bay of Biscay en route to Nelson. Its first premises were built on Town Acre 445, the same block occupied by the museum's present building, with its imposing steel and glass frontage. It houses an excellent local history exhibition, including the largest photographic collection in New Zealand. Open from 10:00 to 17:00, Monday to Friday and 10:00 to 16:30 on weekends and public holidays.

208 Bridge St
Nelson

Suter Gallery

03 548 4699 | *www.thesuter.org.nz*

The 100 year old Suter Gallery has been recently rehoused in a superb new building, where the panoramic windows make as much of a feature of the views out into Queens Gardens as of the art in the airy, light spaces within. The Suter hosts travelling exhibitions, and holds floor and other events to inform the public about the nature and mission of art. Its permanent collection features works by famous local artists John Gully and Toss Woollaston, and has a good array of local ceramics on display. It's a great place to spend an absorbing couple of hours. Open daily, 10:30 to 16:30.

Nelson

Tahunanui Beach

A few minutes' drive to the west of Nelson is the fine, flat, white sand beach of Tahunanui, the seaside playground of generations of the town's residents. There's a very popular (and consequently very hard to book) campground (03 548 5159, www.tahunabeach.co.nz). It's one of the country's safest swimming beaches, with little or no surf or currents. The area behind it has been developed with amusement and sports facilities. There's a skatepark, a BMX track, playgrounds, a roller skating rink, a pool with hydroslides, mini-golf, and a model railway, as well as tennis courts and a petanque course – something, in short, for everyone.

95 Quarantine Rd
Nelson

World of Wearable Arts and Classic Car Museum

03 547 4573 | *www.wowcars.co.nz*

The World of Wearable Arts (WOW) Show (p.63) is held annually and features an indescribable array of costumes, body painting and multimedia craftwork, all designed to be worn and paraded in a curious cross between theatre, fashion show and art exhibition. WOW might have been poached by Wellington, but its spirit lives on in Nelson where it all began in 1987. The WOW and Classic Car Museum, a short drive west of Nelson, features displays of the winning entries from years gone by in one half of the building, and a collection of more than 50 immaculately restored cars and motorbikes in the other. The museum runs a variety of family programmes, and there's an on-site gift shop and gallery specialising in contemporary art. Open daily, 10:00 to 17:00.

South Island Map M3

Tasman District

The Tasman district ranges from the very civilised (its towns have excellent cafes and restaurants where you can drink local wines, and most probably an art gallery or studio to boot) to the very wild (Kahurangi National Park is as close to untouched wilderness as you'll get outside the heart of Fiordland, p.290). Abel Tasman National Park, which preserves some of New Zealand's prettiest coastline, is the big draw but there are plenty of other features that you won't see elsewhere: the Waikoropupu Springs (p.258) and the Riwaka Resurgence, where a river that has been running underground for many kilometres boils up into the daylight again.

South Island Map L2

Kaiteriteri

Kaiteriteri is the region's most popular summer holiday destination. It features a shallow estuarine lagoon flanked by bush-clad islets, opening out to a gorgeous beach of white sand. If you want to stay at the Kaiteriteri Beach Motor Camp (03 527 8010, www.kaiteriteribeach.co.nz), you'd best book well in advance, as much of the custom returns year-in, year-out, merely rolling their bookings over.

Sea kayaks are for hire (Kaiteriteri Kayaks, 0800 252 925), or if paddle power is a little too sedate for you, there's always waterskiing and jetskiing with Kaiteriteri Watersports (0800 66 66 68, www.abeltasmanwatersports.co.nz). Abel Tasman Adventures (0800 000 901) will rent you a self-drive speedboat or small yacht, and skippered charters are available from Kaiteriteri Boat Charters (03 528 6754, www.kaiteriteriboatcharters.co.nz). Excursions to the fur seal colony at Tonga Island depart from Kaiteriteri (0800 25 29 25, www.sealswim.com).

South Island Map M3

Mapua

Mapua, half an hour's drive from Nelson, is a great place to stop off en route to Motueka. The waterfront area in particular has been beautifully developed. There's a photographic museum, mostly devoted to the history of coastal shipping, an aquarium

Tahunanui Beach

Nelson Cathedral

Heading out of Nelson

(Touch the Sea, 03 540 3447, www.seatouchaquarium.co.nz), where you can get close to sharks, stingrays, eels and other aquatic critters, and an award-winning cafe and delicatessen specialising in traditionally smoked food (The Smokehouse, 03 540 2280, www.smokehouse.co.nz). There's also a great patisserie (The Naked Bun, 03 540 3656, www.thenakedbun.co.nz). Like much of the Nelson district, Mapua is overrun with artists and craftspeople. A good selection of local work can be viewed or purchased at The Cool Store Gallery (03 540 3778), and studio tours are available to visit painters, potters and a sculptor working Oamaru stone.

South Island Map L2

Motueka

Motueka was once the hops and tobacco-growing capital of New Zealand. Tobacco is no longer commercially grown, but there are hops and, of course, vineyards. Motueka is the nearest town to the Abel Tasman National Park, so consequently many of the operators servicing visitors to the park are based here. For those interested in the history of the area, Motueka District Museum (03 523 7660) has a good collection of photographs and artefacts. Motueka also has a thriving food, art and crafts market from 08:00 to 13:00 every Sunday. A good spot for pizza is the very hard to find Bakehouse Café (03 528 6111) set back from High Street and indicated only by a footpath sign.

South Island Map L2

Takaka

Situated at the eastern end of the aptly named Golden Bay, Takaka receives a good deal of through traffic from the Abel Tasman National Park (just to the east) and from travellers bound for Farewell Spit (to the west). It's a pleasant little place for a spot of relaxation, nowhere more so than at Anahata Yoga Retreat (03 525 9887, www.anahata-retreat.org.nz).

Takaka's market on Saturday morning is a good place to buy art, crafts and local produce, and a short drive towards Pohara is the recommended Totally Roasted Coffeehouse and Café (03 525 9396, www.totallyroasted.co.nz).

Massacre Bay
Golden Bay was the site of the first, inauspicious contact between Maori and Europeans, when the Dutch explorer Abel Tasman anchored there in December 1642. Four of his crewmen were killed in a skirmish with Maori, prompting him to name the place Murderer's Bay and high-tail it to Indonesia. It was occasionally known by the alternative name 'Massacre Bay until it received its decidedly more marketable name in the 20th century.

About 17km beyond Takaka, you'll find the Mussel Inn (03 525 9241, www.mussel inn.co.nz), a very popular restaurant, microbrewery and bar. The atmosphere is great, and so is the beer, just don't let them see you using a mobile phone. Just before Takaka, up McCallums Road in the Anatoki Valley, you'll find Anatoki Salmon – a freshwater salmon farm that offers you the chance to catch your own fish or simply buy one, fresh, cooked or smoked (03 525 7251, www.anatokisalmon.co.nz).

Takaka Hill

Its nickname, Marble Mountain, sort of gives the game away. Takaka Hill, lying between Motueka and Takaka, is a karst landscape, comprising limestone and marble and incorporating at least three notable geological features: the Riwaka Resurgence, where the Riwaka River reappears from a rocky cleft after running some of its 20km course in a subterranean channel; the Ngarua caves, which are safe and accessible enough for the general public to enjoy and Harwoods Hole, an immense sinkhole 180 metres straight down.

Access to the last is by a short walk from the end of the Canaan Road, a winding, gravel affair that turns off State Highway 60 around 30km from Motueka. There's a viewing platform from which you can see the cave opening up, but unless you mean to abseil into it, approaching the edge is not recommended.

The Ngarua caves are best visited with a guide, and that man is Mike (03 528 8093). The highlight is a magnificent, fluted chamber dubbed the Wedding Cathedral.

The Riwaka Resurgence is found by taking the Riwaka Valley Road (signposted left off State Highway 60 as you travel west from Motueka). The water bubbling up from the cave into the pool at the head of the river is unbelievably clear, and a wonderful place for a swim. The cave itself is also a popular scuba diving site for those with the necessary skills. If you have the wherewithal and desire to stay, there's the upmarket boutique hotel, The Resurgence (03 528 4664, www.theresurgence.co.nz).

Abel Tasman National Park

www.abeltasman.co.nz

Occupying the peninsula that separates Tasman and Golden bays, the 22,530 hectare Abel Tasman National Park is one of New Zealand's most visited attractions, offering spectacular coastal walking and even better boating.

Rainbow Ski
Only an hour and a half's drive from Nelson, Rainbow is a small but excellent skifield. It faces north-east, and on a good day, gets hot sun. There's a decent range of terrain and facilities. Natural snow is boosted by artificial snowmaking. See www.skirainbow.co.nz

There is great road access, but the real park experience is to be had by water or on foot. The 51km Abel Tasman Walkway can be accessed at four points, so it's ideal for day-trippers or those who want to do a section at a time. It gets insanely busy in summer. Bookings are essential, not only for the huts along the route but also for the overflow campgrounds (www.doc.govt.nz or www.abeltasman.co.nz). There have been suggestions in recent years that the park's sanitary facilities cannot cope with visitor numbers, but the Department of Conservation manages visitor pressures carefully. Easily the best time to do the walkway is in the winter, when the crowds and the sandflies (and the mosquitoes at night) are a little thinner on the ground and in the air. The other popular way to see the park is by water, especially by sea kayak.

There are several secluded bays and inlets to explore (many of them too tidal for larger craft), and there's the Tonga Island Marine Reserve, which is home to a fur seal colony and an astounding profusion of underwater life. Take a mask and snorkel if you're visiting. A large, spherical granite boulder, Split Apple Rock (actually lying at the eastern end of Sandy Bay, near Marahau) is a compulsory photo stop for most paddlers. But you'll need plenty of film or memory cards in the Abel Tasman – it's a snapper's paradise.

Marahau

South Island Map M2

Marahau, four kilometres off State Highway 60, exists because of Abel Tasman National Park. More than a dozen businesses based here ply their trade in and around the park's azure water, jewel-like beaches and rugged bushland.

Several sea kayaking operators offer you the guided experience, or the 'freedom paddling' option for a few hours up to several days. The originals are Abel Tasman Kayaks (03 527 8022, www.abeltasmankayaks.co.nz), which is owned by the local iwi (tribe) and offers a cultural dimension to the commentary.

Water taxis depart Marahau for drop-off/collection points in the Abel Tasman at 09:00 and 13:00 each day, returning at 12:00 and 16:30 respectively (Southern Exposure Water Taxis, 03 527 8424, www.southern-exposure.co.nz). There are two other companies offering water taxi services, as well as skippered charters (see www.abeltasman.co.nz for more details).

After a hard day – or hard days – enjoying the park, you could do worse than round it off with a beer and a bite to eat at The Park Café (03 527 8270). The food's basic, but the beer is cold and includes local brews, and there's local arts and crafts for sale too.

Cape Farewell

South Island Map L1

Apart from sand dunes, which form the backbone of Farewell Spit (its Maori name is Te Onetahua, 'piled up sand'), the landscape here is predominantly wetland, and it's one of the country's most prolific wading bird habitats. No fewer than 83 species are represented in spring, so if birding is your thing, sling the bins and the camera in your bag.

Due to the sensitivity of the habitat, access to much of it is strictly controlled. Only two operators, Farewell Spit Eco-Tours (0800 808 257, www.farewellspit.co.nz) and

Kahurangi Nature Experiences (03 525 6044, www.farewell-spit.co.nz), are permitted to take visitors through en route to the lighthouse near the spit's end. The first lighthouse, built in 1870, was once actually at the very tip, but the spit is growing. Tours take a minimum of half a day from Collingwood, and cost between $80 per adult and $110. The no-frills version goes to the lighthouse, which have displays on the area's history. Others allow visitors to walk 30 minutes beyond the light to the large gannet colony near the spit's tip. You can also stop at Puponga (at the north-western limit of Golden Bay), which is a site of considerable significance to Maori and was once a coal mine and port, or go across to Pillar Point and Wharariki Beach, with its immense, weathered arches of granite. If you want a slightly more adventurous way to explore the points of interest of Cape Farewell, there are several tramping tracks and there's an operator who takes horse trekking tours: Cape Farewell Horse Treks (03 524 8031). All of it makes for a unique experience, as this is a landscape quite unlike any other in New Zealand.

South Island Map K2

Kahurangi National Park

Established in 1996 and covering over 450,000 hectares, Kahurangi is one of New Zealand's premier wilderness areas. Much of it is trackless, although there is an extensive network of huts sprinkled throughout the beech forest and tussockland, and trampers, cavers and anglers traverse all but the remotest corners. For those who prefer relatively easy tramping, the Heaphy Track on the western boundary and the more difficult Wangapeka on its southern boundary offer two of New Zealand's best, albeit very different in character. The Wangapeka is a classic river valley route, with steep ridges between catchments, beautiful tracts of beech forest, and several river crossings. It takes four to five days to walk. St Arnaud is a good place to start out from, getting a ride from Nelson Lakes Shuttles (03 521 1900, www.nelsonlakesshuttles.co.nz). The Wangapeka is often combined with the Heaphy to create a round trip.

They main thing they have in common is their almost unbelievable profusion of wasps, which thrive on the honeydew produced by the beech forest.

Kahurangi comprises a number of geological and ecological features: the so-called mineral belt, a band of rock bearing the ores of everything from iron, tin, copper and gold to coal and asbestos; the karst areas of Mount Owen and Mount Arthur, each of which are honeycombed with significant caves and sinkholes (New Zealand's longest cave, the 39km Bulmer Cavern, pierces Mount Owen); and many rare plant and animal species.

The most accessible part of Kahurangi is undoubtedly the Cobb Valley, where an easy day's walk gives you a taste of the Kahurangi experience. Most of the waterways in the park are well-stocked with brown trout, and the wilderness fishing is unparalleled. Tasman Helicopters (03 528 8075, www.tasmanhelicopters.co.nz) is one of several operators who will fly you into the heart of the park, drop you off and return to collect you later in the day.

South Island Map L2

Waikoropupu Springs

The Waikoropupu Springs (or Pupu Springs, as they're known) are renowned as the second most optically pure water in the world, and since you'd have to dive below the Ross Ice Shelf in Antarctica to find the purest, you'd be mad to miss them. Until recently, you could swim here, but the recent outbreak of the destructive alga, didymo, has seen Pupu Springs closed to bathers, divers and fishermen. But all is not lost. There's a clever viewing platform with a periscopic arrangement of mirrors that allows you to stand on dry land and see beneath the water. And, in any case, it's fascinating just watching the muscular percolation of the water which has spent so long underground filtering through the limestone on the surface of the pools.

Area C p.205

Canterbury

The Lowdown

Home to New Zealand's third largest – and most English – city, the imposing presence of the Southern Alps, and the unique landscapes of Mackenzie Country.

The Essentials

Soak in Hanmner Springs, head to the beauty of the Banks Peninsula, tackle Mount Cook. And don't forget the Chathams.

Permanent settlement of Canterbury began with the arrival in 1850 of the Canterbury Association, a league of Anglican gentlemen who dreamed about establishing a model Church of England colony. That colony is now the region's largest city (and New Zealand's third largest population centre), Christchurch.

The character of the region has changed dramatically in the last two decades. Christchurch has become decidedly cosmopolitan compared with the oversized service town it once was, with the makeover of the central city transforming the previously cold, stony heart of the place into a vibrant attraction in its own right. Similarly, the constellation of drab, utilitarian towns up and down the region, from Amberley in the Hurunui district to Timaru in south Canterbury, have been transformed by the new imperative to put the 'style' back into 'lifestyle'. And a day spent 'over the hill' from Christchurch in Akaroa (p.264), one of New Zealand's quaintest towns, enjoying lunch and a glass of local wine on the waterfront, is as good as gets.

Besides the broad, flat alluvial plains, Canterbury has three distinctive areas formed by old volcanic activity – two of which are Banks Peninsula and the Port Hills behind Lyttelton, and the south Canterbury town of Timaru (p.266), built on the weathered lava flows of the evocatively named, long-extinct volcano Mount Horrible. The hot springs at Hanmer and Maruia Springs in the Lewis Pass are a living reminder of the distant volcanic past.

To the west, Canterbury embraces the foothills of the Southern Alps and, past the ramparts of the Dalgety and Four Peaks Ranges, the broad, tussock basin of the Mackenzie Country (p.267), stretching from the glacial lakes that supply much of New Zealand's hydroelectricity to the boundary of Mount Cook National Park (p.268). The snow-capped Alps dominate the view wherever you are in Canterbury; whether you're up in the high country, or they're hovering as a backdrop to your prospect over the plains. The scenery of the foothills area of the Alps formed the backdrop to much of *The Lord of the Rings* movies: the spectacular set for Edoras was constructed in the equally spectacular Mount Somers area. The Alps provide a wealth of recreation opportunities, from the many ski fields in the region to the hiking and mountaineering possibilities of Mount Cook and Arthur's Pass national parks.

South Island Map L5

Hurunui District

Stretching from Kaikoura in the north to the Ashley River in the south, and inland to Hanmer Springs, Hurunui district perches high in the main divide. It has enjoyed a spectacular revival of fortunes on the backs of tourism and viticulture. Waipara boasts more than 20 wineries – its distinctive pinot noir, riesling, chardonnay and sauvignon blanc vintages command respect. Take a wine tour from Christchurch or Kaikoura, see the vineyards aboard a horse-drawn cart drawn (03 314 9001) or get a handle on the terroir at the Waipara Hills Winery Restaurant (03 314 6900). There are good local beaches, notably Gore Bay, which has a good campsite (03 319 8010).

South Island Map L5

Hanmer Springs

Hanmer invites the label of the poor man's Queenstown, not only with its setting but also in the range of activities on offer and the number of tourists it draws. Cafes and handicraft outlets line the main street, backed by the craggy, frequently snow-capped Hanmer and Amuri ranges. Hanmer grew up around the thermal springs discovered here by a Culverden farmer, William James, in 1859. This forms the basis of the thermal resort that delights visitors today. For $12 you can get a single pass to the pools, or you can fork out up to $340 for a package including accommodation, spa, sauna and massage therapies. Contact Hanmer Springs (03 3157 128, www.hanmersprings.co.nz).

Just before you reach the township on State Highway 7A, you'll pass a bridge and a signpost to Thrillseekers Canyon (www.thrillseekerscanyon.co.nz), where a range of adventure activities, including jetboating, rafting, quad biking, bungee jumping, paintball and claybird shooting, are available. Hanmer Springs is close to two small club skifields, the Hanmer Springs Ski Area and Mount Lyford (03 315 6178, www.mtlyford.co.nz). There's no better way to round off a day's skiing than contemplating the snowy peaks from your vantage neck-deep in softly effervescing hot water.

South Island Map L7

Christchurch

At the heart of Christchurch is Cathedral Square, and at the heart of Cathedral Square is Canterbury Cathedral, its spire directing your gaze to heaven. That was the idea, anyway. Of all the various planned immigrant communities Christchurch came closest to realising the purity of the vision: a godly English city away from England. The impression is encouraged by the predominance of Gothic Revival architecture in the older public buildings. Even the city's climate is English, with hard winters and hot summers, although the famed norwester is a hot wind at any time of year. Still, the leafy suburbs of Fendalton (p.140) and Cashmere (p.139) are the closest thing you'll find to English upper class these days.

The centre of the city, still considered one of the most conservative in New Zealand, is now notably arty – the development of the 'cultural precinct' that takes in the Arts Centre, the Art Gallery, Canterbury Museum and the Centre of Contemporary Art (p.266), as well as a number of heritage buildings, has been an inspired move. Christchurch is completely flat, with the sole exception of the Port Hills between the city and the port at Lyttelton. This makes it easy to get around, especially by bicycle. The other striking feature is that it's beautifully planted. Hagley Park (p.263) at the heart of town features rolling lawns, mature trees and Christchurch's superb Botanic Gardens (p.262). The best way to enjoy all this arboreal and floral splendour is to take a punt along the winding course of the Avon River.

Christ's College

Christ's College on Rolleston Avenue (www.christscollege.com) is New Zealand's best-known boys' school. The oldest building, the Big School, dates back to 1863. The chapel is particularly worth a look, if only for its beautiful stained-glass windows. You are welcome to browse the grounds and buildings and, for $5, you can join a guided tour.

Orchard Rd
Christchurch
Map p.508 A3

Antarctic Centre

03 353 7798 | *www.iceberg.co.nz*

The Antarctic Centre celebrates the city's long association with antarctic science and exploration – it's set among the bases of the New Zealand and international research programmes – and gives you as close an encounter with the ice as you're likely to get. Slide down an artificial snow slope, experience an artificial blizzard (the 'snow and ice experience') and go on a 15 minute ride in a Hogglund vehicle. Guides are available, or hire a 'snow phone' ($6, in eight languages). Next to the airport (follow the blue footprints to the terminal), the centre is a great place to spend a few hours before a flight. There's even a left luggage facility ($1.50 an hour for a locker that will hold three big cases, $2.50 for three hours and $3.50 for five). It's relatively pricey though – from $30 to $85 per adult.

Worcester Boulevard
Christchurch
Map p.516 A1 22

The Arts Centre

03 366 0989 | *www.artscentre.org.nz*

The beautiful old stone buildings of the former Canterbury University College campus have been turned into to a thriving arts hub, a leisurely amble from Cathedral Square. The centre is honeycombed with small galleries, studios and crafts shops, theatres and cafes. There are lunchtime concerts on Fridays and live music every day in the summer. Buskers work the crowd outside, food stalls operate in the lane behind and there's a lively arts and crafts market every Sunday. The Court Theatre hosts two venues, the 29 seat Court 1 and 120 seat Forge. The Court's players are the most respected professional theatre troupe in New Zealand.

William Rolleston Statue

Christchurch Museum

Summit Road

Botanical Gardens

Banks Peninsula

Rolleston Av
Christchurch
Map p.515 E1 23

Botanic Gardens

www.ccc.govt.nz/parks/botanicgardens/

These magnificent gardens grew from an oak planted to celebrate an English royal wedding in 1863. Today, the park sprawls across 20 hectares. Gardens Restaurant is open while the gardens are (daylight hours) and it's a fine spot to enjoy a Devonshire tea. The information centre opens weekdays from 9:00 to 16:00, and 10:00 to 4:00 on weekends.

Cathedral Sq
Christchurch
Map p.516 C1 24

Christchurch Cathedral

www.christchurchcathedral.co.nz

The foundations of the cathedral were laid in 1864, but built from locally quarried stone and much of the timber that once grew on Banks Peninsula, it was 40 years and many false starts before it was completed. The original design was by English architect George Gilbert Scott; this was then adapted by Mr Gothic Revival himself, Benjamin Mountfort. There are many points of interest, so it's best to join a guided tour. The cathedral is open to visitors from 9:00 to 17:00 Mondays to Saturdays, and 07:30 to 17:00 on Sundays (or whenever evensong finishes). See the website for service times.

Montreal St
Christchurch
Map p.516 A1 25

Christchurch Art Gallery/Te Puna o Waiwhetu

www.christchurchartgallery.org.nz

The latest addition to – and flagship of – Christchurch's cultural precinct is the fantastic art gallery, housed in a building that's all curved glass and brushed steel. It's as much a work of art as anything hanging on its walls, although the collection rivals most others in New Zealand. It favours new work by Canterbury artists. Open daily from 10:00 to 17:00, and until 21:00 on Wednesdays. Entry is free, although there is a charge for some exhibitions.

New Brighton and Sumner
Map p.508 F4

New Brighton and Sumner Beaches

New Brighton is a popular picnic spot with its long, sandy beach, which is usually safe for swimming (and patrolled in the summer). There's a children's playground as well as excellent toilet and changing facilities. The pier connects with the New Brighton Mall via a cafe and beautiful public library. Fishing is permitted, though restricted to when the pier isn't busy and baitboards are fitted along the pier.

Packed with picnickers and bathers on hot days, and haunted by surfers, kite surfers and windsurfers, the line-up at the Sumner is magical when a norwester combs an easterly swell (although real surfers will tell you you're wasting your time if you're not at nearby Taylor's Mistake). Hang-gliders launch from Scarborough Hill (at the southern end) and the beach forms a handy runway for them. Little blue penguins nest among the rocks, their harsh, eerie cries startling many a romantic couple strolling along the beach at night. In the middle of the beach, a formation named Cave Rock has thrilled generations of Christchurch children.

10 Bridle Path Rd
Christchurch
Map p.508 F7

Christchurch Gondola

www.gondola.co.nz

Voted one of Christchurch's best attractions, the gondola is the easy way to admire the stunning views from the summit of Port Hills. The gondola rises 500m on its 945 metre journey. Passengers are whisked four to a cabin to the top, where you'll find a cafe, upmarket licensed restaurant (Pinnacle) and shops. But you came for the view – over Christchurch, Lyttelton and the Banks Peninsula, towards the Kaikouras and the Alps. Day or night, it's pretty special. It costs $22 for an adult, $10 for a child or $55 for mum, dad and two kids. If you are dining, an adult ticket comes down in price to $12.

7 Tramway La
Christchurch
Map p.516 C2 28

Christchurch Tramway

03 366 7511 | www.tram.co.nz

Trams were the main mode of public transport in New Zealand cities before the second world war. Only Christchurch has preserved part of its tramway, which once extended for 80km throughout the city and suburbs. Today it circuits a mere 2.5km around the centre and takes less than half an hour to complete. The dining car is a classy way to eat while cruising the streets. Groups of 20 or more can book it for breakfast, lunch or morning tea, as well as cocktail functions.

Riccarton Av
Christchurch
Map p.515 D3 29

Hagley Park

www.ccc.govt.nz/parks/hagleypark/

It was an act of vision leaving the heart of Christchurch to parkland. Hagley Park – all 161 hectares – is the envy of other municipalities, extensively planted in mature (mostly exotic) trees and studded with sports grounds. There are few better settings in which to watch a game of club cricket on a Saturday afternoon. Hagley Oval hosts first-class fixtures, plus there are soccer, rugby and hockey grounds, tennis and netball facilities, and even an 18 hole golf course. You'll also find picnic and barbecue facilities, an excellent playground and several toilet blocks. The Avon River offers good punting.

McLeans Island Rd
Christchurch
Map p.508 A2

Orana Wildlife Park

www.oranawildlifepark.co.nz

The highlight at Orana, New Zealand's only open range zoo, is to ride the specially designed transport through the lion reserve at feeding time. With 15 feeding times throughout the day, some critter or another is fed every 40 minutes. Besides the exotic animals, there are several native species, including kiwi and tuatara. A free hop-on, hop-off shuttle circuits the zoo's exhibits and there are free guided walkabout tours at 10:40 and 14:30. It's open from 10:00 to 17:00 daily (no entry after 16:30).

392 Moorhouse Av
Christchurch
Map p.517 D4 31

Science Alive!

www.sciencealive.co.nz

This might seem like the sort of place the geeky member of the gang will try to drag you, but it's actually good fun for all. There are things to look at – ever-changing exhibitions and displays – as well as things to do, such as a climbing wall, slides, a gyroscope and even glow-in-the-dark mini golf. While management reckons kids should be older than six to get the most out of it, you'd really want to take them along when they're slightly older. Prices depend on age: infants are free, adults pay $15 (or $17 if they play mini golf). Open 10:00 to 17:00 Sundays to Thursdays, and from 10:00 to 18:00 on Fridays and Saturdays.

Map p.508 F7

Lyttelton and Around

The quirky port town of Lyttelton has many features that recall its maritime past. The dry dock was built in 1883 and is still in use: you can view it from the lookout in Brittan Terrace, or by arranging a closer inspection with the port company (03 328 8198). The pretty little Timeball Station, perched up on the hill, is one of only a handful of these curious little maritime machines left in the world, and offers glorious views of Lyttelton and Diamond Harbours. Lyttelton Museum (03 328 8972) is entirely devoted to the township's link with Antarctica, most famously Robert Falcon Scott and Ernest Shackleton, who used the port as a base en route to their ill-starred expeditions. Governors Bay is at the tidal head of Lyttelton Harbour and is reached by driving over the Port Hills or around the harbour. It's the site of a hotel that dates to 1870, and still offers accommodation (03 329 9433, www.governorsbayhotel.co.nz). Nearby, you can visit one of Canterbury's most spectacular private gardens, Taunton (03 329 9746, www.tauntongardens.com). There is bed and breakfast accommodation in Jack's Cottage, which dates to 1862.

Around the northern headland of Lyttelton Harbour on the Evans Pass Road is Godley Head. It's honeycombed with defensive fortifications, including a 110 metre tunnel which is good, spooky fun for the kids. And by the foot of the bluffs between Taylor's Mistake and Boulder Bay, you can see the remains of the holiday homes that Christchurch locals once kept in the series of natural caves.

Canterbury's version of New York's Ellis Island, Quail Island was the waypoint for assisted immigrants arriving in the 1800s. It was then used as a quarantine station for livestock – Robert Falcon Scott and Ernest Shackleton both trained their ponies on the beach before heading south on their respective expeditions – and it's now a recreational reserve with a network of walking tracks to explore, plus a former leper colony and 'ships' graveyard' on the western shore, where the remains of eight vessels are visible in the shallows. You can reach the island with the Black Cat Ferry Company (03 304 7641, www.blackcat.co.nz), which will also take you to Diamond Harbour, 10 minutes from Lyttelton. There is a beautiful swimming beach here, with views across to Lyttelton, backed by the moody Port Hills.

The smaller of the two islands in Lyttelton Harbour, Ripapa Island (Mooring Rock) is considered one of the three most sacred Maori sites in the South Island (along with Aoraki/Mount Cook and the tussock basin of Kura Tawhiti).

South Island Map L8

Banks Peninsula, Akaroa & the Outer Bays

Banks Peninsula to the east of Christchurch was formed by the eruption of two massive volcanoes – the remains of their craters form Lyttelton and Akaroa harbours. While many of the long, deep bays that pierce its coastline are shown to be accessible on maps, beware the quality of the roads; they're mostly gravel, steep and winding, not for the faint-hearted or (in many cases) the two-wheel drive. Most visitors head straight to the main settlement of Akaroa, settled by the French in a near-annexation in 1840. Akaroa still bears a discernibly French influence; many of the street names – and some of the local surnames – are French, and many local businesses celebrate the French connection. Lying on the northern shoreline of the long harbour, Akaroa has a picturesque setting. The town is tiny, with narrow streets flanked by weatherboard colonial buildings. Restaurants and cafes abound, as do craft and souvenir shops. The Akaroa Museum (03 304 1013) includes the Langlois-Eteveneaux House, one of the oldest buildings in the South Island.

Needless to say, now as ever, the harbour is Akaroa's greatest asset, and several companies offer tours and cruises, including Black Cat Cruises (03 328 9078, www.blackcat.co.nz) and Dolphin Experience Akaroa (03 304 7726, www.dolphinsakaroa.co.nz).

The so-called Outer Bays of Banks Peninsula are accessible by sea, on foot, by a long, winding and sometimes hairy drive, or by hitching a ride with the Eastern Bays Mail Run (03 325 1334) as it delivers the post. Each bay has its own character. Flea Bay (just to the north of the entrance of Akaroa Harbour) is notable for its population of the rare pohatu, or white-flippered penguin. Pohatu Plunge (03 304 8552, www.pohatu.co.nz) will take you out to the colony. Another option is Le Bons Bay, 15km to the north-east of Akaroa, a pretty spot with a good swimming beach and its own populations of hector's dolphin and pohatu. The local backpackers (in a 130 year old homestead) runs launch trips (03 304 8582, www.lebonsbay.co.nz).

The 10km drive from Okains Bay to Pigeon Bay is wonderfully scenic, with the high ridges alternating with plunging sea cliffs and steep-walled bays. One such bay, Little Akaloa, features one of New Zealand's prettiest churches, St Lukes, built in 1906 entirely by the efforts of a community who had previously been obliged to worship under a tree. Despite its formidable hills, Banks Peninsula is one of Canterbury's most popular cycling destinations. Le Race (www.lerace.co.nz) is an annual cycling event (as fun or serious as you want it to be) that runs from Christchurch to Akaroa.

South Island Map J6

Selwyn District

Selwyn District is named after the river that runs through it from its source high on the eastern flanks of the Alps to Lake Ellesmere and ultimately the Pacific just south of Christchurch. Westward, and leaving the plains with its network of country roads, rivers and streams and service towns, the land climbs through the limestone country (including the spectacular karst landscape of Castle Hill) of the foothills to the main divide proper. Selwyn District contains no fewer than five skifields, and, in Arthur's Pass National Park, one of New Zealand's premier centres for alpine pursuits.

South Island Map J6

Arthur's Pass

Arthur's Pass, at 920 metres the lowest of the three main passes across the main divide, was pioneered in 1864 by surveyor Arthur Dudley Dobson, and bears his name. Low it may be, but the road is still often tricky in winter, and if there's snow in the air, you're well advised to check conditions before tackling it. The tiny collection of buildings just before the true pass – a Department of Conservation office, a railway station, a reasonable cafe and a bunch of accommodation providers (including the Avalanche Creek campground) – is right in the middle of the Arthur's Pass National Park, a swathe of alpine country, including some notable peaks. Walks in the area range from a couple of hours to several days. There are five skifields within a half-hour's drive, and, whether you choose to get among the scenery or not, it's breathtaking to look at.

South Island Map J7

Castle Hill

A small village has grown up at Castle Hill, a little over 100km west of Christchurch on State Highway 73. The principal attractions are outdoor activities, notably rock-climbing and skiing – Castle Hill is within 20km of four skifields, and is adjacent to Cave Stream Reserve. Each entrance to the 362m cave is easily reached by a short walk from the road. The Department of Conservation (www.doc.govt.nz) recommends tackling the tunnel from the downstream entrance. The tunnel is wet, cold and a bit of a scramble, but long enough to be genuinely thrilling.

South Island Map J8

Ashburton District

Bounded by the Rakaia River to the north, the Rangitata to the south and by the ranges to the west, the Ashburton District is spectacular and beautiful by turns. Much of the highcountry area around Mount Somers was used for location shooting for *The Lord of the Rings* trilogy. Mount Somers and the nearby town of Methven are focal points for winter recreation, with several skifields, including one of the southern hemisphere's finest, Mount Hutt, within a half an hour's drive from each.

South Island Map J8

Mount Hutt Ski Area

Mount Hutt skifield boasts the longest ski season in Australasia, with a combination of reliable precipitation, low winter temperatures and sophisticated artificial snow-making machines usually allowing things to get underway in June and lasting the rest of the year. Situated just over an hour's drive from Christchurch, it's very much a local winter playground, as well as a popular destination for Australians exploiting cheap trans-Tasman airfares.

Half the available terrain is suitable for intermediate skiers, but there are beginners' areas and dangerous bits to keep others interested. For those with a genuine death-wish, a bungee jump operates off a bluff in the upper field. On days when snow is due, get a ride on a mountain shuttle rather than risk getting stuck on the road up or having to mess about with chains. The lifts are swift, comfortable and efficient, meaning there's seldom a problem with queues.

South Island Map J8

Mount Somers

Set against the majestic backdrop of the Winterslow Range, Mount Somers is the gateway to the Ashburton District high country, with a collection of lakes and access to the rivers and mountains in which the fishing and hunting excels. The township is small but it's notable for one of the best restaurants in the area, Stonechrubie (03 303 9814) and for the jewellery produced at Rangiatea Station (03 303 9819, www.rangiatea.co.nz) from local shells and minerals.

Mount Somers is also the starting point for the Mount Somers Walkway, regarded as one of the best two-day sub-alpine traverses in New Zealand. Contact the Department of Conservation (www.doc.govt.nz) for more information. There are many shorter walks – from one hour to a full day – for the less adventurous.

South Island Map J9

Timaru & Around

Timaru's name is a corruption of the Maori 'Te Maru', which translates as 'place of shelter'. It was the modicum of shelter from the elements on this fiercely inhospitable coast that caused the settlement to be built up – the town's present-day information centre is housed (along with a bar and a microbrewery) in a bluestone warehouse-cum-boatshed run by one of the surfboat operaters.

Once a derelict port, Timaru is now a very pleasant seaside town that makes the most of its location.

At the top of Stafford Street, with a commanding view of the bay, is Ginger and Garlic (03 688 3981, www.gingerandgarlic.co.nz), widely reckoned to be one of Canterbury's best restaurants. South Canterbury Museum (03 684 7212), one of the finest museums in the South Island, has a great collection focused on South Island local history, and also hosts touring exhibits. The Aigantighe Art Gallery (03 688 4424, www.aigantighe.org.nz), housed in a graceful historic homestead, holds the third largest public collection in New Zealand, with works ranging from 16th century to contemporary and from European and Asian to Pacific Island and local.

South Island Map J8

Geraldine

Situated 130km south of Christchurch at the southern limit of the Canterbury Plains, and spectacularly backed by the grandeur of the Southern Alps, Geraldine is at its best in autumn, when its exotic trees are in bloom. It was once described as the most boring town in New Zealand, and it's hard to deny the locals have plenty of time on their hands when you're confronted by The Giant Jersey (www.thegiantjersey.co.nz) – at three metres from cuff to cuff, two metres high and a metre and a half wide, the largest woollen sweater in the world.

New Zealand artist Peter Caley has a gallery in town (03 693 7278, www.caleyart.co.nz) where you can browse and buy his and other local artists' work. Just outside town, there's the excellent Belanger-Taylor Art Glass Studio, which works with sheet and blown stained glass (03 693 9041, www.belangertaylorartglass.co.nz).

South Island Map J8

Peel Forest

The 773 hectare Peel Forest is the largest remnant of the great podocarp forest that carpeted the Canterbury Plains before the Maori brought fire and European settlers brought axes. It's a popular recreation spot for people from across the region. Situated on the banks of the Rangitata River and at the foot of the Alps, it's a great spot for tramping, fishing, rafting, kayaking, horse riding and cycling within a short radius. There's a DOC campground, and the General Store (03 6963 567, www.peelforest.co.nz) offers accommodation and supplies, as well as a little joint called The Musterer's Bar and Café.

South Island Map H8

Rangitata River

The Rangitata is known as much for its fine salmon fishery as for the fearsome rapids in its upper reaches, which make it one of the great rafting destinations of New Zealand. Rangitata Rafts (0800 251 251, www.rafts.co.nz) operates a full day trip from Christchurch, which you can also join at Peel Forest. There are two Grade 5 sections in the Rangitata Gorge, which are at the limit of commercially rafted whitewater in New Zealand. The season runs from September to May, and costs range from $175 to $185 per person.

South Island Map G8

Mackenzie Country

Surrounded by sheer, snow-capped mountains, and presided over at its north-western extremity by Aoraki/Mount Cook, Mackenzie Country is incredibly beautiful. It's named after a shepherd called James McKenzie who had driven a flock of 1,000 sheep over the basin into a high, broad tussock plain beyond. The little stone Church of the Good Shepherd (p.268) at Tekapo is undoubtedly one of New Zealand's most photographed buildings, such is the grandeur of its setting. But for as long as people have been coming to the district, the main attraction has been Mount Cook (p.268). The Hermitage Hotel (0800 686800. www.hermitage.co.nz) at the entrance to Mount Cook National Park has been the base for sightseers and adventurers since it was built in 1888, although it now nestles in the small township of Mount Cook.

South Island Map G8

Tekapo

Tekapo is attempting to transform itself into a tourist trap and not just a place you pass through en route to Mount Cook. To this end, there's a new winter resort (03 6806 550, www.winterpark.co.nz), incorporating an artificial snow slope, an ice skating rink and hot pools. All gear, including the entire rink, is for hire.

Tekapo is also a natural base from which to explore the surrounding region. Scenic flights are available from Air Safaris (03 680 6880, www.airsafaris.co.nz), which flies fixed-wing aircraft, or from Tekapo Helicopters (0800 359 835, www.tekapo helicopters.co.nz). The latter will take you to the most remote parts of the district. Mackenzie Alpine Horse Trekking (0800 628 269) runs horseback tours in the summer from its base at the foot of Mount John. The lake itself is an excellent venue for watersports (although pretty cold year-round).

Accommodation ranges from the local motor camp (03 680 6825) to the luxurious Godley Resort Hotel (03 680 6848, www.tekapo.co.nz), and there's a very highly regarded Japanese restaurant in town, too: Kohan (03 6806 688).

Mackenzie Country

Lake Tekapo

South Island Map J9

Twizel

Most of Twizel's attractions lie outside the town's boundaries. There are four-wheel drive sightseeing tours – much of this countryside was used as a backdrop to *The Lord of the Rings*. Discovery Tours (03 435 0114, www.discoverytours.co.nz) can provide vehicles, drivers and the local knowledge to show it all off. Thrillseekers will find plenty of terrain to ride mountain bikes over, especially if they catch a helicopter to the top of the steeper bits (see www.helibike.com for details). Sedate kayaking is available on Lakes Pukaki, Ruataniwha and Ohau, the Ohau skifield is 20 minutes' drive, and High Country Auto Services (www.highcountrynz.com) will rent you a jetski. The strange game of golfcross (golf played with an oval ball and goalposts; see www.golfcross.co.nz) is played at Braemar Station on the shores of Lake Pukaki. There's also a freshwater salmon farm (www.mtcooksalmon.com), where you can do a tour from 08:00 to 18:00 daily, feed the fish or buy them to feed yourself.

That's not to say there's nothing to do in Twizel itself. The local picture theatre, Big Sky Movies (03 435 0035), shows new releases, and Poppie's Café (03 435 0848, www.poppiescafe.com) is a good spot for lunch or dinner.

South Island Map G8

Church of the Good Shepherd

Often called the Church of the Lonely Shepherd because of its location on the shores of Lake Tekapo, a photo stop is de rigueur for coach tours. It was built from oak and lake stone in 1935 as a memorial to the runholders of Mackenzie Country. Its window over the altar frames Lake Tekapo and the gothic silhouette of Mount Cook. Services are held on a rotational basis. Nearby, a bronze statue of a border collie pays tribute to James McKenzie's dog, Friday, and the faithful canines that made working the Mackenzie Basin possible.

South Island Map G8

Mount Cook National Park

Whether you intend to climb, walk, ski or just sit still, Mount Cook is a great place to visit, if only to bask in the ineffable grandeur of it all. The park contains several of New Zealand's highest and most formidable peaks, including New Zealand's loftiest, the 3,745m Aoraki/Mount Cook, and a third of the park's total area is under permanent snow and ice. The gaps between the mountains are occupied by glacial valleys, many of them still featuring glaciers; the 27km Tasman Glacier is the longest in the world outside the Himalayas. You can visit the terminal face of the Tasman Glacier by taking a boat across the lake in summer (1 October to 31 May), courtesy of Glacier Explorers (03 435 1077, www.glacierexplorers.com), or the Mueller Glacier by sea kayak (03 4351 890, www.mtcook.com).

This, needless to say, is action man (and woman) country, with the mountaineering, heli-skiing, hunting, fishing and tramping all as good as it gets. For those who prefer to watch, the sightseeing is just about as spectacular, whether from the air, on foot, or the comfort of your own car.

Mount Cook is a funky little village, full of tourists, rabbits and the cheeky native alpine parrot, the kea. Accommodation ranges from the DOC campground at White Horse Hill and the holiday park at Glentanner (03 435 1855, www.glentanner.co.nz), to the luxury of one of New Zealand's best-known hotels, The Hermitage. There are also backpackers, motels and bed and breakfast-style options.

Walking in the area ranges from a 10 minute stroll on the Bowen Track to hikes lasting several hours or a full day (the best of the latter is the walk from the village up to the terminal lake of the Hooker Glacier). Tramping tracks include the popular Ball Pass, Mueller Hut and the Copland Pass over the main divide to Westland. All the customary warnings and advice about mountain conditions apply wherever you are in Mount Cook National Park, only more so. Its altitude and proximity to the coast (just over the hill) make this a dangerous place to be when it cuts up rough. Professional guides are available on all routes. Try Alpine Guides (03 435 1834, www.alpineguides.co.nz), Alpine Recreation (03 680 6736, www.alpinerecreation.co.nz) or High Country Expeditions (03 435 0622, www.highcountrynz.com).

Helicopter flights (including options that will set you down to walk, climb or ski on the snow and ice) are available from The Helicopter Line (03 435 037, www.helicopter.co.nz), and Mount Cook Ski Planes (03 430 8034, www.mountcookskiplanes.co.nz), which has an exclusive licence to land in the park. Some of these companies offer a 'grand traverse' of the main divide, from Mount Cook over to Fox Glacier in Westland, with incomparable views on the way.

Mount Tasman, Mount Dampier, and Mount Sefton (all over 3,000m) attract mountaineers from all over New Zealand and farther afield, and there are other demanding peaks, most notably, of course, the sky-piercer itself, Aoraki/Mount Cook. First climbed in 1884, it's New Zealand mountaineering's greatest challenge, and although it's only a Grade 3 on the scale of difficulty, it has claimed more than 140 lives, see-sawing with the North Island's Mount Taranaki for the title of the country's most dangerous.

South Island Map G8

Mount John

Just outside the township of Lake Tekapo, a short drive or 12km walk along the Mount John Walkway, is the 1,031m Mount John, where Canterbury University's observatory exploits the habitually clear skies. Visitors are welcome: join a guided daylight tour with Earth & Sky (www.earthandsky.co.nz) for $20 (kids $5), or a night-time stargazing expedition for $48 (kids $24). One-hour jaunts set out at 20:00 in winter and 22:00 in summer. The guides are knowledgeable and multilingual. The Astro Cafe's glass walls and ceiling offer spectacular views of the surrounding landscape, and there's also a solar telescope, so you can safely look at the sun. The food, and especially the coffee, is very highly rated.

Chatham Islands

Lying 800km due east of Christchurch, the Chathams are a forgotten outpost of New Zealand, not even included in national weather forecasts on television. It cuts both ways though – Chatham Islanders refer to the mainland as 'New Zealand'. Chatham Island (the larger of the two inhabited islands – there are 10 in all) has a permanent population of fewer than 700 people, while Pitt Island to the south is home to just 50.

Church of the Good Shepherd

The Chathams are an unconventional tourist destination. There's plenty to do, if you like hunting, fishing or photography; beyond that though it's as bleak as the bulk of the landscape. The most significant feature is the 180 sq km Te Whanga lagoon, which is heavily infested with black swans. You can fossick for fossilised shark's teeth on the shores of the lagoon, and at the Hapupuu Reserve at the island's north-eastern tip you can see wooden carvings which are said to be the work of Maori up to 400 years old.

The Waitangi Hotel (03 3050048, www.hotelchatham.co.nz) offers good quality accommodation in a fantastic location right on the water in Petre Bay, and has a remarkably good restaurant, specialising in local seafood. It also runs sightseeing tours of the island. Another option is the Chatham Island Lodge (03 305 0196, www.chathamlodge.net.nz).

The Chathams are serviced by Air Chathams (0508 247248, www.airchathams.com), which flies (noisy) planes from Auckland, Wellington, Christchurch and, occasionally, Napier.

Area D p.205

The Lowdown

Otago has had little choice but to get on with farming and forestry since the goldrush days of the 1860s. Its capital city is a university town (Dunedin), and Oamaru is a kind of living museum.

The Essentials

Wander around Oamaru's whitestone district, visit the blue penguins on Cape Wanbrow, visit the Royal Albatross Centre at Tairoa head, ride the Taieri Gorge Railway.

Otago

Dunedin was little more than 10 years old when gold was discovered in the south of the province at Gabriel's Gully, near present-day Lawrence. An unprepossessing monument depicting a pick and shovel is all that marks the site of the event that irrevocably changed the course of history for the South Island and wider New Zealand.

Other finds swiftly followed, and a mass migration from the spent goldfields of Victoria in Australia ensued, with a range of nationalities pouring into Otago through Dunedin and Oamaru – every one of them in search of their fortune. Regardless of how the individuals fared, Dunedin and Oamaru prospered, as is reflected in their architecture. The magnificent whitestone precinct of Otago, and some of the grand old civic buildings of Dunedin, was built with the proceeds of the sweat and toil of the miners.

Today, Otago is something of a cul-de-sac on the new road to riches: tourism. The bulk of the district is still focused on farming and forestry, but Oamaru receives its fair share of visitors en route to the tourist mecca of Central Otago (p.275), and is striving (with some success) to reinvent itself as a destination. Dunedin, however, remains first and foremost a university town, the vital student body breathing life into its old stone.

This part of the coast was an important trade link between the pounamu (greenstone) sources on the West Coast (p.283) and the main centres of Maori population further north and in the North Island – just as it was later to serve as a hub in the goldrush days. While there were already several whaling sites along the coast, mass European settlement occurred as part of the broad New Zealand Company programme, with the arrival of a Scottish Free Church contingent who settled Dunedin (p.272).

Say Cheese

The produce of Whitestone Cheese (03 434 8098) is internationally famous. It is made according to traditional methods, and ranges from sheep's and goats' milk cheeses to conventional cheddars. You can visit the factory, do a tasting, eat at the cafe (full of Whitestone products plus Central Otago wines) and groups can have the cheesemaker talk them through the process and the range. See www.whitestonecheese.co.nz

South Island Map H10

Waitaki Valley

Two roads follow the course of the Waitaki River inland from the coast: State Highways 82 and 83, which both run parallel for the better part of 60km until they reunite at Kurow. The drive up either road is very scenic. Along the way, at Maerewhenua, just south of Duntroon, 35km from the coastal highway, you pass a curious geological

Penguin coast, Otago

formation named Elephant Rocks – outcroppings of weathered limestone in a flat paddock that look, with a slight stretch of the imagination, like elephants. It was used as a location for the filming of the recent movie version of C S Lewis's *The Lion, the Witch and the Wardrobe*, and it's a great spot for photography. This is on private land, but guided walking company Vanished World (03 4312024, www.vanishedworld.co.nz) has a concession to take visitors. The Waitaki River is an excellent angling spot: salmon run the rapids between January and April. You need a licence (available from most sports stores), or you can use a guide from Waitaki Valley Fishing Guides (03 436 0510).

South Island Map H11

Moeraki

The famous Moeraki Boulders – a collection of almost perfectly spherical rocks lying at the water's edge of a beach 39km south of Oamaru – have excited much speculation down the years, and been interpreted as everything from alien artefacts to the ballast stones of a wrecked 15th century Chinese junk. They are, in fact, septarian concretions, mineral formations accumulated around organic material deposited on a muddy seafloor millions of years ago. They're utterly fascinating to look at, and it helps they're in so picturesque a spot. Some of the broken-up examples make a great photo opportunity, as you can nestle in them as though you're hatching from a great stone egg. There's a visitor's centre and gift shop on the cliff above them.

A little south of the boulders, is the settlement of Moeraki, where you'll find a beautiful campground (03 439 4759) and one of New Zealand's finest restaurants, Fleur's Place (03 439 4480, www.fleursplace.co.nz), which has fantastic views and seafood.

South Island Map H11

Oamaru

Oamaru got a kickstart out of the goldrushes of the 1860s, and the windfall saw it rolling in it by the end of the 19th century. Soon the main street and port areas were lined with grand stone buildings.

The town has a number of attractions besides its architecture; the blue penguin observatory on Cape Wanbrow and the yellow-eyed penguins at Bushy Beach are an eco-tourism drawcard. On South Hill, not far from the blue penguin colony, is Harbour 2 Ocean restaurant (03 434 3400, www.harbour2ocean.com), reckoned by some to be in the top flight of South Island eateries.

Janet Frame's House

New Zealand's most celebrated novelist, Janet Frame, spent much of her life in Oamaru. The little Eden Street house in which she lived is kept these days as a museum in her memory, and there's a trail that takes you by sites of Frame significance.

The area adjacent to Oamaru's port in Tyne Street contains the heart of the town's whitestone area, where an entire block of the original Victorian architecture has been preserved. It's greatly aided by the presence of an eccentric element of the population who not only dresses up in Victorian costume, but get right into the lifestyle.

The area is a powerhouse of creativity, as you'd expect given the renovation of the district was an initiative of the local art society. The restored buildings house a vast array of boutique shops and galleries selling art, crafts and gifts. Of particular note are the studios of Donna Demente (multimedia artist, particularly known for her masks), traditional bookbinder Michael O'Brien (03 434 9277) and Ian Andersen, a sculptor in Oamaru limestone (www.ianandersensculptor.co.nz), and the Grain Store art gallery. There's also a restored Victorian pub, the Criterion (on the corner of Harbour and Tyne Streets), a German bakery, a live music venue and an organ museum. The old Woolstore (1 Tyne St, 03 434 8336) is a good place for a bite to eat.

Waterfront Rd
Oamaru

Blue Penguin Colony

03 433 1195 | *www.penguins.co.nz*

Oamaru Blue Penguin Colony is home to a collection of the smallest penguins in the world, the little blue. The nesting site is among the boulders at the foot of the cliffs of Cape Wanbrow, directly across the harbour from the town. You can learn all about the birds and then observe them when they return to their nests at night from just a few metres' away in the air-conditioned comfort of an observatory. As the birds waddle out of the water at night, it's best to secure your seat about an hour before sunset so that you can get the full commentary. Just over the hill, on the seaward side of Cape Wanbrow, there's a colony of the rare hoiho (yellow-eyed penguin), which can be observed from hides on Bushy Beach, reached by an easy walk from the carpark.

9 Thames St
Oamaru

Forrester Gallery

03 434 1653 | *www.forrestergallery.com*

Named after the architect responsible for the majority of Oamaru's heritage buildings, the Forrester specialises in the works of artists from the Waitaki region and further afield. The gallery is housed in the former premises of the Bank of New South Wales, not in fact designed by Forrester, but rather by his inspiration, Robert Lawson, and completed in 1884. The Grecian temple-style building provides hallowed surroundings in which to spend a couple of hours' browsing. Open daily, 10:30 to 16:30. Entry by donation.

60 Thames St
Oamaru

North Otago Museum

03 434 1652 | *www.northotagomuseum.co.nz*

Housed in the exquisite former premises of the Oamaru Athenaeum, the North Otago Museum has a terrific collection of items charting the history of the Waitaki district. Besides its regular exhibits and displays, it has a huge archival resource for researchers. Open Monday to Friday, 10:30 to 16:30, weekends 13:00 to 17:30. Entry is by donation.

South Island Map H12

Dunedin

The bunch of Free Church of Scotland settlers led by Captain William Cargill and Thomas Burns, a nephew of Robbie, who arrived in 1848 to establish New Edinburgh, found themselves contemplating a bleak, rocky basin, subject to the moody weather that they had left behind.

It didn't deter them – far from it, they took to it with a will, and flourished, especially following the discovery of gold at Gabriel's Gully to the south-west of the city.

Much of the architecture accomplished in the early gold rush days remains: the First Church and Knox Church, the buildings of the University of Otago, Dunedin Railway Station and the bleak but grand law courts and city gaol opposite. All are fine examples of the local stonemasonry, featuring dark volcanic rock edged and trimmed with white Oamaru stone.

Cadbury's Moment
Cadbury's has been supplying chocolate to New Zealanders from its unprepossessing site in Dunedin since the 1930s. You can join guided tours and see how chocolate is made, marvel at a five-storey-high waterfall of chocolate, then buy a truckload of the stuff (03 4677967, www.cadbury.co.nz).

Today, Dunedin is considered a university town. Otago University was New Zealand's first when it was established here in 1869, and the pulse of the city has been inextricably bound up with the rituals and timetabling of the student body ever since. It can seem pretty lifeless and empty during university holidays, but during term, and especially after exams, it's a party town.

The city can be exceedingly cold in the winter, and it's hardly a resort – yet it is full of character, and beautifully set between the hills and the harbour. It's blessed with the surf beaches of St Kilda and St Clair (p.274), and the Otago Peninsula – with more fine beaches and attractions such as the royal albatross colony at Taiaroa – right on its doorstep.

The heart of Dunedin city is Octagon, where several streets converge into what amounts to a giant roundabout. Its flanked by several public amenities, including the magnificent town hall (erected in 1885), the public library and the art gallery.

The Motel on York (03 477 6120, www.motelonyork.co.nz) is the closest to quality hotel accommodation you'll find in the heart of the city. There's also the very exclusive (and expensive) Corstorphine House (03 487 1000, www.corstorphine.co.nz) in Milburn Street. And while there are dozens of restaurants, easily the pick of them is Bell Pepper Blues (03 474 0973).

Otago Beaches
There are some superb beaches along the coastline – Moeraki, Waikouaiti and Dunedin city's beaches – but they are cold in the warm months and bitter in the winter, so more attractive to surfers than to swimmers.

Otago Peninsula

The long peninsula forming the southern headland of Otago Harbour is a great civic amenity for the people of Dunedin. There are several walking tracks, each of which gives splendid views over the harbour, back towards the city and south along the Taieri coast. You can do a seaborne tour along bits or the whole thing with Monarch Wildlife Cruises (03 477 4276, www.wildlife.co.nz).

Around 15 minutes' drive from the Octagon, you'll find the superb Glenfalloch (gaelic for 'hidden valley') Woodland Garden (03 476 1775). Portobello, halfway along the peninsula on its northern side, has been a popular picnic and holiday spot since the city's foundation. There's an excellent campground (Portobello Village Tourist Park, 03 478 0359). There's also a good aquarium associated with the University of Otago's marine sciences department (03 479 5826, www.marine.ac.nz). At the peninsula's tip (50 minutes from the Octagon) is Taiaroa Head, where there's a royal albatross colony with an internationally acclaimed interpretative centre, including the brilliant Richdale Observatory (03 478 0499, www.albatross.org.nz).

For many, the peninsula is synonymous with Larnach's Castle (03 476 1616, www.larnachscastle.co.nz), a great, frilly edifice erected in the 1870s by early conspicuous consumer William Larnach. It was pretty overblown even before Larnach had added every conceivable piece of ornamentation, but while it's all a bit tasteless, it's still a fantastic spot for a view over the harbour and the city, and the gardens are an excellent place to have a picnic in summer.

30 The Octagon
Dunedin

Dunedin Public Art Gallery

03 477 4000 | *www.dunedin.art.museum*

While its collection dates to 1884, the Dunedin Art Gallery is housed in a beautiful new building opened in the centre of town in 1996. The permanent collection includes works by many European masters, notably Claude Monet, and a good cross-section of significant New Zealanders. There's a contemporary emphasis to exhibitions; local luminaries Ralph Hotere and Robin White have both featured. The building also houses an office of the New Zealand Film Archive, and the Nova cafe, which does excellent coffee and good food. Open daily, 10:00 to 17:00.

Anzac Av
Dunedin

Dunedin Railway Station

The sheer, lavish detail of the Railway Station that architect George Troup built for Dunedin in 1906 earned him the nickname of 'Gingerbread George' when it was opened in 1906. Although there's not much in the way of rail traffic using it these days, it's even more available for the admiration of visitors. There are superb stained-glass windows depicting approaching trains, and an impossibly ornate tiled floor. Every available corner, nook and cranny, inside and out, drips ornamentation. These days, the upper floor houses the New Zealand Sports Hall of Fame (03 477 7775, www.nzhalloffame.co.nz), which is open daily 10:00 to 16:00, the ticketing office for Taieri Gorge excursions, and a reasonable buffet restaurant.

410 Moray Pl
Dunedin

First Church

03 477 7118

By contrast with the austerity and self-restraint preached by Dunedin's puritanical founding fathers, the First Church is a magnificent piece of Gothic architecture. So showy was it, in fact, that when it opened in 1873, there were dark mutterings from those among the congregation who preferred their worship without such frills. When the singing of hymns began in 1885, many of these folk formed a breakaway church. They were hard men (and women) in those days; attend a service here on a biting cold Dunedin Sunday and you'll see why the local conditions suited that sort of personality.

Hocken Library

Parry St
Dunedin

03 479 8868 | *www.library.otago.ac.nz*

The Hocken is one of the premier research facilities in New Zealand. Its collections relate to the history and culture of New Zealand, the wider South Pacific and Antarctica, and date from the 17th century to the present. It's designed for the serious researcher rather than the casual browser, although it has regular public exhibitions, including a recent display of the works of early New Zealand photographer Alfred Burton on a South Pacific trip. You'll need to register as a user to access the collections. Call ahead for opening hours.

Otago Museum

419 Great King St
Dunedin

03 474 7474 | *www.otagomuseum.govt.nz*

The Otago Museum's redevelopment in the 1990s has transformed it from a traditionally stuffy and static place to the dynamic, interactive centre you'll find today. One of the first additions was the Discovery Centre, a cross between an amusement park and an educational facility, aimed at children. Activities here range from gazing horrified at tarantulas to playing air-hockey. The opening of dedicated galleries has included the Southern People, Southern Land space in 2002, which covers all aspects of life in the region. The permanent collection is comprehensive in its coverage of local and regional history, and the museum hosts major touring exhibitions. Open daily, 10:00 to 17:00.

Otago Settlers Museum

31 Queens Gardens
Dunedin

03 477 5052 | *www.otago.settlers.museum*

Founded in 1898 and situated next door to the Railway Station, this museum specialises in the social history of Otago, and has one of the finest collections of horse-drawn vehicles in New Zealand. There's also a vivid reconstruction of the sights and sounds (but thankfully not the smells) of the accommodation decks of an immigrant ship, with audiovisual extracts from passengers' diaries. There's a big collection of period costumes, and a dark, rich and frankly overwhelming gallery of portraits of Otago settlers with bare biographical details. Open daily, 10:00 to 17:00.

Speight's Brewery

Rattray St
Dunedin

03 477 7697 | *www.speights.co.nz*

Speight's is an Otago identity, and even more so since the screening of a phenomenally successful series of TV ads celebrating the virtues of the 'southern man'. The Speight's Brewery still operates from the same site it opened on in 1876, and some traditions remain, such as the tap alongside the entranceway where the general public is welcome to fill their own vessels with water from the well used in the brewing process. You can take a brewery tour, and personalise a bottle of Speight's to take away with you. The tour also takes in a beer museum and finishes – predictably – in the Heritage Bar. Open daily, 10:00 to 19:00.

St Clair and St Kilda's Beaches

Dunedin

The beautiful sandy beaches on Dunedin's coastline are great surf spots, and good for hardy swimmers too. Both are patrolled in the summer. For less adventurous swimmers, there's a heated saltwater pool complex at the southern end of St Clair beach. South of St Clair is Tunnel Beach, where Dunedin founder Captain William Cargill had a tunnel driven through the sandstone headland to his family's private beach; it's now a lovely walk to a beautiful surf beach. For less adventurous souls, there's a heated saltwater pool complex at the southern end of St Clair beach.

Area **E** *p.205*

The Lowdown
Once a boomtown, always a boomtown: Central was built on the back of the 1860s gold rushes, and now it's flourishing thanks to the buzz around the heady combination of wine and adrenaline.

The Essentials
Ski at Treble Cone, drink at the Cardrona Hotel, do a bungee jump, tour the Central Otago vineyards (and taste the pinot noir), try panning for gold, ride the Central Otago Rail Trail.

Central Otago

State Highway 8 climbs up and over the Lindis Pass, separating the valley of Ahuriri River from the Lakes District. Once over the other side, there's no mistaking you're in Central Otago (shortened by South Islanders to 'Central'). The landscape is dominated by the wall-like mountain ranges – the Dunstans, Pisa, and Harris mountains – and great lakes, Wanaka and Hawea, Wakatipu and Hayes. This is a landscape unlike any other in New Zealand, with the possible exception of the North Island's Rangipo Desert. The golden breadth of it, with mountains looming on every horizon, imparts a special quality to the light.

Sheep would certainly have outnumbered humans for the better part of its history, had gold not been discovered in 1861 at Gabriel's Gully, near the town of Lawrence, sparking a wave of prospecting throughout the South Island. Gold was just about everywhere; miners poured into the region, the bulk of them along the 175km Dunstan Trail, (which can be retraced in the summer on foot or by bike or with D-Tours (03 488 6177, www.d-tours.co.nz) from Dunedin to Clyde (known then as Dunstan). First tent cities, then towns, mushroomed on the plains and in the valleys of Central – Clyde, Cromwell, Queenstown, Arrowtown all date to the early 1860s. Many original stone buildings have endured as the climate is dry, as have adobe and mud-brick buildings. Life was pretty tough for most. You only need look at the well-preserved Chinese settlement at Arrowtown (p.281) to see for yourself.

As prosperity pushed land beyond the pockets of most, the boom spread to Wanaka. Meanwhile, there was a renewed interest in viticulture. The first grapes had been planted at Clyde in the 1860s. Although the first round of commercial planting didn't begin in the Queenstown area until the 1970s, since the 1990s there has been an explosive increase. The new adrenaline attraction boom that is sweeping the land – still so heavily scarred from the extraction days – is every bit as feverish as the goldrushes (p.280).

South Island Map F10

Climate Change
Central is home to hard winters and scorching summers. Alexandra is consistently New Zealand's hottest town, and Ophir – just 27km away – holds records for being the coldest.

The Maniototo

The spectacular landscape of the Maniototo Basin is better known to most people from the art of South Islander Grahame Sydney, whose paintings are a luminous mixture of photographic realism and spiritualism. Even those en route to Queenstown or Wanaka by-pass the bulk of it, which is a mixture of irrigated farmland, barren tussockland, and tall, stony mountain ridges. The main road skirts it, bending away to the north and following the great arc of the former railway embankment that has been converted to a cycleway, the Central Otago Rail Trail (p.298). It's easily the best way to experience the charms of the Maniototo. Many of the towns that had a bustling self-importance when the rail ran through – Wedderburn, Omakau and Lauder – are little more than dots on the map today.

Blue Pools

But the backwater feel to these places is actually part of the area's charm. It's hard not to be affected by the landscape, the light, the dismal traces of the desperate goldrush years, or its sheer timelessness.

St Bathan's
The Vulcan (03 447 3629) in the gorgeous village of St Bathan's is a great place for lunch and a pint. Afterwards, get a postcard stamped with the unique St Bathan's postmark at the store.

Naseby

A short 14km detour off State Highway 85 north of Ranfurly is Naseby. It's a very pretty town, deserving its occasional nickname 'the jewel of the Maniototo'. There are plenty of visible remnants of its history. Besides the quaint street frontages, there are three museums: the Glenshee Park Museum (03 444 9624), the Maniototo Early Settlers and Jubilee Museum in Earn Street (03 444 9558, open from December to April, 13:30 to 15:30), and the Naseby Motor Museum in the old butcher's shop (open by request, 03 444 9917). All three have eclectic collections from the goldmining and pioneer farming days. Just outside the township itself, in the forestry area, you can see the ruinous remnants of a hillside sluiced for gold.

South Island Map F11

Ophir

About 100m off State Highway 85 at Omakau (and the same distance off the Rail Trail) is the old goldmining town of Ophir. There are several historic buildings to see here – notably the jail and the post office, built in 1886. A good place to stay here if you're on the Rail Trail is Flannery Lodge (03 4474256, www.ophir.co.nz), which can guide you on fishing in the area – brown trout is a speciality of this one.

South Island Map E10

Lakes District

Central Otago is dominated by the three large lakes at its heart: Lake Wakatipu (shortened by locals to 'Wakatip'), Wanaka and Hawea. It wasn't so much the lakes as the rivers feeding and draining them that drove the pattern of population here; the Shotover (one of the richest gold-bearing waterways in history), the Kawarau and the Clutha were all magnets to the fortune-seekers of the 1860s. Queenstown has been transformed from a ski town – sleepy in the winter and all but dead in summer – to a we-never-close adrenaline factory. Something of the same fervour has infused Wanaka, which has experienced a building boom over the last 10 years. The rest of the district is a mixture of wilderness (Mount Aspiring National Park), farmland and vineyard. It's incredibly scenic country, and much of it was used for location and backdrop shooting for *The Lord of the Rings* trilogy.

Wanaka
South Island Map F8

Haast Pass

The pass between the tussock basins and lakelands of Central Otago and south Westland was first crossed in 1861, but it was nearly 100 years later that State Highway 6 was pushed through. It's one of the most scenic drives in the country, giving a cross-section of landforms from the alpine basins to river flats and rainforest that accompany the declining altitude. Toward the Wanaka end of the road, look for a signpost to the Blue Pools. It's a short stroll along boardwalks and through beech forest to a swingbridge that crosses the Makarora River, which has slowed in its journey from its icy source to a series of deep, blue pools in a stony, bush-clad gorge. The clarity of the water is breathtaking.

Central Otago
South Island Map F9

Lake Hawea

Hawea is a pleasant alternative to the bustle and tourist-oriented focus of Wanaka and Queenstown. The lake itself is beautiful, with clear blue water, and it's well-stocked with land-locked trout and salmon, making good fishing. The hunting in the surrounding high country has an international reputation. Lake Hawea Hunting Safaris (03 443 7282, www.hawea-hunting.co.nz) offers 'fair' guided hunting trips and will arrange for trophy animals to be stuffed and freighted to your door.

Wanaka
South Island Map E9

Mount Aspiring National Park

Part of the Unesco World Heritage-listed Te Wahipounamu, the 3,555 sq km Mount Aspiring National Park encompasses some of New Zealand's most impressive landscapes. There are several tramping tracks and routes, including walks up the west and east branches of the Matukituki River from a carpark 40km west of Wanaka township; the former takes you past the Rob Roy Glacier (an easy two-hour walk) to the grand Mount Aspiring hut (an easy half-day). The latter takes you up to the demanding Rabbit Pass on the shoulder of Mount Aspiring (four hard days). There's also the moderately difficult and unforgettably scenic Gillespie Pass out of the Makarora River valley. These and other routes in the park can be done as guided walks (03 443 4476, www.wildwalks.co.nz).
The park is a mountaineer's paradise. The beautiful Mount Aspiring itself (a classic shark's tooth peak) is reckoned a relatively easy mountaineering proposition. Guided climbing and mountaineering trips are available to climbers of all levels of experience from Mount Aspiring Guides (03 443 9422, www.aspiringguides.com) and Adventure Consultants (03 443 8711, www.adventureconsultants.co.nz). All expeditions should be taken seriously, as this is a true alpine environment. Do your homework on whatever walk, tramp or climb you propose. The people to contact are the DOC (www.doc.govt.nz).

Glenorchy

Rees-Dart Track

For many overseas visitors, walking the Rees-Dart alpine valley circuit at the western end of Lake Wakatipu is their taste of the New Zealand wilderness, and it's not a bad one at all. The views of the glacial lower reaches of Mount Aspiring National Park, the beautiful river gorges, the tussock flats and beech forest all make for very pretty walking. While it's rated an easy four to five days, the 'easy' relates to the terrain; you're still walking up to eight hours a day, which can be demanding. If you want to cut down the difficulty a little, a jetboat from Glenorchy will give you a fair head-start up the Dart River; check out Dart River Jet Safari (03 442 9992, www.dartriver.co.nz).

Wanaka

Treble Cone Ski Area

03 443 7443 | *www.treblecone.co.nz*

Treble Cone, 20km west of Wanaka, is one of New Zealand's premier ski resorts. It boasts 550 hectares of skiable (or boardable) terrain, serviced by fast and efficient lifts. It's a spacious but demanding field, with 10% of the groomed area suitable for beginners, and the rest for those of intermediate and advanced abilities. The facilities are top-notch, and the views – over lakes Wanaka and Hawea – are magnificent.

South Island
Map E10

Wanaka

Wanaka lies a little over 50km north of Queenstown. Although it's scarcely recognisable from the village it was 25 years ago, there's still a sleepy feel.
Farming was the major industry until the late 20th century when the skifields in the Cardrona Valley and at Treble Cone opened up tourism. Now it's adrenaline rushes that see large numbers of young visitors passing through.
The lake is an obvious drawcard; it's popular boating and kayaking water (hire with Lakeland Adventures, 03 443 7495, www.lakelandadventures.co.nz). The fishing is excellent and gear and guides are available from several different operators. You can go gold panning in the Clutha River, and combine it with a rafting trip (Pioneer Rafting, 03 443 1246, www.ecoraft.co.nz). Canyoning is popular in season (November to April) with Deep Canyon (03 443 7922, www.deepcanyon.co.nz). There's also paragliding (0800 359 754, www.wanakaparagliding.co.nz) and skydiving (Skydive Lake Wanaka, 03 443 7207, www.skydivenz.com). If you'd prefer to stay in the plane and look at the landscape, several operators offer scenic flights; try Alpine Helicopters (03 443 4000, www.alpineheli.co.nz) or Aspiring Air (03 443 7943, www.aspiringair.com).

The tramping, mountaineering and rockclimbing possibilities of Mount Aspiring National Park (p.277), to which Wanaka is the main gateway, are endless. If that's a little too much for you, there are several easy walks to be done around Wanaka itself. The track to the summit of Mount Iron behind the town gives incredible views of the lake and surrounding mountains. And 4km out of town towards Glendhu Bay, you'll see signposts for the track up Roy's Peak, a stiff two-hour climb rewarded with even more exquisite views.

More sedate pleasures just outside of town include the Wanaka Fighter Pilot's Museum (p.279), Puzzling World (p.279), while sightseeing tours (Wanaka Sightseeing , 03 338 0982, www.wanakasightseeing.co.nz) will point out areas of natural, historical or cinematic history – inevitably, several locations in the area were used for filming *The Lord of the Rings*.

There's a range of accommodation options in the area, from the motor camp at Glendhu Bay (03 443 7243, www.glendhubaymotorcamp.co.nz), 10 minutes' drive from Wanaka, to a number of backpacker and budget hotels. There's also the exclusive waterfront Edgewater Resort (03 443 8311, www.edgewater.co.nz) and the Department of Conservation camp at Albert Town, 8km north of Wanaka. Here you can light a roaring fire right on the banks of the Clutha.

South Island Map E10

Arrowtown

Situated on the Arrow River, 22km north of Queenstown, Arrowtown's main drag is one of the prettiest streetscapes in the world: the buildings, the exotic trees (with all their seasonal colours) and the brooding peaks of the surrounding mountains make for an unbeatable setting.

The Lakes District Museum and Gallery (03 442 1824, www.museumqueenstown.com), attached to the visitor's centre in the main street, details Arrowtown's boom-bust history. It's open from 08:30 to 17:00, daily. A good way to get an appreciation of how hard life was for the miners is to hire a pan from the visitor's centre and try your luck in the icy waters of the Arrow. Then, when you're chilled to the bone, visit the Arrowtown Chinese Settlement on the riverbank where you'll find the well-preserved dirt-floored, stone-walled hovels once occupied by Chinese miners back in the 1880s.

South Island Map E10

Cardrona Valley

The scenic route between Wanaka and Queenstown is over the notorious Crown Range Road. It climbs steadily the length of the beautiful Cardrona Valley, then more steeply to the shoulder of Mount Scott, before descending into the Arrow River valley in a

Lake Wanaka

Arrowtown

series of dramatic hairpin bends. Situated off the Cardrona Valley are two major skifields. On the western wall of the valley, just 25km south of Wanaka, is the Cardrona Skifield (www.cardrona.com). It's a lovely hill, with wide, open, rolling runs, and the best place to brush up on your skills before tackling the more demanding Treble Cone (p.277). Almost opposite Cardrona is the Waiorau Snow Farm and Nordic Ski Area, where you can put those cross-country and telemarking skills to good use, or learn if you are a beginner (03 443 0300, www.snowfarmnz.co.nz). The Snow Farm hosts a variety of winter sports events, including Nordic ski races, and a winter triathlon (including mountain biking on the snow).

For accommodation you could do worse then the Cardrona Hotel (03 443 8153, www.cardronahotel.co.nz), built in 1863 and extensively refurbished in recent years with expanded accommodation and restaurant facilities to go with its famous apres-ski bar.

Wanaka

Base Camp Wanaka

03 443 1110 | *www.basecampwanaka.com*

This magnificent indoor facility gives rock climbing junkies something to do when the weather's closed in on the great outdoors. There's more than 400 sq m of indoor climbing wall, up to 15m high and with 50 square metres of overhang. All gear and tuition is available for hire, you can also buy and rent multisports kit (kayaks, climbing gear and specialist bikes). There's a children's climbing area and playground, plus a cafe and bar.

Wanaka Airport
Wanaka

New Zealand Fighter Pilot's Museum

03 443 7010 | *www.nzfpm.co.nz*

The New Zealand Fighter Pilot's Museum celebrates the fighter aircraft and New Zealanders who have flown them. The collection features several flyable aircraft (including a Hawker Hurricane, Tiger Moth and Chipmunk), as well as static displays, including a Vampire and a first world war biplane. Its excellent exhibitions change regularly. Set to be re-housed in a bigger and brighter building, it is currently open daily from 09:00 to 16:00.

Near Lake Wanaka

Puzzling World

03 443 7489 | *www.puzzlingworld.co.nz*

Stuart Landsborough, who devised this place, must have a pretty warped mind, and so will you after a visit. Outside, there's a mulitlevel maze comprising 1.5km of corridors in which you can happily lose yourself for some time. Inside, several rooms specialise in disconcerting perceptual tricks: there's the Tilted Room, where everything but you is tilted at 15 degrees; Ames Forced Perspective Room (its techniques tricked moviegoers into believing full-sized people were pint-sized Hobbits); the Hologram Room, and very freaky Hall of Following Faces. If you think going to the toilet will offer respite, brace yourself – there's a lifelike mural that makes it seem as though you've strolled into a Roman-style communal latrine. Open daily, 8:30 to 17:30 (17:00 in winter).

Off State Highway 6
Wanaka

Wanaka Transport & Toy Museum

03 443 8765 | *www.wanakatransportandtoymuseum.com*

Probably housing the most eclectic collection of any New Zealand museum, the Wanaka Transport & Toy Museum houses a number of rare and unusual cars, trucks, motorcycles and pieces of military equipment, including a MiG fighter and a huge Russian biplane. There's also an impressive range of toys – from dolls and teddybears to obscure board games – that will give anyone a kick of nostalgia. Open daily, 08:30 to 17:00.

South Island Map E10

Queenstown & Around

Situated on the hip of pretty Lake Wakatipu, and facing the looming Remarkables, Queenstown has always attracted visitors. But with the development of the surrounding skifields and the invention of new attractions such as jetboating, whitewater rafting and bungee jumping, tourism became the new goldrush, and Queenstown boomed.

Today, it's like a town from some resort in the Swiss Alps transplanted into a New Zealand landscape. Gravity is mined for every thrill it can yield, on skis, boards and rubber bands or with parachute cloth.

Queenstown's reputation is mostly built on its winter attractions (as celebrated in its annual Winter Festival, p.62). It has five skifields within an hour's drive. But one activity is indelibly associated with the town: bungee jumping. The home of the bungee is the historic Kawarau River overbridge, site of the Kawarau Bungy Centre run by AJ Hackett (p.341). It's a thrill, if not a cheap one – unless you're over 65 when it's free. Hackett runs three other bungee sites nearby, the biggest and best being Nevis Highwire Bungy, where you jump from a pod suspended over the Nevis River.

Eating in Queenstown

Among the best of the informal restaurants in Queenstown is The Cow (03 442 8588). Practically next door, there's the sophisticated (and expensive) Bunker (03 441 8030), and on Steamer Wharf, Wai Waterfront Restaurant (03 442 5969), specialising in seafood (especially bluff oysters, in season). Out of town a short way (7 km up Gorge Road toward Coronet Peak), you'll find Gantley's (03 442 8999, www.gantleys.co.nz), Queenstown's top restaurant, in the building of an 1863 wayside inn. It's expensive, but the food is superb.

Another of the original adrenaline sports operators in Queenstown is Shotover Jet, which has been running thrilling jetboat excursions on the Shotover and Kawarau rivers for nearly 40 years. At times, it's every bit as near-death as a bungee, but seems like better bang for your buck; an adult gets a ride for $109, and a child for $69, and it lasts longer. There are several operators running the wilder bits of the Kawarau and the Shotover in rubber rafts, including Queenstown Rafting (03 442 9792, www.rafting.co.nz) and Challenge Rafting (03 442 7318, www.raft.co.nz). The most basic trip costs around $150.

Queenstown is, after Wanaka, the gateway to Mount Aspiring National Park (p.277). Three of New Zealand's great walks are here: the Rees-Dart track, the Routeburn and the Greenstone-Caples. There's also fishing, with Lake Wakatipu and its tributaries offering good brown trout angling. Guided excursions are available with Born to Fish (03 248 8890, www.borntofish.co.nz) or Fly Fishing (03 442 5363, www.wakatipu.co.nz).

If you're more interested in merely living it up, the immediate area has plenty of possibilities. There are more than 80 wineries, with around 20 cellar doors. Some of the finest pinot noir in the world is produced here, and the rigours of the climate mean there are also good reislings and sauternes-style wines. The best way to sample is to join a tour; try Queenstown Wine Trail (03 442 3799, www.queenstownwinetrail.co.nz) or Appellation Central Wine Tours (03 442 0246, www.appellationcentral.co.nz). Alternatively you can stay right in town and try it all in the comfort of Wine Tastes at 14 Beach Street (03 409 2226).

Adventure Sports

You can now go surfing down the Kawarau River, with Serious Fun (03 442 5262, www.riversurfing.co.nz), or canyoning at the Twelve Mile Delta (021 507 677, www.xiimile.co.nz) or the Routeburn (03 441 4386, www.gycanyoning.co.nz).

There have always been scenic flights over the greater Lakes District, but there's now a company that will take you along as it does aerobatics over Lake Wakatipu (03 441 4413, www.actionflite.co.nz), another that will take you hot-air ballooning (03 442 0781, www.ballooningnz.com) and several that will strap you to an experienced paraglider and take you along for the ride or rent you a wing if you can handle it yourself (try Queenstown Paraflights, 03 441 2242, www.paraflights.co.nz).

There are even variations on the bungee theme: the Shotover Canyon Swing (operated by AJ Hackett) lets you swing from a point 109m above the river, freefalling at 150kph for 60m. Or you can fly by wire, in a tethered craft that reaches speeds of up to 170kph in the six minutes that you're in the air (03 442 5292, www.flybywire-queenstown.co.nz). And last, but not least, you can jump out of an aircraft and trust the bloke with the ripcord to open the chute (0800 376 796, www.nzone.biz).

If the skifields are too tame for you and you have the disposable income, you can go snowmobiling in the Garvie Mountains with Nevis Snowmobile Adventures (03 445 0843, www.snowmobilenz.com), or heliskiing (or boarding) with Harris Mountain Heli-ski (03 442 6722, www.heliski.co.nz).

Mountain biking seems tame by contrast, but there are some excellent developed trails; Fat Tyre Adventures will point you in their direction and rent you a bike (027 226 2822, www.fat-tyre.co.nz), or even take you to your chosen altitude by helicopter.

Golf in Queenstown
Queenstown has two top golf courses, in Millbrook near Arrowtown, (www.millbrook.co.nz) and Kelvin Heights, on a peninsula in Frankton Arm, off State Highway 6 two kilometres from downtown Queenstown (www.queens towngolf.co.nz).

Coronet Peak

Coronet Peak is 18km from downtown Queenstown, and is probably New Zealand's finest skifield. It has 280 hectares of skiable terrain and the best beginners' facilities of any fields in the area. The great thing about Coronet is the variety of its slopes – everyone can find something to challenge or entertain them.

The facilities, including the lifts, are first-rate. Uniquely among New Zealand skifields, Coronet Peak is equipped for night skiing, with floodlights making some of the easier slopes negotiable. It's not quite the same as skiing in daylight – you lose most of the points of reference that give you your sense of what speed you're doing – but it's exhilarating nonetheless.

Queenstown

Queenstown Gardens

One of the few places in Queenstown where no one tries to sell you anything or tempt you to try a life-threatening activity is the town's gardens. They're beautifully sited on the waterfront and perfect for a picnic or an evening stroll. Still, this is Queenstown, and there has to be an activity – in this case a Frisbee golf course; just bring your own Frisbee.

Queenstown

Bungee

The Remarkables

The beginning of the road up to the Remarkables skifield is just two kilometres from downtown Queenstown, but the 14km gravel road that snakes up the impossibly sheer face of the range takes the better part of 45 minutes to negotiate. It seems incredible that there's anything skiable at the top, but in fact, there's 22 hectares, with 30% of it suitable for beginners. The runs are quite narrow and steep, but, even by South Island standards, the views are spectacular.

Queenstown

Skippers Canyon

The upper reaches of the Shotover River run through a gorge known as Skippers Canyon. Many of the rafting or jetboating trips will bring you up here. Like much of the rest of the interesting bits of New Zealand's geography, parts of Skippers were used as locations for the filming of *The Lord of the Rings* trilogy.

Nomad Safaris (03 442 6699, www.nomadsafaris.co.nz) run four-wheel drive tours and Gravity Action (03 442 5277, www.gravityaction.co.nz) offers mountain bike descents. The road which branches off the access to Coronet Peak is terrifying, unsealed, very narrow and has sheer drops. It's made all the more hair-raising by the volume of large vehicles on it driven by adrenaline sports junkies. Rental car companies tend to exclude Skippers from their insurance cover.

Queenstown

Skyline Gondola

03 441 0101 | *www.skyline.co.nz*

Rearing behind Queenstown, the gondola hauls you up in comparative comfort to the summit of Bob's Peak. There's something slightly old-fashioned about the concept – the gondola, the restaurant, the Maori cultural performances over dinner. But the views over Queenstown and Lake Wakatipu are timeless, and there's the luge (where you ride a three-wheeled plastic cart at insane speeds down a concrete track), a mountain bike trail and a bungee site.

Queenstown

Walter Peak

Diagonally opposite Queenstown to the south-west is Walter Peak, an historic high country sheep station that is still worked, as much for the edification of tourists as for pastoral profit. There's no road access, unless you're prepared to drive most of the way to Te Anau and double back; Walter Peak is reached the same way it's always been – by the TSS Earnslaw steamer. There's a variety of excursions available, ranging in duration and price. The most basic package sees you cruise across, get to see the workings of the farm and enjoy a browse and morning tea in the station's historic homestead. More elaborate packages include a barbeque and horse-trekking. All are put together by Real Journeys (03 249 7416, www.realjourneys.co.nz).

South Island Map D10

Glenorchy

Glenorchy is a pretty little spot, and serves as the gateway to the Rees and Dart river valleys. These are steep-walled, beech-forested gorges with limpid water in stony courses. This countryside starred in *The Lord of the Rings* trilogy in a number of roles, notably as the elven kingdom, Lothlorien. The fishing in all of these rivers, to say nothing of Lake Wakatipu itself, is superb, and there's good hunting in the vicinity too. Dart River Jet Safari (03 442 9992, www.dartriver.co.nz) runs jetboating excursions up the Dart River. There's also the Dart Stables (03 442 5688, www.dartstables.com), who offers horse-trekking in the beech forest lining the Dart Gorge. It pays to be aware that the eating and shopping options are pretty limited in the off-season (summer). Just a few kilometres short of Glenorchy is Blanket Bay (p.36), the site of one of New Zealand's most exclusive accommodation providers.

Area F *p.205*

The Lowdown
Gold, greenstone, coal, glaciers and rain, lots and lots of rain.

The Essentials
Fossick for greenstone then give up and buy some, pan for gold at Shantytown, reflect upon Lake Matheson, fly over the glacier district.

West Coast

From the beautiful coastal walk of the Heaphy Track (p.258) in the north to the awe-inspiring glacier and alpine country in the south, the West Coast is studded with scenic and recreational jewels. The area is blessed with access to five national parks: Kahurangi at the top, Paparoa in the middle, Mount Cook and Mount Aspiring near the bottom and Fiordland at its toe. South Westland (Te Wahipounamu), incorporating much of the southern half of the region, was declared a Unesco World Heritage site in 1990. The rich and colourful history of the coast is proving a drawcard in its own right too, with significant gold and coalmining sites well interpreted to visitors in recent years.

There are some fine restaurants, notably the Bay House Café at Cape Foulwind and Café Nevé at Fox Glacier, some amazing accommodation providers (whether it's the Karamea Domain Campground or the World Heritage Hotel at Haast) and some even more amazing things to do.

But for all its natural beauty – and it's stunning, top to bottom – the West Coast is no paradise. It has the highest rainfall of any region in New Zealand, it gets buffeted by strong westerly winds and, in really nasty weather, waterspouts and tornadoes. And for the most part, the lot of those eking out a living here has been one of unrelenting hardship. None of the main commodities – greenstone, gold, coal and timber – were won without a struggle, and considerable danger. Nowadays the hard-man traditions on which the area is founded have been replaced with 'attraction' industries, such as tourism.

It wasn't until gold was found in the mid 1860s that people settled here in any numbers (a recreation of the kind of life these desperate diggers led in the thrown-together settlements up and down the coast can be seen at Shantytown (p.286), just south of Greymouth (p.285). Once gold petered out, the extraction of coal took over, with miners often going to unbelievable lengths to get at it. And once coal was on the wane, the logging of the magnificent rainforest was the next boom. Maori were also very familiar with the West Coast, even if few chose to live there. It was a highway up and down which pounamu (greenstone, or New Zealand jade) was traded from its sources in south Westland.

Around Westport

South Island Map J4

Cape Foulwind

Ten kilometres west of Westport, Cape Foulwind has a small settlement of baches, a fur seal colony and some of the best surfing on the West Coast. The Bay House Café (03 789 7133) has fantastic views and food to match. It's a great spot to sit with a glass of wine and watch the sun set over the wild Tasman Sea.

South Island Map K4

Denniston & Reefton

The unbelievably hard and isolated lives of those who lived in the tiny coalmining town of Denniston have given this place a kind of cult status. The remains of the settlement and the mine are interesting, and the views (on a clear day) over the coast are superb. There's an excellent museum in the old high school (03 789 9753).

You'd never believe rolling into Reefton these days that it once had its own stock exchange and was the first town in New Zealand to have electric street lighting. The source of all that wealth was, of course, gold, and the town is surrounded by relics of the boom time. A heritage trail, the Reefton Goldfields Journey, starts and finishes in the town and takes in several sites of interest. The Blacks Point Museum has a good collection of goldmining artefacts (03 732 8835). The visitors' centre in Reefton (03 732 8391) incorporates a vivid reconstruction of a goldmine. You can also rent goldmining pans, and staff will direct you to likely spots in the surrounding waterways to try your luck.

South Island Map K3

Karamea

Karamea is adjacent to many of the recreational opportunities of Kahurangi National Park, notably Heaphy and the Wangapeka Tracks and the Oparara Valley. The latter has lately been developed with a network of 27km of mountain bike tracks, based on former logging roads. There's also a cave system known as Honeycomb Hill. Entry is by permit only, or with a guided tour of two to eight people. Bookings are essential (03 782 6652). Kayaking trips in the fabulous limestone gorge of the Oparara River, featuring the highest of three limestone arches, are also available. The excursion lasts five hours, and costs $125 per person. See www.oparara.co.nz for details of this and other tours.

Those emerging from the Heaphy Track find The Last Resort at 71 Waverley Street in Karamea to be a welcome sight. It has a bar, a good restaurant, and a variety of accommodation (www.lastresort.co.nz). There are also two campgrounds, the Karamea Domain Campground (03 782 6069) and the Karamea Holiday Park (03 7826 758).

Punakaiki

Pancake Rocks

The Pancake Rocks, one of the most visited attractions in the South Island, are so-named because they resemble nothing more closely than stacked pancakes. They were formed by the sea eroding different layers of sedimentary limestone at different rates. It's impressive to stand there and feel the swell thundering into the caverns beneath your feet and watch the seawater spurting into the air from the blowholes. You can reach them via a 20 minute walk from a signposted carpark on State Highway 6 near Punakaiki.

Main Rd
Paparoa

Paparoa National Park

03 731 1895 | *punakaikivc@doc.govt.nz*

The 30,000 hectares of Paparoa National Park were set aside in 1987 as the only area in New Zealand where mature rainforest remains in situ over a karst landscape. Some of the park can be explored on foot on the inland track, a two to three-day tramp on a walkway cut in the 1800s to access the goldfields. The area is full of cave and sinkhole systems; the most accessible are the Fox River, a one and-a-half-hour return walk (which includes 30 minutes in the caves) and the Punakaiki Cavern, a short walk inland from Punakaiki. Norwest Adventures (03 788 8168, www.caverafting.com) has the

Franz Josef Glacier

West Coast mountain range

concessions and know-how to show you some of the park's more intrepid caving possibilities. Punakaiki Canoes (03 731 1870) runs half-day kayaking trips along the lovely limestone gorge of the optically pure Porari River.

South Island Map J5

Grey District

The Grey District, comprising the middle of the coast, is the most populous area of the West Coast, with Greymouth alone accounting for more than 40% of the region's population. The beaches along here are stony and littered with the driftwood borne down the rivers; they have a wild charm, but few would contemplate swimming. They are, however, good fossicking sites for semi-precious stones, including pounamu (greenstone). Places of interest include Shantytown, and Hokitika, with its art and craft outlets, some of which specialise in locally mined gold and pounamu. There's also a large craft gallery, Junction Art and Craft Centre (03 736 9333), at Kumara Junction, 18km south of Greymouth. But the neglected jewel of the district is Lake Brunner, which you'll find north of State Highway 73 en route to Arthur's Pass.

South Island Map H5

Greymouth

Greymouth used to have more pubs per capita than any other town in New Zealand. There's one on just about every street corner, although not all of them still serve their original purpose. The town's major industries are tourism (as the West Coast terminus of the Tranz Alpine, p.51, it's the gateway to the West Coast) and fishing.
Greymouth has tended to lag behind the slightly more chic town of Hokitika down the line, but improvements to its waterfront area and the centre of town have closed the gap. There are a number of interesting shops, mostly selling art and crafts, but in the winter they tend to close pretty early. The Left Bank Art Gallery in the old BNZ building at 1 Tainui Street (03 768 0038) is a good place to spend a couple of idle hours browsing; it shows (and sells) contemporary New Zealand artworks including greenstone. Most of Greymouth's cafes and restaurants keep erratic hours in the low season (winter), but a reliable place to get an excellent meal is Priya's Indian Cuisine at 84 Tainui Street (03 768 7377). If you're prepared to head way out of town, Jackson's Historic Tavern (03 768 7377) 45km up State Highway 72 towards Arthur's Pass serves some of the best food on the coast, including a mean pie.

The Flies

Wherever you are on the West Coast, sandflies will always be with you. They're a nuisance in Karamea, they're bad in Greymouth and they're a plague in Jackson Bay.

South Island Map H6

Hokitika

Long before tourism took off on the rest of the West Coast, Hokitika was something of a tourist trap, selling trashy souvenirs to visitors who made it over Arthur's Pass (p.265). Today, it's much slicker, and has an international reputation as the centre of the annual Wildfoods Festival (p.61). Shops specialise these days in the exquisite work being done by local artists with pounamu (greenstone), including the Jade Factory (03 755 8007). A rewarding hour can be spent browsing the shops in Tancred Street, including Ruby Rock (www.nzrubyrock.com), which sells jewellery crafted from the unique New Zealand goodletite, a local mineral in which ruby, sapphire and tourmaline crystals form intricate patterns and swirls.
Have a breather and a bite to eat at the very good Café de Paris (03 755 8933) in the same block. With so much artistic talent around the coast, the Hokitika Art Gallery (03 755 5057) doesn't need to stray far in its search for quality exhibits. A cool place to watch movies is in the boxy little Crooked Mile Theatre (03 755 530, www.crookedmile.co.nz), which specialises in arthouse and New Zealand releases.
The National Kiwi Centre (03 755 5251) in Tancred Street not only features the shy, nocturnal birds, but also a trout pool in which you can try your luck.
Just out of town in Brickfield Street, you'll find Seaforth (03 755 7844), the most attractive private garden on the coast, open Tuesday to Sunday, from 10:00 to 16:00.

Whitebait

The whitebait fritter is considered to be a quintessential New Zealand dish – you can try these, and other, more outlandish offerings, at the annual Hokitika Wildfoods Festival (p.61).

Hokitika is also the hub for the attractions of the surrounding district. Lake Kaniere, 15km inland, is a popular boating and watersports venue, and Due West Canoe Safaris (03 755 6717) offers guided canoeing on Lake Mahinapua (12km south of Hokitika). Scenic flights are available from Wilderness Wings (www.wildernesswings.co.nz) and West Coast Flightseeing (0800 359 937), or if you really want to see the coast in style you could hire a classic sports car from Classic Car Rentals (03 755 6928, www.classiccarrentals.co.nz).

One of the best places to stay in Hokitika is the unprepossessing but supremely well thought-out The Shining Star (03 755 8921, www.accommodationwestcoast.co.nz) just north of town. Its range of accommodation, set among a kind of petting farm full of friendly animals, is right beside the beach.

South Island Map J6

Lake Brunner

One of the little-known attractions of the West Coast is Lake Brunner, off the beaten track some 31km south-east of Greymouth. Covering 40 sq km, set among mature stands of kahikatea forest, the placid lake is not only scenic but full of brown trout. There is a wide variety of accommodation options at Moana, the settlement of mainly holiday homes at the lake's northern end. You can even hire a self-drive houseboat and explore the lake that way (www.houseboats.org.nz). Three kilometres short of Moana as you approach from the north, you'll find Kotuku Pottery (03 738 0082), where the large, coal-fired ceramics are well worth a look.

Rutherglen Rd
Greymouth

Shantytown

03 762 6634 | *www.shantytown.co.nz*

Shantytown is a faithful replica of the type of settlement that mushroomed up and down the coast in the mid 1800s as gold fever swept through, carrying grafters and dreamers with it. The collections of restored and original memorabilia of the coast's hard pioneer days are impressive, as are the photographic archives. Visitors can ride a steam train, and try their luck panning for gold (a find is 'guaranteed', and you get to take your little grains of 'colour' home in a tiny glass jar as a memento). Open daily, 08:30 to 17:00.

South Island Map G7

South Westland

If the coast to the north is good looking, the southern third is exquisite. By the time you reach the glacier district, every view is dominated by the mountains, especially mounts Cook, Tasman and La Perouse. The area is studded with small lakes, their waters stained a deep brown by the leaching of tannin; on a still day these reflect the grandeur of the Alps as faithfully as any mirror.

The two glaciers, Fox and Franz Josef, are among New Zealand's most visited attractions. There are few places in the world where you can approach a glacier so closely by car, and reach it by foot so easily. Beyond the point at which the main highway strikes inland at Haast there is a road south that will bring you to Jackson Bay. It's worth the trip, but only if you've brought insect repellent.

South Island Map E8

Jackson Bay

The population of Jackson Bay is 23, and it's regularly boasted that there are more of the critically endangered Fiordland crested penguins than there are permanent human residents. A local company, Round About Haast (www.roundabouthaast.co.nz), offers boat excursions to view them, and to visit the resident pod of the equally rare hector's dolphins. The penguin colony is reached by a short, attractive walk through a patch of rainforest. Whatever you plan to do, however, take long clothing and the most potent insect repellant known to man – the sand flies here are indescribably voracious.

South Island Map G7

Okarito

Okarito, seven kilometres off State Highway 6 just south of Whataroa, has three major claims to fame. It is home to Keri Hulme, New Zealand's only winner of the Booker Prize for literature; it's a prize whitebaiting spot; and the lagoon has a large resident colony of kotuku (white heron). The best way to get close to the latter is to hire kayaks from Okarito Nature Tours (03 753 4014, www.okarito.co.nz), as you can move across the water unobtrusively and avoid disturbing the birds. It's best to allow a day for the experience, although shorter and longer trips are available. You can also catch a jetboat across the lagoon with White Heron Tours (www.whiteherontours.co.nz). Another local operator (03 7534330, www.okaritokiwitours.co.nz) takes nocturnal tour groups out to spy on kiwis in their natural habitat. This costs $60 per person, with a $15 refund if you don't spot one of the shy critters. If you plan to stay, there's a campground or the comparatively luxurious Okarito Beach House (03 753 4080, www.okaritohostel.co.nz).

South Island Map G7

Franz Josef and Fox Glaciers

The iconic attraction of the West Coast has always been the two glaciers that lie within relatively easy reach of State Highway 6.

Of the two, Franz Josef is more accessible than Fox Glacier, although you can reach them both yourself: Franz Josef by driving just south of Franz Josef township, following the road to a carpark and walking 20 to 30 minutes to the glacier's terminal face; Fox by driving a little over 25km to just south of Fox Glacier township and walking for 30 minutes. Those experienced in glacier travel can go higher – all the way to the neves, in fact – but it's not recommended for everyone else, nor is approaching the terminal faces of either glacier, which are prone to dropping truck-sized ice blocks into their lakes without warning. The safest way to see the glaciers is by joining a guided tour, whether on foot or by helicopter. You'd be mad to pass up the opportunity of a scenic flight if the weather permits. Franz Josef Glacier Guides (03 752 0763, www.franzjosefglacier.com) and The Guiding Company (03 752 0047, www.nzguides.co.nz) both offer half and full-day excursions, and each does helicopter-assisted visits to the very top.

Scenic flights are available from both Franz Josef and Fox; a flight over Mount Cook National Park and south Westland is an unforgettable experience, and the 'grand traverse' – from Fox or Franz Josef to Glentanner and the Mackenzie Basin – over the Great Divide cannot be beaten.

There are a few cafes and restaurants in Franz Josef, but you're better off heading to Fox, and the recommended Café Nevé (03 751 0110).

Pit Stop

If your fuel gauge is nudging empty as you pass a service station on the coast, stop. Many of the smaller centres have a petrol pump in front of the general store, but there's no guarantee there'll be anything in it, especially in summer.

Lake Matheson

One of the most familiar tourist images of the South Island to the connoisseur of postcards is that of Mount Cook reflected in the tannin-darkened waters of Lake Matheson, five kilometres west of Fox Glacier. So sheltered is the little lake by the surrounding bush that you can take a photograph of the mountain and its reflection and be quite unable to tell afterwards which way up it should go.

Pukekura

South Island Map H6

Lake Ianthe

A small lake beside State Highway 6 around 75km south of Hokitika, Ianthe is a classic of south Westland; its tannin-stained waters surrounded and sheltered by tall stands of kahikatea and reflecting the snow-capped Southern Alps. There's a Department of Conservation campground (www.doc.govt.nz), and the lake is popular for boating and trout fishing. About five kilometres before you reach Ianthe, you'll pass the Puke Pub (03 7554008) and The Bushman's Centre. It's hard to miss them; the Bushman's Centre has a large model of a sandfly outside, while there's a model of a possum on the roof of the pub. Puke provides accommodation, and specialises in wild foods – pork, rabbit and, of course, possum – while the Bushman's Centre is a museum of sorts, celebrating forestry and the destruction of possums. You can try your hand at various bushman skills, such as axe-throwing. West Coast eccentricity at its very best.

Area G p.205

Southland

The oldest European settlements are supposed to have been in Southland (both Riverton and Bluff lay claim to the title). More startling, perhaps, is that Maori were well-established here, as it's hard to imagine conditions more remote from their ancestral Polynesia. There's little between the south coast and Antarctica, and winter brings rapidly alternating bands of hail and sleet and a huge, pounding surf.

The best way to experience the charms of Southland is to drive the Southern Scenic Route (p.291), a trip that scribes a lazy arc around the bottom of the South Island, via the picturesque Catlins to Dunedin. However, if you neglect to take a detour to Riverton (p.290) and the gorgeous Te Waewae Bay (p.290), you have officially missed out. Similarly, New Zealanders who claim to know their country without having been across Foveaux Strait to Stewart Island (p.294) can't be taken that seriously.

Like the rest of the South Island, the region was heavily forested before human intervention. Some of the region's most impressive historical sites, such as the Port Craig viaducts on the boundary of Fiordland National Park, and the remains of the bush railways in the Catlins area, are associated with the Southland timber boom.

The coast itself is beautiful, but cold and wild. In the west is the vastness of Fiordland National Park. Created by the effect of massive glaciation, Fiordland is a maze of jagged mountains and deep, steep-walled valleys.

It's unspeakably beautiful, particularly where the landscape meets the sea in the fiords that give the area its name. Most famous of these is Milford Sound (p.292), a long, sheltered waterway presided over by towering mountains including the neat, triangular Mitre Peak. It's one of New Zealand's iconic landscapes and familiar to people the world over. Doubtful Sound and Dusky Sound, while less accessible, are just as beautiful.

The Lowdown

They talk funny down here, but it's friendly, scenic and gets the biggest surf in New Zealand. It includes the neglected paradise of Stewart Island to the south, and the untouchable wilderness of Fiordland National Park to the west.

The Essentials

Cruise Milford Sound, tramp the Hollyford Valley, drive the Southern Scenic Route, admire the petrified forest at Curio Bay, brave a southerly gale on Bluff Hill, eat pizza at the Crazy Fish in Oban on Stewart Island.

The Catlins Coast

South Island Map F13

The stretch of remote, rugged, and remarkable coastline east from Waipapa Point and around to Balclutha (30km south of Dunedin) is known as 'the Catlins', and forms the jewel in the crown of the Southern Scenic Route. It's a mixture of rocky headlands and white sand beaches, some of which receive formidable surf when there's a southerly swell. Residents of Otago and Southland descend in the summer, but it's probably at its best in winter when it's all but deserted. There's a good reason for this, namely the ferocious southerly storms that batter the area, but strike it on a good day and you feel as though you have paradise to yourself. The Purakaunui Falls, a short bushwalk off the main road north of Papatowai, is one of New Zealand's most photographed waterfalls.

Curio Bay

South Island Map E14

Curio Bay is around 50km west of Owaka. You reach the broad, level rock shelf behind the bay by descending a few steps from a carpark. The shelf is actually a 60 million year old fossilised swamp, with the petrified trunks of fallen trees clearly identifiable in the rock. There are good interpretative panels beside the access stairs to alert you to them. Curio Bay is a haul-out spot for hooker's sea lions and the very rare yellow-eyed penguin. These tend to emerge at dusk from the surge channels that lead from the sea and make their way to their nests at the base of the cliffs. They're very shy, and will prefer to stay at sea if they spot people between them and the nesting area.

Nugget Point

South Island Map F13

If you're approaching the Catlins from Balclutha and Molyneux Bay, you'll see the turnoff for Nugget Point shortly after you've passed Kaka Point. It's about a 10km drive to the carpark, and then a 15 minute walk along the ridge to the point where the Nugget Point lighthouse stands. The view from the lookout just beyond the lighthouse is dominated to the south of the point by the Nuggets themselves, a cluster of fantastically eroded rocks, and you can see along the brooding cliffs of the south coast to your right.

South Island Map F13

Pounawea

A small settlement of cribs on an estuary around four kilometres south of Owaka, Pounawea gives access to two typically stunning Catlins beaches: Surat Bay and Cannibal Cove. Surat can only be reached on foot (by following tracks through the dunes; watch out for basking sea lions), and by walking the length of Surat Bay and following a track across the isthmus, you can reach Cannibal Cove. Both are fine surf beaches.

South Island Map E13

Invercargill

Eating in Invercargill
There are plenty of forgettable restaurants in Invercargill, but one which would stand out in much more richly endowed gastronomic territory is The Cabbage Tree (03 213 1443, www.thecabbagetree.com).

Invercargill, the largest town in Southland, is also the world's southernmost city. It's not naturally favoured in its location: it's flat, and close enough to the coast to receive Antarctic blasts. You might think this all adds up to pretty bleak, and you're right. Apart from the attractive streetscape of The Crescent right in the city's heart, and the possible exceptions of the museum and art gallery in Queen's Gardens and the old waterworks nearby, the built environment is unremarkable too.

The successful promotion of the Southern Scenic Route – on which Invercargill is a slight aberration – has meant an increasing number of visitors, however.

The Southland Museum and Art Gallery (03 219 9069, www.southlandmuseum.com) features many items from the whaling and sealing days, and relics from some of the dramatic shipwrecks dotting the south coast.

The exclusive Andersons Park Art Gallery (03 215 7432), which is housed in a stately 1925 vintage Georgian mansion, features regional and national works. Its annual spring exhibition is the highlight of Southland's arts calendar.

South Island Map D14

Bluff

Thirty kilometres south of Invercargill, you come to the little village of Bluff, nestled at the foot of Motupohue (Bluff Hill) and on the shores of a fine natural harbour, from which an intrepid oystering fleet sets out to dredge the beds of wild Foveaux Strait.

Bluff is the end of the line for State Highway 1, and the southernmost point of the mainland road system in New Zealand. An observation point at the top of 265m Bluff Hill gives panoramic views of Ruapuke Island, Stewart Island and a whole lot of empty ocean besides. From here, on the right night, you can admire the Southern Lights (aurora australis), and some spectacular sunsets. It's also the second worst place in the world from which to view a southerly bringing sleet and hail, the worst being Bluff itself, which makes up for the lack of drama with sheer dereliction.

With Riverton, Bluff lays claim to being New Zealand's earliest European settlement. Back down in the township, you'll find the Bluff Maritime Museum (03 212 7534), where you can view exhibits that illuminate the history of the town.

Gore

The quaint town of Gore, situated in the heart of Southland on the convergence of State Highways 94, 90 and 1, is known as the country music capital of New Zealand, and holds an annual bash, the Gold Guitar Awards. The Hokonui Heritage Centre (03 208 9908) is worth a browse. It includes the Gore Historical Museum's collection of colonial-era clothing and the Hokonui Moonshine Museum, which commemorates the district's half-century of illicit whisky distilling from the time of prohibition in 1902 to its repeal in 1952. You can even buy a bottle of Old Hokonui, distilled to the original recipe of the famous 'Hokonui Hooch'. It is rough as guts, but its heritage helps it go down.

Western Southland

Towards the west, Southland prepares itself to become the rugged wilderness of Fiordland. The main centres of population are service towns, with little to detain the visitor for long. However, the south coast, with its scatter of small settlements and spectacular beaches, is one of the South Island's neglected gems.

The little fishing village of Riverton (see below), besides being one of New Zealand's oldest European settlements, is a beautiful place to spend a couple of days, preferably exploring the coastline to the west. Along there, you'll find the geologically interesting Orepuki beach (where you can fossick for precious stones), the achingly beautiful Te Waewae Bay (p.290) and, at its western limit, the historically significant Port Craig.

South Island Map D13

Riverton

Riverton, 30km west of Invercargill on the estuary of the Aparima River, is reputed to be one of New Zealand's oldest settlements and half-ironically proclaimed to be 'the riviera of the deep south'. With a little fishing fleet bobbing at anchor on the calm waters of the estuary, it's undeniably picturesque. The estuary is good for kayaking and swimming in summer, and the town is close to some superb coastline; nearby Cosy Nook is a beautiful, sheltered sandy beach, and The Porridge at Colac Bay (10 minutes' drive west) is a legendary surf break. A great place to stay is the restored hotel, the Riverton Rock Guesthouse (03 234 8886, www.rivertonrock.co.nz), while the BeachHouse Café Bar (03 234 8274) has great views and food, even if the menu is a trifle limited.

South Island Map C13

Te Waewae Bay

The great, lovely sweep of Te Waewae Bay is divided down the middle by the mouth of the mighty Waiau River. At the eastern end, Orepuki is a geologically interesting spot where gold was once mined from the black sands, and gemstones, from semiprecious, such as agates and jaspers, to rare sapphires abound on the beach.

Dolphins, including the rare hector's, and the odd whale can be spotted and it's a great place to ride horses, quad bikes and the occasionally huge southerly swell that thunders in. Port Craig, on Sandy Hill point at the western end of Te Waewae Bay and inaccessible by car, is a fascinating historical site, with four huge timber viaducts from the 1930s timber-milling days still used as footbridges on the Hump Ridge Track (p.294).

South Island Map C11

Fiordland

Fiordland has got it all: rugged good looks, mystery, drama and romance. The 1.2 million hectares of Fiordland National Park are of international significance, as they're one of the world's last, great, relatively untouched wilderness areas. While millions of visitors pass through the park each year, they barely scratch its surface. The vast majority travel to Milford Sound (p.292), one of New Zealand's best-known scenic attractions. You can get there by road (an adventure in itself, particularly in avalanche season), by flying from Te Anau or Queenstown, or by tramping the Milford Track, one of the several famous walks in the park.

Southislanderrr

It's surprising that even in a country as young, small and generally homogenous as New Zealand, there should be obvious regional differences. Yet you always know a Southlander: the accent is characterised by a real 'burr' on the letter 'r' (as though 'burr' was spelled with four 'r's).

Next most popular is the tour to the equally beautiful Doubtful Sound (p.292), reached by taking a boat across Lake Manapouri and then by tour coach along an orphaned road to Deep Water Cove. The truly intrepid can walk the Hollyford Valley to Big Bay on the coast, or the Dusky Track to yet another remote waterway, Dusky Sound.

Many more visitors take scenic flights from Te Anau or Queenstown for a bird's-eye view of Fiordland. The soaring peaks and vertiginous swoops of the valleys make for an exhilarating plane or helicopter ride.

The eastern edge of the park, where the townships of Te Anau and Manapouri are situated, offer a variety of recreational pursuits, notably fishing. The lakes of Fiordland may be fished (with a licence) year round, whereas the rivers are closed for part of the year; check with the Department of Conservation (www.doc.govt.nz).

The Te Anau Wildlife Centre also offers the chance to get up close to one of the world's rarest birds, the extraordinary takahe, which was rediscovered in the second half of the 20th century in the remoteness of Fiordland after being considered extinct for decades.

South Island Map C11

Te Anau

Situated on the boundary of Fiordland National Park, Te Anau is the gateway to the area's many attractions. The local cinema (03 249 8812, www.fiordlandcinema.co.nz) is run by a helicopter company, and its regular feature is a cinematic journey over Fiordland National Park – a great way to whet your appetite. There are seven operators that offer scenic flights over the vast and rugged park, but try Air Fiordland (03 249 7505, www.airfiordland.com).

Te Anau is also a lovely locality in its own right; with the lake (the South Island's largest) sporting scenic charms to rival those of Wakatipu and Wanaka (p.277). You can appreciate its character from the lookout at the end of Ramparts Road.

Lake Te Anau offers excellent fishing with a licence year-round, and there are any number of guides offering to hook you up with local trout (try Outside Sports Te Anau, 03 249 8195, www.sportsworldteanau.co.nz). There are two operators that run scenic cruises: Real Journeys (03 249 7416, www.realjourneys.co.nz), and Cruise Te Anau (03 249 7593, www.cruiseteanau.co.nz). Real Journeys do transfers to the Kepler and the Milford Tracks (p.292).

Across the lake, the Te Anau caves have an impressive glowworm grotto. Real Journeys runs a timetabled service across from the town wharf; it's a 35 minute boat trip, followed by a walk and a silent drift through the main cavern in a small boat.

There are several companies running guided walking trips (whether on the great walks in Fiordland National Park, or on any one of dozens of other local tracks), or you can try horse-trekking, jetboating or even skydiving (New Zealand Skydive Fiordland, 0800 746 754, www.simplifly.co.nz). If you prefer something more sedate, visit the Department of Conservation Visitor Centre (03 249 7920), which is incorporated with the Te Anau Museum. Alternatively you could take a 10 minute stroll along the lake foreshore to the Wildlife Park, to see native birds, including New Zealand's adorably feisty mountain parrot, the kea, and the pin-up bird of the New Zealand wildlife preservation effort, the takahe. Admission is free.

Southern Scenic Route

This iconic drive, which runs from Te Anau down around the southern coast and up to Dunedin, can be done in 10 hours. But to really enjoy it, you should take three days, with two overnight stops en route. For more information, see (www.southernscenicroute.co.nz).

South Island Map C11

Lake Manapouri

Another magnificent Fiordland lake is Manapouri, 20km south of Te Anau. It has 35 large and small islands dotted around, which makes for interesting boating. The best way to see them is by sea kayak. Sea Kayak Fiordland runs guided paddles, or will rent kayaks to those who are sufficiently experienced (03 249 7700, www.fiordlandseakayak.co.nz).

Manapouri is also remarkable for the engineering feat that is the Manapouri Hydroelectric Scheme, which harnesses the 178m fall from the lake to Doubtful Sound through a tunnel to run its turbines. It's a model of unobtrusive industrial development in an ecologically sensitive area, and a surprisingly interesting part of the tour to Doubtful Sound (when it's available).

South Island Map C12

Lake Hauroko

Hauroko means 'windy lake' in Maori and if you're here when a northerly is funneling down the steep-walled valley you'll see why. The lake is situated 130km west of Invercargill via the south coast, the drive taking you past the historic suspension bridge at Clifden.

Hauroko is 40km long, and, at 462m deep, New Zealand's deepest lake. Narrowly disjoined from the mainland is Mary Island, which features a cave where a Maori burial site – reputed to be that of a Maori princess – was discovered in 1967. Some locals will try to spook you with tales of tapu and makutu (curses) that pursue those who set foot here, but Maori scoff at such claims. You're unlikely to infringe any tapu, as a steel grille seals the entrance to the cave. You visit Mary Island, and the lovely

Struan Falls, by taking a cruise with Dusky Track Adventures (03 226 6681, www.duskytrack.co.nz). Lake Hauroko is drained by the Waiaurahiri River, sometimes called 'the longest waterfall in New Zealand', as for most of its two kilometre course it consists of boisterous rapids. Two companies offer jetboat experiences on the river: Luxmore Jet (03 249 6951, www.luxmorejet.co.nz) and Hump Ridge Jet (03 225 8174, www.wildernessjet.co.nz).

South Island Map D10

Milford Sound

Most overseas visitors to New Zealand are already familiar with the vista from the road's end at Milford, out into the sound with the unmistakable silhouette of Mitre Peak rearing above the still water. Few who come with a clear expectation of what they'll see are quite prepared for the grandeur of the scene, however. The best wide-screen digital photography can't quite convey the scale of it. Many of the peaks crowded to the water's edge are 2,000 metres or more, and if you visit in wet weather – with rain falling on 200 out of 365 each year, there's a better than even chance you will – the cliffs will be alive with waterfalls. The largest, Stirling Falls, thunders 146 metres from a notch in the clifftop into the sea.

Most of this is best appreciated from the water, of course. Red Boat Cruises (03 441 1137, www.redboats.co.nz) offers trips complete with classy refreshments and an informative commentary. Real Journeys (03 249 7416, www.realjourneys.co.nz) runs a shorter scenic cruise and an overnight experience.

If you want to get a bit closer to nature, there are two sea kayaking outfits who offer guided paddles or freedom rentals: Rosco's Milford Sound Sea Kayak (3 249 8500, www.kayakmilford.co.nz) and Fiordland Wilderness Experiences (03 2497700, www.fiordlandseakayak.co.nz).

Milford is pretty unique above the waterline, but it's pretty special beneath it, too. As freshwater is stained with tannin leached from the vegetation along its journey to the sea, this layer filters the sunlight and creates the same dim light conditions in the shallows that exist at far greater depth.

Diving in the cold, clear waters of the sound will get you close to organisms (notably the very rare black coral); you just won't see elsewhere without access to a diving bell. Fiordland Expeditions (03 2499 005, www.fiordlandexpeditions.co.nz) runs guided scuba trips. If you fancy a glimpse of this underwater wonderland without getting wet then visit the remarkable floating marine observatory (03 441 1137, www.milforddeep.co.nz) in the heart of the Piopiotahi Marine Reserve at Harrison Cove. So long as you can handle the 10m spiral staircase descent, you'll get to see what the divers do without going to all the bother. Most of the cruises operating on Milford Sound will stop here on request; entry to the observatory is available as an upgrade on Red Boat excursions. It's worthwhile staying at Milford, if only to experience the serenity that descends when the daytime crowds have gone. There's a range of accommodation, from a campground (make sure you've got a warm sleeping bag, and plenty of insect repellent) to lodge-style digs.

Milford Track

This 53km walk can be guided with gear portaged for walkers by guides or even by helicopters. Independent walkers can still do it, but bookings are essential in the summer. The views along the track are magnificent, and then you reach Milford Sound. The track starts on the far side of Lake Te Anau from the township, and climbs steadily over the next three days to the pass. The climbing isn't the hard part, though; it's the descent that gets to most people. You can get access to the start with Real Journeys, (www.realjourneys.co.nz). Ultimate Hikes has the only concession to guide tours along the track (03 441 1138, www.ultimatehikes.co.nz).

South Island Map B11

Doubtful Sound

Less-visited than Milford, and with the distinct advantage of having no permanent settlement, Doubtful Sound is bigger than its glamour-puss relative up the coast and every bit as beautiful. It's reached by a trip across Lake Manapouri (p.290), and a 20 minute coach journey (with a stop at Wilmot Pass, with its commanding and oft-photographed views over the upper reaches of the sound) to Deep Cove. There, you'll board a boat for your short, longer, or overnight excursion out on the water, with the prospect of seeing dolphins, seals and innumerable seabirds. Real Journeys (03 249 7416, www.realjourneys.co.nz) offers the complete package.

Kayaking on Doubtful Sound

Dusky Sound

Waterfall, Milford Sound

Across Milford Sound

Tuatapere

Hump Ridge Track

www.humpridgetrack.co.nz

Southland's Hump Ridge is New Zealand's newest Great Walk, reflected by the level of the facilities along the way. The boardwalks, the benching and water control, and especially the huts and the viewing platforms, are all first-rate and brand spanking new. Numbers are strictly controlled on the walk to preserve the wilderness experience that is in danger of being lost along other New Zealand tramping tracks. The Hump Ridge takes in a wide variety of landscapes, from tussock highcountry to sandy beach, all in a relatively easy day, and you may well sight a rare hector's dolphin en route. A variety of packages are available on the Hump Ridge, from independent walking to the full luxury version, where the hard work is done by helicopters.

Fiordland National Park

Kepler Track

Opened in 1988 as a means to see some the spectacular alpine terrain around Lake Te Anau and Lake Manapouri in Fiordland National Park, the Kepler is a moderately hard three or four days for trampers. It's a 60km circuit starting and finishing at the Lake Te Anau control gates. You can reach this point either by water taxi or through Real Journeys: (03 249 7416). Cruise Te Anau (03 249 7593, www.cruiseteanau.co.nz) offers transfers to the Kepler, by car or by walking. The Kepler can be impassable in winter.

Fiordland

Routeburn Track

This is a world-renowned tramping experience, two to three days spent among some of the most spectacular scenery in the world. A traditional route taken by Maori in pursuit of greenstone, it passes through broad, flat valleys formed through ancient glacial action and now forested in beech, or grassed with tussock. The Routeburn in Fiordland was among the first of New Zealand's Great Walks to be so swamped with walkers that bookings were introduced to control numbers. Access to the track is by water taxi from Queenstown, or an 80km drive. The Routeburn is guided by several companies, including Ultimate Hikes (03 442-8200, www.ultimatehikes.co.nz).

South Island Map D14

Stewart Island

The Maori name for Stewart Island, Rakiura, means 'land of the glowing sky', which is a reference to either the amazing sunrises and sunsets visible at these latitudes or the aurora australis, which frequently lights up the nights here.

James Cook thought Stewart Island was a peninsula when he saw it from afar, but it was left to a shady character by the name of Captain William Stewart, poking about on some errand or another in the early 1800s, to notice Foveaux Strait, the ill-tempered stretch of water between the South Island and the more southerly island that bears his name.

It's comparatively unspoilt, with much of its area given over to national park. A network of approximately 220km of tramping track runs through Stewart Island; it's magnificent (if muddy and often cold) walking, with a variety of terrain to suit all levels of experience. The bush abounds in birdlife now scarce on the mainland: kaka are plentiful, and all it takes to see a kiwi here is the desire and a modicum of patience. Besides tramping, visitors can experience a fisherman's el dorado at Stewart Island, go diving and kayaking, or take a scenic flight or cruise to its remoter reaches. Most of these activities are coordinated through Stewart Island Adventures (03 212 7700, www.stewartislandadventures.co.nz). It's also well worth taking a day trip to Ulva Island, an open wildlife sanctuary at the entrance to Paterson Inlet. Here, you can see some of New Zealand's rarest birds, including the kakapo (of which only 86 survive). Stewart Island Experience will get you there. You reach Stewart Island either by air from Invercargill (Southern Air, 03 218 9129, www.southernair.co.nz) or by boat (Stewart Island Experience, 03 212 7660, www.stewartislandexperience.co.nz).

Tours & Sightseeing

Other options **Activity Tours** p.297

What do you get when you combine the natural entrepreneurial skills of New Zealanders with an innate pride in showing visitors their country? The result is an ever-increasing number of tours and sightseeing options, and because it's New Zealand, the best ones are run with a personal touch and usually include active ways to experience the spectacular New Zealand countryside.

In the North Island, the most interesting tours showcase coastal areas such as Coromandel and the Bay of Islands, explore the wine areas of Auckland, Hawke's Bay and the Wairarapa, and provide straightforward access to mountains, lakes and rivers. Whether it's by sea, by air or on land, and whether it's from the comfort of a vehicle, the relative comfort of a bicycle seat or on your own two feet, sightseeing in the South Island is about as good as it gets anywhere in the world.

And with many of the tourists who have been drawn to New Zealand in recent years being of an adventurous bent, there has been a huge scramble to provide adventure 'destinations', offering activities to the wandering adrenaline-junky.

The stream of sightseers to both islands was given a fillip by the use of much of the natural beauty of the landscape as locations and backdrops to the filming of *The Lord of the Rings* movie trilogy. Many tour companies have added an extra string to their bow showing off sites that have acquired a whole new dimension from their screen roles. To get a feel of the options, contact Wanaka Tours (03 338 0982, www.lordoftheringstours.co.nz).

Activity Tours

Other options **Tours & Sightseeing** p.297

Sea Kayaking

New Zealand is tailor-made for sea kayaking. Sea kayaks are very long compared with the much shorter river kayak, and the extra waterline means they require much less effort to paddle. They're also pretty stable, so you don't have to be that fit or experienced to manage them. Even if you don't feel comfortable hiring one yourself, you can join a guided tour. You'll find someone to rent you a sea kayak just about wherever there's water. There's easily half a dozen operators doing freedom rentals and guided tours in the Marlborough Sounds, and over a dozen in and around Abel Tasman National Park in the Nelson region, easily the best place for sea kayaks in New Zealand. Try Kaiteriteri Kayaks (0800 252 925, www.seakayak.co.nz) or Southern Exposure (03 527 8424, www.southern-exposure.co.nz).

Kayaks for hire

Rafting

While a large number of the rivers of the South Island are commercially rafted, the most notable whitewater can be found on the Buller River, the Rangitata, the Shotover and the Clutha. Ultimate Descents (03 523 9899, www.rivers.co.nz), based in the Buller Gorge, run trips on the Buller; Rangitata Rafts (www.rafts.co.nz) operates on the Rangitata; Pioneer Rafting (03 443 1246, www.ecoraft.co.nz) shoot the rapids of the Clutha, and there are several operators running the wilder bits of the Kawarau and the Shotover: Queenstown Rafting (0800 723 8464, www.rafting.co.nz), Extreme Green Rafting (03 442 8517, www.nzraft.co.nz) and Challenge Rafting (03 442 7318, www.raft.co.nz).

Carry on Camper

A popular way for independent travellers to get around is in a self-catering camper van or in a rental car. Popular camper van companies include Maui (0800 651 080, www.maui.co.nz) and Britz (0800 831 900, www.britz.co.nz). Spaceships (09 309 8777, www.spaceships.tv) are a unique Kiwi invention that combine the drivability of a car with the practicality of a camper fan. Younger backpackers gravitate to the intensely social hop on-hop-off Kiwi Experience bus network (09 366 9830, www.kiwiexperience.com).

Jetboating

Just about every substantial river in the South Island suits commercial jetboating, such is the versatility of the craft.

The pioneering company in the industry is Shotover Jet (03 442 8570, www.shotoverjet.co.nz). On the Buller, try Buller Adventure Tours (03 789 7286, www.adventuretours.co.nz) and on the Haast, try Haast River Safari (03 750 0101, www.haastriver.co.nz). Probably the most conducive waterways in New Zealand are the braided rivers in the east, where you should try Waimak Alpine Jet (03 318 4881, www.alpinejet.co.nz). On Southland's Wairaurahiri River try Luxmore Jet (03 249 6491, www.luxmorejet.co.nz) or Hump Ridge Jet (03 225 8174, www.wildernessjet.co.nz).

Climbing and Mountaineering

For terrain in the Mount Cook area (and for Aoraki/Mount Cook itself), try Alpine Guides (03 435 1834, www.alpineguides.co.nz), or Alpine Recreation (0800 006 096, www.alpinerecreation.co.nz). In Mount Aspiring National Park, you could use Mount Aspiring Guides (www.aspiringguides.co.nz), Adventure Consultants (www.adventureconsultants.co.nz), or Wanaka Rock Climbing and Abseil Adventures (www.wanakarock.co.nz).

Caving

Several areas of the South Island feature kaarst country, where water has sculpted limestone above and below ground into extraordinary shapes and contours. There are significant cave systems scattered all around the island, although the pick of them are in the Nelson area and in Kahurangi and Paparoa National Parks. The Ngarua caves on Takaka Hill are best visited with a guide (03 528 8093). Te Anaroa in Kahurangi is guided by Kahurangi Nature Experiences (03 782 6652). Norwest Adventures have the concessions and know-how to show you some of both Kahurangi and Paparoa's more intrepid caving possibilities (www.caverafting.co.nz).

National Park Alpine Village
Tongariro National Park
Tongariro

Adrift Guided Outdoor Adventures

07 892 2751 | *www.adriftnz.co.nz*

Adrift runs hiking trips, canoeing expeditions and sea kayaking from its base in Tongariro National Park. Fully guided hikes, including all food and accommodation, are a hassle-free way to undertake the park's Tongariro Crossing and Northern Circuit treks. Canoe trips run from one to five days on the Whanganui River, and sea kayaking trips take place further north, around the Coromandel coastline.

Paihia
Bay of Islands

Coastal Kayakers

09 402 8105 | *www.coastalkayakers.co.nz*

The sub-tropical climate of the Bay of Islands is perfect for sea kayaking and Coastal Kayakers' tours explore the best of the area's stunning coast and islands. The one-day trip to Motumaire Island is ideal for beginners, and includes time to sunbathe, swim and snorkel. For moderately fit paddlers, the three-day outer island journey visits hidden coves and quiet, deserted beaches.

Tairua
Coromandel Pensinsula

Epic Adventures

07 864 8193 | *www.epicadventures.co.nz*

Epic Adventures provides the opportunity to catch snapper and tuna around the islands off the Coromandel Peninsula. Island stopovers and multi-day fishing expeditions are a speciality. Accommodation is in luxury lodges or in cabins and campsites on the islands. Skipper Carl can introduce guests to the world-famous Alderman Islands.

Greenlane
Auckland

New Zealand Surf & Snow Tours

09 828 0426 | *www.newzealandsurftours.com*

One-day trips head off to the popular surfing hotspots of Piha and Raglan, and longer five-day road trips continue to the best beaches in Northland. Small group sizes (a maximum of seven) ensure plenty of time for dedicated surfing lessons. Skiing and snowboarding groups visit Mount Ruapehu, and other adventure activities such as skydiving and quad biking can be arranged.

Bicycle Tours

A good place to start is Cycle New Zealand, who offer the country's biggest choice of guided and independent bicycle tours throughout both islands (03 982 2966, www.cyclenewzealand.com). Banbury Tours of Christchurch (www.cyclehire-tours.co.nz, 03 339-4020), will also rent you gear and Adventure South (03 942 1222, www.advsouth.co.nz), who run guided tours of many parts of the South Island, including the rail trails. There are two dedicated cycleways in the South Island: the Central Otago Rail Trail (www.centralotagorailtrail.co.nz), which scribes a 151km arc around the Maniototo Basin and takes four to five days to ride at a steady pace and stopping at the pleasant pubs along the way, and the Little River Rail Trail (www.littleriverrailtrail.co.nz), which follows a 45km section of former railway embankment from Hornby (on the outskirts of Christchurch) to Little River at the base of Banks Peninsula.

Parnell
Auckland

Pedaltours

09 585 1338 | *www.pedaltours.co.nz*

Pedal Tours run cycling trips across New Zealand. In the North Island the eight-day Coromandel Peninsula itinerary includes the beach resorts of Whangamata and Whitianga, and the eight-day Volcano trip visits the natural wonders of Rotorua, Waitomo and Tongariro National Park. Accommodation is in farmstays and hotels, and a back up vehicle is available if the going gets too tough.

Boat Tours

You can charter watercraft, from tiny inflatable kayaks to large yachts, in several locations on both islands, including the Bay of Islands, Marlborough Sounds, the southern Fiords and the alpine lakes. In the Marlborough Sounds, look for Compass Charters (03 573 8332, www.compass-charters.co.nz) and in both the Sounds and in the Nelson region, consider Charterlink (03 573 6591, www.charterlinksouth.co.nz). Skippered charters are available just about everywhere. The beautiful motor-sailing vessels belonging to Real Journeys (03 573 6591, www.realjourneys.co.nz), plying Milford and Doubtful Sounds are fast becoming as iconic.

Bay of Islands

Ecocruz

0800 432 627 | *www.ecocruz.co.nz*

With the 22 metre Manawanui as a comfortable ocean-going base, Ecocruz runs two-night/three-day cruises exploring the Bay of Islands Maritime Park. On board there's room for just 10 passengers and plenty of kayaking, snorkelling and fishing gear to get the most out of visiting uninhabited islands. Fresh seafood is a regular feature of the excellent onboard meals. Trips run from October to April.

15 The Strand East
Whakatane

White Island Tours

07 308 9588 | *www.whiteisland.co.nz*

Fifty kilometres off the coast of the Bay of Plenty is White Island ('Whakaari' in Maori). Trips from Whakatane take around 80 minutes. Upon landing, passengers are given a hard hat and a gas mask - the safety precautions are definitely not for show as White Island is New Zealand's most active volcano. Highlights of the tour include the island's deserted sulphur mining factory, and standing on the edge of the steaming crater.

Brewery Tours

Many boutique breweries will show you their operations: there's Brew Moon (03 593 0088), just outside Amberley in North Canterbury. There's the excellent Founder's Brewery in Nelson (03 548 4638, www.ecobrew.co.nz), and the Mussel Inn (www.mussel inn.co.nz) near Takaka in Golden Bay. The big boys will show you round, too: you can visit the Monteith's Brewery in Greymouth (03 7684149), the Speight's Brewery (www.speights.co.nz) in Dunedin and Dominion Breweries' mainland operation (among its first) in Timaru (03 633 2095). In the lower North Island, try Wild About Wellington (0274 419010), who offer tastings and tours of boutique breweries with a beer expert.

Dolphin & Whale Watching

In Kaikoura in the South Island you can gawk at whales from land, sea, and air: Whale Watch Kaikoura (03 319 6767, www.whalewatch.co.nz) will take you out on the water, while Wings Over Whales (www.whales.co.nz) will fly you over. The three main species of great whale spotted are the Southern Right, the Humpback and the occasional Sperm. New Zealand waters are home to three rare dolphin species: the hector's Dolpin, the dusky Dolphin and the risso's Dolphin. Dolphin Watch Eco-tours (03 573 8040, www.naturetours.co.nz) operate in the Marlborough Sounds and Dolphin Encounter (03 319 6777, www.dolphin.co.nz) in Kaikoura – both will get you close enough to swim with them.

NZ Post Bldg
Cnr of Marsden Rd &
Williams Rd
Paihia

Dolphin Discoveries

09 402 8234 | *www.dolphinz.co.nz*

Dolphin Discoveries pioneered swimming with dolphins in the Bay of Islands in 1991. Its purpose-built catamaran now leaves on twice-daily trips to encounter bottle nose and common dolphins. Wetsuits and snorkelling gear is provided, and trips occasionally spy other marine mammals including Orca and Humpback whales. To avoid impacting on dolphins' natural behaviour such as bonding family groups, some departures are viewing trips only.

Helicopter/Plane Charters		
Aoraki Mount Cook Seaplanes	03 442 3065	www.milfordflights.co.nz
Heletranz	09 415 3550	www.heletranz.co.nz
Helicopter Line	03 442 3034	www.helicopter.co.nz
Heliventures	03 750 0086	www.heliventures.co.nz
Sounds Air	03 520 3080	www.soundsair.co.nz
Southern Alps Air	03 443 4385	www.southernalpsair.co.nz

Helicopter/Plane Charters

The scenic wonders of New Zealand support a lucrative sightseeing industry, not least among aviators, as a quick flyover is a swift, efficient and comfortable way to see a lot of country in a short space of time. It's also a different and humbling perspective. Many of the smaller transport companies offer scenic flights as a sideline – indeed, often getting from A to B is a scenic marvel in its own right. What's more, many 'flightseeing' companies also offer transport to access remote activity areas, such as high off-piste ski terrain or inaccessible mountain-biking runs.

Heritage Tours

PO Box 63-308
Newton
Wellington

Potiki Adventures

0800692 3836 | *www.potikiadventures.com*

Auckland-based Potiki Adventures offer 'tours from a contemporary Maori perspective' and offer a very different experience to the usual combination of folklore and culture at Maori tourist villages in Rotorua. Owners Bianca and Melissa are two young Maori women winning many awards for their innovative and interesting tours. The 'urban Maori Experience' explores Auckland and the West Coast beaches with a context of Maori myths and legends, and the 'Marine Reserve Adventure' travels north for snorkelling and kayaking at Goat Island.

Walking Tours

Bush & Beach (0800 42 3224) run informative eco-tours exploring Auckland's wilder, more natural face including walking tours to bush-clad waterfalls and along black sand surf beaches. Full-day and half-day West Coast tours are available, and the Untamed Island tour spends a busy day exploring Great Barrier Island, 88 kilometres from the mainland.

Guided walking, hiking, tramping or mountaineering is available in the South Island, with most of the more advanced options being region-specific. Many tour operators who get you about by bus will also offer day-trips or even overnight or multi-day excursions into the back- and high-country. Notable amongst these are Flying Kiwi (www.flyingkiwi.com) and Adventure South (www.advsouth.co.nz). Most of the Great Walks and other major tracks have operators who will guide you, and even lug your gear for you or fly it from point to point. Whomever you choose, however, make sure they are licensed and kosher. Fly-by-night operators are becoming a problem for New Zealand's tourism industry.

Wine Tours

Other options **Alcohol** p.368

The South Island boasts four notable wine regions, Marlborough, Central Otago, Canterbury and Nelson whose vintages are recognized on the world wine stage. The largest and best-known of them is Marlborough, where close to 80 wineries have a presence. It's home to the famous Cloudy Bay sauvignon blanc. Close behind it is Central Otago, where the vineyards are as picturesque as the wines – especially pinot noir – are excellent. Vineyard tours are available in each of these regions. In Marlborough region, try Marlborough Wine Tours (03 578 9515, www.marlborough winetours.co.nz) or Wine Tours by Bike (03 577 6954, www.winetoursbybike.co.nz). In Waiapara, you'll find Colmonell Clydesdale Wagon Tours (03 149 001), who can get you from vineyard to vineyard in a horse-drawn wagon. In Nelson, your best bet is JJ's Tours (03 546 5470, www.jjs.co.nz).

11 Pentland Av
Mt Eden
Auckland

Auckland Wine Trail Tours

09 630 1540 | *www.winetrailtours.co.nz*

Tours visit West Auckland's established vineyard scene and the up and coming area of Matakana an hour north of the city. Half-day and full-day tours are available, with plenty of opportunity for cellar door tasting. Transport is in smaller vehicles, ensuring personalised attention, but still allowing room for essential purchases along the way. Full-day tours include lunch in a winery restaurant.

3 Morse St
Napier

Bike D'Vine

06 833 6697 | *www.bikedevine.com*

Bike D'Vine offers a choice of two-wheeled transport including tandems. Four different self-guided tours visit the best of vineyards around the art deco city of Napier, and Havelock North, a pleasant English-style town. Retro scooters are also available for hire either by the hour or the day. A car driver's licence is sufficient to drive the trendy yellow and pink machines.

Martinborough

Martinborough Wine Tours

06 306 8032 | *www.martinboroughwinetours.co.nz*

Small group tours with a maximum of six people visit smaller vineyards around Martinborough's relaxed village. Owners Roger and Jill Fraser have been involved with the development of Martinborough winemaking since the 1980s, and their background ensures plenty of unique behind-the-scenes experiences. Tours also focus on Martinborough's growing gourmet food scene. Duration of tours is from one hour to two days.

Tour Operators

The quality of tour operators in New Zealand is monitored by Qualmark (www.qualmark.co.nz). Each tour or visitor experience that's endorsed by Qualmark has been independently assessed as professional and trustworthy, and tour operators that have passed the assessment usually highlight an official 'Qualmark Endorsed' logo on their websites and promotional literature.

On most tours you can expect professional and knowledgeable service, often infused with a healthy dose of laconic Kiwi humour.

Where organised tours come into their own is to provide access to more inaccessible areas, share costs for more expensive tours such as sailing or kayaking, or provide professional guidance and security when exploring New Zealand's national parks and wilderness areas. Rates are usually non-negotiable, but it's always worth checking websites or asking directly if there are any opportunities for off-season discounts or early booking rates. (New Zealand's tourism industry is busiest from November to April). In major backpacker hubs such as Rotorua, Taupo and Queenstown healthy competition sometimes ensures healthy discounts. Bookings can be made online or through local tourist information offices, (look for the green and white i-SITE logo), and there's normally minimal difference in rates. Nationwide bus tours can also be booked through travel agencies. Link to them from the official tourism websites for each city or region.

Tour Operators

Name	Phone	Web	Speciality
Adventure Consultants	09 0344 3871	www.adventureconsultants.co.nz	Guided climbing, mountaineering, hiking
Alpine Guides	03 435 1834	www.alpineguides.co.nz	Guided climbing, mountaineering, hiking
Amazing New Zealand	09 478 7802	www.amazingnz.com	Package and custom guided or self-guided tours
APT	09 279 6077	www.aptours.co.nz	Nationwide bus tours
Banbury Tours	03 339 4020	www.cyclehire-tours.co.nz	Cycle touring
Bay Tours	06 845 9034	www.baytours.co.nz	Hawke's Bay region
Black Cat Cruises	03 328 9078	www.blackcat.co.nz	Ferry services, sightseeing, dolphin watching
Eco Tours	0800 367 326	www.ecotours.co.nz	Nature tours
First Light Travel	09 360 8320	www.firstlighttravel.com	Package and custom guided or self-guided tours
Fuller's	09 367 9111	www.fullers.co.nz	The islands of Auckland's Hauraki Gulf
Great Sights	0800 744 487	www.greatsights.co.nz	Nationwide bus tours
Guthreys	0800 732 528	www,guthreys.co.nz	Nationwide bus tours
Kaiteriteri Kayaks	0800 252 925	www.seakayak.co.nz	Sea kayaking
Mount Aspiring Guides	03 443 9422	www.aspiringguides.com	Guided climbing, mountaineering, hiking
Naturally Kaikoura	03 319 6767	www.naturalykaikoura.co.nz	Dolphin and whale watching
Newmans	09 623 1504	www.newmanscoach.co.nz	Nationwide bus tours
Northliner	09 623 1503	www.northliner.co.nz	Northland & the Bay of Islands
NZ Travel Pass	0800 339 966	www.travelpass.co.nz	Discount travel pass on Inter-City buses ferries and trains
Scenic Tours	0800 698 687	www.scenictours.co.nz	Nationwide bus tours
Shotover Jet	03 442 8570	www.shotoverjet.co.nz	Jetboating
Taylors	07 332 2223	www.taylortours.co.nz	Bay of Plenty region
Tranzscenic	0800 872 467	www.tranzscenic.co.nz	Tranz Pacific and Tranz Alpine Railways
Tuatara Tours	0800 377 378	www.tuataratours.co.nz	Guided walking

Tel: +971 4 409 4000

Activities

Activities

Sports & Activities

The range of sporting activities in New Zealand could lead you to believe that a love of physical exertion is a prerequisite to calling yourself a Kiwi. But the country also boasts a vast array of more artistic or cerebral pursuits. However, thanks to the magnificent landscape and equable climate, most New Zealanders indulge in some form of outdoor recreation, even if it's just a daily stroll through a leafy park or an amble along a windswept beach.

Current Prime Minister Helen Clark is perhaps a good example of the way many Kiwis mix sport and culture. Clark regularly spends her holidays mountaineering, cross-country skiing and trekking. She's often spotted at sports fixtures and in 2002, she fronted a travel documentary for the Discovery Channel, in which she participated in some of New Zealand's more extreme sports (p.340). She's also minister for arts, culture and heritage and is equally at home at the opera, ballet and theatre or at an art exhibition.

New Zealand's geographical diversity means that just about all outdoor activities are on offer. Most organised sports are termed as either winter or summer sports, but many continue in the off-season with a social league. The relatively mild weather means that many pursuits can be enjoyed all year round, although some are definitely seasonal. In summer, for example, swimmers swarm to the country's innumerable beaches, and this is also peak time for surf lifesaving, a popular club sport with a strong service ethic (p.321). Only the very hardy swim in the ocean during winter, which is when the crowds head to the snow for skiing and boarding (p.332).

Many sporting codes follow a similar administrative set-up, with a national body affiliated to the governing international body. The national organisation oversees regional or provincial bodies, which in turn oversee clubs at a local level. By visiting the website of a national or regional organisation, you can usually find the club nearest you. In most instances, we have listed contacts for the regional associations, rather than individual clubs, as this should be your first point of call to get expert, up-to-date information on sport in the area.

Activity Finder

Regional Sports Trusts

Canterbury West Coast Sports Trust	Christchurch	03 373 5060	www.sportcanterbury.org.nz
Counties Manukau Sport	Manukau City, Auckland	09 269 0066	www.cmsport.co.nz
Harbour Sport	North Shore, Auckland	09 415 4610	www.harboursport.co.nz
Sport Auckland	Auckland	09 815 4710	www.sportauckland.org.nz
Sport Waitakere	Waitakere City, Auckland	09 966 3120	www.sportwaitakere.co.nz
Sport Wellington	Wellington	04 920 4200	www.sportwellington.org.nz

Regional Sports Trusts (RSTs) are a great starting place for anyone wanting to get involved in or find out about recreational activities in the area. Local councils are also good sources of information. They hold lists of all clubs and organisations, which can usually be accessed online. Community noticeboards in the local library are another source of information, as are the free community newspapers that appear through your letterbox each week. The latter two are particularly useful for finding out about one-off events such as weekend workshops, coaching clinics and seminars.

Sugarloaf Reserve, Christchurch

Piha beach

Moorings in Wellington

Indoor rock climbing

Aerobics & Fitness Classes

There are plenty of places where you can raise your heart rate in group classes, from church halls for aerobics-style classes to swanky gyms for step sessions. Generally referred to as group fitness or group training, you'll find classes offering dance, step, circuits, boxing or a combination of these, and more. Elements of yoga and Pilates are often integrated into classes.

A popular new addition is peloton-style cycle training, which is instructor-led interval exercise that simulates a bike ride up hills and down dales. Best of all, it happens indoors and there's loud, inspiring music to keep you pedalling.

Most exercise classes take place in gyms and recreation centres (see Leisure Facilities, p.350), but check noticeboards and newspapers for community classes that may take place in any rented space, such as schools or church halls. Expect to pay between $10 and $15 for a casual class.

Art Classes

Other options **Art & Craft Supplies** p.371

Release the artist within by enrolling in a weekend sculpture workshop, an evening course in carving, or even a full-time fine arts degree. From painting to pottery, stained glass to sketching, there's an art experience for everyone. Community education classes are the most popular places to get together with like-minded people and hone your technique with experienced tutors, but there are also art colleges offering more specialised tuition.

Worcester Blvd
Christchurch
Map p.517 F1 1

The Arts Centre

03 366 0989 | www.artscentre.org.nz

Once the University of Canterbury, the atmospheric neo-Gothic buildings of The Arts Centre are an ideal venue for the promotion of community education and arts and crafts. There are permanent galleries in the complex and every weekend there's a vibrant arts market. The Arts Centre's weekend workshops have an emphasis on small classes, variety and quality teaching.

Ponsonby Rd
Auckland
Map p.486 C4 2

Artstation

09 376 3221 | www.aucklandcity.govt.nz

Auckland City's community arts facility provides art activities for all ages, at all times of the day. Open-access studios include a darkroom, cast glass facility and a print studio, which can be hired by experienced artists. The gallery exhibition showcases art from Auckland's diverse communities and changes every three weeks.

Wellesley St
Auckland
Map p.488 A3 3

Auckland University of Technology School of Art & Design

09 921 9999 | www.aut.ac.nz

This is one of the country's largest providers of art and design education, with programmes ranging from certificate and masters and doctorate level. Popular courses include fashion, printing, graphic design, spatial design and visual arts, as well as computer publishing, fabric printing and a range of other short courses.

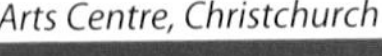
Arts Centre, Christchurch

Madras St
Christchurch
Map p.517 D1 4

CPIT School of Art and Design

03 940 8043 | www.cpit.ac.nz

The Christcurch Polytechnic School of Art and Design is the place to develop your creative and technical abilities. Programmes are offered in fields such as printmaking, graphic design, sculpture, fashion design and photography. Courses are studio-based full and part-time programmes, and include a three-year Bachelor of Design with specialisation in visual arts, and one-year diplomas. There are also short courses on offer.

3 Inverlochy Pl
Wellington
Map p.504 B2 5

Inverlochy Art School

04 939 2177 | www.inverlochy.org.nz

The non-profit Inverlochy Art School is housed in a gracious historic building dating from 1878. The school offers a range of high-quality part-time art classes for all abilities, and classes are taught by practicing artists and artisans. Courses include painting, sculpture, drawing, jewellery, printmaking and fabric arts.

61 Abel Smith St
Wellington
Map p.504 C3 6

Toi Pôneke – Wellington Arts Centre

04 385 1929 | www.wellington.govt.nz

The sprawling community Arts Centre in central Wellington covers 3,000 square metres of space over seven floors, and is a place for people to meet, learn, work and be creative. It has rooms for hire and currently about three dozen artists have studios in the building. A number of arts organisations have offices in the complex and courses are regularly offered. There are also music and dance studios and a darkroom.

Astronomy

Mackenzie District Council in the South Island is pushing for the night skies above the area to be designated a Unesco World Heritage Site. The move is designed to stop light pollution spoiling the magnificent, clear, star-sprinkled skies, but you don't have to go down south to enjoy the Milky Way and Southern Cross. A useful website is www.astronomynz.org.nz, run by the non-profit Phoenix Astronomical Society.

40 Salamanca Rd
Wellington
Map p.502 B3 7

Carter Observatory

04 472 8167 | www.carterobs.ac.nz

The Carter Observatory in Wellington Botanical Gardens is the National Observatory of New Zealand. It has a planetarium, static displays, lecture theatre, visitor gift shop and a range of telescopes, which are all available to the public. Various informative programmes are available. It's undergoing a major refurbishment and is expected to reopen late in 2007.

One Tree Hill Domain
Auckland
Map p.484 C6

Stardome

09 624 1246 | www.stardome.org.nz

The Auckland Observatory and Planetarium goes by the name of Stardome. Its blend of entertainment, education and information makes it a popular place for locals and visitors alike. Well-informed guides present numerous 'edutainment' shows, which change regularly. It is free to become a 'friend of Stardome' and you'll be informed of upcoming events, special deals and new shows.

Ahiaruhe Rd
Wellington
North Island
Map H14

Stonehenge Aotearoa

027 2466 766 | www.astronomynz.org.nz/stonehenge

This unique, open-sky observatory stands in the fields outside the small town of Carterton, about an hour's drive from Wellington. It was built by members of the Phoenix Astronomical Society and was inspired by and built on a similar scale to

Stonehenge in England. It combines modern scientific knowledge with ancient lore from many civilisations, including Maori. Tours are available, but you should book in advance, and special events are held.

Christchurch Arts Centre
Worcester Blvd
Christchurch
Map p.516 C1 10

The Townsend Observatory

03 364 2469 | townsend@phys.canterbury.ac.nz

Based at the Christchurch Arts Centre, The Townsend Observatory is owned by the University of Canterbury. It features a restored 1864 Cooke six-inch refractor telescope, which offers good views of the moon, planets, stars and star clusters and other bright objects. Public viewing is on clear Fridays, during the non-daylight saving time of the year.

Badminton

Badminton is a popular indoor sport and there are plenty of clubs that participate in various leagues and provide coaching. If you're not competitive and just like to play socially, that's okay, because most clubs offer an option for social members. Some centres allow non-members to hire courts on a casual basis and, if you belong to an affiliated club, you will receive a discount on court hire, which ranges from $10 to $20 per hour. The main season runs from March to October.

Badminton			
Auckland Badminton Association	Auckland	09 524 0872	www.auckbad.co.nz
Badminton Canterbury	Christchurch	03 389 8534	www.badminton.org.nz
Badminton New Zealand	Various Locations	04 916 2450	www.badminton.org.nz
Wellington Badminton Association	Wellington	04 386 1689	www.badminton.net.nz

Basketball

If you bump into any super-tall Americans, chances are that they're in the country to show off their skill levels in the main basketball league, the NBL. 'American imports', as they're known, pepper the 10 provincial teams. Basketball enjoys good spectator and participant support and there are leagues, ranging from junior and age-group to elite and mixed social leagues. Basketball is considered a winter sport, but most associations offer a summer league. The national men's team is called the Tall Blacks and the women's side is the Tall Ferns.

Basketball		
Basketball Auckland	09 526 0768	www.basketballauckland.co.nz
Basketball New Zealand	04 498 5950	www.basketball.org.nz
Canterbury Basketball Association	03 982 8459	www.canterburybasketball.co.nz
Wellington Basketball Association	04 389 8004	www.wellingtonbasketball.co.nz

Birdwatching

Other options **Birdwatching** p.308, **Environmental Groups** p.315

When New Zealand drifted away from super-continent Gondwana, no predatory mammals were aboard. Lulled into evolutionary complacency, many birds lost the ability to fly, which made them easy prey when man and other predators arrived. Many species were wiped out and, despite huge conservation efforts, existing native species are under constant threat, including the national bird, the flightless kiwi. However, even those with only a passing interest in our feathered friends will be enchanted by the country's unusual birds, and wowed by the enormous effort being made to protect them. On the government's Department of Conservation website (www.doc.govt.nz), you can read more about birdwatching by clicking on 'parks & recreation' and then 'activity finder'. Serious birdwatchers should contact the Ornithological Society of New Zealand (www.osnz.org.nz) and become members of the centres and reserves listed below.

Lower Styx Rd and Heyders Rd
Christchurch
Map p.508 E1

Brooklands Lagoon

Brooklands Lagoon is a large natural coastal area with a range of habitat types that attract more than 75 migratory and resident species. At the height of the season, there are around 3,000 birds at the lagoon. It is an important wintering site for godwits and swamp birds such as the endangered Australasian bittern. There are wildlife observation platforms and a bird hide.

Waiapu Rd
Wellington
Map p.498 A5

Karori Wildlife Sanctuary

04 920 9200 | www.sanctuary.org.nz

Karori Wildlife Sanctuary, just minutes from downtown Wellington, is a haven for endangered native birds and other wildlife. A predator-proof fence surrounds the 252 hectare site, allowing the birds and forest to thrive without the threat of destructive pests. Volunteer hosts greet visitors at the visitor centre and guided tours and boat cruises are available. Membership costs from $40 per year and grants many special privileges, including access to a regular seminar series.

283 East Coast Rd
Auckland
North Island Map H6

Miranda Shorebird Centre

09 232 2781 | www.miranda-shorebird.org.nz

The Miranda Shorebird Centre is an information and education site located on the Firth of Thames, one hour south-east of Auckland. Thousands of local and migratory wading birds flock to its expansive sand flats and shell banks. The centre has a lodge providing economical accommodation. The public can visit and you can get more involved by joining the Miranda Naturalists' Trust. Membership starts at $35.

Hauraki Gulf
North Island Map G5

Tiritiri Matangi Island

www.tiritirimatangi.org.nz

Located 30km north-east of central Auckland, Tiritiri Matangi Island is an important, exciting conservation project. A massive effort has seen predatory mammals eradicated, 300,000 trees planted and the introduction of many native birds. A ferry service enables visitors to enjoy a day trip, and guided walks are available. The Supporters of Tiritiri Matangi is a non-profit conservation volunteer group, with annual membership costing $20.

Bowling

There are more than 700 lawn bowling clubs in the country and almost every small town and every city suburb will boast a couple of immaculately kept greens and a clubroom that is the focus of social activities. There are serious competitions and tournaments, but bowls is considered a friendly, inexpensive sport that encourages participation by providing free coaching and equipment for beginners. It's a summer activity, but continues on a social basis in the winter. New Zealand has both men's and women's national teams that compete at the highest level.

Bowling			
Auckland Bowls	Level 3, 19 Great South Road, Auckland	09 524 4577	www.aucklandbowls.co.nz
Bowls Canterbury	28a Makora Street, Christchurch	03 351 2070	www.bowlscanterbury.co.nz
Bowls New Zealand	Kalmia Street, Auckland	09 579 5853	www.bowlsnz.co.nz.
Wellington Bowls	Jackson Street, Wellington	04 568 5664	www.bowlswellington.com

Pitching up

Camping

Other options **Outdoor Goods** p.396

New Zealand's great outdoors is never far away – even if you live in the centre of a city you can be in a wilderness area within an hour. A favourite way for New Zealanders to fully experience their country's diverse landscape is to pitch a tent under the stars or park a caravan or campervan. All kinds of camping experiences are on offer, from remote wilderness camps to roadside lay-bys and five-star holiday parks that boast a full range of amenities.

The Department of Conservation (www.doc.govt.nz) manages campsites throughout its network of parks and reserves. Services and facilities range from pit toilets and stream water to grounds with a camp warden, hot showers, lighting and a rubbish collection. You should be self-sufficient and, to preserve the pristine environment, you must leave no trace of your visit. Fees apply, except at informal sites, and some sites are heavily used at different times of the year, so it's advisable to book ahead. Fees range from $3 to $14 per person.

Hundreds of commercial campgrounds are spread throughout the country and, as well as offering powered and unpowered sites, many have cabins, on-site caravans or fully equipped motel-style units to rent. The amenities block usually consists of a kitchen (you provide the food and utensils), showers, toilets and a laundry with coin-operated machines. There may be a games room, swimming pool, playground and other extras. Popular campgrounds will be heavily booked in summer, especially over the Christmas and festive period. Plan ahead or avoid peak times, remembering that things quieten down considerably in the second and third weeks of January. Fees vary, but a powered site for two people will cost about $25.

DOC allows freedom camping in some areas and local councils let campervans pull off the road for the night in certain places. You should always check regulations. Local visitor information centres (i-SITEs) can advise you.

A large number of holiday parks and campgrounds belong to either Holiday Accommodation Parks of New Zealand (HAPNZ, 04 298 3283, www.holidayparks.co.nz) or Top 10 Holiday Parks (0800 867 836, www.top10.co.nz). Both networks have a range of locations and camping experiences, all of which offer affordable, self-catering holiday accommodation and facilities. You can book online or request a print directory of member parks, which are also described on the website.

Canoeing

Other options **Outdoor Goods** p.396

With a long sea coast, sheltered harbours and hundreds of lakes and rivers, New Zealand is the ultimate destination for anyone who loves to paddle. Most Kiwi canoeists and kayakers enjoy the sport for fun and love nothing better than hitting the water alone or with a friend or two. If you're more competitive or would like the support of a group, contact the New Zealand Recreational Canoeing Association (027 2096 101, www.rivers.org.nz). It has several member clubs and is actively involved in conservation and safety. Plenty of operators offer casual canoeing and kayaking experiences.

12 Tamaki Dr
Auckland
Map p.484 D5

Fergs Kayaks

09 529 2230 | www.fergskayaks.co.nz

Fergs Kayaks is owned and operated by Ian Ferguson, who was named Olympian of the Century by New Zealand's Olympic Association for winning one silver and four gold medals in kayaking events at the Olympic Games in the 1980s, not to mention five World Championships. From kayak hire to tuition and retail sales, Fergs is the place to get the low-down on kayaking in New Zealand. There are branches in Auckland and Wellington.

2/7 Pilgrim Place
Christchurch
Map p.516 C4 16

PaddlerZone

03 372 3353 | www.paddlerzone.co.nz

As well as selling every kind of kayak, from multisport to fishing, PaddlerZone offers advice, instruction and guiding services for all forms of kayaking. Whether you're headed to the whitewater or just cruising out for a beach party, it has quality hire equipment and safety gear available for long- or short-term hire.

Climbing

Whether it's scaling towering mountains or bouldering on strange rock formations, you'll find plenty of places to do your Spiderman impersonation in New Zealand. The country's diverse, rugged terrain means there are cliffs and crevices even in the cities. And if the weather is inclement, or you prefer a more controlled environment, there are many indoor climbing walls, including an indoor ice-climbing wall on the west coast of the South Island (see South Island Summits, below).

Climb New Zealand (www.climb.co.nz) is an independent, online resource that provides rock climbing, sportclimbing, bouldering and general information relating to the sport throughout the country. You'll find information on regulations, places to climb, specific climbs in each region, operators who provide climbing experiences, lists of indoor climbing facilities and much more.

Other useful organisations are the New Zealand Sportclimbing Federation (021 242 1995, www.nzsf.org.nz) and the New Zealand Mountain Safety Council (04 385 7162, www.mountainsafety.org.nz).

The New Zealand Alpine Club (03 377 7595, www.alpineclub.org.nz) is an umbrella organisation of clubs throughout the country. It encourages mountaineering, rock climbing and related activities, bringing together people with an interest in the sport. It is also involved in conservation and safety issues and runs an extensive hut system throughout the country.

South Island Summits

Three of the South Island's national parks – Arthur's Pass, Mount Cook (p.268) and Mount Aspiring (p.277) – feature some of the southern hemisphere's best climbing and mountaineering terrain. It's usually challenging, and often dangerous. If your experience or your confidence isn't up to it, you can use a guide. If you're keen to learn a few skills beforehand, there are two brand-new facilities available: the indoor ice-climbing wall at the Hukawai Glacier Centre Franz Josef township (03 752 0600), and the indoor climbing facilities at Base Camp Wanaka (p.279).

Cookery Classes

Fertile soil, clean air and a temperate climate means that fresh meat and produce feature highly in New Zealand cuisine. Add seafood from the pristine waters and you've got a mouthwatering array of ingredients to whip into a culinary masterpiece. Cookery courses range from community classes to weekend workshops with celebrity chefs, some of whom run their own cooking schools. Look in the local paper or news-stand food magazines such as *Dish*, *Cuisine* and *Taste*.

The Food Show (0800 727 469, www.foodshow.co.nz) is a popular annual culinary event held in Auckland, Wellington and Christchurch. Over three days, foodies can sip, sample, browse and buy from a huge number of exhibitors, as well glean tips from seminars and demonstrations run by food experts and celebrity chefs.

1st Floor
22-32 Jellicoe St
Freemans Bay
Auckland
Map p.487 F1 17

Auckland Fish Market Seafood School

09 379 1497 | www.afm.co.nz

The Auckland Fish Market brings fresh seafood, fruit and vegetable retail specialists together on the one site and boasts its own cooking school. It's a modern facility with an auditorium, cooking stations and top chefs dedicated to helping you learn how to prepare all kinds of seafood. Classes are available most nights and cost from $80. You can enrol online.

63 Victoria St
Christchurch
Map p.512 B4 18

The New Zealand School of Food & Wine

03 379 7501 | www.foodandwine.co.nz

Set in the heart of Christchurch's inner-city restaurant and cafe scene, the New Zealand School of Food and Wine is a private training establishment registered with the New Zealand Qualifications Authority (www.nzqa.govt.nz). The director is well-known chef and restaurateur Celia Hay, and the school offers full-time and part-time courses in cooking, hospitality and restaurant management. Options include evening classes, weekend workshops and cooking classes for kids and teens.

41 School Rd
Wellington
North Island
Map G13

Ruth Pretty Cooking School

04 06 364 3161 | www.ruthpretty.co.nz

The Ruth Pretty Cooking School shares recipes, cooking ideas and entertaining tips in a rural setting at Te Horo, north of Wellington. Ruth Pretty is a well-known chef and she arranges for other top cooks and food personalities to give demonstrations to complement her own classes, which run most weekends between March and November and cost $195.

Cricket

There are six major cricket associations responsible for managing and developing cricket in New Zealand. As well as selecting and preparing elite teams, the associations oversee regional cricket, with competitions and tournaments ranging from primary and secondary school competitions right through to senior grades. If you want to get involved as a player, umpire or supporter, the association has contacts and information for each club in the region and you can access this through the relevant website.

Cricket		
Auckland Cricket	www.aucklandcricket.co.nz	09 815 4855
Canterbury Cricket Association	www.canterburycricket.org.nz	03 366 3003
Cricket Wellington	www.cricketwellington.co.nz	04 384 3171

Cycling

Other options **Mountain Biking** p.323, **Sports Goods** p.402, **Cycling** p.312

Learning to ride a bike is a rite of passage for Kiwi kids and you'd be hard-pressed to find a home that doesn't have an assortment of bicycles in the shed. Auckland and Wellington have popular waterfront cycle paths, while the flat terrain in Christchurch makes biking anywhere a breeze.

There are many organised fun rides and even the most gruelling recreational cycle events usually offer shortened courses and team and individual options. Casual bike hire is readily available, often from a local cycle shop. Helmets are compulsory wherever or whatever you ride.

Competitive cycling has a strong following and the sport's profile soared following the success of vivacious Olympic and Commonwealth Games gold medallist Sarah Ulmer. BikeNZ (www.bikenz.org.nz, 04 473 8386) is the umbrella body embracing national bike and cycling organisations, including Cycling New Zealand. It's a good place to find out about any kind of cycling in New Zealand and you'll find links to local clubs.

Christchurch

Explore New Zealand by Bicycle

03 339 4020 | www.cyclehire-tours.co.nz

Christchurch-based Explore New Zealand by Bicycle offers cycling options, from guided tours over several days to casual day hire, allowing you to explore the Garden City on your own. Fully equipped touring bikes are available for short- to long-term hire. Rates start at $35 per day and all information on various local options can be found on the website.

12 Tamaki Dr
Auckland
Map p.484 D5

Fergs Kyaks

09 529 2230 | www.fergskayaks.co.nz

Fergs Kayaks has KMX Karts for hire. These low-profile, three-wheeled trikes are a fun way to explore the waterfronts of Auckland and Wellington. Costs range from $25 per hour to $150 per day. At the Auckland branch, you can hire a more traditional bike from its range of modern cruisers. Hire is $20 per hour or $120 per day.

Parnell Rd
Parnell
Auckland
Map p.489 D4 22

Pedaltours

09 585 1338 | www.pedaltours.co.nz

Pedaltours has been operating for 22 years and offers a large range of cycling experiences. Tours are guided and can last however long you want and be customised for any sized group. Pedaltours allows cyclists to travel at their own pace; there's always a support van on hand for when the going gets tough.

Dance Classes

Other options **Music Lessons** p.324

Not that long ago, a New Zealand man who got kitted up in a frilly shirt and shimmied around a dancefloor could have expected a few sniggers. But popular TV shows such as *Dancing With The Stars* have changed all that, especially since the winner of the first series was former All Blacks strongman Norm Hewitt.

Many traditional dance forms, such as ballroom, ballet, jazz and contemporary, have always been on offer. The Royal New Zealand Ballet, for example, is a well-respected company that tours nationally and internationally. A more recent influence on dance is the changing ethnicity of the population, with Latin forms becoming particularly popular. Perhaps the biggest movement is among the young, who are flocking to hip-hop and street classes in droves.

Whether you're dancing for fun or exercise, or training for a career, New Zealand dance teachers have got it covered and many teach more than one form of dance. DANZ (04 801 9885 or 09 815 1420, www.danz.org.nz) is the national organisation for dance in New Zealand.

260 Queen St
Auckland
Map p.488 A3 23

City Dance & Ballet

09 379 9944 | www.citydance.co.nz

City Dance & Ballet offers everything from ballet, ballroom and belly dancing to flamenco, pole dancing and jazz moves. All classes are open and casual, which means you can start whenever you like. Rates for a one-hour class are $15, and $135 gets you a concession card for 10 classes.

Level 3
Premier Building
2 Durham St East
Auckland
Map p.488 A3 24

Latin Rhythm Dance School

0800 472 572 | www.latinrhythm.co.nz

Auckland's largest salsa school has several locations across the city, offering salsa, Latin and hip-hop classes. The emphasis is on fun and at the school's Club Salsa Nightclub & Bar you can put your moves into action in a social situation. An eight-week salsa or ballroom course costs $100 and hip-hop classes are $5 per session. Private classes start at $40.

Various Locations

Rhythm Nation Dance

03 960 7632 | www.rhythmnationdance.co.nz

Rhythm Nation Dance offers teaching and choreography of various styles of dance in both class and workshop format. Dance forms include jazz, tap, hip-hop, ballet, break-dancing, contemporary and ethnic. All ages and skill levels are catered for. Adult courses start at $95 and private lessons are $35.

15 Witham St
Wellington
Map p.498 C7

Supreme Dance

04 971 1790 | www.supremedance.co.nz

Classes range from beginners through to advanced and are predominantly ballroom and Latin American. Private lessons cost $40 per couple for 30 minutes. An eight-week course costs $100. The school also holds regular social evenings, when you can put your studio learning into practice. Supreme Dance offers dance classes in central Wellington, Tawa and Island Bay.

Diving

If there's one word to describe diving in New Zealand waters, it's diversity. The long coastline stretches from the clear, warm waters of the subtropical far north to the mysterious depths of Fiordland in the South Island (p.290). The surrounding ocean is peppered with dozens of islands and the underwater landscape includes shipwrecks, caves, shallow reefs, steep cliffs and drop-offs, spectacular arches and tunnels. The marine life is an exuberant mix of coral, anemones, kelp forests and fish.

New Zealand Underwater (09 623 3252, www.nzunderwater.org.nz) brings together individuals and groups interested in exploring and enjoying the country's underwater world in safety through diving schools and clubs, spearfishing clubs and underwater photography groups.

Marine Reserves

The Department of Conservation (www.doc.govt.nz) administers numerous marine reserves and parks. Of these, the Poor Knights Islands Marine Reserve is the best known internationally. It's rated one of the top 10 dive sites in the world and offers fascinating shallow dives for novice divers, as well as challenging dives for explorers with more experience. It's reached via the Tutukaka Coast (p.211), three hours' drive north of Auckland.

An hour from Auckland is Goat Island Marine Reserve, which was established in 1975 as the country's first marine reserve. These days, the fish life is so abundant that you don't need to get too deep into the water to experience another world. Anyone with a mask and snorkel can easily float among the fish near the shore.

On the coast north of Wellington, the Kapiti Island Marine Reserve offers clear water and unusual underwater scenery, with the added bonus of connecting to the onshore Kapiti Island Nature Reserve, a pest-free area supporting a wealth of native bird life.

Near Christchurch, the Banks Peninsula Marine Area includes a marine mammal sanctuary, which protects the rare hector's dolphin and other threatened species.

Various Locations

Dive HQ

0800 102 102 | www.divehq.co.nz

Dive HQ is a network of 19 dive franchises, offering everything from dive gear to trips, training, careers and education. There are open water and advanced open water courses, as well as Professional Association of Diving Instructors training. Dive HQ has several outlets in and around Auckland, plus one each in Wellington and Christchurch.

142a Pakiri Rd
Auckland
North Island Map G5

Goat Island Dive

0800 348 369 | www.goatislanddive.co.nz

Goat Island Dive offers scuba diving, snorkelling and kayaking experiences in a variety of locations around Auckland, including Goat Island Marine Reserve and the Hauraki Gulf. Their experienced instructors offer several PADI training courses tailored to individual needs, whether you're a complete beginner or an experienced diver.

Dragon Boat Racing

Legend says that dragon boat racing began around 400BC, when a notable Chinese public figure drowned himself in protest at government corruption. Local fishermen rowed frantically out to save him and, when they realised they were too late, smacked their paddles repeatedly on the water to scare scavenging fish away from his body.

Today, if you attend a dragon boat festival in New Zealand, it won't just be the paddles frightening the fish. Thousands of screaming spectators and beating drums add to the controlled mayhem as teams of 20 fit men and women take to the water to compete in one of the country's most fun and friendly sports.

Regional organisations offer competitions throughout the summer, and major festivals and regattas are held in Wellington, Auckland and Christchurch during February and March. Anyone can get involved. Just contact the New Zealand Dragon Boat Association (email nzdba@paradise.net.nz) or a regional group.

Similar to dragon boat racing is waka ama or outrigger canoe racing. Thanks to the strong Maori and Pacific Island influence in the country, waka ama is gaining a huge following. Waka ama festivals and competitions are exciting, noisy affairs and often great places to experience other aspects of Maori and Pacific culture, such as food, arts and dance. Visit www.wakaama.co.nz or email admin@wakaama.co.nz for more information.

Dragon Boat Contacts

Auckland Dragon Boat Festival Trust
PO Box 100-793
North Shore Mail Centre
Phone: 09 480 4616
Email: info@aucklanddragonboats.co.nz
Web: www.aucklanddragonboats.co.nz

Wellington Dragon Boat Festival
c/o Fergs Kayaks
Phone: 04 471 0205
Email: crew@dragonboat.org.nz
Web: www.dragonboat.org.nz

Environmental Groups

Other options **Voluntary & Charity Work** p.79

New Zealand has many dedicated environmentalists, with groups ranging from high-profile international organisations, such as Greenpeace, to small grassroots affairs. For a comprehensive directory of New Zealand conservation and environmental groups, visit www.greenpages.org.nz or email theteam@greenpages.org.nz. The Department of Conservation (www.doc.govt.nz) runs an extensive series of events and has an active volunteer programme.

Various Locations

New Zealand Trust for Conservation Volunteers

09 415 9336 | www.conservationvolunteers.org.nz

If you would like to get involved in conservation in your area, or even elsewhere in the country or overseas while you're on holiday, NZTCV is the place to start. Established in

1999, it has placed hundreds of volunteers in a wide range of conservation projects around the country. NZTCV also supports and raises funds for training courses and non-profit conservation projects. You can register online.

The Royal Forest and Bird Protection Society of New Zealand

Level One
90 Ghuznee St
Wellington
Map p.504 C2 30

04 385 7374 | www.forestandbird.org.nz

Forest & Bird is the country's largest national conservation organisation. The main objective of this non-profit NGO is to preserve native plants, animals and natural features, and the society is active on many fronts, lobbying at all levels of government. It has 50 branches nationwide, where people from all walks of life and of all ages get involved in local projects. Single/family membership costs $52 per year.

TerraNature Trust

8 Railway St
Newmarket
Auckland
Map p.493 D2 31

09 523 3321 | www.terranature.org

The TerraNature Trust works to preserve and protect native flora and fauna, including the coastline and its marine life and landscape. It's affiliated with the US-based Terra Nature Fund. The Trust operates both at a hands-on grassroots level, through ecological restoration and preservation projects, and at a political level, conducting and supporting national and international campaigns on conservation issues. All work is provided by volunteers and the Trust welcomes new members and donations.

Fishing

Other options **Boat Tours** p.298

With a long sea coast and a plethora of lakes and rivers, it's no wonder that fishing is one of New Zealand's most popular pastimes. Whether it's fishing from boats, jetties, rocks, riverbanks or sandy beaches, or gathering shellfish on the shore, there's a purpose to the typical New Zealand fishing excursion. Kiwis like the idea that they can supplement their diet with fresh seafood, or kai moana as it's known in Maori, and it's a bad day when they don't come home with enough to feed family and friends.
There are strictly-enforced rules on size and bag limit, with stiff penalties for breaching regulations. Most fishing stores carry leaflets outlining rules, and you can brush up via the Ministry of Fisheries (see Saltwater Fishing). You don't need a licence to fish in the sea, but you do need one to fish for trout (see Freshwater Fishing). The best places to get advice on local fishing hot spots are fishing stores, who can also set you up with inexpensive gear.

Saltwater Fishing

The most prized table fish are snapper, tarakihi and gurnard, all of which can be caught surfcasting, as can trevally and the ubiquitous kahawai. Out in boats, the range is obviously greater, with cod, john dory and hapuka (grouper) other common catches. Kingfish are a popular sport fish, as are marlin and tuna. The east coast of the North Island provides the best sport fishing, especially in the Bay of Islands (p.208) and Bay of Plenty. The umbrella organisation for game fishing is the New Zealand Big Game Fishing Council (09 433 9648, www.nzbgfc.org.nz).

Freshwater Fishing

Rainbow and brown trout are found in rivers and lakes all over the country. The best-known spots in the North Island are the Rotorua Lakes, Lake Taupo (p.230) and the Tongariro River, and in the South Island you can try almost any lake or river. Salmon fishing is confined to the South Island, with the Waimakariri and Rakaia Rivers the best-known locations. Fish and Game NZ (www.fishandgame.org.nz)

manages the freshwater fisheries, except in the Taupo region, where they are managed by the Department of Conservation.

Getting Your Licence

Your fishing licence can be purchased from fishing stores or online. It explains all regulations relating to freshwater fishing, including open and closed sections of water, season dates (which vary from region to region) and bag and size limits. Licence options range from 24 hour (adults $18.50, juniors [12 to 17 years] $4.00, children free) to full season (families $120, adults $92, juniors $18.50, children free). You need a separate licence for the Taupo area, available from the Department of Conservation (www.doc.govt.nz).

Sky High
For a different and humbling experience of New Zealand's landscapes, consider a scenic flight (p.299).

Flying

Would you like to fly over an active volcano, an island-studded ocean, a snowy mountain range or a pristine forest wilderness? In compact New Zealand, the chances are you can do all of the above during one morning in the air, as well as take a scenic detour over a city. Flying is a great way to get a different perspective on the country's magnificent landscape and there are dozens of companies offering bird's-eye views of various areas.

Anyone feeling adventurous enough to take the controls of a flying machine will find plenty of places offering lessons. Many New Zealanders can fly small planes, generally having learned at their local Aero Club. These venues offer very reasonable rates, thanks to all assets being owned by members. Aero Clubs provide flight training, from introductory flights through to instructor's ratings. It usually costs less than $100 to join a club and the hourly rate for a trainer aircraft varies from about $100 to $150. Most clubs offer an inexpensive introductory lesson that doubles as a scenic flight, giving you the chance to try and fly before you buy. To find the Aero Club nearest you, contact the umbrella organisation, the Royal New Zealand Aero Club Inc. Freephone 0800 422635; www.flyingnz.co.nz

Air Shows

One major aviation event is Wings Over Wairarapa (www.wings.org.nz, phone 027 477 4717, email info@wings.org.nz), which is held biennially at Masterton, about a 90 minute drive from Wellington. The next one is in January 2009.

Warbirds Over Wanaka (p.61) is held every Easter amid the stunning mountains and lakes of the South Island. The event started in 1988, and is believed to be the biggest event of its kind in the southern hemisphere.

Golf

The country's governing body for golf is New Zealand Golf (www.nzgolf.org.nz, email nzgolf@nzgolf.org.nz, 04 471 0990). Golf is the highest participation sport in New Zealand – it's the number one sport for men and the number two sport for women, with almost half a million adults hooked. Seven million rounds are played annually on 385 courses nationwide, the highest number of courses per capita in the world. Courses range from remote rural clubs, where sheep grazing the fairways are kept off the greens by electric fences, to top-notch championship courses such as Formosa and Gulf Harbour. A useful website is www.golfguide.co.nz.

New Zealand has produced some highly successful golfers, most recently Michael Campbell, who won both the US Open and the HSBC World Match Play Championship in 2005.

Not only is golf in New Zealand incredibly popular and accessible, it's also affordable. Joining a club is not expensive by international standards, although fees vary widely

Golf			
Akarana Golf Club	Auckland	09 620 5461	www.akaranagolf.co.nz
Hagley Golf Club	Christchurch	03 379 8279	www.hagley.nzgolf.net
Karori Golf Club	Wellington	04 476 7337	www.karorigolf.co.nz
Miramar Golf Club	Wellington	04 801 7649	www.miramargolfclub.co.nz
Remuera Golf Club	Auckland	09 524 4288	www.remueragolfclub.com
Waitikiri Golf Club	Christchurch	03 383 1400	www.waitikirigolf.co.nz

between courses and locations. Expect to pay between $400 and $1,800 for full membership. Clubs offer a variety of options and all clubs are listed on the New Zealand Golf website. You don't have to be a member of any club to play a round, although your green fees will be more if you are not a member of an affiliated club. Even then, the average national cost of a round for non-members is $24, while for affiliated members it is $18. Expect to pay more in the cities.

Walking Books
Tramping information is best obtained from the DOC centre closest to the area you intend to walk. That said, general planning can be done in consultation with the DOC website (www.doc.govt.nz), and the New Zealand Tramper website (www.tramper.co.nz), or by using any one of several excellent tramping guidebooks. The best of these is The Bird's Eye Guide to Tramping in New Zealand, *published by Craig Potton Press.*

Hiking (Tramping)

Other options **Outdoor Goods** p.396

In New Zealand, hiking, rambling and bushwalking are called tramping. After you've spent a few hours slogging it out over some hilly terrain, the name will seem entirely appropriate. From well-maintained short trails along the coast and one-day mountain challenges to gruelling multi-day hikes through remote backcountry, you'll find an option to suit you.

Many tramping tracks are in national or regional parks and reserves, although there are some well-known private walks such as the Tora Coastal Walk near Wellington (06 307 8862, www.toracoastalwalk.co.nz) and the Kaikoura Coast Track north of Christchurch (03 319 2715, www.kaikouratrack.co.nz).

The Department of Conservation (www.doc.govt.nz) manages hundreds of tracks and walks throughout the country, including nine Great Walks, which are considered the premier walking tracks. These traverse some of the country's best scenery, and the huts and tracks are of a higher standard than others you might come across. DOC huts are basic but adequate and all have different facilities, so check what's available before you set out. Fees are payable.

Safety should be foremost in your mind when you are preparing for a tramp, even if you are only going for a relatively short time or distance. It's easy to become disorientated in New Zealand's thick bush and climatic conditions can change rapidly. Always tell someone where you are going and when you expect to be back and you should sign in and out of the intentions book if one is provided.

There's an excellent network of tramping, alpine and mountain clubs throughout the country. Membership is inexpensive and all clubs provide a chance to join tramping trips and social events, while some also offer instruction courses, equipment hire and their own huts and lodges. More than 100 clubs are affiliated to the national organisation, the Federated Mountain Clubs of New Zealand (www.fmc.org.nz, email secretary@fmc.org.nz).

Classic tramping

Alpine Sports Club

09 630 5955 | www.alpinesport.org.nz

This outdoor recreation club caters for all ages, with families particularly welcome. The club owns two ski lodges on Mount Ruapehu and a bush lodge in the Waitakere Ranges near Auckland. Activities range from skiing, tramping and mountaineering to camping, kayaking and bushcraft instruction. To join, you must be proposed and seconded by a member and it's recommended that you go to a club night or on a day trip to meet members who will vouch for you. Ordinary membership is $120 per year, families $250.

Christchurch

The Christchurch Tramping Club

03 337 4914 | *www.ctc.org.nz*

This club has members of all ages and runs tramping trips of various levels of difficulty every weekend. It also owns a comfortable hut in Arthur's Pass village in the Southern Alps, and organises instruction courses, with equipment for hire. Before you become a member, you must tramp with a club group for at least three days on at least two different club trips. To sign up for a trip, go along to the weekly club night and add your name to the trip list or phone the trip leader. Ordinary membership is $35 per year.

Wellington

Wellington Tramping & Mountaineering Club

www.wtmc.org.nz

Formed in 1947, this friendly club welcomes everyone from beginners to experienced outdoor enthusiasts. The club owns lodges at Mount Ruapehu and in the Rimataka Ranges near the capital, as well as its own bus. There are activities most weekends and you don't have to be a member to join in. Non-members are also welcome at club nights. If you decide to join, it will cost $59 per year.

Hockey

Hockey is well established in New Zealand and flourishes at club level throughout the country. This energetic, skilful game is played by men and women, with both national sides going by the name Black Sticks. Both teams compete internationally and are often ranked in the top six in the world. A national governing body (www.hockeynz.co.nz, email support@hockeynz.co.nz) aims to promote and develop hockey. Regional associations administer the sport, organising club competitions across all levels. New Zealand's domestic competition is the National Hockey League (NHL), which is played in late winter and early spring.

Hockey		
Auckland Hockey Association	09 576 0683	www.akhockey.org.nz
Canterbury Hockey Association	03 389 9126	www.canterburyhockey.org.nz
Harbour Hockey Association	09 415 7396	www.harbourhockey.org.nz
Wellington Hockey Association	04 389 3337	www.wellingtonhockey.org.nz

Kids' Activities

When people say that New Zealand is a great place to raise kids, they're not just referring to the fresh air and easy access to the outdoors. There is no shortage of organised activities catered specifically for the country's younger residents. Even some events for grown-ups will have attractions such as bouncy castles to keep the kids entertained. Museums and libraries have areas for children and run fun and inexpensive programmes during school holidays, as do galleries, councils and organisations such as the YMCA. Your local council, newspapers and noticeboards are good places to find out about these. Recreation and aquatic centres (see Leisure Facilities, p.350) also run holiday programmes and are inexpensive places to while away a few hours at other times. Many feature a range of depths, wave pools, slides and swings.

Some sporting associations will offer modified versions of sports that are suitable for primary school-age kids upwards, with the emphasis for younger participants being on participation, skill development and fun, rather than winning.

There are plenty of cultural activities on offer, such as dancing, art classes and music lessons. Your council should hold a list of clubs and organisations in the area. Alternatively, ask at the school for ideas and contacts. The *Yellow Pages* is another useful resource, as is the online magazine *Kids Friendly NZ* (www.kidsfriendlynz.com). Of course, you don't need an organised activity or even to spend any money to keep the kids amused. It costs nothing to wander down to the swings and slides at the local park or to make sandcastles on the beach. The Department of Conservation (www.doc.govt.nz) has a list of suggested activities for kids on its website.

Language Schools

Other options **Learning English and Maori** p.186

The number of schools offering English-language courses has risen dramatically in the past decade. More than 1,200 educational institutions have signed up to the government's Code of Practice for the Pastoral Care of International Students, which provides a framework for minimum standards, good practice procedures and a complaints process. Information on the code is available at www.minedu.govt.nz. The New Zealand Qualifications Authority (www.nzqa.govt.nz) approves courses, and sets and reviews standards relating to qualifications and examinations.
Some language schools are standalone private institutions, but the government education system has also embraced international students, with numerous schools actively promoting their English-language programmes overseas. The quality of teaching is generally good and many courses include a recreational element such as skiing or sightseeing. An informative website is www.newzealandeducated.com.
Various other languages are taught at all levels in community classes. Keep an eye on the local paper near the start of each term. Universities and other tertiary institutions also offer specialist language courses and/or degrees.

Various Locations

English New Zealand

www.englishnewzealand.co.nz

English New Zealand has more than 30 member schools throughout the country. All members are approved by the NZQA and are signatories to the Code of Practice for the Pastoral Care of International Students. Also, member schools must have been teaching English as a second language for three years and hold all relevant accreditation and approvals. Many course options are available, so fees vary, but expect to pay about $350 per week for a full-time general English course.

Auckland & Christchurch

Euroasia

0800 387 627 | *www.euroasia.co.nz*

Euroasia offers courses in European and Asian languages, including French, German, Italian, Spanish, Mandarin, Japanese and Korean. Teachers are native speakers and the tailor-made courses feature small, interactive classes. Costs vary, but, as an example, a 10 week evening course in introductory French, consisting of one 90 minute lesson per week, will cost $329.

Various Locations

LCF Clubs

0800 386 000 | *www.funlanguages.co.nz*

Fun Language Clubs teach French, Spanish, German and Chinese to children between the ages of three and 12. The lessons provide informal, fun language experiences in small groups, with activities including art and craft, music, drama and games supported by specialised material. Clubs usually meet once a week and are located in various cities, including Auckland, Wellington and Christchurch.

Libraries

Other options **Books** p.373, **Second-Hand Items** p.400

Every city in New Zealand is well-endowed with libraries, most of which are administered and funded by local government. Libraries are often the focal point for the surrounding community and many people come to read and relax, not just to borrow. The range of books and resources is excellent and, even if you belong to a smaller library, you can borrow from other libraries in the network. Their online catalogues can usually be accessed from home as well as from the library. With the exception of mobile libraries and small branches, libraries have good reference sections and reading rooms, particularly the main ones in each area.

Libraries				
Auckland City Libraries	Auckland	09 377 0209	www.aucklandlibrary.co.nz	A network of 16 community libraries, including the central city library.
Christchurch City Libraries	Christchurch	03 941 7923	www.library.christchurch.org.nz	18 community libraries, plus the central library and a mobile library.
Manukau City Libraries	Auckland	09 262 1819	www.manukau-libraries.govt.nz	14 community libraries, five rural libraries and a mobile library.
North Shore City Libraries	Auckland	09 486 8461	www.shorelibraries.govt.nz	Seven community libraries and a mobile library.
Waitakere City Libraries	Auckland	09 839 0400	www.waitakerelibs.govt.nz	Eight libraries and learning centres, plus a mobile library.
Wellington City Libraries	Wellington	04 801 4040	www.wcl.govt.nz	11 branches, plus the central library.

As well as offering traditional services, modern libraries have a huge range of information available on computers, microfiche, CDs and DVDs and in magazines and newspapers. They also arrange events such as workshops with authors, storytelling, exhibitions, holiday programmes and even concerts. It is usually free for residents to join. Just take along some ID to prove that you live in the area. Most are open six or seven days a week and some offer extended evening hours. The National Library of New Zealand and the Alexander Turnbull Library in Wellington (both at www.natlib.govt.nz) are repositories for important records and reference materials, as is Archives New Zealand (www.archives.govt.nz), also in Wellington. You'll need to make an appointment to visit the latter. The website www.nzlibraries.com has links to all public libraries.

Lifesaving (Surf)

Participants in this exciting, challenging sport may look like they're having a fun day out in the sun, but surf lifesaving has a far more serious side. Every summer, there are deaths by drowning at the country's beaches. If it wasn't for the nation's surf lifesavers, the toll would be far greater. The strong community focus of the sport not only involves rescuing people, but also covers preventative actions, education, national and international competitions and, as a bonus, a strong social scene.

Anyone from the age of seven can join a club, with the junior surf scheme aimed at teaching children skills in a fun environment. To join a club, you can contact your district association, although the easiest method is to head to your local beach and talk to the lifeguards. Anyone over 14 can become a lifeguard, which involves passing an exam and attaining a Surf Lifeguard Award. You'll be taught first aid, resuscitation and practical rescue skills and you must complete a 400 metre swim within a set time limit. Exams are run regularly over summer and, once you've passed, you can join beach patrols and get involved in other aspects of lifesaving, such as driving the inflatable rescue boat.

Surf lifesaving is popular and most surf beaches are patrolled by volunteers from local clubs, usually over the summer between Labour Weekend in October and Easter. There are 71 clubs nationwide and they are affiliated to nine districts, which in turn are governed by the national body, Surf Life Saving New Zealand (04 384 8325, www.slsnz.org.nz). Contacts for all districts and clubs can be found online.

Martial Arts

Many people practise martial arts as an exercise form that combines balance, inner and outer strength and self-defence skills. All well-known forms, such as aikido, judo, ju-jitsu, kung fu and karate, are represented and other popular martial arts are kickboxing, tae kwon do, kendo, and wushu. Some martial arts academies and clubs teach a variety of styles, and classes range from children's and beginner's sessions to self-defence lessons and training for top-level competitions. Useful websites are www.judonz.org, www.karatenz.co.nz, www.itfnz.co.nz and www.combinedmartialarts.co.nz.

Lagoon Stadium
Lagoon Drive
Panmure
Auckland
Map p.484 D6

Fighting Fit Academy

021 448 499 | www.fightingfit.co.nz

Fighting Fit Academy was formed 10 years ago by Mark Stewart, a former world champion in full contact karate. The Academy focuses on the ashihara karate style, but also offers a comprehensive range of fitness and self-development programmes for all age groups. Exercise-style classes include phantom kickboxing, cardio kickboxing, body sculpting and pump.

Level One
25 Home St
Mount Victoria
Wellington
Map p.491 D2 38

Mt Victoria Dojo & Kyokushin Karate

04 384 6345 | www.mvd.co.nz

Mt Victoria Dojo is a purpose-built facility featuring a traditional tatami mat area. The style taught is kyokushin karate and the classes are structured so that people of all ages and fitness levels can join in. Training at the highest level is also available. If you register online, you get two weeks' free training.

Various Locations
Christchurch

Proactive Martial Arts

0800 735 333 | www.selfdefence.co.nz

Proactive Martial Arts has five schools throughout Christchurch and covers a range of martial arts. Regular classes are available and the school also runs specialist workshops and seminars with teachers from around the world. Its kidz kickstart karate programme is designed to teach children martial arts skills in a fun environment. If you register online, you get two free classes.

Mother & Toddler Activities

Drama, dance, art, swimming, gymnastics – you name it, you and your toddler can do it. There's a wealth of activities and experiences designed to entertain and stimulate the very young, while giving parents and carers the chance to interact with others. Almost all council recreation and/or aquatic centres run programmes for tiny tots, as do libraries and YMCAs, which offer Y-Dance and Y-Gymnastics for pre-school-age kids.

1 Lincoln Av
Wellington
Map p.498 C2

Bigair Gymnastics

04 232 3508 | www.bigairgym.co.nz

Bigair Gymnastics is a purpose-built gymnastics facility with classes run by experienced, qualified coaches. Special programmes designed for pre-school children are the 30 minute 'crashmat kids' classes for toddlers aged 18 to 30 months ($6 per session) and 'pocket rockets' for those between 30 months and five years of age (from $90 per term).

Various Locations
Auckland

Drama Queens

09 527 8145 | www.dramaqueens.co.nz

Under-fives get to unleash their imagination during fun programmes aimed at stimulating physical, mental and social development. As well as drama sessions, there are one-hour classes in music and movement, and also storytelling, in which kids get involved in role play. It costs $5 per session.

Various Locations

Jumping Beans

www.jumpingbeans.net

Branches around the country offer fun and physical programmes for newborns and children up to the age of eight. Using specially designed, colourful gym equipment, qualified instructors take children and an accompanying caregiver through a structured class that incorporates movement to music, ball skills, dancing and singing.

Various Locations

Mainly Music

09 629 6025 | www.mainlymusic.org.nz

There are dozens of Mainly Music groups nationwide, each of which offers music, rhythm, rhyme, listening, movement and other music-related activities. Interaction and bonding between the parents and their children is an important part of the programme, so parents and caregivers must participate fully. The 30 minute sessions end with refreshments and a chat.

Motorsports

If you fancy more of a challenge than racing the kids in the dodgems, consider getting involved in motorsports as a volunteer. Clubs are always looking for people to help organise and run events and it's a good way to start the process of becoming a driver. ClubSport events are a good starting point for new drivers. These are competitions usually held on a road, circuit or paddock and include 'basic events', during which competitors, including newcomers, can compete without specialised vehicles and expensive equipment. Events include motorkhana, autocross and sprints. Other events worth joining are competitor coaching and trials.

Member Clubs & Affiliate Member Clubs

In most instances, a competition licence is not required for the above events, but if you want to compete in ClubSport advanced events, you'll need to be a member of either a member club or an associate member club. You also have to be a member to participate in basic sprint events. Both member clubs and associate member clubs are affiliated with and governed by MotorSport New Zealand (www.motorsport.org.nz, MotorSport House, 69 Hutt Road, Wellington 6015, 04 801 9559), but associate clubs don't have the same rights and privileges as full members. Rallying and track-racing are also popular participant events and you can get involved from entry level to championship events. MotorSport New Zealand regulates motorsport, and descriptions and requirements for each racing type are online, as well contacts for clubs throughout the country.

Mountain Biking

Other options **Cycling** p.312

If you look at the terrain of New Zealand, you could easily be convinced that some pedal-pushing super-being had designed it as one huge mountain biker's paradise. It's hilly and rugged – and that's just in the urban areas. Kiwis love their bikes. Their penchant for the fast and furious is reflected in the number of mountain bike tracks and parks around the country. Many are publicly owned (get the information on local parks and tracks from the council or neighbourhood bike shop) and you can ride through a few private parks, too, but national parks are almost all off limits. Sometimes you'll be sharing the track with other recreational users, so follow good safety procedures and show courtesy.

For those who like the thrill of hurtling downhill in the dark, night-riding is becoming increasingly popular and, in winter, the snow-clad mountain slopes are the place to test your mettle. There are many mountain biking events and series throughout the country that nearly always have options for teams and individuals and offer short courses and endurance races. While it's an individual sport, a feature of mountain-biking is the camaraderie between participants, especially in recreational events.

BikeNZ (www.bikenz.org.nz) is the umbrella body that incorporates Mountain Bike New Zealand. Check out the top 10 rides online. Bike NZ also has contact details for mountain-bike clubs around the country.

South Karori Rd
Wellington
Map p.498 A6

Makara Peak Mountain Bike Park

04 499 6376 | www.makarapeak.org.nz

Wellington's most popular riding area is owned by the council, which manages it with the Makara Peak Supporters Group. It's free, but there's a donation box, and volunteers are always needed to maintain and establish tracks. There are currently 8km of four-wheel drive track and 24km of custom-built single track, designed for a range of abilities from beginner to expert.

Port Hills
Christchurch
Map p.508 F7

Port Hills Tracks

03 941 8999 | www.ccc.govt.nz

Christchurch City Council manages this vast network of tracks that connects the city suburbs to the rugged Port Hills and beyond. There are more than 40km of tracks and most of them offer superb views. You can download a PDF map and description, or pick one up from the council or i-SITE.

Restall Rd
Woodhill
Auckland
North Island Map F6

Woodhill Forest Mountain Bike Park

027 278 0949 | www.bikeparks.co.nz

Auckland's most popular purpose-built mountain bike park is 37km from the CBD. There are around 100km of riding over 50 trails to suit all styles and abilities. Night-riding is on Wednesdays and it costs $25 to hire a light. Fees range from free for under 11s to $89 for an annual pass. A day pass is $5 and bike hire starts at $15.

Mountain Biking			
Auckland Mountain Bike Club	Auckland	021 228 8124	www.aucklandmtb.co.nz
Canterbury Mountain Bike Club	Christchurch	03 981 9069	www.canterburymtbclub.org
Wellington Mountain Bike Club	Wellington	na	wgtn.mtbclub.org.nz

Music Lessons

Other options **Dance Classes** p.313, **Music, DVDs & Videos** p.394

From opera to oboe, pop to piano and violin to vocal training, you'll be able to find a teacher to help you make music. You can learn anywhere, from your own home to a university, and your choices will probably depend on whether you want to learn the skill for fun or to progress through the grades and examinations.

The Institute of Registered Music Teachers of New Zealand (IRMTNZ) promotes all aspects of music teaching, and has a database of registered teachers online. (04 479

2722, www.irmt.org.nz). However, just because a teacher isn't registered, it doesn't mean that they won't be able help you along the musical pathway. Ask friends, workmates and acquaintances for recommendations.

140 Barbadoes St
Christchurch
Map p.517 E3 47

Christchurch School of Music

03 366 1711 | *www.csm.org.nz*

Christchurch School of Music was established in 1955, and today has around 90 teaching staff offering a range of tuition to students of all ages. The school focuses on theory and practice and all students are expected to take part in group performances, whether it's an orchestra, band, choir, or ensemble.

Glenfield Leisure Centre
Bentley Avenue
Glenfield
Auckland
Map p.484 C3

Music Education Centre

09 444 5654 | *www.musiceducation.co.nz*

Established in 1981, the Music Education Centre specialises in individual tuition across a range of instruments, including flute, guitar, trumpet and drums. There are two Auckland branches and the centre also runs Music in Schools programmes and sessions for children between 3 and 7 years of age.

Various Locations

New Zealand Modern School of Music

09 570 5843 | *www.modernschoolofmusic.org.nz*

The New Zealand Modern School of Music was established in 1952, and now has 23 branches around the country. Lessons are available to pupils of all ages, including adults. The school's one-to-one lessons are intended to be as fun as possible. Piano, guitar and keyboard are the main instruments taught, but some groups offer electric organ, recorder, brass instruments and vocal training.

5D, K Road Depot
33 Kaiwharawhara Rd
Wellington
Map p.498 C4

World Music Academy

04 472 1688 | *www.worldmusic.co.nz*

World Music Academy offers individual and group music lessons to students of different ages and nationalities in a friendly and creative environment. Qualified instructors specialise in piano, guitar, drums, voice and music theory and, after an initial assessment, each student has a music plan tailor-made for them.

Netball

Every Saturday morning in winter, tens of thousands of girls and women head off to the netball courts to take part in this incredibly popular sport. Kids start playing at primary school and there are many grades of competition, from secondary school to premier leagues. A lot of netball is played outside during the daytime, but, increasingly, games are held indoors, sometimes at night. Netball is a winter sport, but twilight leagues are common over the summer months.

Although it's a high-profile sport (important domestic and international games are televised live), netball clubs don't often have a base with their own clubrooms. Practices may take place on local school courts, gymnasiums or at large netball centres, which are shared by many clubs. Each metropolitan area will have one or more such centre, which administers competitions overseen by the regional association. As a rule, pupils play for their school teams rather than clubs, and adults

Netball			
Christchurch Netball Centre	Christchurch	03 379 4489	www.netballchristchurch.org.nz
Netball Auckland-Waitakere	Auckland	na	www.netballaucklandwaitakere.co.nz
Netball Counties-Manukau	Auckland	09 269 0197	www.netballcm.org.nz
Netball Wellington Centre	Wellington	04 386 0940	www.netballwellington.co.nz

new to the sport or area can join a club and get placed in a suitable team. The best way to start is to contact the regional association to find your closest netball centre and then enquire about the clubs that play there. Your Regional Sports Trust can also help. At the start of the season, grading tournaments are usually held and, after the results are analysed, teams are placed in appropriate leagues.

Orchestras & Bands

Other options **Music Lessons** p.324

The best place for young musicians to advance their skills is at school. Most secondary schools offer tuition in a range of genres, from chamber and orchestral music to jazz and rock. Parents looking to join a musical group will also find school music teachers a good source of information on local options.

Professional or semi-professional orchestras expect a high level of skill and commitment, but more low-key groups encourage amateur participation in a relaxed environment. This is especially true in folk, country, blues and jazz bands and many clubs around the country hold regular club nights either at the clubrooms or at a local bar, where club members and guest artists perform. Ask your local council for a list of clubs and organisations in the area.

Newmarket
Auckland

Auckland Youth Symphony Orchestra

09 309 0280 | www.aucklandyouthorchestra.co.nz

The Auckland Youth Symphony Orchestra is an amateur organisation that for almost 60 years has bridged the gap between secondary school orchestras and adult professional groups. The orchestra trains young adults between 18 and 24 to the highest level and performs and tours nationally and internationally. String, woodwind, brass and percussion players of Grade 8 standard and above may audition.

140 Barbadoes St
Christchurch
Map p.517 E3 52

Christchurch School of Music

03 366 1711 | www.csm.org.nz

As well as offering music tuition, Christchurch School of Music has a wide range of orchestras, bands, choirs, and ensembles, ranging from jazz to symphonic, and orchestra to wind instruments. Students are expected to present concerts and recitals of instrumental and choral music, either alone or with a group. Most students are school age, but the group is open to all.

Various Locations

New Zealand Country Music Association

07 447 2909 | www.nzcountrymusic.org.nz

The New Zealand Country Music Association promotes and supports excellence in country music performance. The organisation incorporates many clubs throughout the country and runs a series of performance awards throughout the year. Friends and family are seen as the core of clubs, which offer fun and friendly environments.

Titirangi
Map p.484 B6

Titirangi Folk Music Club

09 817 7164 | www.titirangilivemusic.co.nz

The Titirangi Folk Music Club has been providing a performance venue for local musicians and singers for more than 40 years, and is a great place to meet new people and hone your musical skills. The range of music covers many genres – as long as it is acoustic. New performers are always welcome and once a month the Friday club night is open to everyone. You can also perform on Saturday nights, and you don't have to be a member or a maestro. Workshops and concerts are also held. The membership fee is $10 per year or $15 for a family.

Wellington

Wellington Scottish Pipes & Drums

04 233 1446 | www.wspd.wellington.net.nz

Wellington Scottish Pipes & Drums formed as an army band in 1932. Today, it plays at various parades and events around the city. Band members range in age and, since it is a teaching band, WSPD caters for players of various levels of ability. New players are welcome, whether experienced or not, and tuition is available. Practices are normally on Wednesday nights from 19:00 until 21:00.

Photography

Whether you're a happy snapper or a professional, photographers have a wealth of impressive subject matter in New Zealand. There are many courses available to those who want to improve their skills and most incorporate tuition in digital post-processing programmes.

Community education courses in basic and advanced photography and associated computer skills are often available as night classes. These may be offered at the local tertiary institution or secondary school. Look in your community newspaper at the beginning of each term to see what's on offer. If you want to take a more in-depth course, there are plenty available. The free monthly magazine, The *Photographer's Mail*, has interesting articles as well as advertisements for courses and equipment. Pick up a copy at your camera shop.

One of the best ways to advance your skills in a supportive, social environment is to join the local camera club or photographic society. These usually meet a couple of times a month and involve field trips, competitions, workshops, peer advice and assessment. They come under the umbrella of the Photographic Society of New Zealand (see below).

The New Zealand Institute of Professional Photography (03 982 2125, www.nzipp.org.nz) represents the professional photographic industry in New Zealand.

Ponsonby Rd
Ponsonby
Auckland
Map p.486 C4 56

Artstation

09 376 3221 | www.aucklandcity.govt.nz

Auckland's community arts facility offers regular evening courses in photography, which are generally held once a week and last for up to three hours. Courses include an introduction to photography using a digital camera, which teaches conventional camera skills, as well as techniques specific to digital photography. There are beginners and advanced camera composition courses, as well as a course covering black and white photography and darkroom skills. Maximum enrolment for each course is seven people. Enrol as soon as possible for an early bird special. You can find more information about Artstation on the Auckland City Council's website.

70 Moorhouse Av
Christchurch
Map p.515 E4 57

Photo Access

03 366 4134 | www.photo.co.nz/photoaccess

Photo Access is a private photographic training facility that offers tertiary tuition to Level 4 on the New Zealand Qualifications Authority (NZQA) framework. Established in 1989, it has been providing a professional course since 1993. The three full-time courses are professional photography, advanced professional photography and digital photography. Part-time evening courses range from travel photography to training in getting the most from your camera. Facilities can be hired by non-students.

22 Raumati Rd
Wellington
North Island
Map G14

The Photo School

04 902 7407 | www.photoschool.co.nz

The Photo School mainly operates from a purpose-built facility at Raumati Beach just outside Wellington, but, because it works in association with Whitireia Community

Polytechnic, some components are delivered on campus. Students can study for certificates in practical or advanced photography, both of which are full-time, 20 week courses. The hands-on courses provide students with a range of photographic, creative and business skills aimed at helping them towards a career in photography. The school also provides seminars to secondary students.

Various Locations

The Photographic Society of New Zealand

www.photography.org.nz

The Photographic Society of New Zealand has been the umbrella organisation for photography in the country for 55 years. It currently boasts 61 camera clubs and photographic societies, as well as individual members, ranging from novices to professionals. There is a variety of events, including conventions, competitions, exhibitions, field trips and workshops for all members to enjoy. It administers a system of photographic distinctions and is affiliated to the Federation Internationale de l'art Photographique. Full adult membership costs $64 per year and you can join online. The website provides links to all clubs.

Pottery

According to national organisation NZ Potters, the proportion of potters and ceramic artists per population is greater in New Zealand than in any other country. Once you've driven around the country, you'll find that easy to believe. It seems that every little town has an art and crafts shop. A high proportion of the wares on sale will be pottery or ceramics produced by local artists, whether they're rustic or functional pieces or fine objets d'art.

If you want to learn the art or hone your existing skills, NZ Potters (www.nzpotters.com) is a good place to start. It's the country's only national organisation for artists and craftspeople who work with clay and it has many affiliated clubs and members around the country. Anyone with an interest in pottery is welcome to join; full annual membership costs $65. The website will also help you to find a club near you. As well as providing a friendly and supportive community, clubs offer use of equipment, training, workshops and workdays, trips, exhibitions and other events.

Other pottery classes are delivered via community education and the best ways to find out about these are either in the local paper around the beginning of term or by asking at the local council, library or community education provider. For those who want to fully extend their sculpting horizons, the Otago Polytechnic School of Art (0800 762 786, www.otagopolytechnic.ac.nz) offers a full-time, two-year diploma in ceramic arts, New Zealand's only specialised programme in ceramic arts at tertiary level.

Rafting in Queenstown

Rafting

Rafting in New Zealand can mean a lot of things. It could involve a family group meandering down a gentle stream or some tough, extreme sports fanatics tackling rapids and waterfalls far off the grading scale. It could be an easy morning excursion with a few exciting mid-grade rapids or a gruelling multi-day challenge on some of the country's wildest and most remote rivers.

In the North Island, the best-known rafting rivers are in the centre and the eastern Bay of Plenty, while the South Island offers dozens of opportunities in the rivers that run from the Southern Alps. River levels change with the weather. From gentle Grade 1 rapids to a Grade 5 challenge, the country has it covered. Wherever you go, you're assured of high safety standards, experienced crew, magnificent scenery and a lot of fun.

Buller Gorge
South Island Map K4

Buller Adventure Tours

03 789 7286 | *www.adventuretours.co.nz*

Buller Adventure Tours has been providing adventures on the west coast of the South Island for 20 years. As well as rafting on the Buller River, it offers jetboating, horse treks, and quad-bike adventures. The three-hour rafting trip takes place on the Earthquake Slip rapids, an entertaining mixture of Grade 3 and 4 rapids. Optional extras include a nine-metre cliff jump, a Grade 2 swim rapid or a rapid run on an inflatable kayak. The trip ends with a barbecue. It costs $110 adult.

Peel Forest
South Island Map J8

Rangitata Rafts

0800 251 251 | *www.rafts.co.nz*

Rangitata Rafts offers a one-day trip on the Rangitata River (p.267), two hours' drive from Christchurch. It includes three hours of rafting, starting with flat water and leading up to Grade 5 rapids in the Rangitata Gorge, with an option to walk around these if preferred. There are opportunities to swim in the clear pools en route and the day ends with hot showers and a barbecue. Lunch and transport to and from Christchurch are included. It costs $185 per person, $175 self-drive. There is also accommodation at the river base.

RD2
Taihape
North Island Map J11

River Valley

06 388 1444 | *www.rivervalley.co.nz*

River Valley is an adventure lodge beside the beautiful Rangitikei River in the central North Island. It provides a variety of rafting experiences. In the gorge above the lodge, there are 10 major Grade 4 and 5 rapids in the 12km run, while below the lodge, calm water and gentle Grade 2 rapids are perfect for a scenic trip. There's accommodation and a cafe and bar, plus a spa facility with sauna and massage. Other activity options are horse trekking, fishing, walking and inflatable kayaking. Both whitewater rafting and scenic/eco-rafting cost $139 per person.

2 White St
Rotorua
North Island Map J8

Wet 'n' Wild

0800 462 7238 | *www.wetnwildrafting.co.nz*

Rotorua-based Wet 'n' Wild has been rafting for 27 years. It offers options on five different rivers, graded from 2 to 5, with trip lengths ranging from 45 minutes to four days. It will also customise group trips. A popular trip is the 45 minute run down the raging Kaituna River, which includes 14 drops, one of which is a seven-metre waterfall ($85). The Lower Rangitaiki trip consists of two hours of relaxing, introductory rafting suitable for beginners, families with young children and those who prefer a less extreme journey (adults $110, children $70, group discounts apply).

Rowing

New Zealand's consistent success at international level has made rowing a popular participant and spectator sport with both men and women. Throughout the country, you'll see rowers practising on calm harbours, glassy lakes and slow-flowing rivers, whether it's a single sculler or a well-drilled rowing eight. The governing body, Rowing NZ (www.rowingnz.com), oversees 65 clubs, 135 schools and seven universities, as well as coordinating thousands of volunteers at regattas around the country. Age-group

Rowing		
Auckland Rowing Association	Auckland	09 815 4717
Canterbury Rowing Association	Christchurch	03 389 3400
Wellington Rowing Association	Wellington	04 463 5055

and secondary-school rowing is very strong, meaning that the sport's popularity is assured in the future.

Lake Karapiro, near Hamilton, is the venue for many major events and will host the World Rowing Championships in 2010. A popular spectator event is the annual Great Race, held on the Waikato River in Hamilton. The two feature races see University of Waikato crews (men and women) challenging an international team, for example from Cambridge or Oxford Universities in the UK or the University of Washington in the US. Off-water festivities are another highlight of the regatta.

As a rule, clubs welcome beginner and experienced male and female rowers of all ages. However, teams differ from club to club, so you may need to contact different clubs in your area until you find one that suits your needs and abilities. If you want your child to be involved in rowing at school, check whether the sport is available at the school before enrolling. Each regional association, club and school has its own page on the comprehensive Rowing NZ website, with a brief description of the club and the contact details.

Rugby

Forget pilots, astronauts and firemen. If you ask a little boy in New Zealand what he wants to be when he grows up, chances are he'll say an All Black. And that little boy might already be pursuing his dream, because New Zealand kids, including girls, start playing rugby at a young age. They even have their own interactive website (www.smallblacks.com) that tells them everything they need to know about getting involved in the game, including contacts for the rugby development officer in their region.

Rugby	
Auckland Rugby Union	www.aucklandrugby.co.nz
Canterbury Rugby Union	www.crfu.co.nz
North Harbour Rugby Union	www.harbourrugby.co.nz
Wellington Rugby Union	www.wrfu.co.nz

In New Zealand, rugby is the game of the masses, drawing players and supporters from all sectors of society and of all levels of ability. As with most New Zealand sports, clubs are part of a provincial union, which in turn is governed by the NZ Rugby Union (www.nzrugby.com). While it may differ from region to region, in general, primary school rugby is administered by clubs rather than schools. It's usual for kids under the age of eight to play non-tackle, barefoot rugby. After that, they are graded by weight and age. At secondary school, most kids play for school-based teams.

Each rugby region has an extensive, well-organised club competition that caters for everyone from social-grade players through to premier league, where players are hoping for selection in representative sides. For a bit less rough and tumble, look for a presidents team for over 30s or a golden oldies side for the over 35s. The NZRU has a community rugby section on its website (www.nzrugby.com), but it is best to contact your provincial union to find a club that suits your needs. Alternatively, get in touch with your regional sports trust or just go to the closest rugby ground during practice nights and ask around.

In summer, tens of thousands of men and women play touch rugby, a fast-paced, non-contact version of the game that's guaranteed to get you fit very quickly. Touch also has a strong social emphasis and there are some winter leagues. To find an organisation near you, visit www.touchnz.co.nz.

Running

Affordability and accessibility make jogging an extremely popular exercise activity among New Zealanders. All you need to do is pull on a decent pair of running shoes, and head out into the fresh air and pound the myriad parks, reserves and walkways. As

A national obsession

well as jogging alone or with friends, most recreational joggers also enjoy participating in the many 'fun run' events that are held regularly throughout the country. These could range from the annual Auckland Round the Bays event which attracts 70,000 participants over the 8.4km course (p.60) to a low-key run/walk organised as a fundraiser for a local primary school. The best way to find out about these events is to read your community newspaper, look on community noticeboards and listen to the local radio station. The independent website www.coolrunning.co.nz has good information relating to events and running in general. If you join a local running club, you'll be kept up to date with event information and can join in club runs and walks.

Sailing

Other options **Boat Tours** p.298

Maori sailed to New Zealand on great ocean-going waka (canoes) and, a few hundred years later, European explorers, whalers and settlers arrived in various wind-driven vessels. Back then, sailing long distances was a necessity, but the exhilaration of crossing a vast ocean with the wind as the only means of propulsion must have worked its way into the settlers' genes, because Kiwis are now among the best sailors in the world. Wherever in the world there's a yachting regatta or race, you're guaranteed to find a large proportion of kiwis among the crew. They are noted for their design and building skills, covering everything from luxury vessels to sleek racing yachts.

It could be said that a boat designed in Whangarei in 1920 is the reason for all this yachting enthusiasm and expertise. The P Class yacht was designed to be safe for children to sail, being easily righted and virtually unsinkable. It turned out to be a perfect learning vessel and children and adults took to the water in their droves. Many of the country's best sailors cut their teeth on the P Class and, despite the advent of many modern classes of yacht, it remains popular.

Thousands of New Zealanders own yachts of varying sizes (Auckland isn't called the City of Sails for nothing) and, while many use them purely for recreation, others belong to clubs that offer competitions, training and social events. Owning a yacht or belonging to a yacht club is not considered elitist and Auckland alone has about 50 clubs, each having its own particular flavour and benefits. Some may be geared towards competitive sailing, while others are more family oriented.

If you are new to the sport, it's essential to have lessons, with many clubs offering adult classes and junior programmes. Some have schemes where newcomers team up with existing boat owners to get a feel for the sport. The best thing to do is browse the descriptions of each club on the website of the national body, Yachting New Zealand (09 361 1471, www.yachting.org.nz), or contact the regional association. Alternatively, you could take some lessons with a commercial sailing school. The Yachting New Zealand website lists clubs that offer lessons, as well as affiliated sailing schools with learn to sail programmes.

Sailing			
Auckland Yachting Association	Auckland	09 302 2030	www.ayba.org.nz
Canterbury Yachting Association	Canterbury	03 348 9074	www.cya.org.nz
Wellington Yachting Association	Wellington	04 388 6795	www.wya.wellington.net.nz

Scouts & Guides

The youth movement established by Robert Baden Powell, author of *Scouting for Boys*, celebrated its 100th birthday in 2006. Scouting began in New Zealand in 1908 and is still going strong – it enjoyed its 18th Jamboree in 2007. The emphasis is enjoying outdoor pursuits, especially camping, so it's perhaps not surprising that the group thrives in such spectacular surroundings. It was a Kiwi, Colonel Cossgrove, who set up the Guides movement following the publication of *Peace Scouting for Girls* in 1910.

Various Locations

Guides New Zealand

0508 46 1461 | *www.guidesnz.org.nz*

Girl Guides groups offer many interesting programmes aimed at helping girls and young women reach their full potential. They offer a supportive environment where girls can develop various skills, self-confidence and self-esteem, while having a lot of fun and making new friends. Guides group activities take place after school, at weekends and during the holidays and include camps and adventure days. The structure starts with 'pippins' for five to six year olds and goes up to 'leaders' for those aged over 17. Use the website or freephone to find a Guides group near you.

Various Locations

Scouting New Zealand

04 471 0720 | *www.scouts.org.nz*

Scouts provide challenging, supportive programmes designed to maximise personal growth. Local scout groups are a great place to make friends, while having fun and learning practical skills. You don't have to be a boy and scouting starts with keas for six- to eight year olds and goes through to rovers for young adults (18 to 26 years). Due to the popularity of water-based activities and the proximity of cities to the coast, there are a number of Sea Scout groups. Use the site to find the group nearest you.

Skiing & Snowboarding

In summer, the roads to the coast are busy with surfboard-laden cars heading for the waves. But from July to October, travellers are heading inland and the roof-rack cargo switches to skis and snowboards.

There are around two-dozen ski fields throughout the North and South Islands, ranging from those with basic but adequate amenities to commercial fields boasting the full range of top-notch facilities.

In the central North Island, the active volcano, Mount Ruapehu (p.280), is the main skiing area, while the South Island boasts a lot of fields clustered between the towns of Fairlie and Hanmer Springs. These less-crowded, inexpensive slopes offer good facilities and you can buy a season Chill Pass (www.chillout.co.nz; 03 318 4830, winter only), which allows you to ski on any or all of them.

The Remarkables, Queenstown

The best-known fields are around Queenstown and Wanaka, with Queenstown in particular swinging into party mode during the winter (p.62). The ski fields aren't crowded by international standards, although it's worth trying to avoid school holidays. If you really want your own space, consider heli-skiing or heli-boarding, where you are whisked away to a remote, pristine location with acres of unspoiled powder, possibly even on one of the country's glaciers.
Larger ski fields invariably offer services such as ski hire, instruction and cafes. Some have on-field accommodation, but it is more common to stay in the nearest town.

Ruapehu Alpine Lifts
Taupo
North Island Map J9

Mount Ruapehu

07 892 3732 | www.mtruapehu.com

The mountain is about a four-hour drive from either Auckland or Wellington and has two ski areas, Whakapapa in the west and Turoa in the south. Between them, the two fields cover 1,150 hectares and offer dozens of groomed and off-piste trails, plus a plethora of lifts to get you there. Ski packages for beginners start at $80 for adults and $55 for youngsters between 5 and 18. These include full-day equipment hire, a 110 minute lesson, a beginners' area lift pass and one sightseeing chairlift ride. An all day lift pass to the upper mountain is $88/$44.

Queenstown
South Island
Map E10

NZ SKI

www.nzski.com

Coronet Peak and The Remarkables (both Queenstown), and Mount Hutt (Methven) are the best-known fields in the South Island. Although they come under one umbrella, they are individually managed and contact details for each are on the website. The fields have different attributes and terrain, but all offer excellent facilities for everyone from beginners through to advanced skiers. A two-day lift pass costs $154 for adults and $79 for seven to 17 year olds and gives unlimited lift access to Coronet Peak (p.281), The Remarkables and Mount Hutt.

Cardrona Valley Rd
Wanaka
South Island
Map E10

Snow Farm

03 443 0300 | www.snowfarmnz.com

This is the country's only cross-country skiing resort. It's open between July and September and offers 55km of groomed cross-country trails. There's direct access to all trails from the on-field accommodation at Alpine Lodge, meaning you can walk out of the front door and ski. Trails have been designed for all levels of skiers and throughout the season there are events catering for the young and old, beginners through to elite racers. A day trail pass costs $30 for adults, $25 for tertiary students and $15 for schoolchildren.

Skydiving

If you've always wanted to take a death-defying leap out of a plane, you'll find plenty of places to do it in New Zealand. After the initial adrenalin rush of freefall, the gentle drift back to earth allows lots of time to enjoy the country's magnificent scenery from a unique perspective. The most popular way to get started is a tandem jump, where you're strapped to a qualified instructor who takes care of all the technicalities while you just enjoy the ride. A tandem jump costs about $245, depending on the location and the height from which you jump. If you can't get enough of the sensation, you can take a series of lessons designed to have you solo jumping in safety. Several operators offer the internationally accepted Accelerated Freefall (AFF) programme for beginners. The New Zealand Parachute Industry Association (NZPIA) website (www.nzpia.co.nz) has links to popular operators.

Control Tower
Wigram Aerodrome
Christchurch
Map p.508 A5

New Zealand Skydiving School

0800 697 593 | *www.skydivingnz.com*

The New Zealand Skydiving School is based at Wigram Aerodrome, 15 minutes from Christchurch, but also runs a tandem skydiving operation from Methven. Tandem jumps from both sites cost $245/$295 for jumps from 9,000/12,000 feet. Wigram is the base for the school's AFF course for novices. If you want to take up skydiving as a career, the school offers the country's only course to attain a diploma in commercial skydiving, which is approved by the New Zealand Qualifications Authority and the NZPIA.

Various Locations

NZ Skydive

0800 865 867 | *www.nzskydive.co.nz*

NZ Skydive operates in the Bay of Islands, Auckland and Queenstown. All locations offer tandem jumps and, in Queenstown and Auckland, experienced solo sport divers can experience magnificent drop zones. The cost depends on the location and the height you jump from. For example, a tandem jump from 9,000 feet costs $220 in the Bay of Islands and $245 in Queenstown and Auckland. From 12,000 feet, it's $260/$295. There are discounts for groups of four or more. Auckland also offers beginners the AFF first-jump course.

Hastings
North Island
Map K11

Sky Sports NZ

0800 759 348 | *www.0800skydive.co.nz*

Sky Sports NZ operates out of Masterton Aerodrome for the Wellington, Wairarapa, Palmerston North and Manawatu areas, and Hastings Aerodrome for Napier and Hawke's Bay. Tandem jumps are offered at both locations. Experienced jumpers are welcome and the company also offers the AFF course for beginners. Bookings are essential and gift vouchers are available.

Soccer

Soccer in New Zealand doesn't have anywhere near the profile of other mainstream sports. In fact, the game has received negative publicity because of administrative, development and performance problems up to the highest level. Participation levels are high among younger players, but retention is a problem because players tend to

Soccer Federations

Name	City	Phone	Website	Regions covered
Capital Soccer	Wellington	04 586 5814	www.soccer.org.nz	Wellington, Horowhenua/Kapiti, Lower Hutt, Porirua, Upper Hutt and Wairarapa
Central Soccer (east)	Napier	06 843 5073	www.soccereast.org.nz	Hawke's Bay, Manawatu and Taranaki
Central Soccer (west)	Taranaki	06 357 5349	www.soccerwest.org.nz	Hawke's Bay, Manawatu and Taranaki
Force Three	Hamilton	07 843 1368	www.forcethree.com	Waikato, Bay of Plenty, King Country Coromandel and Hauraki
Mainland Football	Christchurch	03 355 3595	www.mainlandsoccer.co.nz	Marlborough, Kaikoura, Nelson, Tasman Buller, Greymouth, Westland, Hurunui Waimakariri, Banks Peninsula, Selwyn Christchurch and Ashburton
Soccer South	Dunedin	03 470 3040	www.soccersouth.co.nz	Timaru, McKenzie Basin, Waimate, Waitaki Clutha, Central Otago, Queenstown Dunedin, Gore and Invercargill
Soccer2	Auckland	09 579 0705	www.soccer2.org.nz	Auckland, Manukau, Papakura and Franklin
United Soccer 1	Albany	09 414 3690	www.unitedsoccer1.org.nz	Far North, Whangarei, Kaipara, Rodney North Shore and Waitakere

move on to other sports as they get older. A strategic plan by New Zealand Soccer (09 414 0175, www.nzsoccer.com) has the twin aims of making soccer the leading participation sport in New Zealand across all age groups and helping the national team qualify for and be competitive in all major FIFA tournaments.
Soccer in New Zealand has recently been revamped into seven federations, which are responsible for growing and developing the game at a local level, as well as improving communication and accountability. While they are still under the national umbrella, the federations are largely autonomous and combine coaching, refereeing, playing and administrative functions for all ages, grades, divisions, clubs and schools, whether competitive or social. Each federation is made up of many clubs, so is the best place to get advice on a team that suits your needs.
There are two main domestic premier competitions, the New Zealand Football Championship (NZFC, 09 414 0175, www.nzfc.co.nz) and the Chatham Cup. The newly formed Wellington Phoenix (04 474 2140, www.wellingtonphoenix.com) competes in the stronger Australian A-league. The national team is the All Whites.

Social Groups

Other options **Support Groups** p.176

Social groups in New Zealand tend to be centred on a shared interest such as a sport or cultural activity, so getting involved in a club or society means you'll be interacting socially with like-minded people. International service organisations such as Lions and Rotary are popular, with hundreds of clubs throughout the country. Contact 04 384 7559 or www.lionsclubs.org.nz, or www.rotary.org.nz. If you want to sharpen your public-speaking skills, you'll find more than 200 toastmasters clubs around the country (visit www.toastmasters.org.nz or call 0800 736 753).
If you would like to get together with people of the same ethnic background, the website of the government's office of ethnic affairs is the place to browse. The extensive online community directory has contact details for hundreds of ethnic organisations, from *Al Mujaddid* Islamic newspaper to the Zionist Federation of New Zealand (www.ethnicaffairs.govt.nz, 09 362 7968 for Auckland, 04 495 7200 for Wellington, 03 353 8312 for Christchurch).
If you want company without actually leaving the house, you can join the virtual world at www.socialise.co.nz. But if you want the real thing, try joining The Group (www.thegroup.co.nz, 09 373 3796 for Auckland, 04 499 3309 for Wellington), which organises social events through its branches in Auckland and Wellington.

Squash

Other options **Leisure Facilities** p.350

Many minor sports in New Zealand enjoy a surge of popularity when national representatives are succeeding on the world stage. Squash is no exception, reaching its pinnacle in the 1980s, when Dame Susan Devoy seemed unstoppable in the international game.
The glory days are over, but squash still remains relatively popular, with dozens of clubs around the country enjoying a healthy membership. The national body is Squash NZ (www.squashnz.co.nz; 09 815 0970), and there are 11 district associations.

Squash			
Squash Auckland	Auckland	09 845 4146	www.squashauckland.org
Squash Canterbury	Christchurch	03 341 5438	www.squashcanterbury.co.nz
Squash Wellington	Wellington	04 233 9680	www.squashwellington.org.nz

Auckland waves

These administer the local scene and are good places to find a club suited to your needs. Inter-club competitions cover juniors, social, masters and seniors.

Most people who play squash belong to a club, rather than hiring courts on a casual basis. Indeed, most squash clubs don't hire their courts to casual players, but, if you have a friend who is member, they can sign you in for a game. If you just want to play on an ad hoc basis, some council-owned recreation and leisure centres have courts, as do some YMCAs.

Surfing

In the space of a few decades, surfing in New Zealand has moved from being a fringe activity with a rebellious image to a mainstream sport with more than 200,000 people participating at some level. It's now on the sports menu at many secondary schools. Once almost solely practised by young males, surfing now offers opportunities to both sexes, with plenty of older board-riders still hitting the waves. Many of these mature surfers were once considered rebels, but nowadays their kids are carving up the waves and pushing the surfing boundaries under the watchful eye of their proud parents.

Not all surfers belong to clubs. Many just head out alone or with a group of mates. To learn, most people buy or hire a board and go out on some small waves. If you want to speed up the process, there are plenty of surf schools and instructors around the country.

Wherever you are in New Zealand, you won't be far from some decent waves, from gentle beach breaks to gnarly offshore reef breaks. On the North Island, surfing hotspots include Piha and Muriwai near Auckland (p.218), and Raglan (p.221), Taranaki and Wellington. On the east coast, there's Mount Maunganui, the Gisborne area and the southern Wairarapa. South Islanders also have plenty to choose from, especially down the long east coast.

Surf shops are a good place to find out about local conditions. The umbrella organisation is Surfing New Zealand (www.surfingnz.co.nz), while www.surf.co.nz is a great resource, with everything you'll need to know about surfing, including webcams at popular surf spots and up-to-date surf reports.

Wellington

Mahina Surf School

04 136 5563 | www.mahinasurf.co.nz

Mahina Surf School in Wellington caters to all ages and abilities and provides fun, action-packed lessons around the capital's varied surf beaches. A full-day 'learn to surf' tour costs $120 and will get you out of the city to some of the surrounding beaches. It includes free city pick-up, lessons, surfboard, wetsuit and booties. The four-hour city limits learn to surf lesson costs $80. There's a discount if you bring your own gear. Lessons cater for up to five people.

Muriwai Beach
North Island Map F6

The Muriwai Surf School

09 787 3464 | www.muriwaisurfschool.co.nz

The Muriwai Surf School is located on the west coast, a 35 minute drive from Auckland CBD. The school offers a large range of hire surfboards suitable for everyone from absolute beginners to advanced surfers. Introductory lessons are held daily at 10:30 and 15:00 ($45), while intermediate and advanced tuition are available three times daily ($80). Lessons take 90 minutes and include wetsuit and surfboard hire.

12-14 New Brighton Mall
Christchurch
Map p.508 F4

South Island Surf Company

03 382 6969 | www.surfsouth.co.nz

Based at New Brighton beach in Christchurch, the South Island Surf Company will get you get kitted out and ready for surfing. It's a shop that sells everything from bikinis to boards, and also hires out boards and wetsuits. Lessons for beginner and intermediate surfers are available and can be either for groups or individuals. Two-hour group tuition costs $40 for adults and $25 for children, including wetsuit and board hire. One-on-one sessions are $70 for 90 minutes. Overnight and three-day surf trips can also be arranged.

Swimming

Other options **Leisure Facilities** p.350

Sport & Recreation New Zealand estimates that more than one million people participate in either recreational or competitive swimming each year. With the country's long coastline and abundance of waterways, knowing how to swim is imperative. At primary school, swimming is part of the physical education curriculum and even small primary schools in remote rural areas have their own pool, teaching safety and survival skills in addition to basic swimming. Many parents arrange lessons for their children at an even earlier age, with aquatots classes available at most community pools.

Swimming		
Swimming Auckland	Auckland	09 448 1480
Swim Canterbury	Christchurch	03 348 4153
Swimming Wellington	Wellington	04 567 3269

Most people swim for fitness and health, while competitive swimmers join local clubs, usually in community or school facilities. You can find your nearest club by contacting your regional association. The umbrella organisation is Swimming New Zealand (04 801 9450, www.swimmingnz.org.nz).

Another useful organisation is Swim Coaches and Teachers of New Zealand (03 443 1284, www.nzscat.org.nz), which represents professional swimming teachers, coaches and providers throughout the country. Water Safety New Zealand (04 801 9600, www.watersafety.org.nz) is charged with keeping everyone safe in the water through education.

Tennis

Other options **Leisure Facilities** p.350

Tennis is an extremely popular participation sport, with 320,000 people in New Zealand playing singles and doubles, and numbers split fairly evenly between the sexes. While a large percentage just go out and have a hit with their friends, almost 50,000 people belong to clubs, which are spread the length and breadth of the country. These range from tiny rural outfits that use school courts to huge city organisations that boast a range of top-notch facilities. Contact details are available both from the governing body, Tennis New Zealand (www.tennisnz.com, 09 528 5428), and your regional association.

Each region has dozens of clubs (the combined Auckland regions have about 75) and there'll be a range of competitions on offer, from juniors to mid-week ladies and from

Tennis			
Auckland Tennis	Auckland	09 373 3623	www.aucklandtennis.co.nz
Canterbury Tennis	Christchurch	03 389 6484	www.canterburytennis.co.nz
Tennis North Harbour	Auckland	09 414 5530	www.tennisnh.net.nz
Wellington Tennis	Wellington	04 385 9709	www.wellingtontennis.org.nz

premier leagues to competitions for veterans. Not every club will have a team in every competition, so, to find out if a club suits your needs and abilities, just pop along one day or evening. Social tennis is popular and most clubs offer some form of coaching, whether it's paid lessons with a tennis pro or a voluntary helping hand from an experienced club member.

If you don't want to join a club, you can often use school or community courts for little or no charge. Ask at the school or the council. Some clubs hire out their courts, but members of the public will pay a higher rate than club members and, even if a club's courts can be easily accessed, it doesn't mean anyone can just turn up and play. You should check first to see if they are available for public use. Small clubs will often have honesty boxes for casual players.

Triathlon

There's a multitude of triathlon, duathlon and multisport events held around the country and plenty of chances to test and improve your endurance. Every year, there seems to be a new challenge added to the list.

New Zealanders have embraced triathlon and multisport with a passion. However, the sport isn't just about super-fit athletes slogging it out over a demanding course. Triathlons and duathlons are popular in schools and there's a whole range of gentler events at which people of limited fitness are encouraged to participate to the best of their abilities. You'll find events just for women, just for kids and some just for the downright crazy. Regional sport trusts (see Leisure Facilities, p.350) are the best places to find out about this kind of event. Triathlon NZ is the national organisation (09 524 6959, www.triathlon.org.nz).

Alexandra
South Island
Map F11

Goldrush Multisport Event

03 449 2150 | www.goldrush.co.nz

Goldrush is a friendly and affordable event that follows the old gold trails through the spectacular scenery of Central Otago. The 375km course includes kayaking, mountain biking, running and road biking, and passes through two old rail tunnels, which are pitch black and said to be haunted. The next Goldrush takes place in March 2008.

Taupo
North Island Map J9

Ironman New Zealand

07 303 0193 | www.ironman.co.nz

The gruelling Ironman New Zealand is held in Taupo every summer and attracts many repeat competitors from around the world. Some are elite athletes, but there are no qualifying races, so it's open to anyone who thinks they can handle the course. Taupo is a small town and the event is noted for its friendly atmosphere and community backing.

Manukau Harbour
Manukau City
Map p.484 E7

MORE FM TriWoman Series

www.tri.co.nz

The TriWoman Series probably attracts more participants than any other triathlon series in the country, if not the world. Since its inception in 2003, more than 68,000 women have participated in a supportive, achievable event aimed at everyday women, no matter what their level of fitness. It's held all around the country during the summer.

Christchurch

Speight's Coast to Coast

03 348 3282 | www.coasttocoast.co.nz

This race is said to be the world's premier multisport event. Competitors cross the South Island from west to east, traversing the Southern Alps in a mountain run, kayaking the Grade 2 rapids of the Waimakariri River, and completing some tough cycling routes, too. The event is run every February and there are team and individual options.

Various Locations

Triathlon National Series

09 524 6959 | www.triathlon.org.nz

The Triathlon National Series takes place at a number of spots around the country over the summer. Each venue hosts two races, a Tri My Sport participation race, which caters to first-time competitors, and a medium- to advanced-level race, open to anyone over the age of 18.

Wine Tasting

New Zealand has come of age as a wine-producing nation and it seems that everywhere you turn there's a boutique vineyard. While sauvignon blanc receives the highest international accolades, other styles, both red and white, are being noticed. Wine-growing regions are spread the length and breadth of the country and cover a diverse range of terrain, climate and soil types. This all adds up to a vast number of styles, from pinot noir and merlot to chardonnay, riesling and methode traditionelle. The website of New Zealand wine and grape growers (09 303 3527, www.nzwine.com) provides good background. Wine-tasting opportunities range from a serious workshop or course with an acknowledged expert to relaxed wine tours where the emphasis is on the social side as much as the wine. Some bars and wine shops have regular wine-tasting sessions led by a wine grower and, over spring and summer there are dozens of wine and food festivals where producers set up stalls to show their wares. The best place to find out about courses is the local paper, which is also where you'll see bars and retail outlets advertising wine nights. The New Zealand Wine Tourism Network (www.wtn.co.nz) has information about wineries, tours and festivals.

Bob Campbell

www.bobcampbell.co.nz

Bob Campbell is one of New Zealand's leading wine experts is one of only 257 masters of wine in the world. His popular wine diploma course has been running for more than 20 years. It takes place every five weeks in Auckland and is sometimes available as a one-day option in other locations. The course covers wine and food matching, wine types, wine faults, serving temperatures and much more.

Wellington

Flat Earth

0800 775 805 | www.flatearth.co.nz

Flat Earth's trails cover Hawke's Bay, Wairarapa and Marlborough, areas that are home to hundreds of wineries, cafes and vineyards. The boutique vineyards around Martinborough wine village are easily accessible from Wellington and the company's personalised day tour includes tastings at several award-winning boutique wineries.

63 Victoria St
Christchurch
Map p.512 B4 81

The New Zealand School of Food & Wine

03 379 7501 | www.foodandwine.co.nz

This school offers several full- and part-time wine programmes. These range from an internationally recognised advanced programme for would-be sommeliers wishing to extend their knowledge of wines, spirits, beer and liqueurs to an introductory course for those with little knowledge or experience.

417A Tamaki Dr
St Heliers
Auckland
Map p.484 D5

NZWINEPRO

09 575 1958 | www.nzwinepro.co.nz

NZWINEPRO customises tours to cater for casual visitors as well as serious wine enthusiasts. Full- and half-day tours cover the vineyards around Auckland and there is also an option to visit the numerous vineyards on Waiheke Island (p.111). Wine workshops are available for groups.

Adventure Sports

New Zealand is firmly at the forefront of adrenalin-inducing adventure tourism. Wherever you travel in the country, you'll find people throwing themselves off bridges, bouncing down hillsides inside large plastic balls or racing along sandy beaches on manoeuvrable, lightweight land yachts. Bungee jumping, jetboating, zorbing and land sailing are all Kiwi inventions, but other technologies have also been given a Kiwi makeover to make them bigger, higher, faster, scarier and more accessible than ever before.

Bridge swinging, parasailing, whitewater rafting, skydiving, cave tubing, heli-skiing, quad biking and whitewater sledging are just some of the other activities that will get your pulse rate soaring. Unless they're obviously seasonal, such as skiing, most activities are available all year round – even water-based activities aren't off limits during winter. Rotorua (p.227) and Queenstown (p.280) are acknowledged as adventure centres, but you can get a rush in most parts of the country. And you don't have to travel out of town to get your thrills. Right in Auckland's CBD, for instance, you can take a controlled jump off the Sky Tower (p.216) or bungee off the harbour bridge. In hilly Wellington, you can take an exhilarating quad bike trip over some incredibly rugged terrain, while in Christchurch you can glide over the city and surrounds in a paraglider or a hot-air balloon.

The best place to find out about adventure activities is at local visitor information centres, known as i-SITEs. As well as being clued up about activities in their area, staff can advise you of attractions throughout the country and make bookings for you nationwide.

Blokart Providers

Blown Away	Auckland	09 574 6447	www.blownaway.co.nz
Franklin Country Blokarts	Auckland	09 235 6465	www.franklinblokarts.co.nz
Muriwai Surf School	Auckland	021 4 78734	www.muriwaisurfschool.co.nz

Blokarting

Invented by Tauranga's Paul Beckett, the blokart is best described as a combination of go-kart and land yacht. It's extremely lightweight and can operate in any wind direction. It weighs only 29kg and can be packed or unpacked into its carry-case in a matter of minutes. Its small size and extreme manoeuvrability means it can be used on any hard surface, such as beaches, carparks and tennis courts. It is also very easy to use and suitable for any gender, age or size.

There is a purpose-built track for hire at the blokart headquarters and manufacturing base at Blokart Heaven, 176 Parton Road, Papamoa, Tauranga. Phone 07 572 4256.

Blokarts reach speeds of 90kph and have gained an international following. There are blokart championships in several countries and enthusiasts from around the world often get together for more extreme blokart experiences, such as a 2,000km traverse of the Gobi Desert, attempted in 2007. While the growing band of blokart owners seek out more and more exciting experiences, non-owners can still get a thrill by hiring a blokart for an hour or so. Generally, a hire experience will be on a sealed surface,

Tackling Mount Cavendish

but if you can get a group together you can usually arrange a beach run. Cost will be around $30 for 30 minutes.

Bungee Jumping

Bungee is synonymous with New Zealand and many travellers save their cash to make their jump in the sport's own spiritual home. The inventor of modern bungee, AJ Hackett, is a legend in the land. Along with friend Henry van Asch, he pioneered the unique system that allows people to jump safely from great heights with nothing more than a stretchy cord attached to their ankles. They were inspired by a video of the Oxford University Dangerous Sports Club, whose members tried to emulate the traditional 'land-diving' of Pentecost islanders in Vanuatu.

They received worldwide attention in 1987, when AJ jumped from the Eiffel Tower. The following year, they established the world's first commercial bungee operation at Kawarau Bridge in Queenstown. They were only given a 30 day operating licence but, nearly 20 years later, the original bungee site remains one of the most popular in the world. A jump costs between $100 and $150, more if transport to the site is included.

Mokai Bridge
Queenstown
South Island
Map E10

AJ Hackett Bungy

www.ajhackett.co.nz

There are bungee adventure experiences available in Queenstown and Auckland. The spectacular Kawarau Gorge site provides a 43 metre jump ($150) and you can also take a behind-the-scenes tour. A rugged four-wheel drive trip will get you in the mood for the hair-raising 134 metre Nevis Highwire Bungy jump ($210), while the Ledge Urban Bungy ($150) is right in Queenstown. In Auckland, you can take the bridge climb over the top of the harbour bridge or bungee jump from underneath it ($100). Multi-activity packages are available.

Mokai Bridge
Taihape
Queenstown
South Island
Map E10

Mokai Gravity Canyon

0800 802 864 | www.gravitycanyon.co.nz

Mokai Gravity Canyon is an extreme adventure park, situated beside the beautiful Rangitikei River in the central North Island. At 80 metres, the bungee is the highest bridge bungee in the country and also the highest night-time bungee. The flying fox, shooting out at 160kph from 175 metres above the river, is said to be the most extreme in the world, while at 80 metres, the giant swing is the highest tandem swing. A solo bungee is $125, tandem $250 and a bungee, fox and swing combo costs $280. Open 09:00 to 17:00 daily.

202 Spa Rd
Taupo
North Island Map J9

Taupo Bungy

07 377 1135 | www.taupobungy.co.nz

Taupo Bungy has been operating since 1991. It's located on a scenic bend in the Waikato River, not long after the river leaves Lake Taupo and just before it pounds over Huka Falls. The 47 metre jump is from a cantilevered platform that can hold about 100 spectators. Solo and tandem jumps are available ($99/$198) and water-touch jumps incur no extra cost. The '4-play' deal includes activities offered by Taupo Bungy, Hukafalls Jet, Helistar Helicopters and Taupo Tandem Skydiving. Hours are 09:00 to 17:00 in winter and 09:00 to 19:00 in summer (with bookings).

839 Main Rd
Hanmer Springs
South Island Map L5

Thrillseekers Canyon

03 315 7046 | www.thrillseekerscanyon.co.nz

Thrillseekers Canyon is a 90 minute drive from Christchurch at the junction of State Highway 7 and State Highway 7A, near Hanmer Springs. The 135 year old Waiau Ferry Bridge is the site for the 35 metre bungee jump. There is jetboating and rafting through the attractive Waiau Gorge, as well as quad biking and off-road kart safaris. There is also paintball and claybird shooting available.

Canonying

Canyoning has really taken off in recent times. It's a kind of hybrid of rafting and caving where you pull on a wetsuit, grab a small flotation device (often a boogie board) and jump into a river in order to float through the gorges and shoot the rapids. The South Island's limestone country is ideal for this, where the river has gouged a deep course through the soft rock. But it's not only limestone country that has great canyoning terrain: the gold rivers of Central Otago (p.275) offer unforgettable drifts through sheer-walled chasms. Try Serious Fun (www.riversurfing.co.nz), Mad Dog River Boarding (www.riverboarding.co.nz), Twelve Mile Delta Canyoning (www.xiimile.co.nz) or Routeburn Canyoning (www.gycanyoning.co.nz).

Cave Tubing

If you're not claustrophobic or scared of the dark, cave tubing could be the adventure you're seeking. Cave tubing, also known as blackwater rafting, takes place on rivers that flow deep underground. Your craft is an inflatable tyre tube and you wear a wetsuit and a helmet with headlamp to light your way. Trips involve floating along calm stretches of water, while glow-worms glitter overhead, leaping into the dark over waterfalls and squeezing through narrow underground passages. The most popular place for cave tubing is the Waitomo region and several operators offer experiences in different caves.

8 Whall St
Greymouth
South Island Map H5

Adventure New Zealand

03 768 6649 | *www.nzholidayheaven.com*

Near Greymouth, on the west coast of the South Island, you'll find the Dragon's Cave, where can you float gently under the light of thousands of glow-worms, show someone you care as you drift down the love tunnel and get some thrills on the wild west big wet and greasy, a 30 metre natural hydroslide. It takes five hours and costs $145, or $230 with an abseiling entry to the cave. The company offers many other tours and activity packages. Freephone 050 828 6877 for bookings.

Otorohonga
North Island Map H8

The Legendary Blackwater Rafting Company

0800 228 464 | *www.blackwaterrafting.co.nz*

The Legendary Black Water Rafting Company at Waitomo was New Zealand's first cave tubing operator. It is the only company with access to the stunning Ruakuri cave, which has recently reopened after being closed for 18 years. The three-hour black labyrinth tour is the company's original adventure, costing $90, with five departures daily. The more demanding black abyss trip mixes abseiling, climbing and cave tubing during five hours of underground adventure. It costs $175 and departs four times daily.

Waitomo Caves Village
Waitomo
North Island Map G8

Waitomo Adventures

0800 924 866 | *www.waitomo.co.nz*

Waitomo Adventures pioneered the exciting lost world caving and abseiling adventure and now offers a range of other intriguingly named adventure options, such as the haggas honking holes, St Benedict's cavern and TumuTumu toobing. The tubing trip through TumuTumu Cave also involves walking, swimming and abseiling and takes four hours. Trips depart daily and cost $125.

Jetboating

If anyone typifies the spirit of 'Kiwi ingenuity', it's New Zealander Bill Hamilton, inventor of the waterjet propulsion system. Hamilton, who went on to be knighted, dreamed of a boat that could navigate the South Island's stony, shallow rivers and take him to the wild, inaccessible places beyond.

In 1954, his first boat using waterjet technology successfully negotiated the Waitaki River, and from there the design was improved to make it faster, more powerful, and more efficient. Essentially the waterjet system sucks in water and discharges it at high speed via a pump – the jet unit. This powerful stream of water propels the boat forward, while changing the direction of the water stream steers the boat. This means there's no propeller so jetboats can operate in extremely low water levels, and they're also incredibly responsive and manoeuvrable.

There are dozens of places around the country where you can get a jetboat thrill by skipping over stony river bed covered by a few just a few inches of water, missing a mid-river obstacle by centimetres or doing the famous Hamilton 360 spin.

Whanganui
North Island
Map H10

Bridge to Nowhere Tours

0800 480 308 | www.bridgetonowheretours.co.nz

This four-hour jetboat odyssey heads up the remote reaches of the Whanganui River. Trips follow the historic route of Maori canoes and paddle steamers. At Mangapurua Landing, passengers alight and walk to the famous Bridge to Nowhere. Tours depart twice daily in summer and once a day in winter (adults $105, children 15 years of age and under $50). Canoeing is available and you can opt for a canoe/jet combination. There's lodge accommodation, and jetboat pick-up and drop-off at the area's remote walking tracks. Shorter scenic journeys can also be arranged.

Waimakariri River
Christchurch
South Island Map K7

Jet Thrills

0800 277 729 | www.jetthrills.com

Jet Thrills experiences take place on the Waimakariri River, 15 minutes from central Christchurch (the company provides a free shuttle service on request). Jetboat-only options include the thrilling 30 minute braided blast (adults $70, children $35) and the 60 minute blast plus ($95/65). The jet trek ($105/85) combines a 60 minute horse ride with a 30 minute jetboat trip, while the heli jet ($210/$195) is a 20 minute trip up the river, followed by a 10 minute helicopter ride. Tours depart on the hour during summer months and by arrangement in winter.

Main Town Pier
Rees St
Queenstown
South Island
Map E10

Kawarau Jet

0800 529 272 | www.kjet.co.nz

Established in 1960, Kawarau Jet was the world's first commercial jetboat operation. The one-hour trips depart from Queenstown's Main Town Pier, travelling across Lake Wakatipu into the willow-lined Kawarau River, then into the fast-flowing braids of the Shotover River. Trips depart every hour and include entry to the Underwater Observatory (adults $85, children $45). Combinations with other Queenstown activities are available. Kawarau Jet also operates on Lake Rotorua.

316 State Highway 33
Te Puke
Bay of Plenty
North Island Map J8

Longridge Fun Park

0800 867 386 | www.longridgepark.co.nz

Longridge Fun Park is located at The Junction, an adventure centre two hours south-east of Auckland, near Te Puke. The jetboat experience (adults $89, children $39) races for 12.5km along the Kaituna River, where you see waterfalls, native birds and flora. Rides are customised according to your adrenalin levels and are suitable for all ages. Trips depart on the hour every hour, with a minimum of two people required. Longridge also offers four-wheel drive experiences and a kiwifruit & farm tour. Packages with other operators at The Junction include helicopter rides and rafting.

Whitewater Sledging

If you want to taste the fury of New Zealand's raging rivers, try whitewater sledging. This extreme sport gets you right down to water level and it's almost guaranteed that you'll swallow some river water as you open your mouth to scream. Known also as hydrospeeding, whitewater sledging had its origins in France, but it's perfectly suited to New Zealand conditions.

It's usually practised on the same rivers as rafting, but the individual is totally in control of the craft. Each person has his or her own purpose-built sledge, which is about the size of a boogie board, but it's made of hard plastic and moulded at the front to protect your arms and upper body. You're also supplied with fins and a helmet, wetsuit and lifejacket. After training in calm water, sledgers lie on the board and steer through rapids using body position and fins. You can also drop over waterfalls and, in Taranaki, you can drop over a nine-metre dam (021 461 110, www.damdrop.com). River surfing and river boarding are similar pursuits and are available with Mad Dog in Queenstown (03 442 7797, www.riverboarding.co.nz) and Serious Fun River Surfing, also in Queenstown (0800 737468, www.riversurfing.co.nz).

Roaring Meg Power Station
Queenstown
South Island Map E10

Frogz

0800 437 649 | www.frogz.co.nz

Frogz has been operating for 14 years and offers two daily trips on the magnificent Kawarau River. Its half-day run covers five kilometres of high-volume whitewater, with Grade 3 and above rapids (costing from $135). If you're up for a challenging day out, there's also the full-day gorge trip, which takes in 15km of the river's most powerful rapids ($285). Transport to and from the river from Wanaka, Queenstown or Cromwell is included.

Hells gate, Tikitere State Highway 30
Rotorua
North Island Map J8

Kaitiaki Adventures

0800 338 736 | www.kaitiaki.co.nz

Kaitiaki Adventures is based at the Kaituna River, near Rotorua. As well as offering Grade 5 rafting and sledging on the Kaituna, it operates on several other rivers in the region. Kaitiaki ('guardian' in Maori) has a strong cultural ethos and trips usually begin with a karakia (prayer) to the Maori ancestors of the river. A Grade 3 run on the Kaituna costs $99, while the four-hour Grade 4 Rangitaiki trip costs $189. The latter includes lunch. Combos with zorb and swoop are also available.

Zorbing

It might sound like a pub conversation brainwave that should never have taken off, but there are few more fun – and surreal – experiences than getting inside a giant beach ball and rolling down a hill. Such is the essence of zorbing, which was invented by Kiwis Andrew Akers and Dwayne van der Sluis in the mid 1990s. The giant zorb ball has two skins, and the area between them is inflated, while the inner sphere is open to allow airflow. Zorbonauts, as participants are called, are harnessed starfish-style into the inner sphere, then rolled down hills at speeds of up to 30kph. A variation on the original harness zorb is the hydro zorb, which has a bucket of water (warm in winter) added to the ball. Hydro zorbonauts are not harnessed, so they can slosh around with the water as they roll downwards – and they can also share the washing-machine experience with a friend or two.

Zorbing is currently only available at the original site at the Agrodome in Rotorua (p.227), where you can also indulge in activities such as jetboat sprinting, bungee, swoop (a kind of swing), freefall extreme (skydiving without leaving the ground) and helicopter rides. It's also home of the famous sheep shows. A single Zorb ride costs $45 and three rides $90.

Spectator Sports

For a small nation, New Zealand holds a surprising number of international titles across a range of team and individual sports. Winning is a matter of national pride (beating Australia at anything is particularly satisfying), so even representatives in minor sporting codes will find their prowess – or lack of it – the subject of debate among the nation's armchair experts, media and even politicians.

Whether it's at a pub, club, home or the actual venue, getting together to support anyone wearing the silver fern – the national emblem – is a social ritual enjoyed by men and women alike. Rugby is regarded as the national sport (some might say it's an obsession) and, it enjoys the strongest and most parochial support. Rugby league, cricket and netball also attract good crowds, as do major tennis tournaments, motorsport events and horse racing. These high-profile sports offer good facilities for players and spectators, as do many of the minor sports. New Zealand regularly competes internationally in a range of sports and the country has hosted many international events, including the Commonwealth Games, Rugby and Cricket World Cups and America's Cup yachting regattas. In November 2007, the country will host the Netball World Championships and, in 2011, it hosts the Rugby World Cup.

Cricket

From December to March, the thwack of leather on willow resonates at sports grounds across the country. The national men's team is the Black Caps and, while they're not as dizzyingly successful as the team across the ditch (that's Australia), they generally acquit themselves with aplomb. The Black Caps play tests and one-day internationals against at least one touring side per season and Australia and New Zealand compete annually for the Chappell-Hadlee Trophy, a series of three one-day matches. The national women's team, the White Ferns, compete successfully at international level. The main venues for international cricket are Eden Park in Auckland, the Basin Reserve and Westpac Stadium in Wellington, and Jade Stadium in Christchurch. Hamilton, Queenstown and Napier also host one-day matches. One-day international matches are well-attended, so, if possible, buy a ticket in advance, although you can usually buy test match tickets at the gate with no problem. New Zealand Cricket is the governing body. The website has links to provincial associations and lists schedules and fixtures (03 366 2964, www.nzcricket.co.nz).

Cricket		
Auckland Aces	09 815 4855	www.aucklandcricket.co.nz
Canterbury Wizards	03 366 3003	www.canterburycricket.org.nz
Central Stags	06 835 7617	na
Northern Knights	07 839 3783	www.ndcricket.co.nz
Otago Volts	03 477 9056	www.otagocricket.co.nz
Wellington Firebirds	04 384 3171	www.cricketwellington.co.nz

Six regional teams compete in the domestic State Championship (three-day matches), the State Shield (one-day fixtures) and the short, action-packed Twenty20 series. Women's teams compete in the State League. Even domestic finals only attract modest crowds, so you will have no trouble getting a ticket at the gate to any domestic game.

Horse Racing

'They're racing!' Almost every day of the week, the race commentator's call sets hearts aflutter as sleek thoroughbreds bounce from the starting gates. Horse racing has long been part of the New Zealand sporting landscape and, after a few years in the doldrums, it's currently enjoying a resurgence.

Spring and summer are great times to head to the track, grab a cold beer or glass of wine, gamble a little and soak up the sun. Big race days are a chance for people to dress up in frills and flounces, but no one minds if you rock up in a T-shirt, shorts and flip-flops, because racing in New Zealand is very much a sport for the everyman – and everywoman. From March to November, there's a jumping season featuring hurdles and steeplechases. New Zealand Racing oversees the sport (04 576 6240, www.nzracing.co.nz). The major meetings are in November (New Zealand Cup Week, Riccarton Park, Christchurch, 03 336 0055, www.riccartonpark.co.nz), January (Wellington Cup Carnival, Trentham Racecourse, 04 528 9611, www.trentham.co.nz) and in March (Auckland Cup Week, Ellerslie Racecourse, 09 524 4069, www.ellerslie.co.nz).

Harness Racing

Harness racing is also popular, with well-known tracks being Alexandra Park in Auckland (09 630 6164, www.alexpark.co.nz) and NZ Metropolitan in Christchurch (03 338 9094, www.themet.co.nz). The premier fixture on the harness racing calendar, the New Zealand Trotting Cup, draws crowds of up to 25,000. The governing body is Harness Racing New Zealand (03 964 1200, www.hrnz.co.nz).

Another Black Day

They started the tournament as strong favourites but the All Blacks failed to live up to expectations at the 2007 Rugby World Cup. Despite leading France at half-time in their quarter-final, they lost 20-18 in a thrilling match. The All Blacks will have to wait until 2011 – when New Zealand hosts the tournament – for a shot at redemption.

Motorsports

If you like the great outdoors, laced with a whiff of exhaust fumes and the roar of finely tuned engines, you'll find plenty to get excited about in New Zealand, whether it's the roar of V8 motors around a city circuit, or the protesting whine of a rally car's gearbox on a country road.

MotorSport New Zealand grew out of an association of eight car clubs that were formed in 1947. That unusual alliance of racing drivers, vintage vehicle and car clubs has evolved into a successful organization, which has gained international recognition for New Zealand drivers and events. The likes of Denny Hulme, Chris Amon and Bruce McLaren remain household names after their success in Formula One in the 1960s and 1970s, as does Paul Radisich for his success in World Super Touring Cars in the 90s.

The country went into mourning in 2003, when successful, much-loved rally driver Possum Bourne was killed in a low-speed accident just before the annual race to the sky in the beautiful South Island high country. To New Zealanders who had watched him carve up corners from Africa to Australia, it seemed even more poignant that he should be taken in such an unexpected way.

Ones to Watch

Both racing and rallying attract good crowds and there are circuits for both across the country. Rally series to watch out for include the New Zealand Rally Championships, the Targa Rally series and the New Zealand leg of the FIA Asia-Pacific Rally Champs. Any championship racing events such as the NZV8s make great watching, as does the New Zealand round of the Australian V8 Supercars. In 2007, the New Zealand leg of the inaugural A1GPs proved popular (www.a1nzl.com). Visit www.motorsport.org.nz to find out how, when and where you can get your next fix of fast and furious four-wheel action.

Netball

Take one stadium on a cold winter's night, add a few thousand screaming fans (mostly female), two teams of tall, athletic women and a game that's fast, physical and uncompromising and you've got netball, one of New Zealand's most exciting spectator sports.

The national team, the Silver Ferns, are the current world champions, who also picked up the gold medal at the 2006 Commonwealth Games in Melbourne. Arch-rivals Australia were the beaten finalists on both occasions and, with the next World Championships looming in November 2007, the Silver Ferns will be looking to hold on to their crown. The national teams play a home and away series against Australia every year, usually in July, and host other netball-playing nations on a regular basis. A revamped domestic competition in 2008 will include Australian teams, with five franchises from each side of the Tasman competing in the Tasman Trophy Netball League.

Netball New Zealand (09 623 3200, www.netballnz.co.nz) is the national body for the administration, promotion and development of the game. The website lists fixtures and links to regional franchises.

Rugby League

For many years, rugby league in New Zealand languished in the shadow of rugby union and there was fierce rivalry between the two. You were either a die-hard league supporter or a fanatical union fan and never the twain could meet. Even players were not allowed to switch codes. A lot has changed in the past decade and although union remains dominant many New Zealanders religiously follow both games. Players can now change codes, and several high-profile names, including former All Blacks, have made the switch. The jury will always be out on whether players can adjust and, when a league convert messes up during a rugby game or vice versa, critics won't let it go unnoticed.

The top domestic competition is the Bartercard Cup, which is played between 10 teams, nine of which are from the North Island. It doesn't attract as much spectator support or media coverage as the Warriors games, but, if you want to watch a game, log onto www.nzrl.co.nz, which will give you a schedule of matches, as well as anything else you'll need to know about rugby league in New Zealand. The season is March to October. The national team are the Kiwis and they compete regularly against Australia, with the Anzac Day test (April 25) a traditional fixture. A Tri-Nations series, with Great Britain as the third contender, is held regularly.

Mt Smart Stadium
2 Beasley Av
Auckland
Map p.484 D6

The Warriors

Rugby League's surge in popularity is linked to the establishment of the Auckland-based Warriors (09 526 8822, www.warriors.co.nz), who, since 1995, have been the only New Zealand team in the top Australian competition, the NRL. This makes them a genuine national team and home games at Mount Smart Stadium are packed with patriotic supporters wrapped up against the winter chill.

Rugby Union

It's entirely fitting that the passionate Maori war challenge, known as the haka, is inexorably linked to rugby, because no other sport raises the collective Kiwi blood pressure quite as much as 15-a-side. In fact, the nation's psyche sometimes seems linked to the fortunes of the national team, the All Blacks, with a loss plunging the populace into the depths of despair and a win resulting in national euphoria.

Westpac Stadium, Wellington

Rugby, from club to provincial and international level, is overseen by the New Zealand Rugby Union (04 499 4995, www.allblacks.com). Competitions, fixtures and links to provincial unions are online. Major test matches are played in Auckland, Wellington, Christchurch and Dunedin, while provincial venues occasionally host tests against minor nations. Regional teams in the Air NZ cup are: Northland, Counties-Manukau, Waikato, Bay of Plenty, Taranaki, Hawke's Bay, Manawatu, Tasman, Otago, Southland. The tournament takes place in October.

Jade Stadium

The South Island's premier sporting venue, and one of the world's great rugby grounds, Jade Stadium began life as Lancaster Park in 1880, when it hosted rugby, athletics and cricket. Following its name change in 1998 and an extensive refurbishment completed in early 2002, it's a magnificent facility. A big game here – a one-day cricket international, an All Black test match or any significant match involving the Crusaders Super 14 side – is an exhilarating experience, especially if you're supporting the local team.

All Blacks & The Tri-Nations

All Blacks fixtures include the annual Tri-Nations series between New Zealand, Australia and South Africa (which takes place in June and July), and there's usually a home test series against another rugby-playing nation. The Bledisloe Cup is contested each year between New Zealand and Australia.

The Super 14 and Air New Zealand Cup are major first-class competitions, attracting partisan crowds, with the former involving teams from New Zealand, Australia and South Africa and the latter being played among New Zealand's provincial teams. Popularly known as the 'Log o Wood', the Ranfurly Shield trophy has an almost mystical status and shield challenges result in some of heartland rugby's most legendary battles. The national women's rugby team, the Black Ferns, also competes internationally.

Rugby Sevens

Fast-paced rugby sevens is a crowd-pleaser. During the annual sevens tournament in Wellington (www.sevens.co.nz), the city switches into party overdrive for two days and nights. The tournament is one of eight held around the world as part of the International Rugby Board Sevens series. It involves 16 international teams and the New Zealand tournament is usually held in February.

New Zealand Super 14 Teams

All New Zealand Super 14 teams have a loyal fan base and important home games are often sold out. You can avoid this by purchasing a season pass, which entitles you to other privileges and discounts. Prices are set at the beginning of the season and all tickets can be purchased online. The season runs from February to May.

Auckland

Blues

www.theblues.co.nz

The Blues franchise starts in Auckland city and covers all unions north of the city. The Blues reached the peak of their powers early on in the Super League, winning the inaugural competition in 1996, and making it two in a row the following year. Their third win came in 2003, and they have since made semi-final appearances in 2004 and 2007. Their home base is Eden Park in Auckland and, as the name suggests, they play in blue.

Cnr Tristram & Abbotsford Streets
Hamilton
North Island Map G8

Chiefs

09 839 5675 | *www.chiefs.co.nz*

The Chiefs draw their players from an area south of Auckland and, while the boundaries have changed several times, the current member rugby unions are Waikato, Bay of Plenty, King Country, Thames Valley and Counties Manukau. While they have yet to reach great heights, the Chiefs are always competitive and usually finish mid-table. Their best placing was fourth, in 2004. Their playing colours are black, yellow and red and the home base is Waikato Stadium, Hamilton.

40 Stevens St
Christchurch
Map p.508 D5

Crusaders

03 379 8300 | www.crfu.co.nz

The Crusaders are undoubtedly the most successful team in the competition, having won the title six times and been finalists twice. The franchise of the red and blacks covers the top of the South Island, and the main playing venue is Jade Stadium in Christchurch (see opposite). The Crusaders have produced a large number of All Blacks, including former fly-half Andrew Mehrtens, who was regarded as the most dominant player of his era. Current All Black first-five eighth – and the nation's pin-up boy – is Crusader Daniel Carter.

Carisbrook
Burns St
Dunedin
South Island
Map H12

Highlanders

03 466 4010 | www.orfu.co.nz

The Highlanders franchise covers the southern part of the South Island, uniting three provincial rugby unions south of the Waitaki River. The team colours acknowledge the alliance – gold for north Otago, blue for Otago and maroon for Southland. The Highlanders reached the final in 1999, and have been semi-finalists twice. Their home ground is Carisbrook in Dunedin.

Level 1
113 Adelaide Rd
Newtown
Wellington
Map p.506 C1 100

Hurricanes

04 389 0020 | www.hurricanes.co.nz

Based in Wellington, the Hurricanes franchise is made up of nine member unions in the lower half of the North Island. Their playing colours are yellow and black and their home ground is Westpac Stadium in Wellington. Known for their exciting and open style of rugby, the Hurricanes are always competitive and have been semi-finalists a number of times. Their best result was in 2006, when they lost the final to their old foes, the Crusaders. Former All Black and Hurricanes captain Tana Umaga remains one of rugby's best-liked and most recognisable figures.

Tennis

It's been a long time since New Zealanders have been able to claim a player competing at the highest international level, but that doesn't stop them coming out in droves to play and watch tennis. Summer is peak time for tournaments and the ASB Tennis Centre in Auckland is the place to be in January, when international male and female tennis pros hit the courts.

First up is the country's richest professional women's sporting event, the ASB Classic (09 373 3623, www.asbclassic.co.nz), which has become something of an institution since its genesis in 1986. The 2007 tournament was won by rising Serbian star Jelena Jankovic, who beat Russian Vera Zvonareva in front of record crowds. Men take centre court the following week during the Heineken Open (www.heinekenopen.co.nz), which has been part of the national sporting scene since 1968. Neither tournament attracts the biggest international stars, but many second-tier and emerging players use it as a warm-up and training ground for Grand Slam events.

The New Zealand men's team contests the annual Davis Cup tie, and the women's team competes in the Fed Cup. Wellington's Renouf Centre (04 385 9709, www.wellingtontennis.org.nz) and Wilding Park in Christchurch (03 389 6484, www.canterburytennis.co.nz) are often the venues for these and other significant events.

Tennis New Zealand is the governing body (09 528 5428, www.tennisnz.com).

Leisure Facilities

The Kiwi penchant for fitness and sport is reflected in the range of leisure facilities on offer throughout the country. Facilities in cities and rural areas are often based at the local school. Once school concludes for the day, the hall, gymnasium, pool and classrooms often become the venue for community classes and sports. Metropolitan areas also offer a plethora of other options, ranging from expensive, upmarket gyms to dozens of inexpensive, well-equipped community leisure and aquatic centres funded by the local council, often with the backing of corporate sponsors.

There's a crossover between private and public sports clubs, health clubs, gymnasiums, aquatic centres and leisure centres, with even the spa and beauty market being integrated into the sector. For instance, a community leisure facility may offer wave pools, hydro-slides, indoor and outdoor pools, a diving pool, spa and sauna, a fully-equipped gym, fitness classes and a cafe. Another may not have a pool or gym, but might have a stadium for basketball, volleyball, badminton, aerobics and other indoor sports.

Private Gyms

Community facilities are open to everyone, including visitors, and they are usually just as well-equipped as private concerns. Casual rates are often less expensive at community facilities. However, full membership of, say, a well-equipped community gym will often be on a par with private gyms. A private gym may offer fitness classes, a pool, spa, sauna and steam rooms, plus an on-site hairdresser, massage therapist and physiotherapist who charge separately for services.

Both private and public centres welcome inspection visits, and facilities can generally be used on a casual basis, which is a good way to see if it matches your requirements. Plenty of payment options are available, from casual pay-as-you-go for classes and pool and gym use to concession cards and fully fledged membership for three, six or twelve months. Full membership entitles you to use the facilities as often as you like and clubs usually allow you to pay in instalments.

Health Clubs

Many council leisure centres provide gym facilities and exercise classes of a good standard. Some private gym chains and franchises can be found throughout the country and membership generally entitles you to use facilities in other areas. Each gym will have a large range of membership and payment options tailored to suit individual needs. It's hard to give an accurate summary of fees, but expect to pay between $850 and $1,200 for full annual membership. It will depend on factors such as

Health Clubs

Name	Areas	Phone	Website	Membership
Bodyworks	Two locations in Wellington	04 499 4488	www.bodyworks.co.nz	Membership options from $16.50 per week
CityFitness	Auckland	09 920 2120	www.cityfitness.co.nz	Monthly to yearly packages
CityFitness	Wellington	04 478 6228	www.cityfitness.co.nz	Monthly to yearly packages
Club Physical	Auckland and Wellington	0800 258 248	www.clubphysical.co.nz	Full annual membership $1,193 several other options available.
JustWorkout	Four locations in Auckland	09 379 5300	www.justworkout.co.nz	Membership options from $16 per week (Auckland Central) with Ezipay
Olympus	Christchurch	03 365 6060	www.health-fitness.co.nz	na
Platinum Fitness	Auckland CBD	09 300 6470	www.platinumfitness.co.nz	na
Pro-fitness	Two locations in Christchurch	03 366 2221	www.pro-fitness.co.nz	na
Symmetry	Wellington CBD	04 471 0938	www.symmetryglobal.com	na

age, when you will be using the facilities, your fitness objectives and whether you pay upfront or choose a flexible option. A casual group class will cost between $10 and $15. Some gyms have franchises nationwide. Contact details for regional gyms are listed on the main company websites. Gyms are listed in the *Yellow Pages* under Health & Fitness centres.

Various Locations

Contours

www.contours.co.nz

Contours gyms offer a range of facilities and services designed to help women achieve their health and fitness goals. There are 12 branches throughout the country, including five in Auckland, two in Wellington and one in Christchurch. As well as fitness classes and a supported gym programme, some branches offer additional services such as hair and beauty salons, childcare, sunbeds, physiotherapy and a nutritionist.

Various Locations

Les Mills

www.lesmills.co.nz

Les Mills has been one of the leading gym chains since it was established in 1968 by the New Zealand Olympian of the same name. It has 10 clubs around the country, including three in both Auckland and Wellington and two in Christchurch. The company develops its own group fitness programmes, which are used in its gyms worldwide. The New Zealand Les Mills clubs variously provide women-only areas, early childhood education centres, beauticians, cafes, saunas, spas, nutritionists and physiotherapists.

Various Locations

YMCA

04 568 9622 | *www.ymca.org.nz*

Through its extensive Y-Fitness programme, the YMCA encourages a broad section of the community to become involved in recreational activities. The emphasis in the many well-appointed YMCA fitness and recreation centres is on socialising, fun and acceptance.

Sports Centres

The local council is your one-stop shop for finding out about sports and leisure facilities in the area. Councils throughout the country own and support a huge network of public swimming pools, recreation centres, community stadiums and sports grounds. These provide an extensive range of facilities and programmes designed to support people of all ages and abilities. Each council website has a services, leisure or recreation section with full descriptions of each centre and the services it provides, as well as contact details, hours of operation, location maps and links to websites of various centres. See www.lgnz.co.nz for a list of council websites.

Sports Centres		
Auckland		
Auckland City Council	09 379 2020	www.aucklandcity.govt.nz
Manukau City Council	09 262 5104	www.manukau.govt.nz
North Shore City Council	09 486 8600	www.northshorecity.govt.nz
Waitakere City Council	09 839 0400	www.waitakere.govt.nz
Wellington		
Hutt City Council	04 570 6666	www.huttcity.govt.nz
Porirua City Council	04 237 5089	www.pcc.govt.nz
Wellington City Council	04 499 4444	www.wellington.govt.nz
Christchurch		
Christchurch City Council	03 941 8999	www.ccc.govt.nz

Country Clubs

The traditional country club is a rare thing in New Zealand, but a few have sprung up around the country over the past few years. They are usually based around a championship golf course and an expensive, exclusive hotel or residential facility. Membership options vary and some on-site facilities may be exclusively reserved for the use of residents or guests.

Clearwater Resort

Clearwater Av
Christchurch
Map p.508 B2

03 360 2146 | www.clearwaternz.com

Christchurch's exclusive Clearwater Resort offers upmarket hotel accommodation set in 465 landscaped acres just outside the city. There's a championship golf course, a restaurant and bar, driving range, practice putting greens, tennis courts, walking trails, on-site fly fishing and archery.

Formosa Country Club

Jack Lachlan Dr
Auckland
North Island Map G6

09 536 5895 | www.formosa.nzgolf.net

Auckland's Formosa Country Club enjoys panoramic views over the Hauraki Gulf. There's an exclusive villa-style hotel and facilities include a bar, restaurant and cafe, conference and function rooms and a pro shop. The sports stadium has a squash court, indoor tennis courts, heated indoor swimming pool, a gymnasium, spa pool, sauna and steam rooms. There's also an all-weather driving range.

Gulf Harbour Country Club

Gulf Harbour Dr
Auckland
Map p.484 C1

09 424 0971 | www.gulfharbourcountryclub.co.nz

Just north of Auckland, on the Whangaparaoa Peninsula, Gulf Harbour features a world-class golf course and matching club facilities. Complementing the course are a restaurant, library, squash and tennis courts, billiard room, swimming pool and gym. Golf retail and pro tuition is available.

On the fairway in Christchurch

Well-Being

A few decades back, New Zealanders had a stoic 'she'll be right' attitude to health and well-being, often resisting visiting a health provider unless it was absolutely necessary. Natural remedies and alternative therapists were also seen as hocus-pocus, but times have changed dramatically. The alternative therapies scene is thriving, and many medical practitioners now involve methods, such as acupuncture and massage, in their practice.

Maori Medicines

Maori have always derived remedies from the land and these traditional methods of healing are often incorporated into products and practice. Courses in traditional Maori medicine are taught alongside better-known disciplines such as yoga, ayurveda and aromatherapy. Natural healthcare providers are represented by The New Zealand Charter of Health Practitioners (09 414 5501, www.healthcharter.org.nz), which aims to provide consumers with professional, well-qualified members.

Spa Therapy

Because of the abundance of hot thermal springs, therapeutic spa treatments have always been part of the Kiwi lifestyle. Spa tourism became popular from the late 1800s, with centres such as Rotorua (p.227) and Hanmer Springs (p.259) luring overseas visitors to undergo treatments, some of which seem bizarre with today's knowledge. For most Kiwis, however, a spa treatment just means finding a natural hot spring and soaking away the aches and pains.

Old & New Treatments

With such resources and history, the country was well positioned to move quickly into providing modern health and beauty treatments. Nowadays, you can find just about any treatment you want, often using products unique to New Zealand. A wide range of services and products are available and there is a crossover in terminology used to describe them. For example, beauty therapists often offer spa-style treatments and massage, and health spas offer beauty treatments. Another worldwide trend to hit the country is appearance medicine and there are numerous specialised clinics offering chemical and laser treatments, botox, dermal fillers, dermabrasion and so on. Laser tooth-whitening at dentists is also popular.

Beauty Salons

Other options **Perfumes & Cosmetics** p.398, **Health Spas** p.355

The terms 'beauty salon' or 'beauty parlour' often refer to hairdressing salons; for beauty treatments you're more likely to go to a beautician, beauty therapist or beauty clinic. For a haircut, you'll go to a hairdressing salon or barber – although some hairdressers also provide beauty treatments. Beauty therapists are extremely common and, while many operate out of commercial premises, they're also popular home-based businesses. All the usual treatments are available, such as waxing, lash tinting, facials, electrolysis, make-up, artificial tanning and nail treatments. Most therapists also offer a range of treatments for men and many offer massage and spa-type therapies.

Various Locations

About Face

www.aboutface.co.nz

About Face has five clinics in Auckland, all offering a wide range of skincare and beauty therapy, as well as numerous massage options. The company has a strong loyalty and referral programme, offering free treatments and discounts for clients who visit regularly or refer friends. All clinics, except Mount Eden and Remuera, are open seven days and operate at least two late nights. As an examples of costs, a lash tint will set you back $20, a 60 minute marine facial would be $100 and an 80 minute hot stone massage would cost in the region of $150.

Suite 5
Marsden Village
153 Karori Rd
Wellington
Map p.498 A5

Absolute Bliss

04 476 6664 | www.absolutebliss.co.nz

As well as providing all the regular treatments you'd expect at a beauty clinic, Absolute Bliss provides a range of appearance laser treatments, such as hair removal, body contouring and cellulite treatments. Massage is also on the menu. The opening hours change from winter to summer, but usually it's open from 09:00, six days a week, with late night opening on Wednesdays and Thursdays. A 60 minute aromatherapy massage costs $70 and facials range from $45 to $150.

51 Holmwood Rd
Christchurch
Map p.510 C3 109

Jouvence

03 355 6488 | www.jouvence.co.nz

Jouvence originally opened in 1964, making it one of the oldest beauty therapy clinics in the country. The friendly and professional team provides a large range of treatments in modern, stylish surrounds. The clinic is open Monday to Friday 09:00 to 17:00, with late nights on Tuesdays and Wednesdays by appointment. It's also open by appointment on Saturday from 09:00 to 15:00. A 30 minute French manicure costs $42, while a 60 minute full body skin detox is $95.

Hairdressers

Finding a hairdresser when you move to a new place is fraught with difficulty. Even one recommended by a friend may not be to your taste and, because hairdressers are a transient bunch, even when you find a stylist you like, they may disappear to a salon on the other side of town.

However, there's no shortage of hairdressers and barbers in New Zealand, ranging from the no-appointment-necessary type, offering just cuts, to top salons, for which you'll have to book weeks in advance. Salons are found in shopping malls and suburban shopping centres and on the high street, and there are also home-based and mobile businesses. Check the *Yellow Pages* for listings.

Expect to pay anything between $20 and $80 for a wet cut and style.

Various Locations

Just Cuts

www.justcuts.co.nz

Just Cuts has more than 150 salons around the country, all of which operate on a no-appointment, no-request system – just turn up when you want a cut. The salons specialise in cutting for men, women and children and they don't do any chemical or colouring work. A cut costs $22 and, for an extra $5, you can get a pre-cut shampoo. A dry-off also costs $5 and full blow dry start at $25, depending on length and style. Seniors, students and children get discounts on selected days and cuts have a seven-day guarantee.

Various Locations

Rodney Wayne

www.rodneywayne.co.nz

Rodney Wayne is a franchised hairdressing group with more than 60 outlets spread throughout the country. The salons offer a full range of hair treatments, such as styling and colouring, and there's an emphasis on training and keeping abreast of fashions and techniques. Salons are independently owned and hours and prices differ from salon to salon. There is a handy salon locator on the main website.

Quay Complex
Lambton Quay
Wellington
Map p.503 D2 112

Salon Bausch

04 473 2257 | www.salonbausch.com

Located centrally on Lambton Quay, Salon Bausch is one of the most respected salons in the capital and has been going for 25 years. All stylists are fully qualified, with a minimum of eight years' experience, and all are trained in the latest techniques. Salon Bausch offers a full range of cuts, colours and form treatments, as well as make-up, scalp treatments and body-painting. A shampoo, cut, style and finish costs $65 for women and $45 for men, and colour treatments range from $125 to $200. It's open from Monday to Saturday, with late night opening on Thursdays and Fridays.

Various Locations

Servilles

www.servilles.com

Servilles hair salons were established 20 years ago by Paul Huege de Serville, and are widely regarded as among the best in the country. It offers leading-edge creativity and flair, with Servilles stylists and salons regularly triumphing in competitions. There are six salons and three Servilles barbers in central Auckland, as well as a luxurious day spa at Princes Wharf (09 309 9086). Servilles has a training academy.

203 Tuam St
Christchurch
Map p.516 C3 114

Soho Hair Styling

03 962 0286 | sites.yellow.co.nz/site/soho

Soho Hair Styling is a newcomer on the Christchurch scene and is owned by Michelle Marsh, who also owns Surreal Hair and Beauty (03 365 2215), another top city salon. Soho offers a sophisticated loft-style urban space where you can relax and be transformed by top stylists. The staff are all senior stylists and the salon also employs colour technicians and hair-extension specialists. It's open from Tuesday to Saturday, with late nights on Thursdays and Fridays.

Health Spas

Other options **Massage** p.356, **Leisure Facilities** p.350

The luxury health market has exploded in New Zealand, with so-called spas springing up everywhere from luxury hotels to suburban shopping centres and rural retreats. While some might be more appropriately classed as beauty clinics rather than spas, that doesn't mean you're not going to get a good level of treatment in relaxing surroundings. Most day-spas offer treatments such as facials, wraps and skin detox, and also provide various forms of massage. Some may also have hydrotherapy massages. There may be a steam room, sauna, spa pool and lap pool, as well as a lounge where you can relax between treatments. Spas are no longer the domain of the wealthy and many offer affordable packages, with loyalty and referral programmes offering even greater discounts.

Heritage Building
28 Cathedral Sq
Christchurch
Map p.516 C2 115

Champs-Elysées

03 365 3630 | www.champs-elysees.co.nz

Champs-Elysées offers an extensive spa menu, ranging from basics such as an eyelash tint ($24) to a seven-hour decadent day package, which costs $757 for a plethora of treatments, including a decent lunch. The bubble and steam area offers a 25m heated lap pool, a spa pool and a sauna room. Opening hours are Monday to Friday 08:30 to 20:00; Saturday, 08:30 to 18:00; and Sunday, 09:00 to 17:00.

Various Locations

East Day Spa

www.eastdayspa.com

East Day Spa aims to provide a place of calm and serenity, with a range of treatments designed to stimulate holistic well-being. The spas are located in central

Auckland and Wellington and combine skin, massage and beauty treatments in an exotic, tranquil setting. Facilities include a hydrotherapy room with Vichy shower, steam room, relax room and single and double massage suites. A range of packages is available.

Amuri Av
Hanmer Springs
South Island Map L5

Hanmer Springs Thermal Spa

0800 873 527 | *www.hanmersprings.co.nz*

This spa is part of the Hanmer Springs Thermal Pools complex, 90 minutes' drive from Christchurch. A range of health and beauty treatments is on offer, including Swiss, hot stone and sports massages, body wraps and facials. Water treatments include a steam room, Vichy shower and hydrostorm infusion. A 90 minute 'alpine aqua revitaliser' is $124, while the 'ultimate Hanmer spa experience' is $346 for 150 minutes.

Lyons Road
Pokeno, RD1
Auckland
North Island Map G7

Spa du Vin

0800 772 800 | *www.spaduvin.co.nz*

This upmarket spa provides a Balinese spa experience in an attractive New Zealand landscape just south of Auckland. The spa menu offers a wide range of luxurious treatments for men, women and couples. As an example, the two-hour Tropical Delight package costs $220 for one person, while the three-hour 'ultimate indulgence package' is $550 per couple.

21 Main Rd
Waiwera
Auckland
North Island Map G5

Waiwera Infinity Thermal Spa Resort

09 427 8800 | *www.waiwera.co.nz*

Waiwera Infinity Spa is based in the seaside Waiwera Thermal Complex, just over 30 minutes' drive north of Auckland. To complement its long-established complex of natural hot pools and accommodation, Waiwera has added a day spa utilising the relaxing thermal waters. An extensive range of beauty treatments and massage is available and there's also a medi-spa and dental spa offering more specialised treatments, such as botox, facial peels and dental procedures. Packages are available, some of which include accommodation.

Massage

Other options **Health Spas** p.355, **Leisure Facilities** p.350

While spas, beauty therapists and physiotherapists have got their hands on much of the massage market, other providers specialise in different types of massage. Many are trained in a range of therapies, such as sports massage, relaxation, and Swedish and shiatsu massage. The walk-in style of massage centres hasn't caught on here, but some massage services are mobile and will come and soothe away your stresses at your home or business. Expect to pay $50 for a 30 minute massage. Massage New Zealand (www.massagenewzealand.org, 09 623 8269) is a self-regulated association with a constitution, a code of ethics and a complaints procedure. An online database of practitioners is currently being compiled.

Level 1
230 St Asaph St
Christchurch
Map p.516 C3 120

Canterbury Neuromuscular Clinic

0800 700 775 | *www.massagetherapychristchurch.co.nz*

This complementary medicine clinic in central Christchurch offers massage therapy, herbal medicine and healing body therapies. Well-qualified, professional staff provide therapeutic, Swedish and sports massages, as well as reflexology, neuromuscular therapy and massages for mums-to-be. Other services include workplace massages, acupuncture, chiropractic treatment, herbal medicine and aromatherapy. Most massages cost $45 for 30 minutes and $65 for an hour.

105a Weldene Av
Glenfield
Auckland
Map p.484 C3

Healing Hands Massage Therapy

09 410 0588 | www.healinghands.co.nz

Healing Hands will come to your home or your business, or you can make an appointment at its clinic. The therapists specialise in specific injury treatment, reflexology, aromatherapy, deep-tissue massage, sports massage and lymphatic drainage. Hours are Monday to Saturday, 09:00 to 19:00.

Level 4
Hallenstein House
276 Lambton Quay
Wellington
Map p.503 D3 122

Revitalize Health Practice

04 499 0334 | www.revitalize.net.nz

Revitalize is a natural health clinic in central Wellington with seven massage specialists providing treatments such as relaxation, deep-tissue and sports massages, lymphatic drainage and trigger-point therapy. It also offers numerous therapies designed to assist the well-being of mothers and babies during and after pregnancy. Other therapies available include reiki, shiatsu, reflexology, acupuncture and naturopath services. They also provide a workplace massage service.

Meditation

Meditation is a way of disconnecting from the world and allowing stillness to pervade the body and mind while you remain alert. Once you have learned meditation techniques, applying them at any time can give you a sense of clarity and focus – ideal in the middle of a hectic day. As well as creating inner harmony, meditation is said to reduce stress, lower blood pressure and even slow the aging process.

Meditation

Auckland Shambhala Buddhist Centre	Auckland	09 627 7261	www.shambhala-buddhism.org.nz
Kadampa Buddhism Centres	Various Locations	04 473 3221	www.meditate.org.nz
Self Realization Meditation Healing Centres	Auckland	09 441 9446	www.selfrealizationcentres.org
Self Realization Meditation Healing Centres	Christchurch	03 359 8507	www.selfrealizationcentres.org
Vipassana Meditation Centre	Auckland	09 420 5319	www.medini.dhamma.org

There are several different forms of meditation, some of which are associated with religious teachings like Buddhism. Some forms of yoga involve an element of meditation, while the trademarked Transcendental Meditation (TM) was developed in 1958 by Maharishi Mahesh Yogi, the Indian sage who became a guru to the stars. TM uses mantras or sounds to take the mind and body into a meditative state. Meditation courses are sometimes offered at community classes. See your local paper or contact your local community education provider. Costs at community organisations are reasonable, ranging from $20 to $150 for a six-week course. On the other hand, an extensive TM package can cost in excess of $3,000.

Nail Bars

The advent of artificial nails means that everyone can have glamorous claws these days. There are plenty of places waiting to give you the nails you want and take care of the ones you already have. While beauty therapists are the most common first port of call for a manicure or pedicure, or to get artificial nails, a few nail bars and kiosks have sprung up around the country. They are mainly found in the CBDs of larger cities or in shopping malls.

Nail Bars

Art of Nails	Wellington	04 939 1181
Nail Scene Plus	Christchurch	03 365 6078
Polished	Christchurch	03 341 6747
Sassi Nail Bar	Auckland	09 366 6242
The Makeup & Nail Studio	Wellington	04 389 1026
The Nail Bar	Auckland	09 537 5950
The Paintbox	Auckland	09 978 6464

Nail bars often operate on a walk-in basis, although, as they are often a solo operation, you may have to wait a while. Nail technicians, as qualified staff are known, offer a range of options, such as manicures, pedicures, French polish, artificial nails and nail art. Some may also offer hand and foot massages and artificial tanning. A full manicure will cost about $30 for 30 minutes, while a simple coat of polish should be about $10. For French tip acrylic nails, expect to pay from $75.

Pilates

Other options **Yoga** p.360

Pilates is a body-conditioning system that focuses on strengthening and stabilising the core muscles supporting the spine. It was developed around 80 years ago by Joseph Pilates, who combined elements of other exercise and sport disciplines to help rehabilitate hospital patients. The programme is based on seven principles that are designed to enhance strength and flexibility and balance the mind and body. The method had a strong following among dancers, but Joseph Pilates died before it gained international kudos.

Training to be a Pilates instructor is a long, involved process and there is an ongoing debate about what constitutes real Pilates qualifications. Pilates is popular and you'll find classes in most cities, either at specialist Pilates studios or in gyms. However, many classes, especially in gyms, offer only Pilates mat work. If you want to fully benefit from the system, you should investigate each studio, ask about the qualifications of the instructors and see what equipment is provided.

Pilates purists may not agree with the trend, but the discipline is growing and changing, with practitioners developing and adding new techniques that draw on modern knowledge and equipment.

47 New North Rd
Auckland
Map p.491 F2 123

Absolute Pilates

09 308 8488 | *www.absolutepilates.co.nz*

Absolute Pilates is directed by a former professional dancer who completed her teaching certificate with The Pilates Foundation UK. The studio provides group mat classes and individual sessions in a fully equipped studio. It specialises in a holistic approach to exercise and well-being. Absolute Pilates also provides mobile mat classes to businesses. A mat class is $15 per person and a personal training session is $65.

Level 5
150 Featherston St
Wellington
Map p.503 D3 124

Performance Pilates Limited

04 473 0404 | *www.performancepilates.co.nz*

Performance Pilates in central Wellington offers a range of sessions, from introductory to advanced. Only one class is run at a time and numbers are restricted. For instance, the 75 minute 'studio' and the 60 minute 'studio express' classes only have four participants. Mat classes last for 60 minutes and have a maximum of 10 participants. An initial one-to-one session is $70 and a block of five sessions costs $185.

1 Barrys Point Rd
Takapuna
Auckland
Map p.484 C4

Pilates Natural Fitness Studio

09 489 1987 | *www.pilates.co.nz*

This large studio was opened in 2000, and its owner has qualifications from international Pilates school Stotts. Frequented by several national celebrities, the studio has developed its own form of the discipline, known as Suna Pilates. It follows the pure Pilates method, but incorporates new techniques based on the latest biomechanical and anatomical research. Individual, group and mat classes are available and introductory sessions run throughout the day from 07:00 until 21:00. They cost $45 per person or $60 for two people.

357 Madras St
Christchurch
Map p.513 D3 126

Pilates Personal Fitness

03 377 4649 | www.pilatespersonal.co.nz

This popular Pilates studio was established in 2002, and its clients include some of the region's top sports people. It trains people of all ages and sizes, aiming to improve fitness, strength and posture or provide rehabilitation for pain and movement disorders. There's a choice of one-on-one training through to groups with a maximum of eight. The studio also provides Gyrotonic, a stretching and strengthening system that uses specially designed equipment that can be adapted for all body types.

Reiki

Reiki is a Japanese healing therapy that balances the mind, body and spirit with a transfer of life-force energy between practitioner and patient. The reiki practitioner will pass his or her hands over the patient's body, channelling energy into that person and making them feel relaxed and stress-free. As well as creating a sense of well-being, raising the life-force in this way is said to make the patient stronger and better able to fight off illness.

You don't have to undress for a Reiki treatment and it is recommended that you have several sessions close together when you first start treatment. It's also possible to undergo Reiki training and treat yourself. There is no religious element and anyone can train to be a practitioner, with students learning to attune themselves to the life force and use hand positions to channel it to the patient. The three levels of attainment are Reiki 1st degree, Reiki 2nd degree and master degree.

There are hundreds of Reiki teachers and practitioners throughout New Zealand and many work from home. The national organisation is Reiki New Zealand (www.reiki.org.nz, info@reiki.org.nz), an affiliate member of the New Zealand Charter of Health Practitioners. It was formed in 1994 by a group of Reiki master teachers and has a code of conduct and code of ethics. The website has a contact list of member teachers and practitioners throughout the country.

Tai Chi

The benefits of the ancient martial art of tai chi have long been known in Asia, with millions of people rising early and gathering in public spaces to perform their morning routine. While it's relatively rare to see it being practised outdoors in New Zealand, community halls, recreation centres, gyms and specialised centres all host tai chi groups.

Tai chi is a non-aerobic exercise of slow, graceful movements that come together in a fluid routine under the guidance of a qualified teacher. It's said to have both physical and mental benefits and improves balance, circulation and flexibility. It can be practised by people of any age and its gentle nature makes it a popular exercise choice for older people and those recovering from injury. In fact, the New Zealand Accident Compensation Corporation (ACC, www.acc.co.nz) recommends it for injury prevention for over 65s and subsidises tai chi classes all around the country. Classes are often held as community education courses.

Various Locations
Wellington

Master Shi Mei Lin

www.wutaichi.org.nz

Master Shi Mei Lin provides various classes in venues around Wellington. Shi Mei Lin started training in martial arts at the age of seven and graduated from the Beijing Sports and Cultural University in Chinese Martial Arts. She has toured with Chinese teams and has several national and international tai chi titles. She teaches wu-style tai chi, tai chi sword and shaolin kung fu, and is also a registered acupuncturist. Classes include beginners, intermediate and advanced. Register online.

Various Locations

Sing Ong Tai Chi

www.singongtaichi.com

Sing Ong Tai Chi has groups in more than 20 locations around the country and follows the teachings of professor Yek Sing Ong and his senior students. It teaches tai chi for health and self-defence and new students are always welcome. No previous experience is needed. Just find a class near you on the online directory and contact the instructor to confirm the details.

Yoga

Other options **Pilates** p.358

Yoga practice is widespread in New Zealand. You'll need to research what kind of yoga suits you, whether it's active ashtanga, or the more gentle 'integral' before you commit to a class. Another thing to consider is the amount of spirituality that you're comfortable with. This varies according to the style and your teacher and may include meditation, relaxation, chanting and inspirational readings. Check your community paper or noticeboard for courses. Yoga retreats are also popular. While some follow a strict disciplinary regime, others are more of a lifestyle retreat. These generally include another activity such as art classes, holistic healing workshops or cookery classes. Popular regions for retreats are Northland, Coromandel, Waiheke Island in Auckland and Nelson.

60 Broadway
Newmarket
Auckland
Map p.493 D2 129

The New Zealand School of Yoga

09 524 5432 | www.nzyoga.co.nz

This school was established in 1983, and provides a supportive environment where classical hatha yoga is taught. The principal instructors trained in Iyengar yoga (a form of hatha) at the Iyengar Institute in India and have been practising for more than 25 years. The school's easy-start classes provide an effective building block for those new to the practice ($75 for six classes). A single class costs $20, but there are many discount options. Six-monthly membership is $600 and allows unlimited classes. Three-hour workshops are held regularly and cost $75 (free for members).

Various Locations
Christchurch

Shivjag

03 342 5107 | www.shivjag.co.nz

Shivjag supplies yoga-related products and offers yoga classes at two community venues in the Garden City. Classes are available for all ages and include hatha yoga, meditation, therapy yoga and yoga for youngsters. Traditional Indian head massages, vegetarian cookery courses and yoga retreats are also available. Casual lessons are $12, a 10 lesson term costs $90 for adults and $60 for children, while a five-week meditation course is $25.

190 Federal St
Auckland
Map p.487 F3 131

Yoga Academy

09 357 0750 | www.yoga.co.nz

This school offers both ashtanga and hatha yoga under the direction of well-trained teachers who make regular visits to India to receive further instruction from their guru. Other classes are hatha flow, pregnancy and restorative sessions. Casual classes cost $15, but there are several discount options. Six-monthly membership is $586.

Level 1
21-23 Jessie St
Wellington
Map p.505 D3 132

Yoga in Daily Life

04 801 7012 | www.yogaindailylife.org.nz

This practice is based on classical yoga and is suitable for all ages and levels of physical ability. Classes include beginners, pregnancy, pranayama (breathing) and meditation. A 90 minute class costs $13 and a 45 minute class costs $9. Discount cards are available. The centre also has an event programme that includes dinners, retreats and forums.

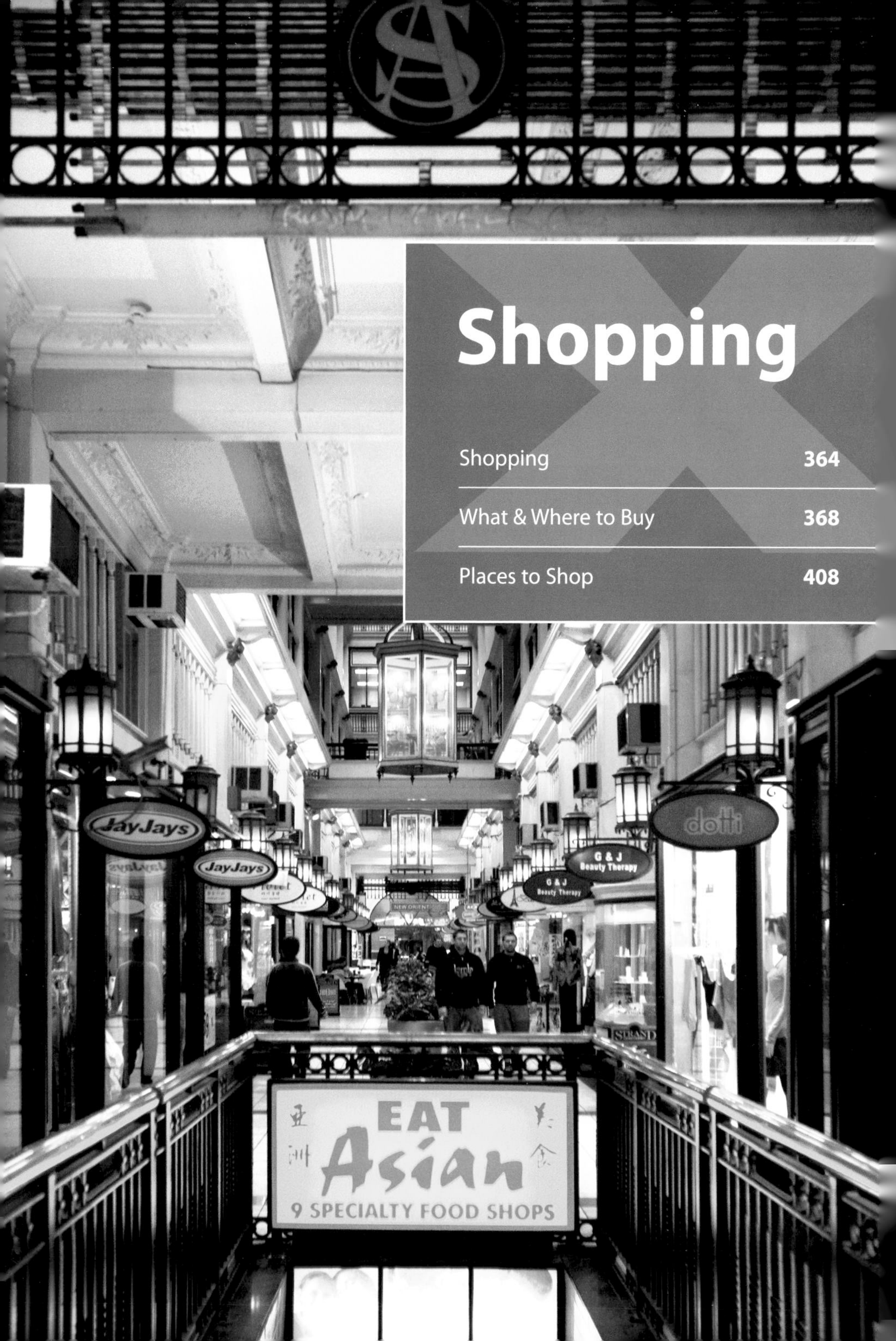
JayJays
JayJays
G & J
Beauty Therapy
dotti
EAT
Asian
9 SPECIALTY FOOD SHOPS

Shopping

Shopping

New Zealand's shopping is becoming increasingly globalised – you'll find all the world-famous brands at internationally comparable prices, including motor vehicles, clothing, electrical and computer equipment. The heyday of New Zealand manufacturing is over, as more production is outsourced, especially to China. However, many niche New Zealand brands are earning a name for themselves for quality and innovation, such as merino-wool knitwear manufacturers Icebreaker and outdoor goods manufacturers Macpac (both have outsourced their production to China but retain head offices in New Zealand).

In 2007, New Zealand's strengthening dollar was starting to have the impact of lowering the cost of imported goods, although the Reserve Bank was intent on curbing this trend. Fresh produce tends to be cheaper than in many developed countries – agricultural and horticultural production is supplemented by imports from around the Pacific Basin.

In worldwide cost of living comparisons, such as those made by Mercer Human Resource Consulting, New Zealand's cities consistently rank at the cheaper end of the scale. In the 2007 Mercer rankings (which include the cost of housing), Auckland came in as the 99th most expensive city in the world, with Wellington the cheapest major city in Australasia, at 111.

Shopping malls filled with major-brand chain stores dominate city shopping in New Zealand, at the expense of local shopping strips – and the malls are getting larger by the year. Department store shopping isn't as popular as in other countries, though each major city has an iconic store. Farmers' markets in country towns and city outskirts are increasing in popularity as colourful and often cheap ways of buying produce – often organic – and cottage-industry products such as jams and preserves. Each city also has a few markets that can be good places to buy fruit and vegetables, and there are good factory shopping outlets selling major clothing brands cheaply (p.376). Parallel importers offer some goods, such as electrical and computer equipment, for slightly cheaper prices, but the competitiveness in the mainstream shopping sector means there's not all that much difference in prices.

Auckland and Wellington are considered the best shopping destinations in the country. By virtue of its larger size Auckland has more shops, but Wellington is considered a more colourful and compact destination, with some strong local clothing brands. While Auckland does have plenty of good independent shops, they tend to be spread out.

Clothing Sizes

Women's Clothing						
New Zealand	8	10	12	14	16	18
Europe	36	38	40	42	44	46
Japan	5	7	9	11	13	15
UK	8	10	12	14	16	18
USA	6	8	10	12	14	16

Men's Clothing						
New Zealand	92	96	100	104	108	112
Europe	46	48	50	52	54	56
Japan	S	na	M	M	na	L
UK	35	36	37	38	39	40
USA	35	36	37	38	39	40

Women's Shoes						
New Zealand	5	6	7	8	9	10
Europe	35	36	37	38	39	40
France only	35	36	38	39	40	42
Japan	22	23	24	25	26	27
UK	3.5	4.5	5.5	6.5	7.5	8.5
USA	5	6	7	8	9	10

Men's Shoes						
New Zealand	7	8	9	10	11	12
Europe	41	42	43	44.5	46	47
Japan	26	27	27.5	28	29	30
UK	7	8	9	10	11	12
USA	7.5	8.5	9.5	10.5	11.5	12.5

Measurements are approximate only; try before you buy

Window shopping

The country's salespeople are usually less pushy – and sometimes less polished – than those in major international cities because New Zealanders don't respond well to that kind of pressure. It pays to know (and be assertive but not aggressive about) your rights as a consumer, as salespeople may not always be fully informed.

The most anticipated sale time is from 26 December to early January but competition in the retail industry means there are bargains to be had year-round. Shop around, as it's a good bet that at any given time whatever you're buying will be on sale somewhere.

Online Shopping

The big name in online shopping in New Zealand is the auction site TradeMe, the local answer to eBay. TradeMe was set up by a canny young entrepreneur with funding by far-sighted investors. It was sold to the Fairfax Media Group in 2006 for $700m. The hugely popular site, www.trademe.co.nz, is dominated by people selling second-hand goods, including cars, but is making inroads into property marketing and the job market. For second-hand goods, delivery or pick-up options are negotiated directly between the buyer and seller.

Retailers are slowly making their goods available online as well as in stores, often for low or no delivery costs, although the take-up isn't nearly as fast as it could be. Some large stores don't even have decent websites, let alone offer online shopping. Technology and niche retailers have been a bit faster off the mark than the larger stores. Telecom's fairly new shopping site www.ferrit.co.nz has the potential for big things, as you can buy goods from a range of retail outlets, but for now the number of outlets are too limited for the site to really come into its own and many major stores aren't participating.

Dozens of online stores specialise in computer gear, electronics and technology. For price comparisons on computers and electrical goods, updated daily, see www.pricespy.co.nz.

You'll struggle to shop online without a credit card, though other options are slowly becoming more popular. Some outlets offer online payments via PayPal or WorldPay, though Paymate is more common in New Zealand. Other traders allow electronic bank deposits, arranged through your bank. TradeMe has its own (optional) payments system called SafeTrader.

Expect to pay up to $10 for delivery of a small item (usually by post or CourierPost, p.159) and up to $60 for prompt delivery of large furniture locally. Many retailers don't charge to deliver expensive items.

Online Shopping

www.ebay.co.nz	Second-hand goods and auction site
www.ezibuy.co.nz	Clothes and some homewares; fairly cheap
www.ferrit.co.nz	A variety of new goods, from clothes to electronics
www.fishpond.co.nz	Books, CDs and DVDs
www.netpharmacy.co.nz	Health and beauty, including medicines
www.shopnewzealand.co.nz	Various, including books, CDs and clothing
www.thedeal.co.nz	Various new goods, including homewares and clothing
www.theperfectgift.co.nz	Homewares
www.trademe.co.nz	Mostly second-hand goods, including cars

If you're buying goods from overseas, you may have to pay GST (12.5%) and import duty, though some goods are exempt, including books and CDs. If the duty and GST come to less than $50, Customs will waive it in most cases. Check what charges you're liable for on www.customs.govt.nz/importers. There's also a list of prohibited imports, which includes animal products, plants and seeds. Many New Zealanders buy brand-name cosmetics from overseas website www.strawberrynet.com.

Refunds & Exchanges

Legally, traders must give you a refund if goods or services are faulty or otherwise fail to comply with the Consumer Guarantees Act stipulations (see Consumer Rights, below). It's wise to keep your receipts for all large purchases, though you don't always need to show a receipt if you have an alternative proof of purchase, such as a credit card record. Many shops voluntarily allow refunds, exchanges and store credits in other circumstances to keep you happy – and retain your custom. Some large stores have a no-questions-asked refund, exchange or credit facility if you return a product within a certain timeframe, usually 14 or 30 days. Normally, the product must be unused and in its original packaging or with labels still attached. Policies vary from store to store so it's best to check, especially if you're unsure about a purchase. If a shop displays a sign stating that it doesn't offer refunds for a change of mind or for goods on sale, it doesn't affect your legal right to a refund for faults.

When you buy under a store finance deal (often called 'hire purchase') you can cancel within a three-day cooling-off period, as long as the product has not been delivered. If you're buying a gift ask for a gift exchange card in case the recipient doesn't like it. Another option is buying on 'appro' (subject to approval). A home decorating shop, for example, may allow you to return a rug if you decide it doesn't match your living room. Sometimes retailers won't process your payment for a few days to give you time to change your mind – but this should be agreed first.

Consumer Rights

Consumers are protected by the Consumer Guarantees Act and the Fair Trading Act. The Consumer Guarantees Act covers goods and services bought for personal or household use, including gifts, but not those bought from private sellers and from auctions. Goods and services must be of acceptable quality, fit for the purpose they are made for, safe, last for a reasonable time, have no minor defects, and be acceptable in look and finish. They must match the description given by the seller and must be the same as any samples you've been shown. Manufacturers and importers must also guarantee that spare parts and repair facilities will be available for a reasonable time. If a product has a minor fault you have the right to ask for a repair; if there's a major fault you can get a refund or replacement.

The Fair Trading Act prohibits misleading and deceptive conduct, false representations and unfair practices by people in trade, for example, misleading advertising. The act covers all advertising and selling of goods and services, but does not cover private sales. If you suffer a loss from being misled, under the Fair Trading Act you can go to the Disputes Tribunal and argue your case. If you have a problem with goods or

services you've paid for, take it up with the trader first, then with the manufacturer, if necessary. If you're still not satisfied try the relevant industry body. You may then be able to take it to the Small Claims Court.
For more information on your rights, contact the Ministry of Consumer Affairs (04 474 2750, www.consumeraffairs.govt.nz), Disputes Tribunal (www.justice.govt.nz/tribunals), your nearest District Court or the Consumers' Institute (0800 266 786, www.consumers.org.nz – advice is for members only).

Shipping

Most stores have their own local shipping and delivery networks, often offered at an extra cost, but for international shipping and for large shipments it's best to shop around. For smaller goods, New Zealand Post is usually the most convenient option. You can send parcels by courier, international track-and-trace, airmail or the cut-price (and slow) sea mail. See the online rate calculator at www.nzpost.co.nz, pop into your local PostShop or call 0800 736 348. An alternative for deliveries within New Zealand is Fastway Couriers (www.fastway.co.nz), or look up your local franchise in the White Pages (www.whitepages.co.nz). To send larger items within New Zealand or overseas get quotes from several freight companies as prices can vary hugely. Start with the comparison website www.intlmovers.com and some of the leading companies, including Mainfreight (09 259 5500, www.mainfreight.co.nz), Crown Relocations (0800 227 696, www.crownrelo.co.nz) or Allied Movers (0800 00 00 22, www.alliedmovers.com). Local removal companies are listed in the *Yellow Pages* (www.yellowpages.co.nz).

How Much In...
If you'd like to do a quick price comparison before you buy, see the exchange rates table on p.53.

How to Pay

New Zealand was an early adopter of electronic debit card payments, called Eftpos. Pretty much every shop in the country, including convenience stores (dairies) and even some market stalls, has an Eftpos machine. Most also take credit cards. The most commonly used are Visa, MasterCard, American Express and Diners Club. Get a pin number for your credit card to avoid having to sign for purchases, speeding things up. It's still handy to carry cash for small purchases, especially if you're shopping in smaller stores or remote places that don't offer credit or debit card payments. New Zealand is reasonably safe and muggings are rare, though you shouldn't leave cash, wallets and handbags in cars. Some traders will charge for small Eftpos transactions or insist on a minimum spend. Personal cheques are becoming less commonly accepted, though some retailers will allow them from customers with a track record or suitable identification, but they will often charge a small cheque fee. While traveller's cheques are valid at many souvenir and tourist stores, you're more likely to cash them at banks or bureaux de change. A few of these places accept overseas currencies but this is rare. Some larger stores, including Farmers and The Warehouse, have their own store credit cards. Many larger shops offer a lay-by facility, which allows you to pay for an item in instalments, though you don't get it until it's fully paid for. An alternative is to buy through a store finance facility – many offer long-term interest-free deals but be sure to carefully check the fine print – and your budget.

Bargaining

Bargaining is not common in New Zealand, except at some markets, but feel free to ask a trader for a discount, especially on a large purchase, a multiple purchase or a cash purchase. There's fierce competition among stores selling goods such as household appliances, computers, electronics and technology – if a trader thinks you might head to the shop down the street you could get a discount. Many stores will match or better their competitors' advertised purchase prices on request. It's also worth asking for a discount on shop-soiled goods or those with defects, however minor.

What & Where to Buy

New Zealand is a great place to shop. You'll find everything from weekend markets with hidden treasures to boutiques stocking the best designer fashion. From paintings to DIY, delis and department stores, you'll find it all below.

What & Where to Buy – Quick Reference

Alcohol

Other options **Drinking** p.429

Less than a decade ago you couldn't buy alcohol in New Zealand on Sundays, supermarkets couldn't sell alcohol at all and the legal drinking age was 20. Now the laws are more liberal. As well as buying from liquor stores, you can get wine and beer (but not spirits) at supermarkets and larger convenience stores. Supermarkets have since cornered the market on wine – most have entire aisles dedicated to it and some have good sale prices – but specialist wine stores are the places to go if you want a bit of guidance about just which sauvignon blanc to serve with your snapper.

Alcohol

Auckland			
Brown's Seriously Fine Wines	287C St Heliers Bay Road	09 528 4847	na
Caro's	114 St Georges Bay Road	09 377 9974	www.caros.co.nz
Ellerslie Wine Cellars	123 Main Highway	09 579 5556	na
Glengarry Victoria Park	118 Wellesley Street	09 308 8346	www.glengarry.co.nz
La Barrique Mt Eden	31 Normanby Road	09 638 5000	www.labarrique.co.nz
La Barrique Remuera	154 Remuera Road	09 524 6666	www.labarrique.co.nz
Liquor King	254 Ponsonby Road	09 360 1580	www.liquorking.co.nz
Peter Maude Fine Wines	33 Coates Avenue	09 520 3023	www.pmfw.co.nz
Wellington			
Cellar-vate	40 Molesworth Street	04 499 0978	http://cellar-vate.co.nz
Centre City Wines & Spirits	2-4 Waring Taylor Street	04 473 7095	www.centrecity.co.nz
Glengarry Thorndon Quay	230-232 Thorndon Quay	04 495 4527	www.glengarry.co.nz
Regional Wines and Spirits	15 Ellice St, Mount Victoria	04 385 6952	www.regionalwines.co.nz
Rumbles Wine Merchant	32 Waring Taylor Street	04 472 7045	na
Vinotropolis	3 Majoribanks Street	04 385 6577	na
Wineseeker	86-96 Victoria Street	04 473 0228	www.wineseeker.co.nz
Christchurch			
Hemingway Fine Wines	51 Chester Street West	03 374 3344	www.hemingwayfinewines.co.nz
Rare Fare	29-31 Main North Road, Papanui	03 352 9047	www.rarefare.co.nz
The Beer Emporium	200 Papanui Road, Merivale	03 356 3040	www.thebeeremporium.co.nz
The Wine Ferret	130C Montreal Street	03 379 1674	www.wineferret.co.nz
Vino Fino	188 Durham Street	03 365 5134	www.vinofino.co.nz
Whisky Galore	797 Colombo Street	03 377 6824	www.whiskygalore.co.nz

Supermarkets and chain stores tend to be cheaper than boutique outlets. You can buy wine at vineyards but it won't necessarily cost you less. Some of the best specialist stores in the main centres are listed here.

You can also buy alcohol online, though you'll need to show proof of age on delivery. Try Liquor King (www.liquorking.co.nz, 0800 746 762), Glengarry (www.glengarry.co.nz, 0800 733 505), The Mill (www.themill.co.nz, 0800 843 6455) or the supermarket Foodtown (www.foodtown.co.nz, 0800 404 040, wine and beer only). The minimum legal age you can buy alcohol is 18 and you can prove you are eligible with a passport, a New Zealand driving licence or a Hospitality Association ID card (application forms available from PostShops and www.hanz.org.nz). Under 18s caught buying alcohol can be fined from $200 and the seller can be fined up to $10,000. Sellers are also banned from serving alcohol to intoxicated people or 'allowing a person to become intoxicated'. This rather unwieldy law is rarely enforced but gives a vendor an excuse to turn someone away if he or she is becoming problematic. Some cities and towns have liquor bans in certain places at certain times – especially on beaches around New Year. These are well signposted.

Home brewing of beer is popular in New Zealand and in any larger city you'll find several specialist retailers. Many supermarkets also sell home-brewing ingredients. Brewcraft, which has several stores in Auckland, also sells online (0508 273 927, www.ebrewcraft.co.nz). Two of New Zealand's popular boutique beers – Monteith's and Macs – make home-brewing kits. It's also legal to distil spirits at home for personal use – you'll find equipment and ingredients at home-brewing stores.

Expect to pay from $15 for a decent bottle of wine (cooking wines sell for as little as $6 a bottle), $25 to $60 for a bottle of vodka and $5 to $15 for a six-pack of beer. You can buy alcohol duty-free if you're going through an international airport.

Art

Other options **Art Classes** p.306, **Art & Craft Supplies** p.371

On Display

There are a number of recommended arts festivals held throughout the country. For the pick of the bunch, see Annual Events, p.58.

New Zealand has a thriving local art industry, with contemporary and abstract works especially popular. The artist spoken of in the most revered terms is the late abstract painter Colin McCahon, whose best moody landscapes fetch up to $700,000. He also produced plenty of other works that sell for considerably less money. Other top-echelon painters are Frances Hodgkins, Gordon Walters, Ralph Hotere, Pat Hanly and Charles Goldie (the latter is known for early 20th century portraits of Maori). To get an idea of the best contemporary and up-and-coming artists, look up the winners of the Wallace (www.wallaceartstrust.org.nz) and Walters (www.aucklandartgallery.govt.nz) art awards. Photography, sculpture and Maori object art are being touted as the next biggest things.

If you want to start a private collection, find out what artists are being bought for public collections, talk to dozens of dealers and build relationships with a few good ones, visit galleries and auction houses, keep an eye on art awards and exhibitions here and overseas, and read books and magazines on art, such as the periodicals *Art New Zealand* and *New Zealand Art Monthly*. The *Australian Art Sales Digest* (www.aasd.com.au) publishes New Zealand's auction house results, which can give you an idea of star performers. Among the best places to start your research – and your collection – are the big auction houses: Webb's (09 524 6804, www.webbs.co.nz, 18 Manukau Road, Epsom, Auckland), Dunbar Sloane (04 472 1367, www.dunbarsloane.co.nz, 7 Maginnity Street, Wellington, and 09 630 9178, 12 Akepiro Street, Mount Eden, Auckland) and contemporary art specialists Art+Object (0800 806 001, www.artandobject.co.nz, 3 Abbey Street, Newton, Auckland).

For less highbrow works, watch out for affordable art fairs in the main centres offering the works of rising artists. Wellington has its annual Affordable Art Show, with a $500 average price for a piece (www.affordableart.co.nz). Auckland hosts the annual Original Art Sale (www.theoriginalartsale.co.nz), with works on sale for $100 to $5,000. The upmarket Ferner Galleries has an affordable art arm called Art for Less with an online store (www.artforless.co.nz, 0800 346 327). Another online outlet is Affordable Art (www.affordable-art.co.nz), with most works priced between $100 and $1,500. Artland (www.artland.co.nz) sells a wide array of prints by New Zealand artists, as does Kina (www.kina.co.nz). Art Nerd (www.artnerd.co.nz) has a good array of prints and paintings. You'll also often find the work of local artists for sale on the walls of cafes and the online auction site TradeMe (www.trademe.co.nz), where you can often find bargains. Some home decor stores and gift stores sell artworks, mainly prints. Listed here are specialist stores selling affordable contemporary art in the main centres. In Auckland, Devonport has several affordable galleries and stores, and is a nice place for a wander. It's always worth popping into galleries in smaller places, too.

Art

Auckland			
Art Bureau	9 Kirk Street	09 360 8002	www.artbureau.co.nz
Art by the Sea	cnr King Edward Pde and Church Street	09 445 6665	www.passionart.co.nz
Art of this World	1 Queens Parade	09 446 0926	www.artofthisworld.co.nz
Corban Estate Arts Centre	426 Great North Road	09 838 4455	www.ceac.org.nz
Flagstaff Gallery	30 Victoria Road	09 445 1142	www.flagstaff.co.nz
Focus Frame Centre & Gallery	718 Dominion Road	09 630 4428	na
Fresh Gallery Otara	46 Fairmall	09 274 6400	na
Kura Contemporary Ethnic Art	188 Quay Street	09 302 1151	www.kuragallery.co.nz
Masterworks Gallery	77 Ponsonby Road	09 378 1256	www.masterworksgallery.com
Pauanesia	5 High Street	09 366 7282	na
Texan Art Schools	366 Broadway	09 529 1021	www.texanartschools.co.nz
Wellington			
Art Bureau	7-11 Dixon Street	04 385 6636	www.artbureau.co.nz
Artbeat	102a Kapiti Road, Paraparaumu	04 298 1670	www.artbeat.co.nz
Avid	48 Victoria Street	04 472 7703	www.avidgallery.co.nz
Emerge Gallery	Cnr Wakefield St and Chaffers St	04 385 2766	www.emergegallery.co.nz
Kura Contemporary Ethnic Art	19 Allen Street, Courtenay Place	04 802 4934	www.kuragallery.co.nz
Lush Design Gallery	18 Raumati Roadd, Raumati	04 902 5874	na
Millwood Gallery	291B Tinakori Road	04 473 5178	www.millwood.co.nz
Pohutukawa Dreaming	2/92 Upland Rd, Kelburn	04 475 9557	na
Roar! Gallery	55 Abel Smith Street	04 385 7602	roargallery@paradise.net.nz
Tamarillo	102 Wakefield Street	04 473 6095	www.tamarillonz.com
Te Papa	Cable Street	04 381 7000	www.tepapa.govt.nz
The Art Shed	3 Mt Cecil Road	04 234 1728	na
Christchurch			
Art World	1/1063 Ferry Road, Ferrymead	03 384 3484	na
Arts en Vogue Gallery	60 Victoria Street	03 377 0260	na
Christchurch Art Gallery	Cnr Worcester St and Montreal St	03 941 7388	www.christchurchartgallery.org.nz
Cultured Gallery	229B Fitzgerald Avenue	03 379 7530	na
Heart of Art	515 Madras Street	03 377 3922	www.artlover.co.nz
The Arts Centre of Christchurch	2 Worcester Street	03 366 0989	www.artscentre.org.nz

Art & Craft Supplies

Other options **Art** p.369, **Art Classes** p.304

Depending on how seriously you take your arts and crafts, you'll either want to frequent specialist stores – usually more expensive and stock higher quality goods – or the cheaper emporiums. The major stationery chains and other more general stores such as The Warehouse (www.thewarehouse.co.nz, 09 489 7000) and Spotlight (www.spotlight.co.nz, 0800 276 222) are also good for creative supplies. Dozens of scrapbooking shops have sprung up across the country. Framing stores also sell equipment, or order online through Art Supplies (www.artsupplies.co.nz). Some of the main city outlets are listed here, or look under 'art supplies' in *Yellow Pages* (www.yellowpages.co.nz).

Art & Craft Supplies

Name	Area	Address	Phone	Web
Archibald's Art Supplies	Wellington	95 Main St, Upper Hutt	04 528 0123	www.archibaldsartsupplies.co.nz
Art of Canvas	Christchurch	8 Dickens Street, Addington	03 339 4322	www.artofcanvas.co.nz
French Art Shop Auckland	Auckland	33 Ponsonby Road	09 376 0610	www.thefrenchartshop.co.nz
French Art Shop Wellington	Wellington	70 Ghuznee Street	04 384 9494	www.thefrenchartshop.co.nz
Gordon Harris The Art & Graphic Store	Various Locations	na	09 520 4466	www.gordonharris.co.nz

Baby, Child & Maternity Items

Two major chains sell a general range of international and local brand baby, toddler and maternity items (but not maternity wear): Baby Factory (0800 222 932, www.babyfactory.co.nz) and Baby City (0800 282 2582, www.babycity.co.nz), with branches throughout the country. Both offer limited online shopping, while Baby Factory also offers a baby shower service and gift registry (shower parties are popular in New Zealand). Chain department stores Farmers (09 272 6996, www.farmers.co.nz), The Warehouse (09 489 7000, www.thewarehouse.co.nz) and Kmart (09 279 4409, www.kmart.co.nz) also stock a good range of baby items and children's clothing. There are several competitive online baby gear stores: try www.kiwibaby.co.nz, www.kiwibaby.com, www.babyonthemove.co.nz, www.winkalotts.co.nz, www.wobble.co.nz and www.babyuniverse.co.nz.

Kids' clothes

The children's wear market is otherwise cornered by chain stores Pumpkin Patch (09 274 2233, www.pumpkinpatch.co.nz), JK Kids Gear (0508 225 555, www.jk.co.nz) and T & T Childrenswear (09 274 8207), with branches nationwide. For upmarket and more expensive children's wear, there's nationwide chain Urban Angel (find your nearest store on www.urban angel.co.nz) and independent boutiques in major cities. Trelise Cooper Kids' (p.382) range of designer children's clothing has raised eyebrows for its cute styles and high prices (Nuffield Street, Auckland, 09 984 6301).

If you're looking for a gift for a baby, Nature Baby (www.naturebaby.co.nz, 09 360 8546), with two stores in Auckland and an online shop, stocks a beautiful – but relatively expensive – range of natural cotton and merino wool baby clothes, toys and so on. Also take a look at the online store www.babybuds.co.nz, which does a range of gift baskets. Pumpkin Patch and JK Kids Gear have a selection of affordable maternity wear. For more upmarket maternity clothes, try Egg Maternity (www.eggmaternity.co.nz, 09 523 0398), with stores throughout the country and online, and Mama Love (www.mamalove.co.nz, 0800 626 256), available at some independent boutiques and online.
Baby food is readily available at supermarkets. Leading brands are Wattie's and Golden Circle. Organic food is also popular – Wattie's has a range, otherwise try Green Monkey or Only Organics, all available in supermarkets.

Beachwear

Other options **Sports Goods** p.402, **Clothes** p.375

You'll have a tough time finding swimwear outside the summer season – which is frustrating if you plan to take a tropical Pacific Island holiday in July – but it's not impossible. There is a handful of speciality stores in the main cities that sell top-quality swimwear year-round – otherwise you may have to settle for more utilitarian training gear from a sports store. In summer, many general clothing stores also sell basic swimwear, often very cheaply, including UV protective suits for children. For maternity swimwear you'll have to go to a specialist maternity wear store (see Baby, Child and Maternity Items). Moontide and Jennifer Dean are popular local brands. Swimwear tends to go on sale towards the end of summer. Surf shops in all major cities and beach towns sell cool beachwear in summer and streetwear all year round – mostly popular international brands such as Ripcurl and Billabong. The most ubiquitous chains are North Beach Surf N Skate, Chances Surf and Streetwear, and Amazon, with plenty of independent stores as well. New Zealanders call swimsuits 'togs'

Beachwear

Auckland	Address	Phone
Aktiv Worx – Swimwear	The Strand	09 489 7335
Beach Hut	13 Hurstmere Rd	09 489 2495
	71 Dominion Rd	09 623 4511
Blue Dude Swimwear	6 Durham St East, Auckland Central	09 309 5017
Grace	Sylvia Park, 286 Mt Wellington Highway	09 580 1081
	Westfield Shoppingtown, St Lukes	09 846 3560
Hot Body	277 Broadway	09 529 2040
U Brassiere & Swimwear	973 Colombo St	0800 834 846
Wellington		
Splash Swimwear	20 Victoria Street	04 387 3122
The Swim Shop	132 Oriental Parade, Oriental Bay	04 385 0362
Christchurch		
Starfish Swimwear	558 Colombo St	03 379 0009

Bicycles

Though relatively few New Zealanders commute by bicycle, cycling is a popular sport – especially mountain biking – so there are plenty of specialist stores selling big international names at competitive prices. Most also service bikes – some will offer complimentary servicing with a new bike. The biggest nationwide chains are Bike Barn, with an online store (0800 245 322, www.bikebarn.co.nz), Hedgehog Bikes (09 444 0644, www.hedgehog.co.nz) and R&R Sport (0800 777 767, www.rrsport.co.nz) but it's otherwise the domain of independent stores, most staffed with frighteningly knowledgeable sales people. Some of the best Auckland, Wellington and Christchurch independent specialist stores are listed here. Approved cycle helmets are compulsory by law, as are lights if night riding. A decent mountain or road bike will set you back about $800 to $1,500, though you can get many cheaper, more basic models, either at the specialist shops or at chain department stores Farmers (09 272 6996, www.farmers.co.nz),

Bicycles

Auckland	Address	Phone	Website
Bicyclette	76 Sale Street, Freemans Bay	09 966 0494	www.bicyclette.co.nz
Calibre Cycles	2 Eden Street	09 522 5427	www.calibrecycles.com
Cycle City	45 Cavendish Drive, Manukau City	09 262 1043	na
Cyco	282 Ponsonby Road	09 376 4447	www.cyco.co.nz
Kiwivelo	122-124 Anzac Street	09 489 5494	www.kiwivelo.co.nz
Mt Albert Cycles	859 New North Road, Mount Albert	09 846 1820	na
Planet Cycles	216 Dominion Road	09 630 6940	www.planetcycles.co.nz
R&R Sport	Cnr Karangahape Rd and Ponsonby Rd	09 309 6444	www.rrsport.co.nz
Wallis Cycles	4/2 Robert Street, Ellerslie	09 525 3117	www.walliscycles.co.nz
Wellington			
Burkes Cycles	16-22 Coutts Street, Kilbirnie	04 387 3036	www.burkescycles.co.nz
Capital Cycles	135 Victoria Street	04 385 6752	www.capitalcycles.co.nz
Cycle Science	120 Featherston Street	04 499 0599	www.cyclescience.co.nz
Johnsonville Cycles and Servicing	11 Burgess Road	04 478 3042	www.jvillecycles.com
Mud Cycles	338 Karori Road	04 476 4961	www.mudcycles.co.nz
On Yer Bike	181 Vivian Street	04 384 8480	na
The Bike Shop	119 Kapiti Road, Paraparaumu	04 297 1499	www.thebikeshop.co.nz
VIC Cycles	461-463 High Street, Lower Hutt	04 569 9854	www.viccycles.co.nz
Christchurch			
Chain Reaction Cycles	114B Riccarton Road	03 343 5040	www.chainreaction.co.nz
Cycle Trading Co	27 Manchester Street	03 366 3760	www.cycletrading.co.nz
Cyclone Cycles	245-247 Colombo Street	03 332 9588	na
John Bull Cycles	Cnr Colombo St and Tuam St	03 366 7408	www.johnbullcycles.co.nz
Laurie Dawe Cycles	838 Colombo Street	03 366 5639	na
Scotty Browns	81 Manchester Street	03 366 3773	www.scottybrowns.com

the Warehouse (09 489 7000, www.thewarehouse.co.nz) and Kmart (09 279 4409, www.kmart.co.nz) – just don't expect any good advice at the department stores. You'll have to factor in the cost of a helmet (from about $50), a lock ($20 to $40), a pump (from $10) and other accessories. For second-hand models, try the auction website TradeMe (www.trademe.co.nz) or a local cycle shop. An online store selling bike parts for competitive prices is Torpedo7 (0800 867 733, www.torpedo7.co.nz).

Books

Other options **Second-Hand Items** p.400, **Libraries** p.321

The book market in New Zealand is dominated by Whitcoulls (www.whitcoulls.co.nz, 09 985 6570), which has about 80 branches nationwide, and Paper Plus (www.paperplus.co.nz, 0800 727 377) and its smaller subsidiary Take Note, with more than 100 stores between them. There are also some excellent independent stores – their pricing is usually competitive and their staff are often far better informed than their peers in the larger stores.

Second-hand books, Devonport

The international Dymocks and Borders chains have a presence in the main cities – Borders' flagship store at 291 Queen Street, Auckland (09 309 3377) is the biggest bookshop in the country, and also sells music and movies. Whitcoulls has an excellent online store and will source pretty much any book for you, though it might take several weeks if the book needs to be ordered from overseas (which doesn't cost you any more than sourcing it locally). The Warehouse also sells a limited selection of latest releases and cut-price books (www.thewarehouse.co.nz,

Books

Auckland			
Children's Bookshop	Cnr Jervois St and St Mary's Road	09 376 7283	www.childrensbookshop.co.nz
Cook the Books (specialising in cookbooks)	405 Mt Eden Road, Mt Eden Village	09 638 4628	www.cookthebooks.co.nz
Paradox Books	26 Victoria Road	09 446 0023	na
Techbooks	378 Broadway	09 524 0132	www.techbooks.co.nz
The Booklover	67 Hurstmere Road	09 489 8836	www.thebooklover.co.nz
The Women's Bookshop	105 Ponsonby Road	09 376 4399	www.womensbookshop.co.nz
Time Out Bookstore	432 Mt Eden Road, Mt Eden Village	09 630 3331	www.timeout.co.nz
Unity Books	57 Willis Street	0800 486 489	www.unitybooks.co.nz
Unity Books	19 High Street	09 307 0731	www.unitybooks.co.nz
Wellington			
Capital Books (specialising in technical books)	110 Featherston Street	04 473 9358	www.capitalbooks.co.nz
Parson's Books & Music	126 Lambton Quay	04 472 4587	na
The Children's Bookshop	26 Kilbirnie Plaza, Kilbirnie	04 387 3905	www.childrensbookshop.co.nz
Christchurch			
Easts Books on High	236 High Street	03 377 0197	www.eastsbooks.com
Scorpio Bookshop	79 Hereford Street	03 379 2882	na

09 489 7000). For online-only stores try www.fishpond.co.nz and www.goodbooksnz.co.nz (the latter's profits go to Oxfam). Academic books can be found at university bookshops. Some good independent and second-hand bookstores in Auckland, Wellington and Christchurch are listed here, many of which have online stores. In Auckland, Devonport has a cluster of good new and second-hand bookshops.

Second-Hand Bookshops

Arty Bee's Books	17 Courtenay Place	Wellington	04 385 1819
Crossroads	110 Featherstone St	Wellington	04 499 5212
Evergreen Books	15 Victoria Road	Auckland	09 445 2960
Hard to Find Bookshop	201 Ponsonby Rd	Auckland	09 360 1741
Hard to Find Bookshop	171 to 173 The Mall	Auckland	09 634 4340
Liberty Books	147 High Street	Christchurch	03 366 4828
Nostromo Books	598 Great North Rd	Auckland	09 360 7323
Smith's Bookshop	133 Manchester St	Christchurch	03 379 7976
The Devonport Vintage Bookshop	81A Victoria Road	Auckland	09 446 0300

Camera Equipment

Other options **Electronics & Home Appliances** p.384

New Zealand is internationally competitive when it comes to the cost of most camera equipment – especially if you buy from smaller online dealers, who are often very responsive to even small changes in exchange rates. They may give you a better deal than you'd get duty-free. Of course, with online stores, you don't get the specialist advice you would at a camera shop (so get your advice from these then price-check widely before you buy). The biggest specialist chain is Camera House (09 309 7537, www.camerahouse.co.nz), with stores in nearly every large shopping mall in the country. Otherwise, look at the many independent stores or the large general electronics chains: Dick Smith Electronics (09 414 2800, www.dse.co.nz), Harvey Norman (0800 422 423, www.harveynorman.co.nz), Betta Electrical (09 444 0720, www.bettaelectrical.co.nz), Bond & Bond (0800 202 066, www.bondandbond.co.nz), 100% Your Electronics Store (0800 107 090, www.100yes.co.nz), Hill & Stewart (0800 221 144, www.hillandstewart.co.nz) or Noel Leeming (0800 444 488, www.noelleeming.co.nz).

To find the best deals, keep an eye on the price comparison website www.pricespy.co.nz. Sometimes the bigger chains will have the best deals – and you can often talk your way into a discount – but often it's a small importer based in Gore (p.289) or somewhere equally obscure. Traders usually provide guarantees and warranties of about a year but always check the fine print. Most stores offer extended warranties of up to five years for an extra cost, or you could try bargaining to get it thrown in for free. You'll end up back at your local camera shop if you need repairs and servicing. If you can resist buying the newest camera out for about six months the price will drop considerably.

Car Parts & Accessories

New Zealanders love their cars and you'll find plenty of businesses selling car parts. The country is following international trends of souping-up cars, in the vein of American TV programme *Pimp My Ride*, so you'll see convoys of boy racers circling the streets at night with their lowered ear-splitting Japanese cars lit up like Christmas trees and booming out rap tracks. A whole industry has sprung up to cater for them. But the police have been given more power to issue fines and demerit points for noisy modified exhausts, cars with noisy exhausts won't pass the compulsory Warrant of Fitness test and more crackdowns are threatened.

There are large nationwide chain stores specialising in car parts: Repco and its subsidiary Appco Auto Parts (0800 800 878, www.repco.co.nz), Partmaster (09 376 7886, www.partmaster.co.nz), Autostop (0800 288 678) and BNT Automotive, (09 414 3200, www.bntnz.co.nz). There are many smaller local dismantlers, too. It's also worth contacting the specialist dealers in particular makes of car. To find the right one, visit www.partsconnection.co.nz. New car dealers have parts and maintenance arms, although these can be a more expensive route. It can be harder and more expensive to find replacement parts for European cars than for Japanese cars.

Clothes

Other options **Beachwear** p.372, **Lingerie** p.392, **Sports Goods** p.402, **Shoes** p.400

Twenty years ago Kiwis flew to Sydney or Melbourne for a weekend to find interesting clothes. Today, though many women still use shopping as an excuse for a girls' weekend across the Tasman, New Zealand more than holds its own. Not only are most of the chain stores in Australia identical to those in New Zealand (thanks, globalisation), but New Zealand's fashion designers and manufacturers are every bit as innovative and productive as their larger neighbours. Unlike Australia, New Zealand's cities don't have large one-stop designer department stores of the calibre of Myer or David Jones, but the designers do tend to congregate in particular areas, and upmarket boutiques in smaller centres stock a range of designers. The more sophisticated department stores have good clothing ranges. Try Smith & Caughey in Auckland (p.410), Kirkcaldie & Stains in Wellington (p.414) and Ballantynes in Christchurch (p.419).

New Zealand doesn't have the same definition of 'high street shopping' as some other countries. Here, those shops are called 'chain stores' and are usually found in malls. Most have migrated over from Australia and very few stock clothes that are made in New Zealand. 'High Street stores' usually refers to the upmarket designer boutiques on High Street in central Auckland. The stereotype of fashionable New Zealand women – especially older women – is that they always wear black.

Designers & Boutiques

New Zealand punches above its weight internationally when it comes to designer fashion. Arguable the queen of New Zealand fashion – certainly the most visible presence – is Karen Walker, who frequently appears at the top international fashion shows. New Zealand also has a grand fashion show, Air New Zealand Fashion Week, held each September. It's not open to the public, which is unfortunate because it's a great introduction to what's around. The next best introduction is a wander around

High Street in Auckland CBD, Nuffield Street in Newmarket, Auckland, or Lambton Quay in Wellington. You won't find too many bargains but you might find a bit of inspiration and entertainment. Some of the biggest local names are listed below, along with their retail stores. Most are also stocked in other stores – check their websites for details. Ricochet (p.382) and Moochi (p.382) are probably the cheapest of these labels.

Factory Shops

There's been an explosion in New Zealand's factory shopping outlets in recent years, with the Dress-Smart malls sucking up many of the outlet stores of the big chains that sell their excess product for sizeable discounts. Dress-Smart (www.dress-smart.co.nz) has malls in Auckland, Hamilton, Wellington and Christchurch. Auckland's is the biggest, with about 100 retail stores, mostly selling clothes, based in Onehunga. There is also a Fox Outlet Centre, with 50 factory shops, in Auckland (www.foxoutlets.co.nz). There are many factory shops outside of these centres. A useful website for locating them is www.factoryshops.co.nz, though it's still in development and lists few stores out of Auckland. Another is www.bargainshopping.co.nz. Otherwise, look up 'factory shops' in your *Yellow Pages* or on www.yellowpages.co.nz, or the websites of particular chains. Auckland Shopping Tours (021 211 6793, www.aucklandshoppingtours.co.nz) takes minibus tours of the city's factory outlets.

Factory Shops

Dress-Smart Auckland	Auckland	151 Arthur Street, Onehunga	09 622 2400
Dress-Smart Christchurch	Christchurch	409 Main South Road, Hornby	03 349 5750
Dress-Smart Hamilton	Hamilton	The Base, Te Rapa Road	07 846 0077
Dress-Smart Wellington	Wellington	24 Main Road, Tawa	04 232 0226
Fox Outlet Centre	Auckland	3 Akoranga Drive, Northcote	09 486 4445

Older Women

Several chain stores cater to the more mature woman, most valiantly ignoring the latest fashion in favour of comfortable clothes designed to suit older frames.

Older Women

Ballentynes Fashion Central	25 stores nationwide, plus online store	04 238 9080	www.bfc.co.nz
Caroline Eve	24 stores in the North Island	0800 227 654	www.carolineeve.co.nz
Kooky	13 stores nationwide	09 489 6395	www.kooky.co.nz
Miller's Fashion Club	26 stores nationwide	09 825 0294	www.millersfashion.com.au

Larger Sizes

Dozens of stores cater to larger people and many general clothes strores have sections for fuller figures. The bigger stores and online stores are listed below, though there are many more small independent stores around the country – try www.realwomen.co.nz for listings. Farmers stores (09 272 6996, www.farmers.co.nz) also have a selection of clothing for larger women, as does Ezibuy (0508 500 500, www.ezibuy.co.nz) and The Carpenter's Daughter (09 624 1715, www.thecarpentersdaughter.co.nz).

Larger Sizes

All Creatures Greater Than Small	na	03 352 3362	www.acfashion.biz
Beggs Big & Tall Menswear	Auckland	0800 42 44 48	www.beggs.co.nz
Big Man Menswear	Auckland	09 276 5434	www.bigmanmenswear.co.nz
K&K Fashion	Various Locations	09 418 4772	www.kandk.co.nz
Precious Vessels	Auckland	09 631 5570	www.preciousvessels.com

Women's Chain Stores

128 Broadway
Newmarket
Auckland
Map p.492 C3 1

Annah Stretton/Annah S

07 889 4053 | *www.annahs.co.nz*

Annah Stretton is an ambitious Waikato businesswoman and designer who also owns and edits women's magazine, *Her*. The clothing, sold through Annah Stretton and Annah S stores nationwide, is interesting, busy, colourful and eclectic, attracting older professional women who want to make a statement. The range is moderately priced – not as cheap as chain stores selling imports, but not as expensive as the more exclusive designer labels.

151 Arthur St
Auckland
Map p.484 C6

David Lawrence

www.davidlawrence.com.au

Another Australian import, upmarket David Lawrence sells mostly high-quality business, evening clothes and casual wear with moderate to expensive pricetags. It has six stores in Auckland, Wellington and Christchurch, including a good outlet shop in the Dress-Smart mall in Onehunga, Auckland (p.411). The website shows its latest styles and prices.

Various Locations

Dotti

www.dotti.co.nz

Dotti targets teenagers and young women with cheap, fun clothing and accessories, including shoes, sunglasses, handbags and jewellery – think Paris Hilton. In its own words: 'Dotti has always been about fashion and that's what totally drives us.' It's another Australian chain, with stores in Auckland, Hamilton, Papamoa, Wellington, Christchurch and Queenstown.

Various Locations

Glassons

03 366 0784 | *www.glassons.co.nz*

Ubiquitous Glassons has cornered the market in cheap, colourful, casual basics. It's one of the most popular stores in the country – you'd be hard-pressed to find a New Zealand woman below the age of 50 who didn't have at least a Glassons singlet (translation: tanktop) in her wardrobe. It also has a limited online store.

Various Locations

Jean Jones

09 273 4910 | *www.jeanjones.co.nz*

Jean Jones sells conservative casual and more formal gear for moderate prices, mostly aimed at stylish older women, though younger woman will find some well-priced basics. It's widespread, with close to 30 stores nationwide, including in many smaller towns, and most of its clothing is made in New Zealand.

Various Locations

Max Fashions

09 307 3339 | *www.max.co.nz*

One of New Zealand's most popular women's clothing stores sells restrained yet good-quality sophisticated, professional and casual clothing, as well as evening wear, for moderate to high prices. You won't have a problem finding a store – they're everywhere: it's not a decent mall if it hasn't got a Max outlet.

555 Colombo St
Christchurch
Map p.516 C4 7

Pagani

03 379 8029

Pagani sells ultra-cheap casual and more formal clothes. The quality's not always the best, but the prices usually are. Its 30 odd stores are scattered around the North Island, including some smaller towns, though it has only one store in the South Island, in Christchurch. For your nearest store, look in the White Pages or on www.whitepages.co.nz.

151 Arthur St
Auckland
Map p.484 C6

Principals

09 630 6900 | *www.principals.co.nz*

Principals sells glamorous clothes, including evening wear, to young women at moderate prices, though it also stocks more casual wear. It has stores in Christchurch and Dunedin and in several North Island centres. Among its eight Auckland stores is a good-value outlet store at the Dress-Smart factory shop mall in Onehunga.

Various Locations

Shanton Apparel

09 295 1010

Long a staple with the budget shopper, Shanton Apparel has a wide range of casual and glamorous clothes for low prices. They have close to 30 stores scattered liberally through the country. There is no website, so to find your nearest store look in your White Pages or on www.whitepages.co.nz or call them.

Various Locations

Staxs

07 578 3120 | *www.staxs.co.nz*

Moderately priced Staxs specialises in classic office wear and more glamorous clothes, including posh evening wear, with 20 stores spread through Auckland, Hamilton, Tauranga, Taupo, Palmerston North, Wellington, Christchurch and Dunedin. It's a fast-growing New Zealand-owned company and is especially well-patronised during school ball season, so don't expect to be the only girl at the ball wearing your Staxs dress.

Various Locations

Supré

www.supre.com.au

A cheap fun, flirty favourite with teenagers, Australian chain store Supré has all bases covered, from casual to more glam gear – though you may catch slightly older women ducking in to buy inexpensive basic singlets, T-shirts and the like. It has 20 stores and you'll find one in most decent-sized cities.

Various Locations

Valleygirl

www.valleygirl.com.au

As you can probably guess, this one's for the teenagers, with fairly large stores selling cheap, fun, colourful clothes that channel the latest American fashions, though it's another Australian chain. It has stores in Auckland, Wellington and Christchurch.

Men's Chain Stores

Various Locations

Barkers Men's Clothing

0800 808 700 | *www.barkersmensclothing.co.nz*

Moderately priced Barkers sells comfortable casual wear: shirts for the pub and the office, suits and coats, including leather jackets. It's recently embarked on an image change, leaning towards smarter, hipper designs with its brand name splashed around less liberally. It has 14 stores throughout the country, plus several outlet stores that are especially good value for money.

Various Locations

Meccano Men's Clothing

07 838 9252 | *www.meccano.co.nz*

Cool Meccano stocks a range of international brands aimed at hip young men, including Levi's, Ben Sherman and Industrie. You'll find casual gear, high fashion and sharp suits. It has stores in Auckland, Hamilton, Tauranga, Palmerston North, Wellington, Christchurch and Dunedin, including outlet stores at Dress-Smart malls in Auckland, Hamilton and Christchurch.

Chain stores NZ style

Various Locations

Munns the Man's Store

03 366 5907

Cue the jokes about men being dressed by their Munns. It tends to ignore the latest fashions and sells reasonably cheap, basic menswear, including suits for people who aren't too fussy about looking like the coolest guy on the street. It also offers suit hire. Stores in Auckland, Hamilton, Wellington, Christchurch and Dunedin.

Various Locations

Rodd & Gunn

0800 188 088 | *www.roddandgunn.co.nz*

Picture yourself sitting in front of the fire in an upmarket lodge after a day's fishing and you'll get the feeling for Rodd & Gunn's style. It has quality, practical, comfortable, moderate-to-high priced clothes and is not a slave to high fashion. It has the contract to dress the All Blacks off the field. Stores in Auckland, Hamilton, Napier, Palmerston North, Wellington, Christchurch, Dunedin and Queenstown.

2 Willis St
Wellington
Map p.503 D3 17

Tarocash

www.tarocash.com.au

An Australian chain that's fairly new to New Zealand, moderately priced Tarocash appeals mostly to men aged 20 to 40 and carries smart casual wear that follows the fashions of the day. At the moment it has only three stores, in Auckland and Wellington, but you can expect to see more of this label.

Unisex Chain Stores

Various Locations

Colorado

www.colorado.com.au

Colorado has moderately priced, fairly conservative casual clothing and footwear for men and women aged about 20 to 40. Despite the name, it's another Australian import. It has 11 stores, mostly in larger malls, in Auckland, Hamilton, Papamoa, Palmerston North, Wellington and Christchurch, including a factory outlet at the Dress-Smart mall in Onehunga, Auckland.

Various Locations

Country Road

www.countryroad.com.au

One of the most established Australian chains in New Zealand, Country Road has a reputation for simple, high-quality casual and office clothing in the moderate-to-high price range. Look out for the periodic sales – it's worth signing up to the mailing list to get in first. Stores in Auckland, Wellington, Christchurch and Queenstown.

Various Locations

Cotton On

www.cottonon.com.au

For cheap T-shirts, singlets, jeans and other wardrobe basics, it's hard to beat new Australian chain Cotton On in price. It's mostly aimed at the younger market but you'll see plenty of older people wearing it, and there are outlets especially for children's wear. Stores in Auckland, Hamilton, Wellington and Christchurch.

Various Locations

Esprit

www.esprit.com

One of the biggest clothing stores in the world, Esprit has long been a presence in New Zealand and sells crisp casual wear and accessories for cheap to moderate prices. It has stores in Auckland, Wellington and Christchurch, as well as a factory outlet at the Dress-Smart mall in Onehunga, Auckland.

Various Locations

Farmers

09 272 6996 | *www.farmers.co.nz*

The ubiquitous Farmers department store sells a wide range of cheap basic clothing, though it's branching out into more upmarket and expensive women's clothes with ranges by Jigsaw and New Zealand designer Liz Mitchell among others. It also has a good selection of men's and women's underwear. Stores nationwide.

Various Locations

Jay Jays

09 579 0744 | *www.jayjays.co.nz*

A good stop for ultra-cheap casual wear and jeans, Jay Jays is targeted at teenagers and people in their early 20s. It also carries accessories including belts, bags, jewellery, hats and basic shoes – mostly street sneakers and jandals (which you might know as flip-flops or thongs). It's yet another Australian chain and has stores nationwide.

Various Locations

Kmart

09 279 4409 | *www.kmart.co.nz*

Kmart department stores stock ultra-cheap men's, women's and children's clothing. Don't expect much in the way of New Zealand-made clothing, quality or the latest fashions, but it could well be possible to fill an entire wardrobe for a couple of hundred dollars if you're not too fussy. It also sells accessories and shoes.

Various Locations

Postie +

03 339 5700 | *www.postie.co.nz*

Once a cheap mail-order company, Postie + now has a major shopfront presence, with 70 stores nationwide selling men's, women's and children's clothes. It caters to all ages, though you'll most often see more mature women browsing the racks, while cool teenagers might not want to admit to shopping there.

Various Locations

The Warehouse

09 489 7000 | *www.thewarehouse.co.nz*

The ubiquitous 'Red Shed' stocks a wide range of ultra-cheap men's, women's and children's clothing. Almost all of it is imported and the quality isn't always very high but there are a few gems hidden on the packed shelves, including some items even the most fashion-conscious teenager might condescend to wearing.

Designers & Boutiques

36 Jervois Rd
Ponsonby
Map p.486 C2 27

Caroline Church

09 377 2680 | *www.carolinechurch.co.nz*

Caroline Church's signature is opulent fabrics in rich colours, such as embroidered silk, made into flowing glamorous skirts and and tops. Most of the designs are intended to be worn on special occasions, though some pieces are casual enough for everyday use. Her flagship store in Ponsonby is especially worth visiting during sale periods, and her designs are stocked by a scattering of stores nationwide, including Unity at 101 Customhouse Quay, Wellington (04 471 1008) and Aria, 182 High St, Christchurch (03 377 1222).

420b New North Rd
Kingsland
Auckland
Map p.490 C4 28

Jane Rhodes

09 846 5661 | *www.janerhodes.co.nz*

Jane Rhodes calls her style 'hip glamour' and says her favourite fabrics are wool and silk. Indeed, it's a good place to look for women's clothing for special occasions, including wedding dresses and bridesmaids' outfits, which the store will make to measure. But there's also plenty of casual separates suitable for the office, and the odd beautifully tailored suit. As well as her own Kingsland store, Rhodes' designs are stocked by about a dozen other stores nationwide, including Hamilton & Murray in Wellington (corner Grey and Featherston streets, 04 472 8872) and Flame in Christchurch (89A Cashel St Mall, 03 374 6990).

6 Balm St
Newmarket
Auckland
Map p.492 C3 29

Karen Walker

09 522 4286 | *www.karenwalker.co.nz*

Karen Walker is probably the most visible presence worldwide in New Zealand designer fashion and specialises in funky outfits, glasses and jewellery for the ultra-hip (and fairly wealthy) young woman about town. She's also done a line of outdoor clothing for Swanndri and even a line of paint colours for Resene. She has another store at 15 O'Connell St, Auckland Central (09 309 6299) and her Wellington store is at 126 Wakefield St (04 499 3558). Her designs are stocked by dozens of other stores nationwide, including Ballantynes in Christchurch (p.419).

47 High St
Newmarket
Auckland
Map p.488 A3 30

Kate Sylvester

09 307 3282 | *www.katesylvester.com*

Kate Sylvester's clothing has an urban, modernist touch. The emphasis is on funky streetwear, though you'll find plenty of dresses for the office among the hoodies, T-shirts and mini-skirts. She has launched a second line called Sylvester, targeted at the younger market, which she describes as Kate Sylvester's 'naughty little sister'. Her other Auckland stores is at 1 Teed St, Newmarket (09 524 8872) and her Wellington store is at 32 Cuba St (04 473 0943). Sylvester's designs are also stocked at more than a dozen outlets nationwide, including Plume at 146 High St, Christchurch (03 366 1663).

Various Locations

Keith Matheson

09 358 0090 | *www.keithmatheson.co.nz*

This is grown-up designer clothing, with a European flavour, for men and women. The emphasis is on sophisticated clean lines and casual chic. This is the place to go if you want to be the best-dressed person in the office. The brand's Auckland stores are at 277 Broadway, Newmarket (09 529 2249), and 41 High St, Auckland Central (09 379 7919); in Wellington at the corner of Lambton Quay and Hunter St (04 499 3944); and in Christchurch at 99 Cashel Mall (03 377 2913).

9 Maidstone St
Ponsonby
Auckland
Map p.491 D1 32

Liz Mitchell

09 360 5047 | *www.lizmitchell.co.nz*

Liz Mitchell's name is most readily associated with a glamorous night out. She offers bridal design and couture as well as a ready-to-wear collection, all for women. There's also a women's corporate clothing label, Tailormade, a more casual Liz Mitchell Essentials range of knitwear and a range of cheaper clothing, Mitchell by Liz Mitchell, available at larger Farmers department stores. Tailormade is also available at Hamilton & Murray in Wellington (corner Grey and Featherston streets, 04 472 8872).

Various Locations

Moochi

07 575 5235 | *www.moochi.co.nz*

Moochi is a fairly new entrant, selling mostly simple but funky casual pieces. The name reflects the company's tenet of 'mooching in style'. Prices are usually a bit more reasonable than most designers, with some good bargains available at sale times, but it's still not a place for the thrifty. It has two stores in Auckland (14 Vulcan Lane, Auckland Central, 09 373 9823, and 246 Broadway, Newmarket, 09 523 4640) and one each in Wellington (111 Custom House Quay, 04 499 3789), Hamilton (25 Ward St, 07 838 0103) and Tauranga (21 Devonport Rd, 07 571 1300).

Various Locations

NOM*D

03 477 7490 | *www.nomd.co.nz*

The leading label NOM*D boasts that it's unaffected by fashion whims and trends, though you'll usually see a hint of the season's wider fashions reflected in the designs (such as patterned tights in 2007). The emphasis is on moody and grungy casual designs for the young and cool of both genders. It doesn't have stores of its own but is stocked in more than a dozen stores nationwide, including Zambesi (p.383) in Auckland and Wellington and Plume at 146 High St, Christchurch (03 366 1663).

Various Locations

Ricochet

09 302 0196 | *www.ricochet.co.nz*

Far cheaper than the other designer stores – especially at sale time – Ricochet is immensely popular with stylish young urban women. It has an accessible collection of knitwear, tailored trousers, jeans and interesting tops, skirts and dresses. It's mostly casual wear but you can also get some good staple pieces for the office or something a bit more glam for a night out. It has two stores in Auckland (35 High St, Auckland Central, 09 379 8558 and 6 Remuera Rd, Newmarket, 09 529 2563) and one each in Wellington (Old Bank Arcade, 233 Lambton Quay, 04 473 7433) and Christchurch (154 High St, 03 377 1643).

536 Parnell Rd
Ponsonby
Auckland
Map p.493 D2 36

Trelise Cooper

09 366 1962 | *www.trelisecooper.co.nz*

Trelise Cooper has a reputation for pretty, feminine clothing – a relatively rare thing in the often fairly dark world of New Zealand fashion – and her designs are often a bit floaty and idiosyncratic. She says the staff at her Newmarket headquarters start the day with a ritual of candle and incense lighting and five minutes of 'beautiful music and uplifting readings'. Cooper's other store in Auckland is at Princes Wharf, Quay St (09 366 1964), and a spin-off children's clothing store, Trelise Cooper Kids, in Nuffield St, Newmarket, Auckland (09 984 6301).

High-end labels

Heels aplenty

Various Locations

Workshop Denim and Helen Cherry

09 303 9290 | *www.workshop.co.nz*

Workshop's staple offering of jeans are a bit of a legend in certain circles in New Zealand. There's no great secret: they'll just well-fitting and fashionable and come in extra-long varieties, which can be hard to find in New Zealand. As well as jeans, Workshop sells cool casual wear while the designs of its partner brand Helen Cherry tend to be a bit more glam. It has two stores in Auckland (corner Vulcan Lane and High St, Auckland Central, 09 303 3735, and 18 Morrow St, Newmarket, 09 524 6844), one in Wellington (corner Customhouse Quay and Hunter St, 04 499 9010) and one in Christchurch (230 Tuam St, 03 379 7305). There are also other stockists nationwide.

Various Locations

World

09 373 3034 | *www.worldbrand.co.nz*

World is one of the leading innovators in New Zealand fashion: this is clothing to wear if you want to be known for a casual but funky and sometimes eccentric style. The emphasis is on the fun, with slogan T-shirts, wry retro throwbacks and splashes of colour. Most of the designs are casual but you'll find some more glamorous offerings. It has three Auckland stores (57 High St, Auckland Central, 09 373 3034, 175 Ponsonby Rd, Ponsonby, 09 360 4544, a menswear store at 47 High St, Auckland Central, 09 377 8331) and a Wellington store (98 Victoria St, 04 472 1595). Stockists nationwide include Honour and Obey in Christchurch (80 Lichfield St, 03 377 6131).

24 Jervois Rd
Ponsonby
Auckland
Map p.486 C2 39

Yvonne Bennetti

09 361 2388 | *www.yvonnebennetti.com*

This is a good place to go to find a dress for a special occasion. Yvonne Bennetti has a large range of women's evening wear as well as more casual offerings. She also stocks a range of shoes but don't expect to find a pair of black loafers; these have more glamorous ambitions. As well as her flagship Ponsonby store, designs are available through stockists nationwide, including Kirkcaldie & Stains (165-177 Lambton Quay, Wellington, 04 472 5899) and Flame in Christchurch (89A Cashel St Mall, 03 374 6990).

Cnr Vulcan La
& O'Connell St
Auckland
Map p.488 A2 40

Zambesi

09 308 0360 | *www.zambesi.co.nz*

One of New Zealand's leading design houses, edgy Zambesi describes itself as 'synonymous with emotional resonance and brooding sensibility'. That usually means a lot of cool, dark clothing. The designs are mostly casual, both men's and women's, with a few dressier pieces on the hangers. It has three Auckland stores (corner Vulcan Lane and O'Connell St, Auckland Central, 09 303 1701; 169 Ponsonby Rd, Ponsonby, 09 360 7391; 2 Teed St, Newmarket, 09 523 1000) and one at 107 Customhouse Quay, Wellington, 04 472 3638. There are about a dozen stockists nationwide, including Plume in Christchurch (146 High St, 03 366 1663).

Computers

Other options **Electronics & Home Appliances** p.384

With nearly three-quarters of New Zealand households owning a computer, New Zealand's computer market is competitive, as it is for all electronic equipment. Fierce rivalry between the suppliers and New Zealand's relatively high dollar of late mean that prices are internationally competitive. All the big international brands are represented, including Apple (try online store Mac Warehouse, www.mac warehouse.co.nz) and it's usually straightforward to get computers repaired.

The biggest computer and technology chain is Dick Smith Electronics (09 414 2800, www.dse.co.nz). The large general electronics chains also sell computers: Harvey Norman (0800 422 423, www.harveynorman.co.nz), Betta Electrical (09 444 0720, www.bettaelectrical.co.nz), Bond & Bond (0800 202 066, www.bondandbond.co.nz), 100% Your Electronics Store (0800 107 090, www.100yes.co.nz) and Noel Leeming (0800 444 488, www.noelleeming.co.nz). The bigger chains often have the best deals and the biggest sales – and you may talk your way into a discount. But it's worth checking out the smaller dealers who might work out of a tiny shop in an obscure suburb with low overheads and do a lot of their trading online. Often these guys will know more about their products than sales people in the more general stores. Check out Computer Lounge (09 368 4818, www.computerlounge.co.nz), Ascent (04 802 3898, www.ascent.co.nz), Supercheap Computers (09 358 0404, www.super cheappc.co.nz) and Software Shop (09 577 3010, www.softwareshop.co.nz). To find the best deals, keep an eye on the electronics price comparison website www.pricespy.co.nz and read *PC World* magazine (09 375 6005, www.pcworld.co.nz). If you hold out on buying the latest computer for six months or more the price usually plummets. You can generally buy one to three-year international warranties or sometimes these will come free with the computer.

Electronics & Home Appliances

Other options **Computers** p.383, **Camera Equipment** p.374, **Mobile Phones** p.394

New Zealanders love buying home appliances, large and small, and there's an international brand available to suit every budget, from the most exclusive Italian imports and the innovative products of local company Fisher & Paykel (09 273 0656) to cheap imports by Chinese companies such as Haier. You can spend as much or as little as you like but you might have to expand your kitchen to fit everything in. When it comes to outfitting the lounge, the same rules apply – buy a 14 inch box television for $180 or a 65 inch plasma for $18,000. Cut-price televisions, DVD players and the like are even sold in larger supermarkets, so you can throw one in next to the veggies. Smaller electronics – MP3 players, mobile phones, gaming devices – are just as popular and just as competitive. They're sold at all the main chain stores listed but it's also worth checking out the smaller technology stores – have a look on www.pricespy.co.nz.

The big players in electronics and home appliances are almost identical in price and selection (in fact Bond & Bond and Noel Leeming are owned by the same company) and you can be pretty much guaranteed that the product you're after will be on sale at one of them at any particular time so always shop around. The 100% Your Electronics Store specialises in Fisher & Paykel products, although it also carries other brands. There are also a few cut-price appliance stores, selling seconds and end-of-line products. Find one near you by searching

Electronics & Home Appliances		
100% Your Electronics Store	0800 107 090	www.100yes.co.nz
Betta Electrical	09 444 0720	www.bettaelectrical.co.nz
Bond & Bond	0800 202 066	www.bondandbond.co.nz
Briscoes	0800 274 726	www.briscoes.co.nz
Bunnings Warehouse	09 978 2200	www.bunnings.co.nz
Dick Smith Electronics	09 414 2800	www.dse.co.nz
Farmers	09 272 6996	www.farmers.co.nz
Harvey Norman	0800 422 423	www.harveynorman.co.nz
Hill & Stewart	0800 221 144	www.hillandstewart.co.nz
Kitchen House	0800 288 288	www.kitchenhouse.co.nz
Kitchen Studio	0800 177 177	www.kitchenstudio.co.nz
Kitchen'Things	0800 574 222	www.kitchenthings.co.nz
Kmart	09 279 4409	www.kmart.co.nz
Mitre 10	0800 4648 7310	www.mitre10.co.nz
Noel Leeming	0800 444 488	www.noelleeming.co.nz
PlaceMakers	09 525 5100	www.placemakers.co.nz
Retravision	0800 473 8728	www.retravision.co.nz
Smiths City	03 983 3000	www.smithscity.co.nz
The Warehouse	09 489 7000	www.thewarehouse.co.nz

on www.bargainshopping.co.nz or www.factoryshops.co.nz. The Warehouse and Kmart carry limited ranges of cheap appliances.

For home appliance rentals, look up DTR (0800 734 735, www.dtr.co.nz) or Mr Rentals (09 579 8122, www.mrrental.co.nz). For second-hand appliances, try the auction website TradeMe (www.trademe.co.nz) or the chain Cash Converters (04 570 3111, www.cashconverters.co.nz).

Home appliances bought in New Zealand can be used in most other countries with the right power plug converter (New Zealand and Australia share the same power points) but you might have trouble in the United States, with its different voltage.

Eyewear

Other options **Sports Goods** p.402

Supplying glasses was once the job of independent optometrists and while there are still plenty around, it's becoming more usual to go to a chain store in a shopping mall to get your eyes tested and glasses made. The biggest players are OPSM (0800 696 776, www.opsm.co.nz) and Visique (0800 847 478, www.visique.co.nz). They have the advantage of being able to stock a good range of frames, including top international brands, at competitive prices. To find an independent optometrist, try the New Zealand Association of Optometrists (0800 439 322, www.nzao.co.nz), or look in your *Yellow Pages* or www.yellowpages.co.nz. Dispensing opticians can make and fit glasses but they don't do eye tests – so few work without an optometrist.

Because optometrists can make a good profit from selling brand-name frames, eye tests are often thrown in for free. Many offer cheap package deals, which include an eye test, a frame, lenses and assembly, but they often don't include a big selection of frames and you'll be tempted to pay more for a better frame, as well as extras like scratch-resistance, anti-reflection coatings or tinted lenses. Most glasses come with one or two-year guarantees. Contact lenses are available from all optometrists – some offer packages for glasses and contacts.

Expect to pay $40 to $80 for an eye check. Frames can cost anywhere from about $40 to several hundred dollars, depending on the brand. Cheap, off-the-shelf glasses are available at chemists, if you have a simple short-sightedness problem.

You can buy prescription or plain glass sunglasses from opticians or optometrists, but you'll often find better non-prescription deals elsewhere. The biggest chain is the mall-dwelling Sunglass Hut (0800 607 895, www.sunglasshut.co.nz). Clothing and surf shops also stock sunglasses, from cheap plastic numbers to expensive brands. Many New Zealanders buy big-name sunglasses duty free or on trips overseas.

Flowers

Other options **Gardens** p.388

New Zealand florists are usually small independents that belong to national or international networks so they can take orders from around the world. Internet-based flower suppliers are becoming big business and many small florists supplement their income with a small online operation. It's handy to check their styles on their websites, as some are still stuck in the past, favouring carnations, gaudy wrappings and loads of gypsophila (better known as baby's breath). Be sure to specify what style of arrangement you want – whether a colourful, modern style for a young mum or a traditional bouquet for your grandmother. Most flowers are available year-round, thanks to the hydroponics industry, but are often cheaper in season. Roses are at a premium around Valentine's Day – not surprisingly, it pays to order well before 14 February. Many petrol stations, supermarkets and plenty of diaries also sell flowers, usually simply packaged and aimed at people shopping for displays in their own homes. To find a florist, look in your local *Yellow Pages* or on www.yellowpages.co.nz, do a web search, or try one of the recommended companies/networks listed here. All offer national deliveries. Inteflora (www.interflora.co.nz) and Teleflora (www.teleflora.co.nz) offer international deliveries.

Flowers

Auckland	Address	Phone	Website
All Seasons Flowers	na	0800 000 080	www.allseasons.co.nz
Bunches	89B Great South Road	0800 505 060	www.bunchesflowers.co.nz
Citywide Florist	Cnr Chancery Lane and Gloucester Street	0800 379 1234	www.citywideflorist.co.nz
Expressions Florist	53 Boulcott Street	0800 367 356	www.expressionsflorist.co.nz
Flowers After Hours	523 Parnell Road	09 303 1038	na
Flowers on Featherston	142 Featherston Street	0800 330 007	na
Interflora	na	0800 808 880	www.interflora.co.nz
Moss	2-10 Nuffield Street	09 523 3310	na
Ready Flowers	na	0800 333 216	www.readyflowers.co.nz
Roses Florist	437 Mount Eden Road	09 630 5369	na
Roses Only	na	0800 908 890	www.rosesonly.co.nz
Send-A-Basket	na	09 622 3555	www.sendabasket.co.nz
Teleflora	na	0800 909 090	www.teleflora.co.nz
The Flower Room	4A Birmingham Drive, Middleton	0800 842 547	www.flowerroom.co.nz
The Wild Bunch	419 Remuera Road	09 529 9547	na
Toi Toi Floral Boutique	214 Jervois Road	09 376 5139	www.toitoi.co.nz
Wild Poppies	3 College Hill	0800 809 453	www.wildpoppies.co.nz
Wellington			
Annabel's for Flowers	53 Boulcott Street	04 472 8124	www.annabels-flowers.co.nz
Black Rose Florist	4 Titahi Bay Road, Porirua	04 237 0585	na
Bunches Floriste	256-262 Lambton Quay	04 473 8813	www.bunches.co.nz
Flowers Rediscovered	289 Tinakori Road	04 471 1021	www.flowersrediscovered.co.nz
Genevieve Flowers	Upper Plimmer Steps, Lambton Quay	04 473 7442	na
WildFlower Florists	80 Mercer Street	04 472 6446	www.wildflowerflorist.co.nz
Christchurch			
Absolutely Flowers	97 Main North Road, Papanui	03 352 6661	na
Andrea's Florist	Avonhead Centre, Withells Rd, Avonhead	03 358 9458	www.andreasflorist.co.nz
Harakeke	16 Poplar Street	03 366 9545	na
Hornby Florist	Hornby Mall, Hornby	03 349 5351	www.hornbyflorist.co.nz
In Water Flower Design Store	Guthrey Centre, City Mall	03 379 3292	na
Julia Gray Florist	154 Hereford Street	03 366 1921	www.juliagray.co.nz
Victoria Florists	107 Idris Road	03 351 7444	www.victoriaflowers.co.nz

Food

Until a few decades ago New Zealanders were known for their stodgy diets of 'meat and two veg' – a serving of red meat, potatoes and an over-boiled green vegetable each night, influenced by their UK roots. Though you'll still find older and rural New Zealanders sitting down to these sorts of meals every night, the large majority have embraced flavours from around the world – Italian, Asian, Spanish, French… Kiwis like to credit themselves with being one of the pioneers of the fusion food movement, mixing in flavours from around the world. An influx of Asian immigrants has led to the easy availability of a wide variety of foods such as noodles, shitake mushrooms and bok choi, especially in the main cities. New Zealand grows many of its own fruit and vegetables, supplemented by more tropical fruits, including bananas and oranges, mostly from Australia, the United States and South America.

Sweets for sale

Fruit & Vegetable Shops

There are plenty of fruit and vegetable speciality shops, especially in larger centres, and prices are often – but not always – lower. If you're passing a small orchard, it's worth popping in and buying straight from the grower – though it's always suspicious if they stock bananas, which don't grow in New Zealand. Fruit World (09 274 0876, www.fruitworld.co.nz) and Orchard & Fields (Auckland only, 09 416 4122) are the biggest chains.

Butcheries

The meat industry has largely been swallowed up (so to speak) by the big supermarkets but it's always worth checking out your local store – if you still have one. Some are gems. The two big chains are The Mad Butcher (09 267 4185, www.madbutcher.co.nz) and Aussie Butcher (North Island only, 09 520 4035).

Bakeries

The biggest bakery chain in New Zealand is Bakers Delight (0800 443 336, www.bakersdelight.co.nz), followed by Brumby's Bakeries (09 522 0062, www.brumbys.com.au). There are also a few mostly mall-dwelling chains, including Michel's Patisserie (09 270 0201, www.michelspatisserie.co.nz) and Muffin Break (09 377 1901, www.muffinbreak.co.nz), but most neighbourhood bakeries are in the hands of independent owners, often Asian immigrants. Among the best high-end bakeries is Pandoro Panetteria (09 621 0088), with stores in Auckland and Wellington. The Baking Industry Association names New Zealand's top bakeries each year, see www.bianz.co.nz.

Speciality Foodmarkets

There are some great speciality food markets in the bigger centres. Farmers' markets selling regional produce are beginning to catch on in the rural areas, as well as the cities. To find a farmers' market in your area, go to www.farmersmarket.org.nz. A list of some of the best delicatessens and speciality foodmarkets in the main centres can be found on p.388. You'll find more under Delicatessens and Gourmet Foods in your *Yellow Pages* or www.yellowpages.co.nz.

Supermarkets

Most New Zealanders stock their pantries almost solely from the large supermarket chains. They buy their meat, fish, fruit and vegetables, dairy, baking, ambient products and even beer and wine, though some hold out against these giants and prefer to patronise their local butcheries, fish shops, delicatessens and fruit and vegetable shops. Asian supermarkets, stocking mostly imported ambient foods and a mixture of imported and local fruit and vegetables, are becoming more prevalent in areas with high Asian immigrant populations, particularly in Auckland. Bigger supermarkets have a wide variety of exotic supplies, though you might have trouble tracking down bok choi in a small town. You'll still have to go to a deli to find some of the more obscure ingredients.

Supermarkets		
Countdown Foodmarkets	0800 404 040	www.countdown.co.nz
Foodtown Supermarkets	0800 404 040	www.foodtown.co.nz
New World Supermarkets	04 527 2510	www.newworld.co.nz
Pak 'n Save Food Warehouses	09 621 0600	www.paknsave.co.nz
Warehouse Extra	09 489 7000	www.thewarehouse.co.nz
Woolworths Supermarkets	0800 404 040	www.woolworths.co.nz

Delis & Speciality Food Shops

Auckland			
Auckland Fish Market Seafood School	22-32 Jellicoe St, Freemans Bay	09 379 1497	www.afm.co.nz
Dida's Food Store	54 Jervois Road	09 361 6157	na
Jones the Grocer	1/143 Carlton Gore Road	09 522 9161	www.jonesthegrocer.com
La Bella Italia	10 Nevis Street	09 566 9303	www.labellaitalia.co.nz
Nosh Food Market	133-135 Apirana Avenue	09 521 1115	www.noshgourmet.com
The Fridge	507 New North Road	09 845 5321	na
The Italian Grocer	54 Ponsonby Road	09 360 2842	na
Zarbo Delicatessen & Café	24 Morrow Street	09 520 2721	www.zarbo.co.nz
Wellington			
Commonsense Organics	na	04 384 3314	www.commonsenseorganics.co.nz
Dixon Street Delicatessen	45-47 Dixon Street	04 384 2436	na
Meat on Tory	5 Lower Tory Street	04 801 6328	www.meatontory.co.nz
Mediterranean Food Warehouse	42 Constable Street	04 939 8105	www.medifoods.co.nz
The Dutch Shop	89 Jackson Street	04 568 9338	www.dutch.co.nz
Wellington Trawling Sea Market	220 Cuba Street	04 384 8461	na
Christchurch			
Copenhagen Bakery	119 Armagh Street	03 379 3935	www.copenhagenbakery.co.nz
Johnsons Grocery	797 Colombo Street	03 366 3027	na
Kapiti Fine Foods	12 Moorhouse Street	03 377 7077	www.kff.co.nz
Temptationz Classic Gourmet Foods	Shop 7, 101 Main North Road	03 354 9640	na

The five biggest supermarket chains in New Zealand are divided between two owners – Woolworths operates Woolworths, Foodtown and Countdown and Foodstuffs owns New World and Pak 'n Save. Cut-price department store The Warehouse is branching out into supermarkets, with stores in Auckland and Whangarei and another planned for Hamilton. Foodtown and Woolworths offer online shopping, at the sites listed. The Consumer's Institute (www.consumer.org.nz) carries out regular price surveys and Pak 'n Save (where checkout bags are not provided) consistently comes out cheapest. In the latest survey the Auckland supermarkets results, in order from cheapest to most expensive, were: Pak 'n Save, Countdown, Foodtown, New World, Warehouse Extra, Woolworths. The larger Foodtown, New World and Woolworths stores tend to have the biggest selections of food, including organic food. Supermarket ready meals aren't nearly as good as those in other developed countries, especially the UK.

Gardens

Other options **Flowers** p.385, **Hardware & DIY** p.389

Gardens

Kings Plant Barn	09 410 9726	www.kings.co.nz
Mitre 10	09 443 9900	www.mitre10.co.nz
Palmers Gardenworld	0800 PALMERS	www.palmers.co.nz
PlaceMakers	09 525 5100	www.placemakers.co.nz
The Warehouse	09489 7000	www.thewarehouse.co.nz

Gardening is said to be the most popular hobby in New Zealand – visit any garden centre on a sunny weekend and you'll believe it. In Auckland, gardening is dominated by a few specialist chains, with major hardware stores and The Warehouse also getting in on the action – though some of its smaller outlets don't stock plants. All sell the same array of products – plants, pots and other accessories – though hardware stores usually stock gardening tools and general furniture stores are the places for outdoor furniture. Outside Auckland, you're more likely to end up shopping at an independent store. Staff at specialist stores offer expert knowledge but you can also pick up basic garden maintenance products at most supermarkets.

Not surprisingly, New Zealand's hardy native plants are popular, but you'll easily find the components for a tropical or cottage garden – however, tropical plants are more successful in the warmer north. It's worth seeking out specialist nurseries in your area as they are usually cheaper than garden centres, especially if you're buying in bulk. Many operate mail-order or online stores. Look up Garden Centres & Nurseries in your *Yellow Pages* or see www.yellowpages.co.nz. The main chains are listed below. For smaller centres see www.garden-nz.co.nz or browse www.gardens.co.nz for nurseries offering mail-order services.

Hardware & DIY

Other options **Outdoor Goods** p.389

Most retail sectors in New Zealand are dominated by big chains – hardware especially so. The big players (listed below) are getting bigger by the year, both in terms of the number of their outlets and their size – and are very competitive. There are few independent general hardware stores. Painting and decorating stores are similarly dominated by big names (and the big hardware stores stock painting and decorating supplies) but there are still many smaller retailers around.

Usually, staff are formidably knowledgeable and many of the bigger stores host workshops. DIY is a hugely popular activity in New Zealand and you'll find shops dedicated to every facet of it – from Knobs 'n Knockers, with four stores in Auckland (0800 652 156, www.knobsnknockers.co.nz), to Well Hung Joinery in Wellington (04 494 7230, www.wellhungjoinery.co.nz) – as well as super stores that stock everything. The cheapest, most readily available – and least glamorous – wood for DIY projects is pine.

Hardware & DIY		
Benjamin Moore Paints	0800 236 666	www.benjaminmoore.com
Bunnings	09 978 2200	www.bunnings.co.nz
Carters	09 272 7200	www.carters.co.nz
Colourplus	0800 733 030	www.colourplus.co.nz
Guthrie Bowron	04 569 8130	www.guthriebowron.co.nz
Hammer Hardware	09 443 9953	www.hammerhardware.co.nz
ITM Building Centre	0800 367 486	www.itm.co.nz
Mitre 10	0800 4648 7310	www.mitre10.co.nz
PlaceMakers	09 525 5100	www.placemakers.co.nz
Resene ColorShops	0800 RE SENE	www.resene.co.nz

Home Furnishings & Accessories

Other options **Hardware & DIY** p.389

There's a gap in the market in New Zealand for an affordable innovative design store such as the international hit IKEA, but the country struggles on gamely with some expensive designer furniture and furnishings – local and imported – available at boutique design stores and plenty of solid (and not-so-solid) offerings at the middle to lower end of the market. Plain old pine is the wood of choice for decent budget furniture, with imported woods usually more expensive. Most of the time the quality of the materials and workmanship improves with price – but not always. Sometimes you can find comparable furniture for widely varying prices. Native timbers – kauri, rimu, matai – are becoming less common but you'll often see 'recycled' native timbers used. Sleepyhead is a popular New Zealand bed manufacturer.

Home Furnishings & Accessories

Auckland		
Bedpost	09 278 1010	www.bedpost.co.nz
Briscoes	0800 274 726	www.briscoes.co.nz
Country Theme	09 522 2626	www.countrytheme.co.nz
Creative Curtains	09 478 9945	www.creativecurtains.co.nz
Curtain Supermarket	0800 287 8246	www.curtainsupermarket.co.nz
Early Settler	09 376 5058	www.earlysettler.co.nz
Farmers	09 272 6996	www.farmers.co.nz
Forhomes Furniture and Beds	09 374 6363	na
Freedom Furniture	0800 373 336	www.freedomfurniture.co.nz
Harvey Furnishings	0800 238 764	www.harveyfurnishings.co.nz
Harvey Norman	0800 422 423	www.harveynorman.co.nz
King Kong Furnishings	09 270 0500	na
McKenzie & Willis	0800 888 999	www.mckenzieandwillis.co.nz
Redpaths Furniture	0800 387 648	na
Spotlight	0800 276 222	www.spotlight.co.nz
Target Furniture	09 623 2910	www.targetfurniture.co.nz
The Warehouse	09 489 7000	www.thewarehouse.co.nz
Wellington		
Beds 'R' Us	04 473 5505	www.bedsrus.co.nz
Big Save Furniture	04 298 4700	www.bigsave.co.nz
Guthrie Bowron	04 569 8130	www.guthriebowron.co.nz

Home furnishing stores usually carry a broad range of designs, though upmarket ones specialise in the more luxurious, expensive ranges. You can spend less than $100 or many thousands on a curtain, a carpet or rug. It's wise to set your budget before you go looking. At the top end of the furniture market are dozens of boutique design stores, featuring local and imported furniture and pieces – in Auckland try Eon Design Centre (09 368 4860, www.eon.co.nz, 20 Beaumont Street, Freemans Bay) or Uno Design (35d Surrey Crescent, Grey Lynn) in Wellington, the cheaper Inhabit Design Store (04 384 5532, www.inhabit.co.nz, 23 Adelaide Road) and in Christchurch Kovacs Design Furniture (03 384 2999, www.kovacs.co.nz, 1000 Ferry Road). These types of stores will often offer interior design services. At the lower end are outlets brimming with (usually) imported mass-produced basics – Target Furniture (in Auckland and Christchurch) is particularly good for a range of styles at affordable prices. For accessories try The Warehouse, which has some ultra-cheap gems among many eyesores, and Briscoes.

Middle market retailers such as Farmers and Harvey Norman have moderately expensive but not very modern ranges, or there's the hipper Freedom Furniture and colonial-inspired Early Settler. The main chains are listed here.

Antiques are popular and mostly the domain of small, independents – look up 'antique dealers' in your local *Yellow Pages* or on www.yellowpages.co.nz. As with most second-

Second-hand furniture

hand goods in New Zealand, the best place for second-hand furniture is the auction website TradeMe (www.trademe.co.nz) though second-hand dealers are also an option. For inspiration and discounts on furniture, furnishings and other goods, brave your nearest home show exhibition. The hectic Auckland Home Show, usually held in September at the ASB Showgrounds in Greenlane, is the biggest. For other centres, see www.homeshows.co.nz.

Jewellery, Watches & Gold

You'll often see locals and tourists sporting intricately carved pendants of jade (called pounamu or greenstone). This is a sacred Maori tradition, though anyone can wear one, and they're traditionally given as gifts rather than bought for yourself. Unfortunately, some of the greenstone jewellery in souvenir shops is just imported cheap copies, so it's best to ask some pointed questions. Anything with the trademark toi iho is fine – it indicates it's an authentic Maori craft, although not all authentic greenstone carries the trademark. Bone carvings are another traditional Maori adornment and paua shell jewellery is also popular. You'll find good offerings at markets.

When it comes to precious stones and gold, there are a few big chain stores (listed below) selling moderately priced jewellery as well as more expensive options. The department store Farmers has an in-store specialist, Prouds Jewellery. But if you're after something special, pop into your local independent jeweller for a chat – they should be able to make something to order for a competitive price. Find one on www.jwnz.co.nz, the website of the Jewellers & Watchmakers of New Zealand. If you're planning an overseas trip, they may be able to sell it to you duty free (you'll collect it from the airport), which can make a big difference to the price. Many jewellers will clean your jewellery for free.

The website www.diamonds.co.nz is a good introduction to the local market. Exclusive overseas brands of the likes of Tiffany and Cartier can be hard to find – try DFS Galleria Customhouse in Auckland (www.dfsgalleria.com, 09 308 0700, corner Custom and Albert streets).

Watches are sold at jewellers, department stores and clothing shops, but if you're buying a major international brand it can pay to wait until you're going overseas and get it duty free.

As cheap costume jewellery goes, women's clothing stores usually stock plenty and there are a few chain stores specialising in costume jewellery – Diva, Equip and Kleins.

Jewellery, Watches & Gold			
Auckland			
Diva	Various Locations	0800 348 269	www.diva.net.au
Equip	Various Locations	na	www.equipyourself.com.au
Fingers	2 Kitchener St, Auckland CBD	09 373 3974	www.fingers.co.nz
Kleins	Various Locations	na	www.kleins.com.au
Michael Hill Jeweller	Various Locations	0800 101 110	www.michaelhill.co.nz
Pascoes The Jewellers	Various Locations	09 377 8351	www.pascoes.co.nz
Stewart Dawsons Jewellery	Various Locations	09 373 2640	www.stewartdawsons.co.nz
Sutcliffe Jewellery	203 Parnell Road	09 309 0127	www.sutcliffejewellery.com
Walker and Hall	Various Locations	09 379 6200	www.walkerandhall.co.nz
Wellington			
Quoil Contemporary Jewellery	149 Willis Street	04 384 1499	www.quoil.co.nz
The Vault Design Store	50 Willis Street	04 471 1404	www.vault-designstore.co.nz
Christchurch			
Form Gallery	Christchurch Art Gallery	03 377 1211	www.form.co.nz
Marocka	His Lordship's Lane, 110 Lichfield Street	03 377 8110	www.marockachch.co.nz
Various Locations			
Prouds the Jewellers	na	09 486 2004	www.prouds.com.au

Sterling silver and cubic zirconia is about as sophisticated as it gets. You'll also find bead shops where you can make your own jewellery from a huge selection of beads and other adornments. Look out for hip New Zealand-made jewellery, using precious stones and cheaper materials.

Leather belts for sale

Lingerie

Other options **Clothes** p.375

A few chain stores specialise in lingerie, but it's largely the domain of independent boutiques, some of them musty, crowded places with names such as Edna's Underwear. They generally stock the same big brands: Bendon, Triumph, Playtex. As well as its own chain, Bendon (an established local company) has several good factory outlets scattered across New Zealand. The department stores Farmers (09 272 6996, www.farmers.co.nz), The Warehouse (09 489 7000, www.thewarehouse.co.nz) and Kmart (09 279 4409, www.kmart.co.nz) stock lingerie. Farmers has the biggest and best-quality selection. More sophisticated department stores such as Smith & Caughey in Auckland (09 377 4770, www.smithandcaughey.co.nz), Kirkcaldie & Stains in Wellington (04 472 5899, www.kirkcaldies.co.nz) and Ballantynes in Christchurch (0800 184 000, www.ballantynes.com) have good ranges. The main specialist chains are listed above.

Lingerie		
Bendon	0800 236 366	www.bendon.co.nz
Bras N Things	09 845 4030	www.bnt.com.au
The Pyjama Co	09 520 5282	www.pyjamacompany.co.nz

Luggage & Leather

Other options **Shipping** p.367

There's one dominant luggage retailer in New Zealand: Australian chain Strandbags, with 21 stores nationwide (www.strandbags.com.au). It sells cheap and moderately priced luggage, wallets, purses, briefcases and so on. As well as other bargain outlets, you could try the department stores Farmers (09 272 6996, www.farmers.co.nz), The

Luggage & Leather			
Auckland			
AK Leather Fashions	Victoria Park Market, 210 Victoria St West	09 309 2909	na
Leather Direct (Christchurch)	Cnr of Colombo St and Tuam Street	0800 392 627	www.leatherdirect.co.nz
Leather Image	34 Fitzgerald Avenue	0800 894 242	www.leatherimage.co.nz
Possum New Zealand	na	09 302 0577	www.possumnz.co.nz
Wellington			
Konev Leather	98 Main Road	04 232 6464	www.konevleather.co.nz
Leather Direct (Wellington)	105 Cuba Street	04 385 8888	www.leatherdirect.co.nz
Christchurch			
Arts Centre Leather Shop	28 Worcester Street	03 366 1143	www.leathershop.co.nz
Canterbury Leather International	na	03 352 4382	www.cantyleather.co.nz
Downunder International	24 Buchan Street	03 377 1966	www.duinternational.co.nz
Florian Leathergoods	202 Madras Street	03 366 7176	na
Lapco	93-97 Clarence Street	03 343 3892	www.lapco.co.nz

Warehouse (09 489 7000, www.thewarehouse.co.nz) and Kmart (09 279 4409, www.kmart.co.nz). Luxury luggage is stocked by upmarket department stores Smith & Caughey in Auckland (03 377 4770, www.smithandcaughey.co.nz), Kirkcaldie & Stains in Wellington (04 472 5899, www.kirkcaldies.co.nz) and Ballantynes in Christchurch (0800 184 000, www.ballantynes.com). Coast New Zealand is a local brand of upmarket canvas bags (0800 454 545, www.coast.co.nz), while Konev makes luxury leather luggage.

Young New Zealanders and tourists tend to prefer backpacks to suitcases and you'll find plenty for sale in NZ. The local outdoor goods manufacturer Macpac (03 338 1106, www.macpac.co.nz) is a world leader and you can buy its products at any outdoors specialist. Alternatively, try one of Kathmandu's 23 outlets (03 373 6110, www.kathmandu.co.nz).

New Zealand has a flourishing niche leathergoods industry, especially strong in the South Island, which uses leathers and skins from cattle, sheep, goats and possums (regarded as a pest). Be warned, a lot of what passes for trendy wear is far from fashionable – some leather manufacturers are blithely stuck in the 1980s and many sheepskin goods manufactured for the tourist market are dated. Long sheepskin boots called ugg boots have been a staple of heat-seeking New Zealanders for decades – and they surprised everyone by becoming an international fashion trend a few years ago. A selection of leathergoods suppliers are listed here – some make to measure. Leather furniture is sold in the more upmarket furniture stores and is usually moderately expensive.

Medicine

Other options **General Medical Care** p.161

Pharmacies are usually fairly easy to find in New Zealand – they're even located in tiny neighbourhood shopping strips. Since the industry was deregulated in 2004 four chains have come to dominate: Life Pharmacy, Amcal, Unichem and Radius Pharmacy, most of which sell online. Smart Pharmacy, a new entrant, is promising to open up to 100 outlets. It's rare to find an independent pharmacy. Pharmacists are university qualified.

Drugs fall into four classifications: 'prescription medicines', available only from a pharmacy with a prescription from a doctor, midwife, nurse or dentist; 'restricted' or 'pharmacy-only' medicines for minor complaints available from a qualified pharmacist without a prescription but not on the shelves; and 'pharmacy medicines' on pharmacy shelves only. You'll find unrestricted 'general sale medicines' – such as basic painkillers – on shelves in pharmacies, supermarkets, dairies, petrol stations or online. Some controlled drugs, such as pseudoephedrine, have additional restrictions – pharmacists must keep a register of people who buy them.

Medicine		
Amcal	0800 275 262	www.amcal.co.nz
Life Pharmacy	09 580 1900	www.lifepharmacy.co.nz
Net Pharmacy	09 373 4485	www.netpharmacy.co.nz
Online Pharmacy	03 477 0049	www.onlinepharmacy.co.nz
Pharmacy Direct	0800 742 762	www.pharmacydirect.co.nz
Pharmacy Express	0800 284 828	www.pharmacyexpress.co.nz
Pharmacy Shop	09 846 6552	www.pharmacyshop.co.nz
Radius Pharmacy	05 0822 8822	www.radiuspharmacy.co.nz
Smart Pharmacy	09 571 9080	www.smartpharmacy.co.nz
Unichem	09 571 9080	www.unichem.co.nz

Prescription medicines are subsidised to different extents by the government's drug agency Pharmac (www.pharmac.govt.nz).

You can find the category of a medicine through Medsafe (www.medsafe.govt.nz, 04 496 2000). Prescription medicines are available online but the prescription must be posted (or in urgent cases faxed by the prescriber) to the online supplier.

Larger centres have after-hours pharmacies (sometimes called 'urgent pharmacies'), usually at hospitals. In other areas, pharmacies extend their hours on a roster system.

Mobile Telephones

Other options **Telephone** p.156

About 80% of New Zealanders have mobile phones (often called cellular or 'cell' phones), so it's a big market, full of all the usual international brands at competitive prices. The biggest catch to buying a mobile phone is that the two coverage providers use different technology. Telecom uses CDMA phones while Vodafone uses GPRS phones, although Telecom plans to phase in GPRS. Until that happens you're best to choose a network before you choose a phone. Both companies operate 3G networks but Vodafone allows for greater international roaming. Both networks have their own retail stores – many of them simple booths in shopping malls – and sell discounted or free phones with contract packages. Your other option is to buy the phone separately, then sign up. There may not be much competition between networks but there's plenty between mobile phone vendors, so always shop around. Mobile phones are sold at all the main electronics chain stores but it's also worth checking out the smaller technology stores – have a look on www.pricespy.co.nz. The big specialist mobile phone stores are Digital Mobile, DS Wireless, First Mobile (selling only Vodafone products), and Leading Edge Communications and Orb Communications (selling only Telecom products). There are also many small independent stores. Telecom and Vodafone both have store directories on their websites, see www.telecom.co.nz and www.vodafone.co.nz.

Mobile Telephones		
100% Your Electronics Store	0800 107 090	www.100yes.co.nz
Betta Electrical	09 444 0720	www.bettaelectrical.co.nz
Bond & Bond	0800 202 066	www.bondandbond.co.nz
Dick Smith Electronics	09 414 2800	www.dse.co.nz
Digital Mobile	0800 434 448	www.digitalmobile.co.nz
DS Wireless	09 520 6483	www.dswireless.co.nz
First Mobile	0800 166 245	www.firstmobile.co.nz
Harvey Norman	0800 422 423	www.harveynorman.co.nz
Hill & Stewart	0800 221 144	www.hillandstewart.co.nz
Leading Edge Communications	0800 LEADING	www.leadingedgegroup.co.nz
Noel Leeming	0800 444 488	www.noelleeming.co.nz
Orb Communications	09 358 0031	www.orb.co.nz
Retravision	0800 473 8728	www.retravision.co.nz
The Warehouse	09 489 7000	www.thewarehouse.co.nz

Music, DVDs & Videos

The music, DVD and video market is dominated by a few chain stores and The Warehouse, with large supermarkets also selling a limited number of latest releases. But there are also a few great independent stores. The price of music has come down in recent years, partly because of increased competition from megastores such as The Warehouse and partly because of the bite downloading has made into the market. You can often find new release music CDs on sale for as little as $25 – the usual retail price is $30 plus. There are a few good online stores and New Zealanders often buy from international internet sites such as Amazon (www.amazon.com) and iTunes (www.apple.com/itunes). New Zealand's DVDs are Region Four compatible.

72 Dominion Rd
Auckland
Map p.491 E3 41

Amplifier

www.amplifier.co.nz

Amplifier is a patriotic legal music downloads site specialising in New Zealand music, including independent releases – it'll accept wares from all sorts of artists, from those signed to international labels to a guy recording in his bedroom. You can listen to music, watch videos and buy MP3 downloads, CDs and merchandise. It also has reviews of local music and profiles of musicians.

291 Queen St
Newmarket
Auckland
Map p.488 A3 42

Borders Books, Music & Movies

www.bordersstores.com

This international chain sells mostly books but has a good sound and video section. It has two stores in Auckland, including its flagship shop at 291 Queen Street, Auckland (09 309 3377), one at 250 Lambton Quay in Wellington (04 471 1900), and one in Christchurch, in the Westfield Mall at Riccarton (03 343 6792).

Various Locations

The CD and DVD Store

www.thecdanddvdstore.co.nz

Another big player in the New Zealand music market, the CD and DVD Store has 31 stores nationwide, most of them in Auckland, Wellington and Christchurch, although some don't actually stock DVDs. It also has an outlet store at the Fox Outlet Centre on Auckland's North Shore, 3 Akoranga Drive, Northcote.

Fishpond

www.fishpond.co.nz

Australasian-wide online store Fishpond is first and foremost a bookshop but has a huge CD and DVD catalogue, selling an enviable selection of new releases and older stock. Shipping costs from $4 for a purchase of less than $29 to $10 for a purchase of more than $500 worth of product.

Queens Arcade
off Queen St
Auckland
Map p.488 D5 44

Marbecks

09 379 0444 | *www.marbecks.co.nz*

Marbecks is a long-established Auckland music shop that now does most of its business online. It has a big range of CDs and DVDs, is proud of its well-informed staff and has a particularly strong classical music section. The retail store is in Queens Arcade, off Queen Street, Auckland Central.

Various Locations

Real Groovy

09 302 3940 | *www.realgroovy.co.nz*

Long a legend among independent music retailers, Real Groovy is becoming a big player in the New Zealand market, with stores in Auckland, Wellington, Christchurch and Dunedin and online. It sells music, DVDs, games and vinyl, new and second-hand. Its Auckland and Wellington outlets are the biggest music stores in the country.

90 Dixon St
Wellington
Map p.504 C1 46

Smoke CDs

04 385 6405 | *www.smokecds.com*

This hip independent online store – with a retail outlet in Wellington – has a great selection of New Zealand music, including small independent labels, as well as all the big international names for competitive prices. Its website also has news, reviews and samples.

Various Locations

Sounds

09 414 1676 | *www.soundsnz.com*

Sounds has more than 40 stores nationwide and, because of its bulk-buying power, often sells new releases at a good discount – around $25 instead of the usual $30 plus. Most of the stores are fairly small but they'll order in any CDs you can't find.

Various Locations

TracsNZ

07 839 4435 | *www.tracsnz.co.nz*

Primarily an online store, Tracs boasts that it has the country's biggest selection of DVDs for sale. Its prices are usually slightly lower than the recommended retail price and it has a wide range of new releases and older titles. It also has retail outlets in Auckland, Rotorua and Hamilton.

Musical Instruments

Other options **Music Lessons** p.324, **Music, DVDs & Videos** p.394

Musical Instruments		
Lewis Eady	09 489 2584	www.lewiseady.co.nz
Music Ways	09 477 0384	www.musicways.co.nz
Music Works	09 523 1426	www.musicworks.co.nz
New Zealand Rockshop	09 379 8609	www.rockshop.co.nz
Piano House of New Zealand	04 384 4400	www.pianohouse.co.nz

The musical instruments market is made up of a few larger stores selling a range of equipment and dozens of smaller operations that specialise in one section of the orchestra – or even one instrument. To find one that specialises in your instrument and type of music, search for 'musical instruments' on www.yellowpages.co.nz, look on www.muzic.net.nz or wholesaler Music Ways' website, www.musicways.co.nz, which has a list of its retailers. The bigger stores are listed above.

Outdoor Goods

Other options **Hardware & DIY** p.389, **Sports Goods** p.402, **Camping** p.310

Very few countries in the world – especially of New Zealand's size – can boast as good a range of outdoor goods. Camping, fishing, hunting, trekking (called 'tramping' in New Zealand), skiing and snowboarding are popular pastimes and well catered for. Sales assistants tend to be extremely knowledgeable, especially in independent stores. Macpac and Fairydown are world-renowned New Zealand brands of outdoor equipment, including tents, sleeping bags, backpacks and clothing. Fairydown was recently bought out by the New Zealand-owned chain store Kathmandu, which stocks a good range of affordable clothing and camping equipment. Ski and snowboarding equipment is a seasonal industry – outside the season many of the dozens of independent specialist stores (mostly based in the main centres and alpine areas) transform into watersports or general outdoors stores. In season many stock second-hand as well as new equipment. Department store chains The Warehouse (09 489 7000, www.thewarehouse.co.nz) and Kmart (09 279 4409, www.kmart.co.nz), as well as the hardware stores Mitre 10 (0800 4 648 7310, www.mitre10.co.nz) and Placemakers (09 525 5100, www.placemakers.co.nz) also stock camping and outdoors equipment in season. Other large specialist stores are listed here.

Ballistics Wake & Snow

72 Barry's Point Rd
Takapuna
Auckland
Map p.484 C4

09 489 4074 | *www.ballistics.co.nz*

As with most independent outdoors stores in New Zealand, Ballistics is run by two very, very keen enthusiasts. They've had their North Shore shop for more than 15 years and specialise in waterski, snowboarding and skiing equipment. They're also very keen wakeboarders and run a wakeboarding camp near Tokoroa in south Waikato (p.219).

Bivouac Outdoor

171 George St
Dunedin
South Island
Map H12

03 477 3679 | *www.bivouac.co.nz*

Bivouac is a bit of a one-stop shop for most basic outdoor activities, including tramping and camping. It also has alpine and rock-climbing gear. Among the brands on offer is New Zealand world leaders Macpac and Icebreaker as well as many leading international names, including North Face, Teva and Leatherman. Bivouac has nine stores nationwide and an online presence.

Cnr Cashel & Barbadoes St
Christchurch
Map p.517 E2 51

Complete Outdoors

03 366 9885 | *www.completeoutdoors.co.nz*

As its name suggests, Complete Outdoors is one of the best places in Christchurch to get kitted out for your outdoor adventure. It has all the camping gear you could ever wish for, as well as a selection of more upmarket luggage and a good array of watersports equipment, including wetsuits.

Level 1
57 Willis St
Wellington
Map p.503 D4 52

Dwights Outdoors

04 528 8245 | *www.dwights.co.nz*

A big player in the Wellington market with four stores, Dwights has been around for almost 30 years. As well as the usual selection of camping and trekking equipment, the store specialises in canvas products, including tarpaulins and awnings, with its own workshop in its Upper Hutt store, and also sells trampolines and equestrian products.

Various Locations

Hunting & Fishing New Zealand

09 298 1556 | *www.huntingandfishing.co.nz*

These hunting, shooting and fishing specialists have been the leading authority in the subject since they opened more than two decades ago. Their stores (all 26 of them) are staffed by experienced hunters and anglers only too happy to pass on their knowledge – both on the products and on local fishing and hunting opportunities. It also stocks clothing and camping and tramping equipment.

Various Locations

Kathmandu

03 373 6110 | *www.kathmandu.co.nz*

Kathmandu is a New Zealand store that's making a bid for a worldwide following, with an increasing shopfront presence in Australia and the UK. It has a wide range of clothing, from casual T-shirts to performance alpine gear, plus tents, sleeping bags and other camping and tramping gear in its 23 stores. It's also a good place to shop for fun, cheap presents for the outdoor enthusiast.

NZ Camp Site

09 337 0633 | *www.nzcampsite.co.nz*

This clever business is targeted at the camping tourist, and offers camping equipment packages for hire or purchase that include everything from tents and sleeping bags to camp cutlery. It can even organise campervan or car rental for you. The website also has tips on how to prepare for your camping adventure.

Various Locations

R&R Sport

0800 777 767

Part bike shop, part outdoors shop, R&R Sport has a wide range of general camping and trekking gear as well as specialist supplies for such sports as climbing, surfing, wakeboarding, waterskiing, kayaking, skiing and snowboarding. The seven stores also carry top general outdoor clothing brands, including Icebreaker, Macpac, Columbia and North Face. It has seven stores across the country.

Various Locations

Snowgum

09 359 9907 | *www.snowgum.com.au*

The New Zealand stores of this popular Australian chain carry a good range of outdoor clothing, but also sells footwear, luggage, travel knick-knacks (including locks and toiletries). It has four stores in Auckland, including a factory seconds outlet at the Dress-Smart mall in Onehunga (p.411), and one store each in Hamilton and Christchurch.

52 Willis St
Wellington
Map p.503 D4 57

Tisdalls

04 472 0485 | *www.tisdalls.co.nz*

An historic Wellington brand, Tisdalls was started more than 110 years ago by a British immigrant as a fishing, hunting and outdoors store. Today its three stores sell a good selection of fishing equipment and lighting and navigation equipment as well as camping and trekking gear and outdoor clothing and footwear. It also has stores in Auckland and Palmerston North.

Party Accessories

Other options **Delivery** p.427

There are a few speciality shops but basic party accessories can be picked up at stationery shops, cheap emporiums, supermarkets and department stores such as The Warehouse (09 489 7000, www.thewarehouse.co.nz) and Kmart (09 279 4409, www.kmart.co.nz). The same places stock Christmas decorations, though a few specialist retailers spring up in the larger centres in season. Christmas trees are on sale at many petrol stations and private homes in December. Catering can be expensive, so shop around. Marquees, crockery, cutlery, tables, chairs, toilets, children's castles, entertainers and even mirror balls are available for hire – but book ahead, especially in summer. Every sizeable town and city has a few costume hire places, though these aren't always cheap. For cakes, try your local bakery and supermarket for basic options, and gourmet bakeries for more elaborate creations. Find local cake makers by looking up 'cake shops and cake decorators' in the *Yellow Pages* or on www.yellowpages.co.nz.

Party Accessories			
Auckland			
Catlor Display and Party Supplies	373 New North Road	09 377 8738	www.catlor.co.nz
Love to Party	na	0800 867 278	www.lovetoparty.co.nz
McEntee Event Hire	Various Locations	0800 244 734	www.mcenteeevent.co.nz
Parties.co.nz	na	0800 727 897	www.parties.co.nz
Party Party	na	09 838 5147	www.partyparty.co.nz
Party Warehouse	133 Blenheim Road	0800 727 899	www.partywarehouse.co.nz
Party Zone	85 Wairau Road	09 442 1442	www.partyzone.co.nz
Wellington			
Party Central	256 Lambton Quay	04 472 5638	www.partycentral.co.nz
Christchurch			
Party World	1063 Ferry Road	03 384 0123	www.partyworld.co.nz

Perfumes & Cosmetics

Top-brand perfumes and cosmetics can be expensive in New Zealand. Many locals buy duty free, from overseas or the international website www.strawberrynet.com. For example, at the time of writing Jean Paul Gaultier's Le Classique Eau de Parfum (50ml) was $157 in one New Zealand pharmacy, $145 in a duty-free store, the equivalent of $115 at United States chain store Sephora and only $80 on Strawberry Net.

A good range of top brands is available – with similar pricing and excellent customer service – at larger pharmacies and the department stores Farmers (09 272 6996, www.farmers.co.nz), Smith &

Lush

Caughey's in Auckland (03 377 4770, www.smithandcaughey.co.nz), Kirkcaldie & Stains in Wellington (04 472 5899, www.kirkcaldies.co.nz) and Ballantynes in Christchurch (0800 184 000, www.ballantynes.com). Supermarkets sell cheaper brands.
The international chains Body Shop (09 377 1428, www.thebodyshop.com) and Lush (0800 587 469, www.lushnz.com) have presences in New Zealand and there are a few good local natural skincare brands. Try Trilogy (04 499 7820, www.trilogyproducts.co.nz) and Living Nature sold in chemists (0508 548 464, www.livingnature.co.nz), as well as the above department stores and health shops. Certain 'professionals only' products such as Dermalogica, Ella Baché and Thalgo are only stocked in beauty clinics and spas. To find a beauty therapist near you see www.beautynz.org.nz, the Association of Beauty Therapists' website, and p.353. There are a few men's beauty therapists in the main centres, but it's not a big market.

Pets

Other options **Pets** p.151

It goes without saying that before you buy a pet you should consider your circumstances. Don't buy a big dog if you live in an apartment or you're away a lot. Dogs are especially closely monitored in New Zealand. They must be registered and any pooches that are first registered after July 2006 must be microchipped. They must also be kept on a leash when in public areas and on your property they must be unable to get out and roam on their own. For more information see www.dia.govt.nz, the Department of Internal Affairs' website. New Zealand is an extremely dog-friendly country. Cats are very popular, too, and you can also buy pet birds, rabbits, mice, frogs, fish, guinea pigs, rats and turtles.
As well as from pet stores (some are listed here) and breeders, you can pick up pets from the SPCA (Royal New Zealand Society for the Prevention of Cruelty to Animals) – mostly dogs and cats (both young and mature) but also rabbits, guinea pigs and other animals. The SPCA recommends that most pets be vaccinated and neutered, and it has a section on its website (www.rnzspca.org.nz) about caring for your pet. It also has a list of its branches nationwide, or you can call 09 827 6094. You can search for dog or cat breeders, respectively on the New Zealand Kennel Club website www.nzkc.org.nz and www.catzinc.org.nz. For an extensive list of pet shops nationwide, see www.petguidenz.co.nz. Most sell food and accessories. For pet grooming services, look up 'pet grooming' in your *Yellow Pages* or online at www.yellowpages.co.nz.

Pets			
Auckland			
Four Seasons Pets	137 Apirana Avenue, Glen Innes	09 528 6337	www.fourseasonspets.co.nz
Lady Gays Pet Centre	18 Anzac Street	09 488 6621	www.ladygayspets.co.nz
Pet Boutique	4/302 Irirangi Drive, Botany South	0800 738 268	www.petboutique.co.nz
Wellington			
Animates	na	04 566 6415	www.animates.co.nz
Hutt Pet Centre	3 Pretoria Street, Lower Hutt	04 569 8861	na
Paws 'n' Claws	Logan Plaza, Main Street, Upper Hutt	04 528 5548	na
Pet Corner	4 Titahi Bay Road, Porirua	04 238 1003	na
Pet Essentials	The Mega Centre, Parumoana Street	04 237 4464	sites.yellow.co.nz/site/petessentialswgtn
The Pet House	16 Coastlands Parade, Paraparaumu	04 296 1131	na
Christchurch			
Animates	467 Papanui Road	03 354 2380	www.animates.co.nz
Critter Kingdom	250 Stanmore Road, Richmond	03 389 2460	www.critterkingdom.co.nz
Papanui Pets	5 Main North Road, Papanui	03 352 8693	na
Pet World	na	03 354 4089	www.petworld.co.nz
Various Locations			
Jansens	na	0508 526 736	www.jansens.co.nz
Pet Corner	na	09 836 3628	www.petcorner.co.nz

Second-Hand Items

Other options **Books** p.373

The auction website TradeMe (www.trademe.co.nz) has become something of a national obsession in New Zealand and though it hasn't exactly killed the second-hand dealers, they've had to adopt the approach of 'if you can't beat em, join em' attitude – most now list their wares on the site. Cash Converters (04 570 3111) is a national second-hand chain specialising in appliances, with 25 stores nationwide – it too has ventured on to the web, with its own auction site (www.cashconverters.co.nz). There are eight Dollar Dealers in Auckland (09 836 6122). Many charities operate little thrift stores, filled mostly with musty clothes and bric-a-brac – you can donate directly to the stores or at charity bins, commonly found at schools and shopping centres. St Vincent de Paul is ubiquitous (04 499 5070). For smaller second-hand dealers, look up 'secondhand dealers' in your *Yellow Pages* or on www.yellowpages.co.nz. Local markets stalls often sell second-hand goods.

Shoes

Other options **Beachwear** p.372, **Clothes** p.375, **Sports Goods** p.402

With hundreds of shoe shops around there's no excuse to go barefoot in New Zealand, unless of course it's high summer and you're on the beach. There are shoes to suit every budget, though you'll find it easier to pick up a pair of jandals (you might know them as thongs or flip-flops) than a pair of Manolo Blahniks. Many moderately priced international brands are readily available. Most shoe retailers are part of a chain, though you'll find some more exclusive stores in places such as Auckland's High Street or Ponsonby Road, as well as small independent stores holding out in a few shopping strips. Unless you count gumboots (wellington boots), there are only a few New Zealand brands – look out for Kumfs (details below), men's manufacturer McKinlays (0800 657 456), and fashionable women's brands Briarwood (09 259 0099, www.briarwood.co.nz) and Minnie Cooper (09 376 3058). The main specialist chain stores are listed below. Department stores – Farmers (09 272 6996, www.farmers.co.nz), The Warehouse (09 489 7000, www.theware house.co.nz) and Kmart (09 279 4409, www.kmart.co.nz) – also have ultra-cheap shoes for sale and many clothing retailers stock small shoe ranges. Sports stores sell big ranges of performance footwear.

Various Locations

The Athlete's Foot

09 271 1593 | *www.theathletesfoot.com.au*

This Australasian chain is a good place to get measured up for sports shoes, especially if you're serious about your sport or have foot problems. Its stores stock major international brands, including Asics, Nike and New Balance, and usually give good advice. There are 10 outlets in Auckland, Wellington and Christchurch.

40-44 Fremlin Pl
Auckland
Map p.484 B6

David Elman Shoes

09 828 8313 | *www.davidelman.co.nz*

A local company, David Elman Shoes manufactures and imports mainly high-quality, moderate to high-priced women's shoes. The range tends towards the more glamorous rather than the casual. It has its own branded stores in Auckland, Tauranga and Hamilton and its shoes are sold through a few other stockists around the country.

Various Locations

Foot Locker

09 845 1412 | *www.footlocker.co.nz*

Foot Locker stocks a wide range of casual and performance sneakers for men and women, including the big international brands – Nike, Adidas, Converse and the like. It also sells big-brand exercise clothing. It has 14 stores in Auckland, Hamilton, Wellington and Christchurch, and staff tend to be reasonably well informed.

Various Locations

Hannahs Shoes

04 237 5499

Hannahs has long been New Zealand's staple shop for affordable footwear and, with 64 stores throughout the country, you won't have to look far to find one. Don't expect to find anything high-end – though Hannahs always sends a nod fashion's way, you'll mostly find cheap variations on latest themes for men, women and children.

Various Locations

Kumfs Shoes

09 633 2000 | *www.kumfs.co.nz*

This venerable New Zealand brand has a reputation for making comfortable shoes for older ladies but is making inroads into changing that image with lines directed at younger buyers. It also sells good-quality men's footwear, mostly suitable for the office. There are 18 Kumfs stores nationwide and the shoes are sold at dozens of other stockists.

10 High St
Auckland
Map p.488 A2 63

Mi Piaci

09 524 5199 | *www.mipiaci.co.nz*

Mi Piaci means 'I like' in Italian, and if you're a woman who prefers your shoes glamorous and fairly expensive, this is the store for you. It has five stores in Auckland and Wellington. It's owned by the larger chain store Overland Footwear and you'll find good deals on Mi Piaci shoes at Overland's outlet store at the Dress-Smart mall in Onehunga, Auckland (p.411).

Various Locations

Number 1 Shoes

09 377 4222 | *www.no1shoes.co.nz*

Want three pairs of shoes for $50? This is the place you're most likely to find them. Number 1 has stacks of ultra-cheap shoes. Sure, some are pretty crap, but if you need a pair of heels for a special occasion that you're not likely to wear again, sneak into a store and don't tell anyone. There are 42 outlets nationwide.

Various Locations

Overland Footwear

0800 683 752 | *www.overlandfootwear.co.nz*

One of New Zealand's most popular – and most visible – footwear chains, Overland stocks a wide range of moderately priced and fashionable men's and women's footwear. It's worth signing up to the mailing list for discounts. There are 27 stores nationwide and online, while its larger stores also sell handbags.

Various Locations

Smiths Sport Shoes

09 626 2097 | *www.smithssportsshoes.co.nz*

As the name suggests, you won't find high heels here – rather a good range of international brands for athletes and casual sportspeople. It's a grandfather in terms of New Zealand shoe shops – the Smith family opened their first store in 1949. There are 12 stores nationwide and they specialise in running, walking and cross training shoes.

Various Locations

Wild Pair

0508 945 372 | *www.wildpair.co.nz*

Targeted at hip young buyers – but not inaccessible for older feet – Wild Pair has a good range of casual and glamorous shoes, including more expensive international names such as Dr Martens and Diesel. It also sells a small range of clothing and accessories, including handbags, jewellery and sunglasses. There are 14 stores nationwide.

Poster for Merino

Souvenirs

Other options **Jewellery and Watches** p.391

Souvenirs to avoid: tacky plastic tiki (made in China), knitted jumpers with sheep and pastoral scenes, cheap paua shell necklaces, Rotorua mud facepacks, All Blacks rugby caps. Souvenirs to covet: good-quality greenstone, bone or paua pendants (see Jewellery and Watches, p.391), stylish merino wool clothing, possum fur products, striking photography or a painting. You won't have difficulty finding a shop stocking New Zealand souvenirs in the main centres and tourist spots, but you might have trouble finding one that offers good-quality products at a fair price. It's wise to avoid souvenir shops in hotels, as the mark-up is usually pretty generous. Airport shops aren't quite so bad and usually have a good range. Markets are always worth visiting, as you'll often come across a small-fry jewellery maker selling his or her wares at a decent price. Most large souvenir stores are fine – they're not nearly as tacky as they once were and many offer internet shopping – but it may pay to shop around, and to seek out local craft shops and gift shops and markets for something unique. As clothing goes, you might be best to check out the brands that locals buy, such as Icebreaker and Swanndri, rather than choose something made especially for tourists, which could be tacky and overpriced (though be aware that a lot of these brands are manufactured overseas). Hokitika, on the South Island's west coast, is the capital of greenstone production and you'll find a lot of authentic products there (p.285). Rotorua has a big greenstone market, too, but some shops are overpriced. Make sure the greenstone isn't imported jade from China. There's a big local market for 'Kiwiana' – coloured tikis, emblazoned tea towels, Buzzy Bee children's toys. Go crazy on it by all means, but remember that it's supposed to be slightly tongue in cheek.

Sports Goods

Other options **Beachwear** p.372, **Bicycles** p.372, **Outdoor goods** p.396, **Shoes** p.400

With its reputation for outdoor and sports activities, New Zealand has a good array of sporting goods shops, both general chain stores and retailers specialising in a

Sports Goods

Name	Phone	Web	Speciality
Cricket Express	09 623 1048	www.cricketexpress.co.nz	Cricket
Elite Fitness	09 441 9277	www.elitefitness.co.nz	Gym Equipment
Fergs Kayaks	09 529 2230	www.fergskayaks.co.nz	Kayaking
FitnessWorks	0800 222 800	www.fitnessworks.co.nz	Gym Equipment
Golf Online	0800 468 888	www.golfonline.co.nz	Golf
Golf Warehouse	09 489 5374	www.golfwarehouse.co.nz	Golf
GolfShop	09 837 0958	www.golfshop.co.nz	Golf
Just Hockey	09 623 1048	www.justhockey.co.nz	Hockey
Pro Tennis	09 373 3623	na	Tennis
Soccer Scene	09 845 6219	www.soccerscene.co.nz	Football
Strung-up Racket Sports	09 827 0650	na	Tennis
Tennis Life	09 410 8804	www.tennislife.co.nz	Tennis
Rugby Post	03 365 4604	www.rugbypostnz.com	Rugby
Soccer Direct	03 981 6571	www.soccerdirect.co.nz	Football
Golf Direct	02 1061 1554	www.golfdirect.co.nz	Golf
Rugby Shop	na	www.rugbyshop.co.nz	Rugby
Sunspots Kayak Shop	07 362 4222	www.kayakshop.co.nz	Kayaking

particular sport. The three big chains are Rebel Sport (www.rebelsport.co.nz, 09 845 0980), Sportsworld (www.sportsworld.co.nz, 0800 999 949) and Stirling Sports (www.stirlingsports.co.nz, 0800 784 754) – all have good ranges, including international brands, at competitive prices. The Warehouse (www.thewarehouse.co.nz, 09 489 7000) and Kmart (www.kmart.co.nz, 09 279 4409) also sells some sporting gear. Individual sport specialists are listed here.

Stationery

Warehouse Stationery, a subsidiary of The Warehouse, has dominated the market for personal, office and school stationery since it opened in the early 1990s. Some of its 40-odd stores are enormous, selling pretty much everything you could want, including office furniture and computers. Office Products Depot, OfficeMax and Cardale's Stationery City (www.fastorders.co.nz) are aimed more at the office stationery market but sell to personal shoppers, too. Otherwise, there are few specialist stationers around, though bookshops – namely Whitcoulls, Paper Plus and its subsidiary Take Note – all stock stationery. Only the bigger city stores have extensive ranges. Most supermarkets and 'dairies' (convenience stores) sell the basics – paper, envelopes, tape and so on. The Warehouse also stocks some stationery.

Stationery

Cardale's Stationery City	09 442 2593	www.cardales.co.nz
Office Products Depot	09 529 1320	www.officeproductsdepot.co.nz
OfficeMax	0800 426 473	www.officemax.co.nz
Paper Plus/Take Note	0800 727 377	www.paperplus.co.nz
The Warehouse	09 489 7000	www.thewarehouse.co.nz
Warehouse Stationery	0800 736 245	www.warehousestationery.co.nz
Whitcoulls	09 985 6570	www.whitcoulls.co.nz

Textiles

Other options **Souvenirs** p.402, **Home Furnishing and Accessories** p.389, **Wedding Items** p.406

Fabric stores and tailors aren't nearly as plentiful as they were before it became far cheaper to buy imported ready-made clothes. There are still some stores holding out, though the ranges aren't always that inspiring. For ultra-cheap fabric try an emporium. The biggest chain stores are Arthur Toye Fabrics (04 473 6942), Global Fabrics (09 366 1991) and Spotlight (www.spotlight.co.nz, 0800 276 222).

As for tailoring, many New Zealanders get clothes (suits especially) made during trips to Asia, but it can be cost-effective (and far more convenient) to get suits made here. Many upmarket menswear stores carry only the most popular sizes on the racks and offer tailoring services, often at no extra cost. You'll have to ask around to find the stores in your city that offer these services.

There are plenty of dressmakers and alteration services. It's common to get off-the-rack clothes altered, but most people will only get clothes made for special occasions such as balls and weddings. You can source your own material or leave that up to the dressmaker. Designers often prefer to come up with a design, while dressmakers are happy to work off a pattern.

For local textiles stores and tailors, look up 'clothing – alterations and repairs', 'fabrics – retail', 'sewing services, 'tailors' or 'textiles' in your *Yellow Pages* or on www.yellowpages.co.nz.

Toys, Games & Gifts

There are a few big chain stores around, but toy and gift shops are often independently owned and many sell over the internet, so it's a case of looking up your local outlets in the *Yellow Pages* or on www.yellowpages.co.nz. There are a few competitive computer game chains. Farmers (09 272 6996, www.farmers.co.nz), The Warehouse (09 489 7000, www.thewarehouse.co.nz) and Kmart (09 279 4409, www.kmart.co.nz) all have good selections of toys, games (including computer games) and gifts. Some electronics chain stores also sell computer games, try Dick Smith Electronics (09 414 2800, www.dse.co.nz), Harvey Norman (0800 422 423, www.harveynorman.co.nz), Hill & Stewart (0800 221 144, www.hillandstewart.co.nz), Bond & Bond (0800 202 066, www.bondandbond.co.nz) and Noel Leeming (0800 444 488, www.noelleeming.co.nz). Some music retailers (see Music, DVDs and Videos, p.394) also stock computer games. Toy and games stores often have sales during school holidays.

Various Locations

EB Games

09 354 4309 | *www.ebgames.co.nz*

Australasia's largest video game retailer, EB Games has 29 stores throughout New Zealand, mostly in shopping malls, and an online store and stocks games for all hardware, including PlayStation, Xbox and PC. It has good regular sales – be prepared to elbow your way into stores and put up with some poor hygiene.

Various Locations

Edex Toys

0800 488 052 | *www.edextoys.co.nz*

Edex Toys gets its name from so-called educational toys but don't let that put your kids off – it's a fun store that also stocks dolls and trucks as well as plenty of more creative and worthy offerings, including science kits and arts and crafts sets. It has 10 stores nationwide and limited online shopping.

Various Locations

Flying Saucers

09 978 6237 | *www.flyingsaucers.co.nz*

The gifts at this Auckland-based chain of five stores aren't always cheap but they're usually interesting and quirky. It stocks mostly gifts for adults but has presents for babies and children too, if you're into spoiling children. There is a particularly good range of funky luggage and a good jewellery selection.

Gameplanet

09 623 2790 | *www.gameplanet.co.nz*

Online store Gameplanet is an excellent internet site for avid gamers, with reviews of games and equipment, forums (including one for buying, selling and trading), downloads of demonstration games and movies and games to play online, as well as an extensive library of games and equipment for sale. It boasts of having the widest selection of games and most knowledgeable staff in the country.

118 Cuba Mall
Wellington
Map p.504 C2 71

Iko-Iko

www.ikoiko.co.nz

Iko-Iko is a small but great funky and affordable shop where you'll find all sorts of unusual gifts and homewares products, and a selection of good-humoured adult goods. It has another branch at 195 Karangahape Road, Auckland. It used to have a great website, with online shopping, but at the time of writing it had been replaced with merely a business card entry.

iQ Toys

0800 478 697 | *www.iqtoys.co.nz*

Family-owned iQ Toys started off as a small home business and now boasts that it's New Zealand's largest online toy store, with about 2,500 products for sale, including toys, books, DVDs, software and outdoor equipment. You can arrange to have a gift wrapped and delivered for a small fee on top of the postage.

Gift store

Various Locations

Living and Giving

0800 548 464 | *www.livingandgiving.co.nz*

A homewares store with, as the name suggests, an emphasis on the gift market, Living and Giving has nine stores nationwide and an online store. It's not always the cheapest place to buy homewares – you might want to price check with less-attractive stores – but it has a good range of quality products, including leading international brands.

Various Locations

Nest

09 355 6160 | *www.nest.co.nz*

Like Living and Giving, Nest is a homewares store that markets itself partly as a gift shop and is a popular wedding registry store. Its products are stylish and elegant and its prices are fairly high – but not astronomical. It has five stores, in Auckland, Wellington and Christchurch, and an online store.

Westfield Plaza
Pakuranga
Auckland
Map p.484 E6

Origin Interiors

09 827 6101 | *www.origininteriors.co.nz*

An interiors shop with a giftware bent, Origin Interiors specialises in moderately priced exotic furniture, homewares and gifts, mostly from Asia, with some stock from as far away as Morocco. It's been around for 30 years but has recently expanded and now has four stores in Auckland and an online store.

Shop 224
Westfield Shopping Centre
Manukau
Auckland
Map p.484 E7

Toys 'R' Fun

09 263 4175 | *www.toysrfun.co.nz*

Toys 'R' Fun has seven stores in Auckland, including two 'mega-stores', in Manukau and St Lukes. It stocks a wide range of international-brand toys, including all the latest fads, at competitive prices. It's also a good place to buy children's bikes, scooters and ride-on cars – especially at the larger stores.

Various Locations

Toyworld

www.toyworld.co.nz

Toyworld has been around for decades and has grown into New Zealand's biggest speciality toy store, with 34 outlets nationwide, including shops in many small towns. It sells a good range of international-brand toys for cheap prices. Children – and parents – will especially love its generous sales, usually timed for school holidays.

Various Locations

Trade Aid

03 385 3535 | *www.tradeaid.co.nz*

Trade Aid is one of those shops where buyer's remorse can be warded off by the knowledge you're buying from a country that needs the money (as well as decorating your house with exotic wares on the cheap). Its 30 stores nationwide specialise in fair trade products and it's also a vocal lobbyist.

Wedding Items

New Zealand's wedding industry is remarkably healthy and hundreds of companies specialise in services for weddings. Couples can easily spend tens of thousands of dollars and some prices are outrageously inflated – mention the W word and watch the price go up – so the number one rule is shop around. Most brides spend between several hundred dollars and several thousand on a dress, while grooms hire scratchy polyester suits for a fraction of the price. You can save money by buying off-the-rack wedding dresses and getting them professional altered to fit – just remember it's far easier to make a large dress smaller than the other way around. Many women travel to the main centres, especially Auckland, to search for dresses but it's always worth approaching a local dressmaker, who might be considerably cheaper. Some of the most prominent stores in the main centres are listed below.

Wedding Items			
Auckland			
Astra Bridal	205 Symonds Street	0800 844 544	www.astrabridal.co.nz
Brides on Thorndon	220 Thorndon Quay	04 472 4717	www.bridesonthorndon.co.nz
Jane Yeh	272 Parnell Road	09 368 1527	www.jane-yeh.com
Modes	176 Broadway	09 520 2730	na
Vinka Brides	242 Queen Street	09 300 3047	www.vinkabrides.com
Wellington			
Ruby Bridal	7 Burma Road	021 888 615	www.rubybridal.co.nz
Christchurch			
Avon Bridal Gowns	Cnr Office Road and Papanui Road, Merivale	03 963 6045	www.avonbridalgowns.co.nz
Gillian Melhop Studio	355 Mt Pleasant Road	03 384 8349	www.dfy.biz
Robyn Cliffe Couturiere	399 Montreal Street	03 365 5200	www.robyncliffe.co.nz

For other wedding dress options – as well as lists of photographers, florists, stationers, shoes, venues, caterers, registries and other companies cashing in on the wedding industry – search the online directories www.weddings.co.nz, www.weddingplanning.co.nz and www.newzealandweddings.co.nz, pick up a copy of one of the wedding magazines that caters to the New Zealand market or look up 'wedding arrangements' in the *Yellow Pages* or on www.yellowpages.co.nz. Brave brides and grooms can get ideas at the hectic annual Bride and Groom Show at Auckland's Ellerslie Racecourse (www.aucklandweddingshow.co.nz, 09 336 1188) or smaller shows around the country (see www.bridal.co.nz for details).

High street boutiques

Queen Street

Auckland

Places to Shop

Auckland is increasingly becoming a city of malls filled with Australian chain stores, each one bigger than the last. And even the malls are part of an Australian chain – the Westfield group. The result is a homogenous mass of almost identical shopping experiences in uninspiring buildings. You might forget which Westfield you're in, let alone where you parked your car. But it is possible – and encouraged – to eschew the malls and take to the streets. Sometimes you'll encounter the same chain stores, just with more natural light, but pick the right spot and you'll discover pleasant streets filled with New Zealand's best innovative designers or second-hand bookshops.

Streets/Areas to Shop

Luckily the predominance of malls in Auckland hasn't harmed its best outdoor shopping precincts. In fact, pulling the chain stores into the malls has brought more diversity and individuality to such streets as Ponsonby Road, Karangahape Road and High Street, and a more relaxed atmosphere to villages such as Devonport. Auckland doesn't have much of the clustering of shops as in other cities – most areas retain a mixture of stores, though Ponsonby Road, High Street and Nuffield Street are dominated by high fashion, Karangahape Road is the domain of the eclectic and Broadway and Queen Street have mostly big-name stores and chains.

Map p.484 D4

Devonport

Though its wharf was rebuilt into an ill-considered characterless mini mall in the late 90s (and is now earmarked to be rebuilt again), Devonport is a pleasant place for a sunny afternoon's stroll. It has a good line-up of bookshops, including some of Auckland's best second-hand stores, galleries and antiques stores. Some highlights are Devonport Antiques and Jewellery at 65 Victoria Road (09 445 1694), Devonport Chocolates at 17 Wynyard Street (09 445 6001), Devonport Vintage Bookshop at 81A Victoria Road (09 446 0300), Evergreen Books at 15 Victoria Road (09 445 2960), Wallis at 75 Victoria Road (09 445 6803) and Paradox Books, 26 Victoria Road (09 446 0023). The almost deserted wharf has found itself a good retail use – a farmers' market each Sunday morning. A ferry links Devonport with the city (see p.45). Parking is usually easy.

Map p.488 A3 79

High Street & the Chancery

High Street and its side streets O'Connell Street and the elegant Chancery off Chancery Lane are collectively one of the best fashion addresses in New Zealand. You'll find an interesting array of mostly upmarket men's and women's clothing stores and some innovative gift shops, including The Vault at 13 High Street (09 377 7665) and Pauanesia at 35 High Street (09 366 7282). Among the best clothing stores are Paris Texas at 33 High Street (09 520 4631), Working Style in the Chancery (09 358 3010), Ricochet at 35 High Street (09 379 8558) and Keith Matheson at 41 High Street (09 379 7919). Unity Books, at 19 High Street (09 307 0731), is a local institution. You won't find many bargains in this area but you will find plenty of unique garments and accessories.

Map p.491 F1 80

Karangahape Road

The eclectic and edgy Karangahape Road (more commonly called K Road) has long been a haven for stores that don't quite fit the mainstream, including a fair share of sex shops and strip joints. It's not the most glamorous of shopping destinations but is colourful and safer than you might think, and there are some good-value restaurants, leading galleries and cool clubs. Some K Road institutions are old-fashioned menswear store Leo O'Malley Menswear (at number 235, 09 377 4191), Asian-inspired interiors shop Buana Satu (229, 09 358 5561), funky gift shop Iko-Iko (193, 09 358 0220), the Auckland Rockshop music supplier (100, 379 8609), streetwear and accessories store Illicit HQ (202, 09 379 2660) and vintage clothing store This is not a Love Shop (290, 09 377 1350). There's a market every Saturday on the motorway overpass towards the western end of the road. Parking can be a challenge. You can take a virtual stroll down the road on its website (www.kroad.co.nz).

Map p.484 C3

Link Drive, Glenfield

Link Drive and its surrounding roads are a mecca for people looking to outfit their homes with wares cheap or expensive. Most of the big homewares and electronics stores have a presence here, so it's a good place to do price comparisons. There is also some good smaller furniture stores, including Samarang, at number 18 (09 443 7788), Java Emporium at 6 (09 443 4744) and Inhouse Furniture at (09 443 2145). A cinema complex, bowling alley and some mostly uninspiring food outlets make up the area's facilities. Parking is usually easy, though it's the done thing to drive between stores so the roads can be busy.

Map p.492 C3

Newmarket

Between Broadway, Nuffield Street and the Westfield 277 Newmarket mall, Newmarket is a fabulous time and money waster. Broadway's tributaries Nuffield, Teed and Morrow streets have some exclusive fashion boutiques and Broadway itself has an upmarket array of fashionable chain and leading brand stores, a branch of glitzy department store Smith & Caughey (p.410) and some unique independent shops, including Briarwood Shoes at number 215 (09 529 1737), Moochi at 246 (09 523 4640) and the Askew gift shop at 178 (09 522 8444).

Pop up Teed and Morrow streets for some good designer clothing, including local stars Workshop (09 524 6844), Zambesi (09 523 1000) and Kate Sylvester (09 524 8872), and turn the corner onto Remuera Road to visit the funky clothing store Ricochet (09 529 2563). The new, small Nuffield Street development has a chic European feel and boasts upmarket stores including an opulent Alannah Hill women's clothing store, expensive designer children's clothing store, Trelise Cooper Kids (09 984 6301) and, further down in Balm Street, popular designer Karen Walker (p.381). The northern end of Broadway has a cinema complex, The Warehouse (09 523 1995), Freedom Furniture (09 976 7900) and the popular Olympic Pools complex (09 522 4414).

Map p.486 C3 83

Ponsonby Road, Ponsonby

Ponsonby Road is one of New Zealand's most revered shopping districts. The street stretches from Karangahape Road to Jervois Road – 1.7km of mostly upmarket men's and women's boutiques, cafes and restaurants. It also has some more modest stores that have become Auckland institutions, including Bhana Bros Fruiterers (09 376 5329), which has been at number 129 since 1940 and sells good quality vegetables, fruit and flowers, and butchers Superior Meat Market (09 376 1862). Some of the street's biggest designer names are Minnie Cooper (for shoes and handbags) at 78 (09 376 3058), World at 175 (09 360 4544) and Zambesi at 169 (p.383). It's an especially pleasant place to stroll along on a sunny day; popping into cafes and boutiques at leisure. Parking is free along most of the street but times are limited. It can sometimes be hard to find a space at lunchtime but perseverance always wins out. You can go for a neat virtual stroll along the road on its website (www.ponsonbyroad.co.nz).

Map p.488 A2-A4

Queen Street

Considering that it's Auckland's main street, parts of Queen Street are downright shabby; populated with discount stores, quiet arcades and dodgy-looking food outlets. But that's the exception. Most of the street, which runs from Karangahape Road to Customs Street, just short of the waterfront, is dominated by chain stores and banks. Some chains, including the bookshops Borders (number 291-297, 09 309 3377) and Whitcoulls (number 210, 09 356 5400), have their flagship stores on Queen Street. Souvenir stores are clustered towards the Customs Street end. But the undisputed queen of the street is the elegant Smith & Caughey department store at number 253-261 (p.410).

Department Stores

261 Queen St
Auckland
Map p.488 A3 85

Smith & Caughey

09 377 4770 | www.smithandcaughey.co.nz

Auckland has only one quality department store, the venerable Smith & Caughey. The elegant large space in an old building on Queen Street and a smaller outlet on Broadway in Newmarket (09 524 8049) sell men's and women's fashion, accessories and cosmetics. Founded in 1880, the flagship Queen Street store has been in Caughey family ownership ever since and boasts Auckland's biggest range of cosmetics and fragrances, a good range of accessories, including handbags, hosiery and jewellery, stationery, fine food, men's and women's clothing and shoes, luggage, children's clothes and toys, homewares and a cafe. It also offers a wedding registry service and duty-free shopping, and you can buy beautiful but expensive food and gift hampers in store or on its website. Its sales are generous and always worth a look.

Markets

Auckland has about half a dozen longstanding markets specialising in a range of wares, from produce to clothing. Each has a vastly different atmosphere, from the Polynesian and Asian-dominated markets of Otara and Avondale to the artsy Titirangi Markets. They can be a good place to buy Maori arts and crafts, including pounamu jewellery (otherwise known as jade or greenstone). Bargaining is not as common as in markets in other countries but is always worth a try, especially if you're buying multiple items. The main markets, all of which have free entry, are listed below. There are several smaller local places, many of which are listed on the website www.urbanboheme.co.nz, and some good farmers' markets – check out www.farmersmarket.org.nz.

Aotea Sq
Queen St
Auckland
Map p.488 A3 86

Aotea Square Markets

In the heart of central Auckland and housed in tents, these markets are dominated by budding clothing manufacturers, and local and imported crafts, food, jewellery, skincare and essential oils. It's a good place to stock your wardrobe with interesting yet affordable designs. Open Friday and Saturday 10:00 to 18:00.

Avondale Racecourse
Ash St
Avondale
Auckland
Map p.484 B6

Avondale Markets

This is the place to stock up your fruit bowl, vegetable crisper and your garden. There's fresh local produce from market gardens, orchards and nurseries for sale, alongside second-hand clothes and bric-a-brac in various conditions. Avondale Markets has a strong Polynesian and Asian influence. Open Sunday 06:00 to 12:00.

Newbury Lane
Auckland
Map p.484 D6

Otara Markets

The colourful Otara Markets were once dominated by Maori and Polynesian residents but now you're more likely to find Asian faces behind the more than 300 stalls. The overwhelming atmosphere, however, is still of the Pacific Islands, as Polynesian music buzzes through the market. You'll find Polynesian art, crafts and fashions – traditional and contemporary – fresh produce and flowers, cheap new and used clothing and tempting food stalls. Open Saturday 06:00 to 12:00.

Anzac St
Takapuna
Auckland
Map p.484 C4

Takapuna Markets

These North Shore markets are a good place to stock up on fresh vegetables, fruit, plants, flowers and second-hand clothes, books and bric-a-brac – some people seem to simply load up their car boots with stuff they don't need and park up at the market. You'll also find a few stalls selling local and imported crafts. Open Sunday, 09:00 to 12:00.

Titirangi War Memorial Hall
500 South Titirangi Rd
Auckland
Map p.484 B6

Titirangi Village Markets

The west Auckland suburb of Titirangi is the traditional hangout of hippies and artists. Despite becoming more of a professional commuter suburb in recent years, it still has a boho reputation, which is obvious on market day. You'll find some good arts and crafts and can get a bite to eat while enjoying the entertainment. The market is held the last Sunday of each month from 10:00 to 14:00.

Victoria Park
Auckland
Map p.487 E3 91

Victoria Park Market

www.victoria-park-market.co.nz

Housed in a former power plant, Victoria Park Market is Auckland's most famous market. It offers a mixture of clothing and accessories, art, new age paraphernalia, souvenir and craft shops and temporary stalls. There's also a foodcourt and a few bars and restaurants. It's open 09:00 to 18:00 every day but is best on the weekend when part of the carpark is given over to stalls (though parking is usually easy enough on the street). The market is mostly patronised by tourists but has plenty to offer permanent residents.

Shopping Malls

Sylvia Park and Botany Town Centre, the two biggest malls at the time of writing (with Westfield's new 100 plus Albany store in development), have more of an atmosphere than most of Auckland's offerings, though they're still filled with much the same array of chain stores. The malls are open seven days and most close late on one or two nights of the week, usually Thursday and/or Friday. The busiest times are, not surprisingly, during the lead-up to Christmas, the post-Christmas sales and the school

Victoria Park Market

Elliot Atrium, Auckland

holidays and, even in the malls with thousands of parking spaces, you can be circling for a long time before finding a spot. But if you visit in the early morning you might be able to do even your Christmas shopping in peace.

Cnr Ti Rakau Dr & Te Irirangi Dr
Botany Downs
Auckland
Map p.484 D7

Botany Town Centre

09 272 3888 | www.botanytowncentre.co.nz

While shopping centres elsewhere in New Zealand occupy impersonal, artificially lit malls, the newish Botany Town Centre has gone the other way. Though the cobbled streets and piazzas feel somewhat contrived, Botany is a breath of fresh air – it's mostly outdoors, save a few mini malls and arcades. With 150 stores, including Auckland's largest Farmers store (09 272 9880), it ranks with Sylvia Park as one of the largest shopping centres in the country. It's got pretty much the same array of chain stores you'll find everywhere, including a good line-up of electronics stores, plus a handful of independent stores – have a look at the innovative children's store Edukidz (09 271 5439) and the gift shop Baby Boutique (09 271 2577). There are cinemas, cafes, a supermarket and a few extras such as a dentist, doctor and library.
Across the road is The Hub, a cluster of homewares stores, including most of the big chains. It is open 09:00 to 17:30 weekdays, except for late nights Thursday and Friday, when it's open until 21:00, and 10:00 starts on Sundays and public holidays. It has 2,400 carpark spaces, most of them outdoors, but even they can fill up at busy times.

4 Main Rd
Auckland
Map p.484 A4

Dress-Smart

09 622 2400 | www.dress-smart.co.nz

Once upon a time Auckland's factory, outlet and seconds stores were scattered across the city meaning shopping involved a lot of research and the burning of petrol while flicking through a dozen map pages. Now most of the factory shops are in a purpose-built 90 store mall in Onehunga's town centre. There are some good bargains to be had at some big-name stores, including Esprit (09 634 5292), Max Fashions (09 636 8417), Glassons (09 636 3924), Barkers (09 634 4100) and Overland Footwear/Mi Piaci (09 622 1188). There are a few cafes and fastfood outlets but the better dining experiences are on the town's nearby main street. It's open 10:00 to 17:00 daily and gets busy at weekends and on public holidays when parking can be scarce (though you can always park on the street). A free shuttle bus connects the mall with Auckland city centre – check the Dress-Smart website for details.

3 Akoranga Dr
Northcote Point
Auckland
Map p.484 C4

Fox Outlet Centre

09 486 4445 | www.foxoutlets.co.nz

A smaller competitor to Dress-Smart, the Fox Outlet Centre on the North Shore has 50 outlet and seconds stores including a few good children's wear shops: Line 7 (09 480 8913) and Snowgum (09 480 4491). It's not as well patronised as its Onehunga rival so its carpark is rarely full. Open daily 10:00 to 18:00.

286 Mt Wellington Highway
Auckland
Map p.484 D6

Sylvia Park

09 570 3777 | www.sylviapark.org

This sparkling new mall, with 200 shops over six and a half hectares, is the place to go for chain store shopping in Auckland. It has three supermarkets, a train station linking it with the central city and south Auckland, a creche, Plunket rooms, a Citizens Advice Bureau, a dental centre and an 'entertainment and leisure precinct' with cinemas, restaurants and electronics stores (nicknamed the 'men's creche'). Its precinct-style layout and size means you should choose your carpark carefully to avoid a long walk.

Don McKinnon Dr
Albany
Auckland
Map p.484 B3

Westfield Albany

09 978 5050 | *www.westfield.co.nz*

The new Westfield Albany, which opened its first stage in early 2007, will eventually have more than 100 stores, including a supermarket, a cinema complex, restaurants and bars. Westfield is promising a town centre-like development, presumably similar to the Botany Town Centre (p.411), perhaps signalling a move away from its typical characterless indoor malls. Westfield Albany is across the road from the popular Mega Centre complex of homewares and clothing stores, which includes a Placemakers hardware store (09 414 0900) and The Warehouse (09 415 2225).

11-19 Custom Street West
Auckland
Map p.488 A2 97

Westfield Downtown

09 978 5265 | *www.westfield.co.nz*

A small but handily placed mall, Westfield Downtown is more of a foodcourt with a few dozen shops attached. It's a good place to pop into during your lunch break if you work in the city, thanks to the presence of The Warehouse and Warehouse Stationery (09 309 6996), a pharmacy, a dry cleaners, a shoe repair stall, an optometrist, a bookshop and a few clothing and footwear stores. Parking in the nearby City Council Downtown building can be expensive but public transport links are good. It's open 08:00 to 18:00 Monday to Friday; 10:00 to 18:00 Saturdays; 10:00 to 16:00 Sundays and 10:00 to 17:00 on public holidays.

Cnr Great South Rd & Wiri Station Rd
Manukau City
Auckland
Map p.484 E7

Westfield Manukau City

09 978 5300 | *www.westfield.co.nz*

The big shopping destination in South Auckland, Manukau City has 146 shops, most of which are chain stores, and a supermarket and foodcourt. It also has a Family Planning Association branch, a dental clinic and a library. Westfield has plans to add 35 new shops, more parking and a new cinema. It gets especially crazy in the lead-up to Christmas. It's open 09:00 to 18:00 most days, except for late closing (21:00) on Thursdays and on Sundays, when it's open 10:00 to 17:30.

Cnr Lake Rd & Como St
Takapuna
Auckland
Map p.484 C4

Westfield Shore City

09 978 6300 | *www.westfield.co.nz*

Shore City's long-held title as the number one shopping destination on the North Shore is being challenged by its sister store in Albany. It's a fairly small but pleasant enough place, dominated by a large Farmers store (09 486 2004) and a foodcourt. It has more upmarket chain stores and fewer shabby discount stores than its neighbouring mall in Glenfield. Parking is high-rise and usually not too much of a hassle. The open-air top deck even has sea views. It has a Les Mills (09 488 9413) gym upstairs. Open 09:00 to 18:00 most days, except for late closing (21:00) on Thursdays and shorter hours (10:00 to 17:00) on Sundays.

80 St Lukes Rd
Auckland
Map p.494 A2 100

Westfield St Lukes

09 978 6000 | *www.westfield.com*

St Lukes is a behemoth, with nearly 200 stores, mostly chain offerings, including a cinema complex, foodcourt and supermarket. It also has an adjacent library and a small Mega Centre across the road, with mostly homewares and electronics stores. What it lacks in architectural splendour it makes up for in patronage; it can take a while to get a carpark space at busy times and unless it's early in the morning it's not a good place to pop into if you're in a hurry. Open 09:00 to 18:00, except on Thursdays and Fridays when it closes at 21:00 and on Sundays, when it's open 10:00 to 17:30.

277 Broadway
Newmarket
Auckland
Map p.492 C3 **101**

Westfield 277 Newmarket

09 978 9400 | *www.westfield.com*

A sparkling upmarket mall in Newmarket's popular Broadway shopping district, 277 has a good selection of clothing and footwear stores, including some high-fashion outlets, such as women's label Sabine (09 529 0142), Laura Ashley (09 529 4975), Oroton (09 523 2434) and Polo Ralph Lauren (09 522 7656). It also has a pleasant foodcourt and a large supermarket. Covered parking is free with a receipt for a purchase of $5 or more. It's open 09:00 to 18:00 most days, except Thursdays and Friday, when it closes at 19:00, and Sundays, when it's open 10:00 to 17:00.

7 Catherine St
Henderson
Auckland
Map p.484 A5

Westfield WestCity

09 978 6700 | *www.westfield.com*

The shopping capital of west Auckland, WestCity is a pleasant enough mall with the usual array of chain stores and discount stores, plus a foodcourt, a supermarket and a cinema complex. Free parking is in the multi-level undercover carpark but, like most malls, it gets hard to find a space at busy times. It's open 09:00 to 18:00 weekdays, except Thursdays and Fridays, when it's open until 21:00, and Sundays, when it's open 10:00 to 17:30.

Westgate Dr
Waitakere
Auckland
Map p.484 A4

WestGate Shopping Centre

09 831 0200 | *www.westgate.net.nz*

An open-air shopping centre, WestGate is a sprawling new area of 70 shops and offices, including a supermarket, cinemas and an outlet centre. Waitakere City Council has big plans to develop an adjacent area into a mixture of civic, retail, residential, recreational and commercial space, but these are in their infancy.

Wellington

Places to Shop

Despite the city's notoriously fickle weather, Wellingtonians don't hang out in indoor malls as much as their Auckland counterparts. Instead, the streets and arcades of the city reign when it comes to shopping, with areas for designer clothing and funkier alternative products.

Streets/Areas to Shop

Wellington's compact CBD is great place to while away a few hours or a few days, ducking in and out of designer stores, alternative clothing, gift and music stores and stopping for the odd break at its great cafes and bars.

Cuba St
Wellington
Map p.505 D1 **104**

Cuba Mall

The pedestrianised Cuba Mall (www.cuba.co.nz) along with Cuba Street and its tributaries make up the cool shopping capital of the capital. The area is dominated by small fashion boutiques, but also has a colourful mix of second-hand stores, music shops, groovy cafes, tattoo artists and sex shops. Pop into gift store Iko-Iko at 118 Cuba Mall (04 385 0977), denim and streetwear shop Area 51 on the corner of Cuba and Dixon streets (04 385 6590), menswear store Mandatory at 108 Cuba Street (04 384 6107), Triangle at 47 Ghuznee Street (04 802 4974) and Fashion HQ (04 803 3349), which stocks the work of budding local designers, in the Left Bank arcade. The arcade is worth exploring in itself – it's small but packed with grungy-cool independent stores and cafes, including vintage clothing store Modern Love (04 499 8805). At the top end of Cuba Street are the music stores Real Groovy (p.395) and Slow Boat Records (04 385 1330), both with excellent collections of vinyl, CDs, T-shirts, posters and other music paraphernalia.

Map p.503 D1-4

The Golden Mile

The Golden Mile is the nickname for Wellington's main shopping area, a great place for a wander whether you're shopping or not. It's actually made up of four streets that loosely link into each other: Lambton Quay, Willis Street, Manners Street (and Manners Mall) and Courtenay Place. The busy pedestrian thoroughfare takes in the elegant Kirkcaldie & Stains department store (p.414), several small malls and arcades, including Capital on the Quay (p.416) and the Old Bank Arcade (p.417) and many big-name brand, independent and designer stores. Shops to look out for include popular Wellington clothing label Starfish at 128 Willis Street (04 385 3722), Unity Books at 57 Willis Street (0800 486 489), Arty Bee's Books at 17 Courtenay Place (04 385 1819) and designer clothing store Voon at 142 Willis Street (04 801 8292). Detour to Customhouse Quay to visit designer clothes stores Zambesi at number 107 (p.383), Unity Collection at 101 (04 471 1008) and Basquesse at 95 (04 499 3012, www.basquesse.co.nz). Blair Street (at the Mount Victoria end of Courtenay Place) has fantastic homewares and clothes shops, including Scotties (04 384 3805), which is stocked with the creations of international designers such as Issey Miyake and Comme des Garcons and locals including Marilyn Sainty and Beth Ellery, and Soup, one of the country's finest vintage designer stores (04 385 4722).

Department Stores

165-177
Lambton Quay
Wellington
Map p.503 D3 106

Kirkcaldie & Stains

04 472 5899 | *www.kirkcaldies.co.nz*

Known to locals as 'Kirks', this gracious old department store has been around since 1863 – a very long time by New Zealand standards, even if the present façade was built in the early 1900s. Inside you'll find a hushed atmosphere, an old-school coffee shop, and a luxurious array of imported and local men's and women's clothing (including Polo Ralph Lauren, Tommy Hilfiger and Versace Collection), posh children's wear, cosmetics, fragrances, lingerie, luggage, books, gifts, stationery (including Mont Blanc), gourmet food, furniture, linen, and homewares. Its impressive (and expensive) food hampers can be ordered online and sent around the world. The services of a personal shopper and wardrobe and fashion consultants are also available.

Kirks has a wedding and gift registry service, an alterations service, lingerie fittings, overseas posting facilities and limited duty-free shopping. It has a great off-shoot cuisine store, Kirkcaldie & Stains Cuisine, in the nearby Harbour City Shopping Centre at the corner of Lambton Quay and Brandon Street, which sells gourmet food, wine, tea and coffee (you can also buy online at www.ferrit.co.nz).

Cuba Street

Kirkcaldie & Stains

Old Bank Arcade

Places to Shop – Wellington

Markets

Wellington has a rather limited range of markets compared with the country's other big cities (one of the main local produce markets doesn't even seem to have a name). The local council is looking at ways to give a stronger presence to the city's markets. In the meantime, the most atmospheric offering is to be found out of the city, at Porirua.

Chaffers Market

Waitanga Park
Te Aro
Wellington
Map p.504 C2 **107**

Chaffers is a fresh produce market that's open Sunday mornings (07:30 to 13:00) in the carpark between Te Papa museum and Waitangi Park. It's not as big as the Vivian Street Markets but has cheap regional fruit and vegetables – even chefs have been spotted buying their ingredients here – plants and bric-a-brac. Parking is reasonable.

Farmers' Market

Ghuznee St
Te Aro
Wellington
Map p.504 C2 **108**

Like Chaffers, this market is held on a Sunday and sells fresh produce, though it accommodates far earlier risers, opening at 04:00 and going through until 14:30. You'll find it at the Victoria Street open-air carpark on the corner of Ghuznee and Vivian streets. There's a particularly good selection of Asian vegetables and herbs. Be aware that parking can be a hassle.

Moore Wilson's Farmers Fresh Market

Porirua
South Island
Map G14

04 237 8329 | *www.moorewilson.co.nz*

The food store Moore Wilson operates a fresh food market every Saturday at its purpose-built building on Kenepuru Drive, Porirua, with local growers and producers selling direct to the public. As well as fruit and vegetables, you'll find pickles, olive oils, baked goods and bread. Open daily 08:00 to 14:00.

Porirua Market

Cobham Crt
Porirua City Centre
South Island
Map G14

This vibrant market has a Pacific Island and Asian atmosphere with about 160 stalls selling produce, ethnic food and crafts and second-hand clothing. You'll have to get up early – it opens at 05:00 every Saturday and closes about 10:00. It is renowned for its good, mostly Asian, food stalls.

Wellington Market

Cnr Taranaki St & Wakefield St
Wellington
Map p.505 D1 **111**

04 801 8991

This weekly market, which lacks a certain atmosphere, sells crafts, souvenirs, clothing and bric-a-brac, but its strongest feature is the ethnic food stalls; you'll be able to take your pick from Thai, Indian, Mexican, Korean, Vietnamese and Chinese offerings. It's open Friday to Sunday 10:00 to 17:30.

Shopping Malls

There are relatively few malls in the capital, which has a reputation for far more stylish shopping than its larger, northerly peer. There are exceptions way out in the suburbs, and the city centre has some small malls but even the indomitable Westfield hasn't got much of a hold on Wellington shoppers yet.

Capital on the Quay

226-262 Lambton Quay
Wellington
Map p.503 D3 **112**

04 499 8899 | *www.capitalquay.co.nz*

Though it has a mere 30 shops, Capital on the Quay ranks as the largest shopping centre in the city centre, with a mixture of women's and men's clothing and accessories, gifts, music, homewares and artwork, and several cafes. A large part of the stylish arcade is occupied by a Borders bookshop (04 471 1900). Capital is open weekdays from 09:00 to 17:30, except for Friday (09:00 to 19:00), Saturday (10:00 to 26:00) and Sunday (11:00 to 16:00).

24 Main Rd
Tawa
Wellington
Map p.498 C1

Dress-Smart

04 232 0226 | www.dress-smart.co.nz

You'll find nearly all of Wellington's factory, seconds and outlet stores at Dress-Smart, including big names such as Barkers (04 232 8402), Max Fashions (04 232 8198) and Amazon (04 232 8301). It has more than 30 stores, most of them selling clothing, as well as a few footwear, accessories and children's wear shops and two cafes. Parking is free and easy and there's a reasonably priced shuttle service from the city. It's open daily 10:00 to 17:00.

Titahi Bay Rd
Wellington
South Island
Map G14

North City Shopping Centre

04 237 5569 | www.northcityshopping.co.nz

This brightly lit suburban magnet has close to 100 stores, including many big clothing chains, branches of Farmers (04 237 5176) and Kmart (04 237 9876), a supermarket and cinemas, making it one of Wellington's biggest shopping destinations. It is notable for its excellent parents' room, complete with microwave for heating food and bottles. It has more than 1,100 carpark spaces and there's a train station nearby. Open most days 09:00 to 17:30, with a late night on Thursday (until 21:00) and shorter hours on Sundays and public holidays (10:00 to 17:30).

233-237 Lambton Quay
Wellington
Map p.503 D3 **115**

Old Bank Arcade

04 922 0600 | www.oldbank.co.nz

Easily the most atmospheric place to shop in Wellington, Old Bank Arcade is located in a heritage building that was once home to a bank. Today it's an enclave of innovative New Zealand designer boutiques, including shoe shop Minnie Cooper (04 473 7946) and clothing stores Ricochet (04 473 7433), Andrea Moore (04 471 2200) and Workshop (04 499 9010). There is also a restaurant and several good cafes. It's open Monday to Thursday 09:00 to 18:00, Friday 09:00 to 19:00, Saturday 10:00 to 16:00 and Sundays and public holidays 11:00 to 15:00. There is no parking.

Main St
Upper Hutt
Wellington
South Island
Map G14

Trentham City Shopping Centre

04 528 2626 | www.trenthamcity.co.nz

This 40 store, two-level shopping mall is Wellington's newest and has mostly chain stores, including Farmers (04 527 2190) and The Warehouse (04 527 7402), selling a good range of clothing and accessories. It's hoped the development will revitalise the drab Upper Hutt city centre. It also has a cinema, gym and foodcourt and there's free parking for 500 cars underground. Opening hours for most stores are 09:00 to 17:30, except for a late closing on Friday (21:00) and shorter hours on Sunday and public holidays (10:00 to 16:00).

Queens Dr
Lower Hutt
Wellington
South Island
Map G14

Westfield Queensgate

04 922 3500 | www.westfield.co.nz

The recently redeveloped suburban Westfield Queensgate – easily Wellington's largest mall – has more than 150 shops, mostly a mixture of chain and discount outlets. It also has a supermarket and cinema complex. Most stores are open 09:00 to 18:00, with later closing on Thursdays and Fridays (21:00) and shorter hours on Sundays (10:00 to 17:30). It has a 1,800 space carpark.

Christchurch

Places to Shop

Christchurch shoppers are a mix of tourists, wealthy farmers, arty types and locals. As a result, you can find it all here: tourist tat, mostly likely made offshore, enormous flat-screen TVs, classic 20th century furniture or cheap-as-chips basics. There's something here for everyone, and its often found in a little cluster.

Streets/Areas to Shop

Forgo the department stalls and malls and get out in the fresh air to experience the most interesting Christchurch shopping, from the designer stores and edgy shops in and around High Street, to the creative lanes of Poplar and His Lordship's Lane and the fascinating offerings of the cultural precinct.

Map p.517 D3 118

High Street

A short stroll south-east of Cathedral Square (p.260) brings you to Christchurch's hippest shopping precinct. Browse high-end clothes at Workshop (230 Tuam Street, 03 379 7305) or, on High Street, Plume (03 366 1663), Ricochet (03 377 1643) or Embellish (03 964 7786). Christchurch's best (and pricey) furniture and home furnishings can be found at McKenzie and Willis (at the corner of High and Asaph streets, 03 379 8980). There are smaller, new stores along High and Manchester Streets stocking lovingly restored 20th century furniture but be warned that this design hub is still in its infancy so opening hours can be limited.

At the apex of High and Tuam Streets is Alice in Videoland, a goldmine for cinephiles (03 365 0615). Around the corner, at 209 Tuam Street, is the Physics Room, for edgy art (03 379 5583, www.physicsroom.org.nz). At 112 Manchester Street, the Brooke Gifford Gallery showcases excellent contemporary New Zealand art (03 366 5288). Several worthwhile second-hand bookshops call this area home. Smith's Bookshop, at 133 Manchester Street (03 379 7976, smiths.bookshop.co.nz), is the place for antique and second-hand treasures, especially New Zealand titles.

Map p.517 D3 119

His Lordship's Lane & Poplar Lane

These small streets deserve special mention. His Lordship's Lane is a compact, up-and-coming little area between Lichfield and Manchester streets known as SOL (South of Lichfield). On His Lordship's Lane is the General Store (03 365 9950), with appealing gifts and homewares from all over the world. For arty jewellery, try Marocka (03 377 8110) next door. Go to narrow Poplar Lane, off Tuam Street near the corner with High Street, for some of Christchurch's best chocolates and most stylish flowers, at Harakeke (03 366 9545). Next door, Blue Earth Galleries has natural, New Zealand-made soap, bath products, skin lotions and massage oils (03 366 9646). If you have any money left, Dusk (03 365 4044) will relieve you of it, in return for quirky 'Kiwiana' and gifts.

Map p.516 A1 120

The Cultural Precinct

A stroll from Christchurch Cathedral along Worcester Street to the Arts Centre at the corner of Montreal Street is one of the great pleasures of a weekend in Christchurch. Leaving behind the gaudy tourist tat of Cathedral Square, you cross the Avon River, with its sloping banks and punting visitors, and meander past heritage buildings to the grand stone Arts Centre complex, which once housed the University of Canterbury. Outside, every weekend (rain or shine), from 10:00 to 16:00, up to 80 stalls display local crafts for sale. This is the place for cosy sheepskin slippers, lavender soap, hand-made jewellery and Maori art printed on hand-made flax paper. Inside the historic Arts Centre (open 10:00 to 17:00 daily) is a wide range of retailers with something for

everyone, including cheap souvenirs, hand-blown glass, leatherwear, paintings, T-shirts, jewellery, woodwork and ceramics. On a rainy weekend, watch craftspeople and artists at work, browse the Arts Centre Bookshop (03 365 5277), which concentrates on New Zealand titles, or make your own jewellery at Beadz Unlimited (03 379 5126). Across the courtyard, where the market is held on weekends, find high-end clothes and homewares at Untouched World (03 962 6551), whose merino knits are delectable and sustainably produced.
During the week, visit shops and galleries inside the Boulevard next to the market site for cafes and shops selling beads, books, souvenirs and crafts. Nearby Canterbury Museum (03 366 5000) has a reasonable gift shop and offers an international, tax-free postal service. For art books and unique gifts and souvenirs, visit the shop at Christchurch Art Gallery (03 941 7370). Form Gallery (03 377 1211, www.culturalprecinct.co.nz), in the art gallery building, deserves special mention for its exhibitions of contemporary New Zealand crafts in glass, ceramics, jewellery and other media.

Moorhouse Av
Christchurch
Map p.516 B4 121

Harvey Norman Centre

Furniture shopping in Christchurch became a little easier when Freedom Furniture (03 983 4000), Harvey Norman (03 983 2712) and Morehouse Furniture (03 961 1490) gathered under the same roof on Moorhouse Avenue between Colombo and Durham streets in the south of the city. There's a cafe and a cinema upstairs and Moorhouse Avenue is also home to numerous car dealerships. The centre is open Monday to Thursday 09:00 to 17:30, Fridays 09:00 to 19:00 and weekends 10:00 to 17:30. There is plenty of parking, mostly open-air, but it gets crowded at the weekend.

Department Stores

Cnr of Colombo St & Cashel Street Mall
Christchurch
Map p.516 C2 122

Ballantynes

0800 184 000 | *www.ballantynes.co.nz*

Ballantynes, the grand old lady of Christchurch shopping, was opened in 1854 as a straw hat retailer and became the site of New Zealand's worst fire tragedy in 1947, when 41 people lost their lives. Fortunately, the store bounced back. Today, it is the city's only remaining independent department store, with branches in Timaru and at Christchurch Airport.
Its flagship shop has cannibalised nearby buildings, and it's easy to get lost – but divertingly so amid extensive collections of cosmetics, dressmaking fabrics, homewares, glassware, furniture, gourmet food and wine, sensible loafers and slippers, stationery, souvenirs, toys, luggage and much more. It has a reasonable selection of clothing for men, women and children, though as menswear goes, it is perhaps best known for practical casual attire for chaps of a certain age. Women will find good stocks of hosiery and lingerie. However, shoppers who are looking for particular labels would probably find a better selection at a boutique store.
Services include personal shopping, a beauty salon, gift wrapping, mail order, duty-free shopping and gift registry. Reluctant male shoppers should use the Colombo Street entrance. Prices are sensible all year round but possibly the best time to visit is during the end-of-season sales. Shoppers parked in the Lichfield Street or Crossing Car Park buildings receive a complimentary hour's parking. There is also plenty of parking nearby. Ballantynes is open Monday to Thursday, 09:00 to 19:00, Friday 09:00 to 19:00, Saturday 09:00 to 17:00 and Sunday 10:00 to 16:00.

Markets

Cantabrians love their markets, which are packed with friendly locals and a source of useful goodies. Every suburb of Christchurch, it seems, hosts a monthly or seasonal fundraising market for a school or other worthy cause. Often held in church halls, these markets can be a good source of natural honey (expect to pay $4 to $7 a jar for comb honey), baking, seedlings and crafts. Look in local newspapers for market announcements or keep an eye open for home-made signs at intersections.

Lyttelton Main School
Oxford St
Lyttelton
Map p.508 F7

Lyttelton Farmers' Market

A pleasant weekend outing from Christchurch is over the Port Hills (or through the tunnel) to the Lyttelton Farmers' Market. It's open every Saturday from 10:00 to 13:00 in the grounds of Lyttelton Main School. After strolling around this non-profit market, take the time to explore quirky Lyttelton (p.263), a port town with an historic ambience.

Riccarton Rd
Christchurch
Map p.508 B5

Riccarton Racecourse Market

03 339 0011

Don't miss the Riccarton Racecourse Market – it is possibly the most multicultural event of the week in Christchurch. Operated by Rotary as a fundraising project, the 300 plus outdoor stalls attract huge crowds. Parking is free and there are facilities including toilets, an ATM and an information office. Apart from people-watching, look out for a range of items including fresh produce, clothing, bric-a-brac, souvenirs, native plants, seeds, books, second-hand goods, chocolates, hot food, gifts, jam, jewellery, furniture and tools. Go early for the best range; go late for the best prices. Open Sunday 09:00 to 14:00.

220 Pages Rd
Christchurch
Map p.508 F4

SuperShed Reuse Warehouse

03 381 6495

Although not strictly a market, no guide to shopping in Christchurch would be complete without a mention of the SuperShed Reuse Warehouse, a football pitch-sized space that is paradise for bargain-hunters, DIYers and creative types looking for inspiration.
The SuperShed, open 09:00 to 17:00 daily, has kitchenware, lighting, crockery (including popular New Zealand brand Crown Lynn), computers, furniture, toys, sports gear, books and magazines, clothes, shoes, bikes, carpets, sports gear, DIY materials, electrical appliances and hardware. It is the ultimate in green shopping, since everything has been 'recovered' after being discarded. Stock is then displayed with supermarket-style simplicity. Nearby, on Pages Road, is a Thursday morning market, with more bric-a-brac, hot food, art and books.

Shopping Malls

Christchurch's suburbs are well served with malls. Unfortunately most of them are identikit, with at least one supermarket, several cut-price clothes stores, coffee shop and foodcourt, a stationery store, a knick-knack or gift shop or two, a two-dollar shop, homewares and often a cinema complex. Although Westfield malls have a presence (in Riccarton's large mall), other shopping centres are independently owned. Nevertheless, they are filled with a similar selection of chain stories. They might be useful for the weekly necessities but fortunately Christchurch still has an array of quirky independent shopping precincts.

409 Main Rd South
Christchurch
Map p.508 B5

Dress-Smart

03 349 5750 | *www.dress-smart.co.nz*

Christchurch's Dress-Smart has 50 stores offering up to 70% off the retail price of seconds, factory and outlet goods. Popular brands include Pumpkin Patch children's clothing (0800 786 754), and clothes for adults by Diesel, Puma and Ripcurl. Other shops stock accessories, shoes, body and hair care, CDs and DVDs. Open daily 10:00 to 17:00, the mall also has food outlets for hungry bargain hunters. Buses run to and from the city centre.

Cnr Linwood Av and Buckleys Rd
Christchurch
Map p.508 D5

Eastgate Shopping Centre

03 982 0800

Eastgate, in the suburb of Linwood, is one of Christchurch's busier malls, and following its recent revamp is now an open-centred, roomy space in which to shop. Recommended among its stores is Four Paws (shop 103, 03 381 2373), a pet shop that stocks gourmet treats for dogs and cats, such as rabbit and venison. Opening hours are Monday and Tuesday 09:00 to 18:00, Wednesday to Friday 09:00 to 20:00, Saturday 09:00 to 18:00 and Sunday 10:00 to 18:00.

Cnr of 189 Papanui Rd and Aikmans Rd
Christchurch
Map p.508 C4

Merivale Mall

03 355 9692 | *www.merivalemall.co.nz*

Merivale Mall lies in the heart of an upmarket suburb amid beauticians and private medical clinics. After a spot of laser resurfacing, the well-heeled hoof it to this compact mall, which has the usual offerings alongside some notable shops. The big attraction is Photo & Video International (03 355 7534, www.photo.co.nz), a nationally renowned source of camera and photography equipment. Staff know what they're talking about and are able to find just about anything photographers might need. But even amateur snappers can take advantage of its top-quality prints at competitive prices. Photo & Video offers a tax-free service for goods shipped overseas. The entrance is off Papanui Road. Ladies who lunch will enjoy eating at one of the mall's casual, sunny eateries, such as Savoire Café (03 355 5645). Open weekdays 09:00 to 18:00 with a later close (10:00 on Thursdays), Saturday 10:00 to 17:00 and Sunday 10:00 to 16:00. Outside the mall, Traiteur of Merivale, at the corner of Papanui and Aikmans roads (www.traiteur.co.nz, 03 355 7750) stocks its own focaccia and prepared gourmet meals, and beautiful cured meats from Europe.

55 Main North Rd
Christchurch
Map p.508 C4

Northlands Mall

03 352 6535 | *www.northlands.co.nz*

Northlands has the usual selection of chain stores, plus Lush (03 354 6513), Trade Aid (03 352 9222) and some specialist shops. An information kiosk offers free wheelchairs and mobility scooters, strollers, and bus and entertainment tickets. There are 1,800 carpark spaces, but weekends can be busy. In the streets around Northlands are bulk stationery and other shops. Opening hours are 09:00 to 18:00, with later closings (21:00) Thursdays and Fridays.

Cnr of Marshlands Rd & New Brighton Rd
Christchurch
Map p.508 E4

The Palms

03 395 3067 | *www.thepalms.co.nz*

The Palms was revamped a couple of years ago, turning its focus to food, fashion and entertainment. It's dominated by big-name chain stores, including Farmers (03 375 7096), Glassons (03 385 9869), Hallensteins (03 386 3456), Max Fashions (03 386 3102), Bond & Bond (03 385 4880) and Noel Leeming (03 385 7957). These days the Palms is a pleasant, airy space with plenty of food options, including a Woolworths supermarket. Parking, some of it undercover, can be tight. It's open most days from 09:00 to 18:00, with late closing Thursday and Friday (21:00) and a later start on Sundays (10:00).

129 Riccarton Rd
Christchurch
Map p.508 B4

Riccarton Westfield

03 983 4500 | *www.westfield.co.nz*

When Christchurch's teenagers dream of a trip to the mall, Riccarton Westfield is their fantasy. This is the city's biggest with 170 stores, including cinemas, a foodcourt, a Pak 'N' Save supermarket (03 348 9727), restaurants, a juice bar and clothes shops galore, including the usual suspects: Glassons (03 348 6999), Max Fashions (03 348 5598), Barkers Clothing (03 341 8812) and Hallensteins (03 348 8775). Most shops are open

Monday to Wednesday 09:00 to 18:00, with late nights Thursday and Friday (until 21:00), and a later start on Sunday (10:00). Although there is a lot of parking, the mall gets hectic Thursday to Sunday, and during the school holidays.

Tower Junction Mega Mall

Entrance off Blenheim Rd & Clarence St
Christchurch
Map p.514 A3 132

The US-style strip mall arrives in Christchurch at Tower Junction, a collection of shops arranged around a large carpark, almost necessitating a 300m drive between shops. Best reason to visit? Raeward Fresh (03 341 1110, www.raewardfresh.co.nz) and its cut-price and good-looking fruit, vegetables and meat. Don't expect to find pomegranates or fennel – everything is standard fare – but at these prices, Christchurch shoppers aren't complaining. Within Raeward Fresh is Pacific Catch fish shop, which has a wide range of fresh and frozen fish and shellfish at low prices. Raeward Fresh is open daily 08:30 to 18:00 (20:00 Thursday). Other Tower Junction tenants include Ezibuy (03 962 7030) and Postie + (03 348 5927) for cheap clothing, Animates pet shop (03 341 2227), a hardware store, a stationery shop and Kathmandu outdoor clothing and equipment (03 348 0152). Parking is plentiful. Most shops are open Monday to Friday 09:00 to 17:30 and weekends 10:00 to 17:00.

Clothes are a reflection...

EXPLORER
The Essential Visitors' Guide
mini
Sydney

Going Out

Going Out

Auckland packs in more opportunities for good times and relaxation than any other city in New Zealand, and while you won't make the mistake of thinking you're in London or New York, you can always discover a few like-minded souls out and about most nights of the week. From Monday to Thursday the bars along Ponsonby Road and at The Viaduct can be quiet, and you're more likely to find Aucklanders enjoying a meal at their favourite Thai or Indian restaurant. By Friday night, the hard-working people of Auckland reckon they've earned the right to breathe out, and the city's cosy pubs and sleek bars are filled with revellers knocking back local and imported beers and good Kiwi wines. It's a relaxed, 'play it by ear' scene, where after-work drinks from 18:00 might segue into a casual meal around 20:00, followed by cocktails, and perhaps a stint on the dancefloor. Saturday night starts later and definitely finishes (much) later.

Favourite DJs begin around 22:00 at bars and clubs in the CBD and along Karangahape Road. The night might start with cruisy Pacific-style dub beats, and then build up after midnight to more energetic sounds through to 05:00. New Zealand has liberal drinking laws and in many inner city places you can truly kick on until dawn.

Prepare yourself also for the surprising versatility of Auckland's eating, drinking and clubbing scene. Your favourite bar for casual, post-work drinks might morph into a dance-on-the-bar place once the cheesy and ironic 1980s hits start to flow, while your preferred underground haunt for chilled lounge beats and skillfully prepared cocktails may surprise you with an excellent Pacific Rim-influenced tapas platter.

Increasingly, going out in Auckland is not just about heading into the centre of the city. In recent years excellent neighbourhood bars (especially in inner suburbs such as Kingsland and Mount Eden) have popped up in old shops, libraries and banks, usually offering a sophisticated and versatile mix of drinking and eating. Drop by in the afternoon for a pint as you watch the 'footie' (usually rugby union), and come back for DJ-led shenanigans after dark. And if you find yourself living across Auckland's Harbour Bridge on 'the Shore', there's a compact array of excellent pubs, bars and restaurants along Hurstmere Road in Takapuna.

According to local folklore, **Wellington** has more bars, restaurants and cafes per head of population than New York. It may be urban legend, but it's undeniable that this compact city still has an eating and drinking scene truly worthy of a nation's capital. The two main areas are bohemian Cuba Street and livelier Courtenay Place. Cuba has traditionally been characterised by cheaper ethnic eateries, but now the focus is shifting to drop-dead-cool places, such as Matterhorn (p.459) and Floriditas (p.451), serving excellent food and superb cocktails. Courtenay Place, a short cab ride away, kicks off a little later (around 21:00) and continues until well after midnight with a

Cuisine List – Quick Reference

combination of intimate cocktail bars, boisterous pubs and clubs. Explore the quieter side lanes of Blair Street and Allen Street for the best of the area's restaurants. Further south, **Christchurch**'s prime eating and drinking opportunities are also focused around two hubs. On Oxford Terrace near the Avon River, the area known as The Strip switches from laid-back restaurants in the afternoon to raucous bars later at night. It's a good place to wander and see what appeals. Just to the east, the area around Colombo Street and Cashel Street is also heavy with opportunities for carousing, ranging from tiny hole-in-the-wall bars to noisy brewpubs. No one has ever claimed that a night out in central Christchurch is a quiet affair, so expect a fair bit of blokey southern humour. If you're after something a little quieter, the port town of Lyttelton (12km away) has a fast developing restaurant and after-dark scene, and is preferred by many locals seeking a more sophisticated night out. On weekend afternoons, consider a long lunch at the restaurants in the French-influenced town of Akaroa (p.264) on nearby Banks Peninsula.

No Smoke Without Fines

Smoking in bars and restaurants is illegal in New Zealand and carries a heavy fine for both the customer and the establishment. Head outside if you want to smoke, and check with the staff if smoking is permitted at outdoor tables.

Eating Out

From weekend brunch in buzzy cafes to authentic flavours cooked by the country's increasingly cosmopolitan population, New Zealanders love to eat. Restaurants and cafes are usually casual and relaxed, and compared to Europe and North America, very affordable. Kiwis are a well travelled bunch, and this wanderlust is reflected in the range of cuisines on offer. Every suburb of Auckland, in particular, is dotted with Thai, Indian, Chinese and Turkish restaurants, and increasingly New Zealand chefs are reflecting global influences on their menus. Many eateries open for breakfast and stay open until late at night, and most places are family-friendly, as a new generation of Kiwis comes to grips with satay and sushi. Bookings are recommended on Friday and Saturday nights, especially during the peak dining time of 20:00 to 22:00. Popular 'eat streets' in Auckland include The Viaduct, Ponsonby Road and Parnell Road, and the inner suburb of Kingsland is an emerging favourite with Auckland foodies in the know. In Wellington, the most popular street in on which to eat (and drink and be merry) is Cuba – you could spend days indulging and not exhaust its charms.

Delivery

Take-out food, or 'takeaways' in local parlance, is part of Kiwi culture, and for many busy households it's the only way to top off a hectic working week. Within days of settling into your new home your letterbox will be filled with flyers from neighbourhood Thai, Indian, Chinese and Italian restaurants offering home delivery. Many upmarket restaurants also deliver, and it's always worth asking your favourite restaurant if they are happy to cater for special occasions. Austin's (09 374 5900, www.austins.co.nz) is a speciality catering company that is a regular fixture at corporate events, but is also good for smaller, more private occasions.

Hygiene

To comply with regulations outlets must register with local authorities and display a hygiene grading certificate in a prominent place. Unregistered premises cannot be forced to close down, but can be prosecuted under council bylaws for trading illegally. Individual councils inspect each premises and then grade them according to their own classification system.

Tax, Service Charges & Tipping

Tipping is optional, but a gratuity from 5% to 10% is appropriate for good service in better restaurants. New Zealand is still largely egalitarian, and many places have a tip jar on the counter which is shared among the staff. There's no rule of thumb, but for outstanding service, round the bill to an appropriate amount or add 10% to 20% –

Explorer Recommended

Alfresco		Dizengoff	p.440	Logan Brown	p.452
Coney Cafe	p.456	Ernesto	p.456	The Green Parrot	p.452
Dockside	p.453	**Fine Dining**		The Tasting Room	p.453
Swashbucklers	p.446	50 on Park	p.464	**Prize Pints**	
Waipara Springs	p.465	Engine Room	p.432	Dux de Lux	p.473
White	p.432	White	p.432	Galbraith's Ale House	p.445
Caffeine Fix		Zibibbo	p.451	Hallertau	p.445
Cafe L'Affare	p.455	**Kiwi Cuisine**		Hawthorn Lodge	p.459
C1 Espresso	p.470	Leigh Sawmill Cafe	p.436	Leuven Beer Cafe	p.459

either way it will be appreciated. Note there are no additional charges over and above food and beverages as GST (Goods and Services Tax) is always included, but on public holidays some spots add a 15% surcharge. To cover higher wage costs, many cafes and restaurants require customers to pay a 15% surcharge on public holidays.

Hidden Charges

Most restaurants and cafes operate with no hidden charges. New Zealand's Goods and Services Tax (GST) is usually included in menu costs, and if glasses of ordinary tap water are offered there should be no additional charge. Many cafes provide jugs of water for customers to serve themselves, but still or sparkling mineral water will be charged additionally. Costs will be detailed on the menu. Bread (often with olive oil) is also charged separately. If you are bringing a bottle of your own wine to a BYO restaurant there will be an additional corkage fee (see p.448).

Restaurant Timings

Most cafes and restaurants are open seven days a week, although some more expensive and exclusive eateries remain closed on Mondays. All are closed on Christmas Day, Good Friday and Easter Sunday, and most do not open until 13:00 on Anzac Day, New Zealand's annual war remembrance day (April 25).

Vegetarian Food

Vegetarian food is an accepted part of New Zealand's restaurant scene, and most places will have a few vegetarian options on the menu. Pasta and salads are the most common healthy diversions in cafes, and the country's wide range of Thai, Indian and Chinese eateries always offer interesting vegetarian choices. An excellent Indian vegetarian restaurant is Rasoi in Auckland (211 Karangahape Rd, 09 377 7781), while nearby Satya (p.434) has several good vegetarian and vegan options. Just over the road the Hare Krishna team at Food for Life (268 Karangahape Rd, 09 300 7585) offers vegetarian delights that are incredibly affordable. Similar cuisine, but with a different philosophy, is on offer at The Blue Bird Cafe (299 Dominion Rd, 09 623 4900). In Wellington, Maranui (p.457) and its sister cafe Deluxe (04 801 5455) aren't purely veggie but offer excellent options for vegetarian, vegan and gluten-free diners.

Local Cuisine

To many New Zealanders local cuisine means fish and chips on the beach, or a leisurely barbecue with friends and family on a lazy summer's afternoon. The humble meat pie is the quintessential Kiwi snacks, and The Fridge in Auckland (p.441) bakes the country's best. To find something a little more unusual you'll have to delve a little deeper. Traditional Maori food can be difficult to find. Several speciality restaurants have disappeared in recent years, meaning your best opportunity to experience a hangi (an earth oven) or to try food such as pork and puha (wild watercress) is with a Maori family. The traditional foods of Auckland's significant Pacific Island community (Auckland is the world's largest Polynesian city) can be enjoyed at the annual Pasifika festival (p.60) or at the weekly Otara Market (p.410). Don't miss the chance to try food cooked in an umu, the Samoan version of a Maori hangi (p.27).

Cafes & Coffee shops

Forget petrol and electricity. Auckland and Wellington's economies actually run on caffeine, and locals take their coffee very seriously. There are international chains such as

Starbucks, Gloria Jean's and Esquires, but most prefer to frequent locally owned, independent cafes or local outfits such as Columbus or Sierra.

Coffee roasters are almost as well known as the cafes, and dependable names to look out for include Roasted Addiqtion, Karajoz and Allpress in Auckland. Those that roast their own in Wellington include Mojo (p.457), Caffe L'Affare (p.455), Havana, Supreme, Fuel, and The Immigrant's Son. Most cafes open at breakfast and serve brunch and lunch options along with tasty counter food such as muffins and paninis. Later at night more than a few are transformed into restaurants with full menus and a selection of beer and wine. Kids are welcome; many places provide toys and play areas for children.

Street Food

If you're looking for a quick and tasty bite after a night out in the bars of central Auckland, you're never far from a good noodle bar or kebab shop. To truly become a local, head to the iconic White Lady, a 'pie cart' (really a caravan) that turns out excellent burgers, toasted sandwiches and fish and chips most nights into the wee small hours. You'll find the White Lady on Commerce Street in Auckland CBD. Make sure you ask for beetroot on your burger.

There are really no street food stalls in Wellington, save the pie cart at the station. There are loads of take-out options, however, covering all cuisines, and all times of the day or night. For fish and chips, try Fish Boys in Petone; for those with a taste for Middle Eastern, Ali Baba. For the seriously late night stop try Haitatai Bakery for pies, Kennys, for everything fried, and for a Chinese buffet at 03:00, J&Ms. No need to worry about food poisoning – if you're dining at one of the latter two the previously consumed alcohol will kill any bacteria.

Drinking

New Zealand has come a long way from the 'Six O'Clock Swill' of the 1960s when drinking establishments had to close by 18:00. Now the country's licensing laws are more liberal and flexible, and the line between bar, cafe, pub and restaurant is becoming increasingly blurred. Around the country you'll always find a friendly pub in the quietest of rural areas, and in the main cities and towns there's everything from sophisticated cocktail bars to specialist brewpubs. Auckland, Wellington and Queenstown have the best nightlife, but often the welcome is warmer in smaller centres. Having a few drinks is an integral part of the Kiwi psyche. On Friday night the emphasis will be on after-work drinks, and on Saturdays the focus often switches to watching live sport. Most pubs and bars are open seven days a week to around midnight, but in Auckland, Wellington, Christchurch and Queenstown a few stay pouring 24 hours a day.

Street snacks

Door Policy

In general, only bars with live entertainment have a cover charge, and even that's becoming less common. Door policies relate to age (you must be at least 18 to get in), state of intoxication, and dress – if there's an official policy in place, it will be strict. Few bars have a members' only policy but a couple have designated members' clubs, and increasingly it seems common for those in the know to join these via MySpace or Facebook.

Going Out

Dress Code

New Zealanders on the whole are both reasonably trend-conscious and eclectic. People take their outfits seriously but mostly because they crave individuality. If there's a dress code for a night, it's fairly logical – wear shirts and shoes and you can't go wrong. It's also worth taking an extra layer as many of the cities sit close to water; even in the height of summer it can get chilly after sun down. As a rule, smart casual covers every occasion.

Bun Fight

Like any major city, Auckland is well-endowed with international burger chains, but a couple of local companies are doing their best to lift the fine art of burger-making. With branches across the city, Burger Fuel (www.burgerfuel.co.nz) and Burger Wisconsin (www.wisconsin.co.nz) are a tasty step up from your everyday quarter pounder. A beef and blue cheese pesto burger might cost a little bit more, but you didn't move all this way for something you could buy in any country of the world, did you?

Nightclubs

It must be that laid-back Kiwi personality. In New Zealand you're more likely to be immersed in the mellow stylings of dub and downbeat than the frenetic pleasures of trance and house, especially in Auckland. Those with a 'go hard or go home' mindset can still find somewhere to party until dawn, but the interesting venues are cruisy spots that are a very cool combination of bar and club. Auckland doesn't have any sprawling 'super clubs' so international DJs such as Armin Van Buren play at the St James Theatre (www.saintjames.co.nz) in Queen Street. The St James also hosts big local shows from populist DJ teams, including Nice'n'Urlich. Expect to pay up to $15 for established local DJs, and around $60 for international gigs. Auckland's an egalitarian town, so come dressed smart casual, and the bouncers (usually easygoing Pacific Island guys), should (eventually) grant you access. See www.mukuna.co.nz and www.viewauckland.co.nz for listings.

In Wellington, see www.texture.co.nz and www.wotzon.com for the most up-to-date details, including the latest on Sandwiches (p.461), voted best nightclub in New Zealand in 2006 by *Bartender* magazine.

Gay & Lesbian

Auckland is a tolerant and cosmopolitan metropolis, and the gay and lesbian communities are well integrated into the city. The cafes, restaurants and bars of Ponsonby Road are popular, and later at night the action moves to nearby Karangahape Road. Urge (www.urge.co.nz) is a popular men-only bar and club on K Road, and nearby Family (270 Karangahape Rd, 09 309 0213) turns the kitsch right up, with karaoke nights and drag divas (keep an eye out for the delectable Miss Ribena). Flirt (www.wannaflirt.co.nz) runs regular women's events at Bacio Bar just across the road (309 Karangahape Rd). Local publications *Express* (www.gayexpress.com), *Out!* (www.out.co.nz) and www.gaynz.com are excellent information sources.

Every February, Auckland's gay, lesbian and transgender communities come out to play at the annual Hero Festival (www.hero.org.nz). Events include 'the big gay out' and 'wigs on the waterfront'.

In Wellington, the scene is more integrated with the fabric of the city – people won't need to seek it out in separate and specific places. That said, Imerst (www.imerst.co.nz) and Our Bar (04 802 4405) are popular spots.

Independent Reviews

All of the outlets in this section have been independently reviewed by food and drinks writers based in Auckland, Wellington and Christchurch. Their aim is to give engaging, informative and unbiased views of each venue. If any have led you astray, or if your favourite local eatery doesn't grace these pages, then drop us a line.

Restaurant Listing Structure

Our Going Out section brings your attention to a cross-section of places in Auckland, Wellington and Christchurch that are definitely worth a visit. Each review attempts to give a good idea of the food, service, decor and atmosphere. Starting with restaurants, categorised by cuisine (in alphabetic order), followed by cafes, bars, pubs and clubs, outlets are listed under their respective city.

Auckland

African

The Yellow Star
The yellow star seen to the right is our way of highlighting places that we think merit extra praise. It might be the atmosphere, the food, the cocktails, the music or the crowd, but any review that you see with the star attached is somewhere a bit special.

475 Khyber Pass Rd
Newmarket
Auckland
Map p.492 C3 1

Sahaa

09 523 4578

Sahaa is Auckland's only north African restaurant, but even if the city was packed with other places offering the cuisine of Algeria, Tunisia and Morocco, this place would probably still be the best. At the heart of the menu are rich and fragrant slow-cooked tagines served simply with fluffy couscous. The region's rich culinary heritage is also displayed through a diverse array of starters; visit with a group of friends and share your way leisurely through the list of robust lamb and chicken brochettes, spicy merguez sausages, or home-made bread dipped in roasted dukkah and zingy olive oil. On the dessert menu the cinnamon icecream is so good it will leave you asking if it's available to take away (it isn't as yet, but if more people ask, who knows?). Upstairs is a private room with cushions, carpets and antiques that create an authentic ambience of the Maghreb region.

Brazilian

137-141 Queen St
Auckland
Map p.488 A2 2

Wildfire

09 353 7595 | *www.wildfirerestaurant.co.nz*

Carnivores of the world unite at Wildfire, a traditional Brazilian churrascaria (steakhouse). After warming up with starters such as sirloin on cassava chips, the fun really begins. At one end of the restaurant stands a huge spit, spinning slowly with giant skewers of meat. When you order your main course, a knife-wielding passador (waiter) visits your table and carves lamb, beef or chicken directly from the skewers onto your plate; once you've had your fill of smoky chorizo sausages and marinated New Zealand lamb, just flip your table marker from green to red to signal enough is enough. It may sound gimmicky, but the prime cuts of meat and the quality of the side dishes and sauces make Wildfire a great night out – just steer clear of the harbour's edge when you leave as you'll sink like a stone. There's a second branch on Auckland's North Shore in Takapuna (428 Lake Rd, 09 489 0489).

Chinese

Other options **Far Eastern** p.433

477 New North Rd
Kingsland
Auckland
Map p.490 C3 3

Canton Cafe

09 846 7888

If you see a group of people loitering around Kingsland's New North Road, there's no cause for alarm; they're just waiting to get a table at Canton Cafe. You can book to avoid the queue, but the super-efficient service (almost too quick if you're planning a relaxed meal) means tables open up on a regular basis so you shouldn't find yourself hanging around for too long. Most of the clientele are Chinese families – always an indicator of a good Chinese restaurant – lured back time and again by the great value authentic food. Don't expect flash decor or witty repartee from the wait staff though; you're here for seafood that's so fresh you may think the king prawns have made their own way to the kitchen, and a good range of vegetarian dishes that use silkily fresh tofu. Bring a few friends and some beers or a bottle of wine, and enjoy Chinese, Auckland style.

European

Other options **Mediterranean** p.435, **Italian** p.434, **Spanish** p.437, **French** p.434

Engine Room

115 Queen St
Northcote Point
Auckland
Map p.488 A2 4

09 480 9052

It has been a quick rise to fame for Engine Room, so be prepared to wait for a few weeks to get a booking. Housed in an old post office in the heritage North Shore suburb of Northcote, a string of good reviews and awards have propelled this new restaurant to the top of Auckland's dining tree. The best description of the cuisine is modern bistro, with the open kitchen turning out exemplary versions of classics such as steak frites and innovative and modern variations on tasty comfort food – such as roast chicken with couscous. Auckland's Asian influences are evident on the menu too, with subtle flavours from Thailand and Vietnam making their mark. The service is relaxed but assured, and with a concise menu (normally just six starters and six mains) that changes regularly, the buzzing Engine Room is definitely a place to add to your 'regulars' list.

Soul Bar & Bistro

Viaduct Harbour
Auckland
Map p.487 F2 5

09 356 7249 | *www.soulbar.co.nz*

Soul gets a hard time from some Aucklanders. True, pop in for Friday night drinks and there is a danger you'll be overwhelmed by crowing property developers and the like. But to dismiss Soul as a hangout for neo-rich yuppies would mean missing out on a great dining spot. This busy restaurant delivers some of Viaduct Harbour's best food in a top location. The spacious dining room in cool neutral tones and a wide, sunny terrace, Soul is perfect for people-watching too. And even if the celebrity sightings are on the slim side, the food is deservedly famous. Innovative starters are divided simply into 'cold' and 'hot', and fresh market fish can be cooked as you like it. Clever twists on meat and poultry dishes, plus a full vegetarian menu, prove that Soul aims much higher than to exist as merely a good seafood restaurant. Service is also slick and considerably better than a few other places on The Viaduct.

White

Princes Wharf
147 Quay St
Auckland
Map p.488 A1 6

09 978 2020 | *www.hilton.co.nz*

Situated right at the end of Princes Wharf's 300 metre stretch into Auckland harbour, the Hilton's signature restaurant has arguably the most dramatic location of any eatery in the city. The minimalist interior is panelled with expansive windows, exposing the changing moods of the ocean and sky, and during summer the spacious deck provides front-row seats for the maritime landscape. The location is matched by the standard of the food, wine and service. Classic and traditional recipes are subtly remodelled, always with an eye on the best seasonal, local produce. Seared scallops are partnered with Israeli couscous and fennel risotto, and warm fig tart is served with honey and lavender. Experience the five-course menu ($165 with wine matches) or keep it simple with the three-course 'white lightning' menu ($45) – ideal for business lunches.

White

Far Eastern

Other options **Malaysian** p.435, **Thai** p.438, **Chinese** p.431, **Vietnamese** p.438, **Japanese** p.435

5 Short St
Newmarket
Auckland
Map p.488 B2 7

East

09 532 5518 | www.east.co.nz

East's simple but stylish decor oozes effortless Zen cool. The menu promises 'tasty, fresh, healthy, modern styled Asian food', and it demands interaction. Choose from 11 main dishes showcasing the diverse noodle and rice styles of Asia and add your own main ingredient – beef, chicken, calamari, prawns or tofu. Or go for the Asian-style tapas (try the duck wraps and the chilli salt squid) to get the taste buds fired up. The minimalist drinks menu features three beers, including Kirin from Japan, and a concise wine list with Asian cuisine-friendly aromatics such as pinot gris and riesling. You can take home the East experience in funky containers, straight out of a New York crime drama, or avoid leaving the house totally with the home delivery service. There are other branches at 596 Remuera Road (09 522 0907) and 4/171 Ponsonby Road (09 360 6085).

Cnr Custom St West
& Lower Hobson St
Auckland
Map p.488 A2 8

Monsoon Poon

09 379 9311 | www.monsoonpoon.co.nz

In a city well endowed with affordable and authentic Asian restaurants, Monsoon Poon is something different. This self-described 'south-east Asian trading house restaurant' presents an eclectic combo of the best of the region. Indian food sits happily beside flavours from Vietnam and Thailand, with Malaysian goodies such as laska and satay also making an appearance. Such a diverse blend could merge into mediocrity, but Monsoon Poon keeps it real with surprising culinary authenticity. The delicious cross-cultural experiment takes place surrounded by quirky Asian decor that combines retro statues of Chairman Mao and televisions showing kung fu movies. Have a few drinks in the wonderfully kitsch bar before moving through to the spacious dining room. Try an irreverently named cocktail (maybe a ping-pong or a buddha bing), or a bottle of Emerson's Organic Pilsner, a local microbrew that's quite possibly New Zealand's best partner for a robust Thai curry.

Fish & Chips

612 Remuera Rd
Auckland
Map p.484 D5

The Fishmonger

09 524 6223 | www.fishmonger.co.nz

Whether you eat in or take out, The Fishmonger is a cut above your standard chippie. Tuck into Kiwi classics such as battered snapper and crumbed scallops in modern surroundings. You can also have your fish prepared with a Mediterranean rub, or blackened cajun-style. Excellent gourmet burgers and interesting side dishes such as Thai fishcakes and shrimp and sweetcorn fritters are also available, and the cosmopolitan mix of salads includes zesty Asian coleslaw and tabouleh. The Fishmonger is also a seafood delicatessen. Stock up on Penang fish curry, seafood chowder or salmon kebabs. The chips are gloriously chunky and crispy, and you should definitely leave room for the kumara (sweet potato) variety with aioli. The restaurant has a second location in busy Parnell (363 Parnell Road, 09 373 4290).

Fancy a Brew?

Beer aficionados should raise a pint to the fact that New Zealand has the world's highest number of microbreweries per head of population. One of the best place to sample the results is at brewery bars such as Galbraith's Ale House (see p.445). Most pubs open mid morning for brunch and stay open until after midnight.

French

210 Symonds St
Auckland
Map p.491 F2 10

The French Cafe

09 377 1911 | www.thefrenchcafe.co.nz

Since making its debut in 1985, The French Cafe has continuously been rated one of Auckland's top restaurants. Open for dinner from Tuesday to Saturday and for lunch on Friday, you may have to plan ahead to secure a booking – but it's definitely worth the forethought. Despite the name, if you visit expecting to be served traditional Gallic fare you'll be disappointed – instead there's a distinct Pacific Rim influence at Auckland's most elegantly formal-but-unstuffy dining room. Pink roasted lamb comes with potato truffle fritters, and crispy roast duckling melts with a mandarin puree. Service is possibly the best in town, while the atmosphere remains relaxed. The French Cafe is not cheap (mains will set you back around $40), but for a special night out it offers consistently excellent value.

462 New North Rd
Kingsland
Auckland
Map p.490 C4 11

Tabou

09 846 3474 | www.tabou.co.nz

By promoting itself as the area's 'newest friendly local', Tabou is selling itself short. It might still be a favourite among the residents of a rapidly gentrifying Kingsland, but lurking within this compact bistro and bar is some of Auckland's best French-influenced food. Relaxed, fun dining is possible at the canteen-style communal tables. Tabou's tasting plates are made for sharing; the crostini with blue cheese and honey tastes delicious, managing to find the perfect meeting point of sweet and savoury. After enjoying a classic cocktail, more formal diners can move to dark and moody leather banquettes for French bistro fare. Be sure to check the blackboard for the interesting food and wine specials.

Indian

271 Karangahape Rd
Auckland
Map p.491 F1 12

Satya South Indian Cafe

09 377 0007

Auckland has plenty of good Indian restaurants, but almost all feature cuisine from the north of the sub-continent. The popular southern Indian-influenced Satya is an exception. The food is generally lighter and healthier than standard northern fare, with less creamy sauces and more vegetarian options. Start with dahi puri, a zingy combination of coriander, home-made yoghurt and tamarind chutney, and move on to the fresh coconut flavours of prawn malabari. With a few token swathes of red silk, Satya's ambience is relaxed. It's not a restaurant you need to get dressed up for – the food is what counts. If you want a drink with your curry don't forget to bring along your own beer or wine, and, in the family-run Satya, don't be surprised to see the children take your order. There's also a much smaller branch in Sandringham (515 Sandringham Rd, 09 845 8451).

Italian

Other options **Mediterranean** p.435

53 Nelson St
Auckland
Map p.487 F3 13

Toto

09 302 2665 | www.totorestaurant.co.nz

Dramatic is the best word to describe Toto. The whitewashed walls are trimmed with retro Italian film posters, and warm timber flows seamlessly from the wooden floors to the glorious bar. Once you do leave the confines of one of Auckland's classiest restaurant bars, you'll be treated to glorious Italian cuisine that treads a perfect line between traditional and innovative. The drinks menu recreates lazy days in Rome, with Italian beers as an aperitif and grappa for after your meal, and the wine selection features the best from New Zealand and Italy. During the day, Toto is a regular haunt of power lunchers from the advertising and media worlds, and egos and opinions sometimes bounce noisily off the plastered walls and wooden floors. Come for a leisurely dinner instead, and, on Thursday nights, the live opera performances.

Mediterranean menu

Japanese

Other options **Far Eastern** p.433

Rikka

53 Davis Crescent
Newmarket
Auckland
Map p.492 C3 14

09 522 5277

This dramatic and slender space is the perfect minimalist stage for Rikka's clean and fresh flavours. The sashimi is beautifully fresh, and the tempura light and crunchy but never oily. During the day it's favoured by busy Newmarket business types and shoppers taking time out from the suburb's retail attractions. Seating is in quiet booths, but the best place to graze on one of Rikka's good value lunch boxes ($19.90) is at the shared canteen-style bench. At night, the pace of eating slows down as diners choose a la carte; the scallop and teriyaki trio are particularly good. Auckland's essential Rikka empire also includes Don Don Rikka around the corner (3D Short St, Newmarket; 09 529 0808) and Sake Bar Rikka (Victoria Park Market, 09 377 8239). The former specialises in tasty kamameshi, a rice casserole, and the latter makes your sake dreams come true in traditional Japanese surroundings.

Malaysian

Other options **Chinese** p.431, **Thai** p.438

KK Malaysian Cuisine

463A Manukau Rd
Epsom
Auckland
Map p.496 C4 15

09 630 3555

If there was an award based on restaurant size and quality of food, the tiny KK would win hands down. The floor plan would only suffice as a walk-in pantry at other, flashier eateries, but the family team here turns out home-style food just like your mother makes – that's if your mum was an industrious Malaysian lady using authentic recipes from her own grandmother. The decor is best described as basic, and you'll need to keep your elbows tucked in, but once the beef rendang, squid sambal and chicken satay start arriving, you won't notice even the closest of neighbours. KK is unlicensed so bring your own cold beer or a good bottle of riesling. The KK empire also stretches to a larger restaurant in nearby Ellerslie (28-34 Robert Street, 09 589 1684) that offers a good value buffet ($23) on Friday nights. Bookings are essential at both branches.

Mediterranean

Other options **Spanish** p.437, **Italian** p.434

La Zeppa

33 Drake St
Auckland
Map p.484 E6

09 379 8167

Warning. Don't go to this restaurant with anyone who's even slightly selfish. Most of La Zeppa's food is made for sharing and you owe it to yourself to sample as many of the tapas-style offerings as possible. La Zeppa is situated in a refurbished warehouse with concrete floors, exposed beams and brick walls in Auckland's Victoria Park Market. Traditionally 'Vic Park' is a touristy wasteland when it comes to good eating, but La Zeppa comes to the rescue in a sophisticated and elegant space. A Mediterranean theme links the menu (try the smoked snapper and Pernod dip with flatbread), but an Asian influence also bubbles away with dishes such as miso-cured pork belly. The wine and beer list is equally eclectic, including Founders' Tall Blonde lager, an excellent South Island microbrew. Servings, albeit delicious, are on the small side, so plan on ordering three or four plates per person.

9 Durham St East
Auckland
Map p.488 A3 17

Mezze

09 307 2029

Mezze is one of those versatile establishments that Auckland does so well. Meet work associates for a breakfast briefing (try the grilled Turkish bread with feta cheese, olives and tomato), or mix and match different tapas plates with Friday night drinks. With bullfighting posters and terracotta hues, the decor is ostensibly Spanish, but Turkish rugs and rough-hewn carpets hint at a wider provenance. A warm and eclectic ambience is reflected on the menu, which travels from Morocco to Asia Minor, calling en route in Spain and Italy. At night a laid-back, bohemian buzz is fuelled by a wine list with good value Spanish reds lurking amid favourites from New Zealand and Australia. Beer fans should try the hard-to-find Green Fern organic lager. If you end up living on Auckland's North Shore, there is another equally good Mezze in Birkenhead (98 Hinemoa Street, 09 480 1598).

Mexican

67 Victoria St West
Auckland
Map p.488 A3 18

The Mexican Cafe

09 373 2311 | *www.themexicancafe.co.nz*

The city's first Mexican restaurant is still its best. Since 1983, The Mexican Cafe has been loosening the inhibitions of Aucklanders with robust food, live Latin music and the city's widest selection of Mexican beers. In the restaurant's earliest days, it had a strong following from Auckland's student population, but now the clientele is more diverse. It's a firm favourite with overseas travellers, so most nights you'll hear an excited (and probably slightly slurred) gaggle of accents and languages. Cuisine happily jumps the border north to include dishes from southern California, and the party atmosphere is best enjoyed with a big group when you can share jugs of margarita. At least 80 different tequilas are on offer, and if you're feeling flush, splash out on a shot of Herradura Seleccion Suprema anejo for $30. Chilli junkies should check out the 'devil's nachos', topped with addictive jalapeno peppers.

New Zealand

142 Pakiri Rd
Auckland
North Island Map G5

Leigh Sawmill Cafe

09 422 6019 | *www.sawmillcafe.co.nz*

After visiting this place on a sunny weekend afternoon, you'll probably leave determined to fast-track your application for New Zealand residency. It doesn't get much better than sitting back with a beer from the Sawmill's own microbrewery, tucking into a pizza crammed with local seafood, and tapping your foot to laid-back dub beats. As the name suggests, the cafe is housed in an old sawmill, an hour from the city, and is a favourite among Aucklanders in the know. Complementing the dub DJs are regular gigs from some of New Zealand's more eclectic bands and solo performers, and international acts also rock this heritage space with increasing frequency. Even if there's no music on offer when you visit, the wine list, featuring the best of local Matakana vineyards such as Ti Point, Heron's Flight and Hyperion, makes the trip worthwhile. If no one is willing to be your designated driver, you can always stay the night at the attached hotel.

Seafood

19 Tamaki Dr
Auckland
Map p.484 D5

Hammerheads

09 521 4400 | www.hammerheads.co.nz

Excellent seafood restaurants in Auckland can sometimes seem few and far between, which is surprising for a city built on two harbours. Hammerheads is one of the exceptions and uses its location along the waterfront on Tamaki Drive to its full advantage. The spacious and stately set up occupies an art deco building that used to house the local coastguard, and a maritime influence lingers within. Superb views of Waitemata Harbour and downtown Auckland lure evening diners, and a space on the sunny deck is a hot ticket during the city's sultry summers. Hammerheads' fresh seafood is treated simply, usually with an astute culinary twist. Try the lemon-scented snapper with pickled green papaya and grapefruit, although the most popular dish is the seafood platter for two, featuring fresh oysters, squid, mussels, prawns, salmon and snapper ($115). Make an afternoon of it with a bottle of crisp Cloudy Bay sauvignon blanc.

Spanish

Other options **Mediterranean** p.435

91 Federal St
Auckland
Map p.488 A3 22

Bellota

09 363 6301 | www.bellota.co.nz

When he's not being executive chef at The Providores in London, Peter Gordon, New Zealand's first (and only) celebrity chef is often back home developing his two Auckland restaurants. Both are located in the Sky City Grand Hotel. The more formal is Dine, but you'll find yourself eating at the relaxed Bellota on a more regular basis. In a city where the word 'tapas' is used and abused, Bellota is the real deal with an authentic array of Spanish treats. Gordon's past is as a champion of Pacific Rim fusion cuisine, but at Bellota he plays it mainly straight with beautifully prepared combinations of imported Spanish ingredients such as chorizo and serrano ham, and stunningly fresh local produce. The wine list presents a surprising range of Spanish varietals rarely seen in New Zealand, and a coolly social atmosphere is reinforced with long, shared tables. Don't be too surprised if you keep ordering 'just one more thing' off the extensive menu.

23 Ponsonby Rd
Ponsonby
Auckland
Map p.487 D4 23

Rocco

09 360 6262 | www.rocco.co.nz

When Rocco first opened in 2000, in a refurbished wooden villa at the quieter end of Ponsonby Road, more than a few restaurants had already come and gone in the same heritage space. Now, Rocco's fusion of sassy, professional service and contemporary Spanish cuisine keeps the place buzzing every night of the week, and it's a favourite lunch spot for corporate types toting company credit cards. Most diners kick off with a shared plate of tapas

The local catch

(always changing and always seasonal), before graduating to favourites such as fideua, a warming Catalan casserole of seafood and squid-ink noodles. The eclectic wine list always surprises, and bookings are highly recommended. Make sure you arrive half an hour early so you can ease into the Rocco experience with a cocktail in the bar. If you're planning a private function, ask about hiring the upstairs room.

Thai

Other options **Far Eastern** p.433

483 New North Rd
Kingsland
Auckland
Map p.490 C4 24

Mekong Neua

09 846 0323

Transport yourself to any Auckland suburb and you'll find a perfectly good Thai restaurant, delivering the country's most popular dishes. At the intimate brick-lined Mekong Neua in Kingsland you can immerse yourself in authentic favourites such as pad thai and green and red curries, as well as Issaan dishes such as larb ped yang, a warm roast duck salad. Adventurous palates should enjoy the goong cha nam pla – raw prawns marinated in chilli, ginger and fish sauce. Food from Issaan is traditionally spicier than other areas of Thailand, but the chefs are happy to turn down the heat when requested. Vegetarians are well catered for, and you can also earn good karma with every mouthful – the restaurant supports a Buddhist monastery in Thailand.

Turkish

3 Park Rd
Auckland
Map p.492 A1 25

Cafe Karadeniz

09 307 3449

Some of Auckland's best Turkish food is hidden away in this tiny place at the edge of the city centre. Cafe Karadeniz (Turkish for Black Sea) is the kind of place you inevitably end up sitting in for longer than planned. The mixed mezze shows off the cafe's winning way with dips, and the light and tender calamari could be Auckland's best. The decor has been kept simple, with the walls adorned with black and white photographs of old Istanbul (including Turkish men with quite improbable moustaches), terracotta tiles and warm kilims. Start the night with Efes beer from Turkey and cap it off with a sweet slice of baklava or loukoum (turkish delight). Thousands of kilometres from Istanbul, Cafe Karadeniz is the next best thing to a sunset crossing on the Bosphorus.

Vietnamese

Other options **Far Eastern** p.433

55 Nuffield St
Newmarket
Auckland
Map p.492 C4 26

Hansan Vietnamese Restaurant

09 523 3988

At the quieter end of one of Auckland's flashiest shopping precincts, Hansan delivers fresh Vietnamese cuisine to fortunate locals. Unlike the more humdrum decor of Hansan's other popular branch in industrial Mount Wellington (525 Mount Wellington Highway, 09 570 6338), the Newmarket restaurant is sleek and modern, and includes interesting friezes of Cambodia's Angkor Wat (owner Mr Han is originally from Cambodia). The huge menu is all affordably priced, with main meals from $9 to $12, and all good. Especially popular are the spring rolls with shrimps, fresh mint and coriander. Service is almost pathologically efficient, but if you want to linger over a bottle of your own wine, the wait staff usually get the message. If you're not drinking wine, try a creamy avocado shake.

Cafes & Coffee Shops

181 Ponsonby Rd
Ponsonby
Auckland
Map p.486 C4 27

Agnes Curran

09 360 1551

For Agnes Curran, think New Zealand circa 1965. Classic Kiwi cakes and home-style baking, such as melting moments and lamingtons (slices of sponge cake dipped in chocolate and rolled in coconut flakes) are served in a tiny space that might remind you of afternoon tea at your grandma's place. It's not just the food that could be from another era either – even the decor may look faintly familiar, with reproductions of famous watercolours and a solitary stuffed pheasant. Despite the playfully kitsch interior, the team at Agnes Curran takes its business very seriously, and the coffee and wide selection of teas are up there with Ponsonby's best. There is a small courtyard if you prefer to indulge in yummy quiches and home-made pies outdoors. The cafe is only open for breakfast and lunch.

Shop 12-14
St Kevin's Arcade
183 Karangahape Rd
Auckland
Map p.491 F1 28

Alleluya

09 377 8424

While other parts of Auckland show a shinier face, Karangahape Road remains a slightly grungy and bohemian slice of history. With vintage clothing stores and cool second-hand book shops, 'K Road's' St Kevin's Arcade is defiantly retro and quintessentially hip. Alleluya occupies the far end of the arcade with an assortment of mismatched 1960s furniture and expansive views to Myers Park, one of central Auckland's smallest and prettiest havens. The coffee is uniformly great and, despite Alleluya being a temple to hipness, it's refreshingly free of pretension. A cross-section of cosmopolitan Auckland comes for everything from freshly baked cakes and cookies to simple meals off the blackboard menu. Beer and wine take over later at night from Thursday to Saturday with a younger, cooler crowd, while on Sunday mornings it's the ideal place to resurrect your weekend with a few shots of java and the newspapers.

New Zealand's favourite fuel

Cnr Blake St and Prosford St
Herne Bay
Auckland
Map p.486 C2 29

Blake St

09 360 6261

Slick and smart, under a block of new apartments, Blake St is the kind of neighbourhood cafe everyone wishes would open near their house, even if the polished concrete tables and modern decor don't really represent the rustic nature of the menu. While too many of Auckland's cafes offer the same sort of stuff for brunch, the innovative team here always pulls out a few surprises. For breakfast there's a great selection of imported meats and cheeses, and the toulouse sausages served with bortoli beans are far more interesting than ordinary bangers. Blake St is part owned by the team behind Rocco in Ponsonby (p.437), and Spanish and Italian influences filter through the menu. The kitchen normally closes around 15:00, but freshly made counter food lures busy locals until 17:30 (20:00 on Fridays).

447 Mt Eden Rd
Mount Eden
Auckland
Map p.495 F2 30

Circus Circus

09 623 3833 | *www.circuscircus.co.nz*

If you're scared of clowns, the decor here could give you nightmares. It doesn't put many people off though – Circus Circus is a popular place, and the cafe's quirky decor suits the ambience of Mount Eden Village. Traditional home baking and breakfasts such as home-made muesli and field mushrooms with scrambled eggs keep customers coming, while local workers love the take-out Roasted Addiqtion coffee, using the spot for informal meetings. The cafe looks small from the front, but inside is a labyrinth of nooks and crannies – great for keeping the kids amused while you take it easy. For lunch and dinner, Circus Circus offers beer and wine and serves eclectic dishes such as Moroccan beefburgers and salmon risotto. It's open from 07:00 to 23:00 every day, and offers friendly service and good value.

129-131 Parnell Rd
Parnell
Auckland
Map p.489 D4 31

Citron Vert

09 377 3080

You can often judge a good cafe by the quality of its reading material; at Citron Vert you won't be disappointed with the copies of the day's newspapers and a diverse array of interesting, up-to-date magazines to hand. On weekday mornings, it's crowded with Parnell office workers grabbing coffee and some of Auckland's best muffins, or tucking into good value brunches. The potato hash with salmon and harissa will set you up for even the longest of working days. Seating in the French-themed interior includes a shared canteen-style table and a few private booths that are good for informal work meetings. For lunch and dinner, Citron Vert's excellent wine list comes into play, with a selection of more than 25 available by the glass. A concise delicatessen selection is also available, including glazed ham and artisanal New Zealand cheeses. Buy a baguette from the adjacent bakery and you're all set for an alfresco lunch in nearby Auckland Domain.

256 Ponsonby Rd
Ponsonby
Auckland
Map p.486 C3 32

Dizengoff

09 360 0108

Ask the residents of Ponsonby who makes the best coffee along Ponsonby Road and the name Dizengoff is bound to come up. With stark white decor and a compact menu, it's a favourite refuelling spot for minor fashionistas and Ponsonby's significant gay population. The menu is kosher and vaguely Israeli-influenced (try the mezze-style Israel plate), but also includes beautifully prepared simple dishes, such as scrambled eggs with salmon, and bagels with avocado and cream cheese. Breakfast is the best time to visit, and on weekends you can expect a more leisurely atmosphere as groups of friends meet for caffeine and conversation. If you're there on your own, Dizengoff offers the city's best selection of fashion, lifestyle and design magazines to read while you sip.

507 New North Rd
Kingsland
Auckland
Map p.490 C4 33

The Fridge

09 845 5321

When food-obsessed Aucklanders drive across town just to buy one of The Fridge's home-made pies, you know they must be good; chicken and mushroom is the most popular, but other variants also have their devoted fans. From a small space, The Fridge has expanded to include a sunny courtyard, not to mention the shop next door. A few too many tables are now squeezed in, but the food easily overcomes such a minor quibble. In both a real estate and a foodie sense, Kingsland is an up and coming suburb, and The Fridge keeps standards high with dangerously strong coffee, tasty wraps, and excellent options for brunch (the home-made hash browns are worth driving across town for). Freshly made salads keep you on track for healthy eating, and when you've sacrificed enough, treat yourself to an indulgent take-out tiramisu.

Discounts

Many cafes operate a loyalty card system (such as 'buy nine, get one free'), so it's worthwhile settling on a local favourite for your daily coffee. Buying an *Entertainment Card* is also a good deal. The book costs $60, but includes a range of significant discounts at many cafes and restaurants across New Zealand making it easy to recoup your initial investment.

23 Edwin St
Mount Eden
Auckland
Map p.491 F3 34

Gala

09 632 1572

Tucked away in the middle of an office complex, the sparse and modern Gala can be hard to find. Once you do eventually make your way there, don't be too surprised if you keep returning. During the week Gala is virtually the staff canteen for the coterie of creative businesses which surround it. A steady stream of excellent coffees is relentlessly shuffled out the door, and, more often than not, a shiny laptop is the focus of intense mini-meetings on most tables. If and when the busy clientele gets around to eating, it's usually simple food done extremely well. Try the surprising Indian flavours of 'mother-in-law's eggs', or Gala's take on mushrooms on toast.

67 Shortland St
Auckland
Map p.488 B2 35

Ima Cuisine

09 373 3787 | *www.thelunchbox.co.nz*

Ima means 'mother' in Hebrew, and the food here is certainly pretty nurturing. A few years ago, the popular City Lunch Box, where Israeli chef Yael Shochat turned out gourmet sandwiches and excellent salads, stood on the same site. Now it's a Mediterranean-inspired cafe that's open for breakfast and lunch seven days a week, and for dinner from Thursday to Saturday. Most meals are traditional, but with a sassy addition. The breakfast grill comes with a home-made potato cake and Yael's special baked beans, while prime beefburgers are partnered with french fries, cut from roasted root vegetables. During the week, the team at Ima welcomes a diverse mix of lawyers, local desk jockeys and student types, while on weekends the high-ceilinged space, with its rustic wooden furniture, morphs into a wine bar.

119 Parnell Rd
Auckland
Map p.489 D4 36

Strawberry Alarm Clock

09 377 6959

Named after a 1960s psychedelic rock group, Strawberry Alarm Clock is a refreshing addition to a part of town that sometimes takes itself a little too seriously. Sit inside and see how many of the foreign 'no-smoking' signs you can understand, or wend your way past the kitchen to the hidden courtyard. The palms and potted plants can be a little overgrown, and it sometimes feels like the grungy back garden of your first student flat, but it suits the well-priced food, which might include cajun chicken focaccia sandwiches and decent eggs benedict. Wash it all down with a coffee or a beer. The fruit smoothies are also good.

Bars

Other options **Pubs** p.445, **Nightclubs** p.447

Bellini

Princes Wharf
147 Quay St
Auckland
Map p.488 A1 37

09 978 2025 | *www.bellini.co.nz*

Part of the Hilton Auckland that stretches 300 metres into the harbour like a cruise-liner, Bellini is a bar made just for special occasions. During the day the glacial white interior can seem a bit spartan, and you'll probably only have moneyed hotel guests as company. After dark, drama makes an appearance as harbour lights reflect off the ocean and onto the bar's pristine blank canvas, while Auckland's smart set comes out to play. You're just metres from the water in one of Auckland's best hotels, so expect to pay for the experience. A namesake cocktail will cost you $18, and champagne cocktails go for an additional ten bucks. Wines by the glass start at $14. Bellini is a great spot for celebrating, and definitely worth it.

Bonita

242 Ponsonby Rd
Ponsonby
Auckland
Map p.486 C3 38

09 376 5670

Many of Auckland's bars and restaurants offer tapas, but Bonita (Spanish for beautiful) is one of the few places in town that wouldn't be out of place in Spain. The authenticity starts with the decor. Distressed plaster walls surround a marble-topped bar, scattered with an array of goodies such as anchovies and olives. Tables are arranged on aged wooden floors, and a selection of simple, open sandwiches are on offer, with toppings including chorizo, cheese and prawns. There are larger meals available, but most customers prefer to stand and graze on the various snacks (at around $3 a plate) with a glass of wine, sherry or port. Bonita is a thoroughly down-to-earth spot and is especially recommended for catching up with friends at the end of a busy day.

Chapel Bar & Bistro

147 Ponsonby Rd
Ponsonby
Auckland
Map p.486 C4 39

09 360 4528 | *www.chapel.co.nz*

Eating and drinking are the big reasons why Aucklanders head to Ponsonby Road, but if you asked the strip's more regular habitués, they'd probably say people watching too. With a prime corner location, Chapel Bar & Bistro fulfils all three reasons in the best possible way. When some of Ponsonby's other bars are quiet, the friendly and relaxed Chapel is always busy. Outside there are plenty of tables to watch the passing parade, and inside the vaguely ecclesiastical decor is softened with lots of leather and dark wood. Loyal regulars are usually in attendance, and on Friday and Saturday nights it can be standing room only. With an excellent wine list, a quirky approach to cocktails (try 'the Pope's breakfast'), and tapas-style food, Chapel covers all the bases.

Cowboy

95-97 Customs St West
Auckland
Map p.488 A2 40

09 377 7778

The interior of the sometimes raucous Cowboy is best described as retro-Americana, with flagstone floors, aged walls that look like they've been imported from Dodge City, and lots of leather and wood. As well as the Monteith's beers on tap, there are a variety of bourbons and tequilas, and wine is served in stemless tumblers – a wise move considering how packed this bar sometimes gets. Despite the occasional crush, Cowboy is always relaxed, testament to the bar's friendly staff. Somehow, the tiny space still fits a kitchen that turns out gourmet pizzas and burgers. Music comes courtesy of retro pop videos that you're sure to remember from your adolescence.

455 New North Rd
Grey Lynn
Auckland
Map p.490 C4 41

Gypsy Tea Room

09 361 6970

Auckland's inner suburbs used to be void of interesting places to have a drink, but now great local bars are popping up everywhere – and 'local' is the key word to describe the Gypsy Tea Room. Arty locals from the heritage suburb of Grey Lynn form the regular clientele, and the bar features a barman who's always up for conversation. It's only been open a few years, but this place still looks wonderfully old. That's old in a 'backstreets of Rome' kind of way. The painted walls look authentically aged and straight from a yet-to-be-made sequel to *The Godfather*. The weathered floors are full of character. More than 30 wines are available by the glass, and the small but eclectic beer list features goodies such as Czech Budvar, and Little Creatures Pale Ale from Australia. Bar snacks include delicious risotto balls and individual tasting plates of paella.

5 O'Connell St
Auckland
Map p.488 A2 42

Honey Champagne Cocktail Bar

09 369 5639 | *www.honeybar.co.nz*

Insurance companies obviously had money to burn in the 1920s – no expense was spared on the lavish and spacious former head offices of Alliance Insurance in which hides one of Auckland's best selections of champagne and more than 60 cocktails. The wordy Honey Champagne Cocktail Bar will mix you up a killer drink; try the 'apple crumble', which blends cinnamon-infused 42 Below vodka (New Zealand's own) with apple juice and fresh lime. The wine list is also one of the city's finest, featuring many New Zealand vintages. Wow visiting friends in the classy bar, crafted from oak and marble and dotted with plush couches amid subdued lighting.

463 New North Rd
Kingsland
Auckland
Map p.491 F2 43

The Ivy

09 815 1535

Is this a bar, a restaurant or a cafe? Does it really matter when it's a warm and welcoming space from early to late every day of the week? And while The Ivy is a sound option for coffee, brunch or lunch, it's really at its best after dark. That's when the sophisticated decor combining moody dark wood, exposed bricks and leather makes the most sense. Late at night is also the perfect time to park yourself at the bar to sample the best of The Ivy's cocktails. The zesty 'ginger mojito' goes well with Asian-inspired bar snacks such as chilli and lemongrass-spiced cashews. The encyclopaedic wine list approaches almost 70 different types and, if you're a beer fan, this is one of Auckland's only bars to have Germany's zingy wheat beer Erdinger on tap.

8 Kent St
Auckland
Map p.492 C3 44

Lone Star

09 522 4004 | *www.lonestar.co.nz*

Lone Star has been a draw for years down south in Christchurch, popular for after-work drinks, relatively inexpensive dinners and a no-nonsense atmosphere, and it's now doing the business in Auckland's Newmarket. American in style and always loud and fun, the bar and restaurant are partially divided, and both are popular. The food comes in expectedly huge portions, with favourites such as the barbecue spare ribs and monster burgers having been on the menu since its conception. While it may be loud and proud and quite crowded at times, it is ideal for a beer or two, as well as for a quick bite – if the kitchen's not too busy, they'll even rustle up a takeaway for you.

Lone Star

Cnr Wolfe St & Federal St
Auckland
Map p.488 A2 45

Mo's

09 366 6066 | www.mosbar.co.nz

One of Auckland's smallest bars is also one of the best. At Mo's you're surrounded by towering, grey office blocks, but inside, you could well be in Havana. The tiny interior is bedecked with vintage photos of Fidel Castro, Che Guevara and members of the Las Vegas Rat Pack. Behind the wooden bar, classic cocktails are mixed with care, and different music genres, from Cuban pop to Sinatra ballads, drift in and out like a 1960s radio station playlist. On week nights, suited businessmen crowd in for the great wine list, featuring the best of local labels, while on weekends a younger, funkier crowd sups on imported beers, including Staropramen and Sol.

309 Queen St
Auckland
Map p.488 A4 46

Nombe

09 379 5152 | www.sakebars.co.nz

Don't come to Nombe expecting to lounge around on comfy furniture – this compact spot in the centre of the city is a tachinomi (drinking while standing up) bar. There are a few stools, but the preferred form is to prop yourself at the bar and work your way through the diverse list of sake, Japanese beer, and Tokyo-style bar snacks. Nombe attracts an urban, hipster crowd, drawn by the bar's minimalist but traditional Japanese decor, and a wildly eclectic music policy. Don't be too surprised to hear vintage ska and britpop, followed by James Brown and Aretha Franklin. Next could be classic country music. You're handily placed for drinks before or after shows at the Town Hall and the Aotea Centre (p.475), central Auckland's two main concert venues.

133 Franklin Rd
Auckland
Map p.487 E3 47

Shanghai Lil's

09 358 0868

Dressed in a silk smoking jacket, with a Mandarin collar (naturally), owner Russell Green is the perfect host here in this 1930s Shanghai bordello-style bar. Most nights, you won't find him serving drinks; he's more likely to be shimmying through the throng asking people how their evening is going. More than anything, a night at Shanghai Lil's is a bit like being a guest at Russell's party. Befitting the bar's status as a regular fixture in the Sunday newspapers' society pages, Shanghai Lil's attracts Auckland's A-list. Don't be put off though – in Auckland the A-list hang-outs are usually pleasantly free of air-kissing darlings.

210 Ponsonby Rd
Ponsonby
Auckland
Map p.486 C4 48

The Whiskey

09 361 2666 | www.whiskeybars.com

Decorated with arty black-and-white photographs of long-gone rock stars such as Jimi Hendrix and Jim Morrison, The Whiskey keeps classic rock music alive along Ponsonby Road's bar strip. Most other places recycle house beats or acid jazz and dub, but at The Whiskey you're more likely to hear The Beatles, Bob Dylan and The Doors. Named after Los Angeles' infamous Whiskey A Go Go nightclub on Sunset Boulevard, The Whiskey is also cocktail heaven. Classics such as cosmopolitans and whiskey sours are most popular, but original twists such as vodkatinis and chocolate martinis are also on offer. A diverse crowd, ranging from 18 year old newbies to middle-aged hipsters, packs the chic, brick-lined space to occasionally sing along to AC/DC and The Rolling Stones – some customers with considerably more irony than others.

67 Shortland St
Auckland
Map p.488 B2 49

Wine Loft

09 379 5070 | www.wineloft.co.nz

Over the last few decades, New Zealand wines have made their mark internationally, and Wine Loft is Auckland's best place to contrast and compare a Marlborough sauvignon with a Martinborough pinot noir. It's a classy but relaxed spot, and the combination of slow-spinning ceiling fans, brick walls and leather couches on wooden floors provides the ideal backdrop for diving into a list of more than 60 wines available by the glass. A few tasters will enhance your knowledge of Kiwi wine, and when you find one you like you can upgrade to a larger glass. An additional 90 varieties are available by the bottle, and they all go well with Wine Loft's pizzas and platters. You can also buy wine to take home.

Pubs

Other options **Bars** p.442

37 Normanby Rd
Mount Eden
Auckland
Map p.492 A3 50

Cardrona Speight's Ale House

09 638 4560 | *www.speightsalehouse.co.nz*

Aucklanders are proud of the down-to-earth farming heritage of New Zealand's South Island, and even though the respect is rarely mutual, it doesn't stop urbanites crowding into this authentic replica of a Central Otago pub. Serving excellent wines, beers from Speight's Dunedin brewery and robust meals such as shearers' shanks (lamb roasted with thyme and garlic), you'd need to cross New Zealand's Southern Alps to find a more authentic-feeling place. The lucky residents of Auckland only have to cross town for good times among lots of natural timber, a roaring open fire, and a garden bar dotted with hardy alpine tussock plants. The location, in a light industrial area, may seem incongruous, but if Auckland's Warriors rugby league team (p.347) are winning on the big screen, there's no other place to spend an afternoon.

2 Mt Eden Rd
Auckland
Map p.491 F2 51

Galbraith's Ale House

09 379 3557 | *www.alehouse.co.nz*

The late Michael Jackson (the well-known beer critic, not the other one) described the various ales at Galbraith's Ale House as 'startlingly good'. The team here brews five different beers in the onsite microbrewery, and supplements these with regular seasonal offerings. The best from New Zealand's other microbreweries are also on tap, including the mighty Emerson's range from Dunedin. The pub is housed in an imposing former library, and it could take you a while to read through the extensive listing of international beers available by the bottle. Loyal regulars crowd in most nights, and Sunday afternoon is recommended for sampling some of Auckland's best pub food.

1171 Coatesville-Riverhead Hwy
Auckland
Map p.484 A3

Hallertau

09 412 5555 | *www.hallertau.co.nz*

Hallertau, in Germany, is the world's biggest hop growing region. It's also a microbrewery in rural west Auckland – an essential detour when you're cruising the area's wineries. Four beers are available year round, with an additional six seasonal offerings. A five-beer 'tasting paddle' is the best way to discover your own personal favourite. Hallertau is also popular with locals, and the tapas-style tasting plates are great for sharing on the deck in the shade of leafy hop vines. If none of Hallertau's brews appeal (which is highly unlikely), the bar also stocks what is easily the region's best selection of microbrewery beers from around New Zealand. There are more than 50 ales on offer from 17 breweries, all available to take home.

470 New North Rd
Kingsland
Auckland
Map p.490 C4 53

The Kingslander

09 849 5777 | *www.thekingslander.co.nz*

Just a drop kick away from Eden Park, the spiritual home of New Zealand rugby, The Kingslander has established itself as one of Auckland's best sports pubs since its opening in 2002. This is probably due to the combination of multiple flat screen televisions and comfy sofas, which make you feel like you're at home. The plentiful supply of craft beers from Monteith's is also a factor, of course, as is a good wine list of Kiwi favourites, and one of Auckland's best chicken burgers. With a weekly schedule of regular events, this former 19th century grain store is always busy. Head down when the All Blacks are playing and you'll find it a sea of passionate rugby fans, while on Tuesday nights The Kingslander hosts Auckland's most competitive pub quiz. A combination of the two is your best bet for a rapid immersion into Kiwi culture.

23-27 Nuffield St
Newmarket
Auckland
Map p.492 C3 54

Nuffield Street Brewbar

09 523 4554

Welcome to the future. Secreted away in a ritzy shopping street, the Nuffield Street Brewbar is an uber-cool, urban update of a traditional New Zealand drinking establishment. On tap is the full range of Mac's beers. Mac's Gold, a traditional lager, is the most popular, although worth trying too are the zingy Great White Wheat Beer, and bold as brass Hoprocker Pilsner. In summer you can enjoy Mac's limited edition Brewjolais, a lively offering made with new season hops from the Marlborough region. Also experimental is Brewbar's approach to dining. Share a selection of tapas cones, or the McCashin's platter, which includes fresh New Zealand seafood and surprising Asian flavours. On Friday and Saturday there are toe-tapping jazzy beats from 20:00.

Cnr Ahuroa Rd & Puhoi Rd
Auckland
North Island Map G5

Puhoi Pub

09 422 0812

In a riverside country setting, about 40 minutes north of Auckland, the Puhoi Pub has been serving good honest pints since 1879. It's especially popular with what's known locally as 'westies'. You probably know the look: black heavy metal T-shirts, big, mean-looking dogs, and perhaps a Harley Davidson as an accessory. Don't worry though – they're usually good family men. They'll make you feel welcome and the rest of their clan will probably be in the spacious garden bar with a bag of hot chips and a can of soft drink. Inside, the heritage pub celebrates the area's original settlers from Bohemia (now part of the Czech Republic), with a host of interesting and arcane memorabilia that covers more than a century of local history. An essential detour on a summer afternoon.

224 Symonds St
Auckland
Map p.491 F2 56

Squid Row

09 379 9344 | *www.squidrow.co.nz*

Decor-wise Squid Row is a bold mix of modern and retro, with a shiny, long bar sitting amid vintage surfing memorabilia. A hard-to-miss screen shows 1960s surfing movies (and the season's biggest rugby matches), and the walls are punctuated with an entire photo album of spectacular black and white surfing shots. An unpretentious, younger crowd comes along for good seafood and hearty meals such as 'surf and turf' (steak and prawns). The tasting platters are good value if you come here with a group, and classic cocktails such as margaritas, caipirinhas and mojitos are just six bucks from 17:00 to 19:00 on Friday and Saturday.

23 Westhaven Dr
Auckland
Map p.487 E2 57

Swashbucklers

09 307 5979 | *www.swashbucklers.co.nz*

Outside at Westhaven Marina, a few hundred million dollars of marine assets are moored, but Swashbucklers has retained its humble origins; the compact bar welcomes everyone from fishermen and weekend yachties to total landlubbers. Don't come expecting a cosmopolitan – the closest you'll get is a shrimp cocktail to go with a glass of oaky Kiwi chardonnay – but be prepared to spend a long time exploring Swashbucklers' eclectic interior. Tables are actually rustic barrels, and there's authentic memorabilia from Team New Zealand's ongoing fascination with the America's Cup. After you've had your fill of folklore, grab a waterfront perch and order a basket of oysters, mussels and chips.

Nightclubs

373 Karangahape Rd
Auckland
Map p.491 F1 58

4:20 & Rising Sun

09 358 5643 | www.420.co.nz

On two floors, with great views over downtown Auckland, this split-venue complex offers something for most revellers. The Rising Sun (a rough inner city pub a decade ago) now presents a regular cavalcade of dub, hip-hop and soul. Park yourself with a beer or glass of wine and take in some reggae as Auckland's lights twinkle in the distance. At the adjacent 4:20 things get a little more raucous, with an emphasis on live rock gigs. The music is different every night, but this place boasts the best views from a nightclub anywhere in Auckland – even if you don't stay long enough to see the sun rise.

1 Fort La
Auckland
Map p.488 A2 59

Flight Lounge

09 309 6569 | www.flightlounge.co.nz

Fort Lane has a New York vibe about it, and it's now the city's fastest growing area for a bit of late night or early morning carousing. Forte Club delivers non-stop house and techno to a much younger crowd. Drawing a (slightly) older crowd than Forte, Flight Lounge pumps house into the small hours for Auckland's professional set. There is nothing vaguely airport-like about the decor, but the combination of retro floral wallpaper and slick 21st-century design is different. It opens Wednesday to Saturday at 21:00, and at the weekends the last departure is 05:00.

160 Queen St
Auckland
Map p.488 A3 60

Fu

09 309 3079 | www.fu.co.nz

Fu is a regular haunt of international DJs, and recent visitors have included Derrick May and Kid Kenobi. The sound system bumps and grinds every night of the week with techno, drum & bass and hip-hop, and the Japanese decor, illuminated by a little too much UV light, reveals a very trendy bar. A pool table is a slight diversion from the bass-heavy distractions. Even on school nights, Fu is open until around 04:00, and on weekends, once you pass the queue and the bouncers, you'll be busy until at least 06:00. Occasionally the turntables are ditched in favour of noisy rock and roll.

17 Galatos St
Auckland
Map p.491 F1 61

Galatos

09 303 1928 | www.galatos.co.nz

When it first opened as a ballroom venue in the 1920s, Galatos was described as the 'fastest dancefloor' in Auckland. Following a stint as a venue for theatre, it reopened in 1999 and now the emphasis is on dancing at a range of speeds to an eclectic variety of music and images. Galatos is managed by The Moving Image Charitable Centre Trust, so amid the live gigs is work by the city's independent film and digital media community. Start your night with a cocktail in the upstairs lounge, and then head down a couple of floors to the performance spaces. An esoteric mix of bands, DJs and multimedia entertains a creative, black-clad crowd.

536 Queen St
Auckland
Map p.487 F4 62

Khuja Lounge

09 377 3711 | www.khujalounge.co.nz

Morocco comes to Auckland in this bohemian space accessed by a rickety staircase or an equally ancient lift. A vaguely north African vibe is instilled thanks to terracotta walls, rustic lampshades and flagstone floors. The dancefloor is pretty small, but that doesn't matter because the people moving to the reggae, dub and old school hip-hop usually overflow into most barely lit corners well before midnight. Some nights, more energised world music infiltrates the proceedings with samba, bossa nova and African beats from either DJs or live bands. Earlier in the night it's a great spot for a drink by candlelight.

Wellington

European

Other options **French** p.449 **Italian** p.450, **Mediterranean** p.451

125 Featherston St
Wellington
Map p.503 D2 63

Arbitrageur Wine Room and Restaurant

04 499 5530 | *www.arbitrageur.co.nz*

There's a cool feel to Arbitrageur that's hard to find elsewhere in the city. Maybe it's the brilliant contemporary New Zealand artwork adorning the walls, the chandeliers dripping from the ceiling or perhaps it's the gorgeous copper table tops; pick one, then add to it what makes it a spot you absolutely shouldn't miss – the perfect marriage of wine and food. The fare at Arbitrageur is European, with unique charcuterie, cheese and delicatessen menus, and there are also an astounding 700 local and international wines in house, more than 60 of them offered by the glass. The wines are kept in a fantastic old glass-door vault that's invariably left ajar so diners can lust after their next pairing. One of the most inspired things about this place is the colour code system that navigates the menu, suggesting structures and styles of wine for every dish. It's the perfect chance to learn a little while imbibing.

Cnr Majoribanks St & Kent Tce
Wellington
Map p.505 F2 64

Capitol

04 384 2855 | *www.capitolrestaurant.co.nz*

Capitol is like a favourite pair of shoes – not just any pair though; we're talking suede Italian loafers – simple, classically stylish, right for all occasions, and supremely comfortable. A European bistro at heart, Capitol is the quintessential local, with regulars filling the striking black banquettes next to the huge glass windows that look down on Courtenay Place. The fare is exactly as it reads on the menu – no mess, no fuss, no fluff, just straight-up local, seasonal, honest, and seriously delicious food. The gnocchi is as light as air, the risotto laden with parmesan, and fried squid with aioli deliciously crisp. Then there's the never-to-leave-the-menu hot soft-centered chocolate pudding with creme fraiche. The wine list is food-friendly, with many offered by the glass and a European cellar list to complement. While service, decor and wine come together in perfect harmony, food is definitely the star of the show.

Far Eastern

Other options **Japanese** p.450, **Malaysian** p.451

12 Blair St
Wellington
Map p.505 E2 65

Monsoon Poon

04 803 3555 | *www.monsoonpoon.co.nz*

With a tagline of 'love you long time' there's no way Monsoon Poon could be anything but a little cheeky. It has a great vibe and a lot of fun without compromising the delicious pan-Asian menu. Specialising in cuisines (and decor) specific to the 'coconut belt' (south India through south-east Asia to the Philippines), chefs at Monsoon Poon use some of the freshest ingredients in town. They cover the classics with ease and have thrown in some great twists with a delicious tom yum laksa (for those who just can't decide on one or the other) and 25 herb and spice Indian lamb curry. Monsoon has an award-winning wine list weighted with intriguing aromatics to complement the fare, while the cocktail list is definitely worth perusing (the sassy 'poon tang' is not to be missed). For those looking for a little 'eatertainment', the Poon is where it's at.

Bring Your Own

BYO – 'bring your own' – is popular with New Zealand diners and is most commonly found in casual and ethnic restaurants. The charge for corkage is minimal (around $5) and most BYO restaurants are also licensed to sell alcohol. Many upscale restaurants are starting to designate one night of the week BYO too. It's also acceptable to bring along particularly old, rare or special wines not already on the list.

French

99 Boulcott St
Wellington
Map p.502 C4 66

Boulcott Street Bistro

04 499 4199 | *www.boulcottstreetbistro.co.nz*

The Boulcott Street Bistro is a Wellington institution. Tucked away inside the city's oldest wooden building, it sits atop Boulcott Street in a spot which started life on the outskirts of a port village but now finds itself in the CBD. The villa surroundings make visiting the venue like being welcomed into a cosy home rather than a restaurant. Inside, Boulcott is classic bistro in every sense – a French influenced menu, smart yet relaxed service, and well-paired wines. With good reason a few dishes have reigned supreme over the last 16 years: fried calamari with garlic and anchovy mayo, braised lamb shanks, fillet bearnaise with pomme frites and, naturally, creme brulee. No craziness, no reinventing the wheel, just good, honest fare that draws you back time and time again.

270 Willis St
Wellington
Map p.504 B2 67

Citron Restaurant

04 801 6263 | *www.citronrestaurant.co.nz*

Citron is seriously tiny. The Citron experience, however, is boundless – in passion, quality of ingredients, picture-perfect presentation, and some of the city's most professional and thoughtful service. It is one of only a couple of restaurants in Wellington to offer degustation menus, with diners offered three, nine or 15 courses, to which inspired wine pairings may be added. With this amount of forethought, you can be sure Citron knows its business; it's skilled in the art of building you up, then traversing you gently towards dessert and petit fours. The only thing to do when presented with such an experience is to become putty – hand yourself over to be rewarded with course after course of delight and entertainment. The cuisine is progressively New Zealand, with a touch of French influence, and the menu is ever evolving, chasing seasons. The only way you could go wrong is if you didn't allow enough time to enjoy such a rare treat.

167 Riddiford St
Wellington
Map p.507 D4 68

Eateria De Manon

04 380 1100

Hiding away in one of Wellington's most eclectic suburbs, Eateria De Manon is one of the city's best-kept secrets. As soon as you walk through the front door, feel the warmth of the open fire and become enveloped in delicious aromas, you just know it's going to be one of those plate-lickingly good dinners. The fare is predominantly French and includes escargot, garlic, parsley butter and parmesan, and grilled crispy half duck with lemon-braised chicory and Drambuie ginger sauce, both of which thankfully never leave the menu. The one thing that may take you by surprise is the decor – it's not particularly Gallic. The space started life as horse stables then went on to become a Swiss-chalet-style restaurant – and that's really where it stayed. While there are French touches, there's no mistaking that someone named Heidi used to work here – very kitsch but, once you know the origins, not so crazy. The wine list is appropriately small with some French gems, and the service wonderfully personal. There's a lot of love that goes into the Manon experience, meaning you can't go wrong.

Indian

5/120 Victoria St
Wellington
Map p.504 C1 69

Roti Chenai

04 382 9807 | *www.rotichenai.co.nz*

If you're looking for some of city's best south Indian and Malaysian cuisine, this is your spot. Roti Chenai has been turning out incredibly tasty meals at great value prices for more than a decade. Students, suits, mothers, buskers – ask almost anyone and they'll not only know Roti Chenai but will have enjoyed one of its trademark $6.50 eponymous lunch specials of bread served with a choice of lamb, chicken or dhal curry. Rookies might order rice but you'll soon learn that it's not necessary – the roti is so good and more than enough to sop up all of the curry. In a city that loves its food, Roti Chenai managed to scoop a 2005 consumer award as one of Wellington's best restaurants; add to this a rave review by Wellington's pre-eminent authority on ethnic foods, David Burton, and you have yourself an eatery well worth visiting.

Italian

Other options **European** p.448 **Mediterranean** p.451

10 Nevis St
Wellington
Map p.498 C2

La Bella Italia

04 566 9303 | www.labellaitalia.co.nz

Take a founder from the Amalfi Coast, a chef from Umbria, 28 varieties of Italian cheese including buffalo mozzarella that arrives every 18 days, great coffee, and an incredible selection of salami, coppa, culatello, prosciutto, olives, pastas and gelatos, and you have Le Bella Italia. Any more authentic and you'd actually be in Positano. Located across the Wellington Harbour in Petone, Le Bella is a fabulous find – it is not only a cafe with a delicious menu kept true to its origins, but is also a mecca for food shoppers with a penchant for Italian fare. Licensed La Bella serves lunch every day and antipasto late into the afternoon. The one dish not to be missed is roasted whole fish cooked with a special sauce of gherkins, Sicilian salted capers, and extra virgin olive oil; it is owner Antonio's father's recipe, and is an absolute treat.

141 Cuba St
Wellington
Map p.504 C2 71

Scopa

04 384 6020

Pizza and pinot meet at Scopa – think relaxed, easy, warm, and addictive. A jazzed-up cafe by day, a dressed-down restaurant by night, Scopa is casual, playful and decidedly reasonable. Not surprisingly the wine list is predominantly Italian, but selections are thoughtful, not taking the New Zealand palate too far from what it knows. The menu easily captures Italian favourites through pizza, pasta, salad – with a couple of dishes, such as pappardelle with wild boar ragout, rarely leaving the menu. Tuesday lunches, featuring half-price margherita pizzas, are crazily busy. Scopa has a natural following within the Italian expat community, with regulars routinely stopping in for an espresso at the bar. As a nod to tradition Sunday night is dominated by a fiddle, a guitar, and a killer rendition of *The Godfather* soundtrack.

Japanese

Level 1
43 Courtenay Pl
Wellington
Map p.505 E2 72

Kazu Yakitori and Sake Bar

04 802 4868 | www.kazu.co.nz

Kazu is one of those funky spots you'll find yourself in time and time again, whether for an evening with friends, after a movie, on an intimate first date, or even alone for a bite and a moment to relax. It's small, cosy and the music playing is a cool mix of jazz and funk. The balance is made up by the great sake list with clear directions for rookies, seating with a view in front of the constantly tended grill, attentive staff, and of course the food. Co-owned Kazu Japanese Restaurant (04 802 5298) is the sushi and sashimi star – this Kazu however is master of the yakitori (chargrilled skewers). The best bet is to try one or two of as many as you're able; definitely don't pass up the imo (thick kumara with butter and salt) or the grilled rice cakes with miso sauce, crispy on the outside, soft inside – absolute heaven.

Malaysian

54 Ghuznee St
Wellington
Map p.504 C2 73

KK Malaysian Cuisine

04 385 6698

Wellington has a number of Malaysian eateries but KK is one of the best. It's one of those places people love to love – it's tiny, inexpensive, fast, and very, very good. Everything on the menu is tasty, but most popular are the laksas (curry, seafood or vegetarian), kung po chicken or beef, mee goring, chicken sambal, coconut rice and roti. Service is quick, getting diners in and out in as little as 30 minutes. Unlike a lot of hole-in-the-wall spots, KK takes reservations, which are a must if you have a group of any size (more than two), or you want to be guaranteed a table. Dine in or take out, any day or night of the week, and you'll be hard pressed to find a more consistently good Malaysian local.

Mediterranean

Other options **Italian** p.450

161 Cuba St
Wellington
Map p.504 C2 74

Floriditas

04 381 2212 | *www.floriditas.co.nz*

From the sing-song name to the delicate old world tea cups, and the natural light streaming through every window to mouthwatering morsels such as linguine, fresh toasted walnuts, mint leaves and parmesan, this cafe by day, restaurant by night, is femininity personified. Floriditas' menu changes daily and flows easily from morning through to evening. Coffee is the constant, and goes well with the wickedly delicious baking such as rhubarb, custard and brown sugar brioches. Simple, local ingredients reign supreme at Floriditas and it's not uncommon for fresh herbs to steal the show. A New Zealand weighted wine list (but with some great imports and nearly 50 by the glass) is the perfect complement to the food. If you're not romanced by anything else, desserts including white chocolate pannacotta and honeyed fresh cranberries will win your heart for sure. Open daily 07:00 to 22:00.

25-29 Taranaki St
Wellington
Map p.505 D1 75

Zibibbo

04 385 6650 | *www.zibibbo.co.nz*

Three words you don't often hear bandied about in the New Zealand restaurant world: 'Michelin starred chef'. But Zibibbo has one – and it's pinned to the whites of owner chef, Adam Newell. The scene stealers at Zibibbo are the sangria, and the tapas selection – nine served atop a board fashioned from rimu timber beams, removed from the old police station building in which the restaurant is housed. And it's an almost impossible choice of nine when you have such tasty offerings as fish marinated in coconut, lime and coriander, globe artichoke fritters, tempura battered and served with salsa verde, and crispy pork belly with apple chutney and balsamic vinegar. If the pressure is too much, retire to the open fire, let the staff (who are super relaxed and completely attuned to the intricacies of the menu), choose your dish, and one of the great European wines, and enjoy.

Zibibbo

Mexican

Cnr of Cuba St & Vivian St
Wellington
Map p.504 C2 76

The Flying Burrito Brothers

04 385 8811

Anyone with a penchant for good tequila should make a beeline for The Flying Burrito Brothers. With more than 100 varieties, it has not only the best sipping selection but can blend them to turn out some fabulously lethal margaritas. A little more LA than Guadalajara, the menu is approachable and really tasty. You'll find classics such as burritos, tostadas, tacos, enchiladas and fajitas, and great twists on originals such as paua (abalone) quesadillas. Don't forget the guacamole, corn chips, salsas, and great sides such as rice and beans either – without them it wouldn't be a true Mexican meal. Staff here are all Latino – heck, some are even Mexican – which in a city the size of Wellington is no mean feat. The service is relaxed, upbeat and fun. Make sure you arrive early enough to take in a drink at the bar before being seated; a margarita slushy will get you off to a flyer.

New Zealand

Cnr Onepu Rd & Wha St
Wellington
Map p.498 D7

Elements

04 939 1292

Lyall Bay is a quiet seaside community in Wellington, home to salt-crusted surfers, young families, characterful locals who have lived there their entire lives, and now Elements, an absolute gem of an eatery. What gets you even before the food is the welcoming hustle and bustle of a spot that consistently bursts at the seams, and the beaming smiles of staff. There are touches of the old butchery in which it is housed but cleverly it stays very pretty with lots of light streaming through into the cafe. The food is more than moreish – with dishes such as home-made fish pie with buttered leeks, and sides such as roasted yams, herbs and pumpkin seeds, and warm fig and apple pudding with caramel sauce. Licensed and bring-your-own, the restaurant is open every day and five nights. The retro comfort appeal is inescapable – a five-star experience in jeans.

16 Taranaki St
Wellington
Map p.505 E1 78

The Green Parrot

04 384 6080 | *www.greenparrot.co.nz*

If you don't go to The Green Parrot when in Wellington you'll have missed the most famous landmark, gastronomically speaking, in the city. The Parrot is the city's oldest (opening in 1926), most colourful and well-frequented late night cafe, serving great diner-style meals from 17:00 to very, very late. The decor is almost as it was in its war-time heyday – perfectly kitsch with a giant painted wall of fame depicting familiar faces. To change the famous neon sign would be as disorientating for regulars as getting rid of the original grill – a monstrous slab of melted down gunmetal, three feet by two feet and half an inch thick. Countless *Flintstone*-sized steaks, gargantuan plates of schnitzel and stacks of white bread served with rock-hard squares of butter have been served over the last 81 years – enough to sink several ships. The people are as much a part of The Parrot legend as the food; politicians, prostitutes, playwrights, and the plain old general population all sitting side-by-side – classic Wellington.

Cnr Cuba St & Vivian St
Wellington
Map p.504 C2 79

Logan Brown

04 801 5114 | *www.loganbrown.co.nz*

Logan Brown has an easy elegance. Its spectacular surroundings, set within a beautifully restored 1920s bank chamber, exact service, a brilliant wine list (bring-your-own on Sunday), and a menu to die for, are all presented without an ounce of pretension. Owners Al Brown and Steve Logan are veritable icons in the New Zealand food world as hosts of television show *Hunger for the Wild* and creators of the famed 'Grillslinger' – the ingenious Kiwi barbecue tool belt. The pair's relaxed approach to life, food and wine sets the stage for the signature VIP cocktail, a mouthwatering mix of passionfruit and citrus with Plymouth gin, vermouth and Pimms, and classics such as paua ravioli. But it doesn't stop there; lovers of interesting and tender morsels will adore the roasted groper throats with cream of fennel and warm chorizo vinaigrette, and hot smoked snapper with sauteed potatoes, basil and crayfish mayonnaise.

2 Courtenay Place
Wellington
Map p.505 E2 80

The Tasting Room

04 384 1159 | *www.tasting-room.co.nz*

Stone walls, an oak bar, leather banquettes, trophy antlers, craft beer and wild food – all that's missing are horses and a campfire. The Tasting Room is one of Wellington's true gastropubs; the perfect partnership between tasty food and great beer. The selection of boutique-brewed Monteith's beers is extensive and suitable for pairing with the menu. Chef Len Baldwin, four-time winner of New Zealand's Wild Food Challenge, has designed a delicious menu, particularly for committed carnivores, featuring rabbit saddle and mushroom pie, and wild Awatere venison back steak – vegetarians should run for the hills. To top off an evening of great fare in a relaxed environment, stay awhile because The Tasting Room is a popular late-night spot.

232 Oriental Parade
Wellington
Map p.498 D5

The White House Restaurant

04 385 8555 | *www.whr.co.nz*

The White House has an old-world regality about it. Over the last 15 years, its quiet manner, gentle formality, stellar service, and classic decor has engendered undying loyalty from many Wellingtonians. Inspired by his travels, owner-chef Paul Hoather quite simply likes to cook what he eats. The menu is focused on seasonality and, where possible, local ingredients. It boasts some beautiful game and has a special place for seafood given the restaurant's proximity to the harbour. Fresh shucked oysters, whitebait with asparagus, grilled venison with mushrooms – all classics and wonderfully delicious. The wine list is thoughtful and well matched to the fare; Sundays are bring your own. A pleasure not to be missed.

Seafood

Shed 3, Queens Wharf
Wellington
Map p.503 E3 82

Dockside Restaurant & Bar

04 499 9900 | *www.docksidenz.com*

The owners of Dockside will happily tell you that it's not a waterfront restaurant if you can't spit in the water. While that practice is not recommended, you certainly could manage such a feat here if you wanted; it's a waterfront haven, sitting not just

The Tasting Room

The White House Restaurant

next to the harbour, but over it. On Friday and Saturday evenings Dockside is one of the busiest bars in town, with the marquee-covered deck jumping to the party atmosphere. For the rest of the week, Dockside transforms into a great seafood restaurant with a varied menu that changes daily. Fresh fish is the speciality, as are Dockside's brunches. In summer, Wellingtonians make the most of dining alfresco next to the water – although you can do the same in the winter, only under toasty warm heaters.

Royal Port Nicholson Yacht Club
103 Oriental Parade
Wellington
Map p.498 D5

Martin Bosley's

04 920 8302 | www.martin-bosley.com

Chef Martin Bosley is the heart and soul of what is possibly New Zealand's finest seafood restaurant, working his magic on the freshest species available. His eponymous restaurant tames almost every ocean creature available; the menu flowing effortlessly from clams to crab, a trio of tartars to tuna. Fish can be enjoyed as a deliciously edible work of art or grilled simply with a splash of lemon and silky mashed potatoes. The kai moana (seafood) tasting platter is stunning and, for those in the know, cedar-planked salmon is a speciality. The fare at Martin Bosley's is delectable to the eye and palate – a treat for those who seek out truly sensory dining experiences. Service is impeccable and the location certainly doesn't hurt either, with the restaurant sitting harbourside between funky old boat sheds on Oriental Parade. Undeniably a special occasion restaurant, the more often you dine at Martin Bosley's the more you'll mysteriously find reasons to be here.

Steakhouses

Other options **American** p.462

129 Willis St
Wellington
Map p.504 C1 84

Crazy Horse

04 801 5152 | www.crazyhorsethesteakhouse.co.nz

Crazy Horse is Wellington's finest steakhouse. The interior is warm, well appointed, rich with leather, and the walls are adorned with great depictions of American Indian history as an ode to the Crazy Horse himself. Steakhouse originals take pride of place, with shrimp cocktail and iceberg wedge served with a blue cheese dressing unlikely to leave the menu. Then there's the steak itself – served in 200g or 300g portions – with stars such as fillet bearnaise, fillet mignon, and a completely decadent eye fillet with Australian king prawns reigning supreme. You'll see the usual suspects in the sides and sauces, which are all intended to complement the main event. Succulent steak and a sexy shiraz to go with it, on a cold Wellington winter night? Yes, please.

Queens Wharf
Wellington
Map p.503 E3 85

Shed 5

04 499 9069 | www.shed5.co.nz

If there were a 'fish whisperer' in town he'd be resident at Shed 5. The restaurant location is unbeatable, situated on the waterfront in an original 1888 woolstore, and guests enjoy a great wine list geared to complement the fare. But it's the seafood that steals the show. Chef Simon Gault routinely has up to 10 fish gracing the menu – all incredibly fresh, arriving whole twice daily and filleted by the city's only in-house fishmonger. To mix it up, the menu also features Alaskan king crab served with a trio of smoked chipotle, ginger and garlic butters; Australian king prawns; Galician octopus salad, and New Zealand's own delicious crispy Akaroa salmon. Carrying the ocean theme to the end, dessert lovers can indulge in delights such as parfait of caramel and sea salt, toasted marshmallows and chocolate sabayon, all of which is deliciously clever.

Cafes & Coffee Shops

159 Lambton Quay
Wellington
Map p.503 D2 86

Astoria

04 473 8500

Astoria is a lot like the suits who dot the tables in meetings over roasted long black coffees. During the day it's cut and thrust, fast, snappy and buzzing (which has earned it moniker Meeting Room One). Come 17:00 the ties loosen, wine shows itself and everything slows down a little. Then there's the weekend when things are positively chilled. With counter service through the day and table service through to the early evening, the menu at Astoria is just plain delicious. Seasonal, fresh, rustic and even a little retro, it offers gems such as a bacon sandwich with mayonnaise and rocket; Lancashire hotpot of lamb, kidney, thyme and potato; Moroccan lamb, chickpea and lentil soup; and always at least one gratin and risotto. Anyone who touts black pudding and potato hash with a poached egg must know what they are doing.

27 College St
Wellington
Map p.505 E3 87

Caffe L'Affare

04 385 9748 | *www.laffare.co.nz*

If Wellington is the coffee capital of the country, Caffe L'Affare has to be the parliament. Bustling hardly begins to describe the feeling when you step inside the cafe-cum-wholesale coffee headquarters. The hubbub is perfectly pitched, with suited meetings as commonplace as fathers wrestling with kids ramped up on 'fluffies' (frothy warm milk dusted with cocoa). Staff are always upbeat, personal and attentive, and, although it doesn't need saying, the coffee is outstanding. L'Affare's menu is a mix of counter and menu, with stars including the most delicious flat Italian panini with gruyere, prosciutto and basil; chunky seafood chowder; railway pie with gravy; and, for the kids, 'brat in a bun'. This is the kind of place you can come to alone or with company – either way you'll get the urge, like many Wellingtonians, to call it your local.

497a Karaka Bay Rd
Scorching Bay
Wellington
Map p.498 F6

Chocolate Fish Café

04 388 2808

Chocolate Fish Café is as iconic as the confectionary after which it's named. You can pick any season, any kind of weather, any daylight hour and the cafe, sitting on Scorching Bay, Wellington's prettiest beach, will be hopping. Before *The Lord of the Rings*, Chocolate Fish was busy, but local production of the film whipped it into a frenzy. Inside, there's funky school chairs, outside, staff in fluorescent roadworkers' vests (to save them from sure peril) dash back and forth across Karaka Bay Road to

Cafe L'Affare

serve customers. Chocolate Fish offers great (and quick) coffee, a massive menu of tasty food, and huge icecreams. Dishes seem only to be added to the menu, never removed, which is lucky when it has developed favourites such as kedgeree with sweet parsnip crisps and gourmet mushrooms with wilted spinach.

Dry River Rd
Martinborough
Wellington
North Island
Map H14

Coney Cafe

06 306 8345 | www.coneywines.co.nz

If wine, music, and good food take your fancy then a trip over the hill to Coney Cafe in Martinborough, Wellington's wine country, is more than worth it. It may not be a five-minute exercise, more like 60, but it's the perfect excuse to get out of the city. And once you've made the trip there's easily a day's worth of exploring to be done. Coney makes delicious wines and a lot of care has been taken to pair them with the jazzed-up cafe fare. Specialties such as the vineyard platter, with local nuts, meats, olives, dips and oils in summer, and heartier comfort dishes in winter, are what make this cafe a worthy destination. Set in the beautiful courtyard among the vines with an open outdoor fireplace, Coney is what wine country is all about.

132 Cuba St
Wellington
Map p.504 C2 90

Ernesto

04 801 6878

Fresh and funky, Ernesto is a grown-up Cuba Street joint with decor reminiscent of the island nation's pre 1950s era. The coffee is insanely good and the cafe fare comes with a Cuban twist; choose anything with beans and you can't go wrong. Staples include super tasty counter salads and delicious baked treats such as sweet squares groaning with caramel and chocolate, while the couscous and tofu wraps with rocket and kalamata olives fly out the door. Service starts at 07:30 with breakfast and flows through to lunch then dinner. Music is the constant, switching to live downbeat lounge on Fridays and Saturdays. The only danger with Ernesto is that although you may think you're dropping in for a quick coffee, once you hit the banquette that runs the length of the cafe and begin to watch the Cuba community go by, you just won't want to leave.

234 Cuba St
Wellington
Map p.504 C3 91

Fidels

04 801 6868 | www.fidelscafe.com

If you've ever wondered what makes a cafe timeless, you should check in with the guys at Fidels. Arising from a community of street artists, lower Brooklyn alternatives and Cuba Street characters, Fidels has the same regulars frequenting it now as it did 10 years ago. The cafe is super laid-back, which is what makes it so inviting. The mood is relaxed and caters to every walk of life, the decor is comfortably worn, and the fare classic cafe with a tasty selection of pizzas. Coffee is sensational – hot, strong, fast, and turned out at all hours of day and night. As the sun goes down a small wine list emerges and, while hiding away inside with a glass is tempting, the absolute best is when you can venture outside on a still night, with images of Fidel himself around to keep a watchful eye over proceedings.

42 Tutere St
Waikanae
North Island
Map G14

The Front Room

04 905 4142

The 45 minutes it takes to drive from Wellington to Waikanae is just enough time to shake off the city. Sure, it's a wee way for cafe fare, but it's definitely worth it. Protected by a sand dune from an often wild Waikanae Beach, The Front Room is relaxed and stylish. There are flax mats on the walls, whitewashed wooden floors, an outside dining area fringed with native plants, warm leather couches and a small TV sitting unobtrusively in the corner for holiday homers who are without. With favourites such as chargrilled beef on potato gratin with grilled field mushroom and spinach, and an incredibly decadent hot chocolate pudding with almond heart and vanilla icecream, the menu definitely errs on the side of delicious comfort food. A treat for food-savvy locals and the influx of Wellingtonian weekenders.

7 Lyall Bay Parade
Wellington
Map p.498 D7

Maranui Café

04 387 2829 | www.maranui.co.nz/cafe

Maranui is one of those cafes where you have to be there as the doors open to beat the locals. The coffee is stellar, the food scrumptious and it is located in absolutely the best spot on Wellington's southern coast, as spectacular on one of the city's best days as it is in a screaming southerly. Self-taught chef Katie Richardson has a proclivity towards organic ingredients and vegetarian and vegan schools of cooking (although not exclusively). Specialities such as brown rice sushi (also a favourite at sister cafe Deluxe Espresso Bar at 10 Kent Street, 04 801 5455), chickpea, quinoa and lentil salads, and the vegetarian victory breakfast have even the most dedicated carnivores dropping their surfboards at the door. Check out the funky artwork throughout by local artist Mark Usher.

23 Kent Terrace
Wellington
Map p.505 E2 94

Mojo

04 385 3001 | www.mojocoffee.co.nz

Operating on the principles of fair trading, Mojo imports more than a dozen varieties of coffee for roasting and blending. With six beautifully designed locations dotted through the central city attracting more than 25,000 customers each week, Mojo draws on an extensive loyalty club and wholesale base. Each cafe offers tasty counter food, plus breakfast and lunch menus. So good is their brew that it was voted Wellington's 'best coffee company' by *Capital Times* – no mean feat in a city openly obsessed with a great cup. Coffee can be a serious business, but these guys have a lot of fun with it.

City Gallery Building
Civic Square
Wellington
Map p.505 D1 95

Nikau Gallery Café

04 801 4168

Nikau Gallery Café is a trap for young players. You think you're coming to the excellent gallery, and maybe you'll grab a cup of coffee when you're finished, but when you get there you see that it's all back to front. What you should be doing is coming to Nikau for the excellent food, and then taking in an exhibition if you still have the energy or the inclination. Whiling away time at Nikau is easy, and rewarding. The menu is small – it knows what it does well and sticks to it. With just cause, the cafe has become particularly well known for its kedgeree. For lunch, try the pan-friend haloumi, and for dinner (Fridays only), the duck confit with brussel sprouts.

107 Customhouse Quay
Wellington
Map p.503 D4 96

Pravda

04 801 8858

Be it breakfast, lunch or brunch on the weekends, Pravda bustles. The decor has an elegant, inner city, distinctly eastern European feel to it; encouraging people to stop in first thing for an espresso, to call back for a speedy yet delicious lunch, and to see the day out with a glass of wine at the bar. The menu is contemporary New Zealand, with highlights such as wild mushroom and chicken risotto with wilted spinach, and manuka smoked salmon on nicoise salad. The coffee at Pravda also deserves a mention as it's the proprietor's own – The Immigrant's Son, and it's seriously good.

Mojo

Bars

Other options **Pubs** p.461, **Nightclubs** p.461

126 Cuba St
Wellington
Map p.504 C2 97

Good Luck Bar

04 801 9950

Your good luck starts as soon as you find this gem. Set in a basement on Cuba St, it can be a little tricky to track down – but the queues are the first giveaway. Stepping inside opium-den inspired Good Luck is like taking a trip through the Orient; it features cute Chinese shades, a floating lantern bar and Cambodian food, all brought to life with seriously good techno, jazz-funk and remixed old school sounds. DJs reign supreme, but some of the best nights include live musicians playing reggae, funk, hip-hop and everything in between. When you make your entrance (it's sufficiently laid-back that no-one will notice), turn left for low-lit tables, right for the dancefloor – straight ahead will take you the bar where staff whip themselves into a frenzy turning out some of the city's best cocktails. If you're looking for a place to listen, imbibe and dance, you'll find fortune at Good Luck.

32a Wigan St
Wellington
Map p.504 C3 98

Havana

04 384 7039 | *www.havana.co.nz*

Once you find the funky yellow shack in the back alley adjacent to Cuba Street you'll be hooked – Havana is cool, laid back and uniquely personal. When you're listening to seriously great sounds and taking in a mojito while you check out the original black and white photos of Cuba, it's easy to forget you're in a bar and not at a close friend's home. Music is central to everything that happens at Havana and there is live Latin on

Havana

Hawthorn Lounge

Jet Bar

Tuesdays, jazz on Wednesdays, jazz funk on Thursdays and DJ hosted funk soul on Fridays and Saturdays. Rum-based cocktails are a must but true to its sense of community, Havana also has a great selection of boutique beers such as Wellington's Tuatara. This bar has been part of the Cuba fabric for just a few years but, with a timeless vibe, expect it to be around for a while.

82 Tory St
Wellington
Map p.505 E2 99

Hawthorn Lounge

04 890 3724 | www.hawthornlounge.co.nz

With a roaring open fire, a mantle with marshmallows waiting to be roasted, and a cocktail list with deliciously original twists on the classics, this 1920s and 30s speakeasy-inspired lounge bar is sexy – Marlene Dietrich sexy. The Hawthorn Lounge opened as a spot for those looking to chill with style, play a little impromptu poker on the card tables, or take a seat at the low lit dining table – all with a capacity of just 50. Select a flavour and a libation, more often than not original, will appear tableside. For the most part, music is Parisian jazz funk but to satisfy those with a penchant for new sounds, the first Wednesday of every month is hip-hop night. The best advice? Arrive early and stay late.

Cnr Allen St & Courtenay Pl
Wellington
Map p.505 E2 100

Jet Bar

04 803 3324 | www.jetbar.co.nz

Jet Bar is unashamedly cool. The decor is funky, bar staff are gorgeous, the cocktail list vast, and if you're still not hooked, the funk, jazz and house sounds are guaranteed to get you moving. Add to this the fact that on any given night you can run into New Zealand's most famous faces and you have yourself a place to be seen. Like so many of Courtenay Place's hotspots, Jet can get a little up close and personal as night turns into morning and for this reason it's great fun, but if you're after a something a little more chilled such as table service or even a quiet game of pool, head along early for one of its signature seasonal cocktails.

135-137 Featherston St
Wellington
Map p.503 D2 101

Leuven Belgian Beer Café

04 499 2939 | www.leuven.co.nz

If you've been inside a beer cafe in Belgium, the Leuven will seem familiar with almost every piece having made its way here from the motherland: old black and white pictures, heavy mirrors, well-worn bar, floor tiles, a whimsical old stove, and a drop box for workers wages from bygone days. With beer as near and dear to the Belgians as wine is to the French, Leuven is predictably serious about not only its beverage of choice but the vessels in which they're served. Nearly 25 beers are imported and all are paired with a uniquely original Belgian menu. Mussels are the biggest hit and who could resist a one kilo pot served with frites and mayonnaise? Come Sundays and Mondays and they'll double your order for free. Breakfast, lunch, dinner and brunch are served on the weekends and on Friday afternoons from 16:00 it's standing room only.

106 Cuba St
Wellington
Map p.504 C2 102

Matterhorn

04 384 3359 | www.matterhorn.co.nz

Matterhorn has known a couple of lives in its time but there's no doubting it's a Cuba Street original. It's an everyday place for everyday people; warm, inviting, and comfortable but with an undeniable edge. Recently awarded fifth best bar in the world by *Australian Bartender* magazine, Matterhorn has the most extensive selection of elixirs in Wellington. More importantly, it knows exactly what to do with them. The same can be said for the restaurant, which serves insanely moreish bites such as feta fried on gorse honey and thyme flowers and brunch, lunch and dinner where you'll find honest, rustic pleasures such as quail, venison with pancetta, and grilled pork fillet. Matterhorn is greater than the sum of its parts. A fantastic bar, stellar service, lush New Zealand modernism in decor, open fires inside and out, live entertainment that flows between jazz, soul and rhythm and blues, and a restaurant that rivals the best in town – individually great, but together, not to be missed.

104 Cuba St
Wellington
Map p.505 D1 103

Mighty Mighty

04 385 2890 | www.myspace.com/mightymightybar

Mighty Mighty is a place where people can be themselves, take in a great selection of drinks and enjoy good times in a casual, art inspired, funky space. It's reminiscent of New Zealand in the 1970s, with beer crates upturned for seating outside, super-kitsch porcelain dogs, pinball, space invaders, 45" records on the wall and the best toasted sandwiches in town. It's easy to spot the essence of a local here, albeit with a little cool to jazz it up. Slightly juxtaposed but not out of place is the Mississippi gin-shack style cabaret area, where local musicians appear at least three of the four nights that the bar is open. In between times the sounds move to eclectic soul, old school and funk.

35 Abel Smith St
Wellington
Map p.504 C3 104

The Southern Cross

04 384 9085 | www.thecross.co.nz

It seems like The Southern Cross has been around since the beginning of time. Its predecessor, the Victoria Hotel, was the meeting place of the Wellington Football Club, where players gathered as early as the 1860s after 'friendly' matches with the 18th Royal Irish Regiment based here for the Land Wars. Having seen so much and commendably, changed with it, it's fitting that The Cross now aims to offer the 'urban Kiwi experience'; loads of local and live music, and hot water bottles for those chilly nights in the garden bar. In its down time The Cross goes out of its way to cater to young families. Sunday is kids' day with a team on hand for face painting and entertainment, while parents enjoy the delicious brunch and bistro menus including stonegrill dining: table cooking on a super-heated volcanic stone.

5 Cable St
Wellington
Map p.505 D1 105

St John's Heineken Hotel

04 801 8017 | www.stjohnsbar.co.nz

Situated in what started life as Wellington's Free Ambulance bay, this space has been transformed into a warm, sleek, stylish bar. It's a hotel, but in the old sense of the word, reminiscent of the publican hotels; you can stay late, but not the night. St John's has a great New Zealand-dominated wine list, and although it sells twice the amount of Heineken as any other bar in the country, the promotion is subtle; the most overt being a faint green glow above the bar. St John's has a bar menu but if you wander down the back you'll discover a restaurant with such dishes as maka whero (pheasant breast with venison fillet wrapped in spinach). Like the music – which is almost all homegrown – dishes like this are an ode to indigenous cuisine.

19 Edward St
Wellington
Map p.504 C1 106

Vivo Enoteca Cucina

04 384 6400 | www.vivowinebar.com

Oenophiles will be elated with the the city's own cellar door. Vivo Enoteca Cucina, hidden away on Edward Street, boasts 700 wines, 60 served by the glass. While its list is weighted towards New Zealand, Vivo has a great selection of Australian (often listing the prized Grange by the glass), Italian and French wines, and an entirely respectable North American offering. Refreshingly, it's as serious about stemware as it is about wine, with revered Riedel glassware and the extra-special sommelier collection for those dining in the Dom Perignon Wine Library. Vivo's fare is Italian with piattini (small plates) and cheeses to pair with wines and a simple but tasty dinner menu for those wanting to stay a little longer. Tuesday nights see winemakers in the house to pour and chat.

General Practitioner

Pubs

Other options **Bars** p.458

88 Willis St
Wellington
Map p.503 D4 107

General Practitioner

04 499 5528

The General Practitioner, or GP as it's more commonly known, is a great play on the origins of the building in which it's housed: a surgery dating from 1903. Today's decor tips its hat to these respectable beginnings, but since then the building has played host to restaurants, bars and a brothel. It's now a fantastic spot to watch the city go about its business, and an easy place to wind down at the end of the week with a glass of wine or one of its craft beers. The GP is a gastropub; the fare not unlike that of its co-owned The Tasting Room (p.453), but with less wild meats and more seafood. That said there might be no better way to spend a chilly Wellington afternoon than with a steak, ale and kidney hotpot served with a pint of Monteith's Black.

Nightclubs

25-29 Courtenay Pl
Wellington
Map p.505 E2 108

Boogie Wonderland

04 385 2242

If you're a disco queen, make Boogie Wonderland your mecca. It's seriously cheesy, but it embraces the fact. From the fluffy ducks and *Saturday Night Fever*-style dancefloor to the incessant flashing lights, Boogie Wonderland is pure, unadulterated fun. There is a $10 cover charge, but it's more than likely that's because there's no time to stop to rehydrate yourself once you're inside, pulling out your best electric slide. For a blast from the past, songs you know every word to, and a shame-free night full of throwing in the actions to those songs, get your platforms down to Boogie Wonderland. The limbering up starts around 23:00.

8 Kent Tce
Wellington
Map p.505 F2 109

Sandwiches

04 385 7698 | *www.sandwiches.co.nz*

Sandwiches is an out-and-out club, closing at the serious party hour of 07:00. A cover charge is standard – expect to pay between $10 and $60 to listen to local and international bands and DJs. You'll hear downbeat jazz and soul in the lounge bar, and a little more dance in the club. Unlike other spots, Sandwiches has a dinner menu – all good, but it's definitely the music and list of 20 original cocktails that pull in the party crowd. In full flight, Sandwiches packs in around 400 clubbers. Decor in the lounge is cool with the central feature being a modern twist on an old favourite, the bar leaner. If you're looking for live, late, (all) night entertainment, this is where you'll find it.

Courtenay Pl
Wellington
Map p.505 E2 110

UU

UU is all about the entertainment factor; entertain yourself, be entertained by others – it really doesn't matter as either way you'll have a fine time. It's a 1980s bar decked out with mirrors and a pole; if you can't have fun with that then really you have no business being out in Courtenay Place. The music is loud, everyone knows the words, the drinks flow fast and people (well, women) can get pretty serious about their pole moves. If your inner thigh muscles can handle it and you haven't knocked anyone out, you can stay on until the wee small hours.

Christchurch

American

479A Papanui Rd
Christchurch
Map p.508 C3

Burger Wisconsin

03 352 4041 | www.wisconsin.co.nz

A burger just isn't straightforward anymore; a bite from the beef-in-a-bun industry these days invariably comes with a twist. Thankfully for Christchurch's meat-and-bread lovers, Without going overboard Burger Wisconsin puts enough into its baps to stand out from the ubiquitous gang of chain restaurants. Gourmet options include the chicken, camembert and cranberry classic burger, and the tempting Thai-style fish, coriander and lime; all are priced between $5 and $10. Try washing them down with the caramel 'real shake' for $4. Conveniently located in both Papanui and Cashmere, these are places for a casual catch-up with friends.

Burmese

808 Colombo St
Christchurch
Map p.512 C4 112

The Bodhi Tree – Cuisine of Burma

03 377 6808

While Christchurch is home to a wide variety of great restaurants, it is hard to find any that are booked out on a regular basis well in advance. That's why it's amazing that The Bodhi Tree, housed in a surprisingly low-key, plain little building, is perpetually difficult to get into. The excellent fantastic is best enjoyed shared with others. Six to seven plates is ideal for a table of four, whereupon each dish can be comfortably tasted by all. While the tea salad or spicy raw fish may sound peculiar, the flavours are distinct and delicious. Plump prawns and light curries are also on the menu. The food here makes up for the rather lacking atmosphere and average service, but the bring-your-own wine option makes dining at The Bodhi Tree an inexpensive night out.

Chinese

Shop 12
376 Ilam Rd
Christchurch
Map p.508 B4

Chopsticks Restaurant

03 351 2618

Restaurants often find it hard to balance busy takeaway orders with a full room of diners, but Chopsticks is experienced at keeping everyone happy. Most nights at this Chinese restaurant are busy, and regulars all seem to state consistency as one of the main reasons for returning time and again. The menu covers a wide range of Chinese dishes, and the friendly staff are happy to recommend the most popular. If you want your kids to try Chinese cuisine, Chopsticks is the ideal place to take them; children and large groups are accommodated without hassle, and it's always loud and cheerful inside.

European

Other options, **Italian** p.466, **Spanish** p.468

7 Tramway La
Christchurch
Map p.516 C2 114

Christchurch Tramway

03 366 7511 | www.tram.co.nz

If you're new to the city, one of the best ways to orientate yourself is the view from New Zealand's only working tram. On a relatively small 2.5km track, it passes by the Botanical Gardens, the Arts Centre and the Art Gallery, to name just a few attractions. What's this got to do with eating, you might ask? Well, the Tramway also operates a dining car – a decidedly classy way to dine while cruising the streets. The menu is gourmet, with a price tag that reflects the upper-class style, and meals range from four to five courses – and of course, the outlook is charming along the way. Groups of thirty or more can reserve the dining car for breakfast, lunch or morning tea, or for cocktail functions, so booking is essential. The tram departs from Cathedral Square at 19:00 every day.

Cnr Ilam Rd & Clyde Rd
Christchurch
Map p.508 B4

Misceo Café & Bar

03 351 8011

Misceo is a pleasant upmarket restaurant in which to dine, but is even more special for those who are restricted to gluten-free diets. The menu is varied and suitable for casual evenings out, with some romantic, more intimate tables tucked away for more formal occasions. The pizza here is ideal for sharing, particularly if you want a fast meal, or even if you just want to enjoy a drink at one of the bar tables rather than a more elaborate dinner. As well as its dedication to providing gluten-free dishes to order, Misceo is more than happy to cater to other specific dietary needs if you advise staff when you arrive. The surroundings here are busy and cheerful, and the bar has a good selection of wine and beer. It can get noisy at times, but this generally just adds to the overall lively atmosphere.

819 Colombo St
Christchurch
Map p.512 C4 116

XYZ Restaurant

03 365 6543

Formerly The Seafood Kitchen, hip XYZ has taken over the stylish setting left by the previous owners and transformed it into an expensive, romantic, European-inspired establishment. While the fare is still largely seafood, other influences have been introduced. Game such as pheasant, rabbit and duck have been added to the small selection of mains, with extremely high-class accompaniments. Stinging nettle sauce, champagne truffle oil and other such unusual flavours accompany virtually every dish, meaning there are no 'safe' choices. XYZ is relatively expensive, but the staff are well trained and make dining a joy, meaning you won't begrudge the bill.

Fish and Chips

177 Victoria St
Christchurch
Map p.512 A3 117

Fishmongers

03 366 3129

Hollywood star Jack Black chose to buy his fish and chips here when he was in Christchurch for the filming of *King Kong* – a claim to fame this place is undoubtedly proud of. That said, this is one restaurant that doesn't really need to rely on celebrity endorsements. A far cry from your average fish and chip shop, Fishmongers has almost managed to eliminate grease from the menu; chips are real slices of potato, the fish comes pan fried with lemon juice, and accompaniments include tempura vegetables and assorted seafood. Although there is a small space to eat in the shop, this fine fare is best enjoyed on a takeaway basis and eaten straight from the box.

London Street

French

2 London St
Christchurch
Map p.513 F2 118

London Street

03 328 7171 | *www.londonstreet.co.nz*

Although open only since early 2006, London Street has already earned several rave reviews from New Zealand food critics. The menu is based on simple flavours, which transform into well-defined meals, and the emphasis is on fresh, locally sourced ingredients. If you find it hard to choose the right wine to accompany your meal, two suggested options are printed beneath each dish on the menu to help you out. The local produce ethos is strong – the belief is that it simply tastes better than imported food – with salad ingredients and herbs picked fresh each morning. Pan-seared groper fillets, wood-fried calamari, and steak are all recommended, and the mains are priced at less than $30 – good value for a decent restaurant in Christchurch. The smart building that houses London Street features exposed brickwork, helping to create a modern, laid back atmosphere.

Greek

Gloucester St & Cambridge Tce
Christchurch
Map p.516 B1 119

Santorini Greek Ouzeri

03 377 7626 | *www.santorini.co.nz*

You don't have to like Greek food to come here, but you do need to like a raucous atmosphere. If you make a booking, expect to be pulled from your seat and danced around the restaurant with a group of other diners (even venturing around the outside of the restaurant on special occasions). The culprits are the Bouzouki Band, two enthusiastic guys on guitar who provide live and loud music every night. By closing, they've usually convinced at least a few people to strut their stuff on top of the tables. You can buy the band's CD afterwards. Santorini is ideal with a group of friends, or for a work party. Staff are always looking to have fun; meaning service is smiley and swift. The menu is long and crammed full of hearty traditional fare, including tyganites (pancakes filled with ground beef and cheese) and psari plaki (marinated and pan-fried gurnard fillets). You are invited to enhance all dishes with a shot or three of Santorini's ouzo.

Indian

71 Ilam Rd
Christchurch
Map p.508 B5

Tandoori Palace

03 343 4405 | *www.tandooripalace.co.nz*

Although Tandoori Palace is more commonly recognised as a takeaway by many locals, the Ilam restaurant has been entirely refitted and is now popular for sit-down meals too. It is fully licensed, as well as allowing bring-your-own wine, and the modern style has created a lively, casual atmosphere. Butter chicken, vindaloo and chicken tikka are all tasty, and each main dish is served with a generous portion of plump rice, with good naan bread available on the side. Tandoori Palace even sells its own popular sauces, in the restaurant and at supermarkets, for fans to make their own versions – all you need to do is add meat to recreate the flavours at home. There are several Tandoori Palaces, so if it's takeaway you're after just track down your nearest branch from the website.

International

The George Hotel
50 Park Tce
Christchurch
Map p.512 A4 121

50 on Park

03 379 4560 | *www.thegeorge.com*

Home to former Salon Culinaire South Island Chef of the Year Guy Stanaway, 50 on Park provides diners with a rather accomplished menu and an experience laced with delicious, New Zealand delicacies. Portions of Canterbury lamb, beef and other local produce are used to inspire the constantly evolving menu. Situated inside internationally renowned hotel The George, the restaurant is stylish and modern, in keeping with its surroundings, and the view across Hagley Park is stunning on a clear night. Servings are small yet sumptuous, staff are knowledgeable, and the wine list is well-matched to the food selection. Popular with affluent locals and visitors, 50 on Park is ideal for an expensive yet well-deserved night out. It has enjoyed the talents of some of the country's best chefs, including well-known names such as Peter Thornley and Rick Rutledge-Manning. A must for special occasions or an evening of indulgence.

State Highway 1
Waipara
Christchurch
South Island Map L6

Canterbury House Winery

03 314 6900 | *www.reservecuisine.co.nz*

If you're keen to spend a whole day away from home, or at least a few hours, head north up State Highway 1 and 40 minutes later you will find yourself in the heart of Canterbury's winemaking territory. Although not as picturesque as vineyards farther north, this is still a lovely area to come to for a day excursion or as a special occasion. American-owned, Canterbury House has long functioned in the Waipara Valley, and enjoys a substantial 50 hectares of planted grapes. The setting is fabulous, with the restaurant located in a big house amid stunning grounds. It's open seven days a week, and rather than just sit and eat lunch with one glass of wine, customers are encouraged to try the various grapes through an informal wine tasting service. The pinos gris and chardonnay are particularly good, and the staff are always more than happy to help you match the correct wine to your choice of food.

209 Cambridge Tce
Christchurch
Map p.512 C4 123

Indochine

03 365 7323

This elegant Asian-inspired restaurant is one of Christchurch's real gems; repeatedly ranked as one of the country's top eateries, Indochine possesses both style and substance. The oriental dark wood interior and bamboo-forest wall frieze gives a flavour of the east before you even eat anything. But it gets even better. Start your dining by sharing some dim sum to whet your appetite and warm up the tastebuds. You can make a meal of just these, but if you're intending to move on to the mains, be careful not to over-indulge at this early stage. The next course offers a range of delicious dishes, including grilled squid salad, seared tuna, and sticky beef ribs. Round it off with a dessert or even a dessert cocktail – who could resist trying a tiramisu martini? Unsurprisingly, Indochine attracts a lot of custom, so make sure you reserve – you wouldn't want someone else getting their hands on your pork dumplings.

189 Papanui Rd
Christchurch
Map p.508 C4

JDV

03 964 3860

This spot, a favourite after-work meeting place for Merivale locals, offers consistently good food and a superb wine selection. The menu is updated seasonally, with regular favourites (such as the risotto) changing on a daily basis. The layout of the restaurant and bar is semi-open plan, and the relaxed atmosphere keeps the punters coming back for more. JDV's courtyard is also a top choice for enjoying summer evenings. There are several other restaurants and bars located close by, making it a happening area, although there's really no need to move on after dark as the lounge bar upstairs is ideal for languid evenings and the cocktail list is excellent. If you want to treat yourself to something a little naughty, round things off with a chocolate martini – dessert in a glass.

State Highway 1
Waipara
Christchurch
South Island Map L6

Waipara Springs Wine Bar & Cafe

03 314 6777 | *www.waiparasprings.co.nz*

Another pick of the north Canterbury winery bunch is the excellent Waipara Springs; a boutique vineyard that boasts a superb array of flavours, from light rieslings and sauvignon blancs to more heavy, full-flavoured merlots. There is no way you could leave without visiting the cellar for at least one bottle to take home. Before ordering from the extensive menu, try sampling some of the wine on offer, including one or two stunning vintage years that are extremely fruity. While the lunch menu is decidedly gourmet, one of the most traditional ways to enjoy an afternoon out here is to order a large platter to share, bursting with cheeses, cold meat and plenty more, all the time sipping wine in the sun. If you head out this way with a group of friends, think about hiring a shuttle, and split the taxi fare – that way everyone can relax and not worry about the drive home.

Italian

Other options, **European** p.462, **Spanish** p.468

182 Oxford Tce
Christchurch
Map p.516 B1 **126**

Portofino

03 377 2454

Although the menu isn't overly expensive, the polished staff at this Italian restaurant treat all diners as VIPs, and are pleased to recommend the best food and wine if you're indecisive. All the old Italian favourites such as spaghetti bolognese and seafood marinara are included on the menu. If you love big pasta dishes, this is the place to go – the rich sauces are a sure-fire winner. Portofino is a lively destination, with the restaurant rarely empty; being able to see through to the kitchen adds another dimension to the atmosphere. Service is fast and attentive, the decor is simple and contemporary, and the overall experience is exemplary. After dinner, if you don't want the evening to stop, Portofino is located a two-minute walk to The Strip, where you can be sure to find plenty of late-night bars.

155 Victoria St
Christchurch
Map p.512 A3 **127**

Spagalimis

0800 113 113 | www.spagalimis.co.nz

Spagalimis, which claims to be Christchurch's original Italian pizzeria, has recently undergone a complete image makeover and refurbishment – but thankfully the food remains unchanged and as reliable as ever. Ideal for families, Spags offers good pizza at an affordable price. The chain has been franchised in multiple destinations throughout Christchurch, but the Victoria Street branch is one of its best. Pick your toppings from the old reliable classics or something a little more adventurous – but make sure to leave room for the fries and home-made tomato sauce, a firm favourite with regulars. The restaurant is licensed, so parents can enjoy a drink while the kids sip on soda. There is a separate entrance for takeaway orders, and a delivery service operates to most suburbs in Christchurch.

192 Papanui Rd
Christchurch
Map p.511 F1 **128**

Tutto Bene

03 355 4744

Tutto Bene ('everything is good') is owned by Italian born Felice and his wife Paulette. It remains true to the culture on which this homely place is based – delicious, Italian meals are plentiful and varied, and nothing is very expensive. Locals flock here for some of the best comfort food in Christchurch. The pizza bases are made fresh and, while the main

Portofino

Spagalimis

kitchen is tucked around the back, toppings are added and placed in the oven for all to see just beside the bar. Frequently busy, Tutto Bene has a welcoming feel. Red and white checked table cloths and wooden chairs set the authentic scene, and the chatter of happy customers makes for an uplifting, buzzing background.

194 Gloucester St
Christchurch
Map p.517 D1 129

Winnie Bagoes

03 366 6315 | www.winniebagoespizza.co.nz

As well as boasting one of the best gourmet pizza menus around, Winnie's is home to a great bar, perfect for a beer or a glass of wine while listening to some of the regular live music gigs or DJs. If you're dining, mouthwatering toppings on offer include chicken, cranberry and brie; salmon and capers, and Moroccan lamb, while pastas and salads are also available. The pizzas are affordable, the vibe is great, and, if you want to burn off some of that indulgence you can even have a game of street basketball in the adjacent half-court at the weekend.

Japanese

85 Riccarton Rd
Christchurch
Map p.514 A1 130

At Tony's

03 341 6608 | www.at-tonys.co.nz

There's no shortage of Japanese options in Chistchurch, but At Tony's is one of the best. Renowned for its tuna belly – a real delicacy and a must-try for the more adventurous diner – At Tony's is popular for lunch and dinner, as well as for its all-you-can-eat menu every Tuesday, Wednesday and Thursday (not for the faint-hearted). The restaurant is small and cosy, and aside from the traditional menu, which includes sushi and sashimi, you don't need to be seated around the long teppanyaki table to enjoy the fresh, authentic food. One of the best restaurants in the suburb of Riccarton (p.144), At Tony's is a great option if you don't want to head into the centre of town.

Crowne Plaza
Christchurch
Map p.512 B4 131

Yamagen

03 365 7799

The first restaurant to offer teppanyaki to Christchurch residents, Yamagen is located inside an upmarket hotel and offers fresh, Japanese cuisine cooked on a hot plate. Although relatively pricey, the food is high quality and the chefs are trained to make cooking for an audience an enjoyable experience. If you haven't booked in advance, and there's no room left at the two teppanyaki tables, you can still order the same food, plus items from the traditional Japanese menu, from one of the regular tables – the fare will still taste as good; all that you'll miss is the showmanship. After dinner, a stroll out into the atrium of the Crowne Plaza provides many options for dessert and coffee, or stay at Yamagen and try a Japanese dessert such as flambeed bananas wrapped in a crepe.

Mexican

42 London St
Lyttelton
Map p.508 D4

Volcano Café & Lava Bar

03 328 7077 | www.volcano.co.nz

You can tell that Volcano is a cheerful place just by looking at the outside of the building, which is adorned with yellows, blues and greens. The inside matches the exterior too, with a deserved reputation for fun service and fine food. This bright Mexican restaurant puts a modern twist on traditional fare; the enchiladas, cajun lamb cutlets and nachos are all delicious. Bright lightshades and paper hang from the ceiling, colourful curtains cover the windows and retro chairs add to the funky vibe. Mains are in the high $20s, making it relatively expensive in comparison to other family-style restaurants, but even if you don't live in Lyttelton, it's well worth the journey.

Moroccan

114 Cashel St
Cashel Mall
Christchurch
Map p.516 B2 133

Simo's

03 377 5001 | *www.simos.co.nz*

For classic Moroccan food with a twist, this is the only choice in Christchurch. The walls are covered in traditional Moroccan wallpaper, creating a warm, comfortable and cosy space. To maintain the authentic style, chef Mohamed (Simo) Abbai, who claims to have opened the first Moroccan restaurant in New Zealand, reigns over the kitchen. Simo is a classically trained chef, and the thoughtful menu is well-planned. Arabian platters, spiced dukkah and fragrant couscous are all recommended. The aromas are rich without being overbearing, and staff are polished when it comes to attentive service – although the prices reflect this upper-class feasting experience. If you like the food and want to try more of it, Simo's also offers cooking classes.

New Zealand

15 Wakefield Av
Christchurch
South Island Map L7

Club Bazaar

03 326 6155

Very much a take on iconic New Zealand history, Club Bazaar's walls are covered with 'Kiwiana'. Old rusty tricycles and signs from the past give locals a trip down memory lane, with the cheap Formica tables and retro chairs creating a relaxed point of difference. Downstairs, wooden surfboards have been converted into tabletops. You get the idea. Children are made to feel at home, with old wall-mounted coin games keeping them entertained. The fare is very family friendly, and consists mainly of pizza and pasta dishes, from hawaiians to a hearty serving of cannelloni. Club Bazaar won't win any awards for service, but offers an inexpensive and diverting night out.

Spanish

Other options **European** p.462, **Italian** p.466

143 Worcester St
Christchurch
Map p.517 D2 135

Pedro's Restaurant

03 379 7668 | *www.pedrosrestaurant.co.nz*

Opened more than 20 years ago, Pedro's has stood the test of time. The interior is traditionally Spanish, and feels light and airy even in deep winter. From large group tables to intimate spots for two, everyone is catered for, while the staff are knowledgeable, and the food reasonably priced. Particularly notable is the lamb shoulder, a huge meal that even owner Pedro would struggle with. A large array of fish and seafood dishes is also on the menu, with the paella recommended. Pedro's is licensed, but bring-your-own is also allowed, for a minimal corkage charge.

Thai

84 Hereford St
Christchurch
Map p.516 B2 136

Mythai Thai Restaurant & Monkey Bar

03 365 1295

Mythai has a deserved reputation as a good, reliable source of authentic Thai food. Many ethnic restaurants often overlook a good wine list, but with the Monkey Bar as part of its set-up, there is a decent selection here. Although the dishes include traditional curries and noodles, the flavour has been kept tangy rather than hot to appealing to Kiwi tastebuds. The fish wrapped in tinfoil is a popular must-try, especially if you're a newcomer to Thai delicacies. Like many other Thai restaurants in town, people come here for good food rather than contemporary surroundings and often as part of a large group.

Drink and dine Kiwi style

Cafes & Coffee Shops

384B Montreal St
Christchurch
Map p.512 A3 137

Blax

03 366 8982

Blax exhibits an international feel and serves excellent coffee; its dedicated barista has his regular customers' drinks orders firmly stored in his head. Even if you only frequent the place on a semi-regular basis, he seems to remember if you like one shot or two. The coffee is nothing short of sublime, and the food is simple yet tasty. It's not the place for a hearty lunch, but is ideal for a mid-morning snack or light fare; small sandwiches, delicate rolls and petit fours are commonplace. Blax has recently opened a deli, which occupies the other half of the building. After lunch, or as a complete diversion, you can buy cheeses and other assorted specialities that you may otherwise be hard pushed to find in Christchurch. Gourmet 'take-home' meals are available, or food can also be purchased frozen – and the price is surprisingly affordable.

Cnr Aikman Rd & Papanui Rd
Christchurch
Map p.508 C4

Brigittes Espresso Bar

03 355 6150

Everyone knows Brigittes, a real icon for coffee, culture and wholesome food in the ever-popular suburb of Merivale. When it's busy here it gets *really* busy, but, despite the tables being slightly too small and crammed together, Brigittes has a real soul. People are always coming and going, from young groups of friends to retirees, and there is a constant sound of the coffee machine churning out smooth brews. There are plenty of tables in the recently renovated courtyard – a real sun trap on a good day and a great place to spend a couple of hours on the weekend. Brunch and lunch are superb, and include classic staples such as eggs benedict, bagels and huge toasted sandwiches. On special occasions, such as Mother's Day, bookings are essential – this is everyone's favourite place to take their mum for lunch.

150 High St
Christchurch
Map p.517 D3 139

C1 Espresso

03 379 1917 | *www.c1espresso.co.nz*

Although the outside isn't much and the inside is dimly lit and slightly grungy, C1 is one of the most popular coffee hangouts in the Inner City. Whether you're here for a quick takeaway pick-me-up before work or an hour flicking through a magazine during the day it's a great spot. Probably more suited to those who enjoy more alternative styles, C1 is full of old coffee paraphernalia, and a varied assortment of photos and knick-knacks litter the walls. The food is substantial and relatively inexpensive, with everything from bagels and sandwiches to macaroni and cheese. Vegan diets are also catered for. The coffee is made by C4, which is housed at the rear of the building, and is a brand that many other cafes prefer. If you like making coffee at home, pick up a bag of freshly roasted beans on your way out.

127 Hackthorne Rd
Christchurch
Map p.508 C6

Cup Cafe

03 332 1270

Perched overlooking the city, high on the Cashmere Hills, Cup is popular with locals trying to satisfy their coffee fix, as well as people who flock to the area come the weekend. It is certainly deserving of a drive across town, for brunch, coffee or lunch, although it's worth noting that it doesn't accept reservations. If you can secure a table, stay a while and savour the view over the city, good even on a drab day, as well as the buzz of people coming and going. Food in the cabinet is appetising, and there's a great brunch menu that includes eggs benedict, a full breakfast, and french toast. Coffee is good too, doubly so if coupled with a tasty muffin.

2 Worcester Blvd
Christchurch
Map p.516 A1 141

Le Café

03 366 7722

Having enjoyed a play or performance at the nearby Court Theatre, people come here to extend their evening. Although it serves good food, Le Café is predominantly recognised for brilliant coffee and cakes, sit-down or takeaway. During the day, locals and visitors are found languishing outside in the sun, or during the colder months tucked away inside by the fire. Le Café is also close to Christchurch Museum, as well as Hagley Park (p.263) and the Botanical Gardens (p.262), and on a weekend it's great to get your coffee here then saunter down for a browse around the Arts Centre (p.475).

165 Victoria St
Christchurch
Map p.512 A3 142

Procope Coffee House

03 379 4299

Victoria Street is a destination that enjoys multiple cafes and restaurants, but this one is worth choosing above the competition for breakfast, brunch, lunch or simply a snack. Aside from the fact it has a designated customer carpark – surprisingly hard to find in this location – Procope has all the vital ingredients for success. Well-trained baristas make exceptional coffee and the food is always fresh and appealing, from large lunches to light snacks. Customers pop in on a weekly basis to have their biscuit or cake tins filled, making a visit to Procope the perfect way to stay prepared for guests or simply to have treats at home. The brunch is popular, with a small, delicious and well-priced menu. All the breakfast essentials are included, with bacon and eggs, french toast and muesli recommended.

286 Lincoln Rd
Christchurch
Map p.508 C5

The Tea Room

03 338 8978

Going to The Tea Room is like taking a trip back in time. Tables are clustered around a corner of treasures for sale, from whitewashed sideboards to crafty trinkets. When you're done browsing, decide on traditional 'high tea' in quaint cups, or opt for a more modern caffeine hit. The menu features huge date scones, home-made muffins, sandwiches and bagels. This is a real girls' cafe; pretty coloured icing on sumptuous cup cakes are very hard to ignore, and perfect with a cup of tea.

502 Worcester St
Christchurch
Map p.508 D5

Under the Red Verandah

03 381 1109

This character house has been transformed into a hearty cafe, and despite its location in Linwood, on the outer edge of Christchurch, bookings are essential for lunch on Fridays and brunch over the weekend. The food is wholesome and served country-style, with the front cabinet well stocked with gourmet pies, huge BLT bagels and home-made slices, almost reminiscent of picnic food. The prices are on a par with other quality cafes around town. If you order from the menu the cost does increase, but the gourmet choices on offer, ranging from large vegetarian platters to seafood bisque, are worth the extra dollars.

132 Victoria St
Christchurch
Map p.512 A3 145

Vic's Cafe

03 366 2054 | www.vics.co.nz

During the week this popular cafe doesn't look like much, but as soon as the weekend lands it's packed. Aside from the fact that it serves good coffee, and has a real point of difference with organic food (from breakfast to lunch, the portions are always generous and wholesome), Vic's has an atmosphere unlike any other. Weekends often see live jazz bands in the courtyard (weather permitting), and the driveway plays host to an organic market every Saturday. Rows of vegetables and fruit are available at modest prices and fresh bread and bagels are sold throughout the week.

Bars

Other options **Pubs** p.473

His Lordship's La
Christchurch
Map p.516 C3 146

Cartel Bar

In the centre of town, in an area that until recently was largely comprised of unused commercial buildings, is His Lordship's Lane – Christchurch's hippest new night-time hangout. One bar that has already become a firm favourite is Cartel, a place reminiscent of an intimate underground New York joint. Inside, affluent young drinkers spill from the small bar to the outside areas – no hardship as a large, roaring fire is located on the exterior wall, with bean bags and a bench providing front row seats for early birds. Gas heaters also help alfresco punters stay warm during colder months. Cartel is possibly not the place for dedicated beer drinkers, but with an extensive wine and spirit selection, it's a smart, funky spot for a stylish night out.

SOL Square
179 Tuam St
South of Lichfield St
Christchurch
Map p.516 C3 147

Fat Eddie's

03 943 2833 | *www.fateddies.co.nz*

Good live music played on a regular basis can be hard to find in Christchurch, but Fat Eddie's has filled a niche for people wanting to be in a crowded, busy bar with good tunes in the background. New York-inspired Fat Eddie's is always swinging, be it to soloists or full-on brass jazz bands. Loft-style and located upstairs, the walls at Fat Eddies are classic brick, and the large veranda is ideal for a breath of fresh air when it's packed inside. In keeping with their music theme, cocktails with names like Mr. Bojangles and Statesboro Blues are on the drinks menu, which does stock a fairly wide selection of wine. Don't expect to get in straight away on a Friday or Saturday night though, you will definitely be expected to wait in line. Check out its website for the latest information on who's playing and when.

4 Mansfield Av
Christchurch
Map p.508 C4

No. 4

03 355 3720 | *www.no4bar.co.nz*

Following a stunning refurbishment, No. 4 has become Merivale's premier bar, and one of Christchurch's best. Because of its popularity among locals, the place is busy from Thursday night through to Saturday.

With rugby so integral to New Zealand culture, No. 4 is the preferred place to watch the game if you can't make it to the match, although it's not a dedicated sports bar, even if it has the quintessential 'man's' restaurant, with sport even playing in the dining area. If you don't want to have a sit down meal, bar food is served. The aroma of the dishes emerging from the kitchen is very tempting, with juicy fillet steaks and lamb worth sampling. The ample outdoor area is great for smokers who don't want to be left out in the cold. A plasma screen television and gas heaters ensure the environment is equal to the atmosphere inside.

14 Bedford Row
Christchurch
Map p.517 D2 149

Sammy's Jazz Review

03 377 8618 | *www.sammys.co.nz*

Slightly off the beaten track, this is the place that brought a much-needed alternative feel to Christchurch's nightlife. This wasn't just your average watering hole; it had a relaxed and slightly boho demeanour.

In summer, the courtyard is packed with people listening to the exceptional live music and nursing a drink. Inside is equally appealing, and the little corner bar offers great drinks, including top shelf spirits, as well as an array of good wines. Dinner is also recommended, and recognised as being as gourmet as the jazz, with delicacies such as ostrich on the menu. It is best to come early though if you want a romantic evening. Later on, the tunes rock the place and dancing is positively encouraged.

Clarendon Towers
Oxford Tce
Christchurch
Map p.516 B1 150

Sticky Fingers Restaurant & Bar

03 366 6451 | *www.stickyfingers.co.nz*

Like many places down The Strip, Sticky Fingers is a regular hangout for locals from Thursday through to Sunday. The difference here is the degree of separation from the general cluster of pubs. While dancing and big tunes are common later on in the evening, it isn't quite so clubby as the likes of Liquidity. More suited to an older crowd perhaps, and a favourite for many 'suits' after work, particularly on Fridays, Sticky Fingers is the kind of bar where beer progresses to food and then wine leads to a very late and enjoyable night out on the town. In summer months, the outdoor tables are jammed, with the front of the bar enjoying the very last rays of early evening sun.

Pubs

Other options **Bars** p.472

Cnr Hereford St & Montreal St
Christchurch
Map p.516 A2 151

Dux de Lux

03 366 6919 | *info@thedux.co.nz*

The Dux de Lux, or just the Dux, is the best place in town for a casual drink with friends, particularly on a sunny afternoon or balmy evening. Christchurch residents clearly think so – they've been coming here in numbers for 20 years. Even though there are a huge number of tables outside, they're always in demand; the bar's courtyard backs onto the Arts Centre (p.475), so there's a buzz about the place, especially at weekends. Live bands regularly play inside the big character-building, and attract a diverse crowd. For a more relaxed night, head upstairs where there are pool tables. If you're peckish, try the Dux's strictly vegetarian menu.

263 Bealey Av
Christchurch
Map p.513 D3 152

Speight's Ale House

03 365 9958 | *www.speights-alehouse.co.nz*

If a simple meeting with friends after work in a classic pub-type atmosphere is on the agenda, this place is one of the busiest and most popular choices around. Speight's Ale House is all about having a beer in a relaxed environment. Music plays at full volume late into the night, and people dress up as if they're all on a first date. In the early hours of the evening, however, you wouldn't look out of place arriving in your work boots and scruffy clothes. Strangely, no other bars have been particularly successful on this site, but Speight's has been jam-packed ever since it opened. The eponymous beer on tap, could be a factor, along with its good range of other ales.

Nightclubs

76 Lichfield St
Christchurch
Map p.516 C2 153

Mansion Luxury Lounge

03 366 0939

Five years ago, the owners of Mansion recognised a need for a more international-style club in Christchurch. It has been the hottest place ever since. It's one of the few places for catching decent house music and the latest touring DJ. Most other bars serve food until dark and then attempt a transformation, but this place is about dancing through to the morning after. The decor is modern and fun, although by the time you get here late in the evening it's all about the music.

Cheers!

Wellington Convention Centre

Cabaret Shows

New Zealand is not really a cabaret kind of place, and the burlesque scene tends more to seedier strip clubs. In Auckland it's centred on Fort Street and Customs Street, and in Wellington around Courtenay Place. If naked women cavorting in giant aquariums are your thing, the Mermaid Bar (09 302 0748) in Auckland and the Mermaid in Wellington (04 385 0552) will fit the bill. The exception to the usual after-dark tawdriness are the entertaining drag shows at Caluzzi (09 357 0778) on Auckland's vibrant Karangahape Road. Don't be too surprised if the most straight-laced looking member of your group is singled out by the charming Buckwheat or Miss Ribena. It's all tacky as hell, but highly entertaining. The food's pretty good, too.

Take Two
Get to grips with the country's celluloid history at the impressive New Zealand Film Archive in Wellington (p.245).

Cinemas

Cinema is very popular in Auckland, and most large shopping malls have modern multiplexes attached. As with most towns and cities in New Zealand, tickets cost around $15, but significant discounts are available on Tuesdays. The most comprehensive listings are in Saturday's *New Zealand Herald* newspaper and on the handy www.flicks.co.nz website. In general, Hollywood blockbusters have the same release dates as the US and UK markets, but other titles may be delayed for three to six months. Auckland also has several excellent arthouse cinemas showing foreign and independent films. Hoyt's Gold Class cinemas and Berkeley's Circle Lounge offer (at a price) larger, more comfortable seats and full food and beverage service. Every July the Auckland International Film Festival is attended by caffeine-fuelled movie buffs. Several smaller, specialised festivals are held throughout the year, especially at the compact Academy Cinema. During the summer, Circus Cinema and Open Air Cinema both show films at a variety of outdoor locations around the country.

Wellington is home to *The Lord of the Rings* director Peter Jackson, so cinema is popular in the city. Mainstream cinemas are gathered around Manners Mall and Courtenay Place, while the Penthouse in Brooklyn and the Rialto complex in Te Aro are best for arthouse flicks. The city is also home to an array of film festivals, and in the inner suburb of Te Aro you'll find the Aro St Video Shop, an excellent source of foreign language, cult and documentary DVDs. Don't miss the beautifully restored Embassy Theatre on Kent Street.

In Christchurch, mainstream movies are shown by the Hoyts and Reading chains, and arthouse titles are best seen at the Rialto complex or the two cinemas at the restored Arts Centre (p.260). Check out their websites for information or the *Christchurch Press* newspaper. Christchurch also celebrates several film festivals, but movie buffs usually have to wait until the festivals finish further north in Auckland and Wellington.

Comedy

New Zealanders have perfected a dry and laconic sense of humour, and the best place for some local laughs is the Classic Comedy Club (www.comedy.co.nz) in Queen Street, Auckland. The garish retro decor looks like your grandma's house, but from Monday to Saturday the cream of Kiwi comedy bravely take the stage. There are also occasional gigs from international laugh merchants, but the best time to spy overseas acts is during Auckland's International Comedy Festival (www.comedyfestival.co.nz). Every May, the Classic is the epicentre of the annual laugh fest, but the humorous shenanigans also overflow into other adjacent venues. Nearby Nombe (p.444) is a great bar that's perfect for reliving your favourite punchlines.

Cinemas

Auckland			
Academy	CBD	09 373 2761	www.academy-cinemas.co.nz
Berkeley	Various Locations	09 488 6006	www.berkeleycinemas.co.nz
Bridgeway	Northcote	09 418 3308	www.bridgeway.co.nz
Hoyts	Various Locations	09 303 2739	www.hoyts.co.nz
Lido	Epsom	09 630 1500	www.lido.co.nz
Rialto	Newmarket	09 369 2417	www.rialto.co.nz
Sky City	Various Locations	09 369 2400	www.skycitycinemas.co.nz
Wellington			
Aro St Video Shop	97 Aro Street, Aro Valley	04 801 7101	www.arovideo.co.nz
Embassy Theatre	10 Kent Terrace	04 384 7657	www.deluxe.co.nz
Paramount	25 Courtenay Place	04 384 4080	www.paramount.co.nz
Penthouse Cinema	205 Ohiro Rd, Brooklyn	04 384 3157	www.penthousecinema.co.nz
Reading Cinemas	Courtenay Place	04 801 4601	www.readingcinemas.co.nz
Rialto	Cnr Jervois Quay and Cable Sreet, Te Aro	04 385 1864	www.rialto.co.nz
Village	Various Locations	na	www.skycitycinemas.co.nz
Christchurch			
Arts Centre Cinemas	Arts Centre, Worcester Street	03 366 0167	www.artfilms.co.nz
Hoyts	Various Locations	na	www.hoyts.co.nz
Reading Cinemas	The Palms, Cnr Marshland Rd and New Brighton Road	03 375 7080	www.readingcinemas.co.nz
Rialto	Cnr Moorhouse Avenue and Durham Street	na	www.rialto.co.nz

Film Festivals

Name		
Auckland International Film Festival	0800 842 53835	www.nzff.telecom.co.nz
Christchurch International Film Festival	0800 842 53835	www.nzff.telecom.co.nz
Cinema Circus	anthonytimpson@xtra.co.nz	www.cinemacircus.co.nz
Documentary Film Festival	09 309 2613	www.docnz.org.nz
Human Rights Film Festival	04 496 9616	www.humanrightsfilmfest.net.nz
Italian Film Festival	enquiries@italianfilmfestival.co.nz	www.italianfilmfestival.co.nz
Open Air Cinema	info@openair.co.nz	www.openair.co.nz
Wellington International Film Festival	0800 842 53835	www.nzff.telecom.co.nz
World Cinema Showcase	09 373 2761	www.worldcinemashowcase.co.nz

Concerts

Other options **Theatre** p.476

Auckland is on the map for major international acts, and new venues such as the Vector Arena make it easier for legends such as U2 and Bob Dylan to pop across the Tasman after concerts in Australia. The biggest gig of the year is the Big Day Out (www.bigdayout.com) festival which has attracted The Killers and Franz Ferdinand in recent years. Both Studio and the Leigh Sawmill Cafe (p.436) host local hotshots and cult international acts, while the King's Arms Tavern (p.475) is the city's best (and sweatiest) rock pub. Pick up *Groove Guide*, a free weekly magazine for listings. Jazz buffs should jump on a ferry to the annual Waiheke Island Jazz Festival (www.waihekejazz.co.nz). Both Opera and classical music are best heard at Auckland Town Hall and the Aotea Centre. The adjacent venues are the base for the Auckland Festival (www.aucklandfestival.co.nz), a biennial celebration of music, theatre, visual arts and dance.

Wellington's live music scene is eclectic and varied. The capital's bands are a fairly laid-back lot, ranging from the rootsy beats of Fat Freddy's Drop to the sleek soundscapes

Concert Venues

Venue	Phone	Website
Auckland		
Aotea Centre	09 309 2677	www.the-edge.co.nz
Auckland Town Hall	09 309 2677	www.the-edge.co.nz
King's Arms Tavern	09 373 3240	www.kingsarms.co.nz
Studio	09 374 4278	www.studiolive.co.nz
Vector Arena	09 358 1250	www.vectorarena.co.nz
Wellington		
Bar Bodega	04 384 8212	www.bodega.co.nz
San Francisco Bath House	04 801 6797	www.sfbh.co.nz
Christchurch		
Issac Theatre Royal	03 377 8899	www.isaactheatreroyal.co.nz
Sammy's Jazz Review	03 377 8618	www.sammys.co.nz

of The Phoenix Foundation. You'll see more than a few of them playing at the biennial Cuba St Carnival (p.59). Bar Bodega is Wellington's longest running live music venue, and also features tasty microbrews from the Tuatara Brewery. For raucous up-and-coming bands head along to the compact space that is Mighty Mighty (p.460). The Matterhorn (p.459) slows things down considerably, usually with a laid-back dub feel. Wellington doesn't get as many international concerts as Auckland, but the occasional big name (including David Bowie and Elton John) has been known to bypass Auckland and play their only New Zealand gigs at Wellington's Westpac Stadium. The San Francisco Bath House has occasional gigs by cult international acts. Check out www.texture.co.nz for Wellington music listings.

Separated from the big smokes of Auckland and Wellington, Christchurch has a no-nonsense approach to live music, with a few good venues dealing in honest jazz, blues and rock. Sammy's Jazz Review (p.472) has good food and live music from Tuesday to Sunday. Dux de Lux (p.473) is both a microbrewery and a jumping live venue, and from Tuesday to Saturday presents everything from reggae to rock. Friday nights can (almost) get too busy. Christchurch is the poor cousin to Auckland and Wellington when it comes to visits from international performers, but its role as the South Island's biggest city still lures a few hardy name acts. Gigs often take place at the Isaac Theatre Royal, or the 8,500 seat Westpac Centre, New Zealand's largest indoor venue. See www.jagg.co.nz for listings of live music events in Christchurch. An old-skool printed copy of Jagg is also available at venues and music shops every fortnight.

Theatre	City	Phone	Website
Auckland Theatre Company	Auckland	09 309 0390	www.atc.co.nz
Bats Theatre	Wellington	04 802 4175	www.bats.co.nz
Circa Theatre	Wellington	04 801 7992	www.circa.co.nz
Downstage	Wellington	04 801 6496	www.downstage.co.nz
Silo Theatre	Auckland	09 366 0339	www.silotheatre.co.nz

Theatre

Alas, New Zealand's actors are usually not regarded with the same respect as rugby's mighty All Blacks. New Zealand's theatre scene is relatively small and largely based in Auckland and Wellington. The Auckland Theatre Company lacks a permanent venue, but uses a variety of venues around town. At the Silo Theatre in central Auckland you'll see more interesting and edgy productions. In arty Wellington, theatre is taken more seriously, and the long-standing Circa on Wellington's waterfront has been a mainstay of the country's theatre scene for several decades. Performances range from classics such as Chekhov to the work of iconic New Zealand playwright Roger Hall. Don't be too surprised if some of the actors look familiar; New Zealand's a small place, and you've probably seen them in a couple of local TV shows earlier in the week. Also in Wellington, Bats Theatre presents interesting works in progress, and the Downstage is often the venue for touring productions. Wellington's biennial International Arts Festival (www.nzfestival.telecom.co.nz) presents local and international plays.

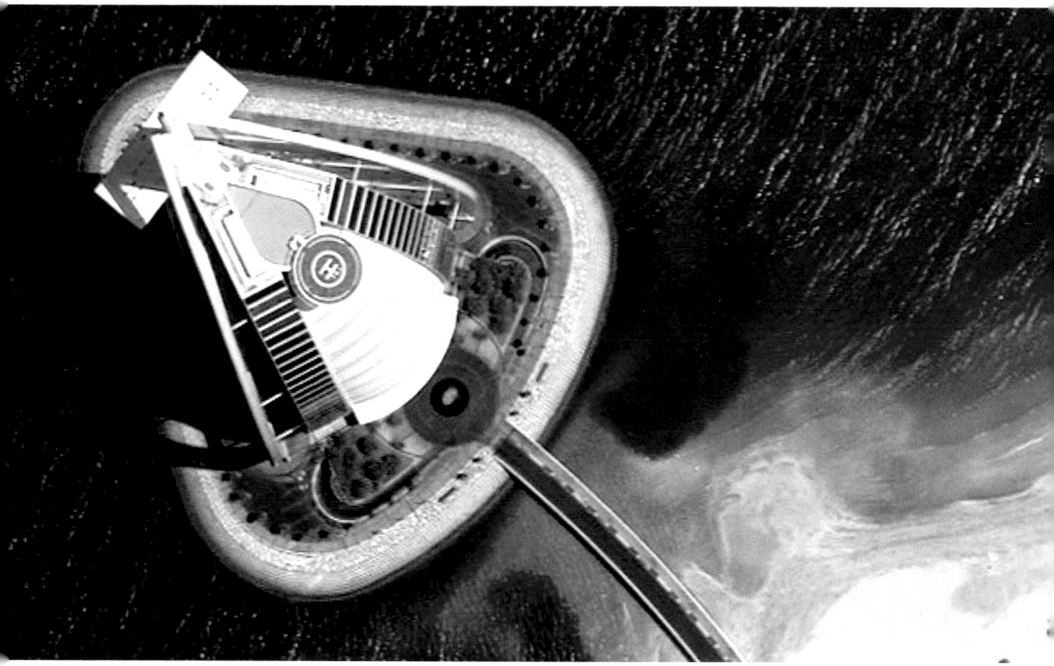

Maps

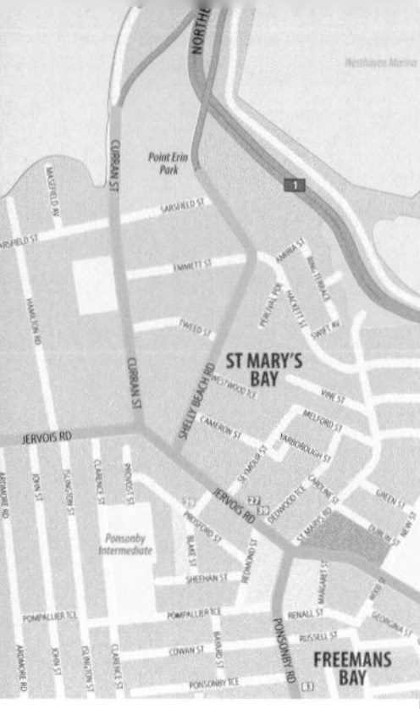

Maps

User's Guide

This section is intended to help you get your bearings when you first arrive, and give a clear idea about all the areas outlined in the book. Provided is an overview of Auckland (p.484), Wellington (p.498) and Christchurch (p.508), a map of New Zealand, a map index and detailed street maps of all three cities. Everything within the cities is covered in the large-scale maps starting on p.486. The sheet maps on pages 485, 499 and 509 show which part of the city each map covers. The map legend below illustrates what the different colours and symbols mean. You may have noticed that some of the places we mention in the guide have map references, like this: ***Map p.000 A1***. The page number (***p.000***) refers to the page that the map is on. The grid reference (*A1*) goes horizontally, then vertically, and the annotation 10 shows exactly where to go. Our annotations are in six different colours, which identify the chapter each item is from. Green annotations are hotels from the General Information chapter, red annotations are bars, cafes, restaurants and other spots from the Going Out chapter and so on. The central margin on each map page gives a full key. Obviously many of New Zealand's attractions are found elsewhere in the country; to locate these and navigate yourself around the North and South Islands see the detailed pull-out map at the back of the book. You'll see grid references to this map throughout the chapters.

New Zealand Maps
Beyond these maps and our own very nifty Auckland Mini Map *(see right for details) there are a number of street directories to be found in bookshops and newsagents across New Zealand. Wises produces a range of city maps and road atlases, while the AA offers basic but useful route maps to its members free of charge.*

Need More?

We understand that this residents' guide is a pretty big book. It needs to be, to carry all the information we have about living in New Zealand. But, unless you've got the pockets of a clown, it's unlikely to be carried around with you. With this in mind, we've created the Auckland Mini Map as a more manageable alternative. This packs the whole city into your pocket and once unfolded is an excellent navigational tool. Visit www.explorerpublishing.com for details.

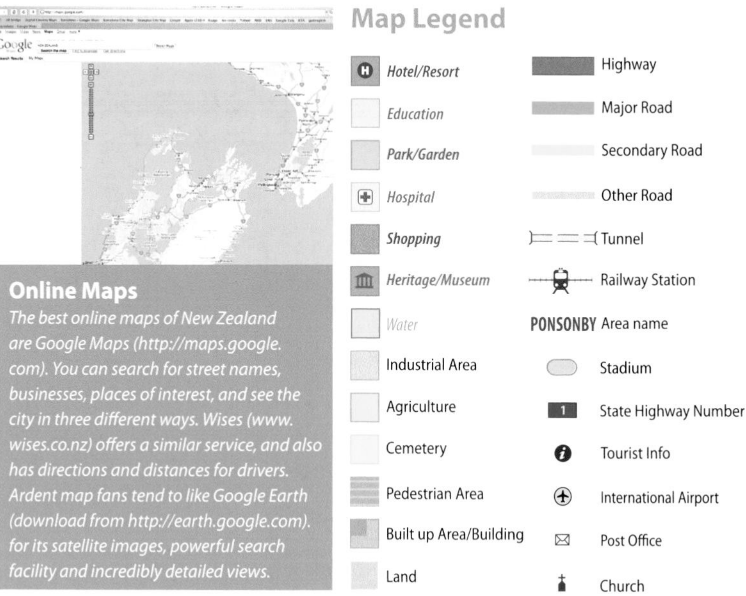

Online Maps
The best online maps of New Zealand are Google Maps (http://maps.google.com). You can search for street names, businesses, places of interest, and see the city in three different ways. Wises (www.wises.co.nz) offers a similar service, and also has directions and distances for drivers. Ardent map fans tend to like Google Earth (download from http://earth.google.com). for its satellite images, powerful search facility and incredibly detailed views.

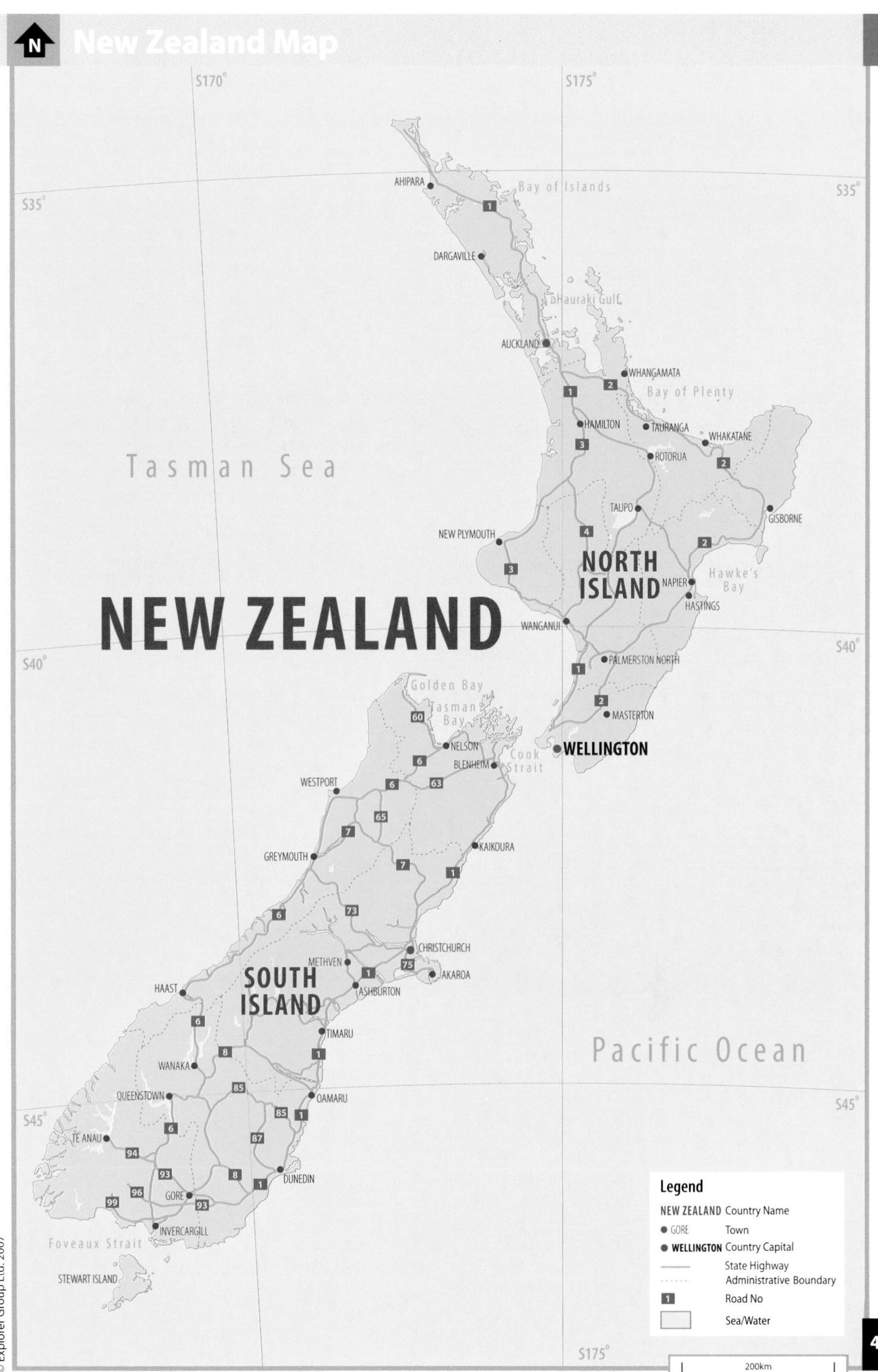
S170°
S175°
S35°
S35°
S40°
S40°
S45°
S45°
S175°
AHIPARA
Bay of Islands
1
DARGAVILLE
Hauraki Gulf
AUCKLAND
WHANGAMATA
1
2
Bay of Plenty
HAMILTON
TAURANGA
WHAKATANE
3
ROTORUA
2
Tasman Sea
TAUPO
GISBORNE
NEW PLYMOUTH
4
2
NORTH ISLAND
3
NAPIER
Hawke's Bay
HASTINGS
NEW ZEALAND
WANGANUI
PALMERSTON NORTH
1
Golden Bay
Tasman Bay
2
MASTERTON
60
NELSON
WELLINGTON
Cook Strait
6
BLENHEIM
WESTPORT
6
63
65
7
KAIKOURA
GREYMOUTH
7
1
73
6
CHRISTCHURCH
METHVEN
75
1
AKAROA
SOUTH ISLAND
HAAST
ASHBURTON
6
TIMARU
8
1
Pacific Ocean
WANAKA
85
QUEENSTOWN
OAMARU
85
1
6
TE ANAU
87
94
93
8
DUNEDIN
1
96
GORE
99
93
INVERCARGILL
Foveaux Strait
STEWART ISLAND
Legend
NEW ZEALAND Country Name
GORE Town
WELLINGTON Country Capital
State Highway
Administrative Boundary
1 Road No
Sea/Water
200km

Auckland Main Streets	Map Ref
Albert St	p.488 A2
Anzac Av	p.488 B2
Auckland Hamilton Mwy	p.492 B3
Auckland Kumeu Mwy	p.491 E1
Balmoral Rd	p.494 B2
Beach Rd	p.488 C2
Bond St	p.490 C2
Britomart	p.488 B2
Broadway	p.492 C4
College Hill Rd	p.487 D3
Crowhurst St	p.492 C3
Curran St	p.486 B1
Customs Street East	p.488 B2
Customs Street West	p.488 A2
Dominion Rd	p.491 D4
Fanshawe St	p.487 E2
Franklin Rd	p.487 D3
Gillies Av	p.492 C3
Gladstone Rd	p.489 E3
Grafton Br	p.492 A1
Grafton Rd	p.488 B4
Great North Rd	p.490 A2
Great South Rd	p.497 D1
Green Lane West	p.496 C4
Greys Av	p.487 F4
Halsey St	p.487 F2
Hobson St	p.487 F3
Hopetoun St	p.487 F4
Jervois Rd	p.486 B2
Karangahape Rd	p.491 F1
Khyber Pass Rd	p.492 A2
Lower Albert St	p.488 A2
Lower Hobson St	p.488 A2
Mayoral Dr	p.488 A4
Ian Mckinnon Dr	p.491 E1
Mt Eden Rd	p.495 F3
Nelson St	p.487 F3
New North Rd	p.490 B4
Newton Rd	p.491 E1
North Western Mwy	p.490 B3
Northern Mwy	p.487 D1
Owens Rd	p.496 A1
Parnell Rd	p.489 D4
Parnell Rise	p.488 C3
Pitt St	p.487 F4
Ponsonby Rd	p.486 C3
Quay St	p.488 A1
Queen St	p.488 A2
Remuera Rd	p.492 C3
Richmond Rd	p.486 A4
Saint Lukes Rd	p.494 A2
Sandringham Rd	p.490 C4

Auckland Main Areas	Map Ref
Albany	p.484 B3
Balmoral	p.495 D2
Beach Haven	p.484 B4
Birkdale	p.484 B4
Birkenhead	p.484 B4
Botany Downs	p.484 E6
Browns Bay	p.484 C3
Devonport	p.484 D4
Eden Terrace	p.491 E2
Ellerslie	p.484 D5
Epsom	p.496 B3
Freemans Bay	p.487 D3
Glen Eden	p.484 B6
Glen Innes	p.484 E5
Green Bay	p.484 B6
Greenhithe	p.484 B4
Greenlane	p.497 F4
Grey Lynn	p.484 C5
Half Moon Bay	p.484 E5
Hauraki	p.484 C4
Henderson	p.484 A5
Howick	p.484 E5
Kelston	p.484 B5
Kingsland	p.491 D3
Laingholm	p.484 A7
Mangere	p.484 D6
Manukau	p.484 E7
Manurewa	p.484 E7
Massey	p.484 A4
Meadowbank	p.484 D5
Mechanics Bay	p.489 E2
Mellons Bay	p.484 F5
Morningside	p.490 B4
Mount Eden	p.495 F1
Mount Albert	p.484 C6
New Lynn	p.484 B6
Newmarket	p.492 C3
Newton	p.491 E1
Northcote	p.484 C4
One Tree Hill	p.484 C6
Onehunga	p.484 C6
Orewa	p.484 B1
Otara	p.484 E7
Pakuranga	p.484 E6
Panmure	p.484 D6
Papakura	p.484 F8
Parnell	p.489 D4
Penrose	p.484 D6
Ponsonby	p.486 C3
Pt Chevalier	p.484 B5
Remuera	p.484 D5
Takapuna	p.484 C4
Te Atatu South	p.484 A5
Titirangi	p.484 B6
Wattle Downs	p.484 D8
West Harbour	p.484 A4
Weymouth	p.484 D8
Whangaparaoa	p.484 C1

Wellington Main Streets	Map Ref
Abel Smith St	p.504 C3
Adelaide Rd	p.506 C3
Aotea Quay	p.501 E2
Aro St	p.504 B3
Bowen St	p.502 C1
Brooklyn Rd	p.504 A4
Buller St	p.504 B2
Cable St	p.505 E1
Cambridge Tce	p.505 E2
Constable St	p.507 E4
Customhouse Quay	p.503 D3
Dufferin St	p.505 E4
Featherston St	p.503 D3
Ghuznee St	p.505 D2
Glasgow St	p.502 A4
Grant Rd	p.500 C2
Hunter St	p.503 D3
Hutt Rd	p.501 D1
Jervois Quay	p.503 D3
John St	p.506 C2
Kelburn Parade Rd	p.502 B4
Kent Tce	p.505 F2
Lambton Quay	p.503 D1
Lennel Rd	p.501 D1
Molesworth St	p.503 D1
Mt Victoria Tunnel	p.507 F1
Mulgrave St	p.503 E1
Murphy St	p.500 C4
Oriental Parade	p.505 F2
Paterson St	p.505 E4
Riddiford St	p.506 C3
Rugby St	p.505 D4
Salamanca Rd	p.502 B4
Sussex St	p.505 D4
Taranaki St	p.504 C4
The Terrace	p.502 C4
Thorndon Quay	p.501 D3
Tinakori Rd	p.500 B4
Victoria St	p.503 D4
Vivian St	p.504 C2
Wakefield St	p.505 E1
Wallace St	p.506 B1
Waterloo Quay	p.501 E4
Webb St	p.504 B3
Whitmore St	p.503 D2
Willis St	p.503 D4

Wellington Main Areas	Map Ref
Breaker Bay	p.498 E7
Brooklyn	p.506 A1
Crofton Downs	p.498 B3
Hataitai	p.498 D6
Highbury	p.498 B5
Island Bay	p.498 C8
Kaiwharawhara	p.498 C3
Karaka Bays	p.498 E6
Karori	p.498 A5
Kelburn	p.498 B5
Khandallah	p.498 D3
Lambton	p.503 E2
Lyall Bay	p.498 D7
Maupuia	p.498 E5
Melrose	p.498 D7
Miramar	p.498 E6
Mornington	p.498 B7
Mount Victoria	p.505 F3
Mt Cook	p.504 C4
Newlands	p.498 E2
Newtown	p.507 D3
Ngaio	p.498 C3
Northland	p.498 B5
Oriental Bay	p.498 D5
Owhiro Bay	p.498 B8
Seatoun	p.498 F7
Te Aro	p.504 C1
Te Kainga	p.498 E3
Thorndon	p.500 C4
Vogeltown	p.506 B4
Wadestown	p.498 C4
Wilton	p.498 B4

Christchurch Main Streets	Map Ref
Antigua St	p.516 A3
Barbadoes St	p.513 E4
Bealey Av	p.512 A3
Blenheim Rd	p.514 A3
Cambridge Tce	P.516 B2
Carlton Mill Rd	p.511 D3
Cashel St	p.516 B2
Cranmer Sq	p.516 A1
Deans Av	p.514 C1
Durham St	p.516 B4
Durham St North	p.512 B3
Fendalton Rd	p.510 A2
Fitzgerald Av	p.513 F3
Glandovey Rd	p.510 A1
Gloucester St	p.517 E1
Hagley Av	p.515 F3
Harper Av	p.511 E3
Hereford St	p.517 F2
Hills Rd	p.513 F1
Idris Rd	p.510 A1
Kilmore St	p.512 A4
Lichfield St	p.516 C2
Lincoln Rd	p.515 D4
Madras St	p.513 D2
Montreal St	p.512 A3
Moorhouse Av	p.515 D4
Oxford Tce	p.516 A3
Papanui Rd	p.511 F1
Park Tce	P.511 F3
Riccarton Av	p.515 E2
Riccarton Rd	p.514 A1
Rossall St	p.510 C1
Salisbury St	p.512 A4
Sherbourne St	P.512 C2
St Asaph St	p.516 A3
Tuam St	p.517 F3
Whiteleigh Av	p.514 A4
Whitmore St	p.513 F2

Christchurch Main Areas	Map Ref
Burnside	p.508 B3
Cashmere	p.508 C6
Diamond Harbour	p.508 F4
Fendalton	p.508 B4
Ferrymead	p.508 F6
Governors Bay	p.508 C8
Halswell	p.508 B7
Inner City	p.516 C2
Lansdowne	p.508 B8
Linwood	p.508 D5
Lyttelton	p.508 F7
Merivale	p.510 C1
New Brighton	p.508 F4
Prebbleton	p.508 A6
Riccarton	p.508 B5
Richmond South	p.513 F2
Shirley	p.508 D4
St Albans	p.508 C4

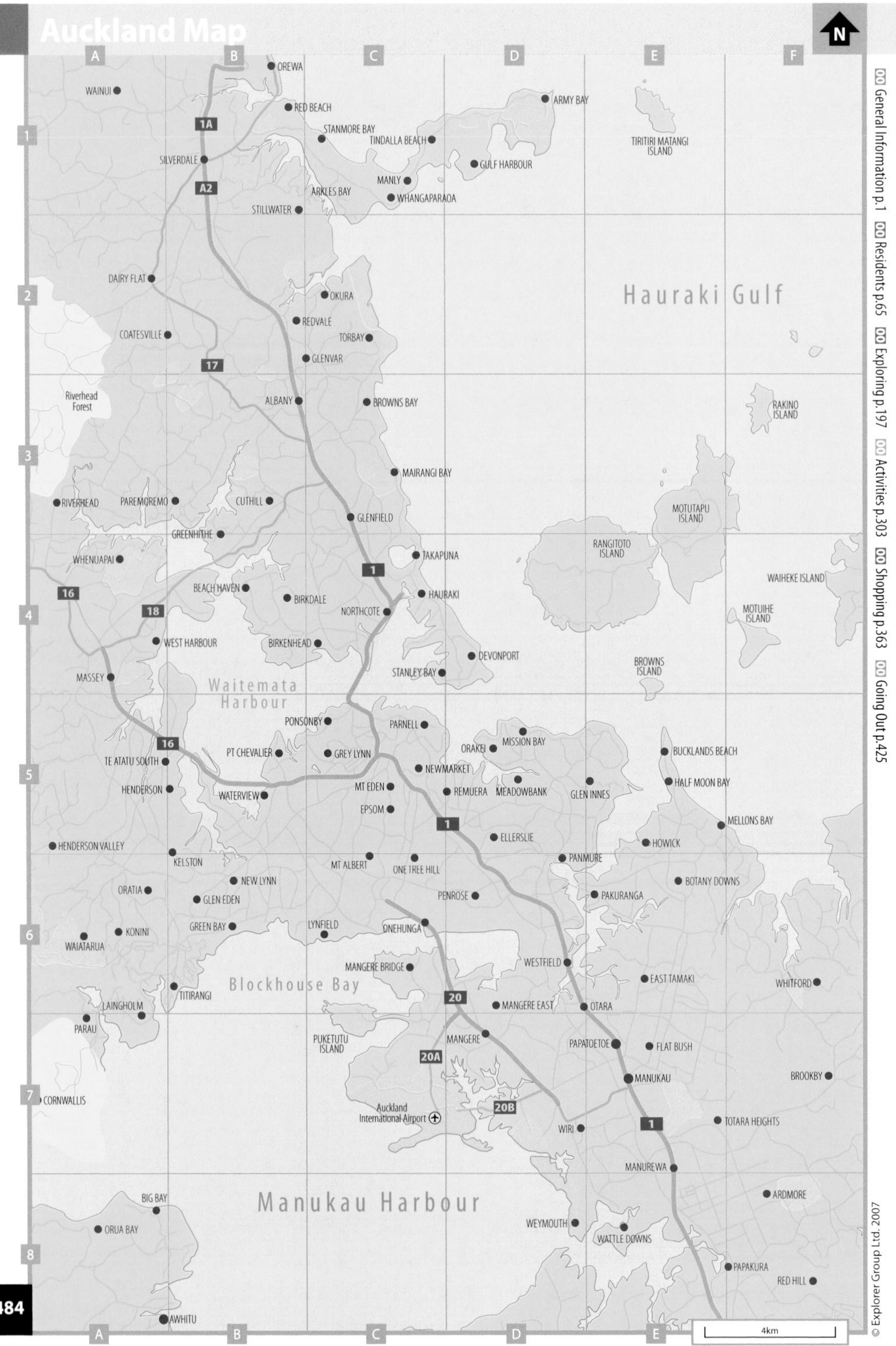

General Information p.1 Residents p.65 Exploring p.197 Activities p.303 Shopping p.363 Going Out p.425

Auckland Sheet Map

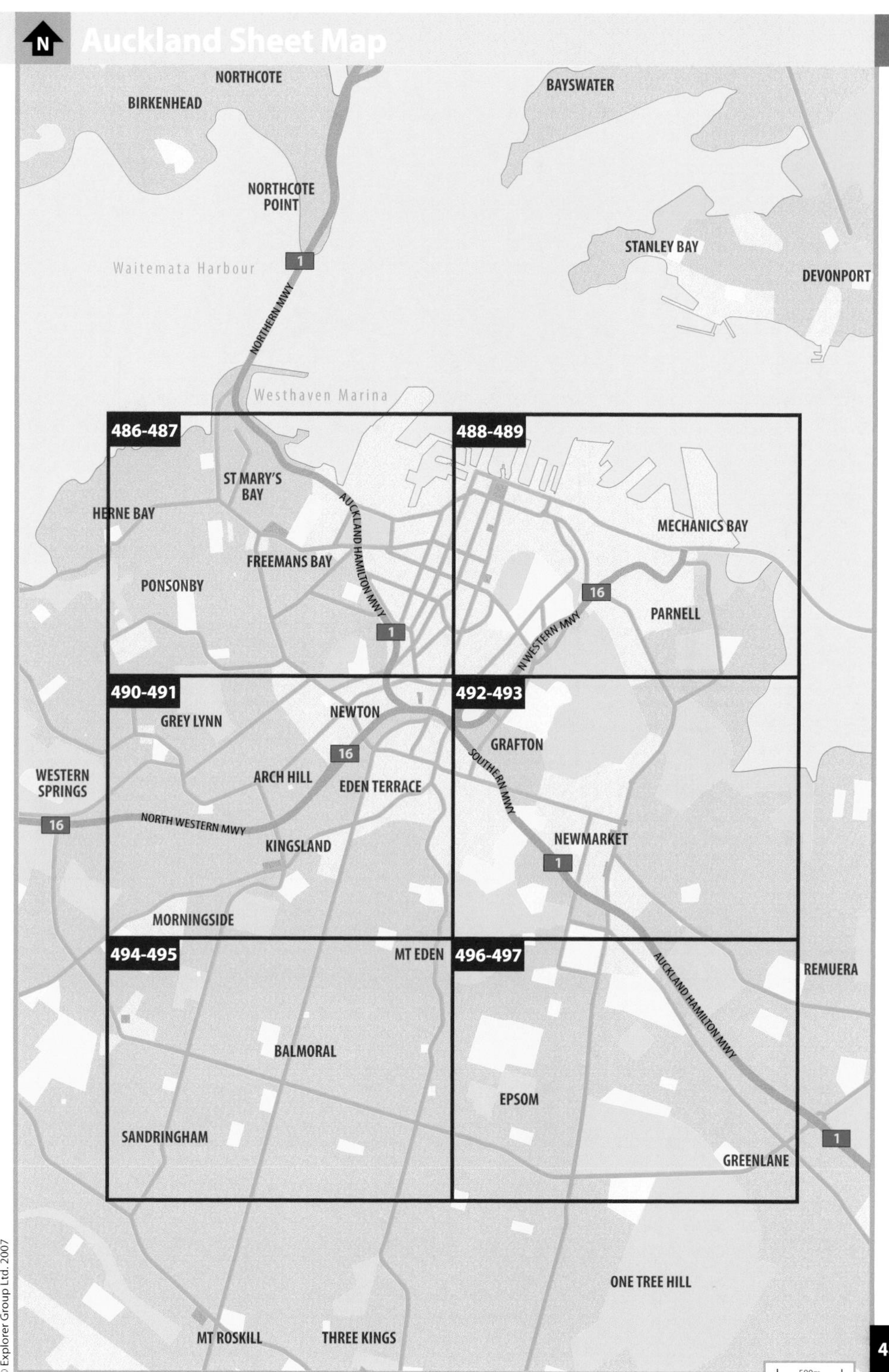

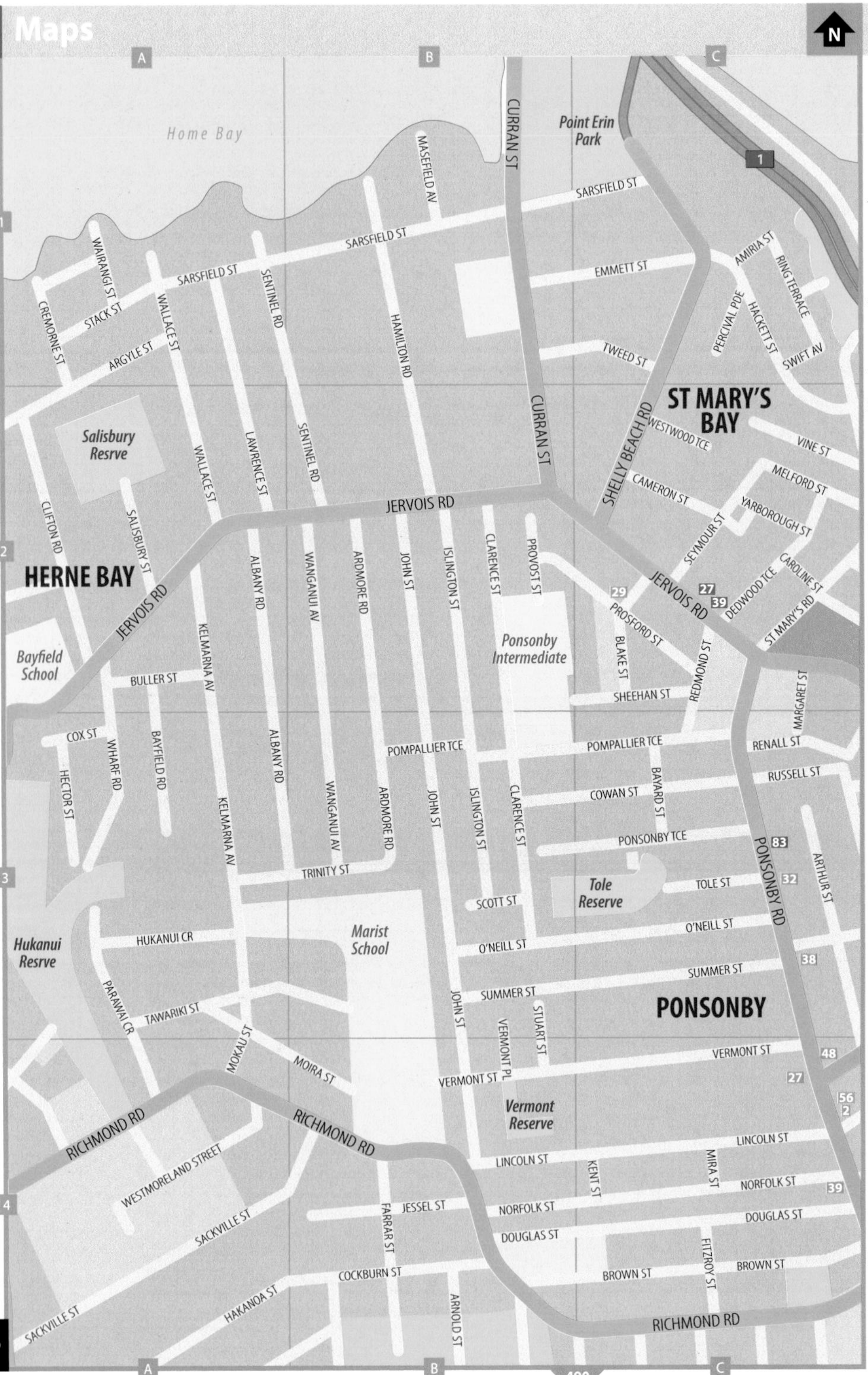

00 General Information p.1 00 Residents p.65 00 Exploring p.197 00 Activities p.303 00 Shopping p.363 00 Going Out p.425

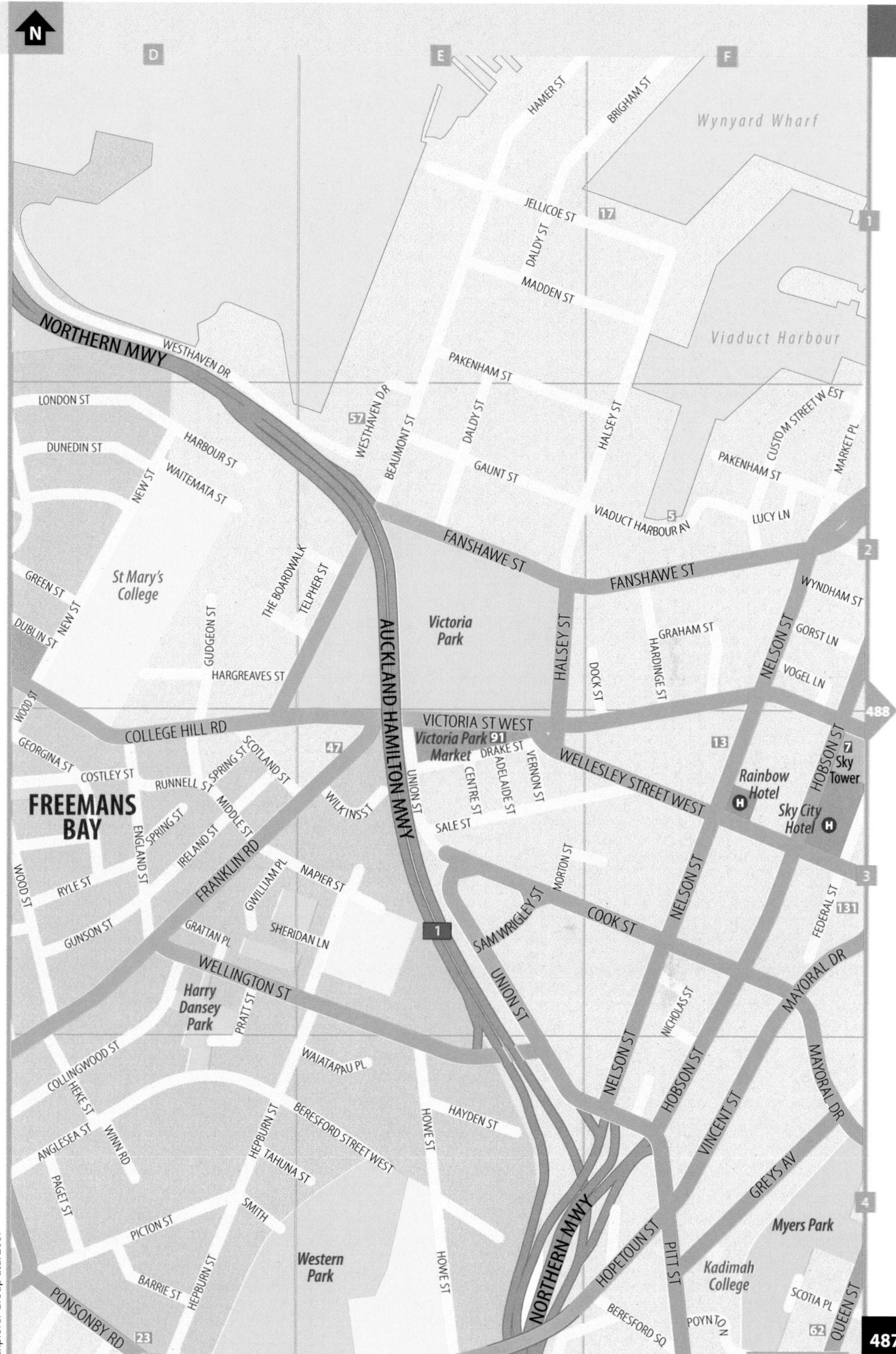
N
D
E
F
Wynyard Wharf
Viaduct Harbour
NORTHERN MWY
WESTHAVEN DR
HAMER ST
BRIGHAM ST
JELLICOE ST
17
DALDY ST
MADDEN ST
PAKENHAM ST
LONDON ST
DUNEDIN ST
HARBOUR ST
WAITEMATA ST
NEW ST
57
WESTHAVEN DR
BEAUMONT ST
DALDY ST
GAUNT ST
HALSEY ST
CUSTOM STREET WEST
MARKET PL
PAKENHAM ST
VIADUCT HARBOUR AV
5
LUCY LN
FANSHAWE ST
FANSHAWE ST
St Mary's College
THE BOARDWALK
TELPHER ST
GREEN ST
NEW ST
DUBLIN ST
GUDGEON ST
HARGREAVES ST
AUCKLAND HAMILTON MWY
Victoria Park
HALSEY ST
WYNDHAM ST
GRAHAM ST
HARDINGE ST
DOCK ST
NELSON ST
GORST LN
VOGEL LN
488
WOOD ST
COLLEGE HILL RD
VICTORIA ST WEST
Victoria Park Market
91
GEORGINA ST
COSTLEY ST
47
SCOTLAND ST
SPRING ST
RUNNELL ST
DRAKE ST
CENTRE ST
ADELAIDE ST
VERNON ST
WELLESLEY STREET WEST
13
Rainbow Hotel
HOBSON ST
7
Sky Tower
Sky City Hotel
FREEMANS BAY
MIDDLE ST
WILKINS ST
UNION ST
SALE ST
ENGLAND ST
SPRING ST
IRELAND ST
FRANKLIN RD
NAPIER ST
GWILLIAM PL
MORTON ST
NELSON ST
3
WOOD ST
RYLE ST
SAM WRIGLEY ST
COOK ST
FEDERAL ST
131
GUNSON ST
GRATTAN PL
SHERIDAN LN
1
WELLINGTON ST
Harry Dansey Park
PRATT ST
UNION ST
NICHOLAS ST
MAYORAL DR
COLLINGWOOD ST
HEKE ST
WAIATARAU PL
NELSON ST
HOBSON ST
MAYORAL DR
VINCENT ST
HAYDEN ST
BERESFORD STREET WEST
HEPBURN ST
HOWE ST
ANGLESEA ST
WINN RD
TAHUNA ST
GREYS AV
PAGET ST
SMITH
NORTHERN MWY
4
Myers Park
PICTON ST
HOPETOUN ST
PITT ST
Western Park
HOWE ST
Kadimah College
BARRIE ST
HEPBURN ST
SCOTIA PL
PONSONBY RD
BERESFORD SQ
POYNTON
QUEEN ST
23
62
491
150m
1
2

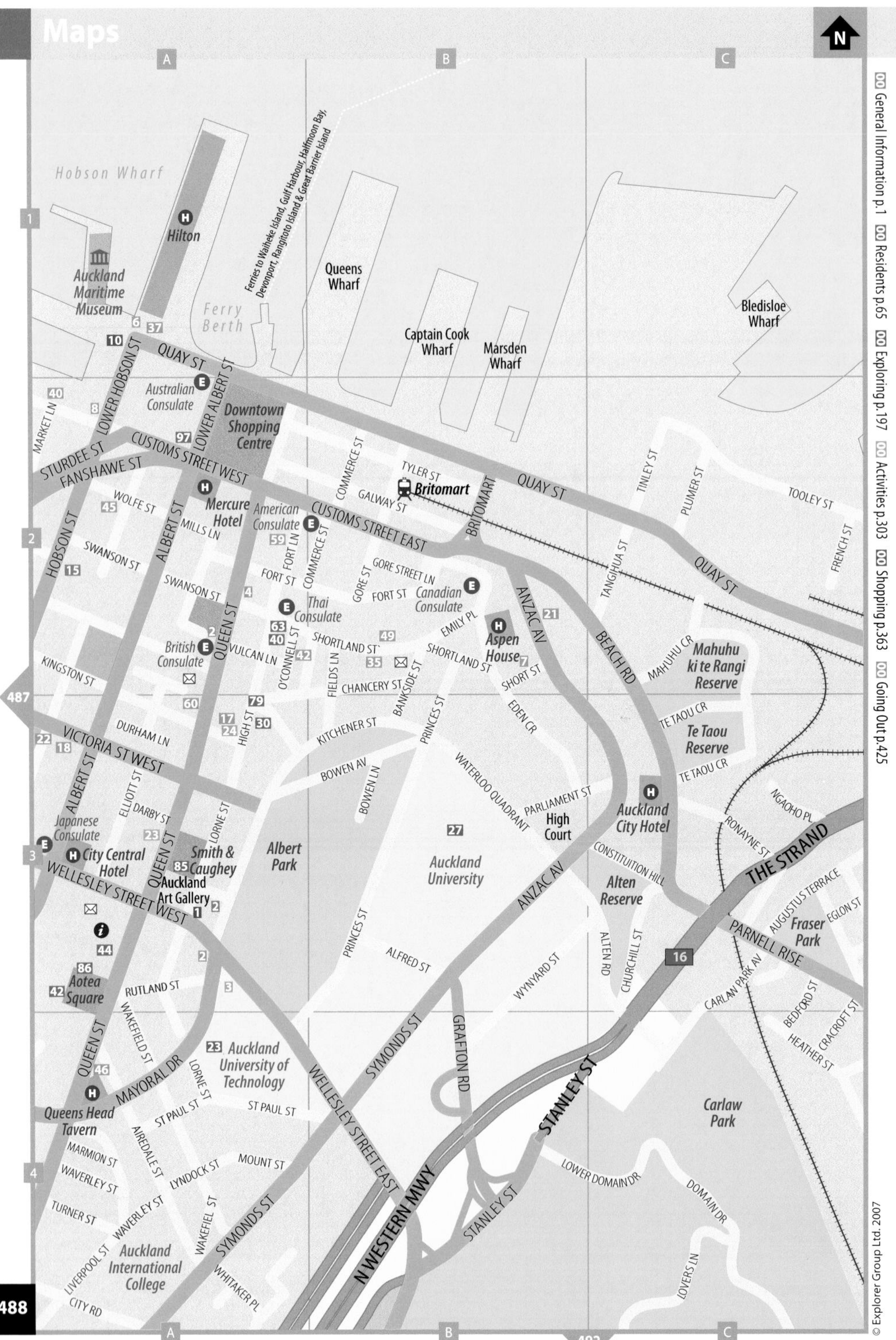

487
492

00 General Information p.1 00 Residents p.65 00 Exploring p.197 00 Activities p.303 00 Shopping p.363 00 Going Out p.425

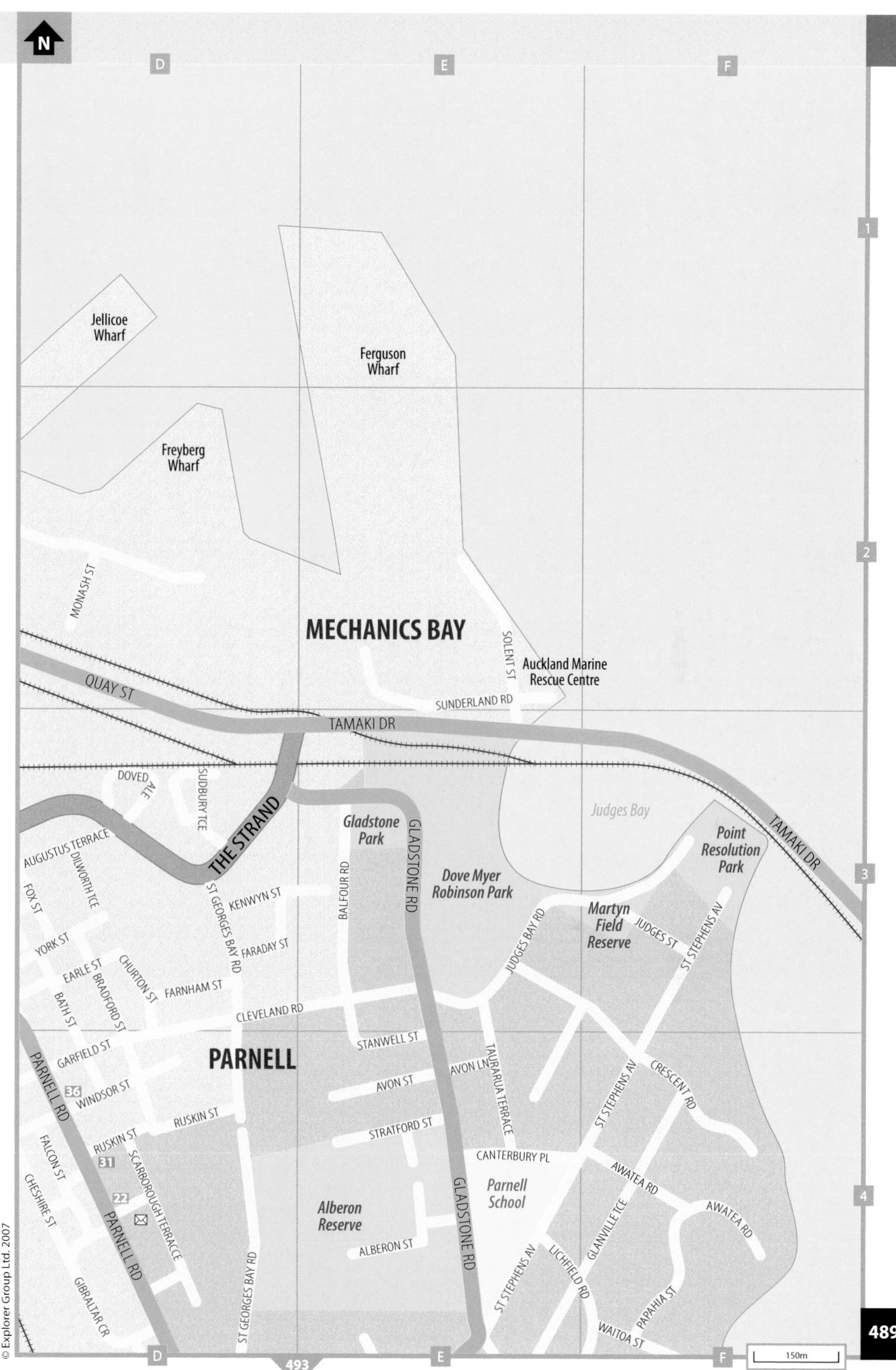
N
D
E
F
1
2
3
4
Jellicoe Wharf
Ferguson Wharf
Freyberg Wharf
MONASH ST
MECHANICS BAY
SOLENT ST
Auckland Marine Rescue Centre
QUAY ST
SUNDERLAND RD
TAMAKI DR
DOVED ALE
SUDBURY TCE
THE STRAND
Judges Bay
Point Resolution Park
TAMAKI DR
Gladstone Park
GLADSTONE RD
AUGUSTUS TERRACE
DILWORTH TCE
FOX ST
ST GEORGES BAY RD
KENWYN ST
BALFOUR RD
Dove Myer Robinson Park
JUDGES BAY RD
Martyn Field Reserve
JUDGES ST
ST STEPHENS AV
YORK ST
EARLE ST
BRADFORD ST
CHURTON ST
FARADAY ST
FARNHAM ST
BATH ST
CLEVELAND RD
GARFIELD ST
PARNELL
STANWELL ST
TAURARUA TERRACE
PARNELL RD
36
WINDSOR ST
AVON ST
AVON LN
ST STEPHENS AV
CRESCENT RD
RUSKIN ST
RUSKIN ST
STRATFORD ST
31
SCARBOROUGH TERRACE
CANTERBURY PL
AWATEA RD
FALCON ST
CHESHIRE ST
22
Alberon Reserve
GLADSTONE RD
Parnell School
AWATEA RD
PARNELL RD
GLANVILLE TCE
ALBERON ST
ST STEPHENS AV
LICHFIELD RD
GIBRALTAR CR
ST GEORGES BAY RD
PAPAHIA ST
WAITOA ST
150m
493

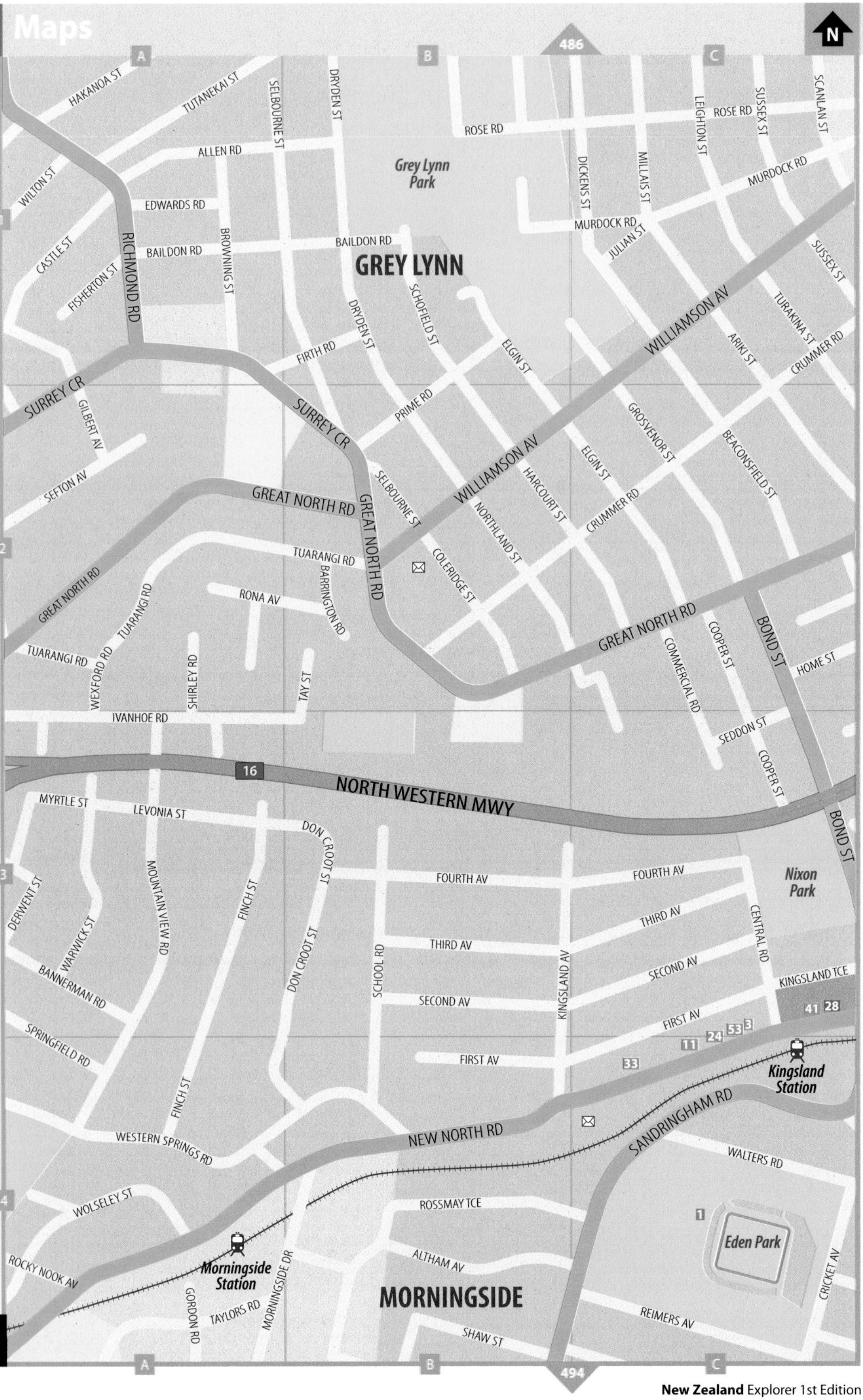

00 General Information p.1 00 Residents p.65 00 Exploring p.197 00 Activities p.303 00 Shopping p.363 00 Going Out p.425

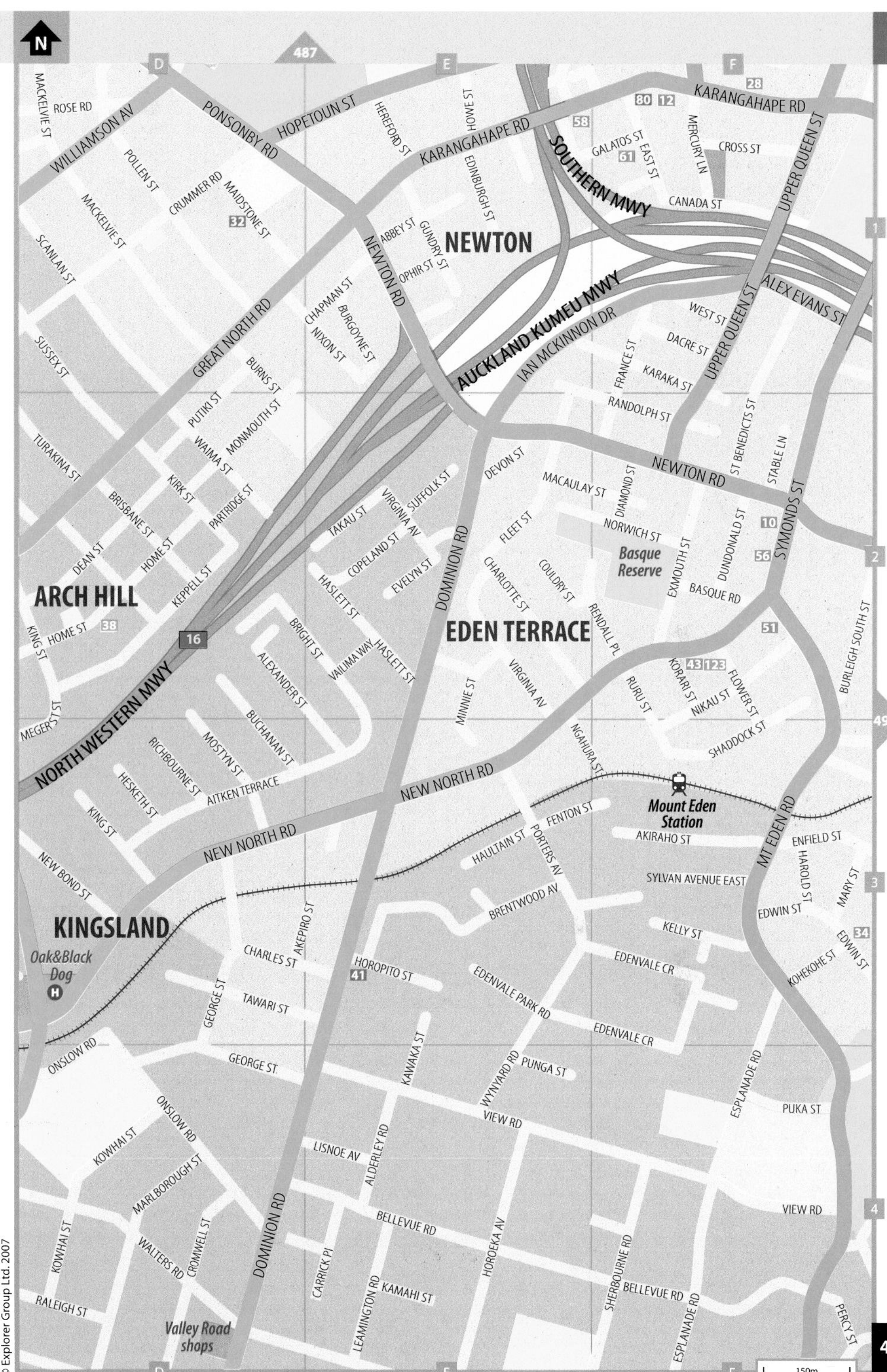
NEWTON
ARCH HILL
EDEN TERRACE
KINGSLAND
KARANGAHAPE RD
PONSONBY RD
HOPETOUN ST
WILLIAMSON AV
GREAT NORTH RD
NEWTON RD
SOUTHERN MWY
AUCKLAND KUMEU MWY
NORTH WESTERN MWY
IAN MCKINNON DR
UPPER QUEEN ST
ALEX EVANS ST
SYMONDS ST
DOMINION RD
NEW NORTH RD
MT EDEN RD
Basque Reserve
Mount Eden Station
Oak&Black Dog
Valley Road shops
150m

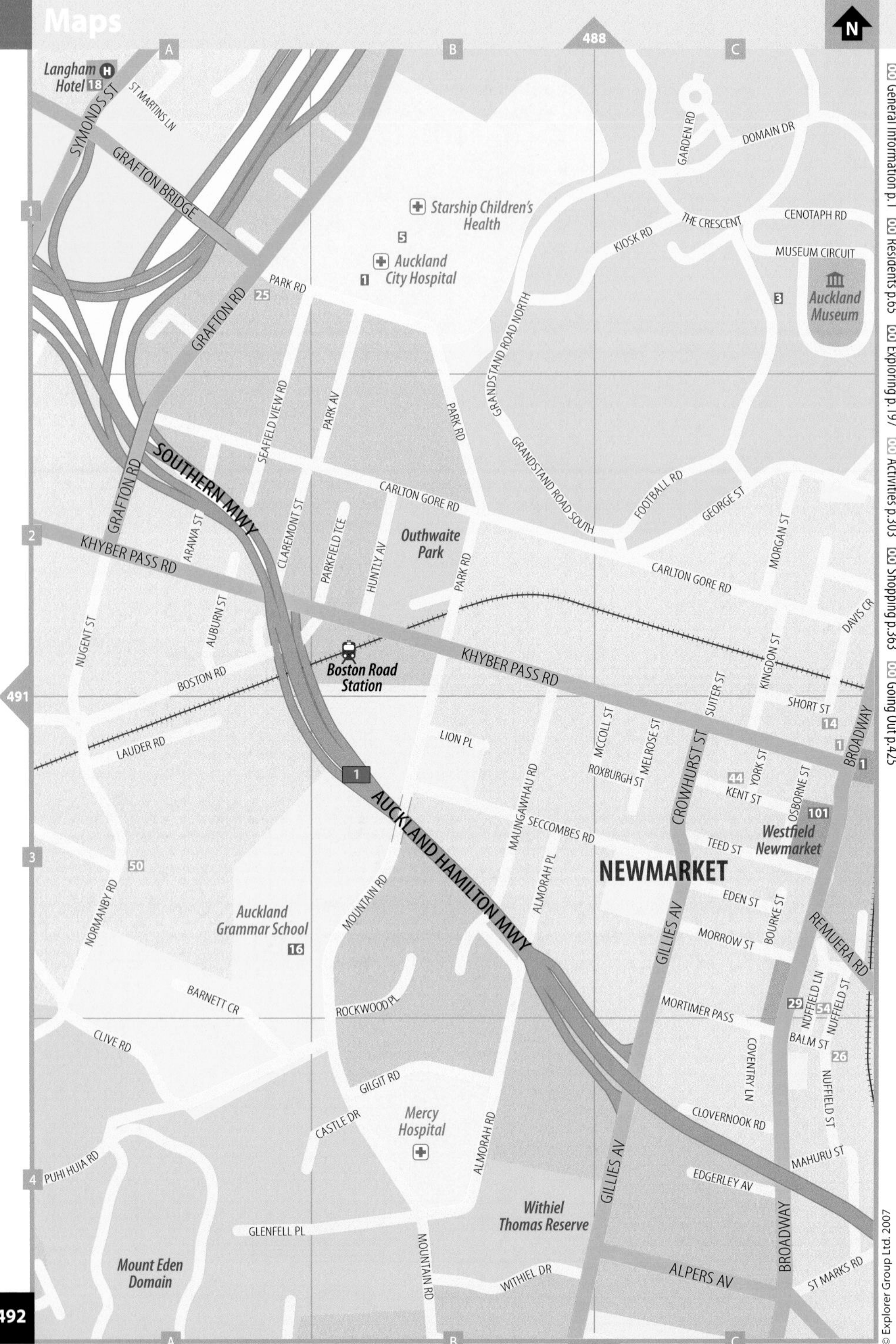

General Information p.1 Residents p.65 Exploring p.197 Activities p.303 Shopping p.363 Going Out p.425

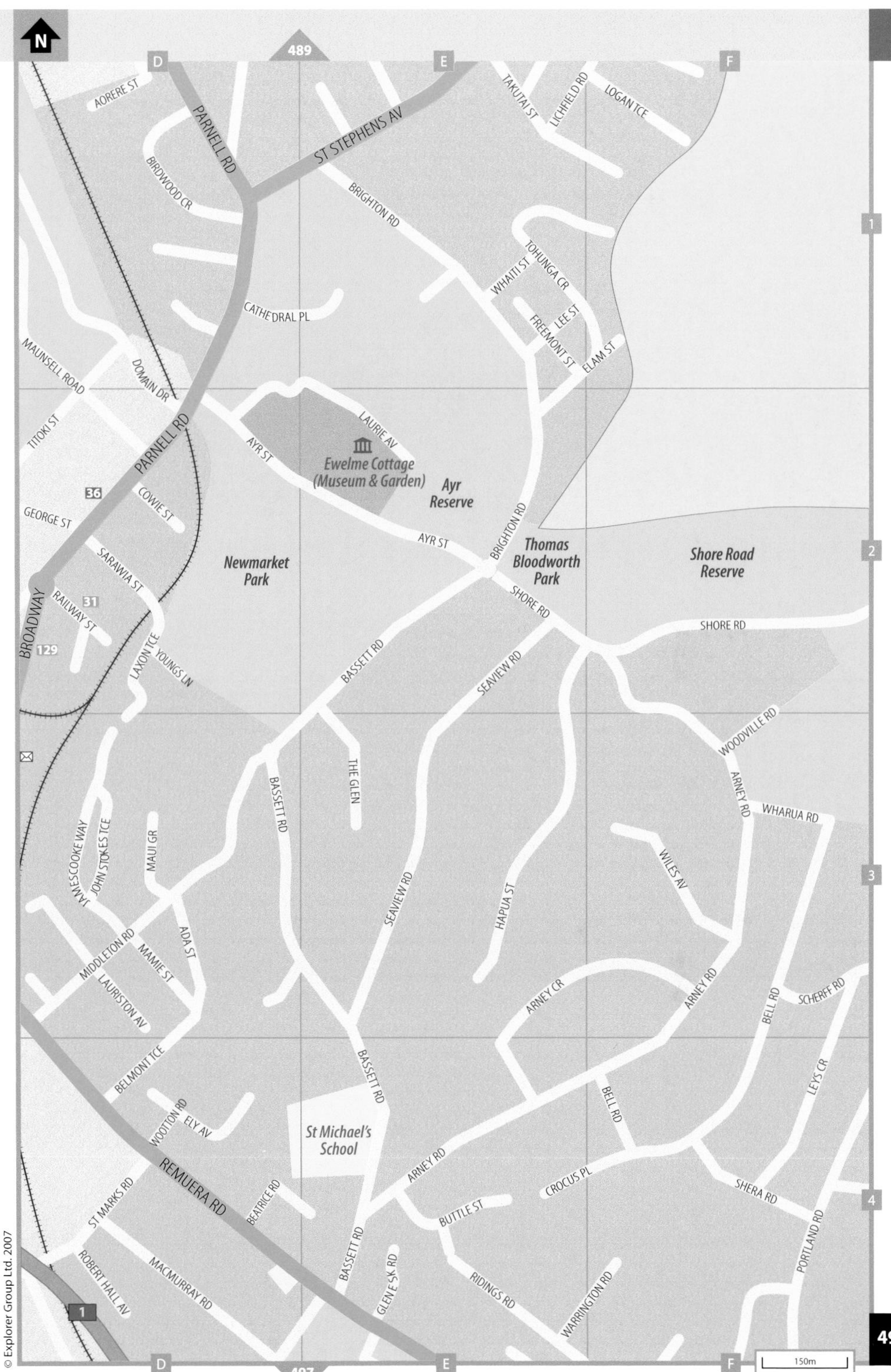
N
489
D
E
F
AORERE ST
PARNELL RD
BIRDWOOD CR
ST STEPHENS AV
BRIGHTON RD
TAKUTAI ST
LICHFIELD RD
LOGAN TCE
1
WHAITI ST
TOHUNGA CR
CATHEDRAL PL
LEE ST
FREEMONT ST
ELAM ST
MAUNSELL ROAD
DOMAIN DR
TITOKI ST
LAURIE AV
AYR ST
Ewelme Cottage
(Museum & Garden)
Ayr
Reserve
36
COWIE ST
GEORGE ST
AYR ST
BRIGHTON RD
Thomas
Bloodworth
Park
Shore Road
Reserve
2
SARAWIA ST
Newmarket
Park
BROADWAY
RAILWAY ST
31
SHORE RD
SHORE RD
129
LAXON TCE
YOUNGS LN
BASSETT RD
SEAVIEW RD
WOODVILLE RD
THE GLEN
BASSETT RD
ARNEY RD
WHARUA RD
JAMESCOOKE WAY
JOHN STOKES TCE
MAUI GR
SEAVIEW RD
HAPUA ST
WILES AV
3
MIDDLETON RD
MAMIE ST
ADA ST
LAURISTON AV
ARNEY CR
ARNEY RD
BELL RD
SCHERFF RD
BELMONT TCE
BASSETT RD
LEYS CR
BELL RD
WOOTTON RD
ELY AV
St Michael's
School
REMUERA RD
ARNEY RD
CROCUS PL
SHERA RD
4
ST MARKS RD
BEATRICE RD
BUTTLE ST
PORTLAND RD
ROBERT HALL AV
MACMURRAY RD
BASSETT RD
GLENESK RD
RIDINGS RD
WARRINGTON RD
1
D
497
E
F
150m

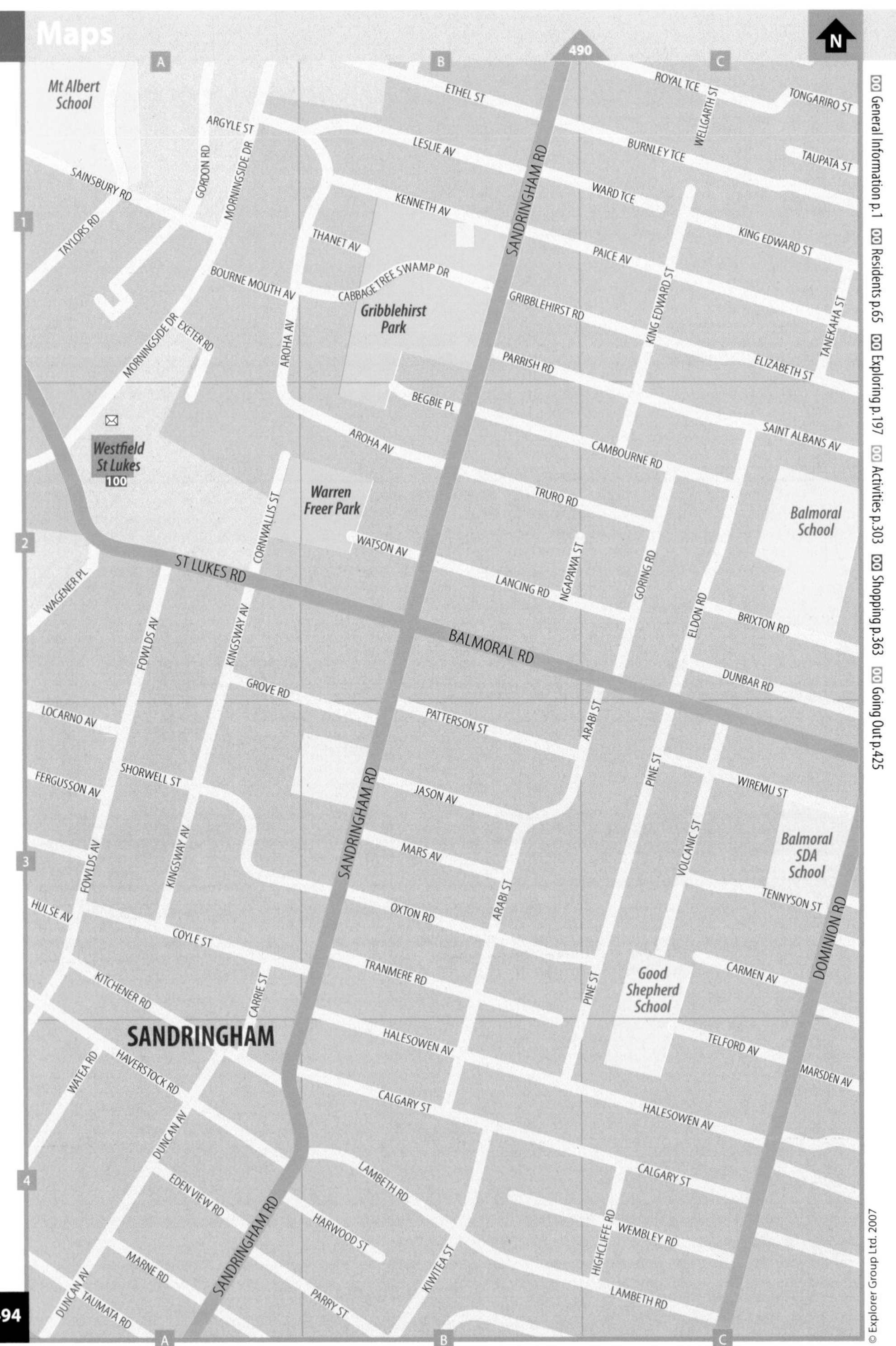

General Information p.1 Residents p.65 Exploring p.197 Activities p.303 Shopping p.363 Going Out p.425

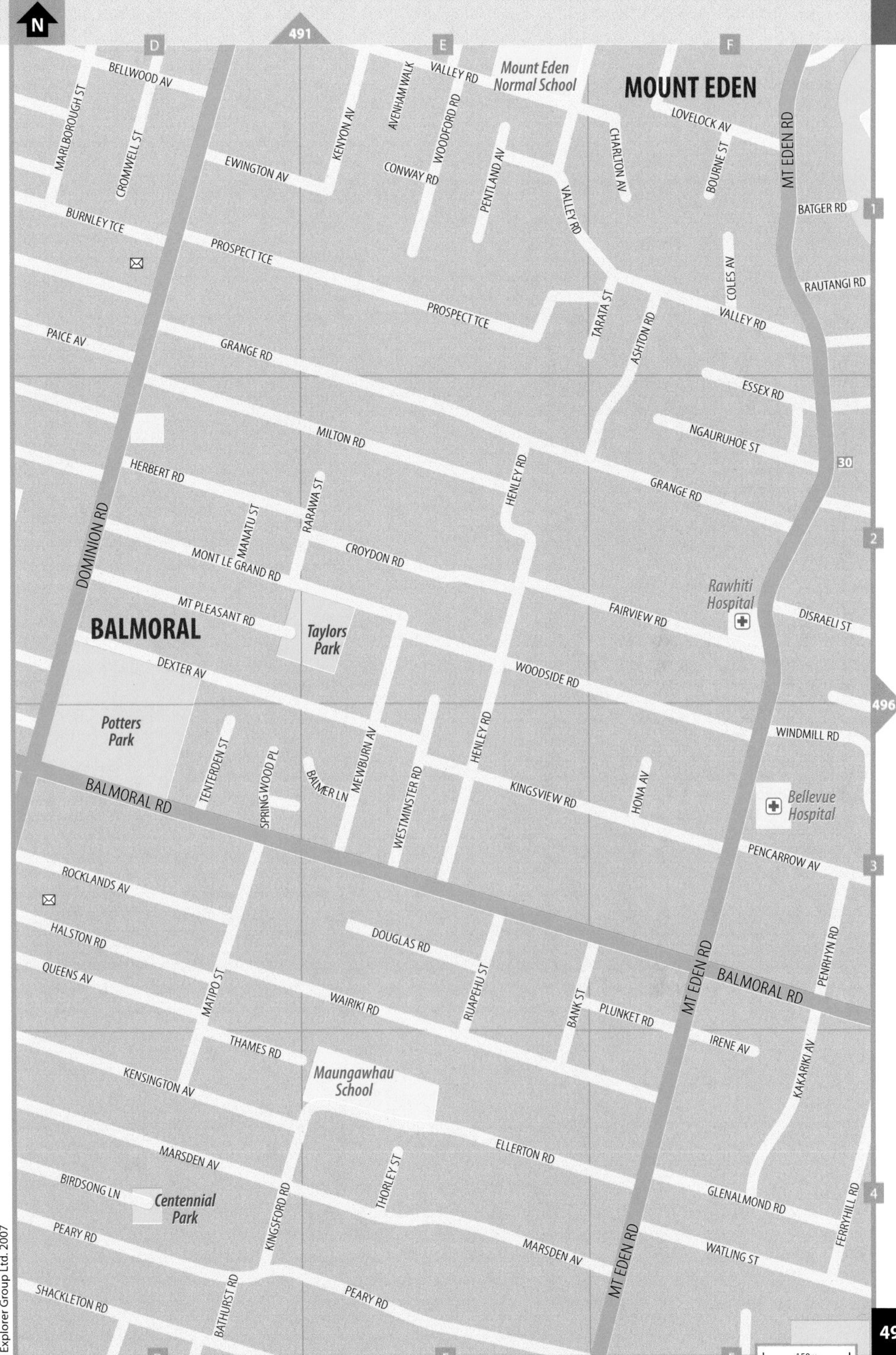
N
491
D
E
F
MOUNT EDEN
BALMORAL
Mount Eden Normal School
BELLWOOD AV
MARLBOROUGH ST
CROMWELL ST
VALLEY RD
AVENHAM WALK
WOODFORD RD
KENYON AV
EWINGTON AV
CONWAY RD
PENTLAND AV
CHARLTON AV
LOVELOCK AV
BOURNE ST
MT EDEN RD
BATGER RD
1
BURNLEY TCE
PROSPECT TCE
COLES AV
RAUTANGI RD
TARATA ST
ASHTON RD
PAICE AV
GRANGE RD
ESSEX RD
NGAURUHOE ST
MILTON RD
30
HERBERT RD
HENLEY RD
RARAWA ST
MANATU ST
DOMINION RD
2
MONT LE GRAND RD
CROYDON RD
Rawhiti Hospital
DISRAELI ST
MT PLEASANT RD
Taylors Park
FAIRVIEW RD
DEXTER AV
WOODSIDE RD
496
Potters Park
WINDMILL RD
TENTERDEN ST
SPRING WOOD PL
BALMER LN
MEWBURN AV
WESTMINSTER RD
KINGSVIEW RD
HONA AV
Bellevue Hospital
BALMORAL RD
PENCARROW AV
3
ROCKLANDS AV
HALSTON RD
DOUGLAS RD
PENRHYN RD
QUEENS AV
MATIPO ST
WAIRIKI RD
RUAPEHU ST
BANK ST
PLUNKET RD
IRENE AV
THAMES RD
KAKARIKI AV
Maungawhau School
KENSINGTON AV
ELLERTON RD
MARSDEN AV
THORLEY ST
BIRDSONG LN
Centennial Park
KINGSFORD RD
GLENALMOND RD
4
FERRYHILL RD
PEARY RD
WATLING ST
BATHURST RD
SHACKLETON RD
150m

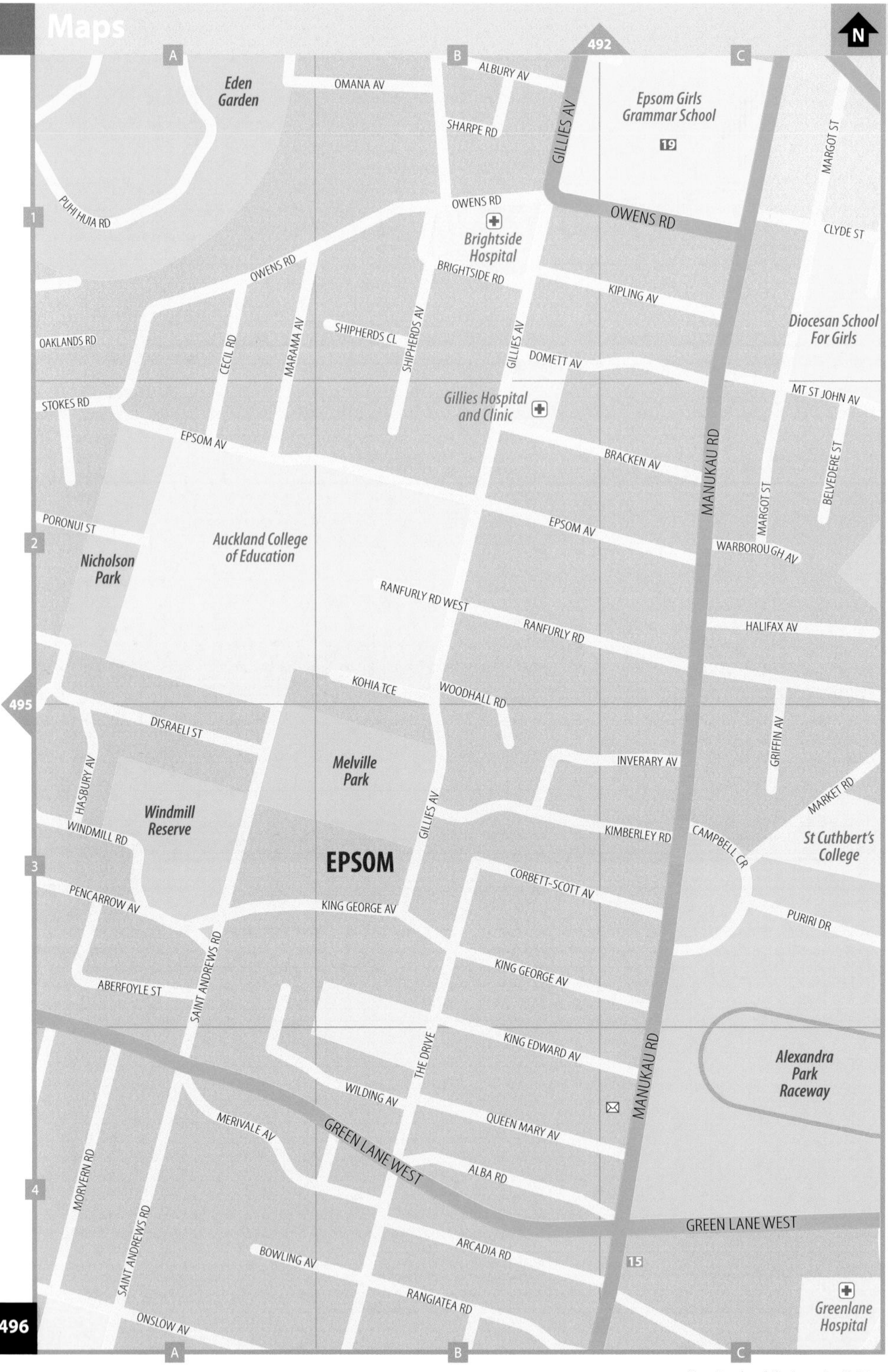
N
A
B
C
492
495
1
2
3
4
Eden Garden
OMANA AV
ALBURY AV
SHARPE RD
GILLIES AV
Epsom Girls Grammar School
19
MARGOT ST
PUHI HUIA RD
OWENS RD
OWENS RD
Brightside Hospital
CLYDE ST
OWENS RD
BRIGHTSIDE RD
KIPLING AV
OAKLANDS RD
CECIL RD
MARAMA AV
SHIPHERDS CL
SHIPHERDS AV
GILLIES AV
DOMETT AV
Diocesan School For Girls
STOKES RD
Gillies Hospital and Clinic
MT ST JOHN AV
EPSOM AV
BRACKEN AV
MANUKAU RD
MARGOT ST
BELVEDERE ST
PORONUI ST
Auckland College of Education
EPSOM AV
WARBOROUGH AV
Nicholson Park
RANFURLY RD WEST
RANFURLY RD
HALIFAX AV
KOHIA TCE
WOODHALL RD
DISRAELI ST
GRIFFIN AV
INVERARY AV
HASBURY AV
Melville Park
MARKET RD
Windmill Reserve
GILLIES AV
KIMBERLEY RD
CAMPBELL CR
St Cuthbert's College
WINDMILL RD
EPSOM
CORBETT-SCOTT AV
PENCARROW AV
KING GEORGE AV
PURIRI DR
SAINT ANDREWS RD
KING GEORGE AV
ABERFOYLE ST
KING EDWARD AV
THE DRIVE
MANUKAU RD
Alexandra Park Raceway
WILDING AV
MERIVALE AV
QUEEN MARY AV
GREEN LANE WEST
MORVERN RD
ALBA RD
SAINT ANDREWS RD
GREEN LANE WEST
ARCADIA RD
BOWLING AV
15
RANGIATEA RD
Greenlane Hospital
ONSLOW AV

General Information p.1 Residents p.65 Exploring p.197 Activities p.303 Shopping p.363 Going Out p.425

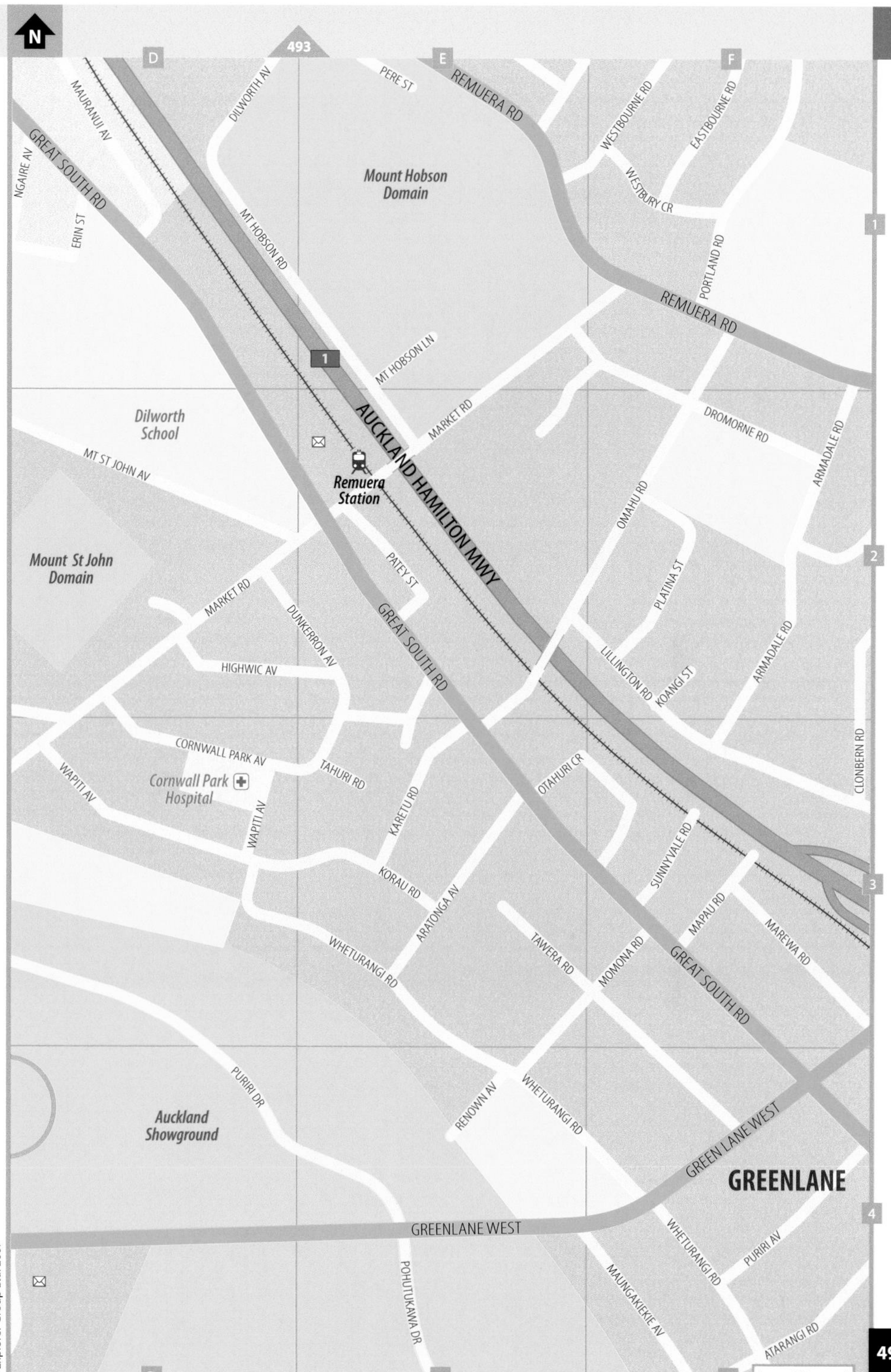
N
493
D
E
F
1
2
3
4
Mount Hobson Domain
REMUERA RD
PERE ST
DILWORTH AV
MAURANUI AV
NGAIRE AV
GREAT SOUTH RD
ERIN ST
MT HOBSON RD
WESTBOURNE RD
EASTBOURNE RD
WESTBURY CR
PORTLAND RD
MT HOBSON LN
MARKET RD
AUCKLAND HAMILTON MWY
Dilworth School
MT ST JOHN AV
Remuera Station
DROMORNE RD
ARMADALE RD
OMAHU RD
Mount St John Domain
PATEY ST
PLATINA ST
MARKET RD
DUNKERRON AV
HIGHWIC AV
LILLINGTON RD
KOANGI ST
CORNWALL PARK AV
TAHURI RD
WAPITI AV
Cornwall Park Hospital
CLONBERN RD
OTAHURI CR
KARETU RD
SUNNYVALE RD
KORAU RD
ARATONGA AV
MAPAU RD
MAREWA RD
WHETURANGI RD
TAWERA RD
MOMONA RD
PURIRI DR
RENOWN AV
Auckland Showground
GREEN LANE WEST
GREENLANE
GREENLANE WEST
POHUTUKAWA DR
MAUNGAKIEKIE AV
PURIRI AV
ATARANGI RD
150m

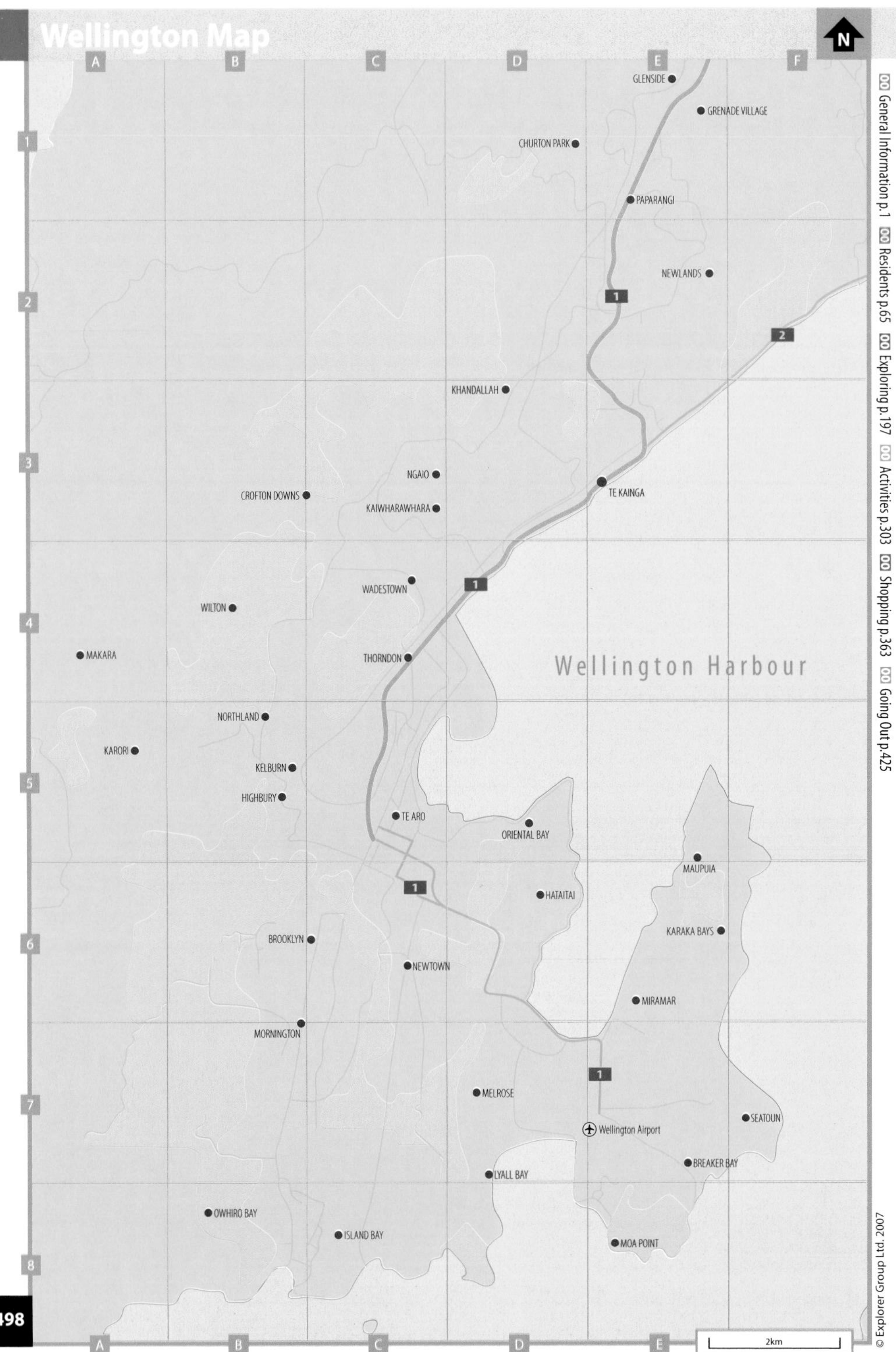

General Information p.1 Residents p.65 Exploring p.197 Activities p.303 Shopping p.363 Going Out p.425

Wellington Sheet Map

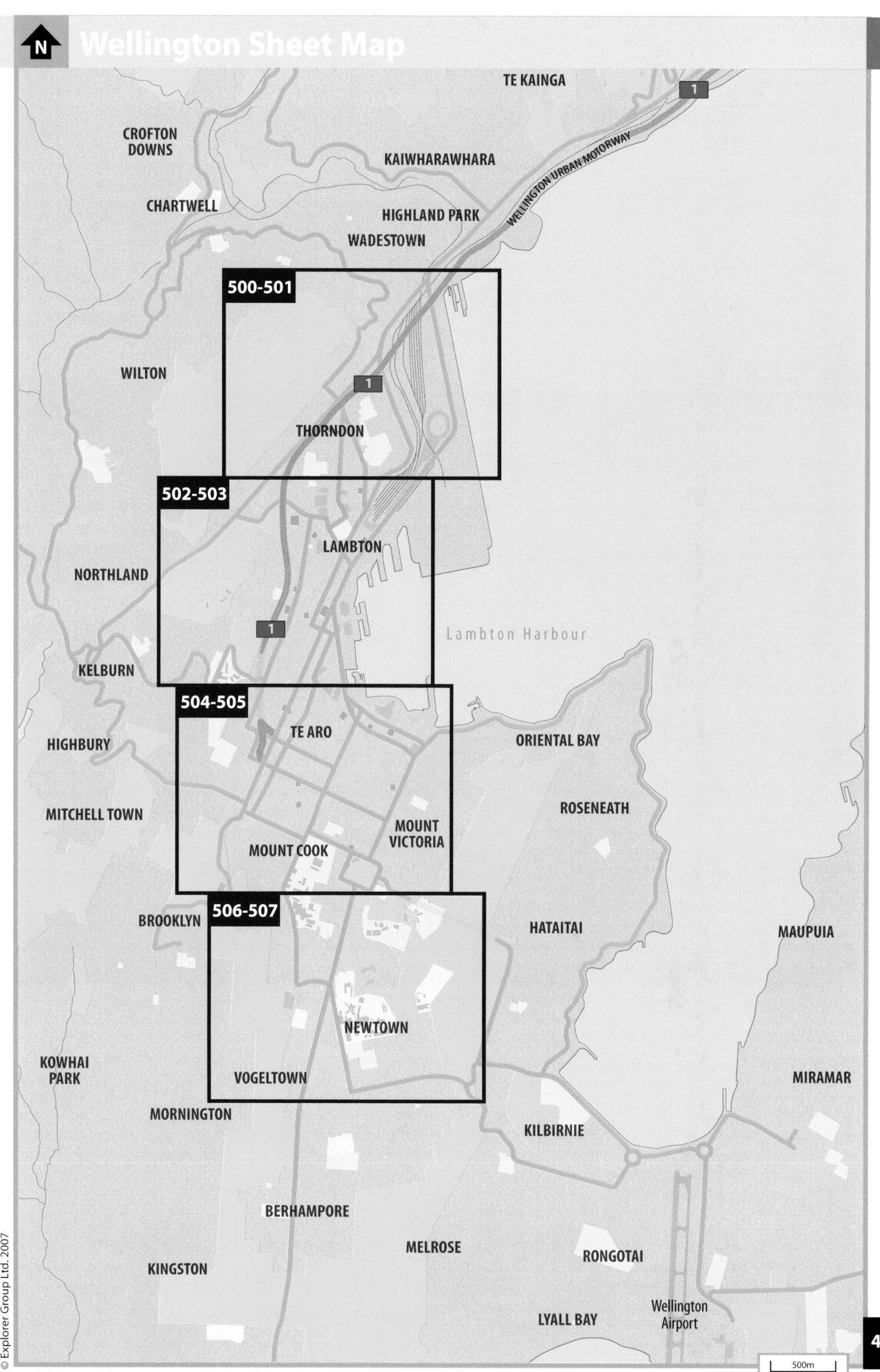

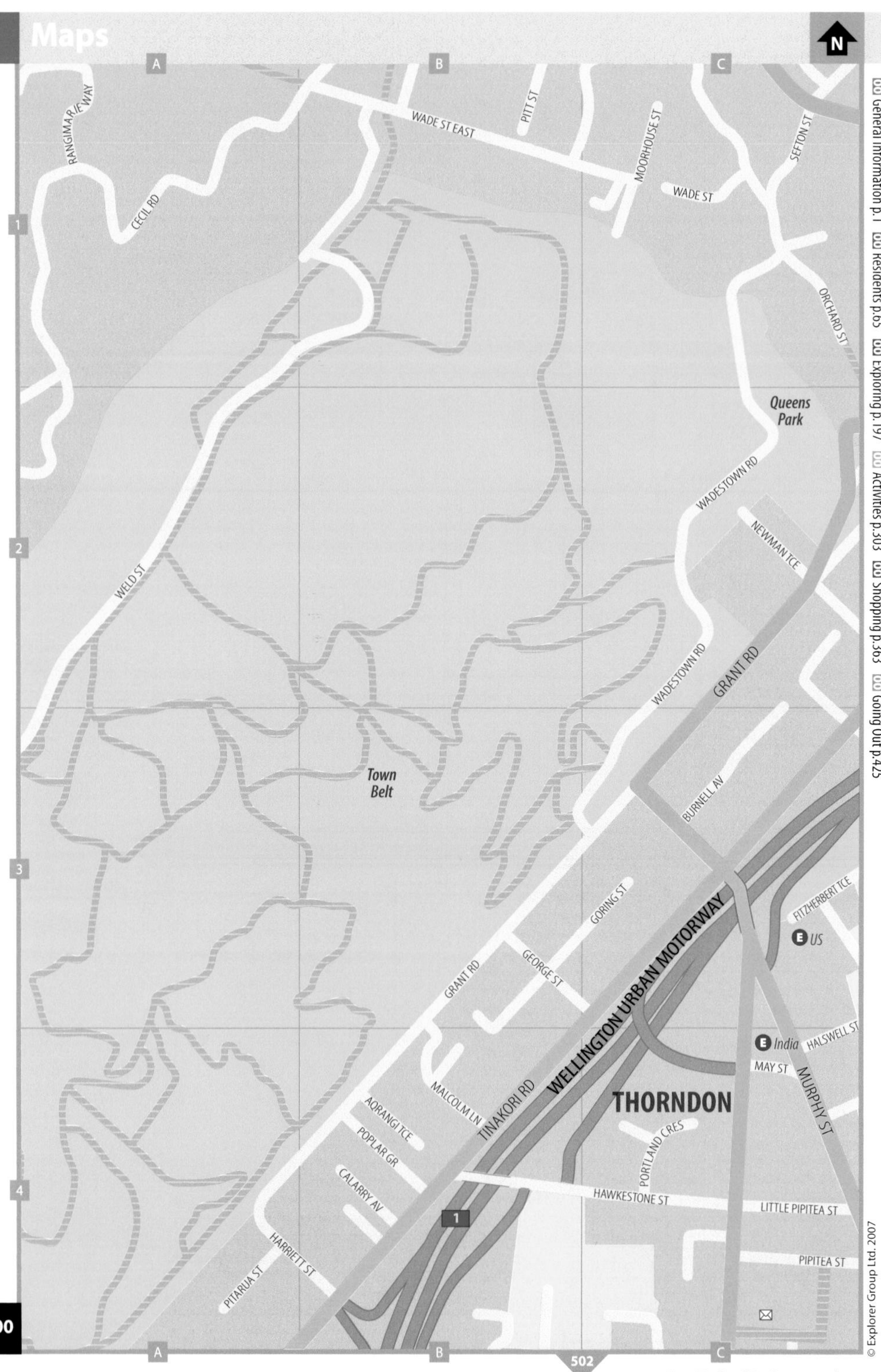

General Information p.1 Residents p.65 Exploring p.197 Activities p.303 Shopping p.363 Going Out p.425

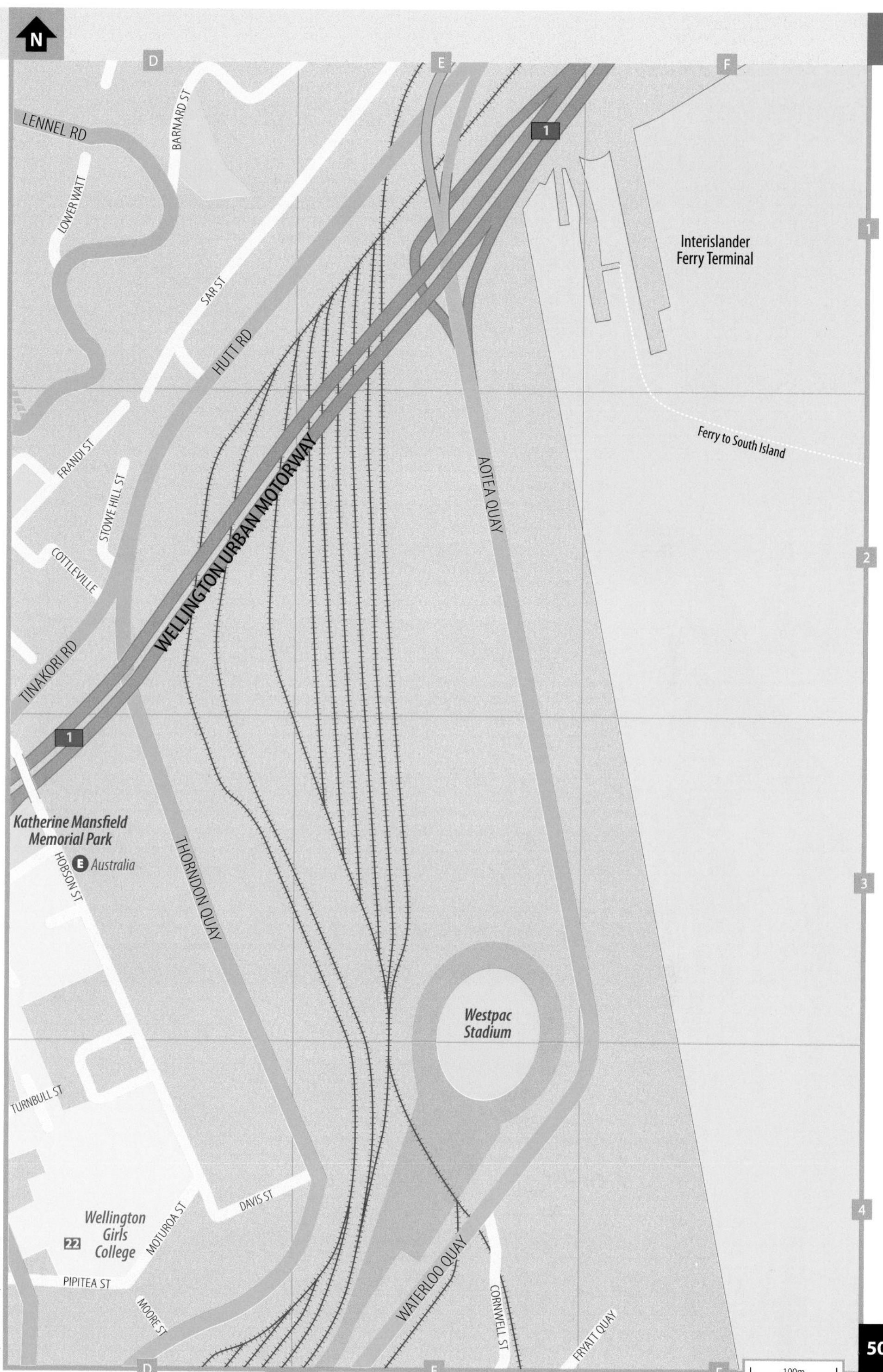
N
D
E
F
LENNEL RD
BARNARD ST
LOWER WATT
SAR ST
HUTT RD
1
Interislander
Ferry Terminal
FRANDI ST
STOWE HILL ST
COTTLEVILLE
WELLINGTON URBAN MOTORWAY
AOTEA QUAY
Ferry to South Island
TINAKORI RD
Katherine Mansfield
Memorial Park
HOBSON ST
Australia
THORNDON QUAY
Westpac
Stadium
TURNBULL ST
DAVIS ST
MOTUROA ST
Wellington
Girls
College
22
PIPITEA ST
MOORE ST
WATERLOO QUAY
CORNWELL ST
FRYATT QUAY
503
100m
1
2
3
4

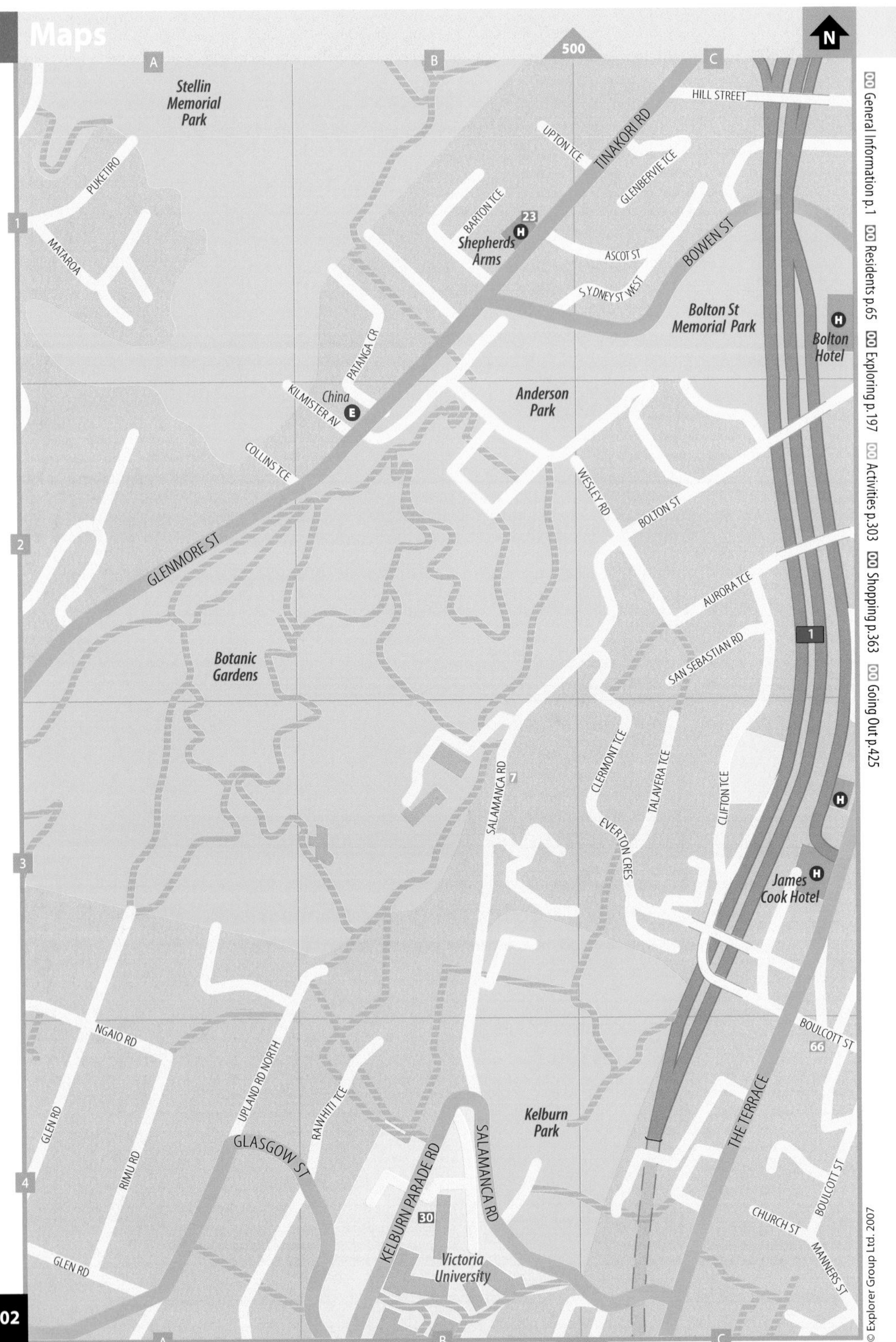

General Information p.1 Residents p.65 Exploring p.197 Activities p.303 Shopping p.363 Going Out p.425

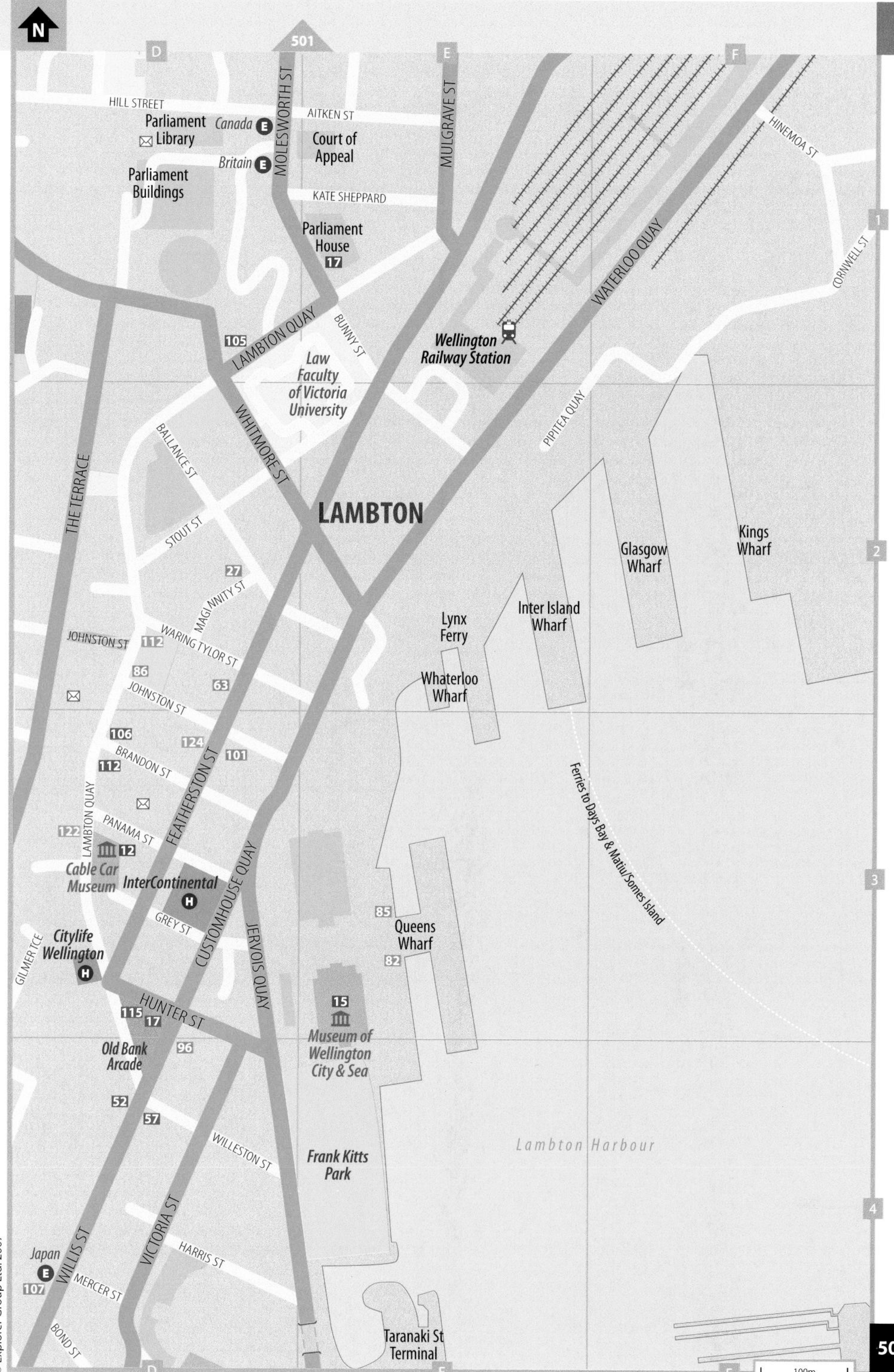
N
501
D
E
F
HILL STREET
Parliament Library
Canada
AITKEN ST
MOLESWORTH ST
Court of Appeal
MULGRAVE ST
HINEMOA ST
Britain
Parliament Buildings
KATE SHEPPARD
Parliament House
17
1
CORNWELL ST
WATERLOO QUAY
LAMBTON QUAY
105
BUNNY ST
Wellington Railway Station
Law Faculty of Victoria University
PIPITEA QUAY
BALLANCE ST
WHITMORE ST
THE TERRACE
LAMBTON
STOUT ST
Kings Wharf
Glasgow Wharf
2
27
MAGINNITY ST
Inter Island Wharf
Lynx Ferry
JOHNSTON ST
112
WARING TAYLOR ST
86
63
Whaterloo Wharf
JOHNSTON ST
106
124
101
BRANDON ST
112
FEATHERSTON ST
Ferries to Days Bay & Matiu/Somes Island
LAMBTON QUAY
PANAMA ST
122
12
Cable Car Museum
InterContinental
CUSTOMHOUSE QUAY
3
85
GREY ST
Queens Wharf
Citylife Wellington
82
GILMER TCE
JERVOIS QUAY
15
HUNTER ST
115
17
Museum of Wellington City & Sea
Old Bank Arcade
96
52
57
WILLESTON ST
Frank Kitts Park
Lambton Harbour
VICTORIA ST
4
Japan
HARRIS ST
WILLIS ST
107
MERCER ST
BOND ST
Taranaki St Terminal
505
100m

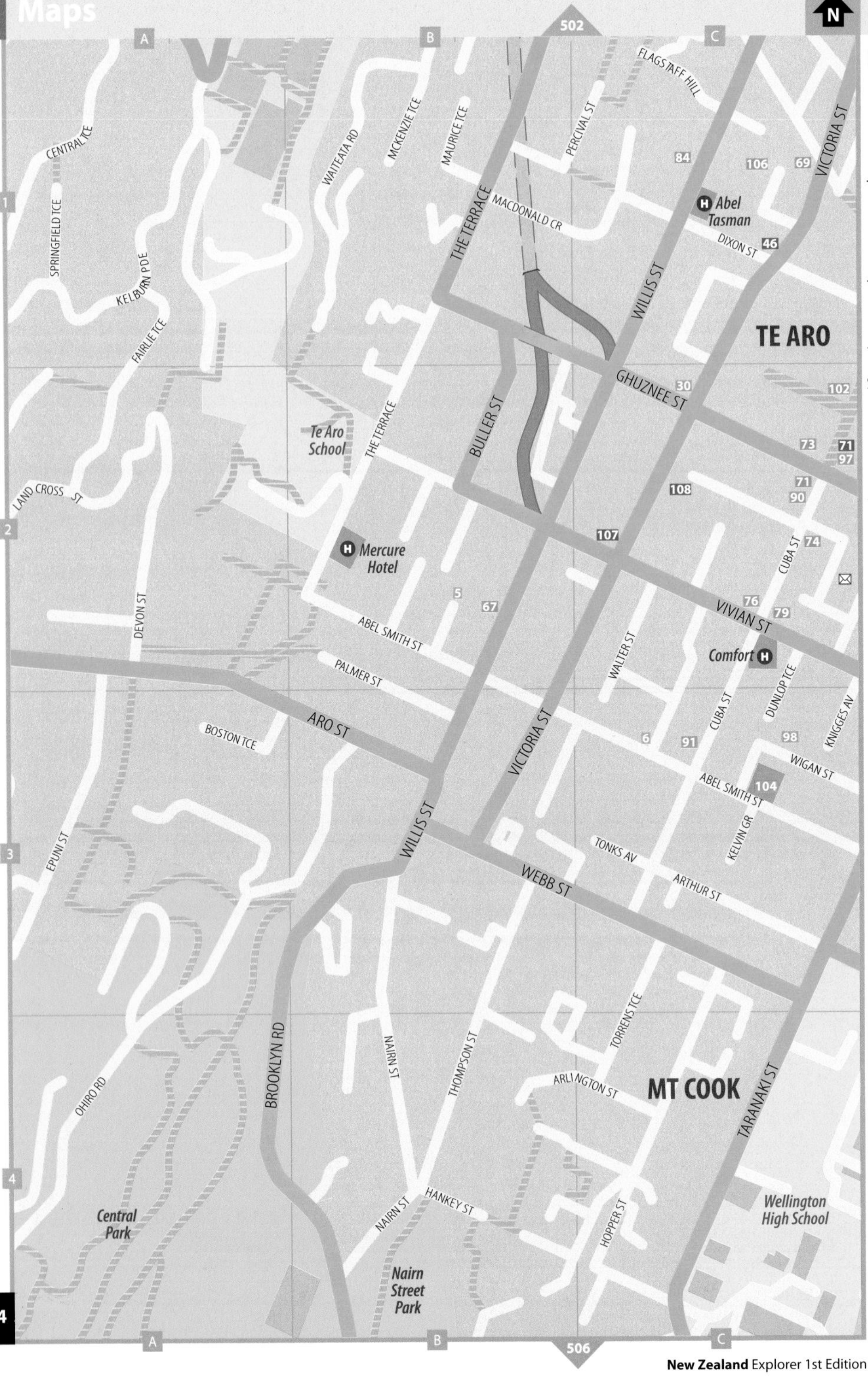

00 General Information p.1 00 Residents p.65 00 Exploring p.197 00 Activities p.303 00 Shopping p.363 00 Going Out p.425

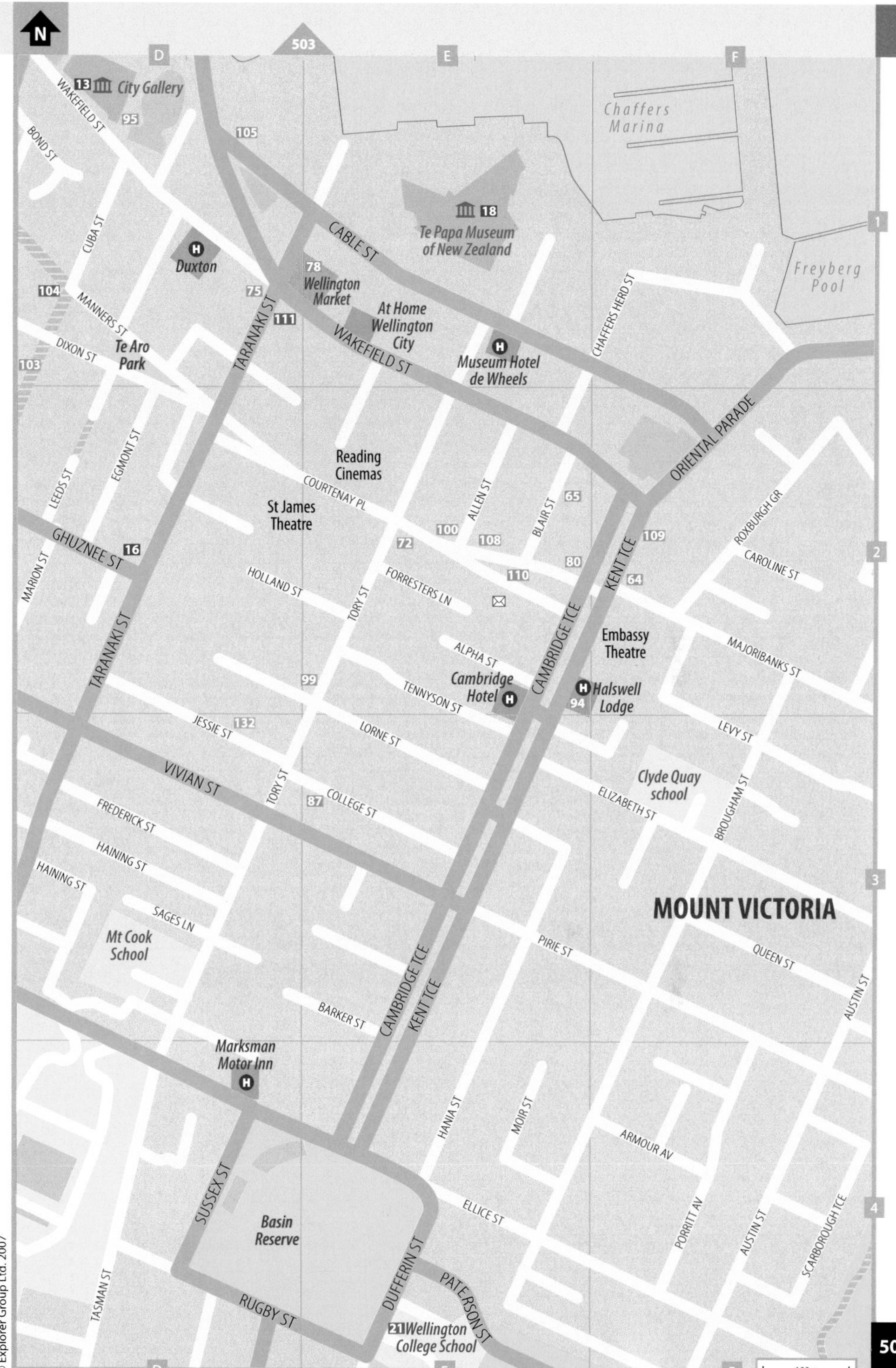

N
503
507
D
E
F
1
2
3
4
13 City Gallery
95
WAKEFIELD ST
BOND ST
105
Chaffers Marina
18
Te Papa Museum of New Zealand
Freyberg Pool
CUBA ST
Duxton
CABLE ST
78
Wellington Market
104
75
MANNERS ST
111
At Home Wellington City
TARANAKI ST
WAKEFIELD ST
CHAFFERS HERD ST
DIXON ST
Te Aro Park
Museum Hotel de Wheels
103
ORIENTAL PARADE
EGMONT ST
Reading Cinemas
LEEDS ST
COURTENAY PL
St James Theatre
ALLEN ST
BLAIR ST
65
100
108
109
GHUZNEE ST
72
KENT TCE
ROXBURGH GR
16
CAROLINE ST
80
HOLLAND ST
FORRESTERS LN
110
64
MARION ST
TORY ST
CAMBRIDGE TCE
Embassy Theatre
ALPHA ST
MAJORIBANKS ST
TARANAKI ST
99
Cambridge Hotel
Halswell Lodge
TENNYSON ST
94
JESSIE ST
132
LORNE ST
LEVY ST
Clyde Quay school
VIVIAN ST
TORY ST
COLLEGE ST
BROUGHAM ST
87
ELIZABETH ST
FREDERICK ST
HAINING ST
HAINING ST
MOUNT VICTORIA
SAGES LN
Mt Cook School
PIRIE ST
QUEEN ST
AUSTIN ST
BARKER ST
CAMBRIDGE TCE
KENT TCE
Marksman Motor Inn
HANIA ST
MOIR ST
ARMOUR AV
SUSSEX ST
Basin Reserve
ELLICE ST
PORRITT AV
AUSTIN ST
SCARBOROUGH TCE
TASMAN ST
DUFFERIN ST
PATERSON ST
RUGBY ST
21 Wellington College School
100m

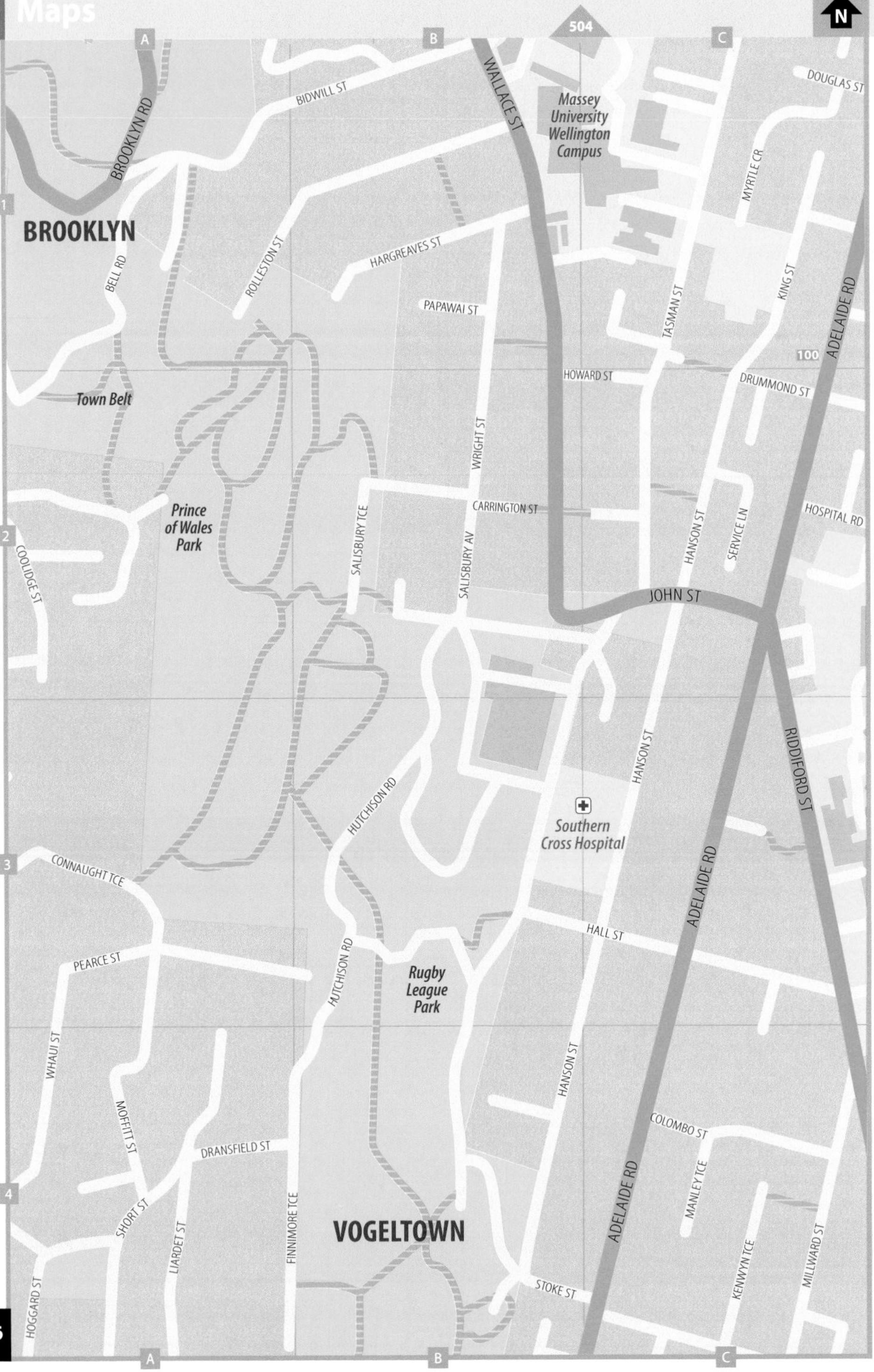

504
100

00 General Information p.1 00 Residents p.65 00 Exploring p.197 00 Activities p.303 00 Shopping p.363 00 Going Out p.425

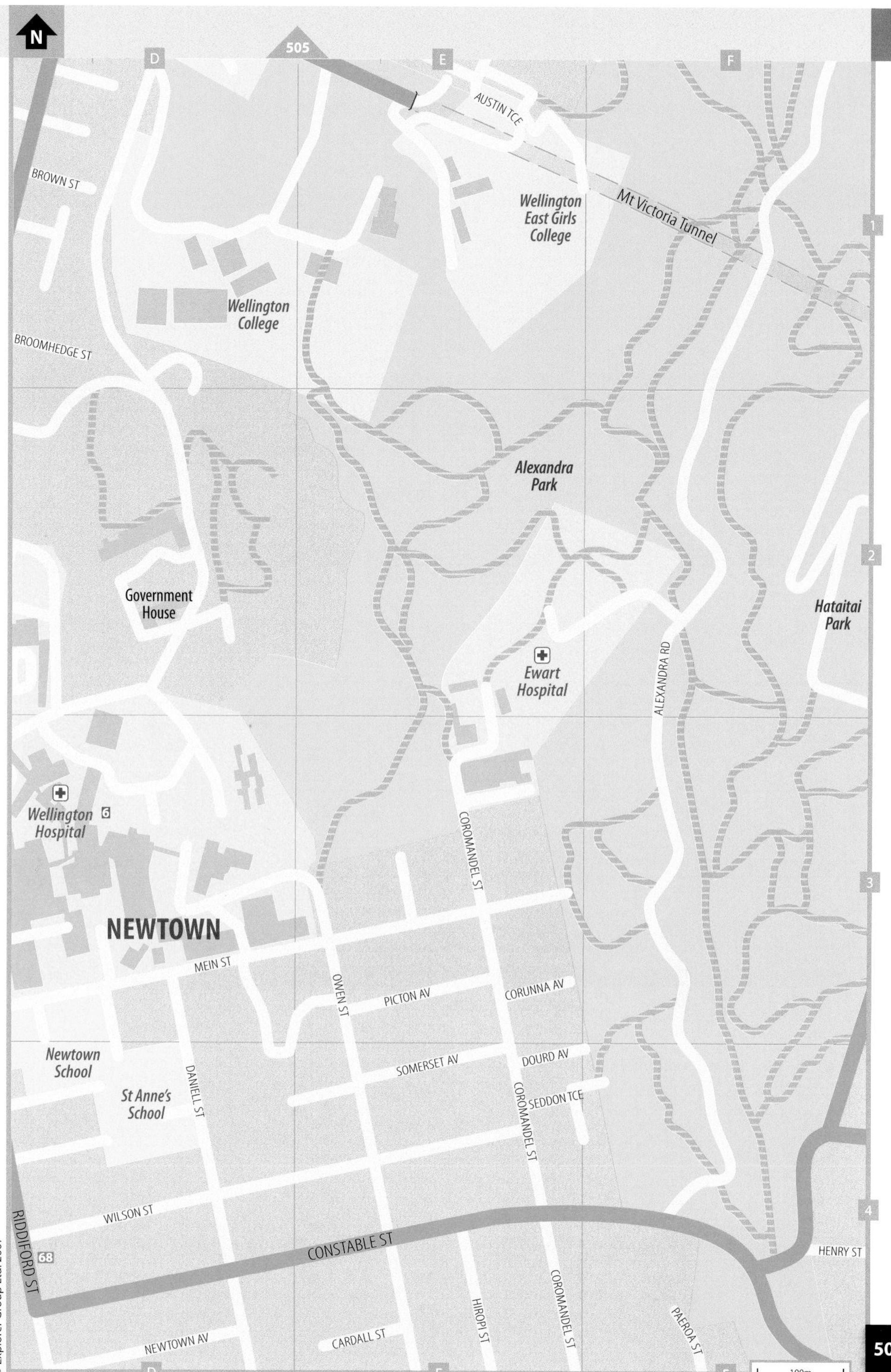
N
505
D
E
F
AUSTIN TCE
BROWN ST
Wellington East Girls College
Mt Victoria Tunnel
1
Wellington College
BROOMHEDGE ST
Alexandra Park
2
Government House
Hataitai Park
Ewart Hospital
ALEXANDRA RD
Wellington Hospital
6
CORОMANDEL ST
3
NEWTOWN
MEIN ST
OWEN ST
PICTON AV
CORUNNA AV
Newtown School
SOMERSET AV
DOURD AV
St Anne's School
DANIELL ST
SEDDON TCE
COROMANDEL ST
WILSON ST
4
HENRY ST
RIDDIFORD ST
68
CONSTABLE ST
COROMANDEL ST
HIROPI ST
PAEROA ST
NEWTOWN AV
CARDALL ST
D
E
F
100m

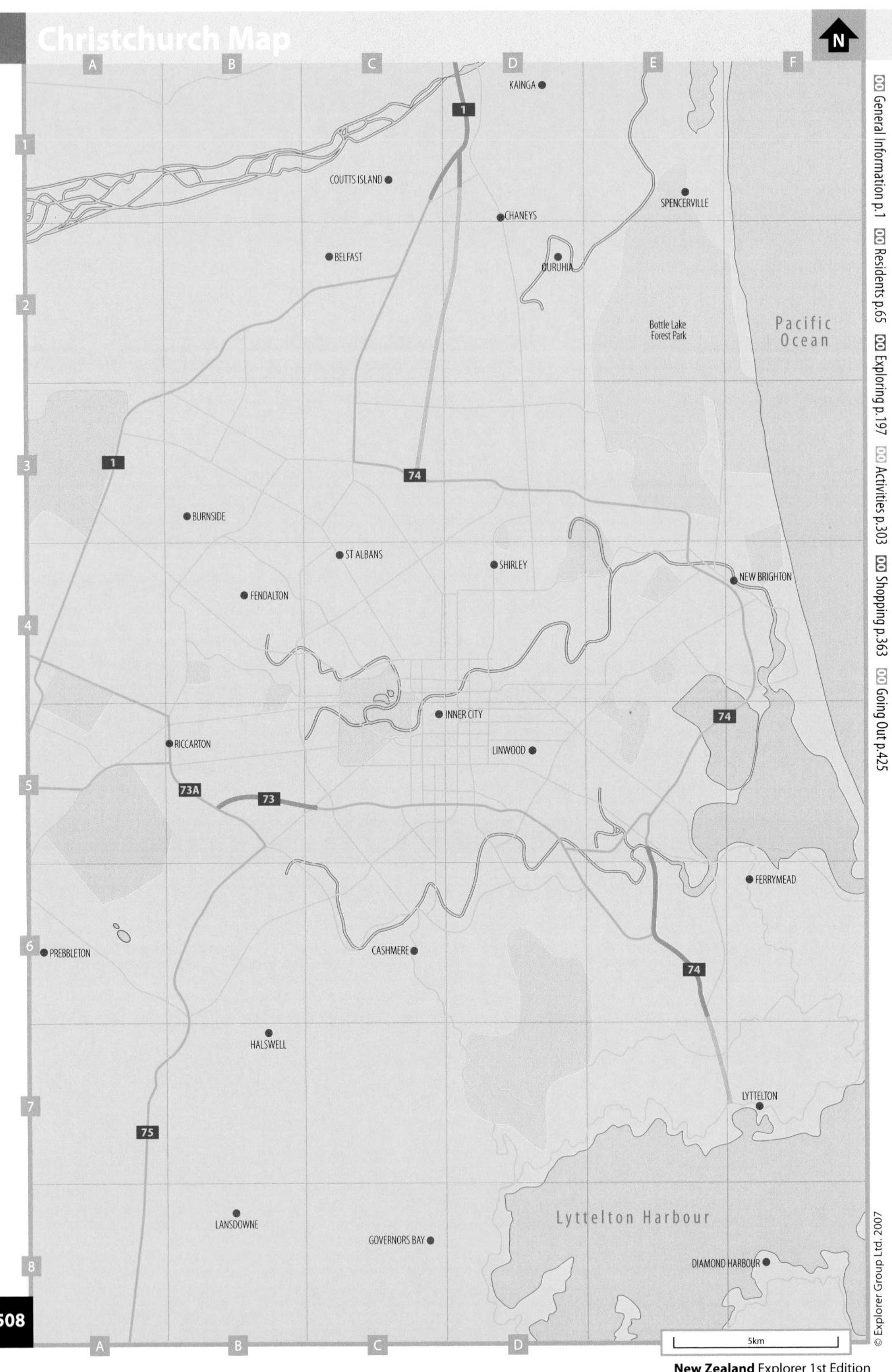

General Information p.1 Residents p.65 Exploring p.197 Activities p.303 Shopping p.363 Going Out p.425

Christchurch Sheet Map

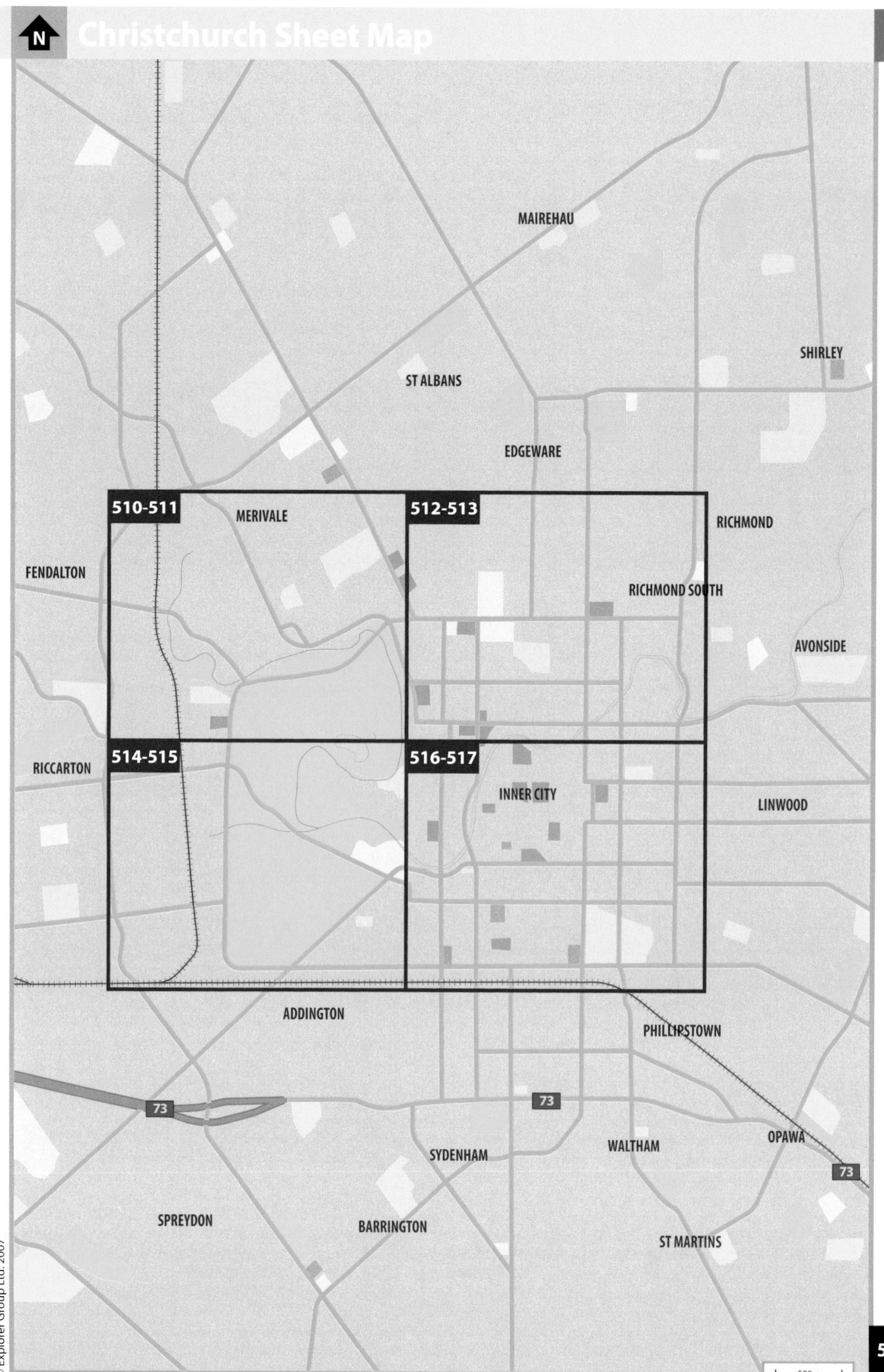

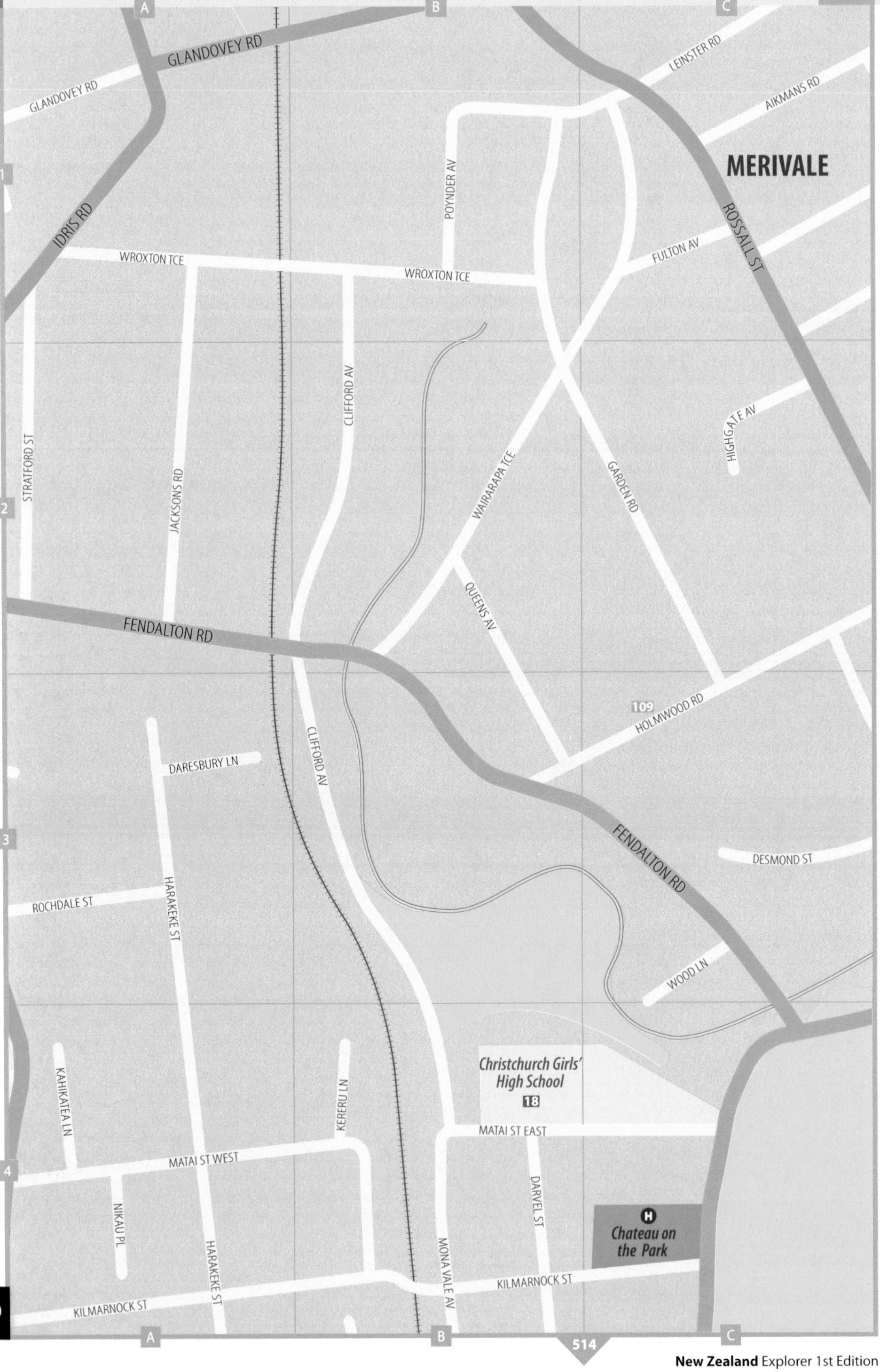

N

A B C

1 2 3 4

GLANDOVEY RD
GLANDOVEY RD
LEINSTER RD
AIKMANS RD
MERIVALE
IDRIS RD
POYNDER AV
ROSSALL ST
FULTON AV
WROXTON TCE
WROXTON TCE
CLIFFORD AV
HIGHGATE AV
STRATFORD ST
JACKSONS RD
WAIRARAPA TCE
GARDEN RD
QUEENS AV
FENDALTON RD
109
HOLMWOOD RD
CLIFFORD AV
DARESBURY LN
FENDALTON RD
DESMOND ST
ROCHDALE ST
HARAKEKE ST
WOOD LN
Christchurch Girls' High School
18
KAHIKATEA LN
KERERU LN
MATAI ST EAST
MATAI ST WEST
DARVEL ST
NIKAU PL
HARAKEKE ST
MONA VALE AV
Chateau on the Park
KILMARNOCK ST
KILMARNOCK ST

General Information p.1 Residents p.65 Exploring p.197 Activities p.303 Shopping p.363 Going Out p.425

514

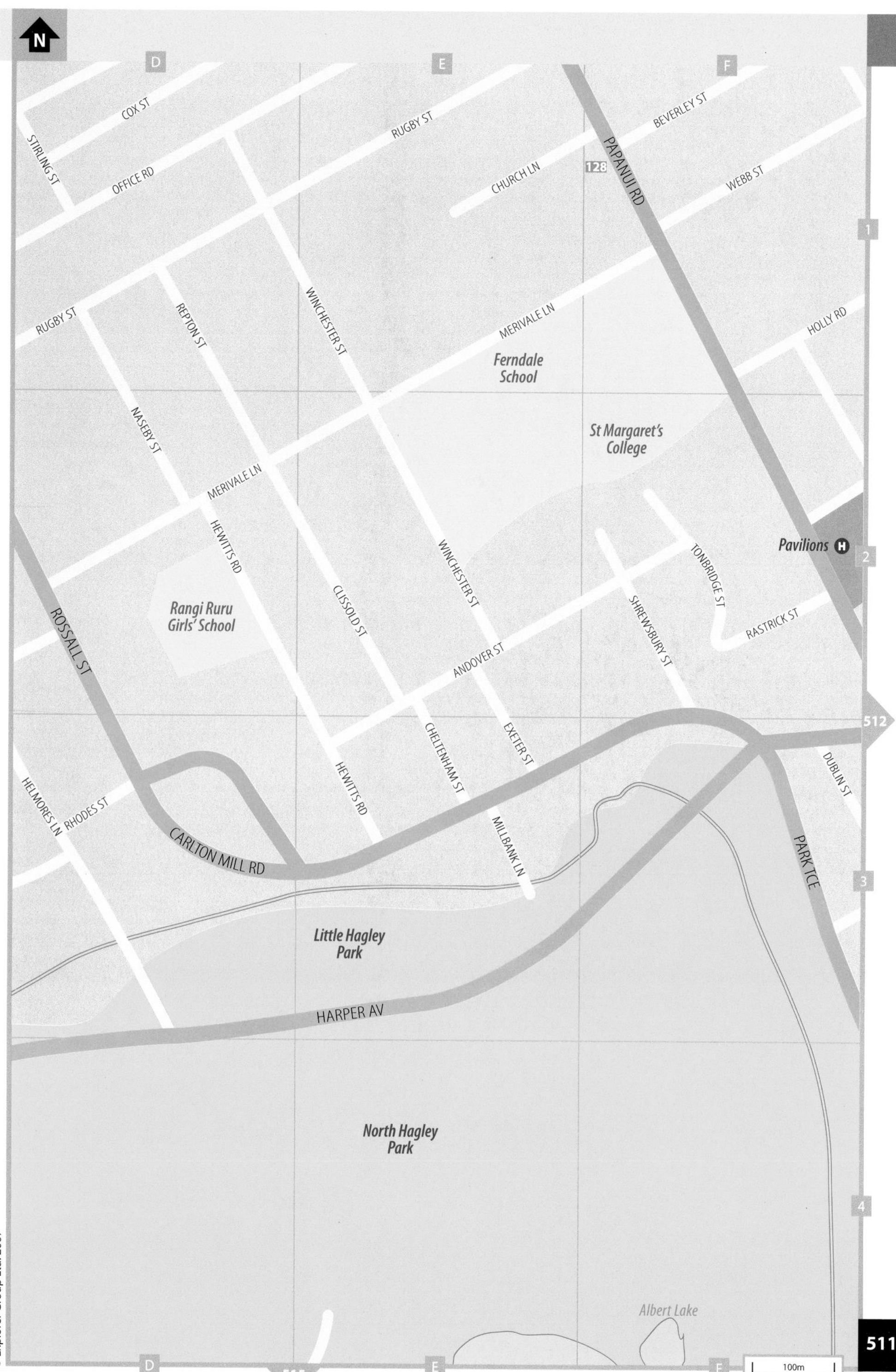
N
D
E
F
COX ST
STIRLING ST
OFFICE RD
RUGBY ST
BEVERLEY ST
PAPANUI RD
128
CHURCH LN
WEBB ST
1
RUGBY ST
REPTON ST
WINCHESTER ST
MERIVALE LN
HOLLY RD
Ferndale School
NASEBY ST
St Margaret's College
MERIVALE LN
HEWITTS RD
WINCHESTER ST
TONBRIDGE ST
Pavilions
2
Rangi Ruru Girls' School
ROSSALL ST
CLISSOLD ST
SHREWSBURY ST
RASTRICK ST
ANDOVER ST
512
CHELTENHAM ST
EXETER ST
DUBLIN ST
HELMORES LN
RHODES ST
HEWITTS RD
MILLBANK LN
CARLTON MILL RD
PARK TCE
3
Little Hagley Park
HARPER AV
North Hagley Park
4
Albert Lake
515
100m
511

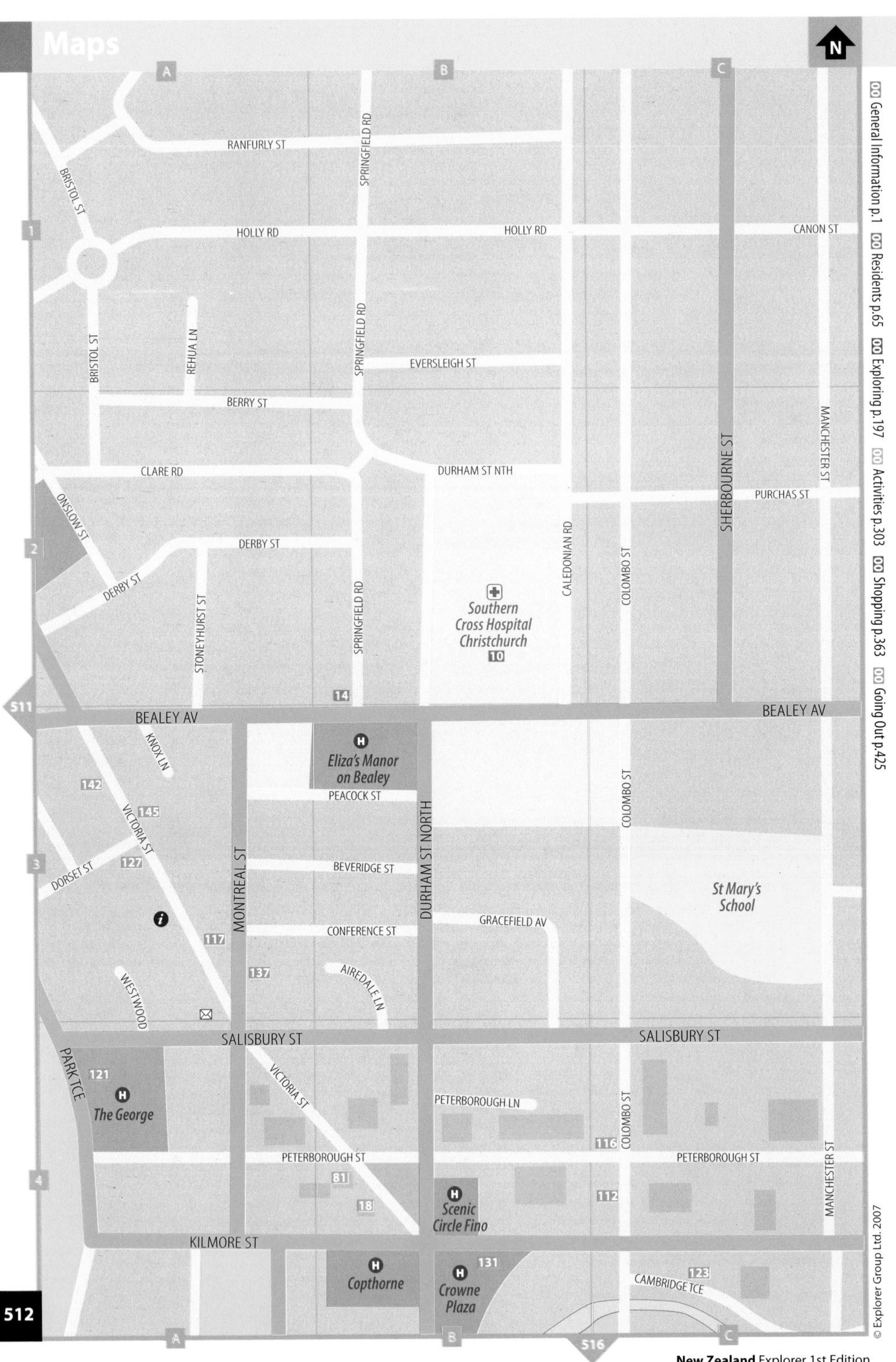

General Information p.1 Residents p.65 Exploring p.197 Activities p.303 Shopping p.363 Going Out p.425

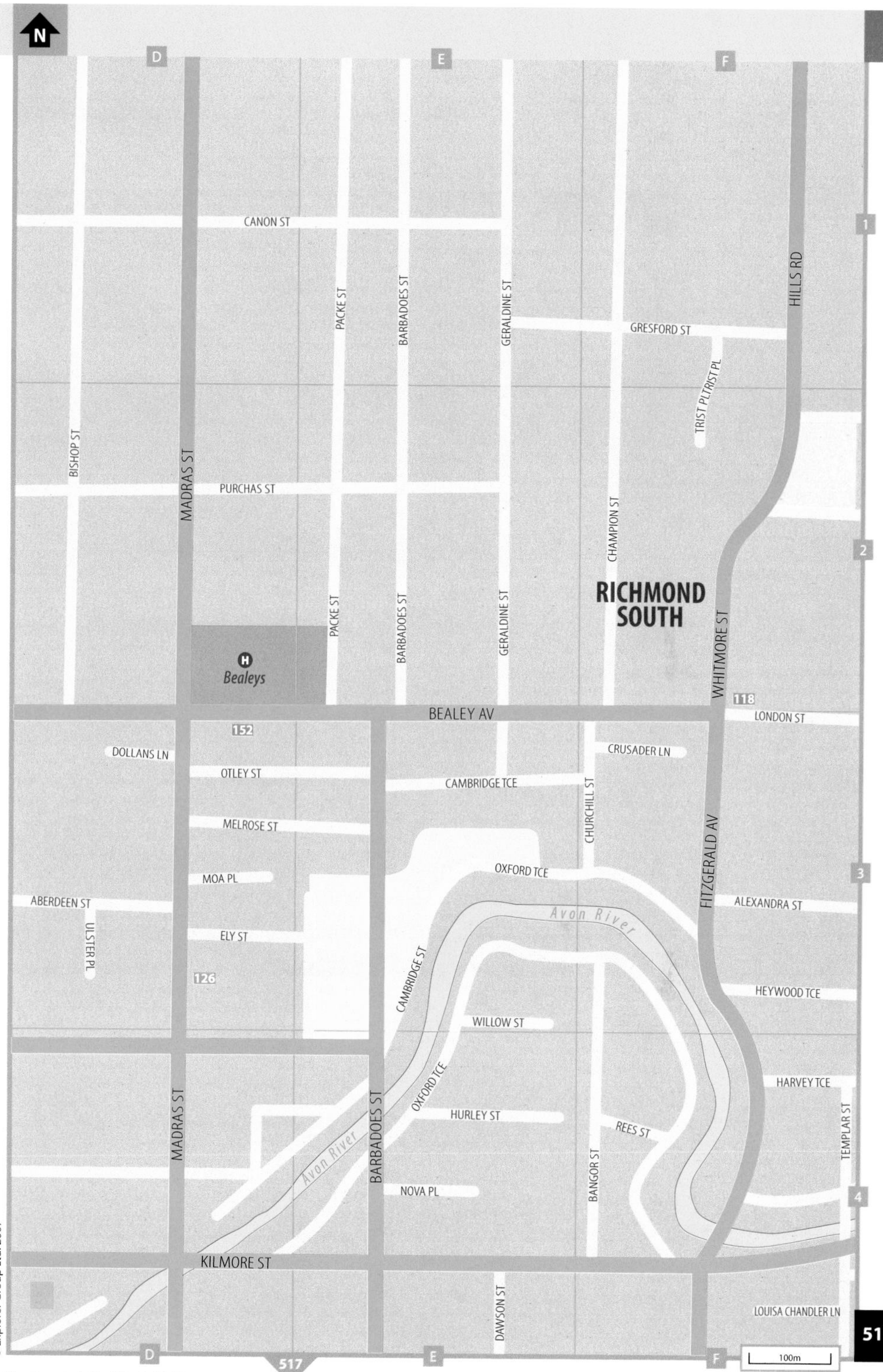
N
D
E
F
1
2
3
4
CANON ST
PACKE ST
BARBADOES ST
GERALDINE ST
GRESFORD ST
HILLS RD
TRIST PL
BISHOP ST
MADRAS ST
PURCHAS ST
CHAMPION ST
RICHMOND SOUTH
WHITMORE ST
Bealeys
BEALEY AV
118
LONDON ST
152
DOLLANS LN
CRUSADER LN
OTLEY ST
CAMBRIDGE TCE
CHURCHILL ST
MELROSE ST
FITZGERALD AV
OXFORD TCE
MOA PL
ABERDEEN ST
ALEXANDRA ST
Avon River
ULSTER PL
ELY ST
CAMBRIDGE ST
126
HEYWOOD TCE
WILLOW ST
HARVEY TCE
OXFORD TCE
HURLEY ST
REES ST
TEMPLAR ST
NOVA PL
BANGOR ST
KILMORE ST
DAWSON ST
LOUISA CHANDLER LN
517
100m

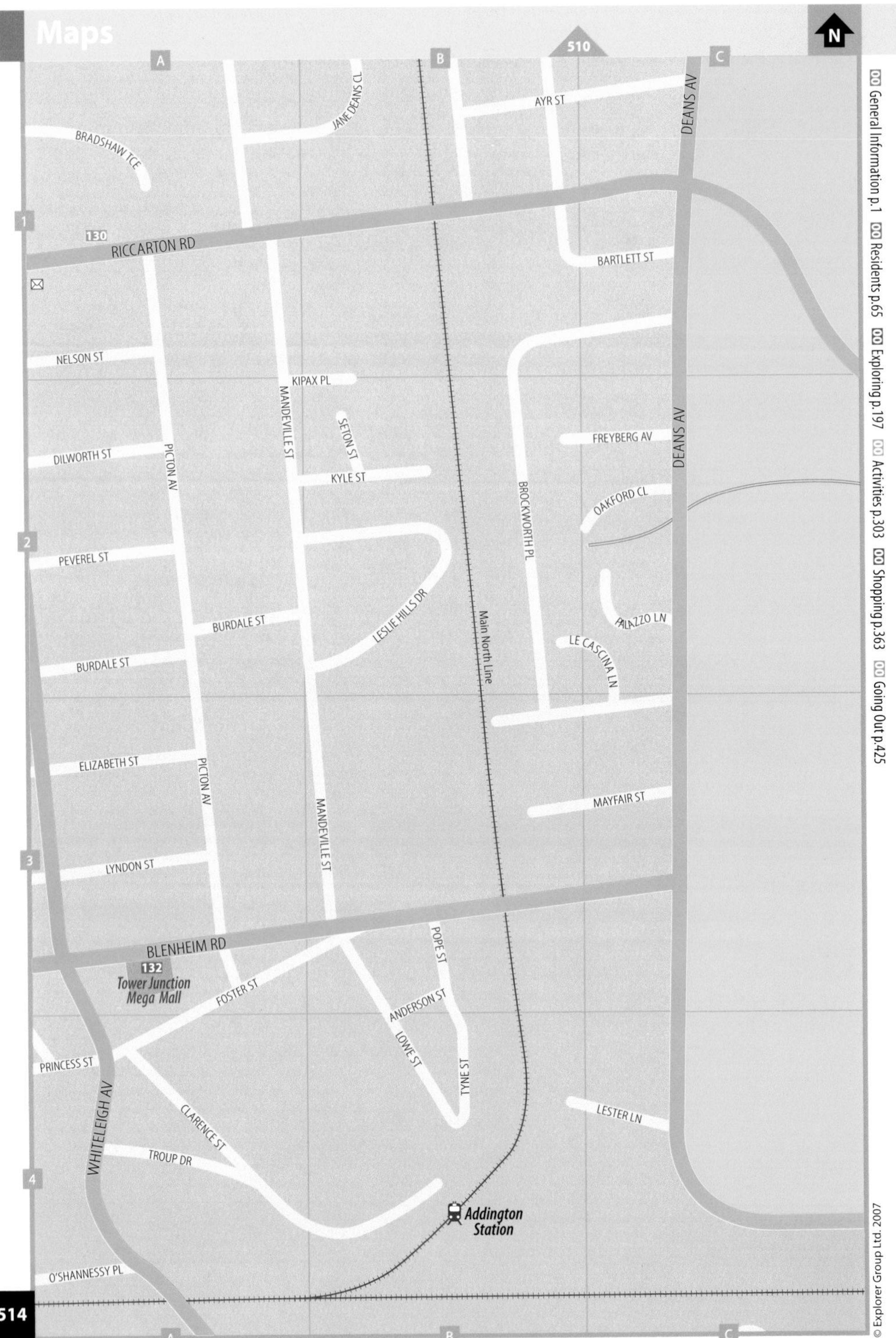

General Information p.1 Residents p.65 Exploring p.197 Activities p.303 Shopping p.363 Going Out p.425

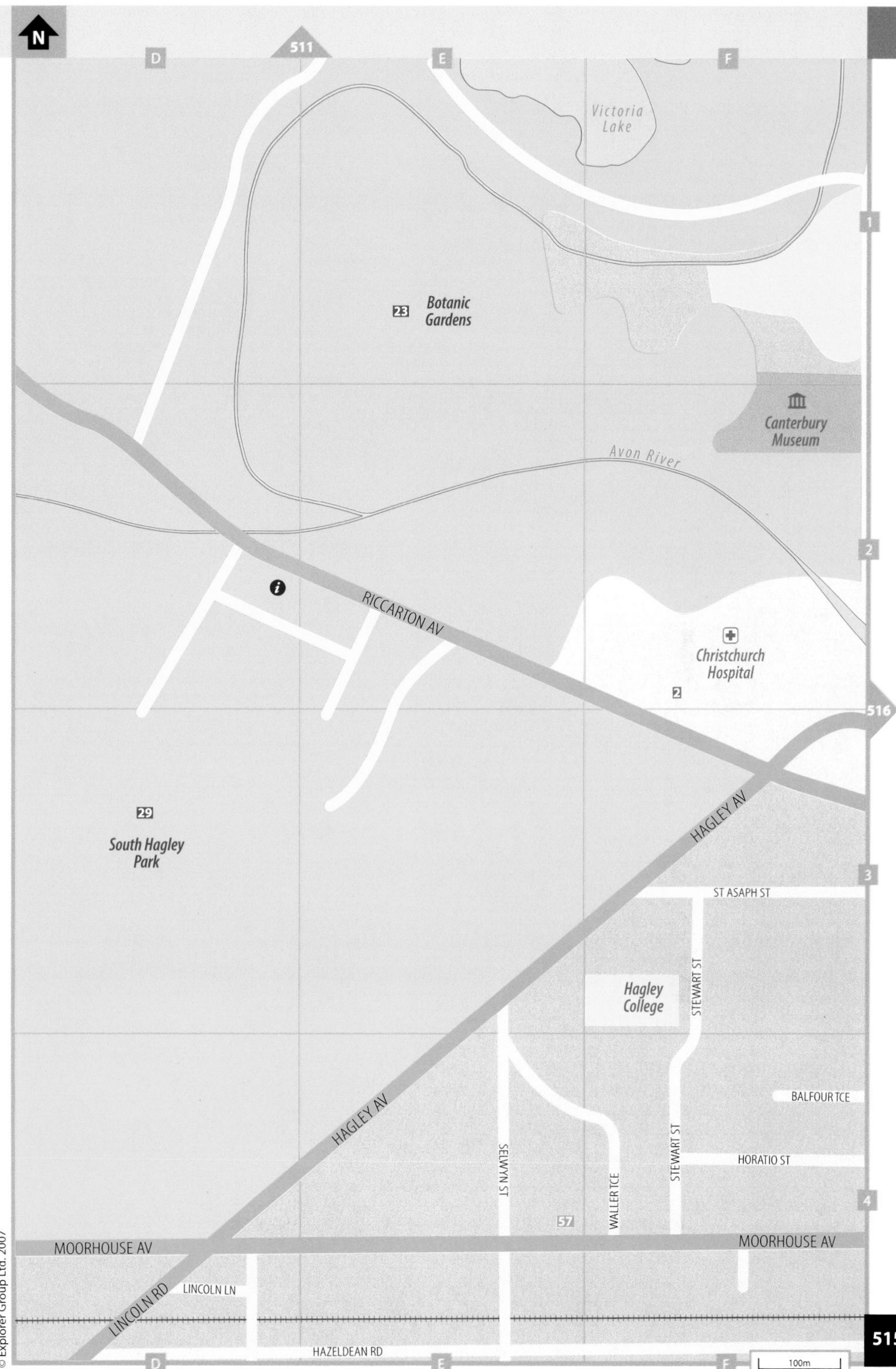
N
511
D
E
F
Victoria Lake
1
Botanic Gardens
23
Canterbury Museum
Avon River
2
RICCARTON AV
Christchurch Hospital
2
516
29
South Hagley Park
HAGLEY AV
3
ST ASAPH ST
STEWART ST
Hagley College
BALFOUR TCE
HAGLEY AV
SELWYN ST
WALLER TCE
STEWART ST
HORATIO ST
4
57
MOORHOUSE AV
MOORHOUSE AV
LINCOLN LN
LINCOLN RD
HAZELDEAN RD
D
E
F
100m

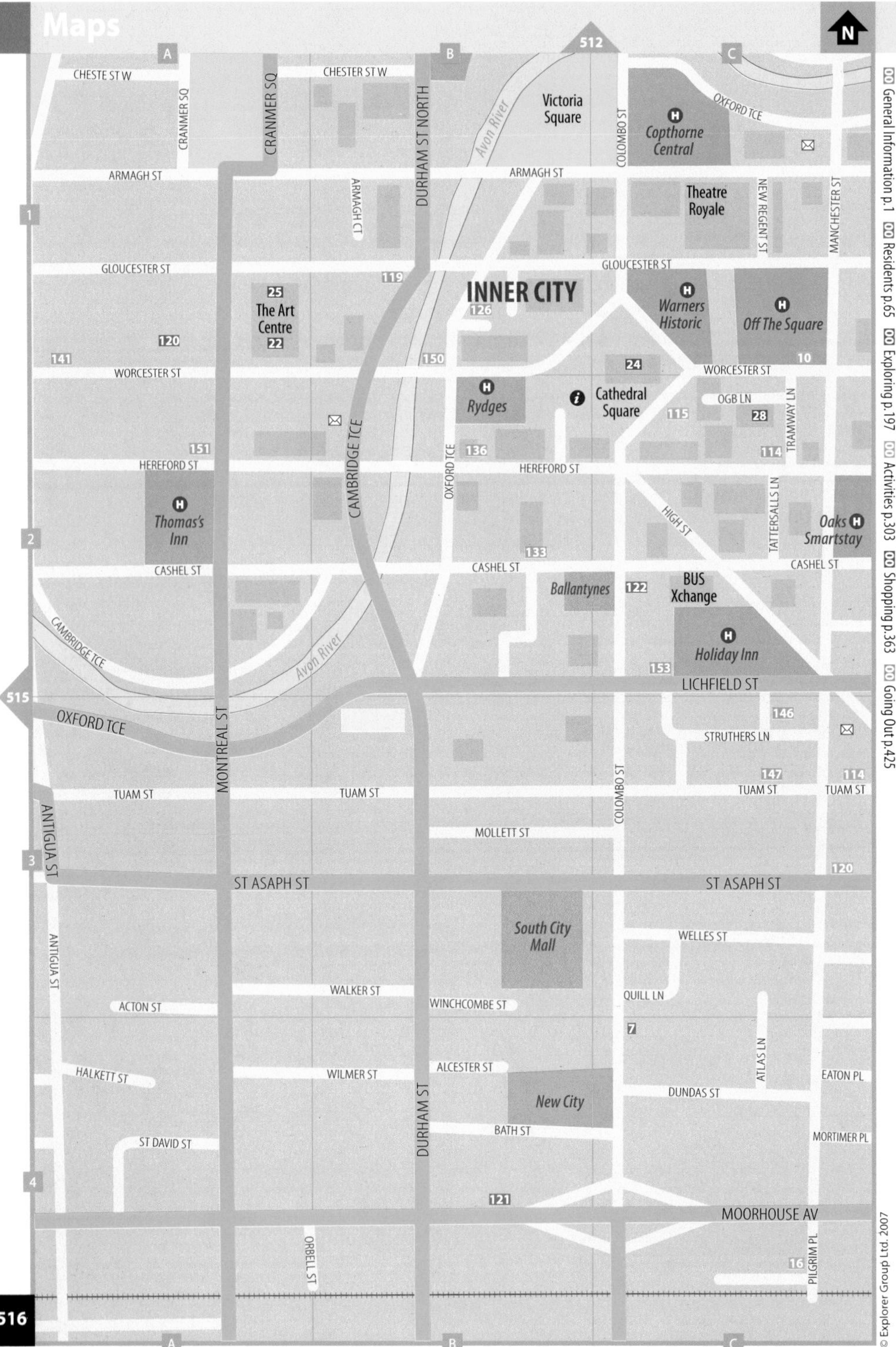

General Information p.1 Residents p.65 Exploring p.197 Activities p.303 Shopping p.363 Going Out p.425

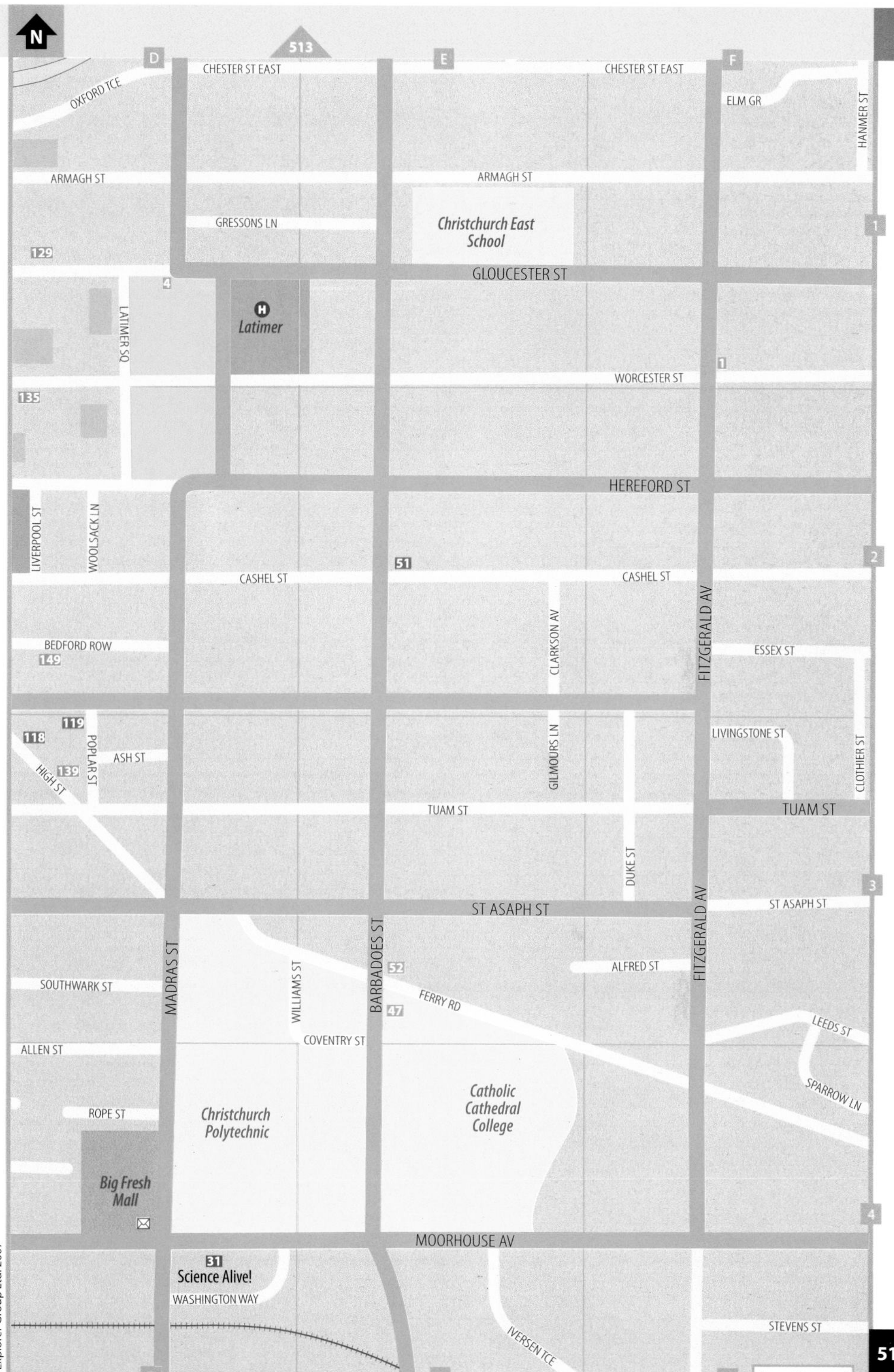
N
513
D
E
F
CHESTER ST EAST
CHESTER ST EAST
OXFORD TCE
ELM GR
HANMER ST
ARMAGH ST
ARMAGH ST
GRESSONS LN
Christchurch East School
129
1
GLOUCESTER ST
4
Latimer
LATIMER SQ
1
WORCESTER ST
135
HEREFORD ST
LIVERPOOL ST
WOOLSACK LN
2
51
CASHEL ST
CASHEL ST
CLARKSON AV
FITZGERALD AV
BEDFORD ROW
149
ESSEX ST
119
118
POPLAR ST
ASH ST
139
HIGH ST
GILMOURS LN
LIVINGSTONE ST
CLOTHIER ST
TUAM ST
TUAM ST
DUKE ST
3
ST ASAPH ST
ST ASAPH ST
FITZGERALD AV
MADRAS ST
WILLIAMS ST
BARBADOES ST
52
ALFRED ST
SOUTHWARK ST
FERRY RD
47
LEEDS ST
ALLEN ST
COVENTRY ST
SPARROW LN
Catholic Cathedral College
ROPE ST
Christchurch Polytechnic
Big Fresh Mall
4
MOORHOUSE AV
31
Science Alive!
WASHINGTON WAY
IVERSEN TCE
STEVENS ST
100m

Index

D

E

F

O

P

Q

R

S

T

U

V

W

Residents' Guides

All you need to know about living, working and enjoying life in these exciting destinations

*

*

*

Mini Guides

The perfect pocket-sized Visitors' Guides

*

*

*

Mini Maps

Wherever you are, never get lost again

*

*

*

Photography Books

Beautiful cities caught through the lens

Calendars

The time, the place, and the date

The Team — The X Files

Ahmed Mainodin
AKA: Mystery Man
We can never recognise Ahmed because of his constantly changing facial hair. He waltzes in with big lambchop sideburns one day, a handlebar moustache the next, and a neatly trimmed goatee after that. So far we've had no objections to his hirsute chameleonisms, but we'll definitely draw the line at a monobrow.

Bahrudeen Abdul
AKA: The Stallion
Having tired of creating abstract sculptures out of papier maché and candy canes, Bahrudeen turned to the art of computer programming. After honing his skills in the southern Andes for three years he grew bored of Patagonian winters, and landed a job here, 'The Home of 01010101 Creative Freedom'.

Ajay Krishnan R
AKA: Web Wonder
Ajay's mum and dad knew he was going to be an IT genius when they found him reconfiguring his Commodore 64 at the tender age of 2. He went on to become the technology consultant on all three Matrix films, and counts Keanu as a close personal friend.

Ben Merrett
AKA: Big Ben
After a short (or tall as the case may have been) career as a human statue, Ben tired of the pigeons choosing him, rather than his namesake, as a public convenience and decided to fly the nest to seek his fortune in foreign lands. Not only is he big on personality but he brings in the big bucks with his bulk!

Alex Jeffries
AKA: Easy Rider
Alex is happiest when dressed in leather from head to toe with a humming machine between his thighs – just like any other motorbike enthusiast. Whenever he's not speeding along the Hatta Road at full throttle, he can be found at his beloved Mac, still dressed in leather.

Cherry Enriquez
AKA: Bean Counter
With the team's penchant for sweets and pastries, it's good to know we have Cherry on top of our accounting cake. The local confectioner is always paid on time, so we're guaranteed great gateaux for every special occasion.

Alistair MacKenzie
AKA: Media Mogul
If only Alistair could take the paperless office one step further and achieve the officeless office he would be the happiest publisher alive. Wireless access from a remote spot somewhere in the Hajar Mountains would suit this intrepid explorer – less traffic, lots of fresh air, and wearing sandals all day - the perfect work environment!

Claire England
AKA: Whip Cracker
No longer able to freeload off the fact that she once appeared in a Robbie Williams video, Claire now puts her creative skills to better use – looking up rude words in the dictionary! A child of English nobility, Claire is quite the lady – unless she's down at Jimmy Dix.

Andrea Fust
AKA: Mother Superior
By day Andrea is the most efficient manager in the world and by night she replaces the boardroom for her board and wows the pants off the dudes in Ski Dubai. Literally. Back in the office she definitely wears the trousers!

David Quinn
AKA: Sharp Shooter
After a short stint as a children's TV presenter was robbed from David because he developed an allergy to sticky back plastic, he made his way to sandier pastures. Now that he's thinking outside the box, nothing gets past the man with the sharpest pencil in town.

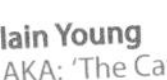

Derrick Pereira
AKA: The Returnimator
After leaving Explorer in 2003, Derrick's life took a dramatic downturn – his dog ran away, his prized bonsai tree died and he got kicked out of his thrash metal band. Since rejoining us, things are looking up and he just found out he's won $10 million in a Nigerian sweepstakes competition. And he's got the desk by the window!

Iain Young
AKA: 'The Cat'
Iain follows in the fine tradition of Scots with safe hands – Alan Rough, Andy Goram, Jim Leighton on a good day – but breaking into the Explorer XI has proved frustrating. There's no match on a Mac, but that Al Huzaifa ringer doesn't half make himself big.

Enrico Maullon
AKA: The Crooner
Frequently mistaken for his near-namesake Enrique Iglesias, Enrico decided to capitalise and is now a regular stand-in for the Latin heartthrob. If he's ever missing from the office, it usually means he's off performing for millions of adoring fans on another stadium tour of America.

Ieyad Charaf
AKA: Fashion Designer
When we hired Ieyad as a top designer, we didn't realise we'd be getting his designer tops too! By far the snappiest dresser in the office, you'd be hard-pressed to beat his impeccably ironed shirts.

Firos Khan
AKA: Big Smiler
Previously a body double in kung fu movies, including several appearances in close up scenes for Steven Seagal's moustache. He also once tore down a restaurant with his bare hands after they served him a mild curry by mistake.

Ingrid Cupido
AKA: The Karaoke Queen
Ingrid has a voice to match her starlet name. She'll put any Pop Idols to shame once behind the mike, and she's pretty nifty on a keyboard too. She certainly gets our vote if she decides to go pro; just remember you saw her here first.

Hashim MM
AKA: Speedy Gonzales
They don't come much faster than Hashim – he's so speedy with his mouse that scientists are struggling to create a computer that can keep up with him. His nimble fingers leave his keyboard smouldering (he gets through three a week), and his go-faster stripes make him almost invisible to the naked eye when he moves.

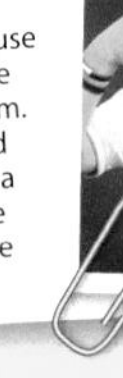

Ivan Rodrigues
AKA: The Aviator
After making a mint in the airline market, Ivan came to Explorer where he works for pleasure, not money. That's his story, anyway. We know that he is actually a corporate spy from a rival company and that his multi-level spreadsheets are really elaborate codes designed to confuse us.

Helen Spearman
AKA: Little Miss Sunshine
With her bubbly laugh and permanent smile, Helen is a much-needed ray of sunshine in the office when we're all grumpy and facing harrowing deadlines. It's almost impossible to think that she ever loses her temper or shows a dark side... although put her behind the wheel of a car, and you've got instant road rage.

Jake Marsico
AKA: Don Calzone
Jake spent the last 10 years on the tiny triangular Mediterranean island of Samoza, honing his traditional cooking techniques and perfecting his Italian. Now, whenever he returns to his native America, he impresses his buddies by effortlessly zapping a hot dog to perfection in any microwave, anywhere, anytime.

Henry Hilos
AKA: The Quiet Man
Henry can rarely be seen from behind his large obstructive screen but when you do catch a glimpse you'll be sure to get a smile. Lighthearted Henry keeps all those glossy pages filled with pretty pictures for something to look at when you can't be bothered to read.

Jane Roberts
AKA: The Oracle
After working in an undisclosed role in the government, Jane brought her super sleuth skills to Explorer. Whatever the question, she knows what, where, who, how and when, but her encyclopaedic knowledge is only impressive until you realise she just makes things up randomly.

The X Files

Jayde Fernandes
AKA: Pop Idol
Jayde's idol is Britney Spears, and he recently shaved his head to show solidarity with the troubled star. When he's not checking his dome for stubble, or practising the dance moves to 'Baby One More Time' in front of the bathroom mirror, he actually manages to get some designing done.

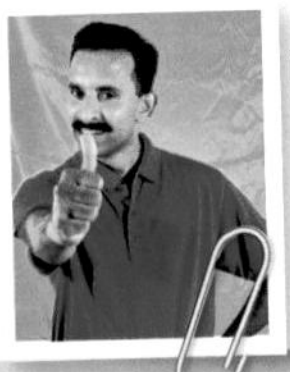

Johny Mathew
AKA: The Hawker
Caring Johny used to nurse wounded eagles back to health and teach them how to fly again before trying his luck in merchandising. Fortunately his skills in the field have come in handy at Explorer, where his efforts to improve our book sales have been a soaring success.

Kate Fox
AKA: Contacts Collector
Kate swooped into the office like the UK equivalent of Wonderwoman, minus the tights of course (it's much too hot for that), but armed with a superhuman marketing brain. Even though she's just arrived, she is already a regular on the Dubai social scene – she is helping to blast Explorer into the stratosphere, one champagne-soaked networking party at a time.

Katie Drynan
AKA: The Irish Deputy
Katie is a Jumeira Jane in training, and has 35 sisters who take it in turns to work in the Explorer office while she enjoys testing all the beauty treatments available on the Beach Road. This Irish charmer met an oil tycoon in Paris, and they now spend the weekends digging very deep holes in their new garden.

Kiran Melwani
AKA: Bow Selector
Like a modern-day Robin Hood (right down to the green tights and band of merry men), Kiran's mission in life is to distribute Explorer's wealth of knowledge to the fact-hungry readers of the world. Just make sure you never do anything to upset her – rumour has it she's a pretty mean shot with that bow and arrow.

Lennie Mangalino
AKA: Shaker Maker
With a giant spring in her step and music in her heart it's hard to not to swing to the beat when Lennie passes by in the office. She loves her Lambada… and Samba… and Salsa and anything else she can get the sales team shaking their hips to.

Mannie Lugtu
AKA: Distribution Demon
When the travelling circus rode into town, their master juggler Mannie decided to leave the Big Top and explore Dubai instead. He may have swapped his balls for our books but his juggling skills still come in handy.

Maricar Ong
AKA: Pocket Docket
A pint-sized dynamo of ruthless efficiency, Maricar gets the job done before anyone else notices it needed doing. If this most able assistant is absent for a moment, it sends a surge of blind panic through the Explorer ranks.

Grace Carnay
AKA: Manila Ice
It's just as well the office is so close to a movie theatre, because Grace is always keen to catch the latest Hollywood offering from Brad Pitt, who she admires purely for his acting ability, of course. Her ice cool exterior conceals a tempestuous passion for jazz, which fuels her frenzied typing speed.

Matt Farquharson
AKA: Hack Hunter
A career of tuppence-a-word hackery ended when Matt arrived in Dubai to cover a maggot wranglers' convention. He misguidedly thinks he's clever because he once wrote for some grown-up English papers.

Matthew Samuel
AKA: Mr Modest
Matt's penchant for the entrepreneurial life began with a pair of red braces and a filofax when still a child. That yearning for the cut and thrust of commerce has brought him to Dubai, where he made a fortune in the sand-selling business before semi-retiring at Explorer.

Michael Samuel
AKA: Gordon Gekko
We have a feeling this mild mannered master of mathematics has a wild side. He hasn't witnessed an Explorer party yet but the office agrees that once the karaoke machine is out, Michael will be the maestro. Watch out Dubai!

Mimi Stankova
AKA: Mind Controller
A master of mind control, Mimi's siren-like voice lulls people into doing whatever she asks. Her steely reserve and endless patience mean recalcitrant reporters and persistent PR people are putty in her hands, delivering whatever she wants, whenever she wants it.

Mohammed Sameer
AKA: Man in the Van
Known as MS, short for Microsoft, Sameer can pick apart a PC like a thief with a lock, which is why we keep him out of finance and pounding Dubai's roads in the unmissable Explorer van – so we can always spot him coming.

Mohammed T
AKA: King of the Castle
T is Explorer's very own Bedouin warehouse dweller; under his caring charge all Explorer stock is kept in masterful order. Arrive uninvited and you'll find T, meditating on a pile of maps, amid an almost eerie sense of calm.

Noushad Madathil
AKA: Map Daddy
Where would Explorer be without the mercurial Madathil brothers? Lost in the Empty Quarter, that's where. Quieter than a mute dormouse, Noushad prefers to let his Photoshop layers, and brother Zain, do all the talking. A true Map Daddy.

Pamela Grist
AKA: Happy Snapper
If a picture can speak a thousand words then Pam's photos say a lot about her - through her lens she manages to find the beauty in everything – even this motley crew. And when the camera never lies, thankfully Photoshop can.

Pete Maloney
AKA: Graphic Guru
Image conscious he may be, but when Pete has his designs on something you can bet he's gonna get it! He's the king of chat up lines, ladies – if he ever opens a conversation with 'D'you come here often?' then brace yourself for the Maloney magic.

Rafi Jamal
AKA: Soap Star
After a walk on part in The Bold and the Beautiful, Rafi swapped the Hollywood Hills for the Hajar Mountains. Although he left the glitz behind, he still mingles with high society, moonlighting as a male gigolo and impressing Dubai's ladies with his fancy footwork.

Rafi VP
AKA: Party Trickster
After developing a rare allergy to sunlight in his teens, Rafi started to lose a few centimeters of height every year. He now stands just 30cm tall, and does his best work in our dingy basement wearing a pair of infrared goggles. His favourite party trick is to fold himself into a briefcase, and he was once sick in his hat.

Richard Greig
AKA: Sir Lancelot
Chivalrous to the last, Richard's dream of being a mediaeval knight suffered a setback after being born several centuries too late. His stellar parliamentary career remains intact, and he is in the process of creating a new party with the aim of abolishing all onions and onion-related produce.

The X Files

Roshni Ahuja
AKA: Bright Spark
Never failing to brighten up the office with her colourful get-up, Roshni definitely puts the 'it' in the IT department. She's a perennially pleasant, profound programmer with peerless panache, and she does her job with plenty of pep and piles of pizzazz.

Sunita Lakhiani
AKA: Designlass
Initially suspicious of having a female in their midst, the boys in Designlab now treat Sunita like one of their own. A big shame for her, because they treat each other pretty damn bad!

Sean Kearns
AKA: The Tall Guy
Big Sean, as he's affectionately known, is so laid back he actually spends most of his time lying down (unless he's on a camping trip, when his ridiculously small tent forces him to sleep on his hands and knees). Despite the rest of us constantly tripping over his lanky frame, when the job requires someone who will work flat out, he always rises to the editorial occasion.

Steve Jones
AKA: Golden Boy
Our resident Kiwi lives in a nine-bedroom mansion and is already planning an extension. His winning smile has caused many a knee to weaken in Bur Dubai but sadly for the ladies, he's hopelessly devoted to his clients.

Shabsir M
AKA: Sticky Wicket
Shabsir is a valuable player on the Indian national cricket team, so instead of working you'll usually find him autographing cricket balls for crazed fans around the world. We don't mind though – if ever a retailer is stumped because they run out of stock, he knocks them for six with his speedy delivery.

Tim Binks
AKA: Class Clown
El Binksmeisterooney is such a sharp wit, he often has fellow Explorers gushing tea from their noses in convulsions of mirth. Years spent hiking across the Middle East have given him an encyclopaedic knowledge of rock formations and elaborate hair.

Shawn Jackson Zuzarte
AKA: Paper Plumber
If you thought rocket science was hard, try rearranging the chaotic babble that flows from the editorial team! If it weren't for Shawn, most of our books would require a kaleidoscope to read correctly so we're keeping him and his jazz hands under wraps.

Tom Jordan
AKA: The True Professional
Explorer's resident thesp, Tom delivers lines almost as well as he cuts them. His early promise on the pantomime circuit was rewarded with an all-action role in hit UK drama Heartbeat. He's still living off the royalties – and the fact he shared a sandwich with Kenneth Branagh.

Shefeeq M
AKA: Rapper in Disguise
So new he's still got the wrapper on, Shefeeq was dragged into the Explorer office, and put to work in the design department. The poor chap only stopped by to ask for directions to Wadi Bih, but since we realised how efficient he is, we keep him chained to his desk.

Tracy Fitzgerald
AKA: 'La Dona'
Tracy is a queenpin Catalan mafiosa and ringleader for the 'pescadora' clan, a nefarious group that runs a sushi smuggling operation between the Costa Brava and Ras Al Khaimah. She is not to be crossed. Rival clans will find themselves fed fish, and then fed to the fishes.

Shyrell Tamayo
AKA: Fashion Princess
We've never seen Shyrell wearing the same thing twice – her clothes collection is so large that her husband has to keep all his things in a shoebox. She runs Designlab like clockwork, because being late for deadlines is SO last season.

Zainudheen Madathil
AKA: Map Master
Often confused with retired footballer Zinedine Zidane because of his dexterous displays and a bad head-butting habit, Zain tackles design with the mouse skills of a star striker. Maps are his goal and despite getting red-penned a few times, when he shoots, he scores.

The *New Zealand Explorer* Team

Lead Editor Sean Kearns
Editorial Assistant Mimi Stankova
Designer Hashim Moideen
Cartographer Noushad Madathil
Photographers Victor Romero, Pamela Grist, Sean Kearns, Andre Zimmermann, Dennis Richardson and Jennie Scotcher
Proofreader Joanna Holden-MacDonald

Publisher
Alistair MacKenzie

Editorial
Managing Editor Claire England
Lead Editors David Quinn, Jane Roberts, Matt Farquharson, Sean Kearns, Tim Binks, Tom Jordan
Deputy Editors Helen Spearman, Jakob Marsico, Katie Drynan, Pamela Afram, Richard Greig, Tracy Fitzgerald
Editorial Assistants Grace Carnay, Ingrid Cupido, Mimi Stankova

Design
Creative Director Pete Maloney
Art Director Ieyad Charaf
Senior Designers Alex Jeffries, Iain Young
Layout Manager Jayde Fernandes
Layouters Hashim Moideen, Rafi Pullat, Shefeeq Marakkatepurath
Junior Layouter Shawn Jackson Zuzarte
Cartography Manager Zainudheen Madathil
Cartographers Noushad Madathil, Sunita Lakhiani
Design Admin Manager Shyrell Tamayo
Production Coordinator Maricar Ong

Photography
Photography Manager Pamela Grist
Photographer Victor Romero
Image Editor Henry Hilos

Sales & Marketing
Area Sales Managers Laura Zuffa, Stephen Jones
Corporate Sales Executive Ben Merrett
Marketing Manager Kate Fox
Marketing Executive Annabel Clough
Retail Sales Manager Ivan Rodrigues
Retail Sales Coordinator Kiran Melwani
Retail Sales Supervisor Matthew Samuel
Merchandiser Johny Mathew
Sales & Marketing Coordinator Lennie Mangalino
Distribution Executives Ahmed Mainodin, Firos Khan, Mannie Lugtu
Warehouse Assistants Mohammed Kunjaymo, Najumudeen K.I.
Drivers Mohammed Sameer, Shabsir Madathil

Finance & Administration
Finance Manager Michael Samuel
HR & Administration Manager Andrea Fust
Accounts Assistant Cherry Enriquez
Administrators Enrico Maullon, Kelly Tesoro
Driver Rafi Jamal

IT
IT Administrator Ajay Krishnan R.
Software Engineers Bahrudeen Abdul, Roshni Ahuja
Digital Content Manager Derrick Pereira

Contact Us

Reader Response
If you have any comments and suggestions, fill out our online reader response form and you could win prizes. Log on to **www.explorerpublishing.com**

General Enquiries
We'd love to hear your thoughts and answer any questions you have about this book or any other Explorer product. Contact us at **info@explorerpublishing.com**

Careers
If you fancy yourself as an Explorer, send your CV (stating the position you're interested in) to **jobs@explorerpublishing.com**

Designlab & Contract Publishing
For enquiries about Explorer's Contract Publishing arm and design services contact **designlab@explorerpublishing.com**

PR & Marketing
For PR and marketing enquries contact
marketing@explorerpublishing.com
pr@explorerpublishing.com

Corporate Sales
For bulk sales and customisation options, for this book or any Explorer product, contact **sales@explorerpublishing.com**

Advertising & Sponsorship
For advertising and sponsorship, contact **media@explorerpublishing.com**

Explorer Publishing & Distribution
PO Box 34275, Dubai
United Arab Emirates
Phone: +971 (0)4 340 88 05
Fax: +971 (0)4 340 88 06
www.explorerpublishing.com

Public Holidays

New Year's Day	1 January
Day After New Year's Day	2 January
Southland	17 January
Wellington	22 January
Auckland	29 January
Nelson	1 February
Waitangi Day	6 February
Otago	23 March
Taranaki	31 March
Anzac Day	25 April
Queen's Birthday	1st Monday in June
Labour Day	4th Monday in October
Hawke's Bay	1 November
Marlborough	1 November
Chatham Islands	30 November
Westland	1 December
Canterbury	16 December
Christmas Day	25 December
Boxing Day	26 December
Good Friday	Varies (21 March 2008)
Easter Monday	Varies (28 March 2008)

City Hotels

Auckland	
Aspen House	09 379 6633
Auckland City Hotel	09 303 2463
City Central	09 307 3388
Esplanade Hotel	09 445 1291
Hilton	09 978 2000
Langham Hotel	09 379 5132
Mercure Hotel	09 377 8920
Novotel Ellerslie	09 529 9090
Rainbow Hotel	09 356 7272
Sky City Hotel	09 363 6000
Spencer on Byron	09 916 6111
Wellington	
Abel Tasman Hotel	04 385 1304
Bolton Hotel	04 472 9966
Cambridge Hotel	04 385 8829
Duxton	04 473 3900
Halswell Lodge	04 385 0196
InterContinental	04 472 2722
James Cook	04 499 9500
Mercure Hotel	04 385 9829
Shepherd's Arms	04 472 1320
Christchurch	
Chateau on the Park	03 348 8999
Copthorne Hotel	03 358 8129
Crowne Plaza	03 365 7799
Elms Hotel	03 355 3577
Huntley House	03 348 8435
Pavilions Hotel	03 355 5633
Rydges Hotel	0800 446 187
The George	03 379 4560

Tourist Information

Auckland (CBD)	09 367 6009
Auckland (Takapuna)	09 486 8670
Christchurch	03 379 9629
Dunedin	03 474 3300
Queenstown	03 442 4100
Wellington	04 802 4860

Embassies & Consulates

Argentinean Embassy	04 472 8330
Australian Consulate	09 921 8800
Brazilian Embassy	04 473 3516
British Consulate-General	09 303 2973
British High Commission	04 924 2888
Canadian Consulate	09 309 3690
Canadian High Commission	04 473 9577
Chilean Embassy	04 471 6270
Chinese Embassy	04 472 1382
Fijian High Commission	04 473 5401
French Consulate	09 522 1410
German Embassy	04 473 6063
Greek Embassy	04 473 7775
Indian High Commission	04 473 7775
Indonesian Embassy	04 475 8697
Israeli Consulate	04 475 7622
Italian Embassy	04 473 5339
Japanese Embassy	04 473 1540
Malaysian High Commission	04 385 2439
Mexican Embassy	04 472 0555
Philippine Embassy	04 472 9848
Polish Embassy	04 475 9453
Singapore High Commission	04 470 0850
Swedish Embassy	04 499 9895
Thai Embassy	04 476 8616
Turkish Embassy	04 472 1290
US Embassy	04 462 6000

Emergency Numbers

Emergency	111
Kidsline	0800 543 754
Lifeline	0800 543 354
Samaritans	0800 726 666
Lost/Stolen Cards	
American Express	0800 722 333
Mastercard International	0800 449 1400
Visa International	0508 600 300
Support Services	
Gay/Lesbian Line	0800 802 437
Victim Support	0800 842 846

Airport Information

Auckland Airport Lost Property	09 256 8968
Christchurch Airport Lost Property	travelinfo@cial.co.nz
Wellington Airport Lost Property	04 385 5124